V&R

Journal of Ancient Judaism
Supplements

Edited by
Armin Lange, Bernard M. Levinson
and Vered Noam

Advisory Board

Katell Berthelot (University of Aix-Marseille), George Brooke (University of Manchester), Jonathan Ben Dov (University of Haifa), Beate Ego (University of Osnabrück), Ester Eshel (Bar-Ilan University), Heinz-Josef Fabry (University of Bonn), Steven Fraade (Yale University), Maxine L. Grossman (University of Maryland), Christine Hayes (Yale University), Catherine Hezser (University of London), Jodi Magness (University of North Carolina at Chapel Hill), Carol Meyers, (Duke University), Eric Meyers (Duke University), Hillel Newman (University of Haifa), Christophe Nihan (University of Lausanne), Lawrence H. Schiffman (New York University), Konrad Schmid (University of Zurich), Adiel Schremer (Bar-Ilan University), Michael Segal (Hebrew University of Jerusalem), Aharon Shemesh (Bar-Ilan University), Günter Stemberger (University of Vienna), Kristin De Troyer (University of St Andrews), Azzan Yadin (Rutgers University)

Volume 8

Vandenhoeck & Ruprecht

Bennie H. Reynolds III

Between Symbolism and Realism

The Use of Symbolic and Non-Symbolic
Language in Ancient Jewish Apocalypses
333–63 B.C.E.

Vandenhoeck & Ruprecht

Bibliographic information published by the *Deutsche Nationalbibliothek*

The *Deutsche Nationalbibliothek* lists this publication in the
Deutsche Nationalbibliografie; detailed bibliographic data available
online: http://dnb.d-nb.de.

ISBN 978-3-525-55035-9
ISBN 978-3-647-55035-0 (e-book)

Cover image:
Achaemenid Golden Winged Lion Roundel
Courtesy of the Oriental Institute of the University of Chicago

© 2011, Vandenhoeck & Ruprecht GmbH & Co. KG, Göttingen/
Vandenhoeck & Ruprecht LLC, Oakville, CT, U.S.A.
www.v-r.de

All rights reserved. No part of his work may be reproduced or utilized in any form
or by any means, electronic or mechanical, including photocopying, recording,
or any information storage and retrieval system, without prior written permission
from the publisher.

Printed and bound in Germany by ⊕ Hubert & Co, Göttingen

Printed on non-aging paper.

To Katrina

רבות בנות עשו חיל ואת עלית על־כלנה
Many women have done excellently, but you exceed them all.

Table of Contents

List of Tables 11
Preface 13
Acknowledgements 17
Abbreviations 21

Chapter 1: Introduction 25
    Plan for this Study 27
    The Genre Apocalypse 28
    Limits of this Study 32
    Methodology 35
    A History of Research 36
    From Lücke to Koch 36
    From Koch to Collins 45
    From Uppsala (back) to Collins 52
    Today 56
    Charting a Way Forward 59
    Symbolism and Realism in Ancient Dream Reports 62
    Structuralist Poetics and Symbols as Conventional Signs 77
    Group Specific Language in the Non-Symbolic Apocalypses? 84

Part 1: Symbolic Apocalypses

Chapter 2: Daniel 2, 7, and 8 93
    The Genre Apocalypse and the Book of Daniel 93
    Daniel 2 94
    The Visionary Redaction of Daniel 2 95
    Language in Daniel 2 100
    Daniel 7–8 111
    Daniel 7 and Ancient Dream Reports 112
    Typical Approaches to Daniel 7–8 115
    The Allegorical/Mythological Approach 115
    The Iconographic Approach 116
    Excursus: Representation in Ancient Near Eastern Art 118
    The Literary Approach 119
    Language in Daniel 7 120

	Between Symbolism and Realism
Excursus: Daniel 7 and the "Model Reader"	141
Language in Daniel 8	144
Findings from Chapter 2	157

Chapter 3: Other Symbolic Apocalyptic Visions 161
    The Animal Apocalypse (1 Enoch 85–90) 161
    Descriptions of Deities, Angels, and Demons 166
    Descriptions of Persons 171
    Descriptions of Ethno-Political Groups 173
    4QFour Kingdoms^{a-b} ar 191
    Descriptions of Deities, Angels, and Demons 193
    Descriptions of Persons 198
    Descriptions of Ethno-Political Groups 199
    Book of the Words of Noah (1QapGen 5 29–18) 207
    Descriptions of Persons 214
    Other Symbols 215
    Findings From Chapter 3 220

Part 2: Non-Symbolic Apocalypses

Chapter 4: Daniel 10–12 225
    Language in Daniel 10–12 227
    Descriptions of Deities, Angels, and Demons 227
    Descriptions of Persons 236
    Descriptions of Ethno-Political Groups 248
    Findings from Chapter 4 261

Chapter 5: Apocryphon of Jeremiah C 263
    Do 4Q383–391 Constitute One Text? 263
    Is Apocryphon of Jeremiah C an Apocalypse? 268
    The Text of Apocryphon of Jeremiah C 273
    Language in the Apocryphon of Jeremiah C 287
    Descriptions of Deities, Angels, and Demons 288
    Descriptions of Persons 293
    Descriptions of Ethno-Political Groups 307
    Findings from Chapter 5 320

Chapter 6: 4QPseudo-Daniel^{a-b} ar 327
    Is 4QPseudo-Daniel^{a-b} ar an Apocalypse ? 330
    The Text of 4QPseudo-Daniel^{a-b} ar 341
    Language in 4QPseudo-Daniel^{a-b} ar 353

           Descriptions of Deities, Angels, and Demons 353
           Descriptions of Persons 357
           Descriptions of Ethno-Political Groups 366
           Findings from Chapter 6 373

Chapter 7: Conclusions 375

Bibliography 389
Indices
     Sources 409
     Persons 415
     Subjects 419

List of Tables

Table 1 Daniel 2 110

Table 2 Daniel 7 140

Table 3 Daniel 8 156

Table 4 Animal Apocalypse 181

Table 5 4QFour Kingdoms^{a-b} ar 205

Table 6 Book of the Words of Noah 218

Table 7 Descriptions of Greece 225

Table 8 Daniel 10–12 252

Table 9 Apocryphon of Jeremiah C and 4Q390 308

Table 10 The Book of Daniel in the Apocryphon of Jeremiah C 321

Table 11 4QPseudo-Daniel^{a-b} ar 370

Table 12 Symbolic and Non-Symbolic Apocalypses 378

Table 13 Symbol Types 382

Preface

This book is a study of the poetics of ancient Jewish apocalypses. As I make final adjustments to the manuscript I am reminded, however, that the relevance of apocalypses and apocalypticism for the field of Religious Studies and the Humanities more generally is hardly limited to ancient history. A few months ago a former student (thanks Mark Lettney) alerted me to an evangelical Christian group based in Oakland, CA that was traveling across the United States to warn people that the judgment day would occur on May 21, 2011.[1] When I realized that the group planned to stop for several days in Jackson, MS I could not resist making contact and setting up an interview. On Monday, March 14th James Bowley (a colleague at Millsaps College) and I sat down to interview two of the group's leaders. While there are incalculable differences between Hellenistic Jews and 21st century American evangelicals, many of their beliefs and exegetical methods are not dissimilar. For example, their repeated emphasis on a fixed, periodized (i.e., dispensationalist), and imminently complete history of the world immediately stood out. Those responsible for texts such as Daniel 2, 7, the *Animal Apocalypse*, the *Apocalypse of Weeks* (as well as several *Sibylline Oracles* and *Testaments*) attempted to remain faithful to traditional practices and beliefs of Judaism by insisting that behind the thin veil of an apparent history in which chaos, suffering, marginalization, and persecution defined them, time functioned according to the perfect order established and guaranteed by YHWH. For a variety of reasons, sometimes self-constructed and sustained, modern American evangelicals also view themselves as marginalized and attempt to re-narrate time in order to see themselves fully enfranchised in God's time and space.

Even more interesting from the perspective of this study is the way Familyradio.com representatives use language to construct identity. In both our interview and their stock literature, they frequently used a set of special sobriquets to define themselves and others – often emphasizing difference and exploiting a kind of dualism. For example, their primary moniker for themselves is "true believers." The expression is intriguing because it does not set them apart from non-believers (e.g., atheists, Buddhists, etc.) so

---

[1] For an exhaustive explanation for the prediction, see Harold Camping, *Time Has an End: A Biblical History of the World 11, 013 BC–AD 2011* (New York: Vantage Press, 2005).

much as it does from other Christians who are mistaken or disingenuous in their beliefs. The founder, owner, and primary bible teacher of the Familyradio.com, Harold Camping, left the Reform Church in 1988 over theological differences. Since then, he has taught his listeners that the "church age" ended in 1988 and that they should no longer have anything to do with any traditional Christian church since all churches are now under the dominion of Satan. This circumstance helps to underscore why the language they use to describe themselves helps specifically to set themselves apart from other Christians. It conforms to Harold Camping's articulation of time (a set and limited number of ages) and provides some psychological tools to cope with estrangement from what has been for most of them a defining sociocultural institution: church.

Other sobriquets used by familyradio.com listeners include "the unregenerate" (a term that can apply to any non-member but is most often used to describe Christians who are not "true-believers"), "the authority" (any organization of Christians with a hierarchy or eldership, i.e., this is their word for "church" and they are commanded not to be subject to "the authority"), "understanding" (a gift God imparts to the few who are able to interpret correctly the true meaning of scripture), and "watchmen" (a term borrowed from Ezek 33 to describe the particular familyradio.com listeners who tour the country in RV's warning of the impending apocalypse). After the interview, we found in their online journal that they even had a sobriquet for us: those "with letters after their name." The expression is one of derision, not respect. Indeed, they contrasted our "unlearned questions" with the insights of a truck driver they met on the same day. The truck driver was suspicious of churches, believed in the concepts of election and predestination, and, most importantly, agreed with their concept of "understanding" (exegesis): "Most people don't realize that God has to open your eyes to understand what the Bible really teaches."[2]

The types of sobriquets used by Familyradio.com representatives are similar to the kind of language used in some of the historical apocalypses analyzed in this study. For example, expressions like הַמַּשְׂכִּילִים "the wise," and עַם יֹדְעֵי אֱלֹהָיו "the people who know their [its] God" from the Book of Daniel, [קריאי]ן "the elect" from 4QPseudo-Daniel[a–b] ar, and המצדקים "those who lead to righteousness" from the *Apocryphon of Jeremiah C* seem to serve precisely the same rhetorical purposes as familyradio.com's "true believers." Similarly, expressions like מַרְשִׁיעֵי בְרִית "the violators of the covenant" from the Book of Daniel and עבדי נאכר "servants of the foreigner" from the *Apocryphon of Jeremiah C* seem to serve rhetorical pur-

---

[2] This information was removed from http://www.familyradio.com/caravan/ms_letters.html on May 23rd, 2011. Indeed, an entirely re-vamped website was launched.

poses similar to familyradio.com's "the unregenerate." The sobriquets establish linguistic boundaries – often binary relationships – that help to define and even construct the countours of the group identity.

I begin this study of ancient texts with an interlude into the modern world not merely to illustrate the ongoing cultural and religious potency of apocalypticism, but to make a methodological point. Those of us who study ancient Jewish apocalypses can reap rewards from the anthropologists, psychologists, sociologists, religionists, and literary critics who delve into the worlds of the Millerites, John Nelson Darby, the Scofield Reference Bible, Hal Lindsey, Edgar Whisenant, the Branch Davidians, Menachem Mendel Schneerson, Marian Keech, Tim Lahaye and Jerry Jenkins, Aum Shinrikyo, John Hagee, Familyradio.com, the Christian Identity movement, Jonestown, the Solar Temple, etc. In sketching the theoretical framework of this study below, I draw on thinkers both ancient and modern in order to best contextualize the language of Jewish historical apocalypses. While the primary audience of this study is specialists in Second Temple Judaism and the Dead Sea Scrolls, I hope that it can be of use to the larger field of Religious Studies and other disciplines who examine apocalypticism. There are portions of this book that are technical and will be of limited use to non-specialists. But it is my hope that the robust theoretical framework constructed in the chapter one will place this study within much broader intellectual conversations and make it intelligible to those attempting to understand apocalypses and apocalypticism from a variety of vantage-points.

In this study I analyze the language of ancient Jewish historical apocalypses. I investigate how the *dramatis personae*, i.e., deities, angels/demons, and humans (both individuals and groups) are described in the Book of Daniel (2, 7, 8, 10–12) the *Animal Apocalypse* (*1 En.* 85–90), 4QFourKingdoms^{a-b} ar, the *Book of the Words of Noah* (1QapGen 5 29–18 ?), the *Apocryphon of Jeremiah C*, and 4QPseudo-Daniel^{a-b} ar. The primary methodologies for this study are linguistic- and motif-historical analysis and the theoretical framework is informed by a wide range of ancient and modern thinkers including Artemidorus of Daldis, Ferdinand de Saussure, Charles Peirce, Leo Oppenheim, Claude Lévi-Strauss, Umberto Eco, and Michael Barkun. The most basic contention of this study is that the data now available from the Dead Sea Scrolls significantly alter how one should conceive of the genre apocalypse in the Hellenistic Period. This basic contention is borne out by five primary conclusions. First, while some apocalypses employ symbolic language to describe the actors in their historical reviews, others use non-symbolic language. Some texts, especially from the Book of Daniel, are mixed cases. Second, among the apocalypses that use symbolic language, a limited and stable repertoire of symbols obtain across the genre and bear witness to a series of conventional associations. Third, in light of the conventional associations present in symbolic language, as well as the specific descriptions of particular historical actors, it appears that symbolic language is not used to hide or obscure its referents, but to provide the reader with embedded interpretative tools. Fourth, while several apocalypses do not use symbolic ciphers to encode their historical actors, they often use cryptic sobriquets that may have functioned as a group-specific language. Fifth, the language of apocalypses appears to indicate that these texts were not the domain of only one social group or even one type of social group. Some texts presume large audiences and others presume more limited and ones. In other words, apocalypticism was not the exclusive domain of a small fringe group even if several small fringe groups appear to have internalized the ideology associated with the genre apocalypse.

Acknowledgments

This book began as a dissertation by the same title at the University of North Carolina at Chapel Hill (2009). I have since changed or adjusted parts of every chapter, but the primary claims of the book remain the same. It is a great pleasure to acknowledge those who have helped me along the way. First, I thank the editors of the *Journal of Ancient Judaism Supplements* for accepting this book for publication and the editorial staff at Vandenhoeck & Ruprecht, especially Jörg Persch and Christoph Spill for their help, patience, and skill.

I thank the University of North Carolina for a University Merit Assistantship as well as a University Dissertation Completion Fellowship. I am also grateful for a travel grant from the Graduate School that defrayed the cost of work done in Vienna, Austria as well as a travel grant from the Department of Religious Studies that allowed me to present some dissertation material at the Annual Meeting of the Society of Biblical Literature in San Diego, California.

John Bullard first introduced me to the academic study of the Bible at Wofford College and he helped me to imagine it as fulfilling vocation. Despite the long hours and frequent wrong-turns and dead-ends in teaching and research, I wake up each morning to do a job that I truly love. Thank you, John. John encouraged me to pursue my interest in Israelite Wisdom literature by going to study at Duke Divinity School with James Crenshaw. I benefited greatly from him in seminars on Job and Qoheleth, but it was a course on "Intertestamental Literature" team-taught with Anathea-Portier Young that formally introduced me to the fascinating world of literature from the late Second Temple Period. I note here that as I finished this manuscript, Thea published a book of her own on Jewish apocalypses: *Apocalypse Against Empire: Theologies of Resistance in Early Judaism* (Eerdmans, 2011). Unfortunately it was not possible to incorporate most of her work into this book, though I have been able to note its relevance on some points.

At the same time as my interest in the Second Temple Period was intensifying at Duke, Armin Lange arrived at UNC and took me on as his first American graduate student. His dual interests in the Hebrew Bible and the Dead Sea Scrolls have surely coined my own research agenda and convinced me that the literature of the late Second Temple Period is not only illuminating for the Hebrew Bible, but inseparable from it. He quickly put me to work on manuscript photographs (a significant departure from the beautifully printed pages of the *Biblia Hebraica Stuttgartensia*) as well as the methods and theories required to analyze ancient texts critically. He has selflessly poured countless hours into my work and has been a uniquely generous *Doktorvater*. It is from him that I have learned best and most in the academy.

So it was at first disconcerting when he announced that he was leaving for a chair in Second Temple Judaism at the University of Vienna while I was preparing for doctoral exams. But his departure provided me with unforeseen opportunities. I had the pleasure of spending much time in the splendid city of Vienna during my last two and a half years of graduate school. I participated in graduate seminars at the University of Vienna and I am especially grateful to Bernhard Palme (Institut für Alte Geschichte) and James Alfred Loader (Institut für Evangelische Theologie) for their hospitality and insights. In Vienna I also benefited from two of Armin's European students, Matthias Weigold and Hanna Tervanotko. I am lucky to count them as my colleagues and friends.

My interests in the Dead Sea Scrolls and Second Temple Judaism have not been limited to texts. I have been fortunate to have Jodi Magness to force me to think not only beyond texts to material culture, but also beyond Syro-Palestine to the world of the Diaspora in Second Temple Times. Similarly, work with Eric Meyers on the archaeology of the Persian, Hellenistic, and Roman Periods in the Levant has helped to contextualize the history and culture that is latent in the texts analyzed in this study. He and Carol Meyers were always helpful to me in Armin's absence and included me in colloquia, etc., of the Hebrew Bible division at Duke. Other Duke faculty have helped me to acquire many of the skills used in this study: Septuagint with Melvin Peters, Aramaic and Syriac with Lucas von Rompay, Ugaritic, Arabic, and Ethiopic with Orval Wintermute, Akkadian with Neil Walls (visiting from Wake Forest Divinity School), and Hebrew with most every Hebrew Bible/Old Testament faculty member. Greg Goering (UVA) held a visiting position in Hebrew Bible at UNC for two years after Armin's departure. I was, by then, finished with coursework, but benefited from conversations with him about Second Temple Judaism.

Those who study the Hebrew Bible have for some time now looked to the East (Mesopotamia) in order to contextualize it. Several of my teachers have also helped me to look for context in the West (Mediterranean). Bart Ehrman and Zlatko Pleše helped me to venture into the worlds of New Testament, Early Christianity, and Greco-Roman religion. I was fortunate to work as a teaching assistant for Bart's Introduction to the New Testament and learn from a true master-teacher. Zlatko improved my Greek considerably but also helped me to engage a world of philosophy and critical theory that has significantly expanded my intellectual horizons. Besides the intellectual debt I owe them, I also thank the five members of my committee (Armin Lange, Eric Meyers, Bart Ehrman, Jodi Magness, and Zlatko Pleše) for the time they devoted to the administrative work involved in minting a new Ph.D. I appreciate it even more now that I've had the opportunity to, e.g., administer doctoral examinations.

Fellow graduate students at UNC and Duke made the journey far more rewarding. Sean Burt and I worked most closely together. I have benefited greatly from him. I have also benefited from coursework and conversations with Erin Kuhns, Jared Anderson, Steve Werlin, Pam Reaves, Carrie Duncan, Ben White, Matt Grey, Chad Eggleston, and Amanda Mbuve.

After completing my Ph.D. I was honored to be hired by the Religious Studies department at UNC. I appreciate the way in which the faculty so generously transitioned me from the role of student to the role of colleague. I would like to thank the students I taught in two seminars on the Dead Sea Scrolls and Rewriting Scripture in Second Temple Judaism for helping me continue to think about some of the issues raised in this book.

In the last year an unforeseen opportunity for my family has moved us to Jackson, MS where I have been fortunate to join the faculty of Millsaps College. All of my colleagues in the Religious Studies department have offered both hospitality and invigorating intellectual exchanges. But I've been especially lucky to work with another Dead Sea Scrolls specialist, James Bowley. We've shared many ideas and beers this year and I'm a much better scholar because of it. I also want to thank my students from a seminar I offered this year at Millsaps: "The Messiah and the Apocalypse: Ancient and Modern Perspectives." We had great fun and I learned a lot from them as we read Daniel and *1 Enoch* alongside modern texts like *Left Behind* and hashed out what apocalypse and apocalypticism mean.

I have profited from many scholars over the last few years. Moshe Bernstein, Hanan (ל״ז) and Esther Eshel, Loren Stuckenbruck, Klaus Koch, John Collins, Daniel Stökl ben Ezra, Maxine Grossman, Matthew Goff, Todd Hanneken, Molly Zahn, Eibert Tigchelaar, Dan Machiela, Hanne von Weissenberg, Moulie Vidas, Alex Jassen, Andy Teeter, and Michael Segal have at various times listened to my ideas and/or responded to my papers and publications by giving helpful feedback, criticism, or encouragement – sometimes saving me from embarrassing errors. I have found in the new generation of scrolls specialists not only a collection of intellects that constantly sharpen each other, but also a community (pun intended) of friends that looks forward to each new conference not only for professional interests, but for the time spent together.

Writing this book was a long and sometimes grueling process, but the support and good humor of my family has helped to insure that the work was never overwhelming. My interest in the Bible began at home at an early age and my mother, father, and sister have always taken a keen interest in what my work now does with those same stories. My two boys, Hilton and Huck, have never known a life apart from their father's work on this book. They have both spent far too many nights and weekends with their father barricaded in the library or glued to his computer screen. Boys, thank you for being patient with your father. As Prov 10:1 predicts, you have both brought me great gladness.

This book is dedicated to my wife Katrina. Such a small gesture hardly acknowledges her love and support for me. She has put up with my long hours of work and my frequent trips to the library (and Austria!) with genuine understanding and patience. She has not only tolerated my consuming work but encouraged me at every turn. She is a model mother to our sons and has achieved great professional success of her own. I truly found an אשת חיל at Wofford College. Her fierce devotion to our family is something to behold, each day giving substance to Shakespeare's definition of love in Sonnet 116: "It is an ever-fixed mark that looks on tempests and is never shaken, whose worth's unknown although his height be taken."

Abbreviations

Primary Sources

1 En.	*1 Enoch*
1QapGen	*Genesis Apocryphon*
1QM	*War Scroll* (*Milḥamah*)
1QpHab	*Pesher Habakkuk*
1QS	*Rule of the Community (Serek haYaḥad)*
4QMMT	*Some Works of the Torah* (*Miqsat Ma'aseh haTorah*)
4QPs-Dan^{a-b} ar	4QPseudo-Daniel^{a-b} ar
Bar	Baruch
CD	*Damascus Document* (Cairo Genizah)
Esd	Esdras
HB	Hebrew Bible
Jub.	*Jubilees*
LXX	Septuagint
Macc	Maccabees
MT	Masoretic Text
NT	New Testament
OG	Old Greek
Sib. Or.	*Sibylline Oracles*
Sir	Sirach
T. 12 Patr.	*Testaments of the Twelve Patriarchs*
Tob	Tobit
Wis	Wisdom of Solomon

Secondary Sources

AAASH	Acta Antiqua Academiae Scientiarum Hunagaricae
AB	Anchor Bible
ABD	Anchor Bible Dictionary
AbrN	Abr-Nahrain

AGJU	Arbeiten zur Geschischte des Spätjudentums und des Urchristentums
ALASPM	Abhandlungen zur Literatur Alt-Syrien-Palastinas und Mesopotamiens
AOTC	Abingdon Old Testament Commentary
AOAT	Alter Orient und Altes Testament
AOS	American Oriental Studies
ASORDS	American Schools of Oriental Research Dissertation Service
BA	Biblical Archaeologist
BASOR	Bulletin of the American Schools of Oriental Research
BETL	Bibliotheca ephemeridum theologicarum lovaniensium
BBR	Bulletin for Biblical Research
BKAT	Biblischer Kommentar Altes Testament
BO	Bibliotheca orientalis
BR	Biblical Research
BZAW	Beihefte zur Zeitschrift für die alttestamentliche Wissenschaft
CBQMS	Catholic Biblical Quarterly Monograph Series
CBR	Currents in Biblical Research
CHANE	Culture and History of the Ancient Near East
CRINT	Compendia rerum iudaicarum ad Novum Testamentum
CSCO	Corpus scriptorium christianorum orientalum
DJD	Discoveries in the Judean Desert
DSD	Dead Sea Discoveries
DSSR	Dead Sea Scrolls Reader
FAT	Forschungen zum Alten Testament
GA	Gesammelte Aufsätze
HALOT	Hebrew and Aramaic Lexicon of the Old Testament
HdO	Handbuch der Orientalistik
HSM	Harvard Semitic Monographs
HR	History of Religions
HSM	Harvard Semitic Monographs
HSS	Harvard Semitic Studies
IEJ	Israel Exploration Journal
ICC	International Critical Commentary
Imm	Immanuel
Int	Interpretation

IOQS	International Organization for Qumran Studies
JAJ	Journal of Ancient Judaism
JAJSup	Journal of Ancient Judaism Supplements
JAOS	Journal of the American Oriental Society
JBL	Journal of Biblical Literature
JJS	Journal of Jewish Studies
JNES	Journal of Near Eastern Studies
JPOS	Journal of the Palestine Oriental Society
JSHRZ	Jüdische Schriften aus hellenistisch-römischer Zeit
JSJ	Journal for the Study of Judaism in the Persian, Hellenistic, and Roman Periods
JSJSup	Journal for the Study of Judaism Supplement Series
JSPSup	Journal for the Study of the Pseudepigrapha: Supplement Series
JSOT	Journal for the Study of the Old Testament
JSS	Journal of Semitic Studies
JTS	Journal of Theological Studies
LCL	Loeb Classical Library
NHMS	Nag Hammadi & Manichaean Studies
NLH	New Literary History
OBO	Orbis biblicus et orientalis
OTL	Old Testament Library
OTP	Old Testament Pseudepigrapha
OTS	Old Testament Studies
RB	Revue Biblique
RBL	Review of Biblical Literature
RevQ	Revue de Qumran
RHR	Revue de l'histoire des religions
SAA	State Archives of Assyria
SBLDS	Society of Biblical Literature Dissertation Series
SBLEJL	Society of Biblical Literature Early Judaism and its Literature
SBLMS	Society of Biblical Literature Monograph Series
SBLRBS	Society of Biblical Literature Resources for Biblical Study
SBLSCSS	Society of Biblical Literature Septuagint and Cognate Studies
SBLWAW	Society of Biblical Literature Writings from the Ancient World
SBT	Studies in Biblical Theology
STDJ	Studies on the Texts from the Desert of Judah
SVTP	Studia in Veteris Testamenti pseudepigraphica

TDNT	Theological Dictionary of the New Testament
TDOT	Theological Dictionary of the Old Testament
TLOT	Theological Lexicon of the Old Testament
TSAJ	Texte und Studien zum Antiken Judentum
UF	Ugarit Forschungen
VT	Vetus Testamentum
VTSup	Vetus Testamentum Supplements
WMANT	Wissenschaftliche Monographien zum Alten und Neuen Testament
ZAW	Zeitschrift für die alttestamentliche Wissenschaft

Chapter One

Introduction

Behold, the fourth beast – dreadful, terrible, and exceedingly mighty. It had great teeth of iron and was devouring and crushing and stomping the remainder at its feet. And it was different from each beast that was before it and it had ten horns. (Dan 7:7)

Daniel 7 describes the ancient kingdom of Greece as a terrifying beast.[1] It also describes individual Greek rulers as particular horns on the beast's head. Apocalypses such as Dan 8 and the *Animal Apocalypse* (*1 En.* 85–90) use the same type of symbolic language. In the research history below I attempt to show that this type of language has led most interpreters to describe symbolic language as a defining feature – a *sine qua non* – of ancient Jewish apocalypses. Recent work, however, has called into question whether or not symbolic language is a ubiquitous feature in the ex eventu prophecies of ancient Jewish apocalypses. While working to categorize the texts from the Qumran library by genre for DJD 39, Armin Lange and Ulrike-Mittmann-Richert noticed that some apocalypses describe historical or heavenly entities in a different manner than one finds in Dan 7.[2] They suggested that ancient Jewish apocalypses were not necessarily symbolic in character and called for further research on the language of apocalypses.[3] Their concern with language can be seen in a comparison of descriptions of Greece in ancient Jewish apocalypses. For example, the writer of the *Apocryphon of Jeremiah C* represents Greece as יון (*Yawan* "Greece").[4] One

---

[1] Strictly speaking, the writer of Daniel depicts the kingdom of Macedonia, not Greece. It is unlikely, however, that the writer appreciated any such distinction in light of the angelic interpretation of the dream vision from Dan 8 (cf. 8:21) and the correlation of Alexander and the מלכות יון "Kingdom of Greece" in 11:2–3.

[2] Armin Lange and Ulrike Mittmann-Richert, "Annotated List of the Texts from the Judean Desert Classified by Genre and Content," in *The Texts From the Judean Desert: Indices and An Introduction to the DJD Series* (ed. Emanuel Tov; vol. 39 of DJD; Oxford: Clarendon, 2002), 120–1.

[3] Lange and Mittmann-Richert, "Annotated List of the Texts from the Judean Desert Classified by Genre and Content," 121. Lange himself performed a preliminary investigation in which he compared descriptions from Dan, the *Animal Apocalypse*, and *Jub.* Armin Lange, "Dream Visions and Apocalyptic Milieus," in *Enoch and Qumran Origins: New Light on a Forgotten Connection* (ed. Gabriele Boccaccini; Grand Rapids: Eerdmans, 2005), 27–34.

[4] Devorah Dimant, "4QApocryphon of Jeremiah," in *Qumran Cave 4 XXI* (ed. Devorah Dimant; vol. 30 of DJD; Oxford: Clarendon Press, 2001), 152–3.

cannot find a more realistic description of Greece than יון in Classical Hebrew. 4QPseudoDaniel^{a-b} ar even mentions the personal names of particular Greek rulers.[5] A careful analysis of the book of Daniel shows that the last and largest apocalypse in that book (chapters 10–12) never uses symbolic ciphers to represent Greece or any other political body. Instead, the explicit term יון is used to describe Greece and titles such as "king of the north" or "king of the south" are used to describe particular Seleucid or Ptolemaic rulers in Dan 11. These descriptions are considerably different than the ones found in Dan 7. The language found in *Apocryphon of Jeremiah C* and 4QPseudoDaniel^{a-b} raises intriguing questions about the language found in better known Jewish historical apocalypses. Is symbolic language really a hallmark of the genre apocalypse? Do all historical apocalypses use symbols to allegorize older myths? Does the symbolic language found in some historical apocalypses serve to conceal or protect resistance groups? If so, does symbolic language indicate that apocalypses were the domain of small, marginal, or fringe groups within Judaism of the Hellenistic Period? If not all apocalypses use symbols, can the explicit language of some historical apocalypses reveal information about the kind of communities for which these texts were important?

In this study I attempt to provide answers for these and other questions by analyzing the language of ancient Jewish historical apocalypses. While apocalypses and apocalypticism have not lacked for scholarly attention in the last four decades, work specifically dedicated to the language of apocalypses has not moved significantly beyond Hermann Gunkel's work in *Schöpfung und Chaos in Urzeit und Endzeit*, a work that is not even specifically concerned with the genre apocalypse.[6] This lack of work on the language of apocalypses obtains in spite of the fact that most students of apocalypses have declared symbolic language to be a *sine qua non* of the genre apocalypse.[7] John Collins highlighted the need for more analysis of the language of apocalypses over twenty-five years ago while most still waged battles over the questions of form: "The literary conventions that determine

---

[5] For example, בלכרוס = Βαλακρος in 4Q243 21 2. Another name that cannot be deciphered is, nevertheless, probably Greek. See John J. Collins and Peter Flint, "4Qpseudo-Daniel^a ar," in *Qumran Cave 4 XVII: Parabiblical Texts, Part 3* (ed. James VanderKam; vol. 22 of DJD; Oxford: Clarendon Press, 1996), 109.

[6] Hermann Gunkel, *Schöpfung und Chaos in Urzeit und Endzeit* (Göttingen: Vandenhoeck & Ruprecht, 1895). Cf. now Hermann Gunkel, *Creation and Chaos in the Primeval Era and the Eschaton* (Grand Rapids, MI: Eerdmans, 2005). I hasten to point out that good work, though not enough of it, has been done on the rhetoric of apocalypses. Cf. Adela Yarbro Collins, *Crisis and Catharsis: The Power of the Apocalypse* (Philadelphia: Westminster, 1984).

[7] A representative statement can be found in David Russell, *The Method and Message of Jewish Apocalyptic* (Philadelphia: Westminster, 1964), 122.. See the history of research below for additional similar opinions.

the manner of composition and the nature of the literature are no less important than the generic framework."[8] I hope that this study will fill in portions of the portrait of Jewish Historical apocalypses that still want for color. Ultimately, I paint a picture of language that is more complex and nuanced than a simple symbolic vs. non-symbolic scheme. But I insist that many of the most important insights about language of apocalypses are only revealed when one begins with the basic binary structure developed by Lange and Mittman-Richert.

Plan for this Study

The remainder of chapter one is divided into two basic parts. In the first part, I sketch a history of research on the language of ancient Jewish apocalypses. In the second part, I attempt to establish a theoretical framework within which to view the language of apocalypses. I divide the history of research into four periods: 1) from Lücke to Koch, 2) from Koch to Collins, and 3) from Uppsala (back) to Collins, and 4) current trends. Several of the questions already intimated in the introduction above are made salient in this review of research.

Conspicuously missing from the many studies that purport to accord great significance to the symbolic language of Jewish apocalypses is any explicit method for understanding the language or any systematic analysis of it. I am not aware of any study that provides explicit criteria for determining whether or not language is symbolic. I show that the concept of explicit, realistic apocalyptic language is all but missing from more than two hundred years worth of research. Thus, while the data from the history of research is accordingly one-sided (i.e., there essentially is no history of those who have found non-symbolic language), it is precisely that one-sidedness that opens the requisite space needed to define symbolic and non-symbolic language in ancient Jewish apocalypses. Accordingly, the history of research is followed by a section that attempts to solve the largest problem encountered in the history of research, the lack of a robust conceptual framework.

In the theoretical framework, I attempt to set the parameters for discussion of the language encountered in the analysis of texts in chapters two through six. I begin by considering work done by Leo Oppenheim on the language of ancient dream reports as well as the logical antecedents of Oppenhiem's work in the *Oneirocritica* of Artemidorus of Daldis. It is

---

[8] John J. Collins, *The Apocalyptic Imagination: An Introduction to Jewish Apocalyptic Literature* (Grand Rapids: W.B. Eerdmans, 1998), 14.

from these works that I derive my basic typology for symbolic vs. non-symbolic language. Next I consider a model of language derived from the work of Ferdinand de Saussure and Charles Peirce and filtered through structuralists like Claude Lévi-Strauss in order to find a nomenclature to describe the conventional relationships encountered in part one of this study. I then consider the notion of group-specific language in order to better understand the texts found in part two of this study. I give attention to several recent studies of language in the sectarian Dead Sea Scrolls as well as more general studies of apocalyptic language such as one finds in Michael Barkun's *Disaster and the Millenium*. With a theoretical framework in place, I proceed to the main body of this study, which is divided into two major sections: symbolic apocalypses (chapters two and three) and non-symbolic apocalypses (chapters four, five and six).

In chapter two I analyze chapters 2, 7, and 8 from the Book of Daniel. In chapter three I compare the evidence from the symbolic apocalypses in the Book of Daniel with three other symbolic apocalypses: *The Animal Apocalypse* (*1 En.* 85–90), 4QFour Kingdoms^{a-b} ar, and the *Book of the Words of Noah* (1QapGen 5 29–18).

In chapter 4 I analyze the language found in Dan 10–12. Chapters five and six are devoted to two texts from Qumran: *Apocryphon of Jeremiah C* and *Pseudo-Daniel*$^{a-b}$ *ar*. I provide a fresh transcription and translation for each of the last two texts. In the case of the *Apocryphon of Jeremiah C*, I provide the first fully combined edition of all fragments. The analysis of both *Apocryphon of Jeremiah C* and *Pseudo-Daniel*$^{a-b}$ *ar* is preceded by a discussion of why each text should be treated as an apocalypse.

The Genre Apocalypse

The terms "apocalypse" and "apocalyptic" are particularly problematic when used to describe texts from the Qumran library.[9] The discovery of the Dead Sea Scrolls preceeded and fueled a scholarly discussion that began in the late 1970's and sought to give greater precision to the terms apocalypse, apocalyptic, and apocalypticism.[10] Many Dead Sea Scrolls were initially given the designation "Apocalyptic" (i.e., the incorrect English nominal approximation of the German *Apokalyptik*) even though they did not appear similar to texts such as Daniel in terms of genre. The resulting confusion

---

[9] Lange and Mittmann-Richert, "Annotated List of the Texts from the Judean Desert Classified by Genre and Content," 120.

[10] The now standard distinctions are summarized by Collins, *The Apocalyptic Imagination*, 1–21.

about the genre apocalypse and contents of many scrolls discovered at Qumran is summarized by Florentino García-Martínez:

The announcement that the most characteristic apocalypses, such as Enoch or Daniel, were abundantly represented in the new finds, the discovery that other compositions previously unknown had characteristics similar to these apocalypses and could therefore be legitimately considered new apocalypses, the awareness that the most typical sectarian writings had a remarkable eschatological dimension and showed a very radical dualistic thinking, and above all the fact that the group from which the manuscripts were supposed to have come was a secluded community, providing for the first time a model for the sociological background of the apocalypses all helped to create a pan-Qumranism in the investigation of apocalypticism.[11]

There are many texts from the Qumran library that one might describe with the adjective "apocalyptic." These texts contain themes, motifs, or other elements familiar from the genre apocalypse but they are not examples of revelatory literature. Examples of the apocalyptic features mentioned above might include 1) a periodized history, 2) dualism, 3) messianism, 4) a final, eschatological battle, or 5) the concept of predestination.[12] Texts like the *War Scroll* (1QM), the *Damascus Document* (D), and the *Pesharim* contain some of these elements. None of these high-profile scrolls, however, share the literary form of apocalypses.

Hartmut Stegemann raised precisely this problem at the 1979 Uppsala Colloquium on Apocalypticism. He noted the *non-sequitor* that an apocalyptic community like the Qumran Essenes had not actually produced any apocalypses.[13] Stegemann's assertion that "the emperor hath no clothes" appears correct on one level. The caves at Qumran may not have preserved a single apocalypse composed by Essenes. But several texts unknown before the discoveries at Qumran have the potential to further illumine the genre apocalypse. Texts that one might describe as apocalypses are *Apocryphon of Jeremiah C*, *Pseudo-Daniel^{a-b}*, 4QHistorical Text A, *Words of Michael*, *Book of Giants*, *New Jerusalem*, 4QapocrDan ar, *The Book of Noah*, 4QFourKingdoms^{a-b} ar, and *Testament of Amram*.[14] Not everyone

---

[11] Florentino García Martínez, "Apocalypticism in the Dead Sea Scrolls," in *The Encyclopedia of Apocalypticism* (ed. John J. Collins; New York: Continuum, 1998), 163.

[12] John J. Collins, *Apocalypticism in the Dead Sea Scrolls* (London: Routledge, 1997), 9–11.

[13] Hartmut Stegemann, "Die Bedeutung der Qumranfunde für die Erforschung der Apokalyptik," in *Apocalypticism in the Mediterranean World and the Near East* (ed. David Hellholm; Tübingen: Mohr, 1983), 495–530.

[14] See Lange and Mittmann-Richert, "Annotated List of the Texts from the Judean Desert Classified by Genre and Content," 120–1. See also John J. Collins, "Apocalypticism and Literary Genre in the Dead Sea Scrolls," in *The Dead Sea Scrolls after Fifty Years: A Comprehensive Assessment* (ed. Peter Flint and James VanderKam; Leiden: Brill, 1989), 403–30. The most recent discussion is found in Jörg Frey, "Die Bedeutung der Qumrantexte für das Verständnis der

would describe these texts as "true" apocalypses. In each case one faces a highly fragmentary text that does not provide sufficient evidence to describe its genre definitively. But part of the problem is the idea that there is such a thing as a "true" apocalypse (i.e., generic realism). This last part of the problem is symptomatic of a more deeply rooted problem that one confronts when analyzing the genre of some of the fragmentary texts from Qumran: some classical research methodologies, such as form criticism, are in a state of flux (or even limbo).[15]

Apocryphon of Jeremiah C is sometimes described as "pseudo-prophecy."[16] I am unaware of what this category means though it does not seem to be coterminus with the more precise category, "literary-prophecy." The use of the genre prophecy or "pseudo-prophecy" to describe either *Apocryphon of Jeremiah C* or *Pseudo-Daniel^{a-b} ar* is highly problematic. In light of the significant evolution of "prophecy" in the imaginations of Jewish writers from the Iron Age to the Hellenistic period, it is crucial to define prophecy before using it to label *Apocryphon of Jeremiah C*. In his recent monograph, *Mediating the Divine*, Alex Jassen makes the point that prophecy was not an extinct concept in the Dead Sea Scrolls/Second Temple Judaism. He also makes the point that the concept of prophecy found in the scrolls is the product of significant transformation and reconceptualization.[17] In particular, regardless of the terminology that is found in some scrolls, Jassen shows that the mediating functions of the Qumran community, for example, are easily distinguishable from the biblical models of prophet and prophecy.[18]

The fact that *Apocryphon of Jeremiah C* makes use of a biblical prophetic figure no more indicates that the text is a prophecy than the use of Jere-

---

Apokalyptik im Frühjudentum und im Urchristentum," in *Apokalyptik und Qumran* (ed. Jörg Frey and Michael Becker; Paderborn: Bonifatius, 2007), 11–62, esp. 23–34.

[15] The most recent treatment of the problems and possibilities of form criticism is the 2009 PhD dissertation of Sean Burt (Duke University). I thank Sean for making available to me a section entitled "The Form-Critical Problem of the Nehemiah Memorial; Or, Reanimating the *Sitz im Leben*." See also Antony Campbell, "Form Criticism's Future," in *The Changing Face of Form Criticism for the Twenty-First Century* (ed. Marvin Sweeney and Ehud Ben Zvi; Grand Rapids: Eerdmans, 2003), 15–31. Erhard Blum, "Formgeschichte – A Misleading Category? Some Critical Remarks," in *The Changing Face of Form Criticism for the Twenty-First Century* (ed. Marvin Sweeney and Ehud Ben Zvi; Grand Rapids: Eerdmans, 2003), 32–45.

[16] The most conspicuous use of the expression "pseudo-prophecy" is found in the title of DJD 30: Devorah Dimant, *Qumran Cave 4 Parabiblical Texts, Part 4: Pseudo-Prophetic Texts* (vol. 30; Oxford: Clarendon Press, 2001). Cf. also Collins, *Apocalypticism in the Dead Sea Scrolls*, 10.

[17] Alex Jassen, *Mediating the Divine: Prophecy and Revelation in the Dead Sea Scrolls and Second Temple Judaism* (STDJ 68; Leiden: Brill, 2007). See also William Schniedewind, *The Word of God in Transition: From Prophet to Exegete in the Second Temple Period* (JSOTSup 197; Sheffield: JSOT Press, 1995).

[18] Jassen, *Mediating the Divine*, 279–308.

miah in *2 Maccabees* makes it a prophecy. If one discovered only a small portion of *2 Maccabees*, it might be tempting to describe it as a prophetic text. It is demonstrably not. While the fragmentary *Apocryphon* might appear at first to be analogous to the biblical book of Jeremiah, I hope to show that some of its features are far closer to ancient Jewish apocalypses than to typical prophetic oracles.

In this study I use the definition of apocalypse from *Semeia* 14 as my working definition:

> A genre of revelatory literature with a narrative framework, in which a revelation is mediated by an otherworldly being to a human recipient, disclosing a transcendent reality which is both temporal, insofar as it envisages eschatological salvation, and spatial, insofar as it involves another, supernatural world.[19]

Numerous proposals have been made to modify this definition. Some have desired to add more specificity and others have desired to make the definition more inclusive.[20] I proceed under the assumption that all generic definitions are imperfect because of the continual innovation and cross-fertilization of genres. Thomas Pavel addresses this issue in one of two issues of the journal *New Literary History* devoted to the notion of genre in 2003:

> With all their instability, generic notions are irreplaceable. Attempts to speak about literature in terms of a single all-encompassing category that would make generic concerns obsolete (the "masterpiece" of the Romantics, the "poem" of the New Critics, and the "text" of poststructuralist criticism) leave aside something essential. Genre is a crucial interpretive tool because it is a crucial artistic tool in the first place. Literary texts are neither natural phenomena subject to scientific dissection, nor miracles performed by gods and thus worthy of worship, but fruits of human talent and labor. To understand them, we need to appreciate the efforts that went into their production. Genre helps us figure out the nature of a literary work because the person who wrote it and the culture for which that person labored used genre as a guideline for literary creation.[21]

The value of definitions, and I believe this is true of the *Semeia* 14 definition, is that they allow us to see more clearly the fine distinctions between

---

[19] John J. Collins, *Apocalypse: The Morphology of a Genre* (Semeia 14; Missoula, Mont.: Scholars Press, 1979), 9.

[20] Cf. Eibert Tigchelaar, "More on Apocalyptic and Apocalypses," *JSJ* 18 (1987): 137–44. The most recent survey is Todd Hanneken, "The Book of Jubilees among the Apocalypses" (Ph.D. Dissertation, University of Notre Dame, 2008) 86–103. See also Lorenzo DiTommaso, "Apocalypses and Apocalypticism in Antiquity (Part 1)," *CBR* 5 (2007): 235–86, esp. 38–47.

[21] Thomas Pavel, "Genres as Norms and Good Habits," *NLH* 34, no. 2 [Theorizing Genres I] (2003): 202. See also Margaret Cohen, "Traveling Genres," *NLH* 34, no. 3 [Theorizing Genres II] (2003): 481–99. Mark Salber Phillips, "Histories, Micro- and Literary: Problems of Genre and Distance," *NLH* 34, no. 2 [Theorizing Genres I] (2003): 211–29.

texts that share general similarities. Nevertheless, generic definitions are always preliminary statements, not final assessments. They indicate a group of texts that might be most profitably read together. They inform the expectations of a reader. Definitions focus on form,[22] but a full study of genre includes elements such as content and theme, language, context, function, material attributes of the text, mode of composition and reception, and the role of tradition.[23] This study looks toward a more complete understanding of ancient Jewish apocalypses by systematically analyzing a feature of the genre that is not included in generic definitions: language.

The Limitations of this Study

This book is a systematic study of the language of Jewish historical apocalypses but it is not a comprehensive one.[24] The number of historical apocalypses is too large to apply a systematic analysis to each text. Moreover, I am especially interested in calling attention to how texts from Qumran should shape our conception of the genre apocalypse. Therefore I have set some parameters that limit the body of evidence I consider. In the first instance, I exclude texts that fall outside of the dates 333–63 B.C.E., i.e., the Hellenistic Period in Syro-Palestine.

The genre apocalypse emerges out of a rich literary seedbed that is exemplified in particular by prophetic texts such as Isa 24–27 and Zech 1–8.[25] It is probably accurate to describe both of these texts as proto-apocalypses,

---

[22] "Generic definitions should focus upon the formal, structural composition of the literary works rather than upon thematology. It may be necessary to keep characteristic motifs in view, but identifications of subject matter are of dubious value, since related subjects may be expressed in several genres." William Doty, "The Concept of Genre in Literary Analysis," in *Society of Biblical Literature, One Hundred Eighth Annual Meeting Book of Seminar paper* (ed. Lane McGaughy; Los Angeles: Society of Biblical Literature, 1972), 439.

[23] Cf., for example, the generic-analytic approach of Kenton Sparks in Kenton Sparks, *Ancient Texts for the Study of the Hebrew Bible: A Guide to the Background Literature* (Peabody, MA: Hendrickson, 2005), 5–21.

[24] Texts such as the *Book of the Watchers* (*1 En*. 1–36) are not included because they are heavenly/otherworldly journeys, not historical apocalypses. A study of the language of heavenly journeys is also highly desirable, but I have chosen historical apocalypses because each text presents a similar chronological scheme and this scheme generates comparable evidence more consistently than do heavenly journeys. In other words, a comparison of the language found in only historical apocalypses is more likely to find "apple-to-apple" rather than "apple-to-orange" data.

[25] Two studies have been most influential in outlining the continuity between post-exilic prophecy and the genre apocalypse: Paul Hanson, *The Dawn of Apocalyptic: The Historical and Sociological Roots of Jewish Apocalyptic Eschatology* (Philadelphia: Fortress, 1975). Peter von der Osten-Sacken, *Die Apokalyptik in ihrem Verhältnis zu Prophetie und Weisheit* (vol. 157; München: C. Kaiser, 1969).

but some of the most important features of literary apocalypses, i.e., intense interest in the angelic world and a robust, imminent eschatology – are not routinely found in post-exilic prophetic texts.[26] Therefore I do not include Hag, Zech 1–8, Ezek 40–48, Isa 24–27, or 56–66 in this study. These texts prefigure aspects of the form and thought of apocalypses, but they are not apocalypses. For many scholars, the socio-historical stage is not fully set for the emergence of the genre apocalypse before the Hellenistic Period and the associated cultural upheavals in Syro-Palestine.[27] While the deep roots of their form and worldview can be detected in texts from the post-exilic period (and even before), many apocalypses are direct responses to events in the Hellenistic period. Some texts like the *Book of Watchers* appear to be general responses, but others such as Dan 7 and the *Animal Apocalypse* appear to respond directly to particular historical circumstances (e.g., the Hellenistic religious reforms of Antiochus IV and the Maccabean revolt, respectively).

A similar situation obtains with Dan 4. It is unclear when the text was written, but it is likely a pre-Maccabean text.[28] The discovery of the *Prayer of Nabonidus* almost certainly indicates that Dan 4 is based on earlier traditions that date to the Persian Period.[29] The *Prayer of Nabonidus* appears to describe the madness of King Nabonidus of Babylon (Nebuchadnezzar in Dan 4) and reports that the king was helped by a young Jewish man.[30] Evidence from the Greek versions of Dan 4 also suggest a date in the Persian Period. Dan 4 may have formed part of the earliest Aramaic Daniel-Book.[31] Finally, Dan 4 does not contain the imminent eschatology or inter-

---

[26] Cf. Collins, *The Apocalyptic Imagination*, 24–5.

[27] Collins, *The Apocalyptic Imagination*, 33–7. This discussion in *Apocalyptic Imagination* summarizes two more substantial pieces on this topic: John J. Collins, "Jewish Apocalyptic Against Its Hellenistic Near Eastern Environment," *BASOR* 220 (1975): 27–36. John J. Collins, "Cosmos and Salvation: Jewish Wisdom and Apocalyptic in the Hellenistic Age," *HR* 17 (1977): 121–42. Both essays are now collected in John J. Collins, *Seers, Sybils, and Sages in Hellenistic-Roman Judaism* (Leiden: Brill, 2001), 59–74, 317–38.

[28] John J. Collins, *Daniel* (Minneapolis: Fortress Press, 1993), 233–4.

[29] For the *editio princeps*, see John J. Collins and Peter Flint, "4QPrayer of Nabonidus ar," in *Qumran Cave 4 XVII: Parabiblical Texts, Part 3* (ed. James VanderKam; vol. 22 of DJD; Oxford: Clarendon Press, 1996), 83–93. See also the discussion in Esther Eshel, "Possible Sources of the Book of Daniel," in *The Book of Daniel: Composition and Reception* (ed. John J. Collins and Peter Flint; vol. 84 of *VTSup*; Leiden: Brill, 2001), 387–94.

[30] Cf. Matthias Henze, *The Madness of King Nebuchadnezzar: The Ancient Near Eastern Origins and Early History of Interpretation of Daniel 4* (JSJSup; Leiden: Brill, 1999). See also Klaus Koch, *Die Reiche der Welt und der kommende Menschensohn: Studien zum Danielbuch* (GA 2; Neukirchen-Vluyn: Neukirchener Verlag, 1995), 83–124. Klaus Koch, *Daniel* (BKAT XXII/6; Neukirchen-Vluyn: Neukirchener Verlag, 2005), 408–15.

[31] The most thorough argument for this theory is Rainer Albertz, *Der Gott des Daniel: Untersuchungen zu Daniel 4–6 in der Septugintafassung sowie zu Komposition und Theologie des aramäischen Danielbuches* (vol. 131; Stuttgart: Verlag Katholisches Bibelwerk, 1988). See

est in the heavenly world that is typical of most apocalypses. For these reasons, I do not specifically analyze Dan 4. The tree imagery used in Dan 4 is discussed, however, in chapter three. Daniel's tree imagery is helpful for understanding the tree imagery in 4QFour Kingdoms^{a-b} ar and the *Book of the Words of Noah*.

On the other end of the spectrum, 4 Ezra is excluded from this study because of its late date (late first century C.E.).[32] The same is true for 2 Baruch. Like 4 Ezra, 2 Baruch presumes the fall of Jerusalem in 70 C.E. (chapters 1–9 detail the fall of Jerusalem).[33] It is possible that 4 Ezra served as a source for 2 Baruch.[34]

Some texts that do not fall outside the period 333–63 B.C.E. are not analyzed individually. There are several texts from Qumran that *may* be literary apocalypses, but so little remains of them that generic classification is highly problematic. These texts include 4QWords of Michael ar (4Q529, 6Q23), 4QVision^a ar (4Q556), 4QpapVision^b ar (4Q558), 4QVision^c ar (4Q557), 4QHistorical Text A (4Q248), 4QapocrDan ar (4Q246), and the *Book of Giants* (the dream of Hahyah).[35] While these texts are not analyzed individually, several of them are discussed in my analysis of other texts.

Finally, I do not analyze the *Book of Jubilees* or the *Apocalypse of Weeks* (*1 En.* 93 + 91:11–17) systematically. There is disagreement over whether or not the *Book of Jubilees* should be described as an apocalypse.[36] The only book-length study of the genre of *Jubilees* concludes that it is an apocalypse that attempts to turn the genre apocalypse on its head by using the literary framework of apocalypses to express a significantly divergent worldview.[37] There is no confusion about the genre of the *Apocalypse of*

---

also L. M. Wills, *The Jew in the Court of the Foreign King* (Minneapolis: Fotress, 1990). Timothy McLay, "The Old Greek Translation of Daniel IV–VI and the Formation of the Book of Daniel," *VT* 55 (2005).

[32] Stone dates the composition to the time of Domitian (81–96 CE) – most likely towards the end of his reign. See Michael Stone, *Fourth Ezra* (Hermeneia; Minneapolis: Fortress, 1994), 9–10.

[33] George Nickelsburg, Jewish Literature between the Bible and the Mishnah: A Historical and Literary Introduction (Philadelphia: Fortress, 1981), 280–7. Gwendolyn Sayler, *Have the Promises Failed: A Literary Analysis of 2 Baruch* (SBLDS; Chico: Scholars Press, 1984).

[34] Cf. Stone, *Fourth Ezra*, 39–40.

[35] Cf. Lange and Mittmann-Richert, "Annotated List of the Texts from the Judean Desert Classified by Genre and Content," 120–1. Collins, "Apocalypticism and Literary Genre in the Dead Sea Scrolls," 403–30. Frey, "Die Bedeutung der Qumrantexte für das Verständnis der Apokalyptik im Frühjudentum und im Urchristentum," 11–62.

[36] Collins, *The Apocalyptic Imagination*, 79–84. Christopher Rowland, *The Open Heaven: A Study of Apocalyptic in Judaism and Early Christianity* (New York: Crossroad, 1982), 51–2. Armin Lange, "Divinatorische Träume und Apokalyptik im Jubiläenbuch," in *Studies in the Book of Jubilees* (ed. Matthias Albani, et al.; Tübingen: Mohr Siebeck, 1997), 25–38.

[37] Hanneken, "The Book of Jubilees among the Apocalypses".

Weeks.³⁸ These texts are excluded primarily for reasons of space.³⁹

A second major limitation of this study is specifically related to the type of data I mine from individual apocalypses. I analyze the expressions used to describe historical actors in the historical reviews, i.e., deities, angels/demons, and humans (both individuals and groups). I choose the category of historical actor because it is consistently represented in all early Jewish apocalypses. Other types of data, such as geographical locales, might also be fruitful.⁴⁰ But they provide a less complete data set for a student who wants to cover the entire genre.

Methodology

This study analyzes the language of Jewish historical apocalypses. The primary methodologies used to do this are linguistic- and motif-historical analysis. In other words, for each expression used to describe a historical actor, I analyze how that term is used 1) within the particular text, 2) within the genre apocalypse in general, and 3) in other Israelite/Jewish and ancient Near Eastern/ancient Mediterranean literature. In some cases, it is necessary to go beyond how a particular expression is used and investigate the literary motif within which the term is embedded. Only by considering the full semantic range of each description is it possible to accurately assess how they function within their individual contexts. Moreover, it is only by considering the full semantic range of each description that one is able to see the linguistic patterns that emerge across the genre apocalypse. For example, if one focuses only on how the "little horn" of Dan 7 refers to Antiochus IV Epiphanes or how the ram with the large horn in the *Animal Apocalypse* refers to Judas Maccabeus, one would miss the larger scheme in which animals are consistently used to describe humans in symbolic apocalypses. In other words, there are at least two levels of symbolism in the text. This observation is important because it recognizes the linguistic constraints placed on a given writer who wants to describe a human being in symbolic cipher. The categorical association animal=human is always

---

³⁸ Collins, *The Apocalyptic Imagination*, 62–5. James C. VanderKam, *Enoch and the Growth of an Apocalyptic Tradition* (vol. 16; Washington, D.C.: Catholic Biblical Association, 1984), 141–60. On the inclusion of *1 En.* 91 with 93, see Matthew Black, "The Apocalypse of Weeks in the Light of 4QEn^g" *VT* 28 (1978).

³⁹ For a preliminary statement about the non-symbolic nature of the language of *Jub.*, see Lange, "Dream Visions and Apocalyptic Milieus," 27–34.

⁴⁰ In this regard, see Maria Leppäkari, *Apocalyptic Representations of Jerusalem* (111; Leiden: Brill, 2006). Daniel Machiela, "Each to His Own Inheritance: Geography as an Evaluative Tool in the Genesis Apocryphon," *DSD* 15 (2008): 50–66.

prior to the choice of which particular animal a writer might use to describe a particular human.

More specialized methodological procedures are carried out at relevant junctures. These include redaction criticism (i.e., source criticism, the attempt to separate originally distinct literary layers), paleography (the analysis of ancient handwriting to date ancient documents), and textual criticism (the endeavor to reach the [most] original version of a text by evaluating extant witnesses).

A History of Research

In this research history I review scholarly conceptions of the language found in early Jewish apocalypses. Since Lange and Mittmann-Richert's call to formally distinguish between non-symbolic and symbolic apocalypses came only in 2002, and since little has been said about it since then, this history of the research is largely one-sided. The first scholars whose work I analyze had no access to the Dead Sea Scrolls. Thus, they never knew a stand-alone non-symbolic apocalypse. They only had access to non-symbolic apocalypses that were parts of literary works that included symbolic apocalypses (perhaps *Sibylline Oracles 3* forms an exception to this rule).

From Lücke to Koch

Critical studies of apocalypses began with Friedrich Lücke's *Versuch einer vollständigen Einleitung in die Offenbarung des Johannes* [Towards a Comprehensive Introduction to the Apocalypse of John], published in 1832. Lücke took the word ἀποκάλυψις from the title of the New Testament Apocalypse of John and used it as a generic term to describe an entire body of texts originally and primarily produced by Jews in the Hellenistic period. Thus, Lücke coined the term "apocalypse" as it is used today. His main arguments about apocalypses still enjoy consensus support in the Academy though, unlike Wellhausen's work on the Pentateuch and Noth's work on the Deuteronomistic History, he is more rarely credited. Lücke believed that *Apokalyptik*[41] was a natural outgrowth of Israelite prophecy. While modern scholars would prefer to see a slightly more nuanced picture of the

---

[41] John Collins has made clear that the word apocalyptic should not and cannot be used as a noun in English. When discussing the work of earlier scholars, however, I keep the terminology used by each individual scholar (for German authors, the noun *Apokalyptik*, and for English authors, the adjective "apocalyptic" in quotation marks). This prevents more recent concepts from being applied anachronistically to older works.

origins of apocalypticism, most agree that the main stream was Israelite prophecy.[42] He also saw eschatology as the leading motif of apocalypses.[43] Tord Olsson construes his most important legacy to be Lücke's emphasis on history:

His emphasis on a particular conception of history as the essential basis of apocalypticism and from which its other characteristics can be generated: visionary form and symbolism, apocalyptic time measuring, pseudonymity, its learned and artificial style, and the conception of an *angelus interpres*.[44]

Lücke's conception of history is of interest to this study – particularly as it affects his understanding of symbolism in apocalypses. He viewed the *Apokalyptiker* as analogous to the prophet. For him apocalypses were not products of communities or schools of thought but products of the solitary, inspired *Apokalyptiker*. In contradistinction to people who view history in three divisions (past, present, and future), the *Apokalyptiker* viewed history as a unity:[45] "*Weder die Zukunft noch die Vergangenheit des göttlichen Reiches liegt für den Apokalyptiker ausserhalb der geschichtlichen Wirklichkeit, sondern in derselben, aber in dem, was in dieser Wirklichkeit das Wahre und Wesentliche, gleichsam der Kern ist, nicht irgendwie Erscheinungsschale.*"[46] Lücke believed that the *Apokalyptiker* saw history as God saw history – a manner he describes as "*wo die zeitlose Wesenheit der Zukunft des göttlichen Reiches mit der zeitlich nach Jahr und Tag*

---

[42] Two influential studies in this regard are Osten-Sacken, *Die Apokalyptik* and Hanson, *The Dawn of Apocalyptic*.

[43] The same thought can be found in Hanson, *The Dawn of Apocalyptic*. Collins, "Apocalypse: The Morphology of a Genre." Collins, *The Apocalyptic Imagination*, 11–2.

[44] Tord Olsson, "The Apocalyptic Activity. The Case of Jamasp Namag," in *Apocalypticism in the Mediterranean World and the Near East: Proceedings of the International Colloquium on Apocalypticism, Uppsala, August 12–17, 1979* (ed. David Hellholm; Tübingen: Mohr Siebeck, 1983), 22–3.

[45] Whether or not ancient Israelites or Second Temple Jews would have viewed history precisely in terms of past, present, and future is unclear. Indeed, "history" itself may be an anachronistic category. John Van Seeters has argued that the Pentateuch should be understood as ancient historiography in the same way that most scholars understand Herodotus to be. For a succinct statement, see John Van Seters, "The Pentateuch," in *The Hebrew Bible Today: An Introduction to Critical Issues* (ed. Steven McKenzie and M. Patrick Graham; Louisville: WJK, 1998), 12. For a more robust treatment, see John Van Seters, *Prologue to History: The Yahwist as Historian in Genesis* (Louisville: Westminser John Knox, 1992). Reading the Pentateuch as ancient historiography, does not, however imply that all of the material involved is historically accurate. Van Seters makes this point emphatically in John Van Seters, *Abraham in History and Tradition* (New Haven: Yale University Press, 1975).

[46] [Neither the future nor the past of the divine realm lies outside of historical reality for the *Apokalyptiker,* rather they are the same [lit. "but in the same"], but what is true and essential in this reality is, as it were, the kernel, not somehow only an empty shell.] Friedrich Lücke, *Versuch einer vollständigen Einleitung in die Offenbarung des Johannes* (Bonn: Eduard Weber, 1852), 37.

bestimmten geschichtlichen Erscheinung zusammenliegt."[47] It is from this divinely inspired view of history that symbolic representation derives. Lücke also believed the *Apokalyptiker* had real, visionary experiences that fleshed out his divinely inspired view of history:

> Der Apokalyptiker, wie in der Vergangenheit, so auch in der Gegenwart und Zukunft des göttlichen Reiches alles einzelne Wirkliche, was er erkennt und anschauet, zu einem, ihm von Gott gewiessenen, andeutenden Erscheinungsbilde, Symbol, von der ganzen Wahrheit und Wesentlichkeit der göttlichen Reichsgeschichte macht, oder, anders ausgedrückt, zum Stücke der Curve, worin die ganze Bahn des göttlichen Reiches für ihn abgebildet ist und worin er diese prophetisch anshauet.[48]

For Lücke, the less clearly an *Apokalyptiker* understood the history revealed to him, the more symbolic his speech became. His symbolic speech was not, however, a covering for history unknown. Quite the opposite: "Je mehr seine Darstellung symbolisch poëtischer Art ist, desto mehr wird sie unbewusst das wahre Sachverhältniss ausdrücken."[49]

The modern theorist would quickly isolate several of Lücke's catchwords, *e.g.*, *Wahre* and *Wesentliche*. Words like "true" and "essential" certainly reflect his historical location. Like virtually any other *Bibelwissenschaftlicher* of his time, he attempted to pare away what he saw as superfluous in biblical (or other ancient) texts and find their essential core. Postmodern theorists have warned us well enough to be wary of those who might peel the layers in search of the "true" onion. But the fact that Lücke's mental categories were inherited from the Enlightenment is no reason to ignore him.

The main interest for this study is Lücke's conception of the language in apocalypses. In the strictest sense, he does not understand there to be any particular representation techniques at work. In other words, the visionary him/herself has very little agency. The use of symbols is not, for example, a literary technique, but a plain and honest reflection of the visionary reality imparted by God. The symbols are not products of the writer's creativity,

---

[47] [Where the timeless character of the future of the divine realm is united with the historical phenomenon of time measured by year and day.] Lücke, *Versuch einer vollständigen Einleitung in die Offenbarung des Johannes*, 37.

[48] [The *Apokalyptiker*, as in the past, so also transforms in the present and future of the divine realm every individual reality that he recognizes and intuits into an apparent image shown to him by God, a symbol, of the entire truth and essence of the history of the divine realm, in other words, [into] the piece of the curve, in which the whole path of the divine realm is mapped out for him and in which he intuits this path in a prophetic manner.] Lücke, *Versuch einer vollständigen Einleitung in die Offenbarung des Johannes*, 38. Thanks to Jonathan Hess for helping to improve this translation.

[49] [The more its portrayal/representation is (of a) symbolic-poetic sort, the more it will unconsciously express the genuine facts.] Lücke, *Versuch einer vollständigen Einleitung in die Offenbarung des Johannes*, 38.

education, conventions, or even his ineptitude at describing reality. Instead one might say that for Lücke the divine view of history that the *Apokalyptiker* experiences is akin to a mural. Individual pieces with individual meanings can be picked out, but the more important concern is how they all work together to form a large – even overwhelming – picture at large. The *Apokalyptiker* uses symbolic language not because he cannot understand individual parts of history but because his grand vista necessitates that they be described in a way that does justice to the whole.

Twenty-five years after Lücke's large tome appeared, Adolf Hilgenfeld concurred that the symbolic ciphers found in apocalypses were products of actual visionary experiences.[50] He also agreed that the use of symbolic ciphers was a ubiquitous feature of apocalypses. He treated the meaning of the symbols at length, but in doing so made the crucial mistake not to distinguish between actual symbolic ciphers and other figures of speech that are not symbolic.[51] In other words, for Hilgenfeld there is no distinction between terms like "king of the south" in Dan 11:40 and "little horn" in Dan 7:8. Both are descriptions of earthly rulers, but I suggest below that the language is significantly different. Hilgenfeld never gives a formal definition of symbolic, but it appears to mean "cryptic" for him. I hope to show that such a conception, while common, misses many of the nuances pregnant in the language of ancient Jewish apocalypses.

R.H. Charles was the first to make a major contribution to the study of apocalypses in the English language. Like Lücke and Hilgenfeld, Charles's view of the visionary (Lücke's *Apokalyptiker*) was central to his understanding of apocalypses. He agreed with Lücke that the visionary was closely related to the prophet and used the very same methods to secure knowledge: dreams, visions, trances, spiritual communion with God. Of these methods Charles writes: "These are *physical experiences, and reflection or rather reason embracing the powers of insight, imagination, and judgment.*[52] Of the reality of such experiences, he goes on to claim, "no modern psychologist entertains a doubt."[53]

Like Lücke, Charles did not really view the language of apocalypses as governed by learned literary conventions. For Charles symbolic description involved human attempts to describe the ineffable. Lücke believed that the visionary would describe things precisely as seen and those images natural-

---

[50] Adolf Hilgenfeld, *Die jüdische Apokalyptik in ihrer geschichtlichen Entwickelung: Ein Beitrag zur Vorgeschichte des Christenthums nebst einem Anhange über das gnostische System des Basilides* (Jena: Friedrich Mauke, 1857).

[51] Hilgenfeld, *Die jüdische Apokalyptik in ihrer geschichtlichen Entwickelung*, 30.

[52] R. H. Charles, *A Critical and Exegetical Commentary on The Revelation of St. John* (1975 [1920]: T&T Clark, 1920), civ. (Charles's emphasis)

[53] Charles, *A Critical and Exegetical Commentary on The Revelation of St. John*, cv.

ly appeared "symbolic" to other humans. It seems that Charles understood there to be more of an active "image-translation" in the writing of the apocalyptic visionary. Charles believed that the visionary was limited in his ability to understand fully a heavenly vision and equally limited in his ability to describe the few things that he did understand from the heavenly vision. He thus employed symbolism as a literary convention of last resort. Charles also concurs with Lücke and Hilgenfeld (and virtually every scholar that follows) that symbolic representation is ubiquitous in apocalypses: "Hence in his literary presentment of what he has seen and heard in the moments of transcendent rapture, the images he uses are symbolic and not literal or pictorial. In fact, symbolism in regard to such subjects is the only language that seer and layman alike can employ."[54]

Interest in apocalypses continued in England with the work of H. H. Rowley. He, like Lücke and Charles, saw a connection between prophecy and apocalypticism, but did not share their strong emphasis on the individual visionary as analogous to the prophet. In particular, he pointed out that the short, terse oracles common to Israelite prophecy are quite different from the extended accounts of apocalyptic visionaries.[55] For Rowley, the genre apocalypse begins properly with the Book of Daniel and was inextricably tied to the upheavals of the Maccabean period.[56]

Rowley represents a new stage in the evolving conceptions of the language of ancient Jewish apocalypses. He considered the use of symbolic language to be a literary technique. In other words, Rowley inserts a bit more of the visionary into the vision. Rowley's visionary has some agency in the process of writing his/her texts. Unlike Lücke, who believed that symbolic language was the presentation of what a visionary actually saw, or Charles who saw symbolic language as a sort of translation of the visionary's experience, Rowley believed that symbolic language was deliberately woven into the fabric of the vision in order to accomplish particular purposes. He understood symbolic language as a "safe" means of encoding a critique of a contemporary power. Symbolic language could help to prevent reprieve from those under critique. He provides an illuminating example from his own time:

We have but to remember that a newspaper in German-occupied Paris during the war published a poem which read superficially as an attack on Britain and in praise of Germany. But divided vertically and red in two stanzas, the meaning was precisely reversed. It would be no harder to whisper the clue in Palestine than in Paris, and

---

[54] Charles, *A Critical and Exegetical Commentary on The Revelation of St. John*, cvii.
[55] H.H. Rowley, *The Relevance of Apocalyptic* (London: Lutterworth Press, 1964 [1944]), See 15–16.
[56] Rowley, *The Relevance of Apocalyptic*, 43.

probably no harder to get past the friends of Antiochus than to get past the Paris censorship.[57]

Rowley's opinion is still influential today and popular opinion still understands the symbolic language of some apocalypses as a mode of protection from political enemies. For example, Paul Hanson's influential study, *The Dawn of Apocalyptic*, draws similar conclusions.[58] Indeed, political scientist James C. Scott's notion of the "hidden transcript" in his classic study of resistance implicitly suggests that one should read the language of apocalypses in this way.[59] Other contemporaries of Rowley voiced different opinions concerning the impetus for the literary devices used in apocalypses.

Martin Noth presumed that writing apocalypses required a significant education in world history. The manifest historical errors made by those who wrote apocalypses cause contemporary scholars to be a bit more hesitant, but he makes a provocative suggestion: apocalyptic visionaries were trained not only in history but also trained to use a particular mode of symbolic representation. Noth held, "Die Apokalyptik hat zunächst allerlei zu ihrer Zeit kursierenden Stoff an Weltzeitalter- und Weltreich-Vorstellungen aufgenommen, vielleicht auch allerlei Stoff an Symbolen für geschichtliche Erscheinungen und Mächte."[60] For Noth as for Rowley, the language of apocalypses had nothing whatever to do with visionary experiences. The language of apocalypses instead reflected, for them, the kinds of literary conventions used by educated professionals. The authors of apocalypses might not have ever experienced dream visions, but they used the literary form of dream visions to accomplish their purposes.

Gerhard von Rad devoted a mere fifteen pages to *"Apokalyptik und Daniel"* in his nearly 1,000 page *magnum opus*, *Old Testament Theology*.[61] While he does not linger about the language of apocalypses, his work is noteworthy for this study. Von Rad parted company with most other scholars by declaring that *Apokaplyptik* did not spring from Israelite Prophecy,

---

[57] Rowley, *The Relevance of Apocalyptic*, 50.

[58] Cf. Hanson, *The Dawn of Apocalyptic*, 252.

[59] James C. Scott, *Domination and the Arts of Resistance: Hidden Transcripts* (New Haven: Yale University Press, 1990). See broader discussion of Scott and his relevance for ancient Jewish apocalypses in Anathea Portier-Young, *Apocalypse Against Empire: Theologies of Resistance in Early Judaism* (Grand Rapids: Eermans, 2011), esp. 31–45.

[60] [*Apokalyptik* initially took up all kinds of contemporary circulating material on world age- and world empire-notions, perhaps also all kinds of material on symbols for historical phenomena and powers.] Martin Noth, *Das Geschichtsverständnis der altestestamentlichen Apokalyptik* (Geisteswissenschaften 21; Köln: Westdeutscher Verlag, 1954), 25.

[61] Gerhard von Rad, *Old Testament Theology: The Theology of Israel's Prophetic Tradition* (trans. trans. D. Stalker; vol. II; New York: Harper & Row, 1965), 301–15.

but from Israelite Wisdom.⁶² Von Rad's desire to see close links between *Apokalyptik* and Wisdom led him to link the literary conventions found in many apocalypses to "figurative discourses" or מְשָׁלִים, a form of teaching traditional to Wisdom.⁶³ The merits of his proposal about "figurative discourses" are not a primary concern. What is important to note is that von Rod's conception of the language of apocalypses continues to follow the scholarly trend that began with Rowley and Noth, i.e., von Rad views the language of apocalypses as learned and conventional. Beyond the use of "figurative discourses" von Rad found other ways in which the language of apocalypse was to be distinguished from the language of prophecy. He saw one such distinction in their varying strategies for describing history:

> The prophets certainly used allegorical code to present historical events of a certain kind (Is. VIII. 5–8, Ezek. XVII 1ff., XXXI. 1ff.): but what they dealt with was isolated events in history, whereas apocalyptic literature tries to take the whole historical process together and objectify it conceptually. To this end it reduced the endlessly varied shapes and forms of history to a number of relatively simple allegorical and symbolical representations.⁶⁴

Von Rad provides a good description of symbolic apocalypses to the extent that he highlights how limited and stable the linguistic repertoire of the writers of ancient Jewish apocalypses was. But von Rad's position fails to explain all the data. Texts like Dan 10–12, *Apocryphon of Jeremiah C*, and 4QPsDan^{a-b} ar cannot be explained by this model of apocalyptic language. To von Rad's credit, he only knew about the first of these texts.

A final important point from von Rad about the language of apocalypses is that the literary conventions used by the writers of apocalypses make some apocalypses malleable and easily appropriated for different times and purposes. While he held that the symbolic ciphers used in Daniel originally referred to particular people or entities, he believed the referents of some symbols changed even within the literary development of the Book of Daniel itself (and certainly in later interpretation). For von Rad, the earliest versions of the Daniel literature's four-kingdom scenario culminated with Alexander the Great. Later the system was adjusted to describe Antiochus

---

⁶² Von Rad's position is well known and often described. His main critique is that the respective conceptions of history in Prophecy and *Apokalyptik* are irreconcilable. See Rad, *Old Testament Theology*, esp., 303–08. Criticisms of von Rad have become more muted since scholars have recognized that the origin of apocalypses cannot be expressed in "either/or" terms. For example, Hans Peter Müller has outlined the important connection between features of apocalypses and Near Eastern mantic wisdom and his argument has been widely accepted. Cf. Hans Peter Müller, "Magisch-mantische Weisheit und die Gestalt Daniels," *UF* 1 (1969): 79–94.

⁶³ Rad, *Old Testament Theology*, 306.

⁶⁴ Rad, *Old Testament Theology*, 304–5.

IV Epiphanes.⁶⁵ Which particular earthly kingdom is described can change with the times – a convenient ambiguity perhaps intentionally worked into the symbolic system.

Three important monographs appeared after von Rad's *Old Testament Theology* and each criticized his view of *Apokalyptik*.⁶⁶ They emphasized the prophetic roots of *Apokalyptik* and singled out eschatology as an issue with which von Rad had not adequately dealt. The two most influential books were Peter von der Osten-Sacken's brief monograph *Die Apkalyptik in ihrem Verhältnis zu Prophetie und Weisheit* and Paul Hanson's *The Dawn of Apocalyptic*.⁶⁷ But these two works do not deal specifically with the language of apocalypses.⁶⁸ The third notable response to von Rad, D. S. Russell's *The Method and Message of Jewish Apocalyptic*, was less influential but it specifically treats the language of apocalypses. Russell's connection of "apocalyptic" and prophecy is less sophisticated than either von der Osten-Sacken's or Hanson's. His overall discussion of what he calls "apocalyptic" is, however, broader and addresses many more questions than do theirs.

Russell concurs with many of his forebears who conclude that symbolic language is an essential part of apocalypses: "The apocalyptists give full reign to their imaginations in extravagant and exotic language and in imagery of a fantastic and bizarre kind. To such an extent is this true that *symbolism may be said to be the language of apocalyptic.*"⁶⁹ Russell's statement highlights several concerns. The most significant is the presumption that all apocalypses are by definition symbolic. In order to reach his conclusion about symbolic language in apocalypses, he must go along with Hilgenfeld's treatment of terms such as "king of the north" from Dan 10–12 as symbolic.⁷⁰ It is important to mention that, unlike most of the scholars

---

⁶⁵ Rad, *Old Testament Theology*, 311.

⁶⁶ It bears repeating that I represent the work of scholars in this history of research by using their own words. Some of those words are now considered imprecise. For example, I would prefer to use the word "apocalypse" here, but that is not all that von Rad meant to indicate when he used the term Apokalyptik.

⁶⁷ Osten-Sacken, *Die Apkalyptik*. Hanson, *The Dawn of Apocalyptic: The Historical and Sociological Roots of Jewish Apocalyptic Eschatology*.

⁶⁸ Hanson later gave some attention to the issue in two dictionary entries: Paul Hanson, "Apocalypse, Genre," in *The Interpreter's Dictionary of the Bible, Supplementary Volume* (ed. Keith Crim; Nashville: Abingdon, 1976), 27–8. Paul Hanson, "Apocalypticism," in *The Interpreter's Dictionary of the Bible, Supplementary Volume* (ed. Keith Crim; Nashville: Abingdon, 1976), 28–34.

⁶⁹ Russell, *The Method and Message of Jewish Apocalyptic*, 122. My emphasis.

⁷⁰ Hilgenfeld, *Die jüdische Apokalyptik in ihrer geschichtlichen Entwickelung: Ein Beitrag zur Vorgeschichte des Christenthums nebst einem Anhange über das gnostische System des Basilides*, 30. Russell never actually cites Hilgenfeld. My connection of their positions is merely a logical one.

discussed thus far, Russell actually had some access to the Qumran library. He provides descriptions of fifteen scrolls, including what he calls the "Pseudo-Daniel Apocalypse" (i.e., 4QpsDan^{a-b} ar). My discussion of Dan 10–12 in chapter four and 4QpsDan^{a-b} ar in chapter six will insist, contra Russell, that symbolism is not always the language of apocalypse.

Russell concurs with Lücke, Hilgenfeld, and Charles that the symbols found in apocalypses are in one way or the other products of actual, visionary experiences had by individuals. The symbols are the only means by which visionaries could express the ineffable. Russell differs, however, in that he believed that actual visions or auditions are only partly responsible for the symbolic language in apocalypses.

Russell believed that "apocalyptic," unlike prophecy, was a literary phenomenon from its inception (thus, he is not in total disagreement with Rowley, Noth, and von Rad). Whether or not a robust oral apocalyptic tradition ever existed in Judea is difficult to know. One can observe that books like *1 Enoch* and Daniel are collections of books that came together over a period of time.[71] Other stories like the *Book of Giants*, *Bel and the Dragon*, *Susanna,* and 4QpsDan^{a-b} ar attest to an active and dynamic tradition of story-telling about the figures who dominate early Jewish apocalypses. Russell holds that while part of the explanation for apocalyptic symbols is to be found in actual visionary experiences, the primary influence derives from, "stereotyped language and symbols which belonged to a fairly well-defined tradition whose roots went back into the distant past."[72] It is difficult to parse Russell's statement since he never defines "symbolic," but his contention that apocalyptic symbols are a literary phenomenon rooted in historical usage is almost certainly correct.

Russell's description of the language of apocalypses begs the question: From which "fairly well-defined tradition" do the "stereotyped language and symbols" of Jewish apocalypses derive? We have seen that Noth already speculated about this and von Rad attempted to provide some explanation for it. Unfortunately, Russell does not adequately answer this question. He ultimately describes the language of Jewish apocalypses as "allegorical." Russell follows the lead of Hermann Gunkel's *Schöpfung und Chaos in Urzeit und Endzeit* in this regard.[73] There is nothing wrong with proposing that Israelite and Jewish literature borrows from earlier Near Eastern myths – sometimes allegorizing myths or even re-allegorizing allegories. Such practices can be readily conceded. Gunkel's methodology is

---

[71] Collins, *Daniel*, 1–70. George Nickelsburg, *1 Enoch 1* (Minneapolis: Fortress Press, 2001), 21–36.

[72] Russell, *The Method and Message of Jewish Apocalyptic*, 122.

[73] Gunkel, *Schöpfung und Chaos in Urzeit und Endzeit*, esp., 41–69.

still valid even if the particular connections he drew between texts like Daniel and Mesopotamian chaos myths are not. The problem is, as modern literary theorists have discovered, that the appropriation of a myth allegorically or the re-appropriation of an allegory is not the same thing as using a symbol or a symbolic system. The former depends on a minimum level of knowledge about the original myth or allegory and maintains the framework of the older story. The latter does not. Moreover, not all apocalypses retell or appropriate older myths. None of the apocalypses I treat in part two of this study can be described as allegories. The way in which Russell situates his discussion of the language of apocalypses within the methodological framework of Gunkel's *Schöpfung und Chaos* is important, however, because it continues to provide the standard methodological framework. One may note, for example, that Collins's discussion of language in *The Apocalyptic Imagination* follows the same pattern (see more below).[74] I do not suggest here a problem with Collins' work. I only seek to point out that there are multiple layers of representation and that language as plot/motif is categorically different than language as poetics.

From Koch to Collins

According to Klaus Koch, the study of "apocalyptic" was brought into the mainstream of Continental scholarship by Ernst Käsemann's 1960 essay, "The Beginnings of Christian Theology."[75] It was the translation of Koch's *Ratlos vor der Apokalyptik*, however, that transformed the study of apocalypses in the English speaking world. His primary contribution was to expose Christian embarrassment over the possibility that Jesus was apocalyptic in his life and thought.[76] A second major contribution was his insistence that if scholars were to understand what was apocalyptic about apocalypses, "A starting point in form criticism and literary and linguistic history is, in the nature of things, the only one possible."[77]

Koch outlined six features integral to the literary type "apocalypse." Koch's fifth feature is of primary interest to this study: "The language takes on a concealed meaning by means of *mythical images rich in symbolism*."[78] Koch discerns a system that he describes as follows: "The forces of world-time are reduced to their outstanding basic characteristics, appearing as

---

[74] Collins, *The Apocalyptic Imagination*, 14–21.
[75] Klaus Koch, *The Rediscovery of Apocalyptic: A Polemical Work on a Neglected Area of Biblical Studies and its Damaging Effects on Theology and Philosophy* (SBT 22; Naperville, Ill.: Alec Allenson, 1970), 14.
[76] Koch, *The Rediscovery of Apocalyptic*, 54–97.
[77] Koch, *The Rediscovery of Apocalyptic*, 23.
[78] Koch, *The Rediscovery of Apocalyptic*, 23.

dangerous, often unnaturally degenerate beasts or as huge trees or rushing waters. The people of God and their leaders are also depicted correspondingly as land or lion or vine."[79] For Koch, the basis of the symbol system is to be located in the Hebrew Bible itself. The writers of apocalypses represented particular entities with particular symbols because of the ability of those symbols to represent the "outstanding basic characteristics" of their referents. Thus, when Koch says "symbol," he means metonym or metaphor. He does not make a judgment about whether or not symbols might be meant to re-mythologize long de-mythologized aspects of religion, but he does hypothesize that symbolic language of apocalypses "suggests a particular linguistic training, perhaps even a particular mentality."[80] In this respect Koch agrees with Noth and von Rad. I intend to join Koch in arguing that the writers of apocalypses appear to have used symbols not randomly, but systematically. I also agree with Koch that, to some extent, the symbolic system has antecedents in texts from the Hebrew Bible. I disagree with Koch on other counts. First, I disagree that the symbolic system he highlights is an essential feature of all apocalypses. I also disagree that the symbols are essentially metaphors.

Paul Hanson's *The Dawn of Apocalyptic* is his most influential work on apocalypses, but he also produced a series of short articles in the New Interpreter's Dictionary of the Bible that are more relevant to this section of the research history. Whereas *The Dawn of Apocalyptic* was primarily concerned with the origins of "apocalyptic" in post exilic prophecy, his IDB articles are more concerned with the linguistic features of apocalypses.

Hanson discusses the genre apocalypse by selecting an exemplar text and then finding other texts that share a large number of features. Like Lücke he selects the New Testament Apocalypse of John as his exemplar on the grounds that it is "the work originally designated apocalypse in antiquity."[81] This move is implicitly criticized by John Collins in his *The Apocalyptic Imagination*. For Collins, the title of a work cannot be substituted for generic classification.[82] In other words, just because a work is titled "apocalypse" does not mean it is one.[83] Even though the modern generic classification "apocalypse" is derived from Lücke's discussion of Revelation, it is not the first (or second, or third, etc.) apocalypse that was written in antiquity. In spite of his methodological slip, many of the "typical features" of

---

[79] Koch, *The Rediscovery of Apocalyptic*, 26.

[80] Koch, *The Rediscovery of Apocalyptic*, 27.

[81] Hanson, "Apocalypse, Genre," 27.

[82] Collins, *The Apocalyptic Imagination*, 3–5.

[83] While this statement might seem imperialistic or dismissive of categories the ancients themselves used, see Thomas Beebee, *The Ideology of Genre: A Comparative Study of Generic Instability* (University Park, PA: Penn State University Press, 1994).

apocalypses that Hanson outlines are useful. Of particular interest to this study is that he shares with Koch the opinion that symbolism is a key feature of apocalypses. Perhaps of even greater interest is that he, unlike most other scholars, acknowledges that symbolic language is not ubiquitous: "Not only is there latitude for either 'direct' description of heavenly events or symbolic description, but the disclosure can occur in a vision or in rapture (or . . . in a dream)."[84] Hanson is, as far as I know, the first scholar to mention the possibility of non-symbolic language in an apocalypse. Unfortunately, he does not pursue this line of thought further except in his attempt to explain the *Sitz im Leben* of apocalypses: "Most of the apocalypses mentioned above seem to stem from settings of persecution within which they reveal to the faithful a vision of reversal and glorification. This is made possible by concentration on heavenly realities, whether given in the form of symbols or in purported direct description."[85] The relative dates of the symbolic and non-symbolic apocalypses make such a claim problematic.

While Koch's survey of the most prominent features of apocalypses included "mythical images rich in symbolism,"[86] and Hanson's list of essential features included "symbolism," John Collins's highly influential "master-paradigm" of the generic features of apocalypses contains nothing about language.[87] Unlike virtually every scholar that precedes him, Collins does not describe symbolic language as a primary constitutive element of apocalypses. In the first instance, this stems from Collins's refusal to mix form and content in his definition. But in order to fully explain the absence of symbolism from Collins's definition, it is necessary to examine a monograph published by Collins two years before his *Semeia* volume. A reading of Collins's *The Apocalyptic Vision of the Book of Daniel* shows that for him, the use of symbols in early Jewish apocalypses is a matter that illumines the motif- and tradition-histories of apocalypses, but not their conventional framework. Thus his "master paradigm" speaks only of "revelation by means of visions" as an essential feature, without further characterizing it.[88] I have already mentioned that Collins adopts Russell's model (e.g., Gunkel's methodology) for understanding the language of apocalypses.

---

[84] Hanson, "Apocalypse, Genre," 27.
[85] Hanson, "Apocalypse, Genre," 28.
[86] Koch, *The Rediscovery of Apocalyptic*, 23.
[87] John J. Collins, "Introduction: Towards the Morphology of a Genre," in *Semeia 14* (ed. John J. Collins; Missoula: Scholars Press, 1979), 6. The "master paradigm" was developed in conjunction with others in the apocalypse group of the SBL Genres Project.
[88] Collins, "Towards the Morphology," 6.

In his *Apocalyptic Vision of the Book of Daniel*, Collins devotes two chapters to the symbols used in the Book of Daniel. He describes Dan 7 and 8 as allegorical vision accounts "formulated in traditional language, much of which is drawn ultimately from ancient Near Eastern mythology."[89] For Collins, the symbols of the beasts in Daniel "acquire their force and richness from their traditional associations."[90] He borrows Peter Wheelwright's words to describe the symbols in Daniel as: "symbols of ancestral vitality."[91]

Collins finds that the use of particular symbols in individual apocalypses owes to the particular Canaanite or Near Eastern myths that they allegorize.[92] While I agree that some of the symbols and mythological scenarios found in ancient Jewish apocalypses are reflexes of Canaanite or Near Eastern myths, I have reservations about this approach. It tends to treat each individual apocalypse by looking for its individual "parent" text or tradition and presumes that every apocalypse is an allegory of an ancient Canaanite or ancient Near Eastern myth. While the approach works well with Dan 7 or 8, it fails when one treats other apocalypses such as Dan 10–12. In what follows, I examine Collins's arguments and attempt to show why his conception of the language of apocalypses – while highly insightful – leaves room for further investigation.

In his treatment of the symbols found in the Book of Daniel, Collins treats Dan 7 as an allegory based on the Canaanite combat myth. I stipulate that he is correct in his assessment. He is probably also correct that, despite its similarities with chapter 7, Dan 8 appropriates a different myth.[93] He locates that myth in Isa 14. In the oracle against the king of Babylon in Isa 14, the figure of הֵילֵל בֶּן־שָׁחַר, "Day-star, son of Dawn," attempts to ascend to the heavens above the stars, set up a throne, and sit in the assembly on *Zaphon*. He is foiled, however, and falls to *sheol*. Some speculate that the text may have originated as a gibe against Sargon II, but I believe Collins is correct that it contains themes familiar to Canaanite mythology. I treat the myth more extensively in chapter two below, but mention for now that

---

[89] John J. Collins, *The Apocalyptic Vision of the Book of Daniel* (HSM 16; Missoula: Scholars Press, 1977), 95.

[90] It is telling that Richard Clifford, who makes the same argument, uses *only* Dan 7 to illustrate it. Clifford's arguments about Dan 7 are perfectly reasonable, but his extrapolation of his results to apply to all early Jewish apocalypses is problematic. Richard Clifford, "The Roots of Apocalypticism in Near Eastern Myth," in *The Encyclopedia of Apocalypticism* (ed. John J. Collins; New York: Continuum, 1998).

[91] Collins, *The Apocalyptic Vision*, 99.

[92] For a similar but independant opinion, see Matthias Delcor, "Mythologie et Apocalyptique," in *Apocalypses et théologie de l'espérance* (*Lectio Divina*; Paris: Les Editions du Cerf, 1977), 143–77.

[93] Collins, *The Apocalyptic Vision*, 106.

Collins sees the scene in Dan 8 where the little horn "felled some of the host and the stars to earth and trampled them" as a reflection of the basic plot found in *Helal ben Shachar*.[94] There are several problems with this identification. I do not disagree with Collins about the way in which Dan 7 and 8 appropriate older myths. But two methodological problems must be raised. First, Collins's analysis is unable to explain most of the language that is found in Dan 7 and 8. Instead, the method primarily points to latent plot-elements. The problem is particularly pronounced in chapter 8 where the myth of הֵילֵל בֶּן־שָׁחַר can only account for *one* of the symbols used in Dan 8: stars. The rest of the symbols in chapter 8 find no antecedents in Isa 14. Collins admits this and locates antecedents for the other symbols elsewhere:

> It has long been realized that the choice of symbols for the kingdoms of Greece and Persia is determined by the astral geography of the Hellenistic age. The ram is the constellation Aries which presides over Persia, according to the astrologer Teucer of Babylon. The goat represents Capricorn in the Zodiac, and according to Teucer, Capricorn presided over Syria. The author of Daniel was obviously familiar with the system of Teucer or one of its antecedents.[95]

In chapter two I argue that the symbols used in Dan 8 were probably not derived from the Zodiac known from Teucer.[96] For now I simply highlight that Collins's primary methodology of understanding the symbolic language of apocalypses is unable to account for most of the symbols in Dan 8 and is almost entirely unable to explain any of the data analyzed in the second part of this study: Dan 10–12, *Apocryphon of Jeremiah C*, and 4QPsDan[a–b] ar. For now I discuss only Dan 10–12.

Collins attempts to trace the use of Near Eastern myths in Dan 10–12 like he did in Dan 7 and 8. "In chs. 10–12, we meet again familiar mythic motifs. Each people on earth is represented by an angelic prince in heaven."[97] His claim for "mythic motifs" is based on the fact that ancient Near Eastern peoples envisioned particular gods reigning over particular geographical areas (much like kings). The most obvious problem with this approach is that this motif is not at all the same thing as a myth – at least not in the way that the Combat Myth or *Helal ben Shachar* is. The language used in Dan 10–12 is significantly different from that used in Dan 7 and 8, but Collins's method does not allow one to take full account of these

---

[94] Collins, *The Apocalyptic Vision*, 107.
[95] Collins, *The Apocalyptic Vision*, 107.
[96] Collins has since softened his position. See the discussion in 2.3.4 below.
[97] Collins, *The Apocalyptic Vision*, 108.

differences.⁹⁸ Collins admits that "the history narrated by the angel in Dan 11 is not described in mythological terms."⁹⁹ In order to deal with this situation, Collins extends his argument about the use of allegories to posit that the texts must also be read as allegories of specific events in human history (not only older myths). He warns against understanding them as "naïve allegories."¹⁰⁰ He does not believe that any of the symbols used in Dan 7–12 should be characterized in the words of Philip Wheelwright as "steno-symbols." In other words, none of the symbols should be read as having an exclusive one-to-one relationship with the thing that is being symbolized. Collins is surely correct about "steno-symbols" – at least on the level of the language that he analyzes, i.e., the particular historical referents of a given description. But he may not be correct on a larger level.

An example of what Collins means by "steno-symbol" is the usage of the symbol π in mathematics to symbolize the precise number 3.14159. The relationship is purely conventional. Collins is correct that the "little horn" cannot be taken as a steno-symbol for Antiochus IV, nor a lion for Babylon. The remains of the literary and material culture available to us from the Near East cannot bear any such claim. But Collins is skeptical that any "steno-symbols" exist in the world of literature. Unfortunately, Collins may set up a false choice between the beasts as "steno-symbols" on the one hand, or "allegorical symbols" on the other. His criticism of Philip Wheelwright's term "steno-symbol" extends to all semiotic approaches to literature. "It is noteworthy that Wheelwright resorts to mathematics for an example of steno-symbols. In fact it is difficult to imagine a literary allegory which can be fully exhausted by one referent, or can be translated without any loss of meaning."¹⁰¹ I disagree with Collins on two grounds. First, the polyvalency of symbols is probably at least as much, if not more, a product of interpretative communities than the language itself. Nietzsche's explanation of how "literal" language came to be literal in the first place illuminates this.¹⁰² Second, Collins's problem with "steno-

---

⁹⁸ I obviously do not claim that Collins is ignorant of these differences – only that his methodology does not bring them to the forefront of his analysis in the way that other methods might.

⁹⁹ Collins, *The Apocalyptic Vision*, 109.

¹⁰⁰ Collins, *The Apocalyptic Vision*, 112.

¹⁰¹ Collins, *The Apocalyptic Vision*, 112.

¹⁰² Nietzsche believed that the most realistic, truthful language that one could find once originated as figurative language. "A mobile army of metaphors, metonyms, and anthropomorphisms – in short, a sum of human relations, which have been enhanced, transposed, and embellished poetically and rhetorically, and which after long use seem firm, canonical, and obligatory to a people: truths are illusions about which one has forgotten that this is what they are; metaphors which are worn out and without sensuous power; coins which have lost their pictures and now matter only as metal, no longer as coins." Friedrich Nietzsche, "On Truth and Lie in an Extra-Moral Sense," in *The Portable Nietzsche* (ed. Walter Kaufmann; New York: Random House, 1980), 46–7. Derrida treats metaphors similarly by quoting Anatole France's Polyphilos "All

symbols" is that he supposes that goats, rams, and other beasts must all constitute individual steno-symbols if they are to be symbols at all. To his credit, Collins's main concern is to refute the arguments of, e.g., Norman Perrin who argues for precisely this unfortunate model of "steno-symbols."[103] As Collins points out, Perrin's contrast between Jesus' "kingdom of God" as a "tensive" symbol and the "steno-symbols" of apocalypses like Daniel, "Shows little appreciation for the allusive and evocative power of apocalyptic symbolism."[104]

Norman Perrin's attempt to apply semiotic theory to Daniel fails because it attempts to understand the meaning of Daniel's symbolism on the wrong level of the text. But there is another level of the text that must be examined. I hope that the discussion of the term "symbol" in the theoretical framework below makes clear that Collins's criticism of Perrin is correct but that his estimation of the value of semiotics for literature is too low. It cannot be used to explain how each beast refers to a particular historical referent, but it might be useful in describing the deeper structures that govern the associations made in symbolic apocalypses, e.g., animal=human or human=angel. The best illustration of my point comes from Collins himself.

In *The Apocalyptic Vision of the Book of Daniel*, Collins admits that his overall method (allegorical/mythological) is unhelpful for interpreting the כְּבַר אֱנָשׁ "one like a human being" in Dan 7. Better stated, the "one like a human being" helps one understand the plot of the story as a kind of allegory of the Combat Myth (in light of the Ugaritic Baʿal myths), but the figure in Daniel is not illuminated by associations with the figure of Baʿal. One is forced to make use of another type of comparison. Collins compares how humans are used in other apocalypses and concludes that in apoca-

---

these words, whether defaced by usage, or polished smooth, or even coined expressly in view of constructing some intellectual concept, yet allow us to frame some idea to ourselves of what they originally represented. So chemists have reagents whereby they can make the effaced writing of a papyrus or a parchment visible again. It is by these means palimpsests are deciphered. If an analogous process were applied to the writings of the metaphysicians, if the primitive and concrete meaning that lurks yet present under the abstract and new interpretations were brought to light, we should come upon some very curious and perhaps instructive ideas." He then uses the theory of language to argue for an corollary in ideology: "White mythology – metaphysics has erased within itself the fabulous scene that has produced it, the scene that nevertheless remains active and stirring, inscribed in white ink, an invisible design covered over in the palimpsest." Jacques Derrida, *Margins of Philosophy* (Chicago: University of Chicago Press, 1984), 211, 13.

[103] See Norman Perrin, "Eschatology and Hermeneutics: Reflections on Method in the Interpretation of the New Testament," *JBL* 93 (1974): 3–14. John J. Collins, "The Symbolism of Transcendence in Jewish Apocalyptic," 19 (1974): 5–22. Collins, *The Apocalyptic Vision*, 112–5. Collins, *The Apocalyptic Imagination*, 16.

[104] Collins, *The Apocalyptic Imagination*, 16.

lypses, humans symbolize angels.¹⁰⁵ In my judgment he is correct in his identification of כְּבַר אֱנָשׁ as an angel precisely because he is able to isolate "human being" as one of the ways in which angels are consistently symbolized in other early Jewish apocalypses (the other way being stars). There is no older myth that will help isolate the identity of כְּבַר אֱנָשׁ.

Only by analyzing how human beings are used in other apocalypses does the pattern become clear. The case of the "son of man" is the only one for which Collins employs such a comparison. It is just this kind of comparative-linguistic approach that I apply in this study.

From Uppsala (back) to Collins

Collins's publication of *Semeia* 14 was a watershed moment in the study of ancient apocalypses. Indeed, much of the work of the last three decades could be fairly characterized as responses and refinements to Collins's work. Just months after the publication of *Semeia* 14, it exerted a commanding presence among leading scholars who gathered in Uppsala, Sweden for an international colloquium to investigate apocalypticism in the Mediterranean world and the Near East. The colloquium's voluminous proceedings were published three years later and reflect keen interest in and engagement with Collins's work. The essays of Jean Carmignac and Lars Hartman are particularly pertinent to the present study.

Jean Carmignac's essay, "Description du phénomène de l'Apocalyptique dans l'Ancient Testament," brings his own definition of the genre apocalypse into conversation with Collins's definition. While Carmignac believes their respective definitions are more alike than they are different, Carmignac's definition places primary emphasis on language. More specifically, Carmignac views symbolic language, an element totally missing from Collins's definition (see above), as a defining feature of apocalypses. Further, Carmignac leaves eschatology out of his paradigm. Collins, like most scholars, emphasizes eschatology. I juxtapose the definitions of Collins and Carmignac below:

Collins

A genre of revelatory literature with a narrative framework, in which a revelation is mediated by an otherworldly being to a human recipient, disclosing a transcendent reality which is both temporal, insofar as it envisages eschatological salvation, and spatial, insofar as it involves another, supernatural world.¹⁰⁶

---

[105] Collins, *The Apocalyptic Vision*, 144–6.
[106] Collins, "Towards the Morphology," 9.

Carmignac

Genre littéraire qui décrit des révélations célestes à travers des Symboles.[107]

The definitions are similar to the extent that they both consider apocalypses to be heavenly revelations. The glaring difference is that Carmignac pushes language to the forefront of his definition while Collins leaves it out entirely. For Collins, language is not part of the generic framework of apocalypses. Carmignac sees language as vitally important, though, as is typical of most of the studies I have reviewed thus far, he does not give a critical definition of "symbol." He does, however, suggest a proper way to understand the symbols. While Collins treats symbols as a product of the use of old myths, Carmignac believes that the use of symbols in apocalypses owes to the origins of apocalypses in dream visions:

Les songes ont souvent été considérés comme des revelations célestes et leur élément irrationnel pouvait facilement donner prise à des interprétations symboliques. A plus forte raison, quand de tels songes sont vraiment des prémonitions, ils passent volontiers pour des prophéties symboliques. N'est-ce pas le récit coloré et dramatique de ces songes qui a donné naissance à des développements, volontiers repris par les prophètes?[108]

Carmignac's view of the symbols in used apocalypses is a useful one. Rather than attempting to find an antecedent for each symbol in an older myth he attempts to relate the overall pattern to the linguistic patterns found in Near Eastern dream reports. His argument is strengthened by the fact that some apocalypses, like Dan 7 and the *Animal Apocalypse*, have the literary form of dream reports and others, like Dan 2, seem to have developed from texts containing dream reports. If he had pushed his thesis a bit further, he would have discovered that not only could the use of symbolic ciphers in dream visions help explain the use of symbolic ciphers in apocalypses, but that non-symbolic representations in dream visions could help explain non-symbolic representations in apocalypses. To Carmignac's credit, the assigned parameters of his article limited his ability to provide a robust explanation for his theory about the relationship between apoca-

---

[107] [A literary genre that describes heavenly revelation by means of symbols.] Jean Carmignac, "Description du phénomène de l'Apocalyptique dans l'Ancient Testament," in *Apocalypticism in the Mediterranean World and the Near East* (ed. David Hellholm; Tübingen: Mohr Siebeck, 1983), 165. This definition is a revision of a slightly less essentialist attempt at a definition in Jean Carmignac, "Qu'est-ce que l'apocalyptique? Son emploi à Qumrân," *RevQ* 10 (1979): 3–33.

[108] [Dreams were often regarded as heavenly revelations and their irrational element could easily provide occasion for symbolic interpretation. More significantly, when such dreams are truly premonitions, they pass readily for symbolic prophecies. Is it not the colored and dramatic account of these dreams that gave birth to developments that were readily appropriated by the prophets?] Carmignac, "Description du phénomène de l'Apocalyptique dans l'Ancient Testament," 169.

lypses and dream visions. Since Carmignac's article, more work has confirmed his inclination to compare the language of dream reports and apocalypses.[109] I return to Carmignac's claim in the theoretical framework below. Before moving on to Lars Hartman's essay, however, I briefly consider another scholar who makes claims similar to those of Carmignac and who also directly responds to Collins.

In his form-critical study of Enoch and Daniel, Stephen Breck Reid accepts Collins's definition of the genre apocalypse but adds to it the following: "The historical apocalypse uses symbols whose key referents are historical personages and events set in some sort of chronological order, though often it is difficult to discern that order."[110] The conviction that symbols are an integral part of the genre apocalypse (or, at least an integral part of historical apocalypses) persists with Reid and is undoubtedly an important insight. But Reid's particular position on the importance of symbols is lacking on two grounds. First, Reid misses the fact that not all apocalypses are symbolic because he treats Dan 7, 8, and 10–12 as one apocalypse and because he does not take into account any of the apocalypses found at Qumran. Second, he mischaracterizes the "symbols" of Daniel by treating them like Perrin's "steno-symbols" – a position Collins had already criticized in at least three publications (see above).

Reid also agrees with Carmignac on the importance of the world of divination for understanding apocalypses. Reid's analysis differs from Carmignac's in that it does not specifically isolate dream reports/dream divination. He speaks more generally of "mantic activity." Whereas Carmignac ties apocalypses to dream visions by a comparison of their literary forms, Reid ties apocalypses to "mantic activity" through a comparison of the sociological settings of the historical apocalypses of the 2nd century B.C.E. He applies form criticism, social theory, and anthropological analysis to Daniel and Enoch and concludes that apocalypses "reflect a type of mantic activity, which entails the use of omens, dreams, auditions, and the like to predict or appear to predict the future."[111] I agree that one can use the world of divination to reconstruct partially the "native competence" of the readers of early Jewish apocalypses. My position is closer to Carmignac's, however, in that I see the crucial link in the stylistic peculiarities of dream reports.

A second important engagement of Collins's work in the Uppsala volume is also one of the few studies that makes a concerted effort to incorpo-

---

[109] Frances Flannery-Dailey, *Dreamers, Scribes, and Priests: Jewish Dreams in the Hellenistic and Roman Eras* (JSJSup 90; Leiden: Brill, 2004).

[110] Stephen Breck Reid, *Enoch and Daniel: A Form Critical and Sociological Study of Historical Apocalypses* (Berkeley: BIBLA, 1989), 4.

[111] Reid, *Enoch and Daniel*, 5.

rate modern literary theory into the investigation of the genre apocalypse. Lars Hartman engages Collins's works in two distinct ways. First, he engages Collins's insistence on discussing a unified genre "apocalypse" over and against claims by von Rad of a *mixtum compositum*. He sides with Collins on the existence of a more or less unified genre called apocalypse.

But Hartman argues that there are two groups of constitutive elements of a genre and that Collins misses one. The first element "concerns the linguistic characteristics of a text and regards its style, vocabulary, and phraseology" and the second, "has to do with the contents of a text, with what may be called its propositional level."[112] While Hartman praises Collins's "master-paradigm" of the genre apocalypse, he also notes that all of the elements of Collins's "master-paradigm" fall under his second group, *i.e.*, propositional constituents. The same holds true for Collins's definition of the genre apocalypse itself. Language, which Collins does not discuss, would fit into Hartman's first group, "linguistic characteristics." Hartman's paper thus indicates on a theoretical level why a deliberate study of language in apocalypses might be helpful.

Collins engaged many of his inquisitors in 1998 with the revised edition of his *The Apolcalyptic Imagination*. He characterizes Carmignac's definition of apocalypse as, "unobjectionable as far as it goes." For Collins's taste, however, the definition is not narrow enough. In particular, he insists that eschatology must be included. "It is true that the scholarly literature has been preoccupied with eschatology to a disproportionate degree and that it is by no means the only concern of the apocalypses. Yet an approach that denies the essential role of eschatology is an overreaction and no less one-sided."[113] He cites Lars Hartman's treatment of the concept of genre approvingly, though he does not answer specifically Hartman's charge that his definition of apocalypse incorporates only half of the necessary criteria.[114] The framework of *The Apocalyptic Imagination* may implicitly answer Hartman in that Collins devotes as much time to language, setting, and function as he does to the generic framework of apocalypses in chapter one.[115]

---

[112] Lars Hartman, "Survey of the Problem of Apocalyptic Genre," in *Apocalypticism in the Mediterranean World and the Near East* (ed. David Hellholm; Tübingen: Mohr Siebeck, 1983), 332–3.

[113] Collins, *The Apocalyptic Imagination*, 10.

[114] Collins, *The Apocalyptic Imagination*, 8.

[115] Cf. Collins, *The Apocalyptic Imagination*, 1–42. Pages 1–13 are devoted to literary framework, 14–21 to language, and 21–42 to setting and function.

Today

In many ways, Collins's revised edition of *The Apocalyptic Imagination* placed a capstone on the sorts of investigations that were kindled by Lücke and ignited by Koch. Beginning primarily in the 1990's, a new trend in the study of apocalypses emerged. The first major study of this type was published by Paolo Sacchi in 1990.[116] Sacchi makes no attempt to present the most accurate account of the elements of which apocalypses are composed. For him, understanding apocalypses is not best achieved by outlining their primary generic characteristics. Instead, he begins with what he believes to be the oldest apocalypse, the *Book of Watchers* from *1 Enoch*, and isolates its dominant theme or concern: the origins of evil. He then attempts to trace how that concern is dealt with in subsequent apocalypses. Sacchi's innovation is in his assertion that, "there must exist some relationship between apocalyptic form (knowledge through vision and symbolic-mythical expression) and the content of the thought."[117] Most would agree with this. Of course, as he observes, "The problem posed this way is no longer literary, or is not only literary."[118] Collins pays tribute to Sacchi's innovation though he does not subscribe to the ultimate usefulness of Sacchi's methodology.[119]

Some of the most recent investigations into Jewish apocalypses have followed Sacchi by limiting interest in the literary questions posed by the apocalypses.[120] The most significant studies in this regard are the trio of monographs published by Gabriele Boccaccini (*Middle Judaism*, *Beyond the Essene Hypothesis*, and *Roots of Rabbinic Judaism*) and Andreas Bedenbender's *Der Gott der Welt tritt auf den Sinai*.[121] In his review of Bedenbender's monograph, Eibert Tigchelaar comments, "One should note the paradigm shift of the past decade: whereas in the '60's and '70's and even beyond "apocalyptic" was described in terms of Old Testament literary genres prophecy and wisdom, studies like Bedenbender's and Boccaccini's

---

[116] Paolo Sacchi, *Jewish Apocalyptic and its History* (vol. 20; Sheffield: Sheffield Academic Press, 1990).

[117] Sacchi, *Jewish Apocalyptic and its History*, 17.

[118] Sacchi, *Jewish Apocalyptic and its History*, 17.

[119] Collins, *The Apocalyptic Imagination*, 10–11.

[120] See Eibert Tigchelaar, "Review of *Der Gott der Welt tritt auf den Sinai: Entstehung, Entwicklung und Funktionsweise der frühjüdischen Apokalyptik* by Andreas Bedenbender" in *JSJ* 32 (2001): 293.

[121] Gabriele Boccaccini, *Middle Judaism: Jewish Thought, 300 B.C.E. to 200 C.E.* (Minneapolis: Fortress Press, 1991); Gabriele Boccaccini, *Beyond the Essene Hypothesis: The Parting of the Ways between Qumran and Enochic Judaism* (Grand Rapids: Eerdmans, 1998); Gabriele Boccaccini, *Roots of Rabbinic Judaism: An Intellectual History from Ezekiel to Daniel* (Grand Rapids: Eerdmans, 2002); Andreas Bedenbender, *Der Gott der Welt tritt auf den Sinai : Entstehung, Entwicklung und Funktionsweise der frühjüdischen Apokalyptik* (vol. 8; Berlin: Institut Kirche und Judentum, 2000).

focus on the differences and interactions between 3rd and 2nd century B.C.E. Jewish movements, especially the Enochic and Mosaic movements."[122] For example, Bedenbender asserts, "Die Probleme der SBL-Definition liegen somit auf der Hand: Bei einer Reihe von Texten greift sie nur mit Mühe (und sieht sich in einem Fall sogar vor ein unlösbares Dilemma gestellt); und als *literaturwissenschaftliche* Begriffsbestimmung (sei sie auch noch so ausgefeilt) ist ihr *geschichtlicher* Erklärungswert begrenzt."[123] Bedenbender's prefers to describe "*Apokalyptik*" in terms of its social setting:

Apokalyptik im unbezweifelbaren Sinne wurde im Früjudentum hervorgebraucht, als eine Gruppierung um den damaligen Hohenpriester von Jerusalem eine mit Waffengewalt vorangetriebene innerjüdische Religionsverfolgung initiierte und in der Auseinandersetzung mit den Altgläubigen des eigenen Volkes dankbar auf die Hilfestellung der heidnischen Welt-macht, des seleukidischen Imperiums, zurückgriff.[124]

It is unfortunate that Bedenbender breathes new life into the macro-term "*Apokalyptik*." While the German word does not suffer from the grammatical problems that the English pseudo-noun "apocalyptic" does, it is just as broad in Bedenbender's usage as is the English pseudo-noun. One understands his concern for broader questions and connections, but when the term is used as a catch-all it becomes difficult to gain a meaningful understanding of any specific piece (e.g., literature, theology, social setting, etc).[125]

---

[122] Tighchelaar, "Review of *Der Gott der Welt*," 293.

[123] [The problems with the SBL definition are obvious: with a group (lit. row) of texts it holds together only with difficulty (and seeing itself in any case set before an unsolvable dilemma) and as a literary-critical definition (it is overly polished [i.e., "narrow"]) its value for reconstructing history is limited.] Bedenbender, *Der Gott der Welt*, 60.

[124] [*Apokalyptik,* in the sense beyond all doubt, was produced in Early Judaism when a group gathered around the then high priest of Jerusalem initiated a military-backed inner-Jewish religious movement and in conflict with the "old-faithful" (?) of their own people, gratefully fell back upon the assistance of the heathen regime, the Seleucid Empire.] Bedenbender, *Der Gott der Welt*, 259.

[125] A similar move has been made recently by Greg Carey. He introduces the category "apocalyptic discourse." As he understands it, "Apocalyptic discourse refers to the constellation of apocalyptic topics as they function in larger early Jewish and Christian literary and social contexts. Thus, apocalyptic discourse should be treated as a flexible set of resources that early Jews and Christians could employ for a variety of persuasive tasks." Greg Carey, *Ultimate Things: An Introduction to Jewish and Christian Apocalyptic Literature* (St. Louis: Chalic Press, 2005), 5. The category has significant heuristic value for introducing the "constellation of apocalyptic topics" to the uninitiated and contains features similar to those in the master paradigm of *Semeia* 14. I note that unlike *Semeia* 14, Carey's list prominently features symbolic language. But as Lorenzo DiTommaso has noted, the category "apocalyptic discourse," functions quite like the English pseudo-noun "apocalyptic" did before the late 1970's. Cf. Lorenzo DiTommaso, "Review of *Ultimate Things: An Introduction to Jewish and Christian Apocalyptic Literature*," *RBL* 12 (2007): 3 (electronic version). In other words, while useful in its own right, Carey's category does

Boccaccini is similarly dedicated to integrating a historical picture of the Hellenistic period in Palestine into any discussion or definition of apocalypses. It is to Boccaccini's credit that he refuses to accept that all apocalypses must reflect the same worldview. Instead of speaking about "apocalyptic Judaism" or "Jewish apocalypticism," as if Hellenistic Jews would have perceived such a category as being one thing, Boccaccini prefers to discuss "Zadokite Judaism," "Enochic Judaism," "Sapiential Judaism," and "Danielic Judaism."[126] It is certainly a positive turn that scholars like Boccaccini have challenged old and romantic assumptions about "the" (i.e., singular) *Sitz im Leben* of early Jewish apocalypses. His proposal has breathed new creativity into the study of apocalypses. But if the essays in Boccaccini's recent collected volume, *Enoch and Qumran Origins*, are any indication, the newer socio-religious categories that Boccaccini relates to early Jewish apocalypses may be just as problematic.

For example, John Collins writes, "The impulse to apply Occam's razor to the identification of groups in second-century Judaism is commendable up to a point, but it can be carried to excess."[127] Of Boccaccini's specific correlation of the Essenes with his category "Enochic Judaism," Collins writes, "Rather than being a splinter movement, an offshoot of a branch, it seems to me that the sectarian movement reflected in the scrolls involved a synthesis of traditions, Enochic and Mosaic, sapiential and apocalyptic."[128] Thus, Collins agrees with Boccaccini's impulse to see a more diverse Hellenistic Judaism, but he expresses caution about the particular religio-sociological groups that Boccaccini proposes. In the same volume, Jeff Anderson concurs, "To speak definitely, however, about Enochic and Zadokite groups, *as groups*, is an oversimplification of the complexities present in these traditions."[129] Similarly, James VanderKam questions Boccaccini's group terminology and points out a significant problem with a term like "Zadokite Judaism:"

---

not seem capable or making a strict enough distinction between texts like *1 En.* and the *War Scroll*.

[126] See especially Boccaccini, *Roots of Rabbinic Judaism*.

[127] John J. Collins, "Enoch, the Dead Sea Scrolls, and the Essenes: Groups and Movements in Judaism in the Early Second Century B.C.E.," in *Enoch and Qumran Origins: New Light on a Forgotten Connection* (ed. Gabriele Boccaccini; Grand Rapids, MI: Eerdmans, 2005), 349.

[128] Collins, "Enoch, the Dead Sea Scrolls, and the Essenes: Groups and Movements in Judaism in the Early Second Century B.C.E.," 350. For Collins's most recent engagement with "Enochic" Judaism, see John J. Collins, "'Enochic Judaism' and the Sect of the Dead Sea Scrolls," in *The Early Enoch Literature* (ed. Gabriele Boccaccini and John J. Collins; vol. 121 of *JSJSup*; Leiden: Brill, 2007), 283–99.

[129] Jeff Anderson, "From 'Communities of Texts' to Religious Communities: Problems and Pitfalls," in *Enoch and Qumran Origins: New Light on a Forgotten Connection* (ed. Gabriele Boccaccini; Grand Rapids, MI: Eerdmans, 2005), 355.

His definition of Zadokite literature illustrates the problem: it includes nearly all the texts that eventually made their way into the Hebrew Bible (exluding late books such as Dan and Esth), with works such as the Letter of Jeremiah, Tob, and Sir. They are Zadokite in the sense that they were "collected, edited, and transmitted" by temple authorities. I wonder whether it would not be better to speak of the common heritage of almost all Jews at this time rather than to put the tag "Zadokite" on all of this literature, which is quite diverse in content. I suspect that Enochic Judaism, too, embraced most of the books that became the Hebrew Bible, even if its earlier adherents gave less prominence to Moses (whose writings they did use) and questioned (at least at times) the purity of the temple cult in Jerusalem.[130]

The collected articles in Boccaccini's *Enoch and Qumran Origins* indicate that Boccaccini's methods in studying Judaism in the Hellenistic are neither unfounded nor unhelpful. But the articles also indicate that the types of investigations that Koch ignited have not been carried out in full enough measure to provide the necessary data for studies like Boccaccini's. Analyses of Jewish apocalypses as literature has not yet yielded sufficient results to make the sorts of claims that Boccaccini and Bedenbender would hope. There is, then, not only room for a study such as the present one, but a need. The move to reconstruct social groups from literary texts has come too quickly. Several important elements of early Jewish apocalypses remain misunderstood and language is one of the most important, especially in terms of its value for understanding social location. I contend that Koch's nearly four decades old suggestion has not lost its import. To understand what is apocalyptic about apocalypses, "A starting point in form criticism and literary and linguistic history is, in the nature of things, the only one possible."[131]

Charting a Way Forward

One of the most significant shortcomings of work done on the language of historical apocalypses has been the failure to incorporate data from the Dead Sea Scrolls. Certain lengthy and well preserved texts such as the *War Scroll* and the *Pesharim* have been discussed alongside apocalypses and, indeed, they should be. These texts contain features that bear witness to an ideology that we can fairly describe as apocalypticism. But there is also a danger in creating a kind of super-genre that contains texts unconnected by any formal features, but rather themes or ideas (as I have indicated above,

---

[130] James VanderKam, "Too Far Beyond the Essene Hypothesis?," in *Enoch and Qumran Origins: New Light on a Forgotten Connection* (ed. Gabriele Boccaccini; Grand Rapids, MI: Eerdmans, 2005), 392.

[131] Koch, *The Rediscovery of Apocalyptic*, 23.

some see this theme-based method as precisely the right direction to pursue). If one *is* interested in a theme or topic, then it makes sense to create a kind of baroque meta-genre in order to assess it across a spectrum of texts. I would place recent introductory textbook by Greg Carey in this category.[132] The breadth of evidence Carey considers is to be applauded and his assessments of the texts themselves are fine, but his Qumran evidence is derived from the *War Scroll*, the *Temple Scroll*, the *Copper Scroll*, the *Rule of the Congregation, Serek haYahad*, the *Damascus Document*, and *Miqsat Ma'ase haTorah*. He never discusses any of the literary apocalypses found at Qumran. The book is a perfectly fine inquiry into his notion of *Apocalyptic Discourse*. But his categories of "symbolism" and "poetry" as controlling features of apocalyptic discourse do not, in my judgment, move past older treatments of the language of apocalypses and do not exploit the Dead Sea Scrolls as profitably as they might.[133] Indeed, the baroque context he creates may obscure some insights into the literary genre itself. If one is interested in the poetics of apocalypse, a serious comparison between the language of texts like *1 Enoch* and Daniel with texts from Qumran that strongly resemble literary apocalypses is imperative for creating appropriate contexts for interpretation. Without comparison with texts like *Apocryphon of Jeremiah C* and 4QPsDan[a–b] ar, the language of Daniel 10–12 remains mischaracterized by categories like "symbolism."

While several of the scholars mentioned above worked before the scrolls were discovered and others had little or no access, some scholars have ignored evidence from Qumran. I hope to remedy the problem by bringing several important apocalypses found at Qumran into the conversation.

A more complex problem that emerges from the research history is a terminological one. Almost every major student of ancient Jewish apocalypses has understood symbolic language to be a *sine qua non* of the genre. Very few, however, provide any critical account of what they mean by "symbolic." Therefore the difference between descriptions such as חֵיוָה רְבִיעָיָה "the fourth beast" (e.g., "Greece") in Dan 7 and יָוָן "Greece" in Dan 11 are not often accounted for. Thus, the most significant question that must be dealt with before moving forward with an analysis of texts is a terminological one: how can one distinguish between symbolic and non-symbolic language? With what models might we understand the poetics of apocalypse?

Most of the earliest commentators viewed symbolic language as a product of genuine visionary experiences. Thus for Lücke, the visionaries mere-

---

[132] Greg Carey, *Ultimate Things: An Introduction to Jewish and Christian Apocalyptic Literature* (St. Louis: Chalice Press, 2005).

[133] Carey, *Ultimate Things*, 6–14.

ly wrote what they actually saw and for others such as Hilgenfeld or Charles, the visionaries used language to imperfectly describe the ineffable content of true heavenly revelations. A significant change in scholarly attitudes towards apocalypses came about with the work of Noth, Rowley, and von Rad in the middle of the twentieth century. These scholars viewed the language of apocalypses as a product of literary conventions and techniques. Noth viewed the language of apocalypses as reflective of a cosmopolitan education. Rowley saw apocalypses primarily as resistance literature and their language as a means of protecting their writers and readers from political retribution, i.e., encryption. Other prominent scholars have shared this opinion.[134] Like Noth, von Rad saw the language of apocalypses as a reflection of an education in older traditions – not so much as a reflection of the security concerns of the writers and readers (*a la* Rowley). More specifically, von Rad saw the language of apocalypses as deeply rooted in the Israelite Wisdom tradition.

Koch's call for a focus on form- and literary-criticism has been answered by many, and form criticism especially has dominated studies undertaken during the last three decades of the twentieth century. Despite a focus on technical issues within the literature, however, no significant attention has been given to language. Like his forebears, Koch sees symbolic language as a basic element of the genre apocalypse. He understands symbolic language as a series of metaphors – largely appropriated from the Bible (Koch does not view the relationships implied in the metaphors as biblical, only the descriptions).

Collins took seriously Koch's call for a focus on form criticism and, accordingly, divorced the concepts of genre and language in his analysis of apocalypses. Rather than viewing language as a constituent piece of the generic framework of apocalypses, Collins appears to view the language of apocalypses primarily in terms of tradition-history (*a la* H. Gunkel's *Schöpfung und Chaos in Urzeit und Endzeit*). The most significant result of this methodology is that the meaning and significance of apocalyptic language is almost always viewed in terms of how a text, motif, or tradition might be appropriated by a given apocalypse. In other words, the language of each apocalypse is normally treated apart from the others since the language is viewed primarily as a function of the literary/tradition history of that particular apocalypse. Much less attention has been devoted to the elements of the language that are common or recurrent in the genre. I do not ignore the literary history of each text, but I focus more on the semantic range of individual expressions – especially within the genre apocalypse itself. This method may give a more accurate picture of how language

---

[134] Hanson, *The Dawn of Apocalyptic*, 252.

functions across the genre – not only within individual texts. It may also illuminate why different apocalypses use the kinds of language they do and/or what sort of social contexts are presumed by the language of historical apocalypses. These are questions on which I hope my analysis will shed some light, but these concerns cannot be addressed before first establishing a theoretical framework for understanding the literary techniques employed in apocalypses.

Entire monographs have been written on the subject of symbolism and many connotations of the word have limited relevance for this study.[135] In the next section of this chapter, I explore several connotations of the term symbol in order to provide a theoretical framework for the textual analysis in chapters two through six.

The basic typological distinction between symbolic and non-symbolic language is borrowed from ancient and modern analyses of dream reports. More specifically, I use the work of the Assyriologist Leo Oppenheim (likely predicated on the ancient Greek writer/diviner Artemidorus of Daldis) to set the basic parameters for the rest of the study. It became clear in the course of my analysis of the texts, however, that this definition could not fully explain all of the evidence. Both the symbolic and the non-symbolic apocalypses contain features that require a more sophisticated nomenclature. For the conventional relationships uncovered in my analysis of symbolic dreams, I turn to a concept of symbolic language adapted from Ferdinand de Saussure's work on linguistics and Charles Peirce's work on mathematics. I contextualize these thinkers in terms of how they have been appropriated for literary analyses by structuralist thinkers such as Claude Lévi-Strauss. My analysis of the non-symbolic apocalypses presented unique problems that required an even broader theoretical foundation, and it became necessary to turn to recent theoretical models that help explain language that is both explicit and, apparently, group-specific.

Symbolism and Realism in Ancient Dream Reports
In the attempt to understand what is and is not symbolic about the language of apocalypses, I suggest that dream reports may be especially helpful for establishing a baseline definition. We have already seen that some scholars, e.g., Carmignac, have highlighted the relationship between dream reports and apocalypses. More work on this relationship has been done recently and I discuss it below. An important aspect of virtually all prominent descriptions of the form of dream reports is the distinction between those that

---

[135] See the survey in Umberto Eco, *Semiotics and the Philosophy of Language* (Bloomington: Indiana University Press, 1984), 130–63.

use language that requires interpretation and those that communicate clear, explicit messages directly to the dreamer. In the same way that Lange and Mittman-Richert divide historical apocalypses into symbolic and non-symbolic examples, dream reports have been conventionally divided into the categories symbolic and non-symbolic since at least the time of Artemidorus of Daldis.[136] In his classic study of ancient Near Eastern dream reports, Leo Oppenheim makes similar distinctions.[137] Thus, there are at least three reasons why reading the language of apocalypses in light of the language of ancient dream reports could be fruitful: 1) the formal similarity of apocalypses and dream reports, 2) the antiquity of the categories for the language of dream reports, and 3) the endurance of the categories. Below I discuss each of these reasons in greater detail and use several exemplar texts to articulate the difference between symbolic and non-symbolic dream reports.

Some general lines of connection between ancient Jewish apocalypses and divinatory literature are now generally accepted.[138] We saw above that scholars such as Jean Carmignac appealed to ancient Near Eastern dream visions to help explain the genre apocalypse.[139] Following Carmignac, Christopher Rowland has argued for the centrality of the dream-form for Jewish apocalypses. For Rowland the genre apocalypse and its thought-world is "concerned with knowledge of God and the secrets of the world above, revealed in a direct way by dreams, visions or angelic pronounce-

---

[136] Artemidorus, *The Interpretation of Dreams (Oneirocritica)* (trans. Robert White; Park Ridge, NJ: Noyes, 1975), 14–18 (1.1–2).

[137] Leo Oppenheim, *The Interpretation of Dreams in the Ancient Near East* (vol. 46.3; Philadelphia: American Philosophical Society, 1956).

[138] The general idea that ancient Jewish apocalypses are related to divinatory literature is not a new one. Building on Gerhard von Rad's insistence that apocalypses should be most closely related to sapiential texts, Hans-Peter Müller suggested that the use of the figure Daniel in The Book of Daniel is itself an invocation of the world of mantic wisdom. Müller, "Magisch-mantische Weisheit und die Gestalt Daniels," 79–94. Cf. also Hans Peter Müller, "Mantische Weisheit und Apokalyptik," in *Congress Volume: Uppsala, 1971* (ed. P. A. H. de Boer; Leiden: Brill, 1972), 268–93. James VanderKam has argued that the figure of Enoch was ultimately derived from the seventh king in the Sumerian king-list: Enmeduranki. Enmeduranki was traditionally held to be the founder of the bārû (a guild of diviners). VanderKam, *Enoch and the Growth*, 33–71. Helge Kvanvig has also argued for the Mesopotamian background of the Enoch figure as well as the "Son of Man" figure. Kvanvig even argued that Dan 7 is based on a particular Near Eastern dream report, the *Vision of the Netherworld*. Helge Kvanvig, *Roots of Apocalyptic: The Mesopotamian Background of the Enoch Figure and of the Son of Man* (vol. 61; Neukirchen-Vluyn: Neukirchner Verlag, 1988). Matthias Albani has investigated the relationship between astronomy in the ancient Near East and the astronomical book of *1 En*. Matthias Albani, *Astronomie und Schöpfungsglaube: Untersuchungen zum astronomischen Henochbuch* (Neukirchen-Vluyn: Neukirchener 2000). Armin Lange has examined divinatory dreams in the Book of Jubilees. Lange, "Divinatorische Traüme und Apokalyptik im Jubiläenbuch," 25–38.

[139] As we saw above, Carmignac is followed – though in more general terms – by Reid, *Enoch and Daniel*.

ments."[140] Collins has said little on the subject, but it is interesting that he does specifically compare the symbolism used in apocalypses with that found in dream visions.[141] The organic (and sometimes genetic) relationship between dream reports and apocalypses is highlighted most emphatically by Frances Flannery-Dailey.[142]

The feature of Flannery-Dailey's study that is of greatest interest to this study is her consideration of the relationship between dream visions in Hellenistic Jewish texts and apocalypses. Naturally, many of the dream visions that she studies are excerpted from apocalypses. These parent texts include: *1 En.* 1–36, 85–90, Dan 7–12, *2 Baruch*, *4 Ezra*, *2 Enoch*, *Testament of Levi*, *Testament of Abraham*, *Ladder of Jacob*, and *Jubilees*. Much of the evidence for dream reports in Hellenistic Judaism is embedded within apocalypses. Flannery-Dailey does not consider this a coincidence. Rather, she speculates that dreams and their literary form provide the metaphysical space needed by the writers of apocalypses in order to express their concept of divine revelation. Her analysis of Jewish Hellenistic dream texts is primarily form-critical and leads her to six important conclusions. I summarize them below:

First, she believes that the pervasive presence of dreams and visions in apocalypses suggests that they may be more integral to the Jewish apocalypse than the SBL Genres Project recognized. Second (and consequently), she believes that Carmignac was correct in asserting that the "apocalyptic worldview" originates within the "dream tradition." She even suggests that the dream form catalyzed the production of the "apocalyptic worldview" because it provided a form that was much less limiting than prophetic oracles or wisdom poems. Third, she extends her conclusion that dreams reflect an overarching priestly and scribal worldview in order to caution against viewing "apocalypticism" as the outlook of a tiny, uniform, disenfranchised group within Jewish society. Fourth, she proposes viewing certain apocalypses as varieties of dreams texts. Such a classification might mitigate the tension between what appears to be two sub-types of apocalypse or even two distinct genres: historical apocalypses and otherworldly journeys. Fifth, because she believes that apocalypses do cohere as a genre and that dreams and visions play an important role in transmitting eschatological secrets to dreamers *and* to readers, she calls for a study that asks about the extent to which eschatological revelation is communicated to or

---

[140] Rowland, *The Open Heaven*, 9–10.
[141] Collins, *Daniel*, 54–5, 323, 402.
[142] Flannery-Dailey, *Dreamers, Scribes, and Priests*. More recently, see Frances Flannery-Dailey, "Lessons on Early Jewish Apocalypticism and Mysticism from Dream Literature.," in *Paradise Now: Essays on Early Jewish and Christian Mysticism* (ed. April De Conick; Atlanta: Society of Biblical Literature, 2006), 231–47.

otherwise known by *the reader* of certain Qumran texts. Finally, Flannery-Dailey cautions against understanding too stark a contrast between the representation of spatial, temporal, and ontological dimensions and reality in Early Jewish texts.[143] Her *resumé* is worth quoting:

> I suggest that it is the very forms of dreams, inherently flexible and allowing for the transcendence of spatial, temporal, ontological and perceptual limits of normal waking reality, which facilitate and/or catalyze the initial literary articulations of apocalyptic and mystical worldviews. In other words, if Hellenistic Judaism is the canvas, then dreams are the paint, and the resulting portraits of myriad dreams imagine access to otherworldly realms through a number of creative formulas, including apocalypses, mystical ascents, and ontological transformations.[144]

If Flannery-Dailey and others are correct about the relationship between dream reports and apocalypses, then a typology of language borrowed from ancient dream reports may hold important insights for the language of Jewish apocalypses.

Flannery-Dailey's form-critical work is based on the categories established by Leo Oppenheim. His study of Near Eastern dream reports remains the standard in the field. Oppenheim's categories are not, however, innovative. Indeed, similar categories were proposed more than two thousand years before by Artemidorus of Daldis in his *Oneirocritica*. The work of Artemidorus is another important factor in my decision to use dream reports as a model to understand the language of apocalypses. Not only is the literary form of dream reports and apocalypses similar (sometimes the same!), but the categories used to describe their language are nearly as ancient as the Jewish apocalypses analyzed in this study. Artemidorus lived and wrote in the second century C.E., but he quotes sources from as early as the fourth century B.C.E..[145] One should not make the mistake of assuming the project of Artemidorus is the same as that of Oppenheim though. Oppenheim studies dreams as literature and brings modern, rationalist notions to bear on the texts. Artemidorus studied dreams (as phenomena, not literature) before the Enlightenment and certainly before Sigmund Freud. Nevertheless, it seems impossible to ignore what may have been an important catalyst in Oppenheim's work. Moreover, including Artemidorus in the discussion emphasizes that the typology used by Oppenheim is hardly an

---

[143] This paragraph distills six points made by Flannery-Dailey. Cf. Flannery-Dailey, *Dreamers, Scribes, and Priests*, 276–8.

[144] Flannery-Dailey, *Dreamers, Scribes, and Priests*, 14.

[145] Specifically, Aristander of Telmessus (1,31). Aristander was a favorite interpreter of both Philip of Macedon and Alexander the Great (i.e., Plutarch 2, 2–3; Ephorus *FGrH* 70, 217; Arrian 1.25.6–8, Curtius 4.2.14, 17.41.7; Artemidorus 4, 23–24, etc.).

anachronistic one – at least for Hellenistic texts.¹⁴⁶ Therefore, I begin by outlining the typology of Artemidorus and then move on to Oppenheim, who best articulates the typology for the purposes of this study.

Artemidorus makes two sets of distinctions among dream reports. The first type of distinction differentiates between dreams that are products of natural phenomena (ἐνύπνιον) and ones that have divinatory value (ὄνειρος).¹⁴⁷ Artemidorus is generally uninterested in ἐνύπνιον and devotes only a few lines to it.

> It is the nature of certain experiences to run their course in proximity to the mind and to subordinate themselves to its dictates, and so to cause manifestations that occur in sleep, i.e., *enhypnion*. For example, it is natural for a lover to seem to be with his beloved in a dream and for a frightened man to see what he fears, or for a hungry man to eat and a thirsty man to drink and, again, for a man who has stuffed himself with food either to vomit or to choke [because of the blockage caused by the food's refusal to be digested].¹⁴⁸

While ἐνύπνιον is merely physiological, ὄνειρος is something different. "*Oneiros* is a movement or condition of the mind that takes many shapes and signifies good or bad things that will occur in the future."¹⁴⁹ The importance of *Oneiros* is that between the dream experience and the realization of the future it predicts, humans are able to use certain techniques to better understand the predicted future and avoid undesirable outcomes. Before moving to Artemidorus' second major division of dream-types, it is worthwhile to note that some Greek thinkers would have made an additional distinction within the category of ὄνειρος.

Jean-Marie Husser notes a category of dreams that was common in the ancient world and explains why Artemidorus leaves it aside. "True to his stoic ideas, Artemidorus does not accept that dreams may have an origin external to the soul. This very 'materialist' position was not very widespread, and generally a third category of dreams is proposed, those of divine origin, described simply as *oracles* (χρηματισμος)."¹⁵⁰ One illustration of this category is found in Macrobius's *Somnium Scipionis*, "We call a dream oracular in which a parent, or a pious or revered man, or a priest, or

---

¹⁴⁶ As far as I know the first scholar to read Jewish dream reports from the Hellenistic Period in light of Artemidorus is Armin Lange, "Interpretation als Offenbarung: Zum Verhältnis von Schriftauslegung und Offenbarung in apokalyptischer und nichtapokalyptischer Literatur," in *Wisdom and Apocalypticism in the Dead Sea Scrolls and in the Biblical Tradition* (ed. Florentino García Martínez; vol. 168 of *BETL*; Leuven: Peeters, 2003), 17–33.

¹⁴⁷ Artemidorus, *The Interpretation of Dreams (Oneirocritica)*, 14–18 (1.1–2).

¹⁴⁸ Artemidorus, *The Interpretation of Dreams (Oneirocritica)*, 14 (1.1).

¹⁴⁹ Artemidorus, *The Interpretation of Dreams (Oneirocritica)*, 15 (1.2).

¹⁵⁰ Jean-Marie Husser, *Dreams and Dream Narratives in the Biblical World* (trans. Jill Munro; Sheffield: Sheffield Academic Press, 1999), 23.

even a god clearly reveals what will or will not transpire, and what action to take or to avoid."¹⁵¹ This category, oracles, is like Artemidorus' category *oneiros* in that both are dreams with divinatory value. The distinction is that some dreams originate with the soul and others with a deity. The apocalypses considered in this study certainly do not follow Artemidorus' materialist thinking. It is clear to the reader that each text presents a revelation imparted by a heavenly being. It is for this reason that I turn to the similar, though slightly more appropriate, categories used by Oppenheim below. But first it is important to show that among dreams with divinatory value, the distinction between symbolic and non-symbolic dreams already obtained in the ancient world.

Artemidorus divides dreams with divinatory value into two categories. There are theoramic dreams (θεωρηματικοὶ) and there are allegorical dreams (ἀλληγορικοί). He defines theoramic dreams as μὲν οἱ τῇ ἑαυτῶν θέᾳ προσεοικότες "those which correspond exactly to their own dream-vision."¹⁵² He gives some examples of what he means by exact correspondence. "For example, a man who was at sea dreamt that he suffered shipwreck, and it actually came true in the way that it had been presented in sleep. For when sleep left him, the ship sank and was almost lost, and the man, along with a few others, narrowly escaped drowning."¹⁵³

Allegorical dreams, on the other hand, are οἱ δι' ἄλλων ἄλλα σημαίνοντες "those which signify one thing by means of another."¹⁵⁴ It is the allegorical dreams that dominate Artemidorus' *Oneirocritica*. He describes allegorical dreams as a phenomenon in which αἰνισσομένης ἐν αὐτοῖς φυσικῶς τι [καὶ] τῆς ψυχῆς "the soul is conveying something obscurely by physical means."¹⁵⁵ He provides copious examples of these dreams – some of which have more certain meanings than others. For example: "If a person dreams that he has hog's bristles, it portends dangers that are violent similar to those which the creature itself, the hog, I mean, encounters."¹⁵⁶ On the other hand, a person whose dream involves a hyena is much more difficult to interpret: "The hyena signifies a hermaphrodite, a woman who is a poisoner, and a base man who is given to unnatural impulses."¹⁵⁷ While it seems obvious that the hyena is an unfavorable omen,

---

[151] Macrobius, *Commentary on the Dream of Scipio* (trans. William H. Stahl; New York: Columbia University Press, 1952), 90 (1.3.8).
[152] Artemidorus, *The Interpretation of Dreams (Oneirocritica)*, 15 (1.2).
[153] Artemidorus, *The Interpretation of Dreams (Oneirocritica)*, 15 (1.2).
[154] Artemidorus, *The Interpretation of Dreams (Oneirocritica)*, 15 (1.2).
[155] Artemidorus, *The Interpretation of Dreams (Oneirocritica)*, 15 (1.2).
[156] Artemidorus, *The Interpretation of Dreams (Oneirocritica)*, 26 (1.20).
[157] Artemidorus, *The Interpretation of Dreams (Oneirocritica)*, 96 (2.12).

one is limited in their ability to avoid the undesirable future if it might manifest itself with a variety of actual outcomes.

One can see from these examples the basic distinction that Artemidorus attempts to make between the two types of dreams with divinatory value (ὄνειρος). The elements of allegorical dreams point beyond themselves to other realities, whereas theoramic dreams do not. Consequently, allegorical dreams require interpretation. Indeed, Artemidorus' whole point in writing *Oneirocritica* was to create a compendium of the interpretations of allegorical dreams – essentially, a textbook.[158]

Artemidorus' distinction between dreams with elements that point beyond themselves (requiring interpretation) and those that do not provides a foundation for my distinction between symbolic and non-symbolic language in apocalypses. As noted above, however, there is a problem with directly importing his categories since he did not believe that any dreams originated outside of the soul. His refusal to attribute dreams with divinatory value to deities is a minority position. Modern, literary-critical work on the form and content of dream reports has taken into consideration a larger spectrum of evidence – including dreams that purport to be direct communication between a deity and a human. Leo Oppenheim's study of ancient Near Eastern dream reports is a classic that continues to prove its usefulness in the Twenty-First Century.[159] Like Artimedorus, Oppenheim makes two basic sets of distinctions between types of dream reports. In the first instance, he distinguishes three types:

Dreams as revelations of the deity which may or may not require interpretation; dreams which reflect, symptomatically, the state of mind, the spiritual and bodily "health" of the dreamer, which are only mentioned but never recorded, and, thirdly, mantic dreams in which forthcoming events are prognosticated.[160]

These categories basically correspond to the first set of distinctions noted by Artimedorus, i.e., the distinction between dreams that do or do not have divinatory value. There are some differences, however, between Oppenheim and Artemidorus. First, Oppenheim's discussion of dream reports is a discussion of literary records. Artemidorus, on the other hand, was inter-

---

[158] The first three books were produced for a certain Cassius Maximus (unknown) and the last two for his son – an apprentice diviner.

[159] Scott Noegel's recent monograph on "enigmatic" dreams in the ancient Near East downplays the importance of the typologies used by Oppenheim. He does not, however, reject them and as I argue below, implicitly adopts a typological model not very far removed from Oppenheim. In other words, despite his distaste for the terms "message" and "symbolic," he nevertheless treats dreams in two basic categories: enigmatic and non-enigmatic, i.e., those that require interpretation and those that do not. Scott Noegel, *Nocturnal Ciphers: The Allusive Language of Dreams in the Ancient Near East* (AOS 89; New Haven: American Oriental Society, 2007), 4–9.

[160] Oppenheim, *The Interpretation of Dreams in the Ancient Near East*, 184.

ested in the dreams themselves and actually recorded reports of dreams and their interpretations from diviners as an eyewitness. In other cases, Artemidorus uses omens from older collections. The purpose of Artemidorus' study is to help the reader understand dreams. The purpose of Oppenheim's study is to help the reader understand the literary form of ancient dream reports. Therefore, Oppenheim distinguishes between revelatory dreams and omens (mantic dreams) not on the substance of the dreams but on the ways that they were respectively collected and used. Revelatory dreams contain divine revelation pertinent to one dreamer. Mantic dreams are dreams gathered into omen-collections that are subsequently used to help interpret similar dreams by other individuals. Revelatory dreams and mantic dreams may, however, be distinguished in form too. Mantic dreams are short, terse, and rigidly consistent in their pattern of protasis (condition) and apodosis (consequence). For example, "If a man is clad in the hide of a goat: an important person will be removed and will die."[161] Revelatory dreams are far more substantial in length and are often found in narrative or monumental contexts. Both of these dream types fit into Artemidorus' category of dreams with revelatory value. Another difference between Oppenheim and Artemidorus was already mentioned above. For Oppenheim, revelatory dreams from the Near East all claim to have divine origin. For Artemidorus, not all revelatory dreams are of divine origin.

Oppenheim's second set of distinctions again closely parallels those of Artemidorus. Among revelatory dreams (i.e., Artemidorus' dreams with divinatory value) Oppenheim distinguishes between "message dreams" whose contents are immediately clear to the dreamer, and "symbolic dreams" whose contents require interpretation in order to be understood. These categories basically correspond to Artemidorus' "theoramic" and "allegorical" dreams. The difference between Oppenheim and Artemidorus is that Oppenheim's message dream (non-symbolic dream) involves a direct communication between a heavenly being and a human. Like Artemidorus' theoramic dream, Oppenheim's message dreams do describe future events in clear, explicit language – but they are always couched in the direct speech of a heavenly being.

The literary framework of message dreams and symbolic dreams is essentially the same.[162] The real difference is the content.[163] In order to illu-

---

[161] Oppenheim, *The Interpretation of Dreams in the Ancient Near East*, 258. (Assyrian Dream Book, col.I)

[162] A typical message (non-symbolic) dream begins by stressing the fact that the dreamer has gone to bed and is asleep. Next, the dreamer transitions into a different level of reality and this change is normally indicated by a description of the dreamer "seeing" something. Invariably, it is reported that a deity "stands" at the head of the dreamer and the contents of the dream are given.

strate Oppenheim's distinction between dreams that require interpretation and those that do not as well as to provide examples with which to compare the apocalypses in chapters two through six, I provide a fresh translation of two of Oppenheim's examples from the ancient Near East. The first example is a message (non-symbolic) dream. It is the report of a dream experienced by the Neo-Babylonian king Nabonidus:[164]

> In the beginning of my eternal reign they dispatched to me a dream. *Marduk*, the great lord, and *Sîn*, the luminary of the heavens and the outer-reaches, both stood (together). *Marduk* spoke with me: "*Nabonidus*, king of Babylon, carry mudbrick(s) on your chariot horse (and) rebuild *Eḫulḫul* – cause *Sîn*, the great lord, to establish his residence in its midst." Fearfully I spoke to *Marduk*, the *Enlil* of the gods. "The temple[165] that you have commanded be rebuilt, the Mede surrounds it and his force(s) are formidable." Marduk answered me: "The Mede of whom you have spoken, he, his land, and his allies,[166] will be destroyed.[167]

The cylinder goes on to provide an account of what happened to the Median king. While the account of the Mede's fate is not part of the dream of Nabonidus, it is included in the dream narrative and bracketed by the final formula that marks the official end of the dream report, "Word of the great lord, *Marduk*, and *Sîn*, luminary of the heavens and the outer-reaches, whose edict is not overturned." In that brief enclosure, the Median king is named specifically as *Astyges*. Furthermore, *Cyrus of Anshan* (not yet Cyrus the Great) is named as *Marduk*'s tool of destruction for *Astyges*. A specific date is given for the downfall of *Astyges*: the third year of Nabonidus' reign (ca. 553 B.C.E.).

In this typical message dream, the last king of Babylon, Nabonidus, is given specific instructions from a god[168] to perform a specific task. The

---

Finally, the dreamer awakes suddenly, i.e., is startled and often becomes troubled. Oppenheim, *The Interpretation of Dreams in the Ancient Near East*, 187–91.

[163] Oppenheim, *The Interpretation of Dreams in the Ancient Near East*, 206.

[164] My translation is based on the Akkadian critical edition found in Hanspeter Schaudig, *Die Inschriften Nabonids von Babylon und Kyros' des Großen: samt den in ihrem Umfeld entstandenen Tendenzschriften; Textausgabe und Grammatik* (vol. 256; Münster: Ugarit-Verlag, 2001), 416–7.

[165] Lit., "house" (É)

[166] Lit., "the kings going with him" (LUGAL^{meš}*a-lik i-di-šu*)

[167] Lit., "will not exist" (*ul i-ba-áš-ši*).

[168] More than one copy of the Sippar cylinder has been found and they contain variant accounts of which particular God stood before Nabonidus. The exemplar housed in the British Museum reads ^{d}EN -EN GAL-*ú* "Bēl, the great lord" (i.e., the common designation for Marduk). The exemplar housed in Berlin reads ^{d}EN.ZU EN GAL-*ú* "Sîn, the great lord." Paul-Alain Beaulieu's interpretation of the Berlin variant seems persuasive, "This variant was very probably intentional, providing one more example of Nabonidus trying to assimilate Marduk to Sîn. In addition, the verbs *is-li-mu* and *ir-šu-ú ta-a-a-ri* in that same sentence are plural: 'they became reconciled and showed mercy.' Therefore the sequence ^{d}EN/ ^{d}EN.ZU EN GAL-*ú* must be interpreted as "Bēl/ Sîn (and) the great lord," the "great lord" being *Sîn* in one exemplar, and Marduk in the other."

precise geographic location of the temple to be rebuilt is given. Political opponents of Nabonidus are explicitly discussed. He is told to build the temple of *Eḫulḫul* and that his work will be troubled by neither the contemporary Median king nor allies of the Median king. While it is difficult to tell whether or not the account of Cyrus' victory is part of the dream itself or an insertion, there can be no doubt that it occurs before the formulary conclusion of the dream. After his dream vision, Nabonidus does not summon his diviners. He has no need for interpretation. Instead, the cylinder reports, he sets out to accomplish the task demanded of him.[169]

One may contrast the language used in the Nabonidus (Sippar) cylinder with a typical example of a symbolic dream. I have excerpted the next dream report from the *Epic of Gilgamesh*. Tablet 4 describes the journey of *Gilgamesh* and *Enkidu* from Uruk to the Cedar Forest (Lebanon). Along the way, *Gilgamesh* has a series of at least five dreams. Each dream greatly troubles *Gilgamesh* and *Enkidu* is required to interpret the meaning of each dream for him. The following text is taken from the first dream sequence (IV:14–33).[170]

$_{14}$*Gilgamesh* rested his chin on his knees. $_{15}$The sleep that cascades over people fell upon him. $_{16}$During the middle watch, he awoke.[171] $_{17}$He got up and spoke to his friend. $_{18}$"My friend, did you not call me? Why am I awake? $_{19}$Did you not stir me? Why am I (so) confused? $_{20}$Did a god not pass through (here)? Why is my flesh paralyzed? $_{21}$My friend, I have seen a dream. $_{22}$And the dream that I saw was totally bewildering. $_{23}$In an alpine steppe . . . $_{24}$A mountain collapsed into . . . $_{25}$and we like . . .[172] $_{26}$The one who was born in the steppe was able to give counsel. $_{27}$*Enkidu* spoke to his friend. He interpreted his dream.[173] $_{28}$My friend, your dream is auspicious. $_{29}$The dream is valuable. $_{30}$My friend, the mountain that you saw . . . . . $_{31}$We shall seize *Ḫumbaba*, we shall butcher him.[174] $_{32}$And we shall toss his remains onto

---

Paul-Alain Beaulieu, "The Sippar Cylinder of Nabonidus (2.123A)," in *The Context of Scripture* (ed. William Hallo and K. Lawson Younger; Leiden: Brill, 2003), 311.

[169] For a complete English translation of the cylinder, see Beaulieu, "The Sippar Cylinder of Nabonidus (2.123A)," 310–13.

[170] My translation is based on the eclectic transliteration found in Andrew George, *The Babylonian Gilgamesh Epic: Introduction, Critical Edition, and Cuneiform Texts* (vol. I; Oxford: Oxford University Press, 2003), 588–90.

[171] Lit., "He reached the conclusion of his sleep."

[172] George's edition reads [*u ni*]-*nu ki-i* nim gi du ki [. . . . .]. Parpola's reading is slightly different: [*ni*]-*nu ki-i* NUM *gi-du ki*-[. . . . .]. "and we like a fly . . . sinew . . ." I have chosen George's more conservative reading. Without the remainder of the line, no additional meaning is gained even if Parpola is correct.

[173] Lit. "His dream he caused him to meet." (*šu-ut-ta-šú ú-šam-ḫar-šú*). The 3ms suffix on the verb could refer either to Gilgamesh or to his dream. The basic sense of the clause does not change in either case. The expected verb, pašāru(m), is used sparingly in the *Epic of Gilgamesh*.

[174] "We shall butcher him" seems an appropriate translation of *ni-nar-raš-šu* in light of the next line. Only the parts of his body that remain intact (*šá-lam-ta-šú*) are thrown onto the field.

the (battle)-field. ₃₃And (the next) morning we shall learn from *Šamaš* an auspicious message.

Unlike Nabonidus, *Gilgamesh* is unable to understand the meaning of his dream. In the dream *Gilgamesh* is in an alpine steppe and witnesses a mountain collapse. Next, some action takes place that is directly related to him and *Enkidu*. No specific names or places are mentioned in the dream. Instead, symbols are used to represent names and places. Enkidu's response, "My friend, the mountain that you saw," indicates that the mountain is intended to have a real-world and real-time referent in their lives. Indeed, the collapsing mountain almost certainly symbolizes Humbaba. *Enkidu* declares that he and *Gilgamesh* will seize and butcher him. The representation techniques used in this dream of *Gilgamesh* are quite different from those found in the Nabonidus (Sippar) cylinder. While the Nabonidus cylinder specifically names Cyrus, the dream of *Gilgamesh* encodes Humbaba as a mountain.

The significance of Oppenheim's categories lies in the way that they cut across cultural and chronological boundaries. They are as useful outside of Mesopotamia as they are inside. They help to illumine Egyptian, Hittite, Hurrian, Greek, and Israelite dream texts. Indeed one of the most significant advances made by Oppenheim in the study of dreams is the way in which he applies his methodology to such a wide spectrum of texts. His categories work just as well when applied to texts from the Hebrew Bible as from Greece or Mesopotamia. Below are two dream reports from the Hebrew Bible. The first is a "message dream" (i.e., non-symbolic dream) and the second is a symbolic dream. These texts, as well as the Mesopotamian texts translated above, will provide a basis for comparison with the apocalypses in chapters two through six below.

A representative example of a message dream (i.e., "non-symbolic dream") is found in the call narrative of the prophet Samuel (1 Sam 3:1–14). Both its form and style are precisely the same as dream reports from ancient Mesopotamian and Egyptian sources: the dreamer is said to be asleep, the apparition "stands" before him, the message is delivered, and the dreamer wakes up in an anxious state of mind.

₁Now the lad Samuel was a servant of YHWH under [the supervision] of Eli. The word of YHWH was rare in those days and visions were not widespread.[175] ₂On a certain day while Eli, whose eyes had begun to dim [so that] he could not see, was lying down in his room ₃and the lamp of God had not yet gone out; Samuel was lying

---

[175] While the sense of אֵין חָזוֹן נִפְרָץ is clear in Hebrew, English translation is difficult. I follow the NRSV here since it seems to sacrifice the least of each word while coaxing them into functioning together in one English clause. חָזוֹן must often be translated into English as a plural (*e.g.*, Jer 23:16, Ezek 13:16, Dan 1:17).

in the temple of YHWH where the ark of God was located. ₄Then YHWH called to Samuel and he said, "Here I am." ₆He ran to Eli and said, "Here I am, for you called me." But Eli said, "I did not call you. Go back and lie down." So Samuel returned and lay down. ₇Again YHWH called to Samuel and he rose and went to Eli and said "Here I am, for you have called me." But Eli said, "I have not called you my son. Go back and lie down." ₇(Now, Samuel did not yet know YHWH and neither had the word of YHWH been revealed to him). ₈Again YHWH called to Samuel, a third time, and he arose and went to Eli and said, "Here I am, for you called me." [At last] Eli understood that YHWH was calling to the lad. ₉Eli said to Samuel, "Go, lie down, and if he should call to you [again], then you shall say, 'Speak YHWH, for your servant is listening." So Samuel went and lay down in his place. ₁₀Then YHWH came and stood[176] and called out this time like the last time, "Samuel, Samuel." And Samuel said, "Speak, for your servant is listening." ₁₁YHWH said to Samuel, behold, I am about to do something in Israel that will make both ears of anyone who hears it ring with pain. ₁₂On that day I shall fulfill against Eli everything that I have spoken against his house from beginning to end. ₁₃I have told him that I shall judge his house forever, on account of the evil about which he was aware, for his sons were blaspheming God and he did not rebuke them. ₁₄Therefore have I sworn to the house of Eli that the wickedness of the house of Eli shall not be covered by sacrifice or offering forever."

In the dream vision of Samuel, the deity delivers a message of judgment and "names names." The precise geographic *locale* of God's upcoming actions is specified: Israel. Eli and his two sons are specifically singled out for judgment. Their specific sins are explained. The dream report is completely straightforward and every element of the text is represented with language that requires no further interpretation on the part of the dreamer. Indeed, Samuel is nervous at the conclusion of his dreams precisely because he knows what he is expected to do and is worried about his ability to complete the task. One may contrast the representation techniques found in Samuel's dream with a dream report found in the Gen 41.

A paradigmatic example of a symbolic dream report from the Hebrew Bible is found in the Pharaoh's dream from the Joseph Novella (Gen 41:1–7).

₁Now it was after two years (lit. days) that Pharaoh dreamt. And behold, he was standing alongside the Nile. ₂And, behold, coming up from the Nile were seven cows of beautiful appearance and fat flesh and they fed on the sedge (marsh plants). ₃Then, behold seven more (lit. other) cows were coming up after them from the Nile, (cows) of terrible appearance and skinny (lit. thin of flesh). And they stood facing (lit. beside) the cows on the bank of the Nile. ₄And the cows of terrible appearance and thin flesh devoured the seven cows of beautiful appearance and fat (flesh). Then Pharaoh

---

[176] In dream reports from Mesopotamia and Egypt, it is conventional for a deity or other apparition to approach the dreamer and "stand" by them (usually at their head). See Oppenheim, *The Interpretation of Dreams in the Ancient Near East*, 189–91.

woke up. ₅Then he fell asleep and dreamt a second time and behold, seven ears of wheat were coming up on one stalk, fat and of good quality. ₆And behold, seven thin ears of wheat scorched (by) the east wind (i.e., Sirocco), sprouted after them. ₇And the thin ears of wheat swallowed the seven fat and full ears of wheat. Then Pharaoh awoke and, behold, it was a dream.

The writer or redactor of the Joseph novella sets the stage for this dream with several others. The reader is first introduced to Joseph's propensity as a dreamer with the reports of two dreams experienced by Joseph. The writer then introduces the reader to Joseph's ability to interpret dreams in a scene from Joseph's imprisonment in Egypt following his unfortunate encounter with the wife of Potiphar. Two cell-mates each have a dream and Joseph is able to give the correct interpretation (פִּתְרוֹן). When the Pharaoh has the disturbing dream of the cows and the wheat, he is unable to find suitable interpretation among his diviners. The former cell-mate of Joseph, for whom Joseph had correctly interpreted a dream, informs the Pharaoh about Joseph's skill and Joseph is called in for interpretation. He is able to tell the Pharaoh what the mysterious cows and ears of wheat represent.

The distinction drawn between dreams like the dream of Gilgamesh and the dream of Pharaoh on the one hand and the dream of Nabonidus and the dream of Samuel on the other hand reflects how I propose to distinguish between apocalypses that are symbolic and those that are non-symbolic. Symbolic dreams include language that points beyond itself and must be interpreted for the dreamer. Non-symbolic dreams are direct revelations from a heavenly being to a human recipient. They use clear, explicit language for which the dreamer requires no interpretation. Individuals may take issue with defining the language of apocalypses with these categories, but it is my hope that this typology can begin a conversation about the language of apocalypses that is far more deliberate than most previous investigations have been. Individuals may choose to refine or replace these categories, but we only develop a clear picture of the language of apocalypses once we begin to use deliberate and transparent terminology to describe it.

One potential problem with a typology based on the work of Artemidorus/Oppenheim should be addressed. S. Noegel's 2007 monograph, *Nocturnal Ciphers: The Allusive Language of Dreams in the Ancient Near East*, demonstrates that the language of many ancient dream reports reflects an interpretative hermeneutic based on punning (wordplay). In other words, the interpretations often included in dream reports suggest that the key to interpreting dreams lay in the transformation of the spoken word of the dreamer to the written word of the tablet. Interpretations were scholarly exercises in wordplay based on some lexical, phonetic, etc., aspect of a key word within the dream report.¹⁷⁷ While he does not eschew the categories of Artemidorus and Oppenheim, he considers them of little use because they cannot completely explain all the evidence.¹⁷⁸ The imperfection of Oppenheim's categories has been mentioned even by those who use them robustly and I, too, have voiced the same concerns above. Nevertheless, in light of the general utility of the typology, Noegel's criticism perhaps goes too far, and I suggest four reasons that Noegel's work should not spell the end of them.

The first reason concerns the terminology that Noegel introduces. He prefers the term "enigmatic" to the standard one, "symbolic." He does so because he claims that the term symbolic, "presupposes that the peoples of the ancient Near East, as we do today, conceptually distinguished symbolic modes of discourse from non-symbolic modes."¹⁷⁹ I am not convinced that Noegel's term "enigmatic" actually relieves the tension between modern and ancient Near Eastern conceptions of discourse. Indeed, it is not clear how Noegel understands the word "symbolic" and as I attempt to show below, there is hardly a consensus about the term in modern Western culture.

Related to Noegel's criticism of the word symbolic and the nature of ancient Near Eastern discourse is his presumption that most dream reports reflect actual dream experiences that are converted into written words and then interpreted using a number of wordplay techniques by scholars (diviners). There seems little doubt that some of the dream reports we possess find their origins in actual dreams (Artemidorus claims to have been an eyewitness to several of the omens that he records). But like the contents of other omen books, it is also likely that many of the omens were literary creations. (Indeed the texts that I consider in the present study are all almost certainly literary creations with no real antecedent in the dream-life of an individual). Thus, at least in terms of texts from the Hellenistic period, Noegel's concerns about mischaracterizing the conceptual framework of ancient discourse may be less well-founded.

Second, he never provides a critical articulation of what exactly he means by "enigmatic." He claims that the word has ancient precedent in the work of Macrobius, but as Jovan Bilbija points out in a *ZAW* book review, "Both Oppenheim (ib., 206) and Noegel (7 n. 15) seem to think, however, that Macrobius actually used (a Latinized version of) the term 'enig-

---

¹⁷⁷ Noegel notes, for example, how the interpretation of a dream (the apodasis of an omen) might often depend on the polyvalency of a cuneiform sign used to record the dream report (protasis). Noegel, *Nocturnal Ciphers: The Allusive Language of Dreams in the Ancient Near East*, 22–3.

¹⁷⁸ See Noegel, *Nocturnal Ciphers*, 274–6.

¹⁷⁹ Noegel, *Nocturnal Ciphers*, 7.

matic' (from the Greek αἴνιγμα 'dark saying', 'riddle'), whereas this is obviously a modern translation of Macrobius' *somnium*."[180]

Third, Noegel's pool of evidence belies his criticism of Oppenheim's typology. If the distinction between message (non-symbolic) dreams and symbolic dreams is not very helpful, it is interesting that he does not include any message dreams in his study. Ultimately his organization of the dream reports in his book implicitly follows Artemidorus and Oppenheim by choosing a subset of dreams (enigmatic dreams) to study. The so-called message dreams (non-symbolic dreams) would not be a fruitful ground for his type of analysis, and therefore the very shape of his monograph indicates that there is, in fact, a basic utility to the symbolic/non-symbolic typology.

I agree with Noegel that the typology of Artemidorus/Oppenheim cannot sufficiently explain every dream report that we now possess, but that is not the point of formal/typological work. Literary forms and linguistic techniques are always changing, evolving, and innovating (this is why discussions of concepts like *genre* are often so heated). The point is not to find a perfect paradigm or metaphor with which to describe all the evidence. The point is to find a heuristic model to organize the evidence. We only understand the deviations by understanding the major patterns. The notion that some texts deviate from the typology of Artemidorus/Oppenheim is only intelligible in light of the typology from which they deviate. In other words, without a general working model of form, etc., many of the nuances within certain literary types are missed because one has not built the necessary literary competence to read the texts. It is a nice idea that every single literary text would be read on its own against all other literary texts – abandoning comparative work that builds categories that are often broad and even superficial. But this is not how humans learn to read. Jonathan Culler makes the point in his discussion of literary competence: "To read a text as literature is not to make one's mind a *tabula rasa* and approach it without preconceptions; one must bring to it an implicit understanding of the operations of literary discourse which tells one what to look for."[181] Indeed, Noegel's own claims about the presence and function of puns in dream reports presumes a similar kind of baseline structure (this time a semantic one) in the texts. In order to isolate a pun one must presume a far more rigid and limited semantic range for the first instance of a key word. A freer, more removed use of the word (or comparable linguistic strategy) is

---

[180] Jovan Bilbija, "Review of Scott Noegel, *Nocturnal Ciphers: The Allusive Language of Dreams in the Ancient Near East*," *ZAW* 98 (2008): 139.

[181] Jonathan Culler, *Structuralist Poetics: Structuralism, Linguistics and the Study of Literature* (London: Routledge, 1975), 113–4.

then employed. But the deviation of a given lexeme from its usual or expected meaning does not really call into question the most widely attested meaning. These exceptions prove the rule and indicate that it is the rule that provides the literary competence that enables readers to venture below the surface level of dream reports.

My fourth reason also relates to Noegel's evidence pool. Noegel eschews texts that might also and/or better be described as apocalypses or ascent visions and uses very little evidence that dates from the Hellenistic period. His choice of evidence is fine as far as it goes – one would not expect an analysis of *every* known dream report from the ancient Near East. But problems arise from his pool of evidence. Any nuances or patterns (or problems for his thesis) that might appear in texts from the Hellenistic Period (especially apocalypses) are missed. Related to this is his distaste for the term "symbolic" as anachronistic (or even imperialistic) in terms of ancient Near Eastern discourse. He eschews the term at some points as modern and at others as Hellenistic.[182] He may be correct about the misapplication of the term to second millennium texts from Mesopotamia. But one should perhaps be more generous in applying the Hellenistic term to Hellenistic texts (and Hellenistic texts are precisely the evidence with which the present study is concerned).

In spite of my criticism of Noegel and my defense of the basic utility of the dream typologies produced by Artemidorus and Oppenheim, I admit that the distinction between symbolic and non-sybmolic (or needing interpretation vs. needing no interpretation) cannot fully explain the evidence that I approach in this study. Noegel's own work on wordplay has surely revealed a treasure trove of information that would have never been found if he relied only on the typology of Artemidorus/Oppenheim to explain the language of dream reports and I greatly admire his innovation. Thus, the conceptual framework I propose begins with the typology of Artemidorus and Oppenheim, but it does not end there.

Structuralist Poetics and Symbols as Conventional Signs
It became clear early in my research that the symbolic/non-symbolic typology outlined above could not fully explain all of the features of the language encountered in part one of this study. More specifically, among the symbolic apocalypses, some finer distinctions require explanation. In light of the typology borrowed from Oppenheim, it is possible to discuss the semiotics of symbols in apocalypses on two levels. The first level involves the way in which each symbol refers to an historical antecedent (i.e., how

---

[182] Noegel, *Nocturnal Ciphers*, 7–8, 275.

the "little horn" of Dan 7 refers to Antiochus Epiphanes). These relationships appear to take the form of several kinds of tropes, i.e., metaphor, synecdoche, metonymy, etc. Thus, my model of "symbol" generally corresponds with the definition used by Umberto Eco. Eco defines a symbol as a kind of textual implicature and uses the following example as paradigmatic:

> Put the wheel of a carriage at the door of a country house. It can be the sign for the workshop of a carriage maker (and in this sense it is an *example* of the whole class of object there produced); it can be the sign for a restaurant (thus being a *sample, pars pro toto*, of that rural world of which it announces and promises the culinary delights); it can be the *stylization* of a stylization for the local seat of the Rotary Club.[183]

Each of the possible interpretations listed by Eco represents a different type of trope (e.g., synecdoche, metonymy, etc.). For him, the word symbol comprises them all. "Here events, gestures, things suddenly appear as strange, inexplicable, intrusive evidence with a context which is too weak to justify their presence. So they reveal that they are there to reveal something else; it is up to the reader to decide what else."[184] It is possible, however, that a more restricted semiotics is at work on a different level of the language.

The Second type of semiotics involved in apocalyptic symbols is characterized by the way in which certain symbol-types consistently name particular referent-types. In other words, most symbolic apocalypses use a limited and stable repertoire of symbols-types and these symbol types appear to have conventional associations with certain referent types. For example, animals are almost always used to refer to humans (regardless of what species of animal might point to which particular human or group of humans) and humans are normally used to refer to angels.[185] In other words, close analysis of the texts turned up a series of conventional relationships. I mentioned in the research history above one failed attempt to read the symbols found in texts like Dan 7 as conventional signs (i.e., "steno-symbols").[186] This theory was rightly criticized by Collins.[187] But I also mentioned in the research history that Perrin failed to consider levels of meaning beyond the strict association between a symbol and its immediate referent and that a broader analysis may yet turn up an important applica-

---

[183] Eco, *Semiotics and the Philosophy of Language*, 162.

[184] Eco, *Semiotics and the Philosophy of Language*, 157.

[185] The first and, to my knowledge, only intentional investigation into this level of the symbolism of Jewish apocalypses is found in Lange, "Dream Visions and Apocalyptic Milieus," 27–34.

[186] Perrin, "Eschatology and Hermeneutics," 3–14.

[187] Collins, "The Symbolism of Transcendence in Jewish Apocalyptic," 5–22. Collins, *The Apocalyptic Vision*, 144–6. Collins, *The Apocalyptic Imagination*, 16.

tion for semiotics/structural linguistics. I now turn to work on symbols as conventional signs in order to establish a nomenclature to describe the data I have encountered.

Modern, critical connotations of "symbol" have evolved from Ferdinand de Saussure's work in linguistics.[188] De Saussure understood all language to be a system of signs. It is important first to note that de Saussure distinguishes between a language and expressions of that language i.e., speech (*parole*) since I use the word language to mean something more narrow than what de Saussure intends. For de Saussure, "A language, as a collective phenomenon, takes the form of a totality of imprints in everyone's brain, rather like a dictionary of which each individual has an identical copy. Thus it is something which is in each individual, but is none the less common to all."[189] The importance of this distinction is highlighted by the problem of the representation of a language in writing. De Saussure points out, for example, that while a language normally operates in a state of constant evolution, writing tends to remain fixed, and as a consequence, to misrepresent language. A simple example would be how the pronunciation of a word may evolve without a corresponding evolution in the orthography of that word – leaving the reader with a representation of the word that is, in De Saussure's words, "absurd." Such is the case with many French words ending in "oi" such as the word for king: "*roi*." De Saussure charts the variation in pronunciation and orthography for *roi* between the eleventh and fourteenth centuries CE:[190]

---

[188] See "Saussure," in *Modern Literary Theory: A Reader* (ed. Philip Rice and Patricia Waugh; New York: Arnold, 1996), 6–15. See also Daniel Chandler, *Semiotics: The Basics* (London: Routledge, 2002), 17–32. Jonathan Culler, *Literary Theory: A Very Short Introduction* (Oxford: Oxford University Press, 2000), 57–61.

[189] Ferdinand de Saussure, *Course in General Linguistics* (Lasalle: Open Court, 1986), 19.

[190] Saussure, *Course in General Linguistics*, 27.

Period	Pronounced	Written
11th c.	*rei*	*rei*
13th c.	*roi*	*roi*
14th c.	*roè*	*roi*
19th c.	*rwa*	*roi*

I highlight the distinction between *langue* and *parole* here because I use de Saussure's theory outside of the context in which he developed it and for purposes that he may not have foreseen. As I shall show below, however, I am not the first to do so. De Saussure's theory of language has been successfully applied in several other contexts.

De Saussure was particularly keen to highlight the conventional relationships that exist in languages and how those conventional relationships belie the notion that all people begin essentially with the same vista into the physical- and thought-worlds within which they exist. In other words, he argued against the (still) common notion that a language is ultimately "a list of terms corresponding to a list of things."[191] One of the most significant problems with this view according to de Saussure is that, "It assumes that ideas already exist independently of words."[192] Jonathan Culler describes de Saussure's language system and its focus on the arbitrary nature of signs:

First, the sign (for instance, a word) is a combination of a form (the 'signifier') and a meaning (the 'signified'), and the relation between form and meaning is based on convention, not natural resemblance. What I am sitting on is called a *chair* but could perfectly well have been called something else – *wab* or *punce* . . . The second aspect of the arbitrary nature of the sign: both the signifier (form) and the signified (mean-

---

[191] Saussure, *Course in General Linguistics*, 65.
[192] Saussure, *Course in General Linguistics*, 65.

Introduction

ing) are themselves conventional divisions of the plane of sound and the plane of thought respectively.[193]

The problem is not that one cannot isolate the kind of correspondences between a list of terms and a list of things in any given language – indeed, for de Saussure the nature of the linguistic sign is precisely the interaction between an idea and the sound that acts as its signal. The problem is that not all languages possess the same list of things and therefore learning a new language is more complex than simply exchanging one list of terms for another.[194] For example, English has no true equivalent for the French word *bouffer* (cf. German *fressen*, i.e., "to eat" – normally used only for animals or in a very informal way for humans). Similarly, English has no specific word for a one-eyed person, but French does: *borgne*. De Saussure holds that we create the world around us with our language. The world itself is qualitatively different for an American speaker of English than it is for a French speaker of French (or even a British speaker of English).

In other words, the "lists" of concepts and things mentioned above exists, but only in the discrete arena of a single language and not because concepts precede their linguistic expression – both sign and signifier function in a symbiotic relationship. Crucial to de Saussure's theory of language is his conviction that any given language is not merely a nomenclature that "provides its own names for categories that exist outside language."[195] To the contrary:

> This is a point with crucial ramifications for recent theory. We tend to assume that we have the words *dog* and *chair* in order to name dogs and chairs, which exist outside any language. But, Saussure argues, if words stood for preexisting concepts, they would have exact equivalents in meaning from one language to the next, which is not at all the case. Each language is a system of concepts as well as forms: a system of conventional signs that organizes the world.[196]

De Saussure's theories help to explain how "face" can be plural in Hebrew (פנים) while it is singular in English. Rather than simply reflecting a reality that is obvious to everyone, our languages create reality. Different groups possess and maintain different linguistic encyclopedias based on their own arbitrary associations between signifier and signified. Therefore the symbols used in any given language depend directly upon intellectual structures present within a given community. These structures are unique to every language though it is possible for some structures to become ubiquitous or nearly ubiquitous. It is important to note that De Saussure works only on

---

[193] Culler, *Literary Theory*, 57–8.
[194] Saussure, *Course in General Linguistics*, 65–70.
[195] Culler, *Literary Theory*, 58.
[196] Culler, *Literary Theory*, 58.

the level of language, broadly conceived. He does not specifically treat manifestations of a given language in a semantically limiting context such as a literary text, e.g., a novel. But others have applied De Saussure's work on structural linguistics fruitfully in other contexts. The American philosopher Charles Peirce applied to mathematics an intellectual model similar to the one de Saussure developed in his work on linguistics. (Both worked around the same time and independently of one another).

Peirce shares with de Saussure the view that every word, spoken or written, is a component of a sign.[197] But for Peirce, a taxonomic enthusiast, signs can be divided into three basic categories: Iconic, Indexical, and Symbolic.[198] Most semioticians recognize the importance of the categories to the extent that they help to nuance de Saussure's concept of the sign as arbitrary.[199] In other words, the relationships between some signifiers and what they signify are more arbitrary in some cases than others.[200] Among the three categories it is the symbolic sign that is most purely conventional.

For Peirce, iconic signs have qualities that resemble the objects they represent.[201] Iconic signs are not as conventional as symbols, but more so than indexes. One can often deduce the relationship between an icon and its referent based on the qualities of the icon itself. For example, the Proto-Sinaitic *mem* (〰) represents water as an iconic sign and it actually has the appearance of water (waves).[202] Other examples would be portraits, literary tropes such as metaphor and onomatopoeia, and "realistic" sounds (i.e., the sound of a lion's roar representing a lion).[203]

Unlike the icon (the object of which may be fictional), an index stands unequivocally for this or that existing thing.[204] For example, a thermometer provides an indexical signification of the ambient temperature. A low barometer with moist air is an index of rain. Smoke is an index of fire. A personal trademark can also be an indexical sign, e.g., the catchphrase of

---

[197] Peirce differs from Saussure in that he sees three rather than two essential components of any sign: the representamen, an interpretant, and an object. See Charles Peirce, *The Collected Papers of Charles S. Peirce* (Charlottesville: InteLex Corporation 1994), 2.228.

[198] Peirce, *The Collected Papers of Charles S. Peirce*, 2.274–308.

[199] Eco criticizes Peirce's restriction of the word symbol for conventional relationships, but he also admits that, at least etymylogically speaking, this definition probably most accurately reflects the meaning of *sumballein* (even if he docs claim that etymologies lie), cf. Umberto Eco, *The Limits of Interpretation* (Bloomington: Indiana University Press, 1990), 8–9. Eco, *Semiotics and the Philosophy of Language*, 130.

[200] Chandler, *Semiotics*, 36.

[201] Peirce, *The Collected Papers of Charles S. Peirce*, 2.276.

[202] The same can probably be said about the pre-exilic Hebrew *mem*, although it is obvious that the form has already began its journey towards being a symbolic (i.e., conventional) sign. I juxtapose pre-exilic and post-exilic examples of *mem* here: מ (Tel Dan), מ (1QIs^a).

[203] Cf. Chandler, *Semiotics*, 37.

[204] Peirce, *The Collected Papers of Charles S. Peirce*, 2.283–91, 305–6.

Santa Claus ("HO HO HO") or Barack Obama ("Yes We Can"). Similarly, in the United States, the song "Hail to the Chief" is an index of the President since it is only played for presidents. Indexical signs are problematic, however, because indexes can and often do morph into symbols over time. Jonathan Culler provides a representative example: "A Rolls Royce is an index of wealth because one must be wealthy to own one, but social usage has led to its becoming a conventional symbol of wealth."[205]

Symbolic signs are characterized by an entirely arbitrary relationship to their referent. That is to say, one cannot deduce a given meaning from a symbolic sign – the correlation between signifier and signified is entirely conventional. Peirce's symbolic sign is what De Saussure meant by "sign." According to Peirce, "All words, sentences, books, and other conventional signs are symbols."[206] The clearest example of a symbolic sign comes from mathematics. In math the term π is used to indicate the number 3.14. Nothing about π can lead one to infer it represents the number 3.14. It is only the conventional relationship between the signifier and the signified that allows one to understand and use π. An example closer to the subject matter of this project can be taken from the post-exilic form of the Hebrew letter 'ayin. It does not bear an iconic relationship to an eye or spring in the way that the Paleo-Hebrew (Phoenician) 'ayin does, e.g., ய ($1QIsa^a$) vs. O (Tel Dan). It is a purely conventional association.

While the concept of the symbol as a representation of a conventional association was developed in contexts considerably removed from Hellenistic Jewish literature, the work done by de Saussure and Peirce has since been fruitfully applied to literary contexts. Most of these fall under the umbrella of Structuralism and, thus, have closer ties to de Saussure than Peirce. Several studies of Roland Barthes are relevant, but perhaps most of all his analysis of the language used in fashion magazines.[207] The work of Claude Lévi-Strauss on mythology is relevant, as is the work of Roman Jakobson on poetics and the work of A.J. Greimas on semantics.[208] Perhaps most

---

[205] Culler, *Structuralist Poetics*, 17. See also Chandler, *Semiotics*, 43.

[206] Peirce, *The Collected Papers of Charles S. Peirce*, 292.

[207] Roland Barthes, *Système de la mode* (Paris: Seuil, 1967). For another work in which Barthes synthesizes his work on fashion with other topics and ties them all to larger theoretical questions of meaning in language, see Roland Barthes, *Elements of Semiology* (New York: Hill and Wang, 1967).

[208] Cf. the four volumes of Lévi-Strauss's *Mythologiques*: Claude Lévi-Strauss, *The Raw and the Cooked* (New York Harper & Row, 1969). Claude Lévi-Strauss, *From Honey to Ashes* (New York: Harper & Row, 1973). Claude Lévi-Strauss, *The Origin of Table Manners* (New York: Harper & Row, 1978). Claude Lévi-Strauss, *The Naked Man* (New York: Harper & Row, 1981). Roman Jakobson, "Linguistics and Poetics," in *Style in Language* (ed. T. Sebeock; Cambridge: MIT Press, 1960). Algirdas Julien Greimas, *Structural Semantics: An Attempt at Method* (Lincoln: University of Nebraska Press, 1984). Algirdas Julien Greimas, *Narrative Semiotics and Cognitive Discourses* (London: Pinter Publishers, 1990).

instructive for the present study, however, is Claude Levi-Strauss's application of structuralism to the notion of "totemism" (i.e., the phenomenon by which certain tribes are associated or described with certain animals). For Levi-Strauss, to explain a given totem is to understand its place in a system of signs – not merely its particular connection to the culture/group it names.[209] In other words, if one culture is named bear, another fish, and another hawk, it is at least as important to understand the relationships between bears, fish, and hawks as it is to understand the relationship between a particular people-group and "bear."[210] Levi-Strauss's work can serve as a kind of paradigm for the sort of linguistic analysis that is needed in order to understand the language of apocalypses. The totality of the symbolic system at work is what allows one to understand how a single example functions. It will be useful to address Lévi-Strauss's work on totemism in chapters two and three below. There I ask not only how a given symbol describes its referent, but also how the symbol-categories interact with each other and across the genre. In other words, I am attempting to apply a semiotics/Structuralist poetics to a different level of the text than has been previously applied.

Group Specific Language in the Non-Symbolic Apocalypses?
In the last sections I turned to several studies in structural linguistics/semiotics in order to obtain a nomenclature with which to describe the data encountered in part one of this study. The data encountered in part two (non-symbolic apocalypses) also present problems that cannot be answered fully or evenly described using the dream report typologies analyzed above. While the non-symbolic apocalypses analyzed in part two do not use language that points beyond itself or for which the visionary requires interpretation, they often employ cryptic expressions and sobriquets that may have been intelligible only to a limited group of people. An example is perhaps found in Dan 12:3: מַצְדִּיקֵי הָרַבִּים "those who lead many to righteousness." The group described with the expression מַצְדִּיקֵי הָרַבִּים is not symbolic

---

[209] By reading into the social structure of several native peoples a basic opposition between nature and culture, Lévi-Strauss describes the relationships between particular tribes and their "totems" in a series of possible relationships. For him, the very idea of totemism is the unfortunate result of an overly simplistic imagination of the relationship between a given tribe and an animal or plant type. "The totemic illusion is thus the result, in the first place, of a distortion of a semantic field to which belong phenomena of the same type. Certain aspects of this field have been singled out at the expense of others, giving them an originality and a strangeness which they do not really possess; for they are made to appear mysterious by the very fact of abstracting them from the system of which, as transformations, they formed an integral part." Claude Lévi-Strauss, *Totemism* (Boston: Beacon Press, 1963), 18.

[210] Lévi-Strauss, *Totemism*, 15–31, esp., 28–9.

according to the basic typology I employ in this study. It is not a figure of speech that points beyond itself and the visionary does not require an interpretation of its meaning. But unlike other group-descriptions that were widely used and understood in the Judaism(s) of the Hellenistic Period (e.g., "Pharisees," "Sadducees," etc.), this expression is intelligible only to the reader/hearer that is privy to insider information.

The use of group-specific language is hardly limited to non-symbolic apocalypses in Jewish literature of the Hellenistic Period. Indeed, the Dead Sea Scrolls have provided scholars with a treasure trove of group-specific language. Enigmatic expressions like מורה הצדק "The Teacher of Righteousness," הכהן הרשע "The Wicked Priest," and איש הכזב "The Man of the Lie" have prompted a lively scholarly debate over their referents.[211] Recently scholars have brought more methodological sophistication to investigations of how identity is encoded and constructed in the texts found at Qumran. Carol Newsom's 2004 monograph, *The Self as Symbolic Space*, is an exemplar.[212] The fifth meeting of the International Organization of Qumran Studies in Groningen, which was convened in the same year that Newsom's study was published, was devoted to a similar topic and resulted in a volume of proceedings that adds significantly to our knowledge of how language was used to construct identity in Judaism of the Hellenistic Period.[213] Examples include Maxine Grossman's attempt to isolate a kind of subterranean level of discourse in the *Damascus Document* that helps sectarians learn that they are sectarians, Carol Newsom's analysis of non-polemical

---

[211] Numerous studies are devoted to the identities of these figures, though significantly less attention has been given to how these types of descriptions function within Jewish discourse in the Hellenistic Period. See Matthew Collins, *The Use of Sobriquets in the Qumran Dead Sea Scrolls* (London: T&T Clark, 2009). Hanan Eshel, *The Dead Sea Scrolls and the Hasmonean State* (Grand Rapids: Eerdmans, 2008), 29–61. Håkan Bengtsson, *What's in a Name? A Study of the Sobriquets in the Pesharim* (Uppsala: Uppsala University Press, 2000). Ida Fröhlich, "Qumran Names" in *The Provo International Conference on the Dead Sea Scrolls: Technological Innovations, New Texts, and Reformulated Issues* (ed. Donald W. Parry and Eugene C. Ulrich; STDJ 30; Leiden: Brill, 1999), 294-305; "From Pseudepigraphic to Sectarian" *RevQ* 21 (2004): 395-406. For a list of group-specific terms used by Essenes, see James Charlesworth, *The Pesharim and Qumran History: Chaos or Consensus* (Grand Rapids: Eerdmans, 2002), 41. See also Armin Lange, "Kriterien essinischer Texte," in *Qumran Kontrovers: Beiträge zu den Textfunden vom Toten Meer* (ed. Jörg Frey and Hartmut Stegemann; Paderborn: Bonifatius, 2003), 65–6. Especially relevant is Devorah Dimant, "The Qumran Manuscripts: Contents and Significance," in *Time to Prepare the Way in the Wilderness. Papers on the Qumran Scrolls by Fellows of the Institute for Advanced Studies of the Hebrew University, Jerusalem, 1989–1990* (ed. D. Dimant and L. Schiffman; vol. 16 of *STDJ*; Leiden: Brill, 1995), 23–58.

[212] Carol Newsom, *The Self as Symbolic Space: Constructing Identity and Community at Qumran* (STDJ 52; Leiden: Brill, 2004).

[213] Florentino García Martínez and Mladen Popović, eds., *Defining Identities: We, You, and the Other in the Dead Sea Scrolls. Proceedings of the Fifth Meeting of the IOQS in Groningen* (STDJ; Leiden: Brill, 2008).

discourse in the *Serek haYahad* and *Hodayot* in light of Bakhtin's theory of language, and Jutta Jokiranta's investigation of the *Psalms Pesher* in light of social identity theories associated
with H. Tajfel.[214] These studies comport with the evidence of material culture at the Qumran settlement.[215]

Matthew Collins's 2009 monograph, *The Use of Sobriquets in the Qumran Dead Sea Scrolls*, is a sustained investigation of some of the most prominent nicknames used in Qumran texts and is important because he attempts to understand more systematically what is signified by these linguistic patterns themselves. He is particularly concerned with the evolution of the expressions over time in sectarian texts from Qumran. Others have expressed similar ideas before.[216] This possible evolution serves to highlight the extent to which the expressions themselves are constructed by the group *and construct* the group. In other words, some may not have strict historical referents, but might have been used at the discretion of the sectarians to refer to numerous persons who fit the requisite criteria. The use of the terms, then, presumes a linguistic competence that comes only with a sustained involvement in the group. As M. Collins puts it, "A sobriquet is a label that can convey positive or negative connotations and which, given the subjective nature of the descriptive element, has validity only within the context of those who share such a viewpoint."[217] He adds, "Its meaning and specific referent may well be clear to those 'in the know' yet perpetually obscure to outsiders. In this sense, a sobriquet is not strictly a codename (though it may seem it to outsiders), but a transparent label obvious to those

---

[214] Maxine Grossman, "Cultivating Identity: Textual Virtuosity and "Insider" Status," in *Defining Identities: We, You, and the Other in the Dead Sea Scrolls. Proceedings of the Fifth Meeting of the IOQS in Groningen* (ed. Florentino García Martínez and Mladen Popović; vol. 70 of *STDJ*; Leiden: Brill, 2008), 1–11. Carol Newsom, "Constructing 'We, You, and Others" through Non-Polemical Discourse," in *Defining Identities: We, You, and the Other in the Dead Sea Scrolls. Proceedings of the Fifth Meeting of the IOQS in Groningen.* (ed. Florentino García Martínez and Mladen Popović; vol. 70 of *STDJ*; Leiden: Brill, 2008), 13–21. Jutta Jokiranta, "Social Identity Approach: Identity-Constructing Elements in the Psalms Pesher," in *Defining Identities: We, You, and the Other in the Dead Sea Scrolls. Proceedings of the Fifth Meeting of the IOQS in Groningen* (ed. Florentino García Martínez and Mladen Popović; vol. 70 of *STDJ*; Leiden: Brill, 2008), 85–109.

[215] Magness highlights how, for example, some of the distinctive ceramic types found at Qumran indicate a community marked by unique *halakhah*. Jodi Magness, *The Archaeology of Qumran and the Dead Sea Scrolls* (Eerdmans: Grand Rapids, 2002), 82–9.

[216] For example, in Florentino García Martínez and Adam van der Woude's understanding of the Qumran community, the expression "wicked priest" would have referred to more than one Hasmonean High Priest. "A 'Groningen' Hypothesis of Qumran Early Origins and Early History" in *RevQ* 14 (1990): 521-542. As Collins notes, this position was already espoused by William Brownlee, "The Wicked Priest, the Man of Lies, and the Righteous Teacher: The Problem of Identity." in *JQR* 73 (1982): 1-37.

[217] Collins, *The Use of Sobriquets*, 19.

among whom it is used."²¹⁸ The last point is important. It may not be that the expressions are designed to be secrets, but it is possible, even likely, that they would seem like secrets to outsiders. Thus, the use of sobriquets is probably less to keep outsiders out as it is to help insiders know (and demonstrate) that they are inside. An example of the evolution of the Qumran sobriquets can be found, according to Collins, in the development of the expression יורה הצדק "One who will teach righteousness" as a future eschatological figure in CD 6 2–11a to a historical מורה צדק "teacher of righteousness" who lived among the community in CD 4 1–11a to a departed and venerated figure permanently cemented into the identity of the group as מורה הצדק "the teacher of rightousness" in 1QpHab.²¹⁹ The fact that the various expressions יורה הצדק , מורה צדק, and מורה הצדק might be easily collapsed into a single historical figure by outsiders (including modern scholars!) highlights the nuanced linguistic competence that might have been necessary to navigate community identity at any interval. Thus, these expressions work in a fundamentally different way than does the language used to depict *dramatis personae* in symbolic apocalypses. In those cases, a rich interaction with patterns and motifs widespread in the culture would have produced a different effect. Rather than serving as a *de facto* barrier to interpretation as sobriquets could have, symbolic descriptions contain within themselves exegetical tools that commend their use among wide audiences.

What makes the present study different from almost every study of group-specific language in the Dead Sea Scrolls is that the texts I analyze in part two are all probably non-Essene texts. Despite their different approaches to discourse, the studies of scrolls mentioned above analyze primarily or exclusively sectarian/Essene texts. The group-specific language used in the non-Essene texts from Qumran may then permit an even clearer picture into how language/discourse was used to construct identity in Essene texts by comparison, but it may shed even more light on the strategies used throughout Judaism of the Hellenistic Period.

To the recent work performed by Qumran specialists, we must also add work by those studying modern apocalypticism. Several important investigations of how apocalyptic groups construct identity can compliment the work done by scholars of the ancient world. The classic study of apocalypticism from a modernist perspective is Michael Barkun's *Disaster and the Millenium*. According to Barkun, the formation of apocalyptic groups is always predicated, at least in the first instance, upon the creation of two distinct spheres: the righteous microcosm and the evil macrocosm. The

---

²¹⁸ Collins, *The Use of Sobriquets*, 19.
²¹⁹ Collins, *The Use of Sobriquets*, 39–47, 53–58, 125–40.

microcosm created by apocalyptic groups is "an insular social world with distinctive norms and goals" and the macrocosm is "perceived as evil, decaying, and doomed."[220] According to Barkun, the microcosm "must be kept separate from its environment, and its activities must be directed toward individual commitment and group cohesion."[221] The natural mileu in which Barkun locates microcosm movements is agrarian society: "Millenarian movements require a complex social ecology for nurturance, one in which cultural motifs, charismatic leadership, disaster vulnerability and occurrence, and isolation interact with one another."[222] Other scholars have rejected this notion and it is obviously problematic for ancient Judaism since some apocalypses contain utopian visions that are distinctly urban.[223] Barkun makes some allowances for the fact that intellectual constructions might be used to substitute a social mythology for true agrarianism and points to possible exceptions such as fourteenth–fifteenth century Florence, Italy, where the city's own myth-history allowed for the development of apocalypticism within "the cult of Florentine greatness."[224]

As Amy Johnson Frykholm says in her study of the readers of the *Left Behind* book series, "The homogeneity that Barkun insists is important need only be imagined, asserted, and then reinforced by physical or symbolic boundaries."[225] Her analysis of *Left Behind* readers emphasizes this appropriation of Barkun: "The separation between microcosm and macrocosm is crucial to the apocalyptic mythology employed by *Left Behind* and evident in broader American apocalypticism. It asks readers to identify themselves with a marginalized minority as 'outsiders' to the evil majority."[226] More specifically, it asks Protestant Evangelicals to do so. Catholic or Mormon readers, for example, often find the text obtuse and impenetrable because of its dependence on specialized terminology that only Protestant Evangelicals typically understand. Frykholm writes, "The books' language is usually too culturally specific, though it makes universal claims, to do the work producers and many readers hope it will. For readers on the outside, *Left Behind* can be interesting because, as one Mormon man says, 'the language is

---

[220] Michael Barkun, *Disaster and the Millenium* (New Haven: Yale University Press, 1974), 91.

[221] Barkun, *Disaster and the Millenium*, 91.

[222] Barkun, *Disaster and the Millenium*, 96.

[223] The contrary point is made well enough for modern apocalyptic groups by the breadth of urban-centered evidence analyzed in Thomas Robbins and Susan J. Palmer, eds., *Millenium, Messiahs, and Mayhem: Contemporary Apocalyptic Movements* (New York: Routeledge, 1997).

[224] Barkun, *Disaster and the Millenium,* 166–99, esp. 170–73.

[225] Amy Johnson Frykholm, *Rapture Culture: Left Behind in Evangelical America* (Oxford: Oxford University Press, 2004), 14.

[226] Frykholm, *Rapture Culture*, 15.

so far out there, to my mind it is almost wacky.'"²²⁷ For example, the characters in *Left Behind* understand a crucial difference between "believing in God" and "accepting Christ" that most Protestant Evangelical readers will immediately recognize. Indeed, one who understands the crucial difference will have their participation in the linguistically-structured world of *Left Behind* validated. Demonstrating discursive competence affirms the reader's identity within the microcosm of *Left Behind*. While the goal of this language is not to leave others out, the language has this effect. A Catholic reader interviewed by Frykholm told her he was bemused as the "Protestant-ese . . . played itself out and tried to pretty itself as entertainment."²²⁸ He is bemused because of the way "Protestant-ese" is spoken by every character in the novel – even the ones that should not, ostensibly, understand it. "All of the Christian characters, whether they are Middle Eastern, Greek, or from the American Midwest, speak in the idiom of American evangelicalism. In the Midst of all of this, Mark wants an acknowledgement that 'other people won't understand.'" ²²⁹ Indeed, one of the most fundamental concepts in the novel, the "rapture," is a recent theological conjecture that is intelligible almost exclusively in American evangelicalism.²³⁰ One evangelical reader tells Frykholm that she expects the rapture to take place within 30 years. Frykholm writes, "The next thirty years places the rapture toward the end of Bobbi's expected life span. For her, the rapture is an event contained within the story of her life, her own life's expected end. Another reader, an older man named Jackson, tells me, 'I don't expect to die before the rapture happens.'"²³¹ Non-evangelical readers, even those well-versed in the Book of Revelation, are effectively pushed outside of *Left Behind's* microcosm because of their linguistic incompetence.

In his study of millennial rhetoric, Stephen O'Leary argues that the rise and importance of the notion of rapture for American evangelicals can be read as a defense mechanism by which obvious and embarrassing failures such as the "Great Disappointment" of William Miller. In other words, it served to preserve linguistically the boundaries of the microcosm at a time when the boundaries were vulnerable:

The doctrine of the rapture, also known as the "any-moment coming," provided at least three observable rhetorical advantages. First, by positing what was in effect a floating "locus of the irreparable," a temporal threshold that would cut the audience off from the chance to avoid the persecutions of the Tribulation, it functioned as a strong incentive for the conversion of non-believers. Second, as I have already

---

²²⁷ Frykholm, *Rapture Culture*, 73.
²²⁸ Frykholm, *Rapture Culture*, 72.
²²⁹ Frykhom, *Rapture Culture*, 72.
²³⁰ The idea began with the 19ᵗʰ century Plymouth Brethren pastor John Nelson Darby.
²³¹ Frykholm, *Rapture Culture*, 108.

shown, the thought of Christ's imminent return for his saints in the rapture functioned as a mechanism of ethical purification by helping believers to maintain their faith and resist temptations. Third, it gave believers hope that they might avoid not only the catastrophic events of the last days, but also their own personal deaths.[232]

O'Leary highlights other instances of this kind of rhetorical shaping and reinforcing of the microcosm. Examples include Hal Lindsey's use of the expression "this generation" (cf. Matt 24:34) in *The 1980's: Countdown to Armageddon* and Pat Robertson's utopian visions of a future American theocracy in which the microcosm *becomes* the macrocosm with God's help.[233]

Lee Quinby has also characterized apocalypticism as a kind of discourse: "The discourse of apocalypse has rules and conventions for establishing meaning, designating the true from the false, empowering certain speakers and writers and disqualifying others."[234] Indeed, Quinby invokes M. Foucault to characterize apocalypticism as a "regime of truth."[235] This politico-rhetorical model, according to Quinby, explains why a nationalistic, apocalyptic citizen of the United States is likely to use expressions like "America" and "Americans" in a way distinct from how others in North and South Amerca might. Their use of the terms reflects, e.g., Ronald Reagan's "empire of ideals" in such a way that citizens of the U.S. are set apart as more true or real Americans than others (e.g., Mexicans).[236] In other words, the discursive equivalent of Barkun's more literal microcosm is constructed by some in an American vision of ongoing manifest destiny. In a case such as this, "America" is hardly a secretive term, but the full implications of its specialized meaning may not be fully obvious to Brazilians or even more circumspect U.S. citizens.

Barkun's model of microcosm vs. macrocosm is applicable to symbolic apocalypses no less than non-symbolic apocalypses. But the poetics used to accomplish this bifurcation is different and may reflect different real or imagined socio-political locations. The kind of cultural and linguistic competence assumed and employed by non-symbolic apocalypses is different than the one presumed by symbolic apocalypses. The examples of group-specific language I have discussed in this section, whether from the *Damascus Document* or *Left Behind*, provide models for understanding the function of language in texts like Daniel 10–12, 4QPs-Dan^{a-b} ar, and the *Apo-*

---

[232] Stephen O'Leary, *Arguing the Apocalypse: A Theory of Millenial Rhetoric* (Oxford: Oxford University Press, 1994).

[233] O'Leary, *Arguing the Apocalypse*, 153–54, 184–89.

[234] Lee Quinby, *Anti-Apocalypse: Exercises in Genealogical Criticism* (Minneapolis: University of Minnesota Press, 1994), xv.

[235] Quinby, *Anti-Apocalypse*, xv.

[236] Quinby, *Anti-Apocalypse*, xviii–xix.

cryphon of Jeremiah C. Both are equally at home in the genre apocalypse. And this diversity tells us something about the inherent flexibility of literary genre apocalypse in the Judaism(s) of the Hellenistic period.

Part One: Symbolic Apocalypses

Chapter Two

Daniel 2, 7, 8

In this chapter I analyze the language found in three apocalypses from the Book of Daniel: chapters 2, 7, and 8. I initially approached the Book of Daniel with the expectation that its symbolic language would provide a foil for the techniques used in *Apocryphon of Jeremiah C* and 4QPseudo-Daniel^{a-b} ar. In some respects this hypothesis has proven accurate, but a far more complex picture has emerged. When read in light of the categories used by Artemidorus and Leo Oppenheim to describe symbolism in dream reports, the apocalypses in chapters 2, 7, and 8 operate somewhere between symbolism and realism. In other words, they contain symbolic visions that must be interpreted, but they also contain explicit revelations from heavenly figures. I categorize them as symbolic apocalypses in order to distinguish them from the texts in part two that do not use any symbolic language. Beyond this general typology, several deeper associations are uncovered. These relationships are illuminated by the theoretical work of de Saussure, Peirce, and Lévi-Strauss, which I outlined in chapter one. A structuralist poetics adapted from de Saussure and Peirce does not help us to discover the antecedent for each symbol (as some have claimed),[1] but it can reveal the deep, conventional, linguistic structures present in many ancient Jewish apocalypses.

The Genre Apocalypse and the Book of Daniel

Daniel is the only fully developed apocalypse in the Hebrew Bible and it has played a disproportionately significant role in most discussions of the genre apocalypse.[2] The discovery of the antiquity of some parts of *1 Enoch* such as the *Book of Watchers* (*1 En.* 1–36) and the *Astronomical Book* (*1 En.* 72–82) has required scholars to recalculate Daniel's pride-of-place

---

[1] Perrin, "Eschatology and Hermeneutics," 3–14.
[2] See Collins, *The Apocalyptic Imagination*, 85. As Collins notes, Daniel's prominence has not always been helpful to the understanding of the genre apocalypse.

within analyses of the genre.³ In light of the Enochic texts, scholars such as Paolo Sacchi and Gabriele Boccaccini have objected to treating Daniel as an apocalypse at all.⁴ A majority, however, continue to view the Book of Daniel as crucial for understanding ancient Jewish apocalypses.⁵ Moreover, since the *Animal Apocalypse* does not appear to predate most of the Daniel apocalypses, Daniel should still be treated as paradigmatic for historical apocalypses.⁶

Daniel 2

Daniel is comprised of many once-independent literary units.⁷ Some of these units are apocalypses and others are not. The tales in chapters 1–6 fit less securely within the apocalyptic umbrella – even if the shape of the canon nudges them closer to an apocalyptic worldview than they would have when treated individually. In the case of Dan 2 I argue that the literary history of the text takes a court tale with a dream report and transforms it into an apocalypse. Not everyone prefers to read Dan 2 as an apoca-

---

³ Both the *Book of Watchers* and the *Astronomical Book* may be assigned a *terminus ad quem* of ca. 200 B.C.E. They date to at least the third century and possibly even earlier. VanderKam, *Enoch and the Growth*, 79–88, 111–14.

⁴ Sacchi predicates his work on two assumptions: 1) *1 Enoch* is the oldest apocalypse and 2) the main theme of *1 Enoch* is the origin of evil/sin. He then treats other texts with an eye towards these assumptions. His postulates are not in and of themselves controversial. More controversial is his use of textual "themes" to determine genre. Sacchi, *Jewish Apocalyptic and its History*, 17. See also Boccaccini, *Middle Judaism*, 126–60. In a more recent work, Boccaccini describes Daniel as a theological middle-road between "Zadokite" and "Apocalyptic" (Enochic) Judaism. Boccaccini, *Roots of Rabbinic Judaism*, 151–201.

⁵ The most recent introduction to apocalyptic literature begins, for example, with a chapter that treats *1 Enoch* and Daniel together as the earliest apocalypses. See Carey, *Ultimate Things: An Introduction to Jewish and Christian Apocalyptic Literature*, 19–49. This hierarchy reflects no real change from the one inherent in other influential studies such as Collins' *Apocalyptic Imagination* where the early Enoch literature and the Book of Daniel are treated first and most exhaustively. See Collins, *The Apocalyptic Imagination*, chapters 2–3. Newsom characterizes Daniel as a "prototypical" apocalypse. See Carol Newsom, "Spying out the Land: A Report from Genology," in *Seeking Out the Wisdom of the Ancients: Essays Offered to Honor Michael V. Fox on the Occasion of His Sixty-Fifth Birthday* (ed. Ronald Troxel, et al.; Winona Lake: Eisenbrauns, 2005), 437–50, esp. 43.

⁶ On the date of the *Animal Apocalypse*, see Patrick Tiller, *A Commentary on the Animal Apocalypse of 1 Enoch* (SBLEJL 4; Atlanta: Scholars Press, 1993), 61–82.

⁷ This literary history is indicated by dissonances within the final MT text, significant disagreements with the Greek versions, and related texts such as the *Prayer of Nabonidus* that may uncover some early literary sources of Daniel. See Collins, *Daniel*, 54. See also Albertz, *Der Gott des Daniel*. McLay, "The Old Greek Translation of Daniel IV–VI and the Formation of the Book of Daniel," 304–23. John G. Gammie, "The Classification, Stages of Growth, and Changing Intentions in the Book of Daniel," JBL 95 (1976): 191–204.

lypse.⁸ In its original context Dan 2 was not an apocalypse – it was dream report set in the literary framework of a court-tale. Ignoring this context is dangerous since there is no convincing evidence that the Daniel tales from chapters 2–6 were written in Maccabean times. The Persian period is a better fit for some of the stories, which can be described as court tales that highlight the successes of a Jew in foreign royal court.⁹ As individual stories, they share strong similarities with works such as *Ahikar* and the biblical stories of Esther and Joseph. When read in the context of the entire book of Daniel, however, a different image emerges – particularly with chapter 2.

In its original context, chapter 2 did not refer to Antiochus IV Epiphanes or the Hellenistic religious reforms[10] though it is almost certainly a product of the Hellenistic period and a response to Greek hegemony.[11] Similarly, in its original context(s), the story is not an apocalypse. But in its redacted, Maccabean context the story is shaped in such a way that it does participate in the critique of the Hellenistic religious reforms and is an apocalypse. Since my position is controversial, however, and since I introduce the language of Dan 2 as evidence in my larger arguments, I begin with a section in which I defend reading Dan 2 as an apocalypse. I then analyze the individual expressions used to describe historical actors.

The Visionary Redaction of Daniel 2

I am not the first to question the literary integrity of Dan 2. Hartman and DiLella propose that verses 13–23 are secondary additions.[12] They expend only a paragraph to make a case for these additions but offer several convincing literary-critical arguments. For example, after the king issues his decree to execute all wise men in the wake of their failure to interpret his dream, the chief executioner, Arioch, goes to Daniel in verse 14 – presumably to execute him. But Daniel carries on a conversation with Arioch in verse 15 and then personally goes to negotiate with the king as if the king knows Daniel and Daniel has rights to an audience. The king grants Daniel sufficient time to divine the solution to his dream.

---

⁸ Collins, *Daniel*, 173–4.

⁹ See Susan Niditch and Robert Doran, "The Success Story of the Wise Courtier: A Formal Approach," *JBL* (1977). Wills, *The Jew in the Court of the Foreign King*.

[10] The last serious attempt to argue for a Maccabean date was H.H. Rowley, "The Unity of the Book of Daniel," in *The Servant of the Lord and Other Essays on the Old Testament* (London: Lutterworth, 1952), 237–68. See Collins, *The Apocalyptic Vision*, 36–46.

[11] The main evidence for this comes from the use of the four kingdoms motif. See Collins, *The Apocalyptic Imagination*, 92–8. Collins, *Daniel*, 166–70.

[12] Louis Hartman and Alexander DiLella, *The Book of Daniel* (vol. 23; Garden City: Doubleday, 1977), 139.

This version of events is contradicted by verse 24 in which Daniel goes to Arioch (not Arioch to Daniel) after the king's execution decree, pleads for his life, and requests an audience with the king. When Arioch complies with Daniel's request, he introduces the hitherto unknown Jew to the king: "I have found among the exiles from Judah a man who can tell the king the interpretation." The Daniel who was well known and highly respected just a few verses before is now a complete stranger to the king.

Yet another discrepancy suggests itself in this sequence of verses. Daniel does not ask for time to ascertain the correct interpretation of the king's dream in the second description of their meeting. He gives the dream and the interpretation on the spot. Furthermore, Daniel's friends play a role in verses 13 and 17 whereas they do not in verses 24–30.[13] From a literary-critical perspective, Hartman and DiLella offer compelling evidence for a redaction.

John Collins addresses Hartman and DiLella's findings in what can only be described as a hesitant tone, "It has been argued that Daniel's intervention and the report of the revelation are secondary elaborations of the narrative."[14] While Collins does not seem entirely convinced about the redaction (or at least of the extent of the redaction), he agrees that their arguments are reasonable and even adds further evidence to Hartman and DiLella's case. He points out that in verse 16, Daniel requests a delay of execution in order to have time to produce an interpretation. This is ironic since the execution decree was originally issued after the king tired of the court diviners' attempts to "buy time": עָנֵה מַלְכָּא וְאָמַר מִן־יַצִּיב יָדַע אֲנָה דִּי עִדָּנָא אַנְתּוּן זָבְנִין "The king answered and said, 'I know with certainty that you are buying time!'" (2:8).[15]

The redaction of Dan 2 may have been even larger than Hartman and DiLella suggest. In his monograph, *Translatio Imperii*, Reinhard Kratz argues for a more wide-ranging redaction of Dan 2. Kratz argues for a redaction comprised of 14–23, part of 28, part of 39, and 40–45 based primarily on the presence of certain "Maccabean accents" and "eschatological accents" in the text.[16] For example, he holds that the term אַחֲרִית יוֹמַיָּא "end of days" in 2:28 is an addition because of the eschatological implications of the expression. Unlike the arguments Hartman and DiLella arugments, this point – one of Kratz's key points – is not based on literary disagreements. It is thus more a more hazardous approach. For example, it is not a fore-

---

[13] See Hartman and DiLella, *The Book of Daniel*, 139.

[14] Collins, *Daniel*, 153.

[15] Collins, *Daniel*, 153.

[16] See Reinhard Kratz, *Translatio imperii. Untersuchungen zu den aramäischen Danielerzählungen und ihrem theologieschichtlichen Umfeld* (vol. 63; Neukirchener: Verlag, 1990), 55.

gone conclusion that the expression אַחֲרִית יוֹמַיָּא has eschatological dimensions. Shemaryahu Talmon has argued that many (if not most) biblical examples of the Hebrew expression אחרית הימים do not have an eschatological force.[17] The situation changes in the Hellenistic period. Annette Steudel has shown that the expression אחרית הימים always has an eschatological force in its uses in the Qumran library.[18] Unlike some biblical uses that point to a vaguely defined future period, אחרית הימים does not always refer to the future, but sometimes to the past and present. According to Steudel, the main difference between uses in the texts from Qumran and biblical uses is that the Qumran uses always designate, "a limited period of time, that is the last of a series of divinely pre-planned periods into which history is divided."[19] The "end of days" does not mark the punctual end of history. Instead it marks the "last period of time directly before the time of salvation covers aspects of the past, as well as aspects of the present time, and of the future."[20] Thus, it is possible that the expression could have been used without eschatological force in the original version of Dan 2, but acquired its eschatological significance after its Maccabean Era redaction.

Kratz's approach to the evidence in this case is not, however, unreasonable. If one starts an examination of Dan 2 with the knowledge that verses 13–23 are almost certainly additions to the text and that these additions bring the text of Dan 2 much closer to the form and the time of Dan 7, it is logical to look elsewhere in Dan 2 for words, expressions, or verses that closely resemble elements from Dan 7.[21] It is the application of Occam's razor. But the evidence may not bear the weight of the argument for redaction in the case of אַחֲרִית יוֹמַיָּא. Yet it is possible to highlight an instance of Maccabean-era redaction linking Dan 2 to 7 that is supported by literary evidence.

The connection I wish to highlight is found in Dan 2:21 and 7:25.[22] In 2:20–22, Daniel extols the character and deeds of God. One attribute of God in the text is that, הוּא מְהַשְׁנֵא עִדָּנַיָּא וְזִמְנַיָּא "he changes times and sea-

---

[17] Shemaryahu Talmon, "The Signification of אחרית and אחרית הימים in the Hebrew Bible," in *Emanuel: Studies in the Hebrew Bible, Septuagint, and Dead Sea Scrolls in Honor of Emanuel Tov* (ed. Shalom Paul *et al*; vol. 94 of *VTSup*; Leiden: Brill, 2003), 795–810. See also Hugh Williamson, *Isaiah 1–27 Vol. 1: Isaiah 1–5* (ICC; London: T&T Clark, 2006), 166, 80–1.

[18] Annette Steudel, "אחרית הימים in the Texts from Qumran," *RevQ* 62 (1993). See also Annette Steudel, *Der Midrasch zur Eschatologie aus der Qumrangemeinde (4QMidrEschat$^{a.b}$)* (STDJ XIII; Leiden: Brill, 1994), 161–3.

[19] Steudel, "אחרית הימים in the Texts from Qumran," 231.

[20] Steudel, "אחרית הימים in the Texts from Qumran," 231.

[21] For other similarities between Dan 2 and 7, see A. Lenglet, "La Structure littéraire de Daniel 2–7," *Bib* 18 (1972). He makes a detailed argument for the literary unity of Dan 2–7 based on the concentric arrangement of the chapters. He notes parallels between chapters 2, 7; 3, 6; 4, 5. See also Collins's cautions about Lenglet's thesis, Collins, *Daniel*, 33–5.

[22] Cf. Kratz, *Translatio imperii*, 26, 258–60.

sons" (2:21). A similar collocation is found in Dan 7. Dan 7 uses the expression to describe the "little horn" of the fourth beast (i.e., Antiochus IV Epiphanes): וְיִסְבַּר לְהַשְׁנָיָה זִמְנִין וְדָת "And he shall attempt to changes the seasons and the law" (Dan 7:25). In the case of chapter 7, the text describes Antiochus IV's religious reforms and is a reference to the disruption of the cultic calendar.[23] If one approaches 2:21 with the knowledge that 2:13/14–23 is a later, Macabbean era redaction, the most convincing reading of the passage is that the redactor borrows language from Dan 7:25 as a polemic and argues that only God – not Antiochus Epihanes – can change "times and seasons."

Another crucial aspect of the visionary redaction of Dan 2 requires comment. The redaction not only interrupts the narrative of Dan 2 and perhaps even adds eschatological/Maccabean themes or elements, it alters the form of the text. Like most dream visions from the ancient Near East, the original dream report from chapter 2 conforms to the *first* part of Collins's definition of apocalypse: "a genre of revelatory literature with a narrative framework, in which a revelation is mediated by an otherworldly being to a human recipient, disclosing a transcendent reality."[24] In a pre-freudian world, all dreams are revelations (whether symbolic or non-symbolic) mediated by an otherworldly being (a deity, angel, etc) to a human recipient.[25] In its original context, however, the dream report does not disclose a transcendent reality or envisage eschatological salvation.

The addition of the visionary redaction (verses 13/14–23) by the writer/editor of Dan 7(–12?), however, changes the situation. Especially important is verse 19: "Then the mystery was revealed to Daniel in a vision of the night, and Daniel blessed the God of Heaven." The dream experienced by Nebuchadnezzar is never given formal articulation as a dream report of the king. Instead, the dream report as well as the interpretation mediated by YHWH is situated within the context of Daniel's "vision of the night." In other words, the same dream is revealed to both Nebuchadnezzar and Da-

---

[23] Collins, *Daniel*, 322.

[24] Collins, *The Apocalyptic Imagination*, 5.

[25] It is true, as we saw in the introduction, that Artemidorus believed dreams originated in the soul. But this was a minority position and is, at any rate, far from Freud's expression of how life experiences and their sub-conscious and repressed reflexes manifest themselves in dreams. In Freud's own words, "If we restrict ourselves to the minimum of the new knowledge which has been established with certainty, we can still say this of dreams: they have proved that what is suppressed continues to exist in normal people as well as abnormal, and remains capable of psychical functioning. Dreams themselves are among the manifestations of this suppressed material; this is so theoretically in every case, and it can be observed empirically in a number of cases at least, and precisely in cases which exhibit most clearly the striking peculiarities of dream-life." Sigmund Freud, *The Interpretation of Dreams* (trans. James Strachey; New York: Avon Books, 1998), 647. See also 37–9 for Freud's assessment of Aristotle, Artemidorus, and Macrobius.

niel, but the text only articulates the version experienced by Daniel. He is not merely a diviner in the redacted version of chapter 2 – he is a visionary. Indeed, he is perhaps explicitly styled as a visionary (not just a diviner) in the redaction of chapter 2 in order to set the stage for chapters 7–12. Chapter 2 – especially the vision content in verses 31–36 – is thus transformed from a dream report into an apocalypse. The addition of verses 13/14–23 and the way in which Daniel's final canonical shape and historical setting influence how a Maccabean (and later) reader can interpret the text.

The basic form of ancient Near Eastern dream reports as articulated by Oppenheim is, whether symbolic or non-symbolic, the same. The major difference is that non-symbolic dreams are intelligible to the dreamer while symbolic dreams require interpretation. The original shape of chapter 2 conforms to the symbolic dream report form. But the final form of chapter 2 bears witness to a confluence of the two types. The content of the dream report as presented to Daniel "in a vision of the night" בְּחֶזְוָה דִי־לֵילְיָה is unintelligible. Rather than consulting a human diviner, however, the revelatory value of the dream is interpreted for Daniel by "the God of heaven" אֱלָהּ שְׁמַיָּה. This form is not unattested. In certain visions of Amos and Proto-Zechariah both an unintelligible message and its interpretation are mediated by YHWH.[26]

Collins's objection to describing Dan 2 as an apocalypse centers on the issue mediation. "In form, apocalyptic visions are always mediated by an angel or supernatural being. That is not the case here, even in Daniel's nocturnal revelation."[27] It is true that no supernatural being has a speaking-role in the text, but one is designated as revealing the mystery to Daniel. Precisely at the point when Daniel and his friends pray to "the God of heaven" (אֱלָהּ שְׁמַיָּה) concerning "this mystery" (רָזָה דְנָה i.e., the interpretation of the dream), the text reports that "the mystery was revealed to Daniel in a vision of the night, and Daniel blessed the God of heaven" (2:19). Moreover, Daniel specifically eschews the possibility that he could interpret the dream with his own mantic skills, "This mystery has not been revealed to me because of any wisdom that I have" (2:30).

Especially noteworthy in 2:30 is the verb גלה. It is a *pe'il* perfect (G passive) 3ms. Daniel does not actively deduce the interpretation of the dream. He is a passive participant in the process, i.e., this is intuitive, not deductive divination. The sense of the sentence would be vastly different if the verb was rendered as a *pe'al* perfect 1cs: ואנה לא בחכנה די איתי בי מן־כל־חייא רזה דנה גלית "As for me, it is not on account of any wisdom in me greater than

---

[26] See Susan Niditch, *The Symbolic Vision in Biblical Tradition* (Chico, CA: Scholars Press, 1983), 12–3.
[27] Collins, *Daniel*, 173.

any other living being that I have uncovered this mystery." But as the text stands, God interprets the text for Daniel. Why אֱלָהּ שְׁמַיָּה should not count as a supernatural being I do not know. I disagree with Collins that this text is better read as a proto-type of an apocalyptic vision instead of a full-blown example since its redaction history places it, chronologically speaking, in the midst of the production of other apocalypses. Dan 2* post-dates Dan 7. The disparity between texts like Dan 2 and 7 seem to me better explained by the fact that Dan 2 was not originally written to be an apocalypse whereas Dan 7 was. The narrative framework of Dan 2 seems to have been adjusted to anticipate Dan 7 by an editor – perhaps the writer of Dan 7.

Language in Daniel 2
The dream vision described in Dan 2 is experienced twice: once by Nebuchadnezzar and once by Daniel. In the final, redacted form of the text, the dream vision is only articulated as an experience of Daniel. The dream vision fits somewhere between Oppenheim's "symbolic" and "message" (i.e., non-symbolic) dream categories. On two occasions, an undecipherable vision is experienced by a dreamer. Both Nebuchadnezzar and Daniel require interpretation to understand the vision. In Daniel's case, the God of Heaven reveals the interpretation. Daniel, in turn, communicates the interpretation to Nebuchadnezzar.

In the vision, the dreamers are shown a large statue divided into four basic parts. The fourth part of the statue is itself subdivided:

This statue was huge, its brilliance extraordinary; it was standing before you, and its appearance was frightening. The head of that statue was of fine gold, its chest and arms of silver, its middle and thighs of bronze, its legs of iron, its feet partly of iron and partly of clay. As you looked on, a stone was cut out, not by human hands, and it struck the statue on its feet of iron and clay and broke them in pieces. Then the iron, the clay, the bronze, the silver, and the gold, were all broken in pieces and became like the chaff of the summer threshing floors; and the wind carried them away, so that not a trace of them could be found. But the stone that struck the statue became a great mountain and filled the whole earth. (Dan 2:31–5, NRSV)

The dream vision functions as an allegory. It tells two stories simultaneously. The basic level of the allegory is the story of a statue made of various metals. The secondary level of the story is a description of the imperial history of the ancient Near East. In other words, the description of the statue paints a word picture of the history of the ancient Near East from the 7th century B.C.E. until the end of the Hellenistic period. It bears some similarities, at least on a structural level, to several objects of ancient Near Eastern art. A notable example is the "tree of life" in the tomb of Khnumhotep II at Beni Hasan.²⁸ In the wall painting five birds sit aloft branches of an acacia tree. Each bird is a different color and all but the last bird face to the East. A common interpretation of the motif is as follows: The first bird is light grey and symbolizes birth. The second bird is red and symbolizes childhood. The third bird is green and symbolizes youth. The fourth bird is blue and symbolizes adulthood. Finally, the fifth bird is orange and symbolizes old age. It is particularly important that the fifth, orange bird gazes to the West while all other birds gaze east. The sun rises in the East and in ancient Egypt East was the direction from which life springs. The orange bird anticipates the end of life by looking towards the direction of the setting sun. Rather than proceeding strictly vertically, they proceed counter-clockwise around the tree.²⁹ The statue in Dan 2 also recalls a common artistic technique from the ancient Near East: register composition.³⁰ While this technique is most common in Egyptian art, it is well attested throughout the ancient Near East in examples such as the Lachish reliefs of Sennacherib or the Taʻanach cult stand.³¹ Each individual register or layer must be interpreted in the construction of a larger political or theological narrative. They function as a unified tableau – not merely a serial progression of panels found in, for example, modern comic books.

The historical narrative in Dan 2 is highly schematic. The gold head represents Babylonia/Nebuchadnezzar, the silver chest/arms represent Media, the bronze thighs represent Persia, the iron/clay legs/feet represent Greece/*diadochoi*, and the stone that becomes a mountain represents an eternal Yahwistic theocracy. Like the Egyptian tree of life painting mentioned above, Dan 2 employs a symbolic system in which each individual symbol belongs to the same overall type. In the Egyptian tree, the overall type is "bird" and each specimen is represented by a different color bird. In Dan 2, the overall type is "metal" and each specimen is a different type of metal. We shall see that this type of symbolic system (i.e., using pairs of

---

²⁸ For a comprehensive study of the tomb, see Janice Kamrin, *The Cosmos of Khnumhotep II at Beni Hasan* (London: Keagan Paul International, 1999).

²⁹ Regine Schulz and Matthias Seidel, eds., *Egypt: The World of the Pharaohs* (Cologne: Könemann, 2000), 123.

³⁰ Cf. John Baines, "Writing, invention and early development," in *Encyclopedia of the Archaeology of Ancient Egypt* (ed. Kathryn Bard; London: Routledge, 1999), 882–5. While the register system was most clearly articulated beginning in the first dynasty, it had significant antecedents in earlier periods. See Whitney Davis, "The Origins of Register Composition in Pre-Dynastic Egyptian Art," *JAOS* 96 (1976): 404–18.

³¹ For the Lachish reliefs, see David Ussishkin, *The Conquest of Lachish by Sennacherib* (Tel Aviv: Tel Aviv University Publications, 1982). See also the photograph and discussion of the Taʻanach cult stand found in Philip King and Lawrence Stager, *Life in Biblical Israel* (Louisville: Westminster John Knox, 2001), 342–4. Cf. the slightly different interpretation in Othmar Keel and Christoph Uehlinger, *Gods, Goddesses, and Images of God in Ancient Israel* (Minneapolis: Fortress Press, 1998), 157–60.

conventional association) is typical of symbolic apocalypses. As we shall see below, several Jewish apocalypses share a basic symbolic system in which, for example, beasts represent human subjects and humans represent angelic subjects (cf. Dan 7, 8, *Animal Apocalypse*). In Dan 2, metal is (in Peirce's terms) a symbol for "kingdom." Readers have the ability to assign different identities to particular metal elements from the dream, but the basic "metal=kingdom" association remains constant and exercises priority over the second-level choice of which metal represents which referent. In some texts systems of conventional symbols do not extend further than the text itself. In the case of Dan 2 this is not so because there is considerable evidence in the Ancient world for the use of a symbolic system in which metals are used to symbolize kingdoms and/or periods of political history.

The metal terminology (דְּהַב gold, כְּסַף silver, נְחָשׁ bronze, פַּרְזֶל iron, חֲסַף clay/, אַבְנָא stone) used in Dan 2 is with one exception composed of common words that do not deviate from their normal patterns of usage. The exception is the lexeme חסף "clay." It does not have a cognate in Hebrew. Its usage in the Aramaic of the Hebrew Bible is limited to Dan 2 and it is comparatively rare in other dialects of Aramaic.[32] It appears to connote primarily terra cotta and not raw clay. A text from the Qumran library helps to illuminate the lexeme in Dan 2.[33]

4QPrNab ar (4Q242) purports to be a first-person account of the suffering of the final king of Babylon, Nabonidus, and his recovery under that care of a diviner who was a Jewish exile. The text is uncannily similar to Dan 4 and many scholars believe it contains tradition-historical background features of the chapter.[34] Direct dependence seems unlikely since, for example, Dan 4 erroneously presumes that Nebuchadnezzar was the last king of Babylon.

In 4QPrNab ar Nabonidus confesses to God that for seven years he, "was praying [to] the gods of silver and gold, [bronze, iron,] wood, stone, clay (חספא), since [I thoug]ht that th[ey were] gods" (4Q242 1–3 7–8).[35] The

---

[32] Jacob Hoftijzer and K. Jongeling, *Dictionary of the North-West Semitic Inscriptions* (HdO 21; vol. 1; Leiden: Brill, 1995), 383. L. Koehler and W. Baumgartner, eds., *The Hebrew and Aramaic Lexicon of the Old Testament* (Leiden: Brill, 2001), 2: 1879.

[33] The lexeme is also found once in another text from the Qumran library: the *Genesis Apocryphon* (1Q20 13 9). The exact meaning of the word is considerably more difficult to understand in the *Apocryphon*. The context is a dream vision experienced by Noah after the deluge and the reestablishment of life on earth.

[34] See Collins and Flint, "4QPrayer of Nabonidus ar," 85–7. This small text has received considerable scholarly attention. See the bibliography in "4QPrayer of Nabonidus ar," 83. See also Henze, *The Madness of King Nebuchadnezzar*, 63–73. Eshel, "Possible Sources of the Book of Daniel," 387–94.

[35] Trans. John J. Collins, "4Q242 (4QPrNab ar)," in *Additional Genres and Unclassified Texts* (ed. Donald Parry and Emanuel Tov; vol. 6 of *DSSR*; Leiden Brill, 2005), 6–7.

types of metals, wood, and earth mentioned by Nabonidus are not descriptions of raw elements, but descriptions of materials fashioned by craftsmen into cultic images. חספא almost certainly connotes a fired and formed clay statue/figurine and that meaning accords well with the image of the brittle clay (תְּהֵוֵה תְבִירָה) in Dan 2:42. The genitive grammatical construction (construct chain) בַּחֲסַף טִינָא in 2:41 indicates a similar conclusion. חסף is the fired ceramic and טִינָא indicates its raw, source-material, i.e., "(fired) tile of clay." Thus translations of בַּחֲסַף טִינָא as "miry clay" in the KJV and RSV and "common clay" (?) in the JPS must be incorrect.[36] The "baked clay" of the NIV or John Collins's "clay tiles" is to be preferred.[37]

If most of the individual terms used to describe historical actors in Dan 2 are not philologically noteworthy, two motifs in which they function are. The "metals of declining value" motif and the "four kingdoms" motif both contextualize otherwise urbane vocabulary in a way that produces important new meanings within the text. The "metals of declining value" motif found in Daniel has profligate and wide-ranging antecedents in the ancient world. It is best known from Hesiod's *Works and Days* (1.109–201). Hesiod narrates five successive ages and all but the fourth are represented by metals: gold, silver, bronze, fourth, iron. Hesiod is normally dated to the late 8th century B.C.E.. If this date is correct one can trace this motif at least that far back.[38] Other examples of the motif are found in the Persian texts *Bahman Yasht* and *Denkard*, and probably also the Cumean sibyl.

In the version of the motif found in the *Bahman Yasht*, Zoroaster sees, "the trunk of a tree, on which there were four branches: one of gold, one of silver, one of steel and one of mixed iron."[39] Each of the metals represents

---

[36] See Koehler and Baumgartner, eds., *The Hebrew and Aramaic Lexicon of the Old Testament*, 2: 1884. Note, especially, that the verb derived from טין in both Aramaic and Arabic describes an action for which wet, malleable clay is a prerequisite, i.e., to "smear" or "coat."

[37] Noegel interprets the significance of the clay another way. He translates פֶּחָד as "clay" instead of "potter" in 2:41 and suggests that פֶּחָד functions as a pun based on the more rare Akkadian meaning "assembly." "In Akkadian *puḫru* can refer to an assembly of people, lands, city-states, and gods, and it is interesting to note that several Babylonian omen texts use the verb *paḫāru* in reference to the assembly of nations. Daniel underscores the allusion to "assembly" when he remarks that the smashing of the פחר means that the king will see his kingdom divided. His "assembly of nations," so to speak, will be smashed to ruins. Noegel, *Nocturnal Ciphers*, 149. It seems to me that Noegel asks far too much from a Hellenistic text in terms of lexicography. If the function of this text is to provide an ideal Jewish figure – a hero or role model for Jews, one presumes the text was intended for a wide distribution. What are the chances that many Hellenistic Jews would be aware of an Akkadian meaning for the root פחר that is rare even in Akkadian?

[38] See Anthony Green, "Hesiodus," in *Brill's New Pauly: Encyclopedia of the Ancient World* (ed. Hubert Cancik and Helmuth Schneider; Leiden: Brill, 2005), 6: 279. Collins suggests that the scheme may be even older and that Hesiod adapts it. It is unclear where Hesiod might have gotten it from if this is true.

[39] From B.T. Anklesaria's, *Zand-I Vohuman Yasn and Two Pahlevi Fragments*, quoted in Collins, *Daniel*, 163.

a period of history (though not explicitly a "kingdom"). The dating of the Persian texts is, however, highly problematic. In their present form, the *Bahman Yasht* and *Denkard* both date to the 9–10th centuries CE.[40] The *Bahman Yasht* is a *Zand* ("interpretation") of the *Avesta* – a text compiled during the Sassanian period (221–642 CE). But elements of the *Avesta* predate the Sassanian period. Most specialists believe the *Gathas* derive from the first millennium B.C.E.. Unfortunately for non-specialists, proposed dates for the *Gathas* range from the tenth to the first century therein.[41]

Geo Widengren has argued that the four ages motif in the *Bahman Yasht* should not be dated to the Sassanian period:

> La date de sa redaction est sans doute post-sassanide. Mais il va de soi qu'il est de mauvaise méthode de confondre la date de la redaction d'un livre avec la date des sources utilisées dans ce livre. Il ne faut pas oublier non plus qu'on droit toujours essayer de replace ruine idée isolée dans son contexte idéologique pour autant que cette méthode soit possible.[42]

Widengren goes as far as to argue that Daniel to is directly influenced by the four ages motif from *Bahman Yasht*. But a problem with Widengren's essay is the assumption that Daniel *must* have been directly influenced by either Hesiod or a source-text of the *Bahman Yasht*. He concludes that a Persian influence (on Daniel) is more likely based on the transmission of Persian traditions from the Indian *Mahabharata* into the Levant via the Syriac Gnostic Bardaisan in the second century CE.[43] In my view his evidence does not support his conclusions. A more realistic conclusion might be that an early date for the four kingdoms motif from *Bahman Yasht* appears more likely than not. I hasten to note that the opinion of Widengren's major inquisitor (P. Gignoux), i.e., that the *Bahman Yasht* was influenced by Dan 2, seems even more unlikely.[44]

---

[40] Anders Hultgard, "BAHMAN YASHT: A Persian Apocalypse," in *Mysteries and Revelations: Apocalyptic Studies since the Uppsala Colloquium* (ed. John J. Collins and James Charlesworth; vol. 9 of *JSPSup*; Sheffield: JSOT Press, 1991), 115, 18–9.

[41] See the warning about dates for Persian texts in Prods Oktor Skjærvø, "Zoroastrian Dualism," in *Light Against Darkness: Dualism in Ancient Mediterranean Religion and the Contemporary World* (JAJSup 2; ed. Armin Lange, Eric M. Meyers, Bennie H. Reynolds III, and Randall Styers; Göttingen: Vandenhoeck & Ruprecht, 2011), 55–91, esp. 76–89.

[42] [The date of the redaction is undoubtedly post-Sassanian. But, of course, it is a poor method to confuse the date of the redaction of a book with the date of the sources utilized by this book. One must not forget either that it is always right to try to replace a ruined isolated idea in its ideological context provided that this method is still possible.] Geo Widengren, "Les Quatre Ages du Monde," in *Apocalyptique Iranienne et Dualism Qoumrân* (ed. Marc Philonenko; Paris: Adrien Maisonneuve, 1995), 23.

[43] Widengren, "Les Quatre Ages du Monde," 24–7, 48–56.

[44] Phillippe Gignoux, "L'apocalyptique iranienne est-elle vraiment la source d'autres apocalypses?," *AAASH* 31:1–2 (1986).

Like Widengren, K. Eddy argues that Daniel was influenced by *Bahman Yasht*. While I do not think he can substantiate this thesis any more than Widengren can, he does present important evidence that the four kingdoms motif from the *Bahman Yasht* can be dated to the fourth century B.C.E..[45] Eddy makes four significant observations. First, he notes that in the text's conception of the return of a divine hero, there is no Persian king on the throne. He concludes:

> This was not the case in Sassanid times, when the powerful dynast of that name not only held sway in Iran, but even challenged the Byzantine Empire for control of both Syria and Anatolia. This requires a post-Sassanid date – universally rejected – or a pre-Sassanid date for the time of the original composition of this apocalypse.[46]

Eddy also points out the similarities between *Bahman Yasht* and the *Oracle of Hystaspes*, a text probably written in the first century C.E. He is correct that the parallels exist, but they are of such a general nature they cannot be considered significant. For example, both texts contain ideas such as the barrenness of the earth, the widespread death of animals, and the darkening of the sun.[47] These ideas are hardly novel. Eddy stands on *terra firma* however, with his linguistic analysis. In the context of foreign invasion, the text twice mentions the name of Alexander and describes him as "destroyer of religion" and "invader."[48] Next, the forces of the invader are referred to as *Yunan* (i.e., Ionians or "Greeks").[49] The references to *Yunan* are especially interesting since Sassanid writers usually referred to Greeks as *Rūmi*.[50] Finally, Eddy argues that the description of forces invading Persia in the period of mixed iron, "The demons with Dishevelled Hair of the Race of Wrath," is a reference to Greeks.[51] While Eddy's hypothesis seems at first unlikely, his art-historical evidence makes it plausible if not probable.[52] Indeed, one could add considerably more iconographic evidence in favor of

---

[45] See also Hultgard, "BAHMAN YASHT: A Persian Apocalypse," 114–34, esp. 19. See also Marc Philonenko et al., eds., *Apocalyptique iranienne et dualisme qoumrânien* (Paris: Maisonneuve, 1995). But see Philippe Gignoux, "L'apocalyptique iranienne est-elle vraiment ancienne?," *RHR* 216 (1999). David Flusser, "The Four Empires in the Fourth Sybil and in the Book of Daniel," *Israel Oriental Studies* 2 (1972).

[46] K. Eddy, *The King is Dead: Studies in the Near Eastern Resistance to Hellenism 334–31 B.C.E.* (Lincoln: University of Nebraska Press, 1961), 17–8.

[47] Eddy, *The King is Dead*, 18.

[48] Eddy, *The King is Dead*, 19.

[49] Eddy, *The King is Dead*, 19.

[50] Eddy notes that the invaders are sometimes described as coming from *Rum*. He dismisses this description as Sassanid-era editing. Eddy, *The King is Dead*, 19.

[51] Eddy, *The King is Dead*, 19.

[52] Eddy, *The King is Dead*, plates I–II.

his opinion.⁵³ A comparison of the depictions of hair not only in Persian, but Mesopotamian and Egyptian art against those depictions found in Greek art reveals a startling contrast.⁵⁴

In spite of Eddy's considerable evidence, I do not think he is any more successful than Widengren at proving Daniel was influenced by the *Bahman Yasht*. What seems certain, however, is that the tradition of the four kindoms in the *Bahman Yasht* predates the Sassanid period and probably derives from the 4th century B.C.E.. This does not prove dependence, but it does prove that the writer of Daniel *could* have had access to the narrative or to a reflex thereof. Other evidence may also be marshaled for the early and widespread dispersion of this motif.

In the case of the Cumean Sibyl, the text no longer exists.⁵⁵ But Servius' commentary on Virgil's fourth Eclogue indicates that she *saecula per metalla divisit, dixit etiam quis quo saeculo imperaret* "divided the world empires (lit. "the heathens") by metals and also declared who would rule over each age."⁵⁶ In this case, the ages of the world number ten, not four or five, but the motif of representing kingdoms or ages with metals remains constant. The Cumean Sibyl is a generic reference for several different prophetesses, but since Virgil can be securely dated (70–19 B.C.E.), there is little doubt that his traditions about the Sibyl would have been current by at least the 2nd century B.C.E..

Dan 2 also participates in another widespread motif that is related to the "metals of declining value" motif: the "four kingdoms" motif. At least two important articles have been written about it, but the most comprehensive statement is probably found in an excursus in John Collins's *Hermeneia* commentary on Daniel.⁵⁷ The motif appears to have its origins in a three-

---

⁵³ See, for example the coins featuring busts of Alexander the Great and some of the *diadochoi* in Urs Staub, "Das Tier mit den Hörnern: Ein Beitrag zu Dan 7.7f.," in *Hellenismus und Judentum: Vier Studien zu Daniel 7 und zur Religionsnot under Antiochus IV* (ed. Othmar Keel and Urs Staub; Göttingen: Vandenhoeck & Ruprecht, 2000), Abbildungen 2–8.

⁵⁴ One could select virtually any image of royalty or military personel from *ANEP*, compare it to the images noted above, and arrive at this conclusion. Note also the description of Alexander's hair in Pseudo-Callisthenes: την δε καιτην λεοντας "the mane of a lion" (1.13.8). See Karl Müller, ed., *The Fragments of the Lost Historians of Alexander the Great: Fragmenta Scriptorum de Rebus Alexandri Magni, Pseudo-Callisthenes, Itinerarium Alexandri* (Chicago: Ares Publishers, 1979), 12.

⁵⁵ Traditions about the Cumean Sybil appear to have been widespread. She appears Lactantius' *Divine Institutes* and Virgil's *Aeneid*.

⁵⁶ Georg Thilo, ed., *Servii Grammatici qui Feruntur in Vergilii Bucolica et Georgica Commentarii* (Lipsiae: Teubneri, 1887), 44.

⁵⁷ Collins, *Daniel*, 166–70. See also Collins, *The Apocalyptic Imagination*, 92–8. The two articles mentioned are J. W. Swain, "The Theory of the Four Monarchies: Opposition History under the Roman Empire," *Classical Philology* 35 (1940). Flusser, "The Four Empires in the Fourth Sybil and in the Book of Daniel," 148–75.

kingdom schema of Assyria, Media, and Persia that may have functioned as a tool of Achaemenid propaganda.[58] The scheme was expanded during Hellenistic-Roman times to include four kingdoms (Assyria, Media, Persia, Macedonia) followed by a fifth (Rome) in, e.g., Sybilline Oracles 4. An important question for the Book of Daniel is when did this expansion take place?

Several texts assembled by Collins can be securely dated after the final compilation of Daniel and contain the motif: "Polybius (38.22), from the late second century B.C.E.; Dionysius of Halicarnassus (1.2.2–4), about 10 B.C.E.; Tacitus (*Hist* 5.8–9), about 100 C.E.; and Appian (Preface, 9), about 140 C.E."[59] Another late source, the Roman historian Marcus Velleius Paterculus (19 B.C.E.–31 CE), contains the same scheme, but its context is an extract of Aemilius Sura. In 1940, Joseph Swain gave Sura a *terminus ante quem* of 171–168 B.C.E. (i.e., the Third Macedonian War) since he marked the end of Macedonia with the death of Philip in 179 B.C.E..[60] If Swain is correct, Sura's account would predate most of the Book of Daniel. But as Collins points out there are several other examples that employ, to greater and lesser degrees, the four kingdom motif. For example, the *Fourth Sibylline Oracle* – in its original version – can be dated between the mid fourth and mid first centuries B.C.E..[61] As Collins notes, however, "In view of the brevity of the rule attributed to the Greeks, the date should be earlier rather than later in this period."[62] Other examples from the period before Daniel was written/compiled include the Persian *Bahman Yasht* and the Babylonian *Dynastic Prophecy*.[63] Considerably closer to the time of Dan 2 is a fragmentary text from Qumran entitled 4QFour Kingdoms ar (4Q552, 4Q553). *Four Kingdoms* is a dream or vision in which an individual observes and converses with four trees (see chapter 3 below). Each tree represents a kingdom. For example, the conversation with the first tree runs as follows, "I asked him, 'What is your name?' and he said to me, 'Babylon [and I said to him y]ou are he who rules over Persia.'"[64] The second tree

---

[58] This point is made by Flusser, "The Four Empires in the Fourth Sybil and in the Book of Daniel," 148–75. One must temper his conclusions with the questions about dating Persian Zoroastrian sources. See Skjærvø, "Zoroastrian Dualism," 76–91

[59] Collins, *Daniel*, 167.

[60] Swain, "The Theory of the Four Monarchies," 2–3. Collins documents the widespread acceptance of Swain's theory. Collins, *Daniel*, 167, n. 46.

[61] John J. Collins, "The Place of the Fourth Sibyl in the Development of the Jewish Sibyllina," *JJS* 25 (1974): 365–70.

[62] Collins, *Daniel*, 167–8.

[63] On the Dynastic Prophecy, see most recently Matthew Neujahr, "When Darius Defeated Alexander: Composition and Redaction in the Dynastic Prophecy," *JNES* 64 (2005): 101–7.

[64] Trans. E. Cook, "4Q552 (4QFour Kingdoms^a ar)," in *Additional Genres and Unclassified Texts* (ed. Donald Parry and Emanuel Tov; vol. 6 of *DSSR*; Leiden: Brill, 2005). The official publication of this text has only recently appeared: Émile Puech, *Qumrân Grotte 4: XXVII: Textes*

appears to represent Greece, but unfortunately the descriptions of the third and fourth kingdoms are not preserved in the text. At least a limited eschatology is implied in a brief passage from 4Q553 10 2: לה רב איל[ניא "to him ruler of the tre[es." A possible interpretation of the line is that one of the trees (the final tree) or perhaps an outside figure is given power over all the other trees.

I doubt that Daniel was directly influenced by any of the texts discussed above. The most important point to take from this glance at the four kingdoms motif, however, is that the motif appears to have been embedded in the cultural memory of the ancient Near East/Mediterranean. It appears early and continues to appear until quite late. One can say that the descriptions of the historical actors in Dan 2 are couched in a conventional framework that constrains how a model reader interprets the text.[65] The description of historical actors in terms of the four kingdoms motif sets up boundaries inside which an ancient Near Eastern reader or hearer might derive meaning from the text.

Whether the three kingdoms motif used by Achaemenid kings or the four kingdoms motif familiar from the *Fourth Sibylline Oracle*, the basic framework of the literary scheme serves political and ideological purposes. The writer begins by highlighting great and powerful cultures of the past. These kingdoms provide an illustrious peer group for the final kingdoms in each particular example of the motif – placing the final kingdom on an elite short-list of the most imperious nations that the earth has seen. The first kingdoms on the list provide not only peers for the final kingdom, however, they can also provide foils for it. The dawn of the final kingdom is rarely treated as a matter of course. It often marks the advent of the last major political upheaval on earth, not just the latest example in a list that continues into the future *ad infinitum*. This upheaval is not necessarily apocalyptic (i.e., not every example of the *eschaton* involves the heavenly world or the end of earth), but the final kingdom is often understood as one upon which the sun shall never set. The motif is a political statement that serves as propaganda for the final kingdom or against the penultimate kingdom in any particular articulation of the scheme.

The focus of this study is on the "actors" within apocalyptic historical reviews. Close attention to the actors in Dan 2 (and 7) reveal significant insights about the use of the four kingdoms motif in these texts. Like other

---

araméens deuxième partie 4Q550–4Q575a, 4Q580–4Q587 et appendices (vol. 38 of DJD; Oxford: Clarendon Press, 2009). No articles have been devoted to it but it has garnered a few words in discussions of Dan 2 and 4. See Ida Fröhlich, *Time and Times and Half a Time: Historical Consciousness in the Jewish Literature of the Persian and Hellenistic Eras* (JSPSup 19; Sheffield: Sheffield Academic Press, 1996), 37. Collins, *Daniel*, 224.

[65] For the term model reader, see the excursus on "Daniel 7 and the Model Reader" below.

texts such as *Sibylline Oracles 4*, Daniel 2 updates the four kingdom scheme by adding a fifth kingdom to its outline of history. In the case of *Sibylline Oracles 4*, the fifth and final kingdom is Rome. A redactor added the portions about Rome in approximate 80 C.E. – ostensibly in order to make the text relevant for a time after which Alexander, his generals, and their descendants had lost control of the world.[66] The way Dan 2 (see also Dan 7 below) updates the motif is noteworthy among examples in the ancient Near East/Mediterranean in that it posits a fifth kingdom that has yet to appear on earth during the writer's lifetime. In other words, both Dan 2 and 7 explicitly eschatologize the four kingdoms motif. Dan 2 does not serve as propaganda for a regime that is already in power, but for a regime that it hopes will come to power: "And in the days of those kings the God of heaven will set up a kingdom that shall never be destroyed, nor shall this kingdom be left to another people. It shall crush these kingdoms and bring them to an end, and it shall stand forever" (Dan 2:44).

Another interesting aspect of the "actors" in Dan 2's history is the absence of Israelite/Jewish elements before the arrival of an eschatological kingdom ruled over by the God of Israel. As we shall see later, some ancient Jewish apocalypses make copious use of elements from Israel's historical traditions in their *ex eventu* prophecies. For example, in the *ex eventu* history found in the *Animal Apocalypse*, Near Eastern kingdoms such as Babylon have a considerably lower profile than do figures such as Noah or Moses. It is interesting to note that Dan 2 was almost certainly written (and perhaps even redacted) before the Maccabean revolt. Thus, it may articulate a vision of history that cannot imagine independent Israelite/Jewish actors in history. For the writer of Dan 2, Israel plays no role on the stage of world history until the *eschaton*. It may be that some measure of political independence gained during the Maccabean revolt and held during the Hasmonean Period allowed Jewish visionaries to imagine a history in which Israel played an independent, or even pivotal role before the *eschaton*.

Raw Data – Daniel 2

Citation		Allegorical Elements	Referent	Symbol	Symbol-Referent

---

[66] The text is aware of the eruption of Vesuvius in 79 CE. See Collins, "The Place of the Fourth Sibyl in the Development of the Jewish Sibyllina," 365–80. Flusser, "The Four Empires in the Fourth Sybil and in the Book of Daniel," 148–75.

2:32, 35, 38	דְהַב טָב	Gold	Babylonia/Nebuchadnezzar	Metal	Kingdom
2:32, 35, 39, 45	כְּסַף	Silver	Media	Metal	Kingdom
2:32, 35, 39, 45	נְחָשׁ	Bronze	Persia	Metal	Kingdom
2:33, 35, 40, 45	פַּרְזֶל	Iron	Greece	Metal	Kingdom
2:33, 35, 41-3, 45	פַּרְזֶל חֲסַף	Iron/Clay	Greece/ διαδοχοι	Metal/ Earth	Kingdom
2:34, 35, 45	אַבְנָא→ טוּר רַב	Stone→ Mountain	Yahwistic theocracy	Stone	Kingdom

Daniel 7–8

In chapter one I indicated why applying categories developed primarily for dream reports to Ancient Jewish apocalypses might make sense. In particular, I highlighted how Frances Flannery-Dailey's study *Dreamers, Scribes, and Priests* has shown an even closer relationship between the dream reports and apocalypses than most have been willing to admit. The Book of Daniel testifies to this relationship in a clear way. Dan 2 – at least in its original form – unquestionably contains a dream report (so too chapter 4). Characterizing Dan 7 and 8 is slightly more problematic. Both apocalypses employ dream visions, but combine the usually distinct symbolic and non-symbolic (i.e. "message") dream forms into a new form. It might still be described as a hybrid dream-form nevertheless. Each text begins with a symbolic vision, but ends with a non-symbolic revelation that interprets the vision. Thus while Dan 7 and 8 are normally described as highly symbolic, they actually operate somewhere between symbolism and realism.

As we have already seen, it is not unusual for a dreamer to be given a message directly from an apparition, but those cases are always non-symbolic (i.e., "message") dreams. Examples include the dreams of Nabonidus and Samuel discussed in chapter one. The message is perfectly intelligible and needs no further explanation by means of interpretation/divination. Closer parallels to the form of the visions in Dan 7 and 8 would be some passages of Ezekiel and especially Proto-Zech. The form of the visions in Daniel is not simply a prophecy with imminent eschatology and it cannot merely be laid at the feet of the Israelite prophetic tradition based on the antecedents in, for example, Proto-Zech. Susan Niditch points out that visions may have more in common with dream reports than prophecy and, until Proto-Zech, are comparatively rare in prophetic books as compared to non-prophetic books.[67] Indeed, the use of dreams and visions is rare among Israelite literature extant from the period of the supposed hey-day of Israelite prophecy (i.e., 8th–7th centuries B.C.E.). Thus, even though the form of Dan 7 and 8 has much in common with the vision form familiar from, for example, Proto-Zechariah, I hesitate to see in Dan 7 a major influence of "prophecy," since the relevant prophetic texts (i.e., Proto-Zechariah) seem themselves to be aberrations within the prophetic corpus. Instead, I hope to highlight an element of Dan 7's form that reflects its close relationship to dream reports/divinatory literature.

Daniel 7 and Ancient Dream Reports
Each of the main texts in this study use representation techniques that can be illuminated by the form and style of dream reports. The Book of Daniel's relationship to dream reports is especially close and has not gone unrecognized. Studies of dream reports in the Bible or the ancient Near East typically discuss the book of Daniel. Chapters 2 and 4 are often held up as exemplars of the "symbolic dream" type and are presumed to have been influenced by the dream reports found in the Joseph Novella, especially Gen 41.[68] On the other hand, chapters 7 and 8 have always fit somewhat less comfortably into discussions of dream reports even if the introductory formula in Dan 7:1–2 clearly indicates that Daniel was asleep in his bed

---

[67] Niditch, The Symbolic Vision in Biblical Tradition, 12–3.
[68] Husser, *Dreams and Dream Narratives in the Biblical World*, 118–22.

when he experienced the vision.[69] So before analyzing the language of Dan 7, I want to focus on a neglected element of its form that makes my use of Oppenheim's categories all the more appropriate *vis a vis* the text.

Dan 7 is not normally treated in studies of symbolic dream reports. For some scholars, ignoring chapter 7 (and 8) has to do with certain notions about Israelite religion. For example, Oppenheim claims that, "Symbolic dreams are, in the Old Testament, reserved for the "gentiles.""[70] He explains:

> The Bible, that is, the Old Testament, offers an illuminating contrast to all other civilizations of the ancient Near East by actually favoring reports of "symbolic" dreams in historical settings. Yet a specific restriction can be observed: all these "symbolic" dreams are experienced by the "gentiles"; to his own people the Lord speaks in "message"-dreams and not in "dark speeches (Num. 12:8).[71]

The problems with such a conception are self-evident. Other scholars bracket Dan 7 as a result of too strict a distinction between the categories "dream" and "night-vision." It is in my judgment far too easy to overstate the differences between "dreams" and "night-visions." For example, Jean-Marie Husser's definition of a "vision of the night" is essentially the definition of a non-symbolic (i.e., "message") dream according to the terms Artemidorus and Oppenheim. It is still a dream vision whether or not it requires interpretation. Furthermore, the idea that Dan 7 must be *either* a dream *or* a vision involves a strict application of an outdated generic-realism.[72]

The classic form-critical articulation of ancient Near Eastern non-symbolic (message) dream reports established by Oppenheim and employed by Flannery-Dailey in her study of dreams in Hellenistic Judaism is as follows: the dreamer is said to be asleep, the apparition "stands" before him, the message is delivered, and the dreamer wakes up in an anxious state of mind. Symbolic dreams differ in that the dream itself contains symbols and that the dreamer seeks interpretation once he wakes up in an anxious state. In Dan 7 all of the basic elements of dream reports are present, but one of them has not, to my knowledge, been recognized.

Unlike most dreams that require interpretation, Daniel's dream is interpreted by the apparition that first appeared to him. Husser emphasizes Daniel's interaction with an angel as a departure from the normal form of dreams – placing Dan 7 in the undefined category of "vision." But a close

---

[69] While manuscript evidence calls into question many readings in Dan 7, including six significant issues in the first verse alone, the words "on his bed" are not in question.

[70] Oppenheim, *The Interpretation of Dreams in the Ancient Near East*, 207.

[71] Oppenheim, *The Interpretation of Dreams in the Ancient Near East*, 209.

[72] See Noegel, *Nocturnal Ciphers*, 263–9.

examination of the description of the so-called "angel" reveals a significant, formal *similarity* with ancient Near Eastern dream reports. The "angel" that interprets Daniel's dream is not described as a מלאך. It is literally חַד מִן־קָאֲמַיָּא "one of the standing-ones."

Oppenheim's second element of dream reports (i.e., an apparition stands before or over the dreamer) has not, to my knowledge, been associated with the חַד מִן־קָאֲמַיָּא ("one of the standing ones") from with Dan 7. One must take seriously, however, that the *angelus interpres* is introduced with neither conventional angel terminology nor with the symbolic ciphers normally used to describe angels (e.g., humans or stars; see below). Instead, the "angel" is described as "standing" (חַד מִן־קָאֲמַיָּא). One may compare this with descriptions of apparitions that appear conventionally in ancient Near Eastern message (i.e., non-symbolic) dreams. The dream of Nabonidus (see chapter one) begins: "In the beginning of my eternal reign they dispatched to me a dream. *Marduk*, the great lord, and *Sîn*, the luminary of the heavens and the outer-reaches, both *stood* (together)."[73] A dream of *Djoser* reported on the Hunger Stela opens: "While I was sleeping in life and happiness I found the god *standing* before me."[74] The motif is also found in Greek sources. Herodotus (2:139) records the following report: "Afterwards, therefore, when Sennacherib, king of the Arabians and the Assyrians, marched his vast army into Egypt, the warriors on and all refused to come to his (Sethos') aid. Upon this the monarch, greatly distressed, entered into the inner sanctuary and, before the image of the god, bewailed the fate which impended over him. As he wept he fell asleep, and dreamed that the god came and stood at his side."[75] Unlike most Near Eastern dream reports, Dan 7 does not explicitly state that the "standing one" is present from the inception of the dream. But the conversation between Daniel and the standing one presumes as much. For example, when Daniel inquires about the fourth beast, there is no need for the "standing one" to ask Daniel, "what beast?" as if he was not present for the initial events. There is no standard, technical terminology for "standing" that cuts across the lexicography of the ancient Near East and the ancient Mediterranean.[76] But the role of the "standing ones" is ubiquitous in Mesopotamian, Egyptian, and Hittite dreams and often occurs in Greek dreams.

It is similarly important to note that it is not unusual in ancient Near Eastern dream reports for the dreamer to converse with the apparition that stands over" him in the same way that Daniel converses with the "standing

---

[73] See above. My translation, my emphasis.
[74] Oppenheim, *The Interpretation of Dreams in the Ancient Near East*, 251. My emphasis.
[75] Oppenheim, *The Interpretation of Dreams in the Ancient Near East*, 252.
[76] See Oppenheim, *The Interpretation of Dreams in the Ancient Near East*, 245–55.

one." Consider the following excerpt from a dream of Nabonidus:

> The attendant said to Nebukadnezzar: "Do speak to Nabonidus so that he can report to you the dream he has had!" Nebukadnezzar was agreeable and said to me: "Tell me what good (signs) you have seen!" I answered him saying: "In my dream I saw with joy the Great Star, the moon and the planet Jupiter (literally: Marduk) high up in the sky and it called me by name [ ]."[77]

It is specious to claim that the experiences of the Babylonian king in chapter 2 and the experiences of Daniel in chapter 7 may be rigidly distinguished on formal grounds – even if Dan 2* and 7 offer innovation to the traditional forms. Dan 7's combination of the symbolic and non-symbolic forms of dream reports only serves to highlight the imaginative way in which the text remains faithful to the ubiquitous form of dream reports in the ancient Near East. Rather than attempting to distinguish between Dan 2 and 7 on formal grounds (i.e., dream vs. vision), distinctions are most fruitfully made on the levels of 1) the individual dreamers and 2) the articulation of eschatology. Husser acknowledges a precedent for imaginative innovation within dream forms (i.e., an assimilation of dreams and visions) in *1 En.* (83:1–7, 85:1–90:40). He attempts to dismiss the problem by claiming that, "in the apocalyptic writings, the apologetic concern to distinguish the pagans' dream from the inspired visions of loyal Jews was no longer relevant."[78] This is an astounding claim in view of the fact that the *Animal Apocalypse* was almost certainly written or updated around the same time as Dan 7–12.[79] The apocalypses in Dan 2 and 7 are best understood when viewed in the context of dream reports.

Typical Approaches to Daniel 7 and 8
The Daniel apocalypses have received disproportionate attention in the secondary literature compared to the other texts in this study. Chapter 7 is surely the most commented-on apocalypse from Ancient Judaism. Jürg Eggler's book-length research history of just thirteen verses (7:2–14) makes the point emphatically.[80] In order to avoid allowing my textual analysis to degenerate into a research history, I begin by outlining, from a methodological perspective, three typical approaches to the language found in Dan 7

---

[77] Oppenheim, *The Interpretation of Dreams in the Ancient Near East*, 250.
[78] Husser, *Dreams and Dream Narratives in the Biblical World*, 122.
[79] See George W.E. Nikelsburg, *1 Enoch 1* (ed. Hermeneia; Minneapolis: Fortress Press, 2001), 360–1. See also Tiller, *A Commentary on the Animal Apocalypse*, 70–9.
[80] Eggler highlights hundreds of variations on more than twenty basic models in *Influences and Traditions Underlying the Vision of Daniel 7:2–14*. To his list it is possible to add another interpretation of the fourth beast: an Indian rhinoceros. See David Flusser, *Judaism and the Origins of Christianity* (Jerusalem: Magnes Press, 1988), 176–83.

and 8: 1) the allegorical/mythological approach, 2) the iconographic approach, and 3) the literary approach. These approaches are distinct but they are not mutually exclusive and many scholars use more than one. My analysis of the language of Dan 7 and 8 will necessarily involve these approaches. This introductory overview will prevent the need for lengthy digressions in my textual analysis.

The Allegorical/Mythological Approach

The first approach may be labeled the "allegorical/mythological" approach. It interprets each dream report as an allegory of an older myth. This approach essentially began with H. Gunkel's study of Gen 1 and Revelation 12: *Schöpfung und Chaos in Urzeit und Endzeit*.[81] Gunkel argued that Dan 7 was an allegory of the "Chaos Myth," i.e., the Babylonian account of Marduk defeating Tiamat. Most modern scholars reject Gunkel's specific results but retain his method. The current consensus theory treats Dan 7 as an allegory or at least a reflex of the Canaanite Combat Myth – especially as seen in the Ugaritic *Ba'al Cycle*.[82] The *Ba'al Cycle* describes *Yamm* (Sea) or sometimes *Nahar* (River) rising up to challenge the divine council. The council is fearful and El (the high god) agrees to hand over his son, *Ba'al* to the chaotic waters.[83] But *Ba'al* prevails over *Yamm* (or variantly the sea-serpent *Lotan*) with the help of two magical clubs. *Ba'al* is then enthroned as king of the gods. The defeat of the beasts from the sea in Dan 7 and the consequent ascendancy of the כְּבַר אֱנָשׁ "one like a human being" with the help of the עַתִּיק יוֹמִין "ancient of days" are viewed as iterations of the same basic myth.[84]

The allegorical/mythological approach is a useful one, but there are two problems with it. First, it is problematic to the extent that it is not equally useful for all apocalypses. In other words, while many apocalypses are concerned with primordial events, they do not all allegorize an ancient

---

[81] Gunkel, *Creation and Chaos in the Primeval Era and the Eshchaton*, 205–14.

[82] See John J. Collins, "Stirring up the Great Sea: The Religio-Historical Background of Daniel 7," in *The Book of Daniel in the Light of New Findings* (ed. Adam van der Woude; vol. CVI of *BETL*; Leuven: Leuven University Press, 1993), 121–36. For the Baal cycle itself, see Mark Smith, "The Baal Cycle," in *Ugaritic Narrative Poetry* (ed. Simon Parker; vol. 9 of *SBLWAW* Atlanta: Scholars Press, 1997), 80–180. The combat myth is exemplified in other texts such as *Lugal*-e, *Anzu*, *Enuma Elish*, Exod 15, and several Psalms.

[83] On this motif, see also Jon Levenson, The Death and Resurrection of the Beloved Son: The Transformation of Child Sacrifice in Judaism and Christianity (New Haven: Yale University Press, 1993), 3–35. See also Andrew Angel, Chaos and the Son of Man: The Hebrew Chaoskampf Tradition in the Period 515 B.C.E. to 200 C.E. (London: T&T Clark, 2006).

[84] Helge Kvanvig has applied Gunkel's basic methodology to reconnect Dan 7 to Mesopotamia through *The Vision of the Netherworld*. See Kvanvig, *Roots of Apocalyptic: The Mesopotamian Background of the Enoch Figure and of the Son of Man*, 346.

myth. For example, while the allegorical/mythological approach produces meaningful results when applied to Dan 7 and 8, it is unhelpful for understanding 10–12. I note that Collins claims that Dan 10–12 can be read in light of the allegorical/mythological model: "In chs. 10–12, we meet again familiar mythic motifs. Each people on earth is represented by an angelic prince in heaven."[85] But one is *not* confronted by the same kinds of mythic motifs found in Dan 7 or 8. I argue in chapter four that the language of Dan 10–12 explicitly moves the text out of the mythic realm in which chapters 7–8 operate. Chapters 10–12 do not use the same kind of language found in Dan 7–8.

A second problem with the allegorical/mythological approach is that it prioritizes data in a way that obscures some important insights. We might compare this to the study of totemism mentioned in chapter one. One of the important insights gained from Lévi-Strauss's study on totemism is that most scholars were content to examine the relationship between a particular tribe and a particular animal in order to understand the phenomenon of totemism. For Lévi-Strauss it was equally important to understand the relationships between the different kinds of animals used in the totemic system. The allegorical/mythological approach to the language of Dan 7 (or other apocalypses) focuses too heavily on the tradition history of the text without making wider linguistic comparisons within the genre.

The Iconographic Approach

The second major approach to interpreting Daniel's dream reports might be described as the "iconographic" approach. This approach attempts to locate each symbolic cipher from the book of Daniel in a particular example or type from ancient Mediterranean/Near Eastern material culture. One identifies the referent of a given cipher based on the location(s) at which such objects are prevalent. Unlike the allegorical/mythological approach, this approach compares the material history of cultures rather than the history of literature. Joining material culture to the history of literature is a move to be praised, but it must be executed with circumspection.

J. G. Herder was the first to link the *mischwesen* from the Bible with the with wall sculptures discovered at Persepolis – though he does not, as J. A. Montgomery seems to imply, make a specific link to Daniel.[86] Most scholars have attempted to identify the winged lion with art from Babylon or

---

[85] Collins, *The Apocalyptic Vision*, 108.
[86] See J. G. Herder, *The Spirit of Hebrew Poetry* (vol. 1; Burlington: Edward Smith, 1833 [1782]), 17–83. Cf. J. A. Montgomery, *A Critical and Exegetical Commentary on the Book of Daniel* (ICC; Edinburgh: T&T Clark, 1927), 287. See also Collins, *Daniel*, 296.

Assyria.[87] Similar attempts have been made with all beasts found in Dan 7 and 8.[88]

Like the allegorical/mythological approach, there are benefits to the iconographic approach. The hybrid beasts of Daniel reflect not only literary traditions from the ancient world, but also a material world of art that is no less important. There are, however, at least two problems with an iconographic approach to the symbolic ciphers of Early Jewish apocalypses. First, it is rarely possible to conclusively prove that a Jewish scribe living in Hellenistic Judea would or could have had access to specific manifestations of foreign material cultures. The only sure confirmation can come from the discovery of like objects *in situ* in Israel. Second, some of the symbols are ubiquitous in the material culture of the Ancient Mediterranean/Ancient Near East and that makes it difficult to tie those symbols exclusively to one culture or figure in history. In the cases of Dan 7–8, this second problem is underscored by a special exhibition of the Bible Lands Museum Jerusalem put on in 2004.[89] The number of hybrid animals similar to those found in Dan 7–8 is significant and these examples are diffuse both geographically and chronologically in the material culture of the ancient Near East. It is difficult to argue that, for example, winged lions can function as a reference to Babylon in and of themselves.

Excursus: Representation in Ancient Near Eastern Art
Since I acknowledge the limited usefulness of the iconographic approach, it is necessary to say a few words about the nature of art in the Ancient Near East. In this section I highlight an influential theory of Near Eastern art that compliments my literary arguments about the model reader of Dan 7 below: Emma Brunner-Traut's concept of *Aspektische Kunst*. Traut's work is almost exclusively on Egyptian art, but it is relevant to other Near Eastern cultures.

The most basic paradigms of "aspective art" were laid out by Heinrich Schäfer in his *Principles of Egyptian Art*.[90] Schäfer used the terms *geradvorstellig* ("based on frontal images") and "pre-Greek" to describe Egyptian art but was unhappy with both. He did not intend the term "pre-Greek" in a purely chronological sense. For example, he would characterize modern

---

[87] See the summary by Jürg Eggler, *Influences and Traditions Underlying the Vision of Daniel 7:2–14: The Research History from the End of the 19th Century to the Present* (vol. 177; Göttingen: Vandenhoeck & Ruprecht, 2000), 43–4.

[88] Eggler, *Influences and Traditions*, 42–54.

[89] For the resulting catalogue, see Joan Goodnick Westenholz, ed., *Dragons, Monsters, and Fabulous Beasts (דרקונים מפלצות ויצורי פלא)* (Jerusalem: Bible Lands Museum, 2004).

[90] Heinrich Schäfer, *Principles of Egyptian Art* (Oxford: Griffith Institute, 1986 [1919]).

children's drawings as both "pre-Greek" and *geradvorstellig*. Emma Brunner-Traut introduced the term "aspective" to overcome some of the acknowledged problems with Schäfer's terminology.

Brunner-Traut defines aspective art primarily by contrasting it with perspective art. Perspective is a personal viewpoint from which "the object is seen in the context of mankind's separation from the inanimate world."[91] Aspective art does not take a personal perspective. Rather, "an Egyptian renders what he is depicting part for part as it really and ideally *is*, always, everywhere, and for everybody."[92] She uses the example of a square surface to highlight the differing modes of depicting an object. For an Egyptian, "a square surface is shown as an equal, right-angled quadrilateral. Greek or Western renders the same original as it *appears* to the viewer, an arbitrary individual at a random point in time in a particular spot chosen by him and in whatever lighting chances to be."[93] The differences between perspective and aspective approaches to a subject result in significantly different pieces of art. "Depending on where the viewer places himself the sides are foreshortened, the angles are distorted, and the line becomes finer as distance increases; in painting the colours and the shadows change, while an aspective artist will normally only render local colours without shadows."[94] She develops this theory futher in her *Frühformen des Erkennens*.[95] I cannot improve on Jan Assman's summary:

> Brunner-Traut postulates a psychological, cognitive basis for certain especially striking peculiarities of Egyptian art, which she sets in parallelism with other Phenomena in Egyptian culture, as well as with the art of other primitive peoples and with forms of children's art. She groups these peculiarities together under the rubric of the 'aspective.' This erudite concept, which is the opposite of "perspective," designates a purely additive stringing together or aggregating of elements without organizing, structuring principles that would make them appear to be parts of a superordinate whole.[96]

In the excursus below on Dan 7 and the "model reader" I argue that the first three beasts of Dan 7 provide more of a foil than a context for the fourth beast. Rather than forming an organic whole, most of the beasts in Dan 7 are of limited significance. Brunner-Traut's work on aspective art indicates

---

[91] Emma Brunner-Traut, "Epilogue: Aspective," in *Principles of Egyptian Art* (Oxford Griffith Institute, 1986), 426.

[92] Brunner-Traut, "Epilogue: Aspective," 424.

[93] Brunner-Traut, "Epilogue: Aspective," 424.

[94] Brunner-Traut, "Epilogue: Aspective," 424.

[95] Emma Brunner-Traut, *Frühformen des Erkennens: Aspektive im Alten Ägypten* (Darmstadt: Wissenschaftliche Buchgesselschaft, 1992).

[96] Jan Assman, *Death and Salvation in Ancient Egypt* (Ithaca: Cornell University Press, 2005), 26.

that such depictions are typical of ancient Near Eastern art and, perhaps, the "word art" found in the Book of Daniel.

The Literary Approach

A third, less common, but noteworthy approach is represented primarily by Paul Porter's *Metaphors and Monsters: A Literary Critical Study of Daniel 7–8*. This literary-critical examination is of particular interest to the present study. Porter examines the symbolic language of Dan 7–8 through the lens of Max Black's interaction theory of metaphor. He argues that the beasts function primarily as metaphors that draw upon and reflect the "root metaphor" of the "shepherd king."[97]

Porter's location of a "root metaphor" that functions across the genre apocalypse is helpful even if I disagree with his specific results. He importantly exposes how some literary features might function across a wide range of texts in the genre apocalypse. I argue that some of the symbols found in Dan 7, 8, and the *Animal Apocalypse* work on a meta-level that transcends each text and communicates between each text. My problem with Porter's identification of the "shepherd king" as the root metaphor of Jewish apocalypses is based on methodological considerations. For example, he does not observe the critical distinctions that many scholars make between symbols and metaphors.

Even though he quotes Black's understanding of the "frame and focus" of metaphors, Porter's textual analysis reveals that he examines metaphors only in their largest possible sense (i.e., as "figures of speech"). One can make meaningful distinctions between kinds of figures (i.e., metonymy, synecdoche, metaphor, symbol, sign). The purpose of these subgroups is not simply classification but clarification. Symbols and synecdoche may be classified together as types of tropes but they do not function the same way. The lack of distinctions on Porter's part is all the more striking since, in my reading, Black treats metaphor primarily in its restricted sense. Many of Porter's arguments are thus problematic to the extent that he ignores Daniel's restricted metaphors and treats "symbols" as if they were metaphors in the restricted sense. Still, Porter has done the field an important service by highlighting the value of viewing Daniel's literary devices as interacting and communicating across a larger field of texts.

Rather than locating a single "root metaphor," I locate a set of symbols (i.e., pairs of conventional associations) that function across the genre apocalypse and elsewhere in the literature of ancient Judaism and the ancient

---

[97] Paul Porter, *Metaphors and Monsters: A Literary-Critical Study of Daniel 7–8* (Motala: CWK Gleerup, 1983), esp., 61–120.

Near East. Rather than testifying to a "root metaphor," these symbols bear witness to a portion of the socio-cultural encyclopedia that the writers of early Jewish apocalypses maintained.[98] They teach the model reader how to understand the text by functioning as guide-posts – hermeneutic tools woven into the literary fabric of the text.

Language in Daniel 7

The language used in Dan 2 is largely unremarkable from a lexical standpoint. One finds a different situation in Dan 7. Dan 7 presents a fantastic vision couched in the same four-kingdoms framework as Dan 2. Instead of using metals to represent kingdoms, Dan 7 uses beasts: a lion, a bear, a leopard, and a fourth beast (perhaps a kind of elephant?). This combination of beasts is not novel. Several biblical passages associate lions and bears or lions and leopards. Prov 28:15 compares a wicked ruler's oppression of the poor to, "a roaring lion or a charging bear" (אֲרִי־נֹהֵם וְדֹב שׁוֹקֵק).[99] Jer 5:6 depicts ravenous beasts on the outskirts of Jerusalem as YHWH's agents of divine retribution against sinful Judah: "A lion from the forest shall kill them, a wolf from the desert shall destroy them. A leopard is watching against their cities." Indeed leopards are mentioned in the Bible only in association with lions.[100] Daniel's animal-language is set apart from most other descriptions in the Hebrew Bible, however, because none of the beasts are natural; they are all hybrids (or, *Mischwesen*).

כְּאַרְיֵה וְגַפִּין דִּי־נְשַׁר "Like a lion but with the wings of an eagle"

The first instance of symbolic language used in the historical review is a beast described as "like a lion but with the wings of an eagle." The *angelus interpres* informs both Daniel and the reader that the beast represents the first in a series of four earthly kingdoms. Leonine imagery is common in the Hebrew Bible and other Near Eastern literature. Brent Strawn's study of leonine imagery in the Hebrew Bible and the ancient Near East analyzes both naturalistic and metaphorical uses of the lion.[101] When used as a metaphor, the lion is used to describe four different kinds of referents: 1) the self/righteous (e.g., 2 Sam 1:23), 2) the enemy/wicked (e.g., Ps 22:14), 3)

---

[98] For the linguistic notion of "encyclopedia," see Eco, *Semiotics and the Philosophy of Language*, 46–84.

[99] See also 1 Sam 17:34, 36–7, Amos 5:19, Hos 13:8,

[100] See Isa 11:6, Jer 5:6, Dan 7:6, Hos 13:7, Sir 28:23. The same holds true in the NT. Rev 13:2 probably reflects Dan 7.

[101] Brent Strawn, *What is Stronger than a Lion? Leonine Image and Metaphor in the Hebrew Bible and the Ancient Near East* (OBO 212; Göttingen: Vandenhoeck & Ruprecht, 2005).

the monarch/mighty one (e.g., Prov 20:2), and 4) the deity (e.g., Job 10:16). Strawn finds several nuances within these basic categories of metaphorical usage: "It is more positive in tone when applied to insiders, unqualifiedly negative when applied to outsiders, mixed when applied to the monarchy/mighty one and to God."[102] In spite of these nuances, Strawn argues that in all cases, whether metaphorical or naturalistic, "The lion image bespeaks power and threat, even and especially fear."[103]

The lion found in Dan 7 is different from almost every other lion in the Hebrew Bible. Daniel's lion is a hybrid beast. Besides Daniel, only Ezekiel presents a hybrid beast couched in leonine terminology. In Ezek 1:10, one feature of the כְּבוֹד־יְהוָה "glory of YHWH" is a beast composed of predominantly human features. The beast has wings and four faces – one of which is the face of a lion. While this type of hybrid imagery is novel in the Hebrew Bible, it is not novel in the material culture of the ancient Israel and the ancient Near East.

Hybrid creatures are richly attested in ancient Mesopotamian and Egyptian art. Many of these objects are prominently displayed in many of the world's leading museums and some, such as the Egyptian Sphinx of Giza, carry wide-ranging currency in popular culture.[104] Winged lions are attested in both Assyrian and Babylonian art, though as Collins points out, they are not nearly as well attested as is sometimes claimed.[105] For example, it might be tempting to read Dan 7 against images of *lamassu*, sphinx, *Anzû*, or even griffin, but the winged lion of Daniel 7 is different from these creatures.[106] In order to further explore Collins's claim that winged-lions, strict-

---

[102] Strawn, *What is Stronger than a Lion?*, 66.

[103] Strawn, *What is Stronger than a Lion?*, 66.

[104] A few of the most easily accessible collections are found in Paris's Louvre, London's British Museum, New York's Metropolitan Museum of Art, Vienna's Kunsthistoriches Museum, and Berlin's Pergamon Museum. The cultural currency of the Sphinx of Giza – at least in the U.S. – is made obvious by its appropriation in contexts such as Disney's *Alladin*, *The Simpsons* television show, and Las Vegas architecture.

[105] Collins, *Daniel*, 297.

[106] Cf., for example, treatments of *lamassu* as winged lions: Hugo Gressman, *Altorientalische Bilder zum alten Testament* (Berlin: Walter de Gruyter, 1927), 378, 81. Mathias Delcor, *Le Livre de Daniel* (Paris: SB, 1971), 145. For the basic distinctions between hyrbrid creatures in the ancient Near East, see F.A. M. Wiggerman, "Mischwesen A," in *Reallexikon der Assyriologie und Vorderasiastischen Archäologie* (ed. Erich Ebeling and Bruno Meissner; Berlin: Walter de Gruyter, 1997), 222–46. A. Green, "Mischwesen B," in *Reallexikon der Assyriologie und Vorderasiatischen Archäologie* (ed. Erich Ebeling and Bruno Meissner; Berlin: Walter de Gruyter, 1997). See also Christof Uehlinger, "Mischwesen," in *Neues Bibel-Lexikon*. (ed. M. Görg and B. Lang; Zürich/Düsseldorf: Benzinger, 1995), 817–21. In terms of high-quality images the 2004 exhibition, *Dragons, Monsters, and Fabulous Beasts* at the Bible Lands Museum, Jerusalem (and the resulting exhibition catalogue), sheds considerable light on the types of beasts sometimes associated with Daniel's winged lion.

ly speaking, are not as common as they might appear, I highlight the features of one of the most common mistaken identities: *lamassu*.

The Akkadian term *lamassu* indicates a protective spirit.[107] In modern times the word is often used to describe a kind of hybrid beast referred to in Akkadian as *aladlammû*: a bull (or lion) colossus with a human head that may or may not have wings.[108] The association of *lamassu* with *aladlammû* is not entirely haphazard since *lamassāti* were often considered doorway or "boundary" spirits. But *aladlammû* should not be associated with the first beast in Dan 7. *Aladlammû* does not always have wings and the eagle's wings are a key feature of Daniel's first beast. More importantly, *aladlammû* always has a human head and face. There is no indication that the first beast in Dan 7 has a human head or face. In light of Daniel's detailed descriptions, a connection with *aladlammû* seems inappropriate.

The lion-beast in Dan 7 also bears some similarities to the *Anzû* (a lion-headed eagle), the Griffin (an eagle-headed lion), and the Sphinx (a human headed lion often depicted in a seated or prone position)[109] But Daniel's detailed descriptions of its beasts make close associations with any of these mythical creatures problematic. Pure winged lions are considerably less well represented in the material culture of the ancient Mediterranean / Near East, but those that have survived fill out the socio-cultural encyclopedia of Dan 7 in a different way than is normally characterized.

First, of the examples found in Mesopotamia, all post-date the Neo-Babylonian Empire.[110] From the Achaemenid period a Persian roundel (Oriental Institute in Chicago) depicts a pure winged lion and dates to the reign of Artaxerxes II (404–359 B.C.E.) and a gold *rhyton* in the shape of a winged lion (Tehran, National Museum) dates from the fifth century

---

[107] See "lamassu," in *The Assyrian Dictionary of the Oriental Institute of the University of Chicago* (ed. M. Civil, et al.; Chicago: The Oriental Institute, 1973), 60–6. *Lamassu* should not be confused with the lion-demoness *lamaštu*. See "lamaštu" in *The Assyrian Dictionary*, vol. 9, 66–7. Westenholz, ed., *Dragons*, 30–1. F.A. M. Wiggerman, "Lamaštu, Daughter of Anu: A Profile," in *Birth in Babylonia and the Bible: Its Mediterranean Setting* (ed. M. Stol; vol. 14 of *Cuneiform Monographs*; Groningen: Styx Publications, 2000), 217–52.

[108] "aladlammû," in *The Assyrian Dictionary of the Oriental Institute of the University of Chicago* (ed. Ignace Gelb, et al.; Chicago: The Oriental Institute, 1964), 286–7. Westenholz, ed., *Dragons*, 36–7. Prominent examples include the doorway guardians of the palaces of the Assyrian kings Ashurnasirpal II (Nimrud) and Sargon (Khorsabad). See Dominique Collon, *Ancient Near Eastern Art* (Berkeley: University of California Press, 1995), figs. 12, 113. High-quality, zoom-capable digital images of one *lamassu* from Ashurnasirpal's palace may be found online in the New York Metropolitan Museum of Art's Ancient Near East Department at www.metmuseum.org.

[109] See Westenholz, ed., *Dragons*, 32–7, and figs., 56–57, 59–76, 78, 89–126.

[110] A close examination of the lions from the Ishtar Gate reveals that they are not winged. The depictions of the manes mirror well the patterns of real lions. There are, to be sure, other *mischwesen* depicted on the wall.

B.C.E..[111] Second, some examples show extensive Egyptian influence. An example is a fifth century Achaemenid silver bowl with applied winged lions whose faces appear to have been stylized to resemble the Egyptian god *Bes*.[112] A bas-relief from 'Ain Dara in northern Syria (1000–900 B.C.E.) depicts winged lions together with mountain-gods, bird-men, and bull-men. Stylistic features of the relief indicate Hittite or Neo-Hittite production.[113] The largest number of lion-images in the ancient Near East and Mediterranean appear to be sphinxes, but in some cases the sphinx lacks wings and in most every case it has a human face.[114] In other words, it does not match Daniel's first beast in detail.

If one did not have access to Dan 2, it would be tempting to assume that the first beast refers to the Neo-Assyrian empire (followed by Babylonia, Persia, and Greece). Given the prominent place of the Median kingdom in Dan 2 and 8, it seems most prudent to assume that the animal like a lion with eagles wings refers to Babylon. The language used to describe the first beast, however, does not imply any specifically Babylonian (or even Mesopotamian) elements. But it is able to attach succinctly certain characteristics to Babylon that בבל could not do alone. These characteristics are undoubtedly those described by Strawn above: power, threat, and fear. The addition of the wings indicates speed. Babylon is a swift predator. But the attribution of these qualities is secondary to the deeper and more basic association between beasts and humans (kingdoms), i.e., Babylon does not merely or even primarily name a geographical region.

חֵיוָה אָחֳרִי תִנְיָנָה דָּמְיָה לְדֹב וְלִשְׂטַר־חַד הֳקִמַת וּתְלָת עִלְעִין בְּפֻמַּהּ בֵּין שִׁנַּיהּ
"Another beast, a second one, like a bear, but raised up on one side, and with three tusks in its mouth among its teeth."

The second beast is described as, "like a bear" (7:5). Bear terminology is much less prevalent in the Hebrew Bible than lion terminology and bear

---

[111] For the former, cf. http://oi.uchicago.edu/museum/ and the cover of *Near Eastern Archaeology* 68 (2005). For the latter, see Seton Lloyd, *The Art of the Ancient Near East* (New York: Frederick A. Praeger, 1965), fig. 210.
[112] Collon, *Ancient Near Eastern Art*, fig. 148.
[113] Westenholz, ed., *Dragons*, fig. 32.
[114] Cf. Heinz Demisch, *Die Sphinx: Geschichte ihrer Darstellung von den Anfängen bis zur Gegenwart* (Stuttgart: Urarchhaus, 1977), 1–100. Demisch provides examples from Greece and Phoenicia that are especially relevant for the Hellenistic Period. Armin Lange also pointed out to me a fifth century example from Israel (black-figure pottery, Tel Jemmeh). Cf. Ephraim Stern, *Material Culture of the Land of the Bible in the Persian Period 538–332 B.C.* (Jerusalem: Israel Exploration Society, 1982), 139. It is consistent with similar scenes on fifth century black-figure vessels from Greece. The problem with using these examples is that each of them depicts a beast that is hardly ferocious or violent.

iconography is similarly less well attested in ancient Near Eastern art. In the Hebrew Bible bears connote the same basic ideas that lions do: power, predation, savagery, and threat.[115] The most common scenario describes the rage of a mother-bear whose cubs have been stolen. For example, in Hosea 13:8, YHWH threatens retribution to Israel in the following terms: "I will fall upon them like a bear robbed of her cubs, and will tear open the covering of their heart."

Depictions in Near Eastern art are rare and variable. Only one piece clearly indicates an attacking bear. Others depict scenes such as bears being hunted by humans or gathering fruit from trees.[116] H. Junker asserted in 1932 that the bear does not function as a mythological creature in Near Eastern art and his position has been the consensus opinion ever since.[117] Junker is almost certainly correct that the bear did not function as a mythological creature in the ancient Near East and, accordingly, that the bear hybrid does not participate, on an individual level, with some larger mythological framework. But there is anoher sense in which Daniel's bear-hybrid does contain mythological overtones. While none of the individual beasts call on a particular mythological framework, their nature as hybrids or *Mischwesen* alert the reader to the allegory embedded within the vision. The hybrid nature of the beasts brings the mythological framework of the vision itself into focus quickly for the reader by using language that immediately takes the reader out of natural, everyday experiences and places him/her into an alternate reality coined by legend.

We find, then, that there are at least two levels involved in the symbolic language of Dan 7. The first level involves the basic allegory in which kingdoms are represented by beasts. The beasts need not be *Mischwesen* in order for the scenario to work. But in order to show the reader that the allegory functions not only in the earthly sphere, but the heavenly sphere, the beasts are described in terms that alert the reader to the parallel events going on outside the boundaries of his/her terrestrial domain.

---

[115] Cf. 1 Sam 17:34, 36–7, 2 Sam 17:8, 2 Kgs 2:24, Isa 11:7, 59:11, Hos 13:8, Amos 5:19, Sir 25:17, Lam 3:10, Prov 17:12.

[116] For the references, see Eggler, *Influences and Traditions* 45–7.

[117] H. Junker, *Untersuchungen über literarische und exegetische Probleme des Buches Daniel* (Bonn: Peter Hanstein Verlagsbuchhandlung, 1932), 36–40. Those who follow Junker's basic position are W. Baumgartner, "Ein Vierteljahrhundert Danielforschung," *ThR* 11 (1939): 218. A. Jeffrey, "The Book of Daniel," in *The Interpreter's Bible* (ed. G. A. Buttrick; Nashville: Abingdon, 1956), 454. Noth, *Das Geschichtsverständnis der altestestamentlichen Apokalyptik*, 22. A. B. Rhodes, "The Kingdoms of Men and the Kingdom of God: A Study of Daniel 7:1–14," *Int* 15 (1961): 411–30. Collins, *Daniel*, 297. R. Bartelmus, "Die Tierwelt in der Bibel II: Tiersymbolik im Alten Testament – examplarisch dargestellt am Beispiel von Dan 7, Ez 1/10, und Jer 11, 68," in *Gefärten und Feinde des Menschen. Das Tier in der Lebenswelt des alten Israel* (ed. B. Janowski, et al.; Neukirchen-Vluyn: Neukirchener Verlag, 1993), 293.

One more aspect of the bear should be mentioned. Besides having three large tusks, the bear is described as לְשְׂטַר־חַד הֳקִמַת "raised up on one side." Noth, followed by Collins, argues that Daniel's description of the bear refers to posture, i.e., a bear on its hind legs ready to attack.[118] This reading is possible, but it is required neither by the iconographic evidence nor the language in Dan 7. In the first instance, there are as many images of docile bears raised on their haunches as there are vicious ones.[119] In the second instance, the *hop'al* form may indicate something about the bear that is permanent – not an action it takes or movement it makes. If we use an analogy with the *hop'al* form of קום in 7:4, it would not appear that the beast itself is in physical control of its "raised-up" position. The description, "raised up on one side," may instead describe a basic feature of the hybrid-bear's anatomy. In other words, the bear might have had, for example, an extended neck *a la* the creature found in bas-reliefs on the *Ishtar Gate* (Sirrush) or the way a centaur's body extends up on one side. The bear is not, after all, a natural bear, but a hybrid creature. It represents Media. The relationship cannot be established based on any particular quality of the bear or based on any literary or material connections with Media. The basic key to the interpretation of the bear comes in the angelic interpretation of the beasts in Dan 8:21. The bear functions must like the lion did. It attaches notions of power, strength, and predation to Media in a way that מָדַי cannot do alone.

כִּנְמַר וְלַהּ גַּפִּין אַרְבַּע דִּי־עוֹף עַל־גַּבַּיהּ וְאַרְבְּעָה רֵאשִׁין

"Like a leopard, and it had four wings of a bird upon its back and four heads"

If bears are less well represented than lions in the art and literature of the ancient Near East, leopards are even less so. As indicated above, they occur infrequently in the Hebrew Bible and only in direct association with lions.[120] The same holds true in the New Testament. Leopards are also found with lions (and eagles) at *Qasr el-Abd* in *Iraq el-Amir*, a Hellenistic Palace built by the Tobias Hyrcanus.[121] While these leopards are naturalistic and therefore different than Daniel's hybrid animals, *Qasr el-Abd* is still potentially important for understanding the imagery of the Book of Daniel. Andrea Berlin points out that, "though the sculptures are not very distin-

---

[118] Noth, *Das Geschichtsverständnis der altestestamentlichen Apokalyptik*, 22. Collins, *Daniel*, 298.

[119] Eggler, *Influences and Traditions*, 47.

[120] Isa 11:6, Jer 5:6, Dan 7:6, Hos 13:7, Sir 28:23

[121] Unlike some other sites or objects, the leopards and lions are easily distinguishable at *Qasr el-Abd*. I am grateful to Jodi Magness for sharing her digital images of the site with me.

guished artistically, they are, first and foremost, representational art in the Greek tradition, and they adorn a building constructed by a member of the Jewish elite."[122] In other words, *Qasr el-Abd* provides a clear example of a Hellenistic Jew imagining animals through the lens of Greek art.[123] Nevertheless, Daniel's leopard is not a naturalistic one. It is described as having, "four wings of a bird on its back and four heads" (7:6). Several abortive attempts have been made to locate such a beast in ancient Near Eastern art. The most significant parallel has not, to my knowledge, been mentioned – though it too is an imperfect match. An incised shell from southern Mesopotamia (ca. 2500–2400 B.C.E.) depicts a deity on one knee before a seven-headed leopard.[124] One can be sure that the beast is a leopard because of its spots. It has seven heads, not four. The most important point is not, however, finding a perfect match. Even if the beast did have four heads, the provenance of the shell would make any association between it and the Book of Daniel highly doubtful. The shell may depict the battle between the Sumerian god Ninurta and the seven-headed serpent, and accordingly it may reflect a genuine mythological background. If the identification of the Sumerian shell with the myths of *Lugale* and *Angimdimma* is correct, it does not have any implications for Daniel. The supernatural elements of the beasts in Dan 7 do not appear to be specifically derived from particular, mythological, narrative contexts (even though the scene as a whole is almost certainly a reflex of the Canaanite Combat Myth). Instead, the supernatural features of this leopard help train the reader to understand the two levels on which the vision is being narrated.

The significance of the four heads and four wings is debated. The view that they represent the *diadochoi* (Hippolytus, Jerome, Rashi, Calvin) must be rejected since Greece is represented by the fourth beast (see below). Collins outlines two prominent views among modern scholars that are not mutually exclusive:

Modern scholars who identify the third beast as Persia often note that Daniel 11:2 implies only four Persian kings. Alternatively (or simultaneously), both the four

---

[122] Andrea Berlin, "Archaeological Sources for the History of Palestine: Between Large Forces: Palestine in the Hellenistic Period," *BA* 60 (1997): 12.

[123] This association should not be pushed too far since the writer of Daniel and the Tobiads were probably of different opinions about Greek culture. Nevertheless, cultural phenomena such as Hasmoneans taking Greek names indicates that there was no strict divide between Hellenizers and non-Hellenizers. In every case it is a matter of degrees.

[124] Westenholz, ed., *Dragons*, fig. 160. See also Noveck in O. Muscarella, *Ladders to Heaven: Art Treasures from the Lands of the Bible* (Toronto: University of Toronto Press, 1981), 75–6. (*ANEP* 671)

wings and the four heads can be taken to represent the four corners of the earth and thus the universality of the Persian Empire.¹²⁵

It is probably not possible to decipher what, if any, special significance might be attached to the number of wings. We have seen above that neither the lion nor the bear, nor any of the features attached to them have specific associations with their historical referents. The same is probably true here.

חֵיוָה רְבִיעָיָה "A fourth beast"

The base-species of the fourth beast is not specifically designated. The first three beasts are hybrids but their admixture is described in terms of a dominant species. Rather than a species designation, the fourth beast is described with three adjectives: דְּחִילָה וְאֵימְתָנִי וְתַקִּפָה יַתִּירָא "dreadful, terrible, and exceedingly mighty" (7:7) The animal's teeth are "great" (רַבְרְבָן) and made of iron (פַּרְזֶל). During Daniel's dream he sees the animal, "Devouring and crushing and stomping the remainder (of things) at its feet" (7:7). Perhaps the most significant aspect of this animal-symbol, however, is its horns. The fourth beast has ten horns (וְקַרְנַיִן עֲשַׂר לַהּ). In an upheaval three of the horns are displaced by an eleventh horn that is much smaller.

Horns are a common symbol of divinity in the ancient Near East.¹²⁶ Deities such as *Ba'al* are normally depicted wearing horned-headgear.¹²⁷ Far more rarely are kings are depicted wearing horned-crowns.¹²⁸ Especially noteworthy, then, are the numerous depictions of Alexander the Great and the *diadochoi* wearing horned crowns.¹²⁹

---

¹²⁵ Collins, *Daniel*, 298. Collins notes that, "The only Persian kings known from the Bible were Cyrus, Ahasuerus (Xerxes), Artaxerxes, and 'Darius the Persian' (Neh 12:22)."

¹²⁶ Jean Bottéro, *Religion in Ancient Mesopotamia* (Chicago: University of Chicago Press, 2001), 65. Kristian Kristiansen and Thomas Larsson, *The Rise of Bronze Age Society: Travels, Transmissions, and Transformations* (Cambridge: Cambridge University Press, 2005), 63, 65, 68, and section 5.6.

¹²⁷ For *Ba'al* see Olivier Binst, ed., *The Levant: History and Archaeology in the Eastern Mediterranean* (Cologne: Könemann, 2000), 42, 51. See also *ANEP* # 490. Similar iconography is used in Egyptian art. For example, see depictions of Hathor in Schulz and Seidel, eds., *Egypt: The World of the Pharaohs*, 221, 310, 31.

¹²⁸ The most notable may be *Naram-Sin*. See Kristiansen and Larsson, *The Rise of Bronze Age Society: Travels, Transmissions, and Transformations*, 63. Joan Aruz et al., *The Royal City of Susa* (New York: The Metropolitan Museum of Art, 1993), 166. Joan Oates, *Babylon* (London Thames and Hudson, 1986), 41.

¹²⁹ Montgomery is normally credited as the first to make a correlation between depictions of horned Seleucid rulers and the fourth beast in Dan 7. J. Montgomery, *A Critical and Exegetical Commentary on the Book of Daniel* (ICC; Edinburgh: T & T Clark, 1927), 291. S. Morenz took up Montgomery's suggestion and explored it with more numismatic evidence. See S. Morenz, "Das Tier mit den Hörnen, ein Beitrag zu Daniel 7 7f.," *ZAW* 65 (1951): 151–53.

Urs Staub, building on work done by S. Morenz, has amassed an impressive collection of images that depict Macedonian, Seleucid, and Ptolemaic rulers wearing horned headgear. In light of his pan-hellenic evidence, Staub disagrees with Morenz that horns were a motif peculiar to Seleucid kings.[130] He argues that horns were a conventional symbol for all Hellenistic rulers. He also holds that the fourth beast should be associated with the Seleucid war-elephant.[131] The main problem, which Staub acknowledges, is a large gap in the evidence. The latest coin he cites dates from 280 B.C.E.. – more than 100 years before Dan 7 was written. He attempts to work around the gap by pointing to a possible connection with Ptolematic Lagidic coins depicting a horn of plenty.[132] The coins featuring a horn of plenty strengthen the overall picture he paints, but it is doubtful that they can fill in the evidence-gap. As Eggler points out in citing Goodenough: "There is not a single instance of a cornucopia on a Seleucid coin before a series of seven bronze coins minted by Demetrius I, Soter (162–150 B.C.E.)."[133] Two pieces of art that no one has considered may, however, solve or atleast mitigate the problem with Staub's evidence. In the offerings chamber of an Egyptian temple in Edfu, there is a relief dating to the time of Ptolemy IV (221–204 B.C.E.) that depicts Ptolemy IV making an offering to Horus. In the relief, Ptolemy wears a horned crown.[134] A similar motif is found at the temple of Isis in Philae. In this relief dating to the reign of Ptolemy XII (80–51 B.C.E.), Ptolemy offers Horus the corpses of his enemies. He wears a horned crown similar to the one found in the Edfu refief.[135] It is unlikely that a Palestinian Jewish writer would have ever visited these temples, but that kind of direct influence is not the claim I wish to make. The main point one can sift from this Ptolemaic evidence is that horns *were*, as Staub claims, a pan-hellenic motif that was closely associated with Macedonian, Seleucid, and Ptolemaic rulers in a way that was novel in the ancient Near East/Mediterranean. The first relief described above attests that the motif was in use near the time when the Book of Daniel was written and the second proves that it continued to be used by Greek rulers in the East until the end of the Hellenistic period.

The Ptolemaic reliefs do not provide any additional evidence that the fourth beast of Daniel should be associated with war elephants. Staub's

---

[130] Staub, "Das Tier mit den Hörnern: Ein Beitrag zu Dan 7.7f.," 39–85.

[131] Staub, "Das Tier mit den Hörnern: Ein Beitrag zu Dan 7.7f.," 70–84.

[132] For these coins, see Reginald Poole, *Catalogue of Greek Coins: The Ptolemies, Kings of Egypt* (Bologna: A. Forni, 1963).

[133] Eggler, *Influences and Traditions* 51. See also E. R. Goodenough, *Jewish Symbols in the Greco-Roman Period.* (37; New York: Pantheon 1958), 107.

[134] Schulz and Seidel, eds., *Egypt: The World of the Pharaohs*, 307, no. 32.

[135] Schulz and Seidel, eds., *Egypt: The World of the Pharaohs*, 307, no. 33.

war-elephant theory is an intriguing one, but since the first three beasts are all *Mischwesen*, it seems unlikely that the fourth beast should be regarded as conventional. Staub's argument that horns were a pan-Hellenic motif and that horns of the fourth beast should point a savvy reader towards Hellenistic rulers, however, seems entirely appropriate. In this sense, we might read horns as functioning according to Peirce's view of the symbol, i.e., a trope that represents its referent on an entirely conventional basis. In other words, it seems a safe assumption that in the Hellenistic period, horns served as conventional symbols for Hellenistic kings. But iconography is hardly the only basis on which to associate Daniel's fourth beast and Hellenistic rulers.

The fourth beast is described as having "eyes like the eyes of a human" and "a mouth speaking arrogantly" (וּפֻם מְמַלִּל רַבְרְבָן). Daniel describes the eleventh ("small") horn of the beast waging war against "holy ones" (קַדִּישִׁין). The most crucial information about the fourth beast is provided in the attendant's detailed explication of the fourth beast in 7:25:

> And he will speak words against the most high and will afflict the holy ones of the most high. He will intend to change sacred seasons and the law[136] and they will be given into his hand for a time, times,[137] and half a time.

Verse 25 is the linchpin for interpreting not only the fourth beast but the entire dream report. It is from verse 25 that one is able to work backwards with confidence and identify the antecedents of the other beasts. Daniel's attendant explains that the little horn of the fourth beast will attempt to change "sacred seasons and the law." The meaning of this expression is illuminated by 1–2 Maccabees. Details of the Hellenistic religious reforms instituted by Antiochus IV in Judea are found In 1 Macc 1 and 2 Macc 5–6. Two passages from these texts are particularly relevant to Dan 7:25 and help to date the text precisely: 1 Macc 1:44–46 and 2 Macc 6:1–6. The passage from 1 Maccabees reads, "And the king (Antiochus) sent letters by messengers to Jerusalem and the towns of Judah; he directed them to follow customs strange to the land, to forbid burnt offerings and sacrifices and drink offerings in the sanctuary, to profane Sabbaths and festivals, to defile the sanctuary and the priests."[138] 2 Maccabees gives a specific report of the שקוץ שמם:

> Not long after this, the king sent an Athenian senator to compel the Jews to forsake the laws of their ancestors and no longer to live by the laws of God; also to pollute the

---

[136] Following the NRSV for זִמְנִין וְדָת

[137] The conjunction is not translated in idiomatic English. It is missing is 4QDan^a and S. The phrase seems plausible with or without it.

[138] Unless otherwise noted, translations of 1–2 Macc are taken from the NRSV.

temple in Jerusalem and to call it the temple of Olympian Zeus, and to call the one in Gerizim the temple of Zeus-the-Friend-of-Strangers, as did the people who lived in that place. Harsh and utterly grievous was the onslaught of evil. For the temple was filled with debauchery and reveling by the Gentiles, who dallied with prostitutes and had intercourse with women within the sacred precincts, and besides brought in things for sacrifice that were unfit. The altar was covered with abominable offerings that were forbidden by the laws. People could neither keep the Sabbath, nor observe the festivals of their ancestors, nor so much as confess themselves to be Jews. (2 Maccabees 6:1–6, NRSV)

The little horn's effort to "change sacred seasons and the law" is a reference to some – but not all – aspects of Antiochus IV's religious reforms described by 1–2 Maccabees. It is important to note that the שקוץ שמם, the placement of Zeus Olympias in the holy of holies, is not mentioned in Dan 7. Thus we may date Dan 7 rather precisely to a time after the Hellenistic religious reforms had begun but before the שקוץ שמם had taken place. In light of the description of the actions of the little horn, the fourth beast must be identified with Greece and each individual horn should be identified as a particular Greek/Seleucid ruler. Unlike the other beasts in this vision, some evidence points to the possibility that the fourth beast might bear a specific relationship to Greece to the extent that horns might have functioned as a pan-hellenic symbol for rulers of Greek extraction. Nevertheless it seems to me that such a connection could have at best provided a hint to readers – not a definitive interpretation. It is the description of the little horn's actions that settles the identification definitively. The fourth beast participates in the same symbolic system as the other beasts in Dan 7. Beasts are used to represent kingdoms. The fourth beast adds another element to the symbolic systems at work in ancient Jewish apocalypses. Horns are used to represent rulers/kings. It is hardly a new idea that the horns represent individual kings though there is considerable disagreement over which particular rulers the writer might have had in mind.[139] We shall see below that the same kinds of associations are made in other apocalypses such as Dan 8 and the *Animal Apocalypse*.

כְּבַר אֱנָשׁ "One like a human being"

The "one like a human being" is probably the most commonly commented upon feature of chapter 7 if not the entire Book of Daniel.[140] The largest percentage of ink is spilled, however, investigating how the expression

---

[139] See most recently Andreas Blasius, "Antiochus IV Epiphanes and the Ptolemaic Triad: The Three Uprooted Horns in Dan 7:8, 20 and 24 Reconsidered," *JSJ* 37 (2006): 521–47.

[140] Klaus Koch, "Der "Menschensohn" in Daniel," *ZAW* 119 (2007): 370. See also Koch, *Die Reiche der Welt und der kommende Menschensohn: Studien zum Danielbuch*, 156–64.

relates to the New Testament term ο υιος του ανθρωπου "the son of man." This study does not examine the reception of the expression כְּבַר אֱנָשׁ in the New Testament. But two basic points of grammar are worth emphasizing in light of the shadow cast by the New Testament's use of the term "ο υιος του ανθρωπου."[141] First, the noun אֱנָשׁ is in absolute form and accordingly the entire expression is in absolute form. Without the definite article, the expression כְּבַר אֱנָשׁ does not name a particular referent, but one belonging to a class of referents: human beings. This meaning is established by considerable comparative evidence. In pre-Targumic Aramaic, the expression occurs in the third *Sefire* inscription, 1Q20 VI 9, 20, XIX 15, XXI 13, 4Q201 Iiii 18, 4Q206 Ixxii 1, 4Q212 Iv 25–6, 4Q531 14 4, 11QtgJob 9 9, 26 2–3.[142] Most of these cases are plural, i.e., בני אנוש, and connote "humanity." The vast majority of comparative evidence is derived from the Hebrew expressions בן אנוש and בן אדם. The Hebrew expression בן אדם is used 93 times in the Book of Ezekiel as YHWH's normal form of address for the prophet, וַיֹּאמֶר אֵלַי בֶּן־אָדָם עֲמֹד עַל־רַגְלֶיךָ וַאֲדַבֵּר אֹתָךְ "He said to me: O Mortal, Stand up on your feet, and I will speak with you" (Ezek 2:1). Here the meaning of the expression is "human." Other notable uses are those that construct an explicit synonymous relationship between the expression בן־אדם and אישׁ: "God is not a human being (אישׁ) that he should lie, or a mortal (בן־אדם), that he should change his mind" (Num 23:19).[143] Among the non-biblical Hebrew texts from Qumran בן אדם (most often plural: בני אדם) is found 42 times and always designates "humanity."[144] In the construction בני אדם the issue of definiteness must be raised since אדם can function as a proper noun. Many of the examples of the expression, however, contain one or more parallelisms that indicate that אדם functions in its more general sense. For example, within the final hymn appended to *Serek haYahad*, the psalmist writes, "Upon the eternal has my eye gazed – even that wisdom hidden from men (מאנ'ש), the knowledge and wise prudence (concealed) from humanity (מבני אדם). The source of righteousness, well of power, and spring of glory (hidden) from fleshly counsel (מסוד בשר)."[145] In this pas-

---

[141] For a concise and thorough treatment of the expression כְּבַר אֱנָשׁ, see the excursus, "One Like a Human Being," in Collins, *Daniel*, 304–10.

[142] It is perhaps odd to use the expression "pre-Targumic Aramaic" and then list 11QtgJob, but 11QtgJob is not considered a part of the traditional corpus of Targumim. For the *Sefire Inscription*, see J. Gibson, *Textbook of Syrian Semitic Inscriptions* (3vols.; Oxford: Clarendon, 1971–82), 2:48.

[143] Other references include Jer 49:18, 33, 50:40, 51:43, Isa 51:12, 56:2, Ps 8:5, 80:18, 146:3, Job 16:21, 35:8, and Dan 8:17. For the similar expression בן אנוש see Ps 144:3.

[144] With 8 instances, 1QH^a has the highest concentration of usage. Behind 1QH is 1QS with 4 references. Interestingly, however, all of the references in 1QS derive from the hymn appended to the end of the work (i.e., IX 26b–XI 22) – the same formal context as 1QH.

[145] 1QS XI 5–7. Here I adapt elements of the translations found in *DSSSE*, 97 and *DSSR*, 41.

sage אנוש, בני אדם, and סוד בשר are used synonymously. In order to foreshadow a point that will become important below, I add that this psalmist proceeds to describe how members of the *Yahad* (i.e., those *not* like the majority of humanity – at least in their own opinion) have been made heirs with the קדושים "holy ones," i.e., angels.

The second grammatical point involves the the preposition כְּ.[146] The preposition indicates that the figure being described is not human, but "like" a human. Thus, it is problematic to read the expression כְּבַר אֱנָשׁ as a title in Daniel. Collins also rejects reading the expression as a title, nevertheless, I must disagree with his judgment that, "The 'one like a human being' is a symbol of the same order as the Ancient of Days – a mythic realistic depiction of a being who was believed to exist outside the vision."[147] The semiotics of the expression "one like a human being" functions differently. Like the beasts and the horns in Dan 7, the "one like a human being" points to a reality beyond itself and that reality is linguistically structured. The code "human" instructs the reader to read "angel" no less than the code "beast" instructs the reader to read "kingdom." The angel's interpretation does not function to inform Daniel that the beasts represent kingdoms, but to help him understand *which* kingdoms are being described. As Collins himself points out, humans are common symbols for angels in apocalypses and other dream visions.[148] We will see below that humans are used to represent angels in both Dan 8 and the *Animal Apocalypse*. The use of humans to represent angels is also familiar from other literary contexts such as the visitation of Abraham in Gen 18:2, Joshua's encounter with the שַׂר־צְבָא־יְהוָה "commander of the army of YHWH" in Josh 5:13–14, and the revelation to Manoah and his wife that Sampson will be born to them (Judg 13). Humans also represent angels in the Book of Ezekiel. In 8:2, an angel is described as דְמוּת כְּמַרְאֵה־אֵשׁ "a figure that looked like a human being."[149] Unlike the anomalous case in which a human represents the Deity in Ezek 1:26, the figure in 8:2 is almost certainly an angel since, as Collins comments, "his function is to transport the visionary into the presence of the glory of the Lord (v.4)."[150] In Ezek 9–10 the main character is a figure described as הָאִישׁ לְבֻשׁ הַבַּדִּים "the man clothed in linen." 9:3 makes clear that this figure is not YHWH, but one of his angelic instruments: וַיִּקְרָא

---

[146] For a comprehensive treatment, see Ernst Jenni, *Die hebräischen Präpositionen: Die Präposition Kaph* (Stuttgart: Kohlhammer, 1994).

[147] Collins, *Daniel*, 305.

[148] Collins, *Daniel*, 305–6.

[149] Reading איש for אש with the OG (ανδρος).

[150] Collins, *Daniel*, 306. Some identify the figure in Ezek 8 with the representation of the Deity in Ezek 1. See Christopher Rowland, "The Vision of the Risen Christ in Rev. i.13ff: The Debt of an Early Christian to an Aspect of Jewish Angelology," *JTS* 31 (1980): 4–5.

אֶל־הָאִישׁ הַלָּבֻשׁ הַבַּדִּים "And he [the God of Israel] called to the man clothed in linen." Humans also represent angels in the visions of Proto-Zech (cf. 1:8–13).

It is hardly a stretch to suggest that, especially in visionary/revelatory literature, humans function as standard ciphers for angels. The association works on a categorical level.[151] The particular identity of individual angels must be determined based on other evidence within the text. The category "human," however, points the savvy reader to the category "angel." The pair is a conventional association that forms part of the socio-cultural encyclopedia of ancient Israel and this differentiates the "one like a human being" from the "ancient of days" in terms of the linguistic strategies employed by each.

עַתִּיק יוֹמִין "Ancient of Days"

An abrupt shift in the language of Dan 7 is marked with the entrance of the *Ancient of Days*. For the first time in the vision, a character is described with language that does not point beyond itself – at least not in a categorical way. We have seen in the foregoing analysis that with the possible exception of the fourth beast's horns, no individual beast bears a specific relationship to the kingdom it represents. The more compelling aspect of the semiotics of each beast is the way in which they participate in a pair of conventional association. The category "beast" points the reader to the category "kingdom," the category "horn" to the category "king," and the category "human" to the category "angel." The semiotics of עַתִּיק יוֹמִין functions on a different level. It is probably a title or epithet of El, but functions in Dan 7 as a divine name synonymous with El. It is not a trope.

Clues to the meaning of the expression might be derived, in the first instance, from the literary framework of the Canaanite Combat Myth.[152] In the Ugaritic Ba'al Cycle, Ba'al is enthroned after defeating *Yamm*. But it is *El*, the head of the pantheon, that calls for Ba'al's enthronement. El declares to Athirat:

wn.in.bt.lb 'l/km.ilm.

whzr.kbn.atrt.

For Ba'al has no house like the gods, no court like Athirat's so[ns.]

A few lines later, he commands:

---

[151] The first intentional venture into the deep, structural associations found in some apocalypses is found in Lange, "Dream Visions and Apocalyptic Milieus," 27–34.

[152] Clifford, " Roots of Apocalypticism in Near Eastern Myth," 3–38. Collins, "Stirring up the Great Sea: The Religio-Historical Background of Daniel 7," 121–36.

ybn.bt.lbʻ l/klmilm.

wḫẓr.kbn.aṯrt.

Let a house be built for Baʻal like the gods, a court, like Athirat's sons.[153]

One may note that even after Baal is enthroned, El retains the position of high god. The account of Baal's death at the hands of Mot and his eventual resurrection underlines that El never relinquishes his position even as Baal's star rises. The Ancient of Days figure plays the role of the high God El in this Jewish reflex of the Canaanite Combat Myth.

Philological evidence from *Baʻal* and other Ugaritic texts also helps to illuminate the meaning of עַתִּיק יוֹמִין. In many cases, divine names are joined to or function as part of epithets that describe the relative age of the deity. For example, El is sometimes described as *ab.šnm* "father of years."[154] That *ab.šnm* is the semantic equivalent of עַתִּיק יוֹמִין was recognized long ago by Albright and Cross's discussion of the linguistic relationship in his widely read *Canaanite Myth and Hebrew Epic* has not found serious challengers.[155] Another epithet of El functions similarly: *drd[r]* "ageless one."[156] Both locutions indicate the seniority of the deity in the pantheon. They name the original or high god. In the case of Daniel, the title indicates that the Ancient of Days has generational priority over the figure described as "one like a human being."

I should like to point out that other, similar designations are found among the Ugaritic corpus and they might also shed light on the locution עַתִּיק יוֹמִין in a more schematic way. Forty-nine times the name of the goddess Anat is modified with the epithet *bṯlt*, "adolescent."[157] The adjective qualifies her age not in human terms (years), but in terms of her place in the pantheon. She belongs to the younger generation of the gods. Similarly,

---

[153] Transcription and translation of Smith, "The Baal Cycle," 128–9. (*CAT* 1.4.IV:50–1, 1.4.IV:62–V:1)

[154] *CAT* 1.4.IV:24 (=1.1.III:24, 1.2.III:5, 1.3.V:8, 1.5.VI:2, 1.6.I:36, 1.17.VI:49), 1.2.I:10. See Aicha Rahmouni, *Divine Epithets in the Ugaritic Alphabetic Texts* (HdO I:93; Leiden: Brill, 2008), 18–21.

[155] William F. Albright, "The North-Canaanite Epic of ʼAlʼêyân Baʻal and Môt," *JPOS* 12 (1932): 197. Frank Moore Cross, *Canaanite Myth and Hebrew Epic: Essays in the History of the Religion of Israel* (Cambridge: Harvard University Press, 1997), 236–7.

[156] *CAT* 1.10.III:6. See discussion in Mark Smith, *The Early History of God: Yahweh and Other Deities in Ancient Israel* (Grand Rapids: Eerdmans, 2002), 32–43.

[157] See Gregorio del Olmo Lete and Joaquín Sanmartín, *A Dictionary of the Ugaritic Language in the Alphabetic Tradition* (I: 67; 2 vols.; Leiden: Brill, 2003), 1:250. The traditional translation is "virgin." While the technical, sexual sense of that word sometimes utilized in the Ugaritic tablets, it rarely has such a meaning in the present context. The following examples from *Baʻal* are representative (i.e., devoid of sexual impliations): *CAT* 1.3. II:32, III:11, IV:21, 53, V:19, 29, 1.4.II:14, 24, III:33, 39, V:20, 25, 1.6.III:23, IV:6, 21. For a list of all occurrences and up-to-date discussion, see Rahmouni, *Divine Epithets in the Ugaritic Alphabetic Texts*, 134–41.

the god *Ḥôrānu* is described as *ġlm* "the youth" and the goddess Nikkal is referred to as *ġlmt* "the maiden."[158] In spite of the relative obscurity of an epithet such as עַתִּיק יוֹמִין in Aramaic, it appears to fit into conventional naming patterns known from elsewhere in the ancient Near East.[159] The expression is just one among many examples of how ancient writers often encoded the deity's age/status into his or her name by means of an epithet. The motif-historical relationship between Dan 7 and the Combat Myth makes this philological comparison compelling.

This kind of language, i.e., adjectival rather than symbolic description, has an important function in several of the apocalypses I consider below. It is typical of Dan 10–12, *Apocryphon of Jeremiah* C, and *Pseudo-Daniel*[a–b] *ar*. This kind of language also dominates the angel's interpretation of Daniel's dream in this chapter and the next. Two descriptions in particular are noteworthy: עֶלְיָא "the Most High" and קַדִּישֵׁי עֶלְיוֹנִין "the Holy Ones of the Most High."[160]

עֶלְיָא "The Most High"

"The Most High" is sometimes an epithet, but often functions as a proper name. It is used over 150 times in the Hebrew Bible and the Apocrypha – often as a synonym for YHWH: יַרְעֵם מִן־שָׁמַיִם יְהוָה וְעֶלְיוֹן יִתֵּן קוֹלוֹ "YHWH thundered from heaven, the Most High gave forth his voice" (2 Sam 22:14).[161] The name probably also functioned to designate the high god of the Israelite pantheon as opposed to other, local manifestations of El (i.e., El-berith in Judg 9:46, El-bethel in Gen 35:7, El-paran in Gen 14:6, etc). For example, Melchizedek, the king of Salem, is described as a priest of אֵל עֶלְיוֹן "God, most high" (Gen 14:18). In the context of Dan 7, the term "Most High" functions as a proper name since it does not modify another description of the Deity. The term is treated in more detail in chapter three below where I argue that the name functions as a synonym for "God of Heaven" in Jewish writings of the Hellenistic Period. I make a few observations here though. The semiotics of the "Most High" is considerably different than the descriptions of historical actors that we have encountered

---

[158] Rahmouni, *Divine Epithets in the Ugaritic Alphabetic Texts*, 266–70.

[159] Thanks to Jodi Magness for pointing out to me that this tradition continues in the Hekhalot literature, where one of the titles of Metatron is נער, i.e., "the youth." Cf. Andrei Orlov, *The Enoch-Metatron Tradition* (TSAJ 107; Tübingen: Mohr-Siebeck, 2005), 135–6.

[160] The Masoretes propose the *qere* עליאה for the *ktib* עליא. The original, plural form is to be preferred in light of the plural (majestic) form עליונין found elsewhere is Dan 7.

[161] This association is attested across a wide chronological spectrum. See Wis 5:15, 6:3, and Sir 39:5, 47:5. Sir also associates υπιστου "the most high" with the Jerusalem temple (50:7) and νομον ον ενετειλατο ημιν Μωυσης "the law that Moses commanded to us" (24:23).

so far. The description does not point the reader beyond itself. It does not participate in a pair of conventional association (i.e., beasts = kingdoms). Instead it is an explicit name. The "holy ones" connected with the Most High, however, is a symbolic description that functions like the majority of the language we have encountered in Dan 7.

קַדִּישִׁין "The Holy Ones"

In one of the cogent excurses typical of his *Hermeneia* commentary, John Collins mounts considerable evidence in defense of an angelic interpretation of the קַדִּישִׁין in Dan 7. [162] An angelic or divine meaning is attested already in the fourteenth century B.C.E. in the cognate Ugaritic expression *bn qdš*.[163] This meaning is found continually in West Semitic inscriptions throughout the Iron Age.[164] In the Hebrew Bible, "holy ones" almost always indicates angelic beings. For example, the psalmist writes, "Let the heavens praise your wonders, O YHWH, your faithfulness in the assembly of the holy ones (קדשים)."[165] A synonymous parallelism is drawn in this bicolon between שמים "heavens" and קהל קדשים "assembly of the holy ones" indicating that the abode of the holy ones is heaven. The holy ones are unambiguously angels. In terms of lexicography the texts from Qumran are also important for understanding "holy ones" since many of the texts are very close in date to Daniel.

C. Brekelmans lists twenty passages in which the expression is used, though six of the cases he considers doubtful candidates for an angelic meaning and in seven cases he entirely rejects an angelic meaning.[166] L.

---

[162] Collins, *Daniel*, 313–7. This view first gained a significant following after it was expressed by Martin Noth, "The Holy Ones of the Most High," in *The Laws in the Pentateuch and Other Essays* (London: Oliver and Boyd, 1966), 215–28. (First published in the *Festschrift für Sigmund Mowinckel* in *NTT* 56 (1955): 146–57. A notable objection to the angelic interpretation is found in Hartman and DiLella, *The Book of Daniel*, 91. Cf. W. Sibley Towner, *Daniel* (Atlanta: John Knox, 1984), 117–8.

[163] See *CAT* 1. 2.I:21, 38, 1.17.I:4.

[164] See the 10th century Yehimilk inscription from Byblos (*KAI* 1.4.5, 7 and Gibson, 3.18), the 7th century Arslan Tash Inscriptions (*KAI* 1.27.12, Gibson 3.82), and the fifth century inscription of Eshmunazzar of Sidon (*KAI* 2.19.9, Gibson 3.106). For the *Words of Ahikar*, see A. E. Cowley, *Aramaic Papyri of the Fifth Century B.C.* (Oxford: Clarendon, 1923), 215.

[165] Cf. Ps 89:6, 8 [Heb.], Job 5:1, 15:15, Prov 3:30, Zech 14:5, Deut 33:2–3 and perhaps Exod 5:11 if one reads with the OG. Cf. also αγιαις in Jude 1:14.

[166] Brekelmans lists the following passages as examples in which an angelic meaning for "holy ones" is clear: 1QM 1:16, 10:11–12, 12:1, 4, 7, 15:14, 1QS 11:7–8, 1QH 3:21–2, 10:35, 1QDM 4:1, 1QSb 1:5, 1Q36 1:3 1QapGen 2:1. See C. Brekelmans, "The Saints of the Most High and Their Kingdom," *OTS* 14 (1965): 305–29. Brekelmans lists six other disputed passages (1QH 4:24–5, 11:11–12, 1QM 12:8–9, 18:2, CD 20:8, 4QFlor 1:4) and seven that he believes refer to the sect (1QM 3:4–5, 6:6, 10:10, 16:1, 1QSb 3:25–6, 4:23, 4QShirShabb 403.1.i.24). As Collins points out, the passage 4QShirShabb should be considered a reference to angels definitively in

Duqueker has shown, however, that an angelic meaning is at least possible in all the cases.[167] For example, Brekelmans lists 1QM 12 8 as a doubtful case. But the parallelism between קדושים and מלאכים in this passage indicates an angelic interpretation: "For holy is the Lord, and the King of Glory is with us. The nation of his holy ones (קדושים) (are) [our] mighty her[oes and] the army of angels (צבא מלאכים) are enlisted among us."[168] I am able to add even more texts to the list of evidence in favor of Deqeuker's position: 1Q22 Iiv 1, 1Q28b IV 1, 4QInstruction^c 2 I 17 (4Q417), 4QInstruction^d 81 1, 4, 11–2 (4Q418), 4Q457b II 5. One of theses passages requires comment.

In 4QInstruction^d 81 4–5, the sage admonishes, "In this way shall you honor him: by consecrating yourself to him as though he has established you as a holy of holies (לקדוש קודשים) [over all] the earth and among all the [g]o[ds] [א]ל[ים])) he has cast your lot." In this passage "holy of holies" does not refer to the inner-sanctum of the temple or even metaphorically to the pious individual as part of a spiritual temple *a la* the מקדש אדם "temple of man" in 4QMidrEschat^a 1 6 (4Q174). Here the expression means, "an angel among the angels." This meaning is indicated by the parallelism between קדוש קודשים and אלים. A good translation for לקדוש קודשים here might be "as a holy one among the holy ones." It is interesting that unlike texts like 4QShirShabb, the wise ones addressed in this text do not *actually* share communion with the angels, but are admonished to consecrate themselves *as if* God had granted that privilege (later in the same fragment, they are admonished to sing songs to the "holy ones" – a group they yearn to be a part of but yet are not).

The vast majority of examples of "holy ones" Qumran are plausibly explained as angels. In a large percentage of these cases, the evidence demands an angelic interpretation. I cannot agree with Collins, however, that, "There is no undisputed case in this literature, however, where the expres-

---

light of consistent usage in the text. See Carol Newsom, *The Songs of Sabbath Sacrifice: A Critical Edition* (27; Atlanta: Scholars Press, 1985), 24. See also Koch, *Die Reiche der Welt und der kommende Menschensohn: Studien zum Danielbuch*, 142–55.

[167] Luc Deqeuker, "The Saints of the Most High in Qumran and Daniel," *OTS* 18 (1973): 108–87. Deqeuker also adds passages to the list of evidence: 11QMelch 1 9, 4Q181 1 3-6. Collins points out that numerous passages from the 4QShirShabb should be added to the list. See Newsom, *The Songs*, 24–5.

[168] See Deqeuker, "The Saints of the Most High in Qumran and Daniel," 157–9. It is possible, as Deqeuker argues, that עם in this passage should be translated as the preposition. In that case an angelic meaning would be even clearer. Internal evidence is ambiguous, but I favor reading עם as a noun (nation, multitude). עם does not in and of itself demand a human interpretation. Indeed one must keep in mind, as Collins points out, the construction עם קדושי ברית "the people of the holy ones of the covenant." In this case the writer has taken pains to make a human meaning unambiguous. See Collins, *Daniel*, 315.

sion "holy ones" in itself refers to human beings."[169] One might consider 1QM 9 7–8. "When the slain fall, the prie[st]s shall continue blowing at a distance, and they shall not enter in the midst of the slain so as not to be defiled with their impure blood, for they are holy (קדושים)." In this passage priests are referred to as "holy ones." It is because they are קדושים that they may not come in contact with impure blood. This usage is hardly surprising given the frequency with with the adjective "holy" is used to describe aspects of the cult in the Hebrew Bible. For example, the priest wears בגדי הקדש "the holy vestments" and makes offerings in הקדש "the holy place."[170]

Evidence from the Apocrypha/Pseudepigrapha is more mixed. Several texts treat "holy ones" unambiguously as angels.[171] But others, such as the *Aramaic Levi Document,* use the expression "holy ones" to refer both to angels and humans, e.g., קדישין מן עמא "the holy ones from the people" (4QLevi[b] ar 3–4 7).[172] Unlike the ambiguous expression עם קדשים (1QM 12 8), the syntax of the phrase קדישין מן עמא leaves no doubt about a human interpretation. Precedent for a human interpretation can also be found in Ps 34.[173] Moreover, the fact that the adjective "holy" is applied to humans in the Hebrew Bible (cf. Exod 19:6 גוֹי קָדוֹשׁ "a holy nation" and 29:21 וְקָדַשׁ הוּא וּבְגָדָיו "Then he and his garments (will be) holy") would have provided sufficient precedent for an author to develop a substantive use (cf. *Similitudes of Enoch,* 1 Corinthians 14:33, Philippians 1:1). In spite of these human-uses I agree with Collins that when all the evidence is prioritized, the strongest case emerges for an angelic interpretation in Dan 7.

---

[169] Collins, *Daniel,* 316.

[170] Cf. Exod 34:10 and Lev 14:13 as well as all of Lev 23.

[171] Collins lists seven places where the קדיש "holy one" is used substantively in conjunction with עיר "Watcher:" *1 Enoch* 1:2, 22:6, 93:2, 106:19, 4QEnGiants[c] 1:6, 1QapGen 2:1, 4QMessAr 2:18. "Holy ones" are also angels in *1 Enoch* 1:2, 9:3, 14:23, 25, 12:2, 93:6, 103:2, 106:19, 108:3. *1 Enoch* 100:5, however, uses "holy ones" to describe both angels and humans. An angelic meaning for "holy ones" is found in Sir (42:17, 45:2), *Jub.* (17:11, 31:14, 33:12), Tob (8:15), and *Ps. Sol.* (17:43).

[172] The reference to holy ones as angels is not extant in the Aramaic text, but is reconstructed by Greenfield, Stone, and Eshel based on the Athos inscription: קדישיא for των αγιων. The second reading (human meaning) is clear in the Aramaic from Qumran, but Greenfield, Stone, and Eshel note that the it might not actually belong to the *Aramaic Levi Document.* Procedures such as paleography produce inconclusive results. Regardless of the status of fragment 3–4, neither the reading nor the interpretation of קדישין מן עמא is disputed. Jonas Greenfield et al., *The Aramaic Levi Document: Edition, Translation, Commentary* (19; Leiden: Brill, 2004), 60–1, 219–22. Both meanings are also found in Wis (see 5:5, 10:10, and 18:9) and the *T. 12 Patr.* (angels: *T. Levi* 3:3, human: *T. Levi* 18:11, 14, *T. Iss.* 5:4, *T. Dan* 5:11, 12). A human meaning is found in 3 Macc 6:9 and numerous times in the *Similitudes of Enoch.*

[173] The majority of the evidence from the Hebrew Bible points in the other direction. Cf. Ps 89:6, Job 5:1, 15:15, Zech 14:5, and perhaps Deut 33:2 and Exod 6:11 if the OG reading is more original.

Two pieces of evidence must be treated as paramount. First is the use of the term "holy ones" in 7:27a: "The kingship and dominion and the greatness of the kingdoms under the whole heaven shall be given to the people of the holy ones of the most high (לְעַם קַדִּישֵׁי עֶלְיוֹנִין מַלְכוּתֵהּ)." Dominion is not given to the "holy people of the Most High," but to a group of people whose lot is with the "holy ones of the Most High." עַם does not agree with "holy ones of the most high" in number. The people and the holy ones are distinct. Of similar importance is the use of קַדּוֹשׁ "holy one" in Dan 8:13. During his vision, Daniel listens to a conversation between two "holy ones" that are unambiguously heavenly beings. These two pieces of internal evidence from Daniel indicate that the term "holy ones" in Daniel functions in the same way that most other examples from ancient Jewish literature indicate. They are angels.

If the angelic interpretation is correct, then one may observe a considerable difference in representation techniques between the vision and the angelic interpretation in Dan 7. The expression "holy ones" does not participate in a symbolic system in the same way that many other descriptions of angels do (i.e., human = angel). The expression "holy ones" does not point beyond itself. The expression is perhaps not as transparent a description of angels as is, for example, מלאכים, but neither is it a trope. The semiosis of "holy ones" involves transparency, not transference. We shall see that descriptions like this one dominate the non-symbolic apocalypses in chapters four to six. We can thus see in the angelic interpretation of Dan 7 (and 8) some of the earliest evidence of the language that dominates texts such as *Apocryphon of Jeremiah C* and *Pseudo-Daniel*$^{a-b}$ *ar*. The language is realistic – even if the referent of particular descriptions is not always immediately obvious.

Raw Data – Daniel 7

Citation			Historical Referent	Symbol	Symbol-Referent

7:4	כְּאַרְיֵה וְגַפִּין דִּי נְשַׁר	Like a lion with eagles wings	Babylonia	Animal	Kingdom
7:5	דָּמְיָה לְדֹב וּתְלָת עִלְעִין	Like a bear with three tusks	Media	Animal	Kingdom
7:6	כִּנְמַר וְלַהּ גַּפִּין אַרְבַּע דִּי־עוֹף עַל־גַּבַּיהּ וְאַרְבְּעָה רֵאשִׁין	Like a leopard with four avian wings (on its back) and four heads	Persia	Animal	Kingdom
7:7, 19	חֵיוָה רְבִיעָיָה	Fourth Beast:	Greece	Animal	Kingdom

7:7–8, 11, 20–27	וְקַרְנַיִן עֲשַׂר לַהּ	Ten horns	Greek/Seleucid Rulers.	Animal-Horns	King
7:7–8, 11, 20–27	קֶרֶן אָחֳרִי זְעֵירָה	another little horn	Antiochus IV Epiphanes.	Horn	King
7:13–14	כְּבַר אֱנָשׁ	One like a human being	Angel	Human	Angel

Excursus: Daniel 7 and the "Model Reader"

My analysis of Dan 7 shows that much of the language does not fit within Umberto Eco's concept of the symbolic mode, i.e., language whose surrounding context is too weak to support a dominant interpretation. But the evidence from Dan 7 does seem to be greatly illuminated by another of Eco's theoretical concepts: the model reader. Many literary critics of the last three decades have attempted to extricate a text's meaning from the realm of the "author's intention" and relocate a text's meaning solely with the reader. Umberto Eco was for a time a major voice among those literary critics. His more recent work has turned in another direction, more than once making a caricature of the mores of reader-response approaches to literature.[174] His new direction addresses the concept of meaning to the text itself by positing the concept of the "model reader." He claims that:

> To organize a text, its author has to rely upon a series of codes that assign given contents to the expressions he uses. To make his text communicative, the author has to assume that the ensemble of codes he relies upon is the same as that shared by his possible reader. The author has thus to foresee a model of the possible reader (hereaf-

---

[174] "Contemporary textual Gnosticism is very generous, however: everybody, provided one is eager to impose the intention of the reader upon the unattainable intention of the author, can become the *Übermensch* who really realizes the truth, namely, that the author did not know what he or she was really saying." Umberto Eco, *Interpretation and Overinterpretation* (Cambridge: Cambridge University Press, 1992), 39.

ter Model Reader) supposedly able to deal interpretatively with the expressions in the same way as the author deals with them.[175]

There are numerous ways that a reader can discover the *intention operas* of a text – i.e., to become a model reader.[176] One way would be to understand the stylistic conventions of the text. As Eco observes, "If a story starts with, 'Once upon a time,' there is a good probability that it is a fairy tale and that the evoked and postulated model reader is a child (or an adult eager to react in a childish mood)."[177] Texts can construct a model reader by direct appeal or even by implicitly presupposing a specific encyclopedic competence.[178] Below, I apply the concept of "model reader" to Dan 7.

The four beasts found in Dan 7 should not share equal value for a model reader. To presume that each individual beast must have something historically specific, useful, or even interesting to tell the reader is not necessarily correct – especially when the text gives the reader very clear clues about where the model reader's attention should be focused. A model reader of Dan 7 will focus quickly and intently on the fourth beast and will arrive at the fourth beast equipped with the necessary competence to unpack its meaning. C. Caragounis has already made a similar argument though he did not specifically call on Eco's theory of the model reader and he used a limited number of criteria.[179] I hope to build on his work both in theory and in data.

How does the Dan 7 turn a model reader's interest to the fourth beast? There are several ways. First, in the initial dream report, the description of the fourth beast makes use of 79 words.[180] One may compare that with 23, 21, and 20 words respectively for the first three beasts. 145 more words (vs. 19–27a) are dedicated to the fourth beast outside of the initial dream report. The disproportionate percentage of text dedicated to the fourth beast is one indication of its importance to the reader.[181]

---

[175] Umberto Eco, *The Role of the Reader: Explorations in the Semiotics of Texts* (Bloomington: Indiana University Press, 1979), 7.

[176] Eco, The Role of the Reader: Explorations in the Semiotics of Texts, 7.

[177] Eco, *Interpretation and Overinterpretation*, 65. As Eco also notes, judging the stylistic conventions of a text is not necessarily a facile matter – a writer's use of the conventional expression 'Once upon a time,' could be an invocation of irony.

[178] "Encyclopedic competence" here denotes the particular socio-cultural knowledge base that is part and parcel of any culture on earth.

[179] C. Caragounis, "History and Supra-History: Daniel and the Four Empires," in *The Book of Daniel in the Light of New Findings* (ed. Adam van der Woude; vol. CVI of *BETL*; Leuven: Peeters, 1993), 387–97.

[180] Word counts are taken from BHS.

[181] Cf. Caragounis, "History and Supra-History: Daniel and the Four Empires," 389. Caragounis also highlights the disproportionate number of words with which the fourth empire is described in Dan 2. I will pick up that argument below in my analysis of the suspense-plot created by the "four kingdoms" schema.

The rhetoric of the dream report (7:1–14) also indicates the premier importance of the fourth beast. The fourth beast is described with a litany of strong adjectives: "dreadful, terrible, and exceedingly mighty" דְּחִילָה וְאֵימְתָנִי וְתַקִּיפָה יַתִּירָא (7:7). No other beast is described with such strong adjectives. No other beast is described with an adjective at all.

Another important rhetorical device is the statement that the fourth beast, "was different from each beast that was before it" וְהִיא מְשַׁנְּיָה מִן־כָּל־חֵיוָתָא דִּי קָדָמַיהּ (7:7). This statement is important not only because it singles out the fourth beast but because it compares the fourth beast to the other three beasts in the aggregate. None of the other beasts warrant individual comparison with the fourth beast. This rhetorical trend continues throughout the chapter and sets the fourth beast apart in the mind of the reader. The first three beasts are lumped together into one collective group: "the rest of the beasts" וּשְׁאָר חֵיוָתָא (7:12). The fourth beast is the only one that is described individually after the initial dream report.

A final noteworthy rhetorical move is found in Daniel's conversation with the *angelus interpres* in 7:19. After the angel interprets Daniel's dream, Daniel is unsatisfied and appeals for more information about the fourth beast: "Then I desired to be certain concerning the fourth beast, which was different from all of the others – exceedingly dreadful. Its teeth were of iron and its claws were of bronze. It consumed, crushed, and trampled with its feet" (7:19). Daniel exhibits no continued interest in the first three beasts. Indeed, verse 19 may constitute a direct appeal to the reader more than a rhetorical strategy. Either way it is clear that the meaning of the entire chapter hinges on the fourth beast. Daniel's interests direct the interest's of the model reader.

Thus far I have explored ways in which the rhetoric of Dan 7 directs its model reader to focus attention on the fourth beast. The text uses other literary devices to accomplish this. One is the basic suspense-plot set up by the four-kingdoms motif. The four-kingdoms motif appears several times in Jewish literature of the Hellenistic period. It is found in *Sibylline Oracles* 4 and Dan 2, and 4QFourKingdoms. Other examples might include the *Dynastic Prophecy*, *Bahman Yasht*, and *Testament of Naphtali*. There are some indications that *Pseudo-Daniel*[a–b] *ar* could have employed this scheme, but the text is too fragmentary to use it as serious evidence. The motif is designed to prepare a reader's expectations and induce a sense of suspense about how a given application of the motif will turn out. In all cases, the fourth kingdom is the kingdom that is contemporary with the writer (and the intended readership). Greece is normally the fourth kingdom but in some cases like *Sibylline Oracles* 4, a section on Rome is appended later.[182]

In the plot's dénouement, a fifth, eternal kingdom (ruled by God or his chosen representative) arises. Thus, each example of the four kingdom schema offers a unique perspective on how the mighty will fall, oppression shall be reversed, and the righteous shall be rewarded. The model reader of the four kingdom scheme follows the suspense of the scheme throughout history to the oppression (whether real or perceived) of their own day, to the climax found in the decisive defeat of the fourth kingdom and, finally, to the dénouement in the advent of an eternal kingdom. The focus and the climax of the story is always the fourth kingdom – the contemporary situation. The fourth beast offers the reader a(n authoritative) perspective on what will happen in his or her lifetime. When the plot is combined with direct appeal, rhetoric, and disproportionate textual representation, a strong case can be made for reconstructing the model reader as one who should focus on the fourth beast.

Language in Daniel 8

The kind of language that dominates Dan 7 is also found in Dan 8. Like chapter 7, Dan 8 combines a symbolic vision and an explicit/non-symbolic revelation into an integral whole. Unlike Dan 7, chapter 8 does not explicitly describe the initial vision as a dream. Its introductory formula states only "In the third year of the reign of King Belshazzar a vision appeared to me, Daniel, after the one that had appeared to me first" (8:1). Nevertheless, two features of the text indicate that the form of chapter 8 should be read as an example of the same sort of dream report hybrid found in Dan 7. In the first instance, the vision is explicitly linked to Dan 7 by the introductory formula in 8:1. Second, like Dan 7, it employs a description of the heavenly being that reveals information to Daniel as עֹמֵד לְנֶגְדִּי "one standing before me" (8:15). As I highlighted above, this type of description is a hallmark of (non-symbolic) dream reports in the ancient Near East. Dan 8 presents even more innovation over typical dream reports than does Dan 7. The features of symbolic and non-symbolic dream reports are found in Dan 7, but they are divided into two parts: a symbolic vision and a non-symbolic revelation/interpretation. Both symbolic and non-symbolic language is found in Dan 8, but they are not strictly divided between the vision and its

---

[182] Technically, the four kingdom schema is a *five* kingdom schema but convention controls the terminology. The label "four kingdoms" is reasonable since there are always four *earthly* kingdoms.

angelic interpretation. Non-symbolic descriptions are incorporated into the initial symbolic vision report.

The symbolic systems uncovered in Dan 7 using Peirce's theory of symbols (i.e., conventional associations) are found in Dan 8 – though with slight variation. For example, Dan 8 uses animals to symbolize earthly kingdoms and horns to symbolize individual rulers of kingdoms, but once uses horns to symbolize kingdoms (rather than kings). Dan 8 also uses human beings and heavenly bodies (stars) to symbolize angels.

Like Dan 7, chapter 8 narrates a symbolic *ex eventu* history of the ancient Near East, but it departs from the familiar "four kingdoms" motif in two ways. The history includes only three primary kingdoms and does not predict a final eschatological kingdom and/or age of righteousness. The most wicked gentile ruler is defeated, but the vision ends abruptly and vaguely with his demise, "He shall be broken, and not by human hands" (8:25). This account of history is considerably less triumphalistic than the one in Dan 7. At the very same time that the language of this vision offers even clearer or more precise description of the actors in history, it gives a more opaque picture of what the future holds for those under persecution.

אַיִל אֶחָד "A ram"

The first actor in the vision of Dan 8 is a ram (8:3). The most prominent aspect of this ram, when read in the context of Dan 7, is that it is naturalistic. Like any other ram, it has two horns (וְלוֹ קְרָנַיִם). It lacks any of the additional features by which the hybrid beasts of Dan 7 are characterized. The only unusual feature of the ram is that its horns grow while Daniel watches it. In Dan 7, beasts represent kingdoms and horns represent individual rulers of those kingdoms. The same holds true in Dan 8, but with slight variations. Each of the ram's horns represents the ruler of a distinct kingdom. The angel Gabriel interprets the vision for Daniel: "As for the ram that you saw with the two horns, these are the kings of Media and Persia" (8:20). Above I applied Charles Peirce's theory of symbols to Dan 2 and 7 to find a symbolic system comprised of several categorical associations (e.g., beasts = kingdoms). The two-horned ram of Dan 8 is a crucial piece of evidence for substantiating my interpretation because it indicates that individual beasts should not always (if ever) be read as specific references to specific kingdoms. For example, Koch holds that each beast is used on the basis of the characteristics it shares with the particular kingdom it represents.[183] Perrin considers each beast to be a conventional sign ("ste-

---

[183] Koch, *The Rediscovery of Apocalyptic*, 26.

no-symbol") for a particular kingdom.[184] But the single ram from Dan 8 represents two different kingdoms. This duality of meaning poses significant problems for those that argue that each beast has a specific relationship with its referent. The use of one beast to represent two kingdoms confirms the generic or categorical relationship between beasts and kingdoms in the Daniel apocalypses. The same type of categorical relationship is also found in *1 Enoch*'s *Animal Apocalypse*, 4QFourKingdoms[a–b] ar, and one of Noah's dream visions in the *Book of the Words of Noah* (see chapter 3).

The angel's interpretation of the ram and two horns uses the same type of non-symbolic language that one finds in angelic interpretation of Dan 7, but it is considerably more precise. For example, the angel in Dan 7 uses terms like מלכו "kingdom" and מלכין "kings:" "As for the ten horns, out of this kingdom ten kings shall arise, and another shall rise after them" (7:24a). Dan 8 employs the same descriptions but adds to them specific ethno-political designations, i.e., מַלְכֵי מָדַי וּפָרָס "the kings of Media and Persia" (8:20). This level of specificity has not prevented some readers from developing interpretations entirely removed from the context of Second Temple Judaism and the ancient Near East, but such bastardizations of descriptions like "the kings of Media and Persia" are not compelling since they presuppose, for ideological/theological reasons, that the Book of Daniel addresses a period in the future from the perspective of modernity.[185]

צְפִיר־הָעִזִּים "A male goat"

The second beast that appears in the vision of Dan 8 is a male goat (8:5). The locution צְפִיר־הָעִזִּים appears repetitive since either noun could connote a male goat without help from the other (cf. צְפִירֵי in Ezra 8:35 and עֵז in Lev 3:12). The combination is not without precedent, but is normally formed with שָׂעִיר rather than צָפִיר in the Hebrew Bible: "Once the sin that he has committed is made known to him, he shall bring as his offering a male goat (שְׂעִיר עִזִּים) without blemish" (Lev 4:23). צָפִיר is an Aramaic loanword that it is the functional equivalent of Hebrew שָׂעִיר (צָפִיר is an Aramaic isogloss that probably developed from the Semitic root שער).[186] It only occurs five

---

[184] Perrin, "Eschatology and Hermeneutics," 3–14.
[185] See Samuel Núñez, *The Vision of Daniel 8: Interpretations from 1700 to 1900* (Berrien Springs, Michigan: Andrews University Press, 1989). Popular conceptions of the little horn in the late nineteenth century included the papacy and Islam. These types of readings are not without adherents today.
[186] See *HALOT* I: 804–5, II: 1048, 1341–2. The most basic meaning of צָעִיר is "hairy." "Goat" is a derived meaning. Widespread comparative evidence suggests that the root שער is the most ancient. See Patrick Bennett, *Comparative Semitic Linguistics: A Manual* (Winona Lake: Eisenbrauns, 1998), 167. The lexeme ṣpr appears in Ugaritic, but with a different and unrelated meaning. See Lete and Sanmartín, *A Dictionary of the Ugaritic Language*, 788–9.

times in the Hebrew Bible and four of those instances are found in texts partially composed in Aramaic.[187] The presence of this Aramaism supports the position that Dan 7 and 8 are products of the same circles.[188] It also suggests that the language transition present between Dan 7–8 is original. It is possible to read Aramaisms as a sign of an Aramaic original, but there is another, more compelling way to read the evidence.[189] If Dan 8 was originally composed in Aramaic, why wouldn't the translator have used a Hebrew expression instead of an Aramaic one (i.e., שָׂעִיר for צְפִיר)? The expression צְפִיר־הָעִזִּים suggests precisely that Dan 8 was not composed in Aramaic. The Hebrew dialect reflected in Dan 8 reveals a writer who was probably fully conversant in both Hebrew and Aramaic. When linguistic features such as this are combined with evidence from the biblical Daniel manuscripts found at Qumran, the case for an Aramaic original of 8(–12) becomes very difficult to defend. Every copy of Daniel that preserves the relevant sections of the book (i.e., 2:4b and 8:1) confirms the bilingual nature of the text (1QDan^a, 4QDan^a, 4QDan^b, and 4QDan^d). The transitional passages are not extant in 4QDan^c, but it is worth noting that the manuscript dates to ca. 125 B.C.E. – perhaps less than fifty years after the autograph.[190]

The male goat appears at first naturalistic, with one horn בֵּין עֵינָיו "between its eyes." The description of the goat, "coming across the whole earth without touching the ground," (8:5) might at first seem to imply the same cosmic dimensions found in Dan 7. But it may smply reflect the artistic motif of the "flying gallop" that is nearly ubiquitous in ancient Near Eastern art (indeed, world-art up until the end of the nineteenth century).[191] Ultimately, the description might be better read as a Hebrew idiom for speed. Isa 41:2b–3 uses similar language to describe campaigns of Cyrus

---

[187] The passages are Dan 8:5, 8, Ezra 6:17, 8:35, and 2 Chron 29:21. It is likely that the usage in 2 Chron is influenced by the language in Ezra. While some hold to the common authorship model for Ezra and Chron, I am more convinced by the view that one (or more) common redactors might have reworked the Ezra-Neh-Chron material. See Gary Knoppers, *1 Chronicles, 1–9* (AB 12; New York: Doubleday, 2004), 72–100, esp. 93–00.

[188] For a list of other Aramaisms in the Hebrew of Daniel, see Collins, *Daniel*, 20–1.

[189] The most prominent supporters of an Aramaic original for Dan 8–12 are Hartman and DiLella, *The Book of Daniel*, 14–15, 221, 26. Harold Ginsberg, *Studies in Daniel* (14; New York: Jewish Theological Seminary of America, 1948), 41–61.

[190] Eugene Ulrich, "Daniel," in *Qumran Cave 4.XI: Psalms to Chronicles* (ed. Eugene Ulrich, et al.; vol. XVI of DJD, ed. Emanuel Tov; Oxford: Clarendon, 2000), 240, 56, 70, 80.

[191] Examples are legion. Several can be found in the frescos at Dura-Europas. See Ann Perkins, *The Art of Dura-Europas* (Oxford: Clarendon, 1973), nos. 16 and 26. Bowls deocated with hunting scenes from Cyrpus and Ugarit also provide good examples. Cf. Sabatino Moscati, ed., *The Phoenicians* (New York: Rizzoli, 1999), 191, 494. A turning point was reached in art when cinematography pioneer Eadweard Muybridge demonstrated with photography that it is physically impossible for a horse to achieve the "flying gallop" position in which it was so often depicted.

the Great, "He delivers up nations to him, and tramples kings under foot; he makes them like dust with his sword, like driven stubble with his bow. He pursues them and passes on safely, scarcely touching the path with his feet" (אֹרַח בְּרַגְלָיו לֹא יָבוֹא). The only deviation from nature occurs when the goat's horn is broken. Four new horns grow in its place and a fifth, smaller, horn emerges from one of the four (8:8–9). But the goat's unnatural protuberances hardly qualify it as a *Mischwesen*.

The male goat and its horns participate in the same symbolic system of categorical associations that were introduced above. The goat represents Greece, but there is nothing about the goat that specifically invokes Greece. Only within the immediate context of Dan 8 can the reader associate Greece with a goat.[192] One would not assume that goats appearing in other texts must refer to Greece. The association is not a standard one. The starting point for interpretation is the recognition of the categorical association of beasts and kingdoms. The association between horns and rulers seen in Dan 7 also holds true for chapter 8. Some argue for specific associations between the ram and the goat and their antecedents based a zodiak text attributed to Teucer of Babylon.[193] Each of the signs in the zodiac is associated with a particular nation. The ram corresponds to Persia and the goat to Syria. In his first monograph on Daniel, Collins accepted this interpretation, but he expresses more skepticism in his *Hermeneia* commentary.[194] He lays out two specific concerns: 1) The association of goat and Syria is problematic since in Daniel, the goat represents the Greek (Macedonian) kingdom of Alexander, and 2) There is serious doubt as to whether this specific astral geography was known in Palestine in the 2nd century B.C.E.[195]

Several pieces of important evidence may be added to the critique of

---

[192] It is true that some connection might be drawn between Greece and a goat based on the god Pan, who has the hindquarters, legs, and horns of a goat. But there are problems with this association. The goat in Dan 8 is not a *Mischwesen* like Pan and Dan 7 makes clear that *Mischwesen* are in the repertoire of the writer. Moreover, the goat of Dan 8 does not act in ways characteristic of Pan. Finally, it is noteworthy the goat is also a familiar symbol within other cultures of the ancient Near East. I make this point below in the discussion of the zodiac, but a few other connections might be mentioned here. Goats function in the Song to describe the lover's hair (4:1, 6:5), and goat-demons appear four times in the Hebrew Bible (Lev 17:7, 2 Chron 11:15, Isa 13:21, 34:14).

[193] This position was first suggested by Franz Cumont, "La Plus Ancienne Géographic Astrologique," *Klio* 9 (1909). Those who accept it are: Aage Bentzen, "Daniel 6: Ein Versuch zur Vorgeschichte der Märtyrlegende," in *Festschrift A. Bertholet* (ed. Walter Baumgartner, et al.; Tübingen: Mohr, 1950), 69. André Caquot, "Sur les quatre Bêtes de Daniel VII," 5 (1955). Martin Hengel, *Judaism and Hellenism: Studies in Their Encounter in Palestine During the Early Hellenistic Period* (2vols.; Philadelphia: Fortress, 1974), 1:184. Norman Porteous, *Daniel: A Commentary* (Philadelphia: Westminster, 1965), 122. Jürgen Lebram, *Das Buch Daniel* (Zurich: Theologische Verlag, 1984), 97–8.

[194] Collins, *The Apocalyptic Vision*, 107. Collins, *Daniel*, 329–30.

[195] Collins, *Daniel*, 330.

Cumont's position. Other astrological texts that may be just as early as the zodiac attributed to Teucer present altogether different pictures – normally separating Persia and Media. For example, Marcus Manilius (1st century C.E.) associates both Syria and Persia with Aries and Macedonia with Leo (*Astronomica* 4:744–817).[196] Dorotheus of Sidon (1st century C.E.) associates Media with Taurus, Greece with Leo, but does not use Persia at all.[197] The zodiac in Acts 2:9–11 does not associate any sign with Persia, Greece, Macedonia, or Syria. This evidence indicates that there was hardly a strong tradition of association between the ram and Persia or the goat and Greece/Syria. In the words of G. Goold, "The Greek astrologers contradict one another to a degree one would have thought positively embarrassing."[198] The significant variation between zodiacs dating to roughly the same period indicates that even if a second century Palestinian Jew was conversant with Hellenistic astrology, he/she would have hardly recognized a conventional association between the entities proposed by Cumont.[199] We have already seen in Dan 7 that only one of the beasts might have realistically functioned as a conventional symbol for a particular kingdom. There is no reason to expect a greater level of intentionality on the part of the writer of Dan 8. But there is a small textual issue that complicates my system of conventional associations in this case.

The MT text of Dan 8:21 (the angelic interpretation of the goat) reads, וְהַצָּפִיר הַשָּׂעִיר מֶלֶךְ יָוָן "The male goat is the king of Greece." No one doubts that the text actually *means* to imply that "The male goat is the kingdom of Greece." One can feel certain about the implied meaning since in the very same verse, the angel explains, "The great horn between its eyes is the first king." The angel then explains that each of the other five horns represent kings. The large horn cannot represent the king of a king, but a king of a kingdom. One possible explanation for the MT reading is that the text might have originally preserved an Aramaism in the form of the Aramaic word for kingdom (מלכו) rather than מלך. There is no doubt that other Aramaisms are found in Dan 8. The disappearance of the ו from the text could be explained in two ways. First, a construction like מלכו יון would provide an easy opportunity for haplography. ו and י are often very similar

---

[196] G.P. Goold, ed., *Manilius: Astronomica* (*LCL*; Cambridge: Harvard University Press, 1977), 280–9. On Manilius, see also S. J. Tester, *A History of Western Astrology* (Suffolk: Boydell Press, 1987), 30–56.

[197] David Pingree, ed., *Dorotheus Sidonus: Carmen Astrologicum* (Leipzig: Teubner Verlagsgesellschaft, 1976), 427–8. Greek text is preserved in Hephaestion of Thebes'*Apotelesmatikōn* I:1–218.

[198] Goold, ed., Manilius: Astronomica, xci.

[199] See Mladen Popovic, Reading the Human Body: Physiognomics and Astrology in the Dead Sea Scrolls and Hellenistic-Early Roman Period Judaism (STDJ 67; Leiden: Brill, 2007), 130. Tester, A History of Western Astrology, 72.

in the Jewish scripts of the Hellenistic period.[200] In this case the final ו of "kingdom" would be followed by an initial י for "Greece." Indeed, there are four consecutive characters of highly similar shape and style between the two words. Another possibility is that a copyist perceived an error and left out the final ו – rendering the Aramaic word for kingdom into the Hebrew word for king. These possibilities are, however, speculation with no manuscript support. Ultimately, one expects that the text should square with the obvious meaning of the text.

The first horn represents Alexander the Great and the next four horns represent the *Diadochoi*, the generals of Alexander who divided his kingdom after his death. Finally, the small horn represents Antiochus IV Epiphanes. The little horn, "took the regular burnt offering away from him and overthrew the place of his sanctuary" (8:11). These actions correspond with the actions of Antiochus IV detailed above from 1 Maccabees 1:44–6 and 2 Maccabees 6:1–6. Dan 8 details an action of Antiochus, however, that Dan 7 does not. In the midst of the little horn's rampage, Daniel overhears two angels ("holy ones") talking. One asks, "How long is this vision concerning the regular burnt offering, the transgression that makes desolate (הַפֶּשַׁע שֹׁמֵם), and the giving over of the sanctuary and host to be trampled" (8:13)? The expression הַפֶּשַׁע שֹׁמֵם describes the same event as the expression שִׁקּוּץ שֹׁמֵם "the desolating abomination" from Dan 12:11. Both refer to the erection of the image of Zeus Olympias in the holy of holies of the Jerusalem temple.[201]

---

[200] Some of the most impressive instances of this phenomenon are found in manuscripts in which ו and י are distinguished. One might compare the form יהי in 1QS 2 24 with forms like והיה in 1QS 2 12 and והלויים in 1QS 2 12 where they are normally formally distinguished. The connection of ו and sometimes י with the ligatures of letters such as ת is also important for this discussion. Cf. the discussion of ונתתו/ונתתי in 4Q388 7 5 below in chapter 5. Numerous scholars have discussed the problem. Cf. Frank Moore Cross, "Palaeography and the Dead Sea Scrolls," in *The Dead Sea Scrolls after Fifty Years: A Comprehensive Assessment* (ed. Peter Flint and James VanderKam; Leiden Brill, 1998–9), 390. Emanuel Tov, *Textual Criticism of the Hebrew Bible* (Minneapolis: Fortress, 2001), 244. Steven Fassberg, "The Linguistic Study of the Damascus Document: A Historical Perspective," in *The Damascus Document: A Centennial of Discovery. Proceedings of the Third International Symposium of the Orion Center for the Study of the Dead Sea Scrolls and Associated Literature, 4–8 February 1998* (ed. Joseph Baumgarten, et al.; vol. 34 of *STDJ*; Leiden: Brill, 2000), 53–67. Ada Yardeni, "A Draft of a Deed on an Ostracon from Khirbet Qumran," *IEJ* 47 (1997): 234. Elisha Qimron, "The Distinction between Waw and Yod in the Qumran Scrolls," *Beth Mikra* 18 (1973): 112–22. Al Wolters, "Paleography and Literary Structure as Guides to Reading the Copper Scroll," in *Copper Scroll Studies* (ed. George Brooke and Philip Davies; London: Continuum, 2004), 311–34.

[201] Cf. Βδέλυγμα ἐρημώσεως in 1 Macc 1:54 and το Βδέλυγμα in 1 Macc 6:7.

קָדוֹשׁ / עֹמֵד לְנֶגְדִּי כְּמַרְאֵה־גָבֶר
"A holy one" / "One standing before me, having the appearance of man"

Dan 8 shows remarkable variation in its descriptions of angels. Five different expressions are used though each does not present a different representation technique. These descriptions are notable not only because of their variety, but also for where they are employed in the apocalypse. In Dan 7, angels are described in two different ways. One description is symbolic and the other is explicit. In the context of the initial symbolic vision, an angel is described as כְּבַר אֱנָשׁ "one like a human being" (7:13). We saw above that human beings are frequently used as ciphers for angels and the categorical association between humans and angels is a recognizable feature of ancient Jewish literature.

In the dream's interpretation, which includes a flashback that extends the vision, angels are described without symbolic cipher. They are referred to as קַדִּישֵׁי עֶלְיוֹנִין "the holy ones of the most high" (7:22, 25, 27). In light of other uses of the expression "holy ones" (see above), the description must be understood as a direct reference to angels. The term may have originated as an adjectival description, but "holy ones" should probably be regarded as an explicit description in Daniel – tantamount to מלאכים. Dan 8 uses both of the representation techniques described above. While Daniel attempts to understand the vision of the ram and the goat on his own, a figure appears עֹמֵד לְנֶגְדִּי כְּמַרְאֵה־גָבֶר "standing before me, having the appearance of a man" (8:15). Any doubt that the figure might not be an angel is dispelled when Daniel overhears a קוֹל־אָדָם "human voice" calling to the figure who appeared to him: "Gabriel, help this man understand the vision" (8:16). The one "having the appearance of a man" is the angel Gabriel.

The more explicit description, קָדוֹשׁ, is also used in chapter 8 though unlike Dan 7, it only appears in the singular and it is never modified by עֶלְיוֹן "Most High." More interesting than the grammar and syntax, however, is its placement in the apocalypse. The explicit description of angels takes place during the vision itself. In Dan 7, explicit descriptions are only used after the vision is clearly over and the interpretation has begun. It is true that in a flashback (7:19–22), Daniel uses the expression, "holy ones of the Most High," but this is only after the *angelus interpres* has already told him that, "The holy ones of the Most High shall receive the kingdom and possess the kingdom forever – forever and ever" (7:17). While still experiencing the vision in Dan 8 the protagonist overhears אֶחָד־קָדוֹשׁ מְדַבֵּר "a holy one speaking" (8:13). Thus we find a non-symbolic description in the midst of a symbolic vision. Symbolic representation techniques are also used to describe angels in Dan 8.

הַכּוֹכָבִים / צְבָא־הַשָּׁמַיִם / שַׂר־הַצָּבָא
"The stars" / "The host of heaven" / "Commander of the host"

In both Dan 7 and 8 angels are described symbolically as human beings. Dan 8 also uses another categorical association to describe angels: stars. Part of the description of the little horn's desecration of the Jerusalem temple details the cosmic implications of its earthly actions: "It grew as high as the host of heaven (צְבָא הַשָּׁמַיִם). It threw down to the earth some of the host (מִן־הַצָּבָא) and some of the stars (מִן־הַכּוֹכָבִים), and trampled on them. Even against the prince of the host (שַׂר־הַצָּבָא) it acted arrogantly" (8:10–11a). Each of these terms should be understood in terms of celestial bodies or stars and there are significant and wide-ranging associations between stars and angels in ancient Jewish literature.

In one of the earliest pieces of Hebrew literature, the Song of Deborah (Judges 5), the poet describes a battle between some of the tribes of Israel and the kings of Canaan. YHWH also engages in the battle. He and his angels engage the Canaanites: "The stars fought from heaven, (מִן־שָׁמַיִם נִלְחֲמוּ הַכּוֹכָבִים), from their courses they fought against Sisera" (5:20).[202] If Israel associated stars and angels/heavenly beings from its very earliest times, those associations only grew stronger during the late 8th to early 6th century when the Assyrian astral cult exerted influence on their religion.

Deities and other heavenly beings are consistently represented as the sun, moon, and stars in Assyrian iconography. In their *Gods, Goddesses, and Images of God in Ancient Israel*, Othmar Keel and Christoph Uehlinger present a compelling case for what they call "the astralization of the heavenly powers" in Iron Age IIC in Israel under Assyrian influence.[203] Numerous cylinder seals discovered in Israel and dating to Iron IIC contain the same motif: an Assyrian king as loyal servant of the heavenly power (as depicted by the sun, moon, and stars).[204] Stamp seals and cylinder seals from the period typically depict the goddess *Ishtar* in a nimbus of stars and often she is presented with the Venus star and/or the Pleiades.[205] The ico-

---

[202] Cf. also the Letter of Jeremiah 1:60. For the date of the Song of Deborah, see Frank Moore Cross and David Noel Freedman, *Studies in Ancient Yahwistic Poetry* (Grand Rapids: Eerdmans, 1997 (1975)), 3–14. Cross, *Canaanite Myth*, 100–1. David Robertson, *Linguistic Evidence in Dating Early Hebrew Poetry* (SBLDS 3; Missoula: Scholars Press, 1972), 153–6.

[203] Keel and Uehlinger, *Gods*, 283–372. Bernd Janowski, "JHWH und der Sonnegott: Aspekte der Solarisierung JHWH's in vorexilischer Zeit," in *Pluralismus und Identität* (ed. Joachim Mehlhausen; Gütersloh: Kaiser, 1995), 214–41. Smith, *The Early History of God: Yahweh and Other Deities in Ancient Israel*, 148–59. William Dever, *Did God Have a Wife? Archaeology and Folklore in Ancient Israel* (Grand Rapids: Eerdmans, 2005), 232–6. Carol Meyers, *The Tabernacle Menorah* (ASORDS 2; Missoula: Scholars Press, 1976), 145.

[204] Keel and Uehlinger, *Gods*, 287–90.

[205] Keel and Uehlinger, *Gods*, 292–6.

nographic evidence is corroborated by textual evidence from the Hebrew Bible. For example, in Jer 7:18 YHWH speaks to the prophet and mocks the population of Jerusalem with these words, "The children gather wood, the fathers kindle the fire, and the women knead dough, to make cakes for the Queen of Heaven (לִמְלֶכֶת הַשָּׁמַיִם); and they pour out drink offerings to other gods, to provoke me to anger."[206]

In Dan 8 the terms כּוֹכָבִים and צְבָא הַשָּׁמַיִם are synonymous. They attest to an association that has a considerable history in ancient Judaism. A passage from Deuteronomy addresses precisely their association as well as the apparent propensity of some Israelites to worship stars as celestial beings/deities: "And when you look up to the heavens and see the sun, the moon, and the stars (הַכּוֹכָבִים) – all the host of heaven (כֹּל צְבָא הַשָּׁמַיִם), do not be led astray and bow down to them and serve them, things that YHWH your God has allotted to all peoples everywhere under heaven" (Deut 4:19). Other parts of the Deuteronomistic History highlight the same theological concern (cf. 2 Kgs 23:5, 11). Centuries later the *Wisdom of Solomon* ridicules those who suppose that, "Either fire or wind or swift air, or the circle of stars, or turbulent water, or the lumenaries of heaven were the gods that rule the world" (13:2). Thus there were ancient Jews who both approved and disapproved of the association between stars and angel/heavenly beings, but both types appear to be equally aware of the conventional association between the two.

The stars of heaven also play a liturgical role in YHWH's heavenly court. In YHWH's (in)famous response to Job from the whirlwind, he demands of Job, "Where were you when I laid the foundation of the earth . . . when the morning stars (כּוֹכְבֵי בֹקֶר) sang together and all the heavenly beings (כָּל־בְּנֵי אֱלֹהִים) shouted for joy" (38:4a, 7).[207] The psalmist writies, "Praise him sun and moon; praise him all you shining stars (כָּל־כּוֹכְבֵי אוֹר)" (Ps 148:3).[208]

The foregoing examples illustrate the extent to which a conventional association between stars and angels was rooted in ancient Israelite/Jewish culture. One further example illustrates not only this conventional association, but provides a specific mythological context within which to read a major motif present in Daniel's vision in chapter 8. Isa 14 contains a reflex of a Canaanite myth about the gods *Šahar* and *Helel*.[209] *Šahar* (Dawn) is

---

[206] Cf. Jer 44:17–19, 25, 2 Kgs 23:5, 11, Ezek 8:16.
[207] Cf. Bar 3:34
[208] Cf. Pr Azar 1:41
[209] M. Albani argues that Isa 14 does not reflect a Canaanite myth, but rather "alludes by way of criticism to the royal notion of the postmortal apotheosis of the king." Albani explains *Helel* as a divine epithet rather than a divine name, but he omits entirely a discussion of *Šahar* – a figure that is unquestionably a god in Ugaritic myth. See Manfried Dietrich et al., *The Cuneiform Alpha-*

one of the sons of *El*. He and his cousin *Šalim* (Dusk) are born simultaneously and are always mentioned together in the texts from Ugarit.[210] *Helel* is an astral deity, often translated as "moon," but if texts like Isa 14 (see below) are not wholesale innovations, then "Venus" might not be an inappropriate translation. In Ugaritic, the name is used primarily as part of an epithet for *Helel*'s dauthers. He is mentioned several times in close proximity to the Daniel figure in *Aqhat*:

dn[.]il. bth.ymġyn/

yštql.dnil.lhklh/

'rb.bbth.ktrt.

bnt/hll.snnt.

Daniel comes to his house,

Daniel arrives at his palace.

The Katharat (goddesses) enter his house,

The daughters of Helel – the gleaming ones.[211]

Shahar and Helel are never mentioned together in the Ugaritic texts, but Isaiah transmits a portion of a myth that understands Helel to be the son of Shahar:

How you are fallen from heaven, O Day Star, son of Dawn! (הֵילֵל בֶּן־שָׁחַר) How you are cut down to the ground, you who laid the nations low! You said in your heart, 'I will ascend to heaven; I will raise my throne above the stars of God (כּוֹכְבֵי־אֵל); I will sit on the mount of assembly on the heights of Zaphon; I will ascend to the tops of the clouds, I will make myself like the Most High (עֶלְיוֹן).' But you are brought down to Sheol, to the depths of the pit. (Isa 14:12–15).[212]

---

betic Texts from Ugarit, Ras Ibn Hani and Other Places (8; Münster: Ugarit-Verlag, 1995), 1.23:52, 1.100:52, 1.07:43, 1.23:11. Matthias Albani, "The Downfall of Helel, the Son of Dawn: Aspects of Royal Theology in Isa 14:12–13," in *The Fall of the Angels* (ed. Christoph Auffarth and Loren Stuckenbruck; Leiden: Brill, 2004), 62–86.

[210] Cf. Theodore Lewis, "The Birth of the Gracious Gods," in *Ugaritic Narrative Poetry* (ed. Simon Parker; Atlanta: Scholars Press, 1997), 205–14. Not every instance of *Šahar* is used as a divine name. See Lete and Sanmartín, *A Dictionary of the Ugaritic Language*, 2: 812–3.

[211] My adaptation of the translation in Simon Parker, "Aqhat," in *Ugaritic Narrative Poetry* (ed. Simon Parker; Atlanta: Scholars Press, 1997), 56. (*CAT* 1.17 II: 24–7, cf. lines 28–40). My translation of *snnt* as "gleaming ones" (cf. Parker's "radiant daughters") rather than "swallows" is warranted because of the relationship of the goddesses to *hll*, an astral deity, and because of the verb used to describe their entry into Daniel's house. *'rb* has specific astronomical connotations and is used, for example, to describe how the sun "enters" (i.e., "sets"). See Lete and Sanmartín, *A Dictionary of the Ugaritic Language*, 179–81.

[212] Not only the divine names used in this passage (*Helel, Šahar, El*, and *Elyon*), but the location of the divine assembly on Zaphon indicate that this myth owes to a Canaanite heritage. The

As a celestial body whose father is Dawn, Helel is the morning star (i.e., Venus). Most specialists acknowledge that the myth of *Helel ben Shahar* provides the framework for the allegorical description of Antiochus IV's desecration of the Jerusalem temple in Dan 8:9–12.²¹³ So the language used in Dan 8, like chapter 7, draws not only on conventional, categorical associations present throughout ancient Judaism and the ancient Near East, but specifically on Canaanite myth.²¹⁴ If the writer already had one well-known symbolic system by which to depict angels, however, why might he have switched to another associated pair: stars and angels? Collins offers an intriguing solution. "The ambiguity as to whether the stars are the angels themselves or their visual representation facilitates the transition from the allegorical imagery of the he-goat to the realistic account of v 11."²¹⁵ While his comments address the use of star terminology generally, Collins's suggestion perhaps also indicates a possible rationale for the variety of star terminology one finds in chapter 8. The semantic range of expressions such as צְבָא הַשָּׁמַיִם and שַׂר־הַצָּבָא necessarily also carry hints of the human (and military) realm. Thus, the *Sinnplus* achieved with the use of terminology like שַׂר־הַצָּבָא might not only semantically link two otherwise distinct symbolic associations with angels (i.e., humans an stars), but might also facilitate the transition to the realistic description of the desecration of the Jerusalem temple and the even more realistic angelic interpretation in 8:18–25.

---

theme of cosmic rebellion or usurpation (by an astral deity!) can be found in the *Ba'al* traditions. After *Ba'al*'s death at the hands of *Mot*, *Athirat* promotes her son as successor, "So let us make Athtar the Strong king, Let Athtar the Strong be king. Then Athtar the Strong ascends the summit of Sapan, sits on the throne of Mightiest Ball." Smith, "The Baal Cycle," 154. (*CAT* 1.6.I:54–61) *Athtar* is found wanting, however, and driven by her extreme grief, *Ba'al*'s sister/wife *'Anat* tortures *Mot* until he releases *Ba'al* to again reign as king.

²¹³ See Hartman and DiLella, *The Book of Daniel*, 236. Klaus Koch, "Vom profestischen zum apokalyptischen Visionsbericht," in *Apocalypticism in the Mediterranean World and the Near East: Proceedings of the International Colloquium on Apocalypticism – Uppsala, August 12–17, 1979* (ed. David Hellholm; Tübingen: Mohr-Siebeck, 1983), 413–46. Collins, *Daniel*, 332–3.

²¹⁴ The writer of Dan 7 and 8 was certainly not reading texts in Ugaritic, but the not insignificant attestation of Canaanite themes and frameworks in books like Pss and Isa indicate an active conveyor-belt of cultural tradition. Indeed, in light of modern reconstructions of earliest Israel as a Canaanite-successor culture, one should be rather surprised not to find that Canaanite traditions had a significant purchase in Ancient Israel and even during the Second Temple Period.

²¹⁵ Collins, *Daniel*, 333.

Raw Data – Daniel 8

Citation			Historical Referent	Symbol	Symbol-Referent
8:3–4, 20	אַיִל אֶחָד	Ram	Media/Persia	Animal	Kingdom
		two horns	Kings of Media/Persia	Horn	King
8:5, 21	צְפִיר־הָעִזִּים	Male Goat	Greece	Animal	Kingdom
8:5, 8, 22	קֶרֶן	One Horn	Alexander the Great	Horn	King
8:9–12, 23–25	אַרְבַּע	Four Horns	διαδοχοι	Horn	King
	קֶרֶן־אַחַת מִצְּעִירָה	A Little Horn	Antiochus IV Epiphanes	Horn	King
8:10	צְבָא־הַשָּׁמַיִם	Host of Heaven	Angels	Stars/heavenly body	Angels
8:10	הַכּוֹכָבִים	Stars	Angels	Stars/heavenly body	Angels

8:11	שַׂר־הַצָּבָא	Prince of the Host	Arch-Angel	Star/Heavenly Body	Angel
8:13	קָדוֹשׁ	A Holy One	Angel	–	–
8:15–16	כְּמַרְאֵה־גָבֶר	Like a human being	Angel	Human	Angel

Findings from Chapter 2

One

The literary forms of Dan 2*, 7, and 8 have roots in dream reports, but they present a significant innovation over the standard models highlighted by Oppenheim. We saw in chapter 1 that the two categories used by Oppenheim/Artemidorus divide revelatory dreams into 1) those which require interpretation and 2) those that do not. The pre-redaction form of Dan 2 would have fit into Oppenheim's first category (symbolic dreams) without problems. But the post-redaction form includes, as do Dan 7 and 8, both an undecipherable vision and an explicit revelation from a heavenly figure. I indicated that this combination of symbolic and non-symbolic features has antecedents in texts like Proto-Zechariah, but as Susan Niditch has argued, proto-Zechariah is hardly a typical example of Israelite prophecy."[216] Symbolic visions are not ubiquitous or even standard features of Israelite prophecy, but have a separate literary history that sometimes encounters and interacts with prophetic literature.[217] For example, the symbolic vision in Jer 24 is hardly typical of the forms of prophecy found in the rest of the book. Rather than attempting to understand symbolic visions as primarily prophetic phenomena, one should contextualize them within the larger world of divination. Prophecy is, of course, also best contextualized in the

---

[216] Niditch, *The Symbolic Vision in Biblical Tradition*, 12–3.
[217] On the unique nature of the visions in Zech 1–8 compared to the rest of the corpus of Hebrew prophecy, see Carol Meyers and Eric Meyers, *Haggai, Zechariah 1–8* (AB 25B; Garden City: Doubleday, 1987), lvii–lx.

world of divination – so it is hardly a surprise that different elements of that world (prophecy and dreams/visions) might collide. The problem is using prophecy as the umbrella term rather than divination. Therefore, Dan 2*, 7, and 8 ultimately provide examples of texts that have deep roots in the literary expression of dreams in the ancient Near East, but that offer innovation over the standard forms. Their proximity to the symbolic visions familiar from prophetic texts such as Proto-Zechariah appear to attest less to a dependence on prophecy than to a literary innovation that was adopted or adapted to function across several literary genres and that become especially pronounced during the late Second Temple period.

Two

In chapter one, we encountered several models of the symbol that can be helpful for describing the language of ancient Jewish apocalypses. The concept of symbol as conventional sign (i.e., de Saussure, Peirce, etc.) is useful for excavating the deep structures of signification in Dan 2*, 7, and 8. Peirce treats a symbol as a signifier and a signified working together in a purely arbitrary relationship. I side-stepped past mistakes of those who attempted to apply this kind of semiotics to the individual symbols used in the Daniel apocalypses. Instead I used it to excavate the underlying pairs of conventional association hidden in the texts. Peirce's work on symbols does not help us understand, for example, the identity of the winged lion in Dan 7. It helps us to understand the symbolic structure that underlies that symbol and gives it meaning. For example, we have seen that beasts are used to symbolize kingdoms, horns are used to symbolize kings, and humans and stars are used to symbolize angels. These conventional pairs were found numerous times in Daniel and we shall see in chapter three that they function similarly in other ancient Jewish apocalypses. Thus, a structuralist poetics helps us to see the symbolic structures that function across a spectrum of texts. The symbol systems also help to reveal another difference between Jewish apocalypses and Israelite prophetic texts. In terms of representation techniques, the Daniel apocalypses appear to use symbols in a completely different way than one finds in prophetic visions such as Jer 24 (good figs and bad figs) or Zech 5 (flying scroll). The symbolic language of these prophetic texts is entirely dependent upon its immediate context. In contrast, the symbolic language of the Daniel apocalypses participates in a considerably larger and more stable system of signification. Immediate context is still key for understanding the specific antecedent for each symbol in Daniel, but the symbolic structures (i.e., angel = human) that underlie the language make the text far more accessible to a much larger audience.

Three

The very same analysis that revealed the conventional associations at work in the Daniel apocalypses also revealed that many of the associations and the motifs in which they are often framed have deep roots in the cultural memory of ancient Judaism and the ancient Near East. In many cases the symbolic language of Daniel is couched in traditions and motifs that would almost certainly have provided the reader/hearer with a significant number of "built-in" tools for interpretation. Thus, in spite of being largely "symbolic," i.e., using words that point beyond themselves, the apocalypses in Daniel 2*, 7, and 8 should have been easy for many Hellenistic Jews to interpret. In other words, while the symbols might seem to a modern reader to provide obstacles to interpretation, the conventional associations present in the symbols as well as the motifs and traditions in which they are framed should have made their meaning all the more obvious to ancient Jews. The language of the Daniel apocalypses is at every turn pregnant with elements of the socio-cultural encyclopedia of ancient Judaism. In spite of their symbolic language, these texts were not written to hide or conceal information, but to disperse it to the largest possible audience. Their language is so deeply rooted in widespread mythological, iconographic, and linguistic contexts from the ancient Near East/Mediterranean that the realm of possible interpretations is significantly constrained for a model reader. I attempt to show in chapters four through six that, ironically, it may be the non-symbolic apocalypses that functioned as "group-specific" literature, i.e., literature *not* produced (or, at least, not useful) for mass consumption.

Chapter Three

Comparative Evidence: Other Symbolic Apocalyptic Visions

In chapter two I analyzed the types of language used to describe deities, demons, angels, humans, and nations in Dan 2, 7, 8. While some variation exists in those apocalypses, I concluded that each apocalypse uses language that points beyond itself, i.e., language that requires interpretation both for the ostensible visionary (a literary construct) and for the reader. Within the basic observation that Dan 2, 7, and 8 are symbolic apocalypses, more subtle patterns emerged. Each apocalypse presumes a system of conventional relationships. Indeed, several of the apocalypses appear to share the same set of conventional relationships. Examples of these conventional pairs include the use of humans to represent angels or the use of animals to represent humans/kingdoms. In this chapter I provide a control for chapter two by surveying three symbolic apocalypses: the *Animal Apocalypse* (*1 En.* 85–90), 4QFour Kingdoms^{a-b} ar, and Noah's second dream in the *Book of the Words of Noah* (1QapGen 5 29–18 ?). I follow the same primary methodologies used in chapter two: linguistic- and motif-historical analysis. In several instances in the *Animal Apocalypse*, however, a fruitful linguistic analysis is not possible because one cannot reconstruct the original Aramaic words with certainty. In these cases an intra-textual analysis must suffice. I hope to show that the basic categories and associations proposed in chapter two are upheld by the evidence from several non-danielic apocalypses.

The Animal Apocalypse (*1 Enoch* 85–90)

The *Animal Apocalypse* (*1 En.* 85–90) is the larger of two dream reports found in *1 Enoch*'s *Book of Dreams* (*1 En.* 83–90). Both the *Animal Apocalypse* and its sister work, *Vision of the Earth's Destruction* (*1 En.* 83–84), are portrayed as dreams experienced by Enoch and recounted to his son Methuselah. The language used in the two texts could not be more different. The *Vision of the Earth's Destruction* does not use symbolic language.

The *Animal Apocalypse* surely uses more symbolic language than any other Jewish text from the Hellenistic Period.

In its present form, the *Animal Apocalypse* probably dates to the early stages of the Maccabean Revolt. The *terminus ante quem* is established by 4QEn^f, which J. T. Milik dates to 150–125 B.C.E..[1] P. Tiller reports that Frank Cross has indicated to him, however, that the fragment cannot be dated earlier than 100 B.C.E. (i.e., closer to the date proposed by K. Beyer).[2] The dates proposed by Cross and Beyer are more convincing if 1) the text makes mention of Judas Maccabeus (see below) and 2) the manuscript from Qumran is not an autograph. In other words, one would expect some modest amount of time to pass between the writing of the text and its appearance in copies at Qumran.[3]

The *terminus post quem* is considerably more difficult to ascertain. Tiller offers a first-tier date based on comparison with the *Book of Watchers* (*1 En.* 1–36).

The *An. Apoc.* makes use of the story of the fall and judgment of the Watchers as found in *1 Enoch* 6–11, though in a slightly different form. Since the *Book of Watchers*, or at least the section containing chapters 6–11, was probably written in the third century, the *An. Apoc.* must have been written no earlier than the third century.[4]

This first-tier date places the text well within the bounds of this study (333–63 B.C.E.) Depending on how one interprets the referents of some symbols used in the *Animal Apocalypse*, however, one can reach a more precise *terminus post quem*. The most significant symbol in this regard is the ram with the large horn in 90:9–16. Most identify the ram as Judas Maccabeus, but there is a disagreement over whether or not the reference to Judas is original or a later addition to the text.[5] The disagreement centers around the literary integrity of 90:13–19. In this study I follow Milik, Black, VanderKam, and Tiller who argue that there is insufficient/equivocal evidence for

---

[1] J. T. Milik, *The Books of Enoch: Aramaic Fragments of Qumrân Cave 4* (Oxford: Clarendon, 1976), 244.

[2] Tiller, *A Commentary on the Animal Apocalypse*, 61. Klaus Beyer, *Die aramäischen Texte von Toten Meer* (Göttingen: Vandenhoeck & Ruprecht, 1984), 228.

[3] Here I concur with Tiller, *A Commentary on the Animal Apocalypse*, 61. Milik held that the scribe of 4QEn^f (also responsible for 4QTestLevi^b) was a contemporary – or if not only a generation removed – from the author of the *Book of Dreams*. Cf. Milik, *The Books of Enoch*, 244.

[4] Tiller, A Commentary on the Animal Apocalypse, 61.

[5] For representative presentations of each side, see Tiller, *A Commentary on the Animal Apocalypse*, 61–79. Nickelsburg, *1 Enoch 1*, 396–8. For a summary of research on this topic see Daniel Assefa, *L'Apocalypse des animaux (1 Hen 85–90) une propagande militaire? Approches narrative, historico-critique, perspectives théologiques* (JSJSup 120; Leiden: Brill, 2007), 207–21, esp. 18–21. Assefa holds that the *Animal Apocalypse* is pre-Maccabean, but allows for the possibility that 90:13–15 could be a redaction that refers to Judas.

a doublet in 90:13–19.[6] It seems then, that the text was probably composed sometime between 165 and 160 B.C.E. – a time frame that suits the military activities of Judas Maccabeus as described in the text.[7]

The *Animal Apocalypse* is highly symbolic and employs the same basic type of language found in Dan 2, 7, and 8.[8] It is similar to Dan 2, 7, and 8 in several other important ways. First, the *Animal Apocalypse* narrates an *ex eventu* history of real and perceived events in the Near East. Second, Dan 7, 8, and the *Animal Apocalypse* allegorize an older myth/narrative.[9] In the case of Dan 7 the underlying tradition in the Canaanite combat myth. In the case of Dan 8 it is the "Day-Star, Son of Dawn" myth. The basis for the allegory in the *Animal Apocalypse* is Jewish traditions preserved in Gen, Exod, and other books in the Hebrew Bible.[10] There is a prominent scholar who rejects the description of the text as an allegory. In her review of Patrick Tiller's *A Commentary on the Animal Apocalypse of 1 Enoch*, Devorah Dimant criticizes him for describing the basic literary motif as an alle-

---

[6] See Milik, *The Books of Enoch*, 44. Matthew Black, *The Book of Enoch*, or, *1 Enoch: A New English Edition with Commentary and Textual Notes* (vol. 7; Leiden: Brill, 1985), 276–7. VanderKam, Enoch and the Growth, 162–3. Tiller, *A Commentary on the Animal Apocalypse*, 61–79. The most important contemporary voices using this passage to argue for a Maccabean Period redaction rather than a Maccabean Period composition are Jonathan Goldstein, *I Maccabees* (vol. 41; Garden City: Doubleday, 1976), 41–2. Nickelsburg, 1 Enoch 1, 396–8. Nickelsburg argues for a date that is either 1) in the last decade of the third century B.C.E. or 2) after the death of Onias III (169 B.C.E.) if 90:8 refers to Onias' death. Most recently, see Assefa, L'Apocalypse des animaux.

[7] Tiller, *A Commentary on the Animal Apocalypse*, 78–9. Stuckenbruck refrains from making a definitive judgment about the potential redactional layers. He assigns the text a *terminus ad quem* of 160 B.C.E.. Stuckenbruck's analysis of the various stages at which animals' eyes are opened (i.e., divine revelation is disclosed to a privlileged group) indicates that the final events of chapter 90 are carefully integrated into the overall narrative. Loren Stuckenbruck, "Reading the Present in the Animal Apocalypse (1 Enoch 85–90)," in *Reading the Present in the Qumran Library: The Perception of the Contemporary by Means of Scriptural Interpretation* (ed. Armin Lange and Kristin De Troyer; vol. 30 of *Symposium*; Atlanta: SBL, 2005), 91–102.

[8] The basic outline of these results has already been anticipated by Lange, "Dream Visions and Apocalyptic Milieus," 27–34. In his brief essay Lange asks if the representation techniques common to the Book of Daniel and the *Animal Apocalypse* might not point to a common apocalyptic milieu. This literary mileau might help to explain how, if there was not one homogenous apocalyptic movement in 2nd century B.C.E. Judah, texts so similar in imagery and visionary techniques could have been produced.

[9] Here I use the word allegory in its conventional English sense and do not imply the Greek concept of *allegoresis*. Assefa makes a critical distinction between allegory and *allegoresis* and determines that the *Animal Apocalypse* should be described as "une allégorie de l'histoire de l'humanité et de l'histoire d'Israël." Assefa, *L'Apocalypse des animaux*, 163–74. The most basic characterization of the *Animal Apocalypse* might be to say that it is a para-text (or, "parabiblical"). But the specific way in which the *Animal Apocalypse* appropriates Jewish scripture is different than the way that, for example, *Jub.* does. *Jub.* retells episodes from Gen with a different rhetoric. The *Animal Apocalypse* retells Gen with a different language.

[10] Cf. the discussion in Assefa, *L'Apocalypse des animaux*, 163–89.

gory. "Tiller's assertion that the 'Animal Apocalypse' constitutes an allegory (pp. 21–22) is, in my opinion, unfortunate. The concrete, realistic character of the symbols employed and their biblical background militate against such a definition."[11]

Dimant specifically criticizes Tiller for missing numerous associations that are, in her judgment, explicitly dependent on books of the Bible. "The biblical background ... of the various symbols for the Gentiles, passed over in silence by Tiller, confirms the impression that they were drawn from disparate contexts. Thus, for instance, dogs as symbols for the Philistines come from 1 Sam 17:43; Edom as wild asses stems from Gen 16:12 together with Jer 2:24 and Job 24:5; and lions for Babylonians accords with Jer 4:7."[12] Dimant argues that specific, concrete associations also exist for the other animals used in the text. Part of the problem with Dimant's criticism is her understanding of the word allegory. Neither she nor Tiller uses the term in the Greek sense of *Allegoresis*. Tiller clearly intends the standard meaning of the word in English, i.e., a story that functions on two (or more) levels, one of which is (often) derived from an external source.[13] Even if Dimant is right about the origins of the particular terminology that Tiller uses, it is unclear why this would not meet the definition of allegory in standard English usage. But I suggest that Dimant is overconfident about how "concrete" the associations between the animals in the *Animal Apocalypse* and the Hebrew Bible are. In my analysis of the symbols below, I consider the specific associations proposed by Dimant and conclude that she may only be correct about one of them.

Despite their similarities, there are also some significant differences between the *Animal Apocalypse* and Dan 2, 7, and 8. It is worthwhile to highlight four of them. First, the history presented in the *Animal Apocalypse* is far more wide-ranging than the ones presented in Dan 2, 7, and 8. Daniel's symbolic apocalypses begin with the rise of the Neo-Babylonian Empire. The *ex eventu* history found in the *Animal Apocalypse* begins not long after the creation of the earth (Adam and Eve are described in 85:3). Second, the history presented in the *Animal Apocalypse* is far less schematic than those found in Dan 2, 7, and 8. Unlike the symbolic apocalypses in Daniel where history is divided into a small number of discrete periods, the flow of histo-

---

[11] Devorah Dimant, "Review of *A Commentary on the Animal Apocalypse of 1 Enoch* by Patrick Tiller," *JBL* 114 (1995): 727.

[12] Dimant, "Review of A Commentary on the Animal Apocalypse of 1 Enoch by Patrick Tiller," 728.

[13] Tiller, *A Commentary on the Animal Apocalypse*, 21–8. On the concept of Allegory in the English language, see Angus Fletcher, *Allegory: The Theory of a Symbolic Mode* (Ithaca: Cornell University Press, 1964). J. A. Cuddon, ed., *Dictionary of Literary Terms and Literary Theory* (Fourth Edition ed.; London: Penguin, 1999), 20–3.

ry presented in the *Animal Apocalypse* is based on a kind of *Heilsgeschichte*. It begins with Adam and Eve, moves to the saga of the Watchers and their judgment, continues with the legends of Noah and the flood, the birth of the twelve tribes of Israel, sojourn in Egypt, the Exodus, conquest, construction of the temple, the united and divided monarchies, etc. The use of discrete, schematic periods does not really begin in the *Animal Apocalypse* until the Neo-Babylonian period. Despite its ultimate reversion to a schematic, periodized history (beginning in 89:65), the model of history presented in the *Animal Apocalypse* more closely resembles those presented in the second half of this study: non-symbolic apocalypses.

Third, and related to the *Heilsgeschichte* model of historiography just highlighted, the *Animal Apocalypse* centers on Jewish history and Jewish issues from the very beginning of the work. In the symbolic apocalypses from Daniel, Jewish history and Jewish issues appear only at the very end of the texts (the end of history!). The historical account in the *Animal Apocalypse* is based on Jewish scriptural traditions that closely resemble Genesis, Exodus, and Kings (or Chronicles).

Fourth, the role of the angelic interpreter in the *Animal Apocalypse* is far more subtle than in Dan 7 or 8.[14] It is clear from 90:31 that angels accompanied Enoch during his vision: "After that, those three who were clothed in white and who had taken hold of me by my hand, who had previously brought me up (with the hand of that ram also taking hold of me), set me down among those sheep before the judgment took place."[15] But after Enoch wakes from his dream the reader is informed only that he was disturbed. No angel appears and explicitly interprets the dream for him.

The textual history of the *Animal* Apocalypse makes an analysis of its text more complicated than those performed on the Daniel apocalypses above. The book of *1 Enoch* is only fully extant in Ethiopic (Ge'ez) in copies preserved in the Ethiopic Orthodox Tewahedo Church. I follow VanderKam, Nickelsburg, and others in assuming that the (individual) books of *1 Enoch* were originally composed in Aramaic and then translated into Greek before being translated (from Greek) into Ethiopic.[16] The Aramaic text is preserved only in fragments from Qumran.[17] The Greek text is

---

[14] Assefa, *L'Apocalypse des animaux*, 7.

[15] Trans. George Nickelsburg and James VanderKam, *1 Enoch: A New Translation* (Minneapolis: Fortress Press, 2004), 135.

[16] James VanderKam, "The Textual Base for the Ethiopic Translation of 1 Enoch," in *Working with No Data: Studies in Semitic and Egyptian Presented to Thomas O. Lambdin* (ed. D. M. Golomb; Winona Lake: Eisenbrauns, 1987), 247–62. Nickelsburg, *1 Enoch 1*, 15–6.

[17] The most recent editions of these fragments can be found in Donald Parry and Emanuel Tov, *Parabiblical Texts* (DSSR 3; Leiden: Brill, 2005). For detailed discussion see Milik, *The Books of Enoch*.

also highly fragmentary and only a few verses relevant to this study are extant.[18] Fortunately, numerous Ethiopic manuscripts exist and scholars have the benefit of multiple critical editions.[19] In the analysis below I follow a general three-tier system for citation of the text. I give priority to the Aramaic text whenever it is extant. If the Aramaic text is not extant, I use the Greek witnesses if they are available. If neither Aramaic nor Greek witnesses are extant I use the Ethiopic text and provide my own translations.[20] In most cases I must rely on the Ethiopic text. Each of the chapters of Daniel examined above presented a limited number of symbols and I examined them in the order they appear in the text. Beginning with the *Animal Apocalpse*, however, the texts under consideration present a considerably larger amount of data are require a more schematic organization. For most of the texts considered from this point on I divide the evidence into three categories: 1) descriptions of deities, angels/demons, 2) descriptions of individual persons, and 3) descriptions of ethno-political groups.

Descriptions of Deities, Angels, and Demons
Only one deity exists in the universe described in the *Animal Apocalypse*: the "Lord of the Sheep" (cf. *1 En.* 90:18, 20, 29, etc.) The Aramaic description survives partially in 4Q206 4ii 21: מֹ[רא ענא]. There is no reason to expect that other Aramaic expressions are used since the standard description preserved in Ethiopic (አግዚአ አባግዕ *ᵉgziʾ ʾabāgᵉʿ*) does not change in the text.

The Aramaic title מרא "lord" is used in a variety of contexts. For example, in Dan 4:16, 21, Daniel addresses Nebuchadnezzar as מָרְאִי (*Qere* מָרִי) "My lord." Similarly, the opening address of the Saqqara Inscription (6th Century B.C.E.) begins אל מרא מלכן פרעה "To the lord of kings, Pharaoh."[21] It does not seem to be used for non-royals in the way that titles such as שר and בעל are in Hebrew. מרא is also used as a title for deities and perhaps as a divine name. For example, Daniel describes his God as מָרֵא־שְׁמַיָּא "The

---

[18] See Matthew Black, *Apocalypsis Henochi Graece:* (Leiden: Brill, 1970), 36–7.

[19] For a convenient summary of the witnesses, see Nickelsburg, *1 Enoch 1*, 17. The critical editions are Michael Knibb, *The Ethiopic Book of Enoch: A New Edition in the Light of the Aramaic Dead Sea Fragments, 2 Vols.* (Oxford: Oxford University Press, 1978). Black, *The Book of Enoch, or, 1 Enoch: A New English Edition with Commentary and Textual Notes.* S. Uhlig, *Das Äthiopische Henochbuch* (JSHRZ V/6; Güterlsoh: G. Mohn, 1984). One can find a transliterated edition of the text in Tiller, *A Commentary on the Animal Apocalypse*. Finally, Daniel Assefa has recently reproduced Tiller's critical text in Ethiopic characters and made comparisons with other critical editions. Assefa, *L'Apocalypse des animaux*, 28–41.

[20] I follow the Ethiopic text found in Knibb, *The Ethiopic Book of Enoch*. I do not always agree with the base-text of Rylands Ethiopic MS. 23.

[21] Gibson, *Textbook of Syrian Semitic Inscriptions*, 2: 110–6.

Lord of the Heavens" in Dan 5:23. "Lord of the Sheep" should not be considered an idiom for "shepherd" for two reasons. First, as mentioned above, the word does not appear to be as pliable as titles like שר or בעל in Hebrew (e.g., שַׂר־הַטַּבָּחִים "captain of the guard" in Gen 37:36). Second, another more specific term is used for "shepherd" elsewhere in the text (cf. ኖላውያን *nolāw^eyān* in 89:59, etc.). It is possible that the term "Lord of the Sheep" is intended as a divine name, but I am not inclined to accept such an interpretation since it would contradict every other depiction of an "actor" in the history narrated in the *Animal Apocalypse*. It makes more sense to read the description in royal terms, i.e., the "king of the sheep." The deity is depicted in human terms. We saw above that angels are often described as humans and it appears that deities can also be described in these terms.

Angels play a robust role in the *Animal Apocalypse*. Two kinds of linguistic techniques are used to describe them. Some angels are depicted as humans and others are depicted as stars. For Tiller, the use of humans represents a break-down in the allegory, but this is because he does not associate it with the use of humans to represent angels in other texts.²² For example, the use of both humans and stars to represent angels is found in Dan 7–8. The *Animal Apocalypse* and the Book of Daniel share the same representation techniques.

The first angels to appear in the text are the fallen angels or "watchers" described in the Hebrew Bible as *nephilim* (הַנְּפִלִים, cf. Gen 6:4). The *Animal Apocalypse* first describes the fall of one star (ኮከብ *1 kokab*) in 86:1. Then in 86:3 many more stars fall. 4Q206 4i 11 preserves a fragmentary reading of the Aramaic noun from 86:3 (וכביא[כ). It is clear from this reading that the original Aramaic of 86:1 must have been כוכב (חד). These stars procreate with cows (i.e., human women, see below) and produce offspring. Not long afterward another set of heavenly emissaries arrives on earth. Seven beings with the appearance of "white humans" (ሰብእ ፀዓዳ *sab' ḍā'ādā*)²³ execute judgment on the stars and their offspring. The white humans represent the seven archangels described in the *Book of Watchers* who are commissioned to punish the angels who procreate with human

---

²² Tiller, *A Commentary on the Animal Apocalypse*, 24.

²³ The ፀ in ፀዓዳ (*ḍā'ādā*) is smudged and only partially legible in Rylands Ethiopic ms 23. See Knibb, *The Ethiopic Book of Enoch*, 293. This reading does not present the expected orthography. Cf. Wolf Leslau, *Concise Dictionary of Ge'ez (Classical Ethiopic)* (Wiesbaden: Otto Harrassowitz, 1989), 232. Dillman's text has the expected ጸ. Cf. August Dillman, *The Ethiopic Text of 1 Enoch [Das Buch Henoch, 1853]* (Eugene, Oregon: Wipf & Stock, 2005), 62. Nevertheless reading the consonant ፀ instead of ጸ in ፀዓዳ is consistent with the other examples of the word in the Rylands Ethiopic MS. 23 (Knibb). See, for example, the discussion of the figure Abraham below. The interchange is understandable – the distinction between ፀ and ጸ does not exist in the Hebrew dialects of the Bible where the two proto-Semitic consonants have collapsed into צ.

women. The story in the *Animal Apocalypse* follows the plot found in the *Book of Watchers* relatively closely at this point. The seven archangels are Uriel, Raphael, Reuel, Michael, Sariel, Gabriel, and Remiel (*1 En.* 20:1–8). Indeed, the enumeration of the archangels as "four . . . and three with them" in the *Animal Apocalypse* (*1 En.* 87:2) is a specific reflection of the lists of angels found earlier in the *Book of Watchers* (*1 En.* 9–10). Within the group Michael plays a preeminent role – a role that is also depicted in the *Similitudes* and the *War Scroll* (see more on Michael in chapter four). The seven archangels reappear in the *Animal Apocalypse* at *1 En.* 90:21 where they preside over the final, eschatological judgment. In precisely the same way that Dan 7 and 8 used human beings to describe angels, the *Animal Apocalypse* represents angels in human terms.

Besides the seven archangels, two other angels in the *Animal Apocalypse* are described as humans – though they do not begin in human state. These two figures are Noah and Moses. I discuss Noah here and reserve the discussion of Moses for the next section. *1 En.* 89:1 describes Noah first as an animal who is taught secrets by one of the seven archangels and who eventually becomes human:

And one of those four [white-humans] went to one of the white bulls and taught it a mystery – trembling as it was. It was born a bull (ላህም *lāhm*) but became a man (ሰብእ *sab'*). And he built himself a vessel and dwelt in it, and three bulls dwelt with him on that vessel, and the vessel was covered and roofed over them.

The description of the boat precludes any possibility that the white bull is not Noah. The transformation from human to angel described in *1 En.* 89:1 is not reflected in the biblical account. Gen 9:29 reports simply, "and he died." It is noteworthy, however, that Utnapishtim (Atrahasis), a literary forerunner of Noah in the *Epic of Gilgamesh*, does attain immortal status. In tablet 11 of the *Epic of Gilgamesh*, Utnapishtim tells Gilgamesh how, after he survived the flood, Enlil declared to him, "Hitherto Utnapishtim has been a human being, now Utnapishtim and his wife shall become like us gods, Utnapishtim shall dwell afar-off at the source of the rivers."[24]

It is clear from two manuscripts of the *Book of Giants* found at Qumran that Gilgamesh (at least as an individual figure) was a part of the cultural memory of Hellenistic Jews.[25] In the *Book of Giants*, Gilgamesh is depicted

---

[24] Trans. Benjamin Foster, "Gilgamesh," in *The Context of Scripture. Canonical Compositions from the Biblical World* (ed. W. Hallo and K. Lawson Younger; Leiden: Brill, 2003), 450.

[25] There is also evidence for the material presence of the *Epic of Gilgamesh* in the land of Israel, though it dates to a time before Israel existed as such. A Late Bronze Age fragment of the *Epic of Gilgamesh* has been found at Mediddo. It contains part of the text of the dream of Gilgamesh discussed in chapter one. See Wayne Horowitz and Takayoshi Oshima, *Cuneiform in Canaan: Cuneiform Sources from the Land of Israel in Ancient Times* (Jerusalem: Israel Exploration Society, 2006). I do not insinuate that a Hellenistic Jewish Scribe might have been reading

as one of the giants. In 4Q530 2ii +6–12 2 the giant *Ohya* reports to other giants a message he received from Gilgamesh and in 4Q531 22 9–12, one perhaps finds the prelude to that message in Ohya's report to Gilgamesh of a disturbing dream. 4Q531 22 12 may present the beginning of Ohya's dream with a formulaic declaration about whether or not the dream is favorable. If the figure of *Gilgamesh* functions in the cultural memory of Hellenistic Jews then it is possible that the *Epic of Gilgamesh* (in some form) was too. Indeed, the biblical flood stories both represent developments of a common literary tradition that probably goes back the third Millennium Sumer. Therefore, it is possible that aspects of the stories of Noah and Atrahasis could be combined or switched in variant accounts/expressions of the tradition. Apart from a correlation with Atrahasis, the notion of Noah attaining immortality (as an angel) in the *Animal Apocalypse* is unprecedented in the second century B.C.E.

Angels reappear in the *Animal Apocalypse* in human form in 89:59. These angels appear as seventy shepherds: "And he summoned seventy shepherds (ፖናላውያነ 70 $n\bar{o}l\bar{a}w^ey\bar{a}na$), and he left those sheep to them, that they might pasture them. And he said to the shepherds and their subordinates, 'Every one of you from now on shall pasture the sheep, and everything that I command you, do.'" God dispatches four groups of shepherds to pasture the sheep. The first group of twelve shepherds judge until the Babylonian Exile (89:65–72a). Next a group of twenty-three shepherds judge until the arrival of Alexander (89:72b–90:1). Another group of twenty-three shepherds judge from the time of Alexander's arrival into the second century B.C.E. (probably the Hellenistic religious reforms; 90:2–5), and finally a group of twelve shepherds judge until the end time (90:6–19). Commissioned at the same time as the seventy shepherds is one additional angel described only as "another one" (ካልእ $k\bar{a}l^{e\prime}$). It is not clear if the figure is another shepherd, but he is charged with cataloguing the excesses of the seventy shepherds who, according to the Lord of the Sheep, "will destroy more of them [the sheep] than I have commanded them" (89:61). It is his assignment as heavenly scribe by which he is characterized throughout the rest of the text (89:70, 76, 90:14, 17, 22). For example, on the cusp of the *eschaton* in 90:17 Enoch sees "that man who wrote the book at the word of the Lord (ዝኩ ብእሲ ዘይጽሕፉ መጽሐፈ በቃለ z^ekku $b^{e\,\imath e}s\bar{\imath}$ $zay^es^eh^ef\bar{a}$ $maṣ^ehafa$ $baq\bar{a}la$), until he opened the book of destruction that those last twelve shepherds worked, and he showed before the Lord of the sheep that they had destroyed more than those before them." Immediately afterward

---

Akkadian texts. I only suggest that the physical presence of the text in the land of Israel in addition to the mention of Gilgamesh in the *Book of Giants* only increases the likelihood that the text and/or its characters were part of the cultural memory of Jews in the Hellenistic period.

the Lord of the sheep ceases to judge the sheep and empowers them to fight their enemies.

Tiller makes an important connection between the seventy shepherds and a group of angels described in *Apocryphon of Jeremiah C* and 4Q390 as "Angels of Mastemot." In other words, the shepherds should not be viewed as an expression of the oft proposed "seventy guardian angels of gentile nations" scheme.[26] Instead the shepherds should be seen as demonic forces. These wicked angels (demons) are different from the fallen angels, but facilitate the expression of a motif by which at least part of the violence perpetrated on earth must be explained by an external impetus. Tiller compares the fallen angels (stars) who arrive before the flood with the shepherds (wicked angels) as follows:

Both groups are disobedient angels and both wreak havoc on the earth. This is one of the primary means in the narrative of the *An. Apoc.* by which we are meant to understand the troubles and dangers of this life from the perspective of the ancient, mythical past. Just as the tremendous evil and violence that led up to the Deluge was at least in part caused by demonic forces, so the troubles that beset exilic (and postexilic) Israel are caused in part by demonic forces.[27]

Dimant, who first pointed out the relevance of 4Q390 to Tiller, concurs with his assessment.[28] She prefers to push a bit further and suggests that the shepherds be associated with the rule or Belial or Mastema, who are depicted as ruling the forces of darkness in several scrolls found at Qumran (e.g., 1QS III 18–25).[29]

There are some differences between the demonic angels in the *Animal Apocalypse* and *Apocryphon of Jeremiah C* and 4Q390. I discuss the latter texts in detail below, but I note for now that while the shepherds (wicked angels) appear in the *Animal Apocalypse* in advance of the Babylonian exile (89:65–72a), they appear in *Apocryphon of Jeremiah C* – it seems – only after the arrival of Alexander the Great (see the combined edition of the text, lines 57–64 below). Similarly, in 4Q390, the angels appear during the seventh jubilee of the land (cf. 4Q390 1 7–11). The date of the seventh jubilee depends on when one begins the count. Obvious choices would include 597 and 586 B.C.E.. But these choices only make modest changes to the date – the seventh jubilee must occur in the Hellenistic period and, more specifically, in the third century B.C.E.. A date before the Babylonian exile is im-

---

[26] As Tiller points out, Charles long ago expressed hesitation about the concept of guardian angels of the Gentiles. Cf. Tiller, *A Commentary on the Animal Apocalypse*, 53.

[27] Tiller, *A Commentary on the Animal Apocalypse*, 53.

[28] Dimant, "Review of A Commentary on the Animal Apocalypse of 1 Enoch by Patrick Tiller," 728.

[29] Dimant, "Review of A Commentary on the Animal Apocalypse of 1 Enoch by Patrick Tiller," 728.

possible. The difference over the arrival time of the wicked angels may indicate that, despite the hints of deuteronomic theology in *Apocryphon of Jeremiah C*, its critique of Hellenistic culture may be even stronger than the one found in the *Animal Apocalypse*. In other words, it traces the violence and evil experienced in Judea no further back than the arrival of the Greeks. The arrival of the Greeks also marks the arrival of a new throng of wicked angels on earth. These angels, like the watchers before them, portend tragedy.

Before moving on to the next section, I briefly summarize this one. The supernatural beings in the *Animal Apocalypse* are described with precisely the same type of language found in the symbolic apocalypses from the Book of Daniel. These similarities function on both general and specific levels. In general terms, the language used to describe supernatural beings in the *Animal Apocalypse* points beyond itself, i.e., it is symbolic in my appropriation of the terminology of Artemidorus and Oppenheim. On the specific level, the particular descriptions used to describe supernatural beings make use of several conventional pairs that are also found in the Book of Daniel. For example, both humans and stars are used to represent angels. We can see, then, an emerging picture of some deep structures within the language of Ancient Jewish apocalypses.

Descriptions of Persons

I noted above that the scope of the history presented in the *Animal Apocalypse* is considerably broader than those found in the apocalypses analyzed in chapter two. Nowhere is this breadth more evident than in the range of actors that play parts in the history. Since this chapter primarily provides a control for evidence presented in chapter two, it is not necessary to discuss every description (all are documented in the chart of raw-data below). Instead, I survey a representative sample of the techniques used to describe persons in the *Animal Apocalypse*. Specifically, I look at figures from Noah to Moses.

Noah is mentioned above in the discussion of angels since he is transformed into an angel in the *Animal Apocalypse*. Noah only attains an angelic state, however, at the end of his life. Noah is first described as a bull (ላህም *lāhm*) who, at the instruction of an angel, "built himself a vessel and dwelt in it, and three bulls (፫ አልህምት *3 'alh^{e}mt*) dwelt with him on that vessel, and the vessel was covered and roofed over them" (*1 En.* 89:1). The three additional bulls are Noah's sons Ham, Shem, and Japhet. That both Noah and his sons are all described as bulls makes clear that no specific relationship exists between Noah and "bull" or Ham and "bull," etc. In other words, the bull is not used to describe Noah as a metaphor because

Noah shares certain recognizable characteristics with bulls. Neither is Noah described as a bull because there exists a conventional association between Noah and bulls in ancient Jewish thought. Instead, the text makes use of a technique whereby humans are represented with animals. The conventional association is the pairing of animals and humans. The specific description of Noah as a bull is an entirely secondary choice for the writer. It is predicated on a primary decision to use animals to represent all humans. Depictions of other humans in the *Animal Apocalypse* follow suit.

In *1 En.* 89:10–11 Abraham appears as a white bull (ላህም ፀዓዳ *lāhm ḍā'ādā*)[30] and his two sons, Ishmael and Isaac, are described as a wild donkey (አድገ ገዳም *'adgī gadām*) and a white bull (ላህመ ፀዓዳ *lāhma ḍā'ādā*) respectively. This passage illustrates an important feature of the language used in this text. A direct, genealogical line is drawn between Adam and Isaac with the use of bovids. Offspring who do not participate in this line are described with other animals (cf. Ishmael above as a wild donkey). Isaac's sons, Essau and Jacob, are described as "a black wild boar and a [white] ram of the flock" (חזי[ר̇ אכום ודכר די עז).[31] With Jacob a new genealogical scheme begins. Now the scheme focuses on sheep rather than bovids. Jacob (the white ram) sires twelve sheep. All Israelites, Judahites, and their ancestors after Jacob are described as sheep. The text then employs the same linguistic technique and draws a direct genealogical line from Jacob to contemporary Judeans by means of sheep. Jacob marks a pattern change not only in terms of the species used for a particular genealogical line, but in other ways.

Between Abraham and Jacob, only one son is allowed to carry the species-specific genealogical line from his father. All of Jacob's sons, however, are described as sheep. This is a way that the text may mark the distinction between a family lineage and the growth of a nation. The bulls represent a family-line, but the sheep represent a nation. This follows suit with Jacob's name-change in Gen 35:9, "God said to him, 'Your name is Jacob; no longer shall you be called Jacob, but Israel shall be your name.'" As for the actual descriptions of Jacob's sons, 4Q205 2i 27 preserves only the number twelve in Aramaic, but Milik's reconstruction is hardly adventurous: עשר]תרי.[32] The Ethiopic text reads ፲ወ፪ አባግዕ (*10wa2 'abāg^e'*

---

[30] Like the example of the seven white humans in the section above, one finds ፀዓዳ (*ḍā'ādā*) spelled with a ፀ instead of a ጸ. In this case, there is no question about the reading in Rylands Ethiopic MS. 23 (Knibb). For the expected root cf. Leslau, *Concise Dictionary of Ge'ez (Classical Ethiopic)*, 232. I presume all instances of the orthography ፀዓዳ instead of ጸዓዳ represent a phonetic interchange. The latter (expected) reading is the original one.

[31] 4Q205 2i 26

[32] Parry and Tov, *Parabiblical Texts*, 468–9.

"twelve sheep").³³ The twelve sheep are Reuben, Simeon, Levi, Judah, Issachar, Zebulun, Dan, Naphtali, Gad, Asher, Joseph, and Benjamin. Only one of these sheep is given an individual description: "When those twelve sheep had grown up, they handed over one of themselves to the wild asses." The sheep handed over to the wild asses is Joseph (cf. Gen 37). Eventually the eleven sheep are reunited with the one. A description of this transition (1 *En*. 89:14) is partially preserved in Aramaic in 4Q205 2i 29: "And the ram [Jacob] led forth the eleven sheep (אמריא עְשַׂר ל[ח]ד) to dwell with it [Joseph] and to pasture with it among the wolves."

Like the twelve sons of Jacob, Moses is described as a sheep. 4Q206 4ii 20 preserves the Aramaic description of Moses as a sheep from *1 En*. 89:16: "And a sheep (אמר) that had escaped safely from the wolves fled and went off to the wild donkeys." Like Noah, however, Moses does not remain in animal form. He becomes a human (=angel). The transition is preserved only in Ethiopic. At the moment in history just prior to the entry into Canaan, Moses is described as, "that sheep (ዝኩ በግዕ *z*ᵉ*kku bagg*ᵆ) that had led them, that had become a man (ብእሴ *b*ᵉᵆ*sē*)" (*1 En*. 89:38). The two transitions from animal to human in this text are important for illustrating the fundamental associations between animals/humans and humans/angels.

Descriptions of Ethno-Political Groups
Ethno-political groups provide the most complex scenarios in terms of the representation techniques used in the *Animal Apocalypse*. While the descriptions of ethno-political groups conform generally to the same patterns one finds elsewhere in the text, some more specific associations also obtain. These specific associations are not, however, consistent in the text. The general technique used to describe individual humans is also used to represent groups of humans (whether their association is political or otherwise). Beginning with the twelve sons of Jacob, Israel is represented as sheep. This designation holds whether the particular referent is Israel, Judah, or even the inhabitants of Jerusalem.

A group of Midianites appear as wild donkeys at 89:13a when they purchase Joseph on their way to Egpyt: "When those twelve sheep had grown up, they handed over one of themselves to the wild donkeys (ערדיא)."³⁴ The relationship between Midianites and wild donkeys is not conventional – one is able to deduce it only based on the similarity of this narrative with Gen 37. Indeed, Midianites are not the only ones described as wild donkeys.

---

³³ Reading with the variants in Tana 9 and BM 491 based on the orthography in 89:13. See Knibb, *The Ethiopic Book of Enoch*, 301.
³⁴ 4Q205 2i 28. The Ethiopic is አዕዱግ *'a*ᵆ*dumā*.

Ishmaelites are also described as wild donkeys – though there is some variation in the orthography of the descriptions in Ethiopic. For example, Ishmael is described as a wild donkey (አድጊ ገዳም '*adgī gadām*) in 89:11 and the Midianites are described as "wild donkeys" (አዕዱማ '*a^{e}dumā*). The difference (besides number) involves the interchange of an '*ayin* (ዐ) for a *gaml* (ገ). The variation in Ethiopic may be of little consequence since the Ishmaelites and Midianites are both described exactly the same in 4Q205. עדריא is used in both 4Q205 2i 25 and 28.

Combining Ishmaelites and Midianites into one ethnic group is strange, but it accords with the account of the sale of Joseph in Gen 37:25–28. Therein יִשְׁמְעֵאלִים "Ishmaelites" and מִדְיָנִים "Midianites" are used interchangeably. The association is nevertheless strange because Ishmael and Midian are sons of Abraham by different wives (Hagar and Keturah respectively) and have distinct genealogies. Ishmael's genealogy is located in Gen 25:12–18 and Midian's in 25:1–6. It is perhaps this genealogical conundrum that led the writer of *Jubilees* to create the following scenario: "Ishmael, his sons, Keturah's sons, and their sons went together and settled from Paran as far as the entrance of Babylon – in all the land toward the east opposite the desert. They mixed with one another and were called Arabs and Ishmaelites" (*Jub.* 20:12–13).[35] The question of the relationship between the Ishmaelites and Midianites in ancient Jewish sources must be deferred for now. The important point is that the *Animal Apocalypse* clearly associates Ishmaelites and Midianites with the same ethno-political designation. The association of either of these groups with wild donkeys is a matter of convention only for this text. It does not have precedent elsewhere in Ancient Jewish writings and this presents problems for Dimant's case that all the symbols of the *Animal Apoclypse* have concrete associations with language from the Bible. The next few examples illustrate this point even more clearly.

The Egyptians are described as wolves in the second half of verse 89:13: "And those wild donkeys, in turn, handed that sheep over to the wolves (አዝእብት '*az^{e}bt*), and that sheep grew up among the wolves." The Ethiopic ዝእብ *z^e^{e}b* normally indicates "hyena," but 4Q206 4iii 14 makes clear that the Aramaic original was based on the root דאב ("wolf") since when they drown in the Reed Sea, the Egyptians are depicted as ד[בי‍א.[36] (See also 4Q206 4ii 17 where דבי "wolves" are used to describe Egyptians).

The Hebrew cognate זְאֵב is used several times in the Hebrew Bible to mean wolf (Ezek 22:27, Hab 1:8, and Zeph 3:3). Tiller's explanation for

---

[35] Trans. James VanderKam, *The Book of Jubilees* (CSCO 511; Louvain: Peeters, 1989), 119.

[36] It is also possible for the Aramaic דאב to indicate a bear, but that meaning is highly unlikely in this context.

the use of an Ethiopic root meaning "hyena" is logical: "Presumably, since the Aramaic דב could have been understood either as wolf or as bear, the Greek must have read λύκοι ("wolves"), and the translator into Ethiopic, possibly a Syrian, used the Ethiopic cognate of זאב (Hebrew), דאב (Aramaic), etc. instead of the Ethiopic word that means wolf."[37] One could also explain the use of ዘእብ $z^{e\,\gamma e}b$ by arguing that the Ethiopic translator must have been working with an Aramaic original. In this scenario the translator would have made the simple mistake of employing a false cognate. When one considers the evidence from *1 En.* as a whole, however, this possibility seems less likely.[38]

Another important point connected with the discussion of allegory above is the usage of the lexeme זְאֵב in the Hebrew Bible. It is never used in connection with the Egyptians. For example, Ezek 22:27 describes Judahite officials in Jerusalem as, "like wolves (כִּזְאֵבִים) tearing the prey, shedding blood, destroying lives to get dishonest gain." Zeph 3:3 also uses wolves to describe corrupt Jerusalem elites: "The officials within it are roaring lions; its judges are evening wolves (זְאֵבֵי עֶרֶב) that leave nothing until the morning." A different association is found in Hab 1:8. The horses of the Neo-Babylonians are compared to wolves, "More menacing than wolves (מִזְּאֵבֵי) at dusk their horses charge." In no instance are Egyptians described as wolves or compared to wolves in the Hebrew Bible. This evidence is problematic for Dimant's assertion that the imagery in the *Animal Apocalypse* is derived from concrete associations from the Hebrew Bible.[39] There is not a conventional association between Egypt(ians) and wolves in ancient Jewish literature.

A cluster of ethno-political descriptions is found in 89:42–49: dogs, wild boars, and foxes. The setting of the passage is the time frame between the Israelites' entry into the land and Solomon's building of the temple. It is clear that the ethno-political groups are enemies of Israel and that Saul and David (both rams) combat them. Some biblical associations may be behind the choice of animals in this section of the history, but this is far from certain. The primary enemy, dogs (οἱ κύνες), is almost certainly a reference to the Philistines.[40] There is one biblical passage that could provide the background for this description. When David approaches the Philistine Goliath in 1 Sam 17:43 Goliath chides him, "Am I a dog (כֶּלֶב) that you come to me with sticks?" This verse could provide the impetus for the association of

---

[37] Tiller, *A Commentary on the Animal Apocalypse*, 272.
[38] VanderKam, "The Textual Base for the Ethiopic Translation of 1 Enoch," 247–62.
[39] Dimant, "Review of A Commentary on the Animal Apocalypse of 1 Enoch by Patrick Tiller," 728.
[40] This and all references to the Greek text of *1 Enoch* 89:42–47 are from Codex Vaticanus Gr. 1809 found in Knibb, *The Ethiopic Book of Enoch*, 310–12.

Philistines with dogs in the *Animal Apocalypse* and according to Dimant it does.⁴¹ But is it really a "concrete association" as Dimant claims? The term applies only to Goliath in 1 Samuel and is specifically rooted in the narrative context of the military contest. One would have to presume it was applied by the writer of the *Animal Apocalypse* as a kind of synecdoche (i.e., using a part to describe the whole). More compelling evidence that dogs are used to represent Philistines is found within the *Animal Apocalypse* itself when the ram that represents Saul is killed by the dogs (89:47, cf. 1 Sam 28, 31). But even if one does assume that the mention of the word dog in the same sentence as the mention of a Philistine (1 Sam 17:43) did provide the impetus for the writer of the *Animal Apocalypse* to describe Philistines as dogs, how does that make the *Animal Apocalypse* any less of an allegory? To claim that this verse establishes a standard, conventional relationship between Philistines and dogs strains the evidence to a breaking point. "Dog" is not a concrete, explicit description for Philistines in ancient Judaism. Indeed, there are far closer associations between dogs and Israelites in the Bible. For example, in Judg 7:5, the majority of Gideon's troops are compared to dogs. "So he brought the troops down to the water, and YHWH said to Gideon, 'Every one that laps the water with his tongue as a dog (הַכֶּלֶב) laps, you shall set by himself.'" In 2 Sam 9:8, Mephibosheth, grandson of Saul, compares himself to a dog. Hazael compares Elisha to a dog in 2 Kgs 8:13. No concrete relationship between dogs and Philistines is established by the Hebrew Bible.

A matrix of evidence points to a far more conclusive identification of the wild boars (οἱ ὕες) that appear alongside the dogs (Philistines) in 89:42. I indicated above that Esau is described as a wild boar (חזי[ר אכום]).⁴² In Gen 36:12–16 Amalek is twice listed among descendants of Esau. He is the son of Eliphaz, Esau's firstborn, by Timna his concubine. Since the Amalekites are listed among those with whom Saul did battle and since their genealogy indicates that they should be described with wild boars, it makes sense to identify the boars of 89:42–46 with the Amalekites.⁴³ The relationship is only established by presuming that there is an allegory at work. The description "wild boar" is nowhere equated with the Amalekites in the Hebrew Bible.⁴⁴

---

⁴¹ Dimant, "Review of A Commentary on the Animal Apocalypse of 1 Enoch by Patrick Tiller," 728.

⁴² 4Q205 2i 26

⁴³ Saul claims to have killed all but the king of the Amalekites. That claim is complicated by descriptions of David's battles with Amalekites much later. Cf. 1 Sam 14:47–48, 15:1–34 for Saul's interaction with the Amalekites and 1 Sam 27:8, 30:1, 18, 2 Sam 1:1 for David's interaction with the Amalekites.

⁴⁴ The only mention of boars in the Hebrew Bible is Ps 80:13.

The foxes (οἱ ἀλώπεκες) in 89:42 are more problematic. With the Philistines and the Amalekites out of the way, there are at least two other major enemies of earliest Israel (Ammonites and Edomites) and several minor ones (cf. 1 Sam 14:47–48).[45] A possible association between the Ammonites and foxes may be found in Neh 4:3. In response to the construction of city walls in Jerusalem, Tobiah the Ammonite is purported to have said, "That stone wall they are building – any fox going up on it would break it down." It is entirely possible that a verse like Neh 4:3 could have provided the impetus for the *Animal Apocalypse* to associate the Ammonites with foxes. But the association is hardly a concrete one. It is unclear whether Tobiah actually uses the term שׁוּעָל (fox) as a metaphor for "an Ammonite." Furthermore, it must be emphasized that Tobiah may have been a Jew who was referred to by Nehemiah as an "Ammonite" as term of derision. Ammon may have simply been the place Tobiah lived. Any attempt to infer a concrete association between Ammonites and foxes from the Hebrew Bible is highly problematic. Therefore I am sympathetic to Tiller's position. He claims that both Moab and Ammon should be grouped together as foxes. It is important to note that genealogies from Genesis support his position. "Since Moab, along with Ammon, was a descendent of Lot (Gen 19:37–38) it is likely that Moab should be included with Ammon among the foxes."[46] Since many of the associations already seen are predicated on genealogies, this is no small point.

Three more mammals remain to be identified: lions, leopards, and hyenas. They appear together with wolves (Egyptians) and foxes (Amon and Moab) in 89:55 as tools of divine retribution against the kingdoms of Israel and Judah.[47] The lions are most easily identified. They appear isolated from the other beasts in the next verse and the narration makes clear that they destroy the Jerusalem temple: "And I saw that he abandoned that house of theirs and their tower, and he threw them all into the hands of the lions (አናብስት '*anābs^{e}t*) so that they might tear them in pieces and devour them – into the hands of all the beasts" (*1 En.* 89:56).[48] There is little doubt that the lions are Babylonians and the events described as those of the early sixth century B.C.E.. In this particular case Dimant is on much stronger ground in claiming that the symbol is predicated on a concrete association

---

[45] Minor enemies like the Geshurites or Girzites (1 Sam 27:8) seem to be less likely candidates.
[46] Tiller, *A Commentary on the Animal Apocalypse*, 33.
[47] The "wolves" in passage are also technically "hyenas" in Ethiopic. The orthography changes in this instance (አዝብት instead of አዝአብት, i.e., an interchange of *ayin* and *alef*). See the discussion of wolves above for the rationale in translation of አዝአብት.
[48] On the identification of the Jerusalem temple in the *Animal Apocalypse*, see Devorah Dimant, "Jerusalem and the Temple in the Animal Apocalypse (*1 Enoch* 85–90) in the Light of the Ideology of the Dead Sea Sect [Hebrew]," *Shnaton* 5–6 (1982): 177–93.

from the Hebrew Bible.⁴⁹ As indicated in chapter 2, Babylon is described as a lion in Dan 7:4. Unlike many of the so-called biblical associations highlighted above, Dan 7 describes Babylonia as a lion. It does not merely mention Babylonia and lions in the same sentence. But even in the case of Dan 7 the description of Babylon as a lion is not exactly the same as what one finds in the *Animal Apocalypse*. As indicated in chapter two, all the beasts in Dan 7 are *Mischwesen*. Daniel describes the first beast as "like a lion and had eagles' wings" (7:4). Thus, while there is considerably more evidence for associations between Babylonia and lions, I am not prepared to accept the idea that lions were a standard, conventional symbol for Babylonia in the ancient Near East/ancient Mediterranean.

Two mammals remain: leopards (እናምርት '*anām^e^rt*) and hyenas (አፃብዕት '*aḍāb^eʿ^t*).⁵⁰ These mammals appear with lions, foxes, and wolves in 89:55, but no description is provided for their individual actions or characteristics. Their identification is difficult. Tiller identifies them as Assyria and Aram respectively based on the general time-frame of their appearance and those enemies of Israel that appear in the Book of Kings during the same putative time period. The associations are not altogether satisfactory even to Tiller, but at least there exists a logical rationale for the low profile of Assyria. "That Assyria is not prominent in the *An. Apoc.* is understandable since it only fruitlessly threatened Judah in 2 Kgs 18–19 and required tribute money in 2 Kgs 16 and 18."⁵¹ The situation is different for Aram. "The low profile of Aram in the *An. Apoc.* is strange. Aram was a major enemy of Israel during the reigns of David and Solomon (2 Sam 8; 10; 11), but these wars are omitted from the *An. Apoc.*"⁵² What is clear is that the Hebrew Bible does not provide the rationale for using leopards (እናምርት '*anām^e^rt*) and hyenas (አፃብዕት '*aḍāb^eʿ^t*) to represent their referents. The identification of Assyria and Aram (or any other people group) as the referents of the leopards and hyenas can only be derived by viewing the text as an allegory and by seeking referents in other literature on that model.

The final category of animals used to represent ethno-political groups is birds. Four different kinds of birds are mentioned and they are described

---

⁴⁹ Dimant, "Review of A Commentary on the Animal Apocalypse of 1 Enoch by Patrick Tiller," 728.

⁵⁰ Here I am reading with ms Tana 9 vs. Rylands Ethiopic ms 23. See the apparatus in Knibb, *The Ethiopic Book of Enoch*, 316. Even the orthography in Tana 9, however, is not what one expects (i.e., አፃባዕት). Cf. Leslau, *Concise Dictionary of Ge'ez (Classical Ethiopic)*, 237. The fact that Rylands Ethiopic ms 23 uses ዕዕብ rather than ዕብዕ would seem to support Tiller's suggestion that the Ethiopic translator of the text had זאב (Hebrew) or דאב (Aramaic) in mind when working with the words for "hyena" and "wolf" in Greek (see the discussion of wolves above).

⁵¹ Tiller, *A Commentary on the Animal Apocalypse*, 35.

⁵² Tiller, *A Commentary on the Animal Apocalypse*, 35.

Other Symbolic Apocalyptic Visions 179

collectively as አዕዋፈ ሰማይ *'a^{e}wāfa samāy^e* "the birds of heaven" (*1 En.* 90:2). They appear together in *1 En.* 90:2 and in different combinations throughout 90:3–19. The four individual species are eagles (አንስርት *'an-s^{e}rt*), vultures (አውሥት *'awš^{e}t*),[53] kites (ሆባያት *hōbāyāt*),[54] and ravens (ቋዓት *q^{w}ā'āt*). The eagles are the most important in that they lead all the other birds (90:2). The time period during which the birds of heaven appear makes clear that they are probably all Greek. The individual identifications are more difficult. It is disconcerting that, as Nickelsburg notes, a specific mention of Alexander the Great is conspicuously missing.[55] Nickelsburg, at the suggestion of Goldstein, identifies the eagles as Ptolemies. "The eagles are the easiest to identify and almost certainly represent the Ptolemies, whose coins regularly display an eagle on their reverse side."[56] He is correct that Ptolemaic coins often feature eagles on their reverse.[57] But the association may not be so simple. We saw in chapter 2 a significant connection between Macedonians (especially Ptolemies) and horns. Indeed, many of the coins cited by Nickelsburg feature a Ptolemaic ruler wearing a horned helmet or crown on the obverse.[58] Furthermore, many coins feature not an eagle on the reverse, but a horn of plenty.[59] Indeed, the use of horns in connection with Ptolemaic rulers is not limited to numismatic evidence, but is also found in other artistic expressions (see above). So are there reasons not to identify the eagles with the Ptolemies? Perhaps so. First, such an identification would strongly contradict the patterns of association used in the *Animal Apocalypse*, i.e., the associations between particular types of animals and their particular referents are virtually never conventional. Virtually none of the associations have precedents in Jewish literature or material culture. Moreover, one would be surprised for the Ptolemies to be characterized as most important among Greeks/Macedonians in a Jewish document written during the 2nd century B.C.E..

Tiller proposes to read the eagles as Macedonians generally and the other "birds of heaven" as kingdoms that arose after the death of Alexander and the dismemberment of his empire.[60] In this scenario, the ravens would be

---

[53] The reading in Rylands Ethiopic ms 23 contains an interchange of a ሥ (*shaut*, cf. ሠ) for the expected ሰ (*sit*, cf. ሠ/ሰ). The expected ሰ is found in the Berlin ms, but its reading contains a different variant with the expected form. It uses an *'ayin* preformative instead of the expected *'alef* (i.e., the designation of the plural number).

[54] Here I read with ms Tana 9 against the singular form (ሆባይ *hōbāy*) "kite" found in Rylands Ethiopic ms 23 for 90:2. All other birds in the list are plural in form.

[55] Nickelsburg, *1 Enoch 1*, 396.

[56] Nickelsburg, *1 Enoch 1*, 396.

[57] See Poole, *Catalogue of Greek Coins*.

[58] Poole, *Catalogue of Greek Coins*, plates I, III, V, VI, XII, XV, XVII, XXIII, XXXII.

[59] Poole, *Catalogue of Greek Coins*, plates VIII, XII, XIII, XV, XVII, XXIV, XXX, XXXII.

[60] Tiller, *A Commentary on the Animal Apocalypse*, 346.

Seleucids and the kites would be the Ptolemies. Tiller omits the vultures as either a translation doublet or an Ethiopic doublet of similarly spelled words.[61] He finds internal evidence for his emendation to the extent that, "(1) The vultures do not appear in the list of animals in 89.12 although all other animals (except for the asses which appear in the following verse do; (2) the vultures have no independent function and appear only in the phrase "eagles and vultures."[62] Another explanation, however, that would explain both the presence of the vultures and their exceptionally low-profile is the possibility that they represent the kingdom of Lysimachus. Seleucus and Ptolemy were not the only *Diodochi*. Lysimachus founded Lysimachia in 309. He ultimately controlled Lydia, Ionia, Phrygia, and the north coast of Asia Minor. Lysimachus was never, however, a major player in the politics of the Levant.[63]

Dimant agrees that the eagles are Macedonians (Greeks in her terminology), though not for the same reasons. According to Dimant, "The choice of eagles to symbolize the Greeks seems to have been based on ancient exegetical tradition, attested by the pesher on Habakkuk (=1QpHab). The Qumranic pesher applied the simile of the eagle (Hab 1:8) to the *Kittim*."[64] The *Kittim* in the *Pesharim* are almost certainly Romans. Dimant argues, however, that *Kittim* is used elsewhere to refer to Greeks. I fully agree with Dimant that there are examples, especially from the Dead Sea Scrolls, where *Kittim* I used as a designation for Greeks.[65] But I cannot agree with her that *Kittim* refers to Greeks in Dan 11:30. There is a general scholarly consensus that this passage refers to the famous confrontation between Antiochus IV and Popilius Laenas (168 B.C.E.).[66] This event is discussed in more detail in chapter four. It is only the immediate literary context that makes clear who the eagles are in the *Animal Apocalypse*.

---

[61] Tiller, *A Commentary on the Animal Apocalypse*, 346.

[62] Tiller, *A Commentary on the Animal Apocalypse*, 346.

[63] Günther Hölbl, *A History of the Ptolemaic Empire* (London: Routledge, 2001), 9–35, esp., 13, 15, 18, 25, 35. It is true that there were others who inherited parts of Alexander's empire. But a ruler as far away as Macedonia, for example, would appear to have had far less influence, etc., in the Levant.

[64] Dimant, "Review of A Commentary on the Animal Apocalypse of 1 Enoch by Patrick Tiller," 728.

[65] The use of Kittim in Daniel and the *War Scroll* is treated in chapters four and five below. For now I refer to the most recent and significant discussion: Hanan Eshel, "The Kittim in the War Scroll and in the Pesharim," in *Historical Perspectives: From the Hasmoneans to Bar Kokhba in Light of the Dead Sea Scrolls. Proceedings of the Fourth International Symposium of the Orion Center for the Study of the Dead Sea Scrolls and Associated Literature, 27–31 January 1999* (ed. D. Goodblatt, et al.; vol. 37 of *STDJ*; Leiden: Brill, 2001), 29–44.

[66] Hölbl, *A History of the Ptolemaic Empire*, 146–8. Collins, *Daniel*, 384. Donald Gowan, *Daniel* (AOTC; Nashville: Abingdon, 2001), 149–50.

Raw Data from the Animal Apocalypse.[67]

Citation	Description	Referent	Symbol-type	Symbol-Referent
85:3	White bull and heifer	Adam and Eve	Animals	Humans
85:3, 4	Black calf, red calf	Cain and Abel	Animals	Humans
85:5	black bull and heifer	Cain and his wife (cf. Gen 4:17)	Animals	Humans
85:5	many cattle	Enoch, Irad, Mehujael, Methushael, Lamech, Jabal, Jubal Tubal-cain (cf. Gen 4:18–24)	Animals	Humans
85:6	(first) cow, first bull	Adam and Eve	Animals	Humans
85:6	Red cow	Abel	Animal	Human

---

[67] I have not made an entry for every use of every description. Generally, I only make additional entries for a given description if a different meaning or nuance of meaning is intended. Thus, the textual citation in the first column may be the first but not the last time the particular description appears in the text.

85:7	First bull	Adam	Animal	Human
85:8	another white bull	Seth (cf. Gen 4:25)	Animal	Humans
85:9	many white cattle	descendants of Seth, specifically Enosh, Kenan, Mahalalel, Jared, Enoch, Methuselah, Lamech, Noah, Shem, Ham, and Japheth (cf. Gen 5:6–32)	Animals	Humans
86:1	a star fell from heaven	the Nephilim (Watchers, cf. Gen 6:4)	Heavenly Body	Angels
86:1	cattle	Women the "sons of God" impregnated	Animals	Humans
86:4	elephants, camels, asses	the "giants" or heroes of old (cf. הַשֵּׁם הַגִּבֹּרִים אֲשֶׁר מֵעוֹלָם אַנְשֵׁי in Gen 6:4)	Animals	Humans
87:2–3	seven beings like white men (four plus three)	archangels	Human	Angels

88:1–3	one of the four	Michael	Human	Angel
89:1	bull who became a man	Noah	Animal	Human→Angel
89:1	three bulls	Noah's sons: Ham, Shem, and Japheth	Animals	Humans
89:9	white bull, red bull, and black bull (more specific rendering of 89:1)	Shem, Ham, and Japheth	Animals	Humans
89:9	white bull that departed	Noah	Animal	Human
89:10	numerous species	descendants of Noah's sons	Animals	Humans
89:11	white bull	Abraham	Animal	Human

89:11	wild donkey	Ishmael	Animal	Human
89:11	white bull (sired by previous white bull)	Isaac	Animal	Human
89:12	black wild boar	Essau	Animal	Human
89:12	white ram	Jacob	Animal	Human
89:12	twelve sheep	Jacob's sons	Animal	Human
89:13	one of the twelve sheep	Joseph	Animal	Human
89:13	wild asses	Midianite traders (cf. Gen 37:25–28)	Animals	Humans
89:13	wolves	Egyptians	Animals	Humans
89:14	many flocks of sheep	descendants of Joseph enslaved in Egypt	Animals	Humans

89:16	sheep that escaped	Moses	Animal	Human
89:18	another sheep with that sheep	Aaron	Animal	Human
89:21	sheep that went out from the wolves	the Exodus of the children of Jacob	Animals	Humans
89:36	sheep that became a man	Moses	Animal→Human	Human→Angel
89:39	two sheep[68]	Joshua, Aaron	Animals	Humans
89:42ff	dogs, wild boars, foxes	Philistines, Amalekites, Ammonties	Animals	Humans
89:42ff	ram from among the sheep	Saul	Animal	Human
89:45	this sheep	Samuel	Animal	Human

---

[68] See Nickelsburg, *1 Enoch 1*, 369.

89:45ff	another sheep appointed to be ram	David	Animal	Human
89:48b	little sheep who became ram	Solomon	Animal	Human
89:51	sheep who killed other sheep	Ahab	Animal	Human
89:52	Sheep who escaped	Elijah	Animal	Human
89:53	Many other sheep	Israelite/Judahite Prophets	Animals	Humans
89:53	Those sheep	Israelites/Judahites	Animals	Humans (Kingdom)
89:54	The Lord of the Sheep	YHWH	Human	Deity
89:54	Those sheep	Israelites/Judahites	Animals	Humans

Other Symbolic Apocalyptic Visions 187

89:55	Lions, leopards, wolves, hyenas, foxes	Babylonia, Assyria, Aram, Egypt, Ammon and Moab	Animals	Humans (Kingdoms)
89:56	lions	Babylonians	Animals	Humans
89:57	The Lord of the Sheep	YHWH	Human	Deity
89:57–8	Beasts (x2)	The beasts referred to in 89:55	Animals	Humans (Kingdoms)
89:59–74	Seventy shepherds	Wicked Angels	Humans	Angels
89:59–64	Sheep	Judahites/Judeans	Animals	Humans (Kingdoms)
89:65–72a	Twelve Shepherds	Angels	Humans	Angels
89:65–72a	Sheep	Judahites (specifically Jerusalemites)	Animals	Humans

89:65–6	Lions, leopards, wild boars	Babylonians and neighboring kingdoms that do not assist Judah (cf. Obadiah)	Animals	Humans (Kingdoms)
89:70	One who was writing	Angelic scribe	Human	angel
89:70	Lord of the Sheep	YHWH	Deity	Human
89:72b–90:1	Twenty-Three Shepherds	Wicked Angels	Humans	Angels
89:72b	Three of those sheep	Zerubbabel, Joshua, Sheshbazzar (or perhaps Nehemiah)	Animals	Humans
89:72b	Wild boars	Local enemies of a reorganized Judah (different lists appear in Neh. And Ezr.)	Animals	Humans
89:75–6	Lord of the Sheep	YHWH	Deity	Human
89:76	One who was writing	Angelic scribe	Human	angel

89:72b–91	sheep	Judahites both in Israel and exile	Animals	Humans
90:2–5	Twenty-Three Shepherds	Wicked Angels	Humans	Angels
90:2–19	Birds of heaven: eagles, kites, ravens[69]	Various expressions of Greek identity, probably eagles=Macedonians, kites=Ptolemies, and ravens=Seleucids		
90:2–5	sheep	Judeans	Animals	Humans (ethno-political group)
90:6–19	Twelve Shepherds	Wicked Angels	Humans	Angels
90:8	One lamb	Onias III	Animal	Human
90:6–19	Ram with one horn	Judas Maccabeus	Animal	Human
90:6–19	Sheep/rams	Judeans; sometimes specifically Maccabees	Animals	Humans (ethno-political group)

---

[69] Omitting vultures as a doublet, see Tiller, *A Commentary on the Animal Apocalypse*, 346.

90:6–19	Lord of the Sheep	YHWH	Human	Deity
90:6–19	Man who wrote	Angelic scribe	Human	angel
90:20	The Lord of the Sheep	YHWH	Human	Deity
90:21	First seven white men; first star; stars	Archangels and other angels	Humans; Stars	Angels
90:26	Blinded sheep	Disobedient Jews (Judeans)	Animals	Humans
90:31	Three clothed in white	Angels	Humans	Angels
90:37	White Bull[70]	Messiah (second Adam, cf. 85:3)	Animal	Human

---

[70] I presume that this animal is the same one described in 90:38 with black horns. This is not, however, the only option. See the discussion in Tiller, *A Commentary on the Animal Apocalypse*, 386–9. Nickelsburg, *1 Enoch 1*, 403.

4QFour Kingdoms^{a-b} ar

4QFour Kingdoms^{a-b} ar (4Q552–553) is an Aramaic apocalypse found in two or three manuscripts at Qumran. Most of what is left of the text describes a vision experienced by an unknown person. Several English translations exist, but the *editio princeps* only appeared in 2009.[71] For my analysis I have consulted photos (microfiche) of the text as well as the translation of E. Cook in *DSSR* 6.[72] This section was written before the publication of DJD XXXVII, but I have since consulted it. Significantly, Puech has divided the manuscript 4Q553 into two distinct manuscripts, 4Q553 and 4Q553a. He is unsure if all of the fragments of his new 4Q553a all belong together (or even in the *Four Kingdoms* text). This new organization is possible, but I am not yet fully convinced since 1) none of the fragments of the new manuscripts have more than a few letters, 2) their script is clearly the same as the script used in the 4Q553 fragments, and 3) fragment 7 of his 4Q553a clearly includes the רב איל]ניא "ruler of the trees" (4Q553 10 2) (i.e., the fragment is clearly related to the vision about trees encountered in the other manuscripts). I concede that not all of the fragments of 4Q553 may belong to the *Four Kingdoms* text, but the presence or absence of most of them makes little difference because they contain so little content. Puech is correct that a unified 4Q553 would demonstrate a mixed orthography, e.g., both כול and כל. This is unfortunate, but not unprecedented. Moreover, if I am correct that 4Q553 significantly predates 4Q552, this could help to explain 5Q552's consistent full orthography. Only in one case does this question really bear on my main concern, so a more detailed engagement must wait for another time.

A preliminary *terminus post quem* for the text can probably be established at 333 B.C.E.. I argue below that the second of four trees that appear in the vision should be identified as Greece (or Macedonia). If I am correct that the third and fourth trees should be identified as Ptolemaic Egypt and Seleucid Syria (see below) then one may bring the *terminus post quem* down to the beginning of the third century B.C.E.. A *terminus ante quem* may be established more precisely by the paleographic dates of the manuscripts.

4Q552 (ms a) is the easiest to characterize. It is a late Herodian formal script and it dates to ca. 50 CE. Other manuscripts found in this script are

---

[71] Émile Puech, ed., *Qumran Cave 4.XXVII: Textes araméens, deuxième partie: 4Q550–575, 580–582* (DJD XXXVII; Oxford: Clarendon, 2009), 57–90.

[72] The photos are from Emanuel Tov, *The Dead Sea Scrolls on Microfiche: A Comprehensive Facsimile Edition of the Texts from the Judean Desert* (Leiden: Brill, 1995), 43.576, 43.79. See Donald Parry and Emanuel Tov, eds., *Additional Genres and Unclassified Texts* (vol. 6 of DSSR; Leiden: Brill, 2005), 76–81.

4QDeut^j and a non-symbolic apocalypse analyzed later in this study, 4QPseudoDaniel^{a–b} ar.[73] 4Q553 (ms b) may be dated considerably earlier and is therefore the most important manuscript for establishing a *terminus ante quem*. The script is undoubtedly a semicursive script.[74] Especially noteworthy in this regard is the ת. The well defined loop in its left-most vertical stroke is closest to those found in 4QpapMMT^c (4Q398) – a late Hasmonean script that dates to ca. 50–25 B.C.E.. The loop has antecedents as far back as the Nash Papyrus, but the form in 5Q553 is clearly distinct from such earlier examples. Some of א characters in 4Q553 are close to those of earlier semi-cursive scripts such as the 4QXII^a (4Q76), which dates to ca. 150–100 B.C.E. and the ש almost never has the characteristic "tail" of semi-cursive scripts. But the less stylized ש would not make 4Q553 exceptional among other examples of the late Hasmonean semiformal hand.[75] Moreover, other characters such as the ט, (final) ף, and מ move 4Q553 much closer to the late Hasmonean semi-cursive hand. 4Q553 is, if not a perfect match for the late Hasmonean semi-cursive hand, close enough to warrant a date in the first century B.C.E. – most likely later than earlier. Therefore based on content and paleography, 4QFour Kingdoms^{a–b} ar must have been written between approximately 305 and 25 B.C.E.. This large span of time is unsatisfactory, but I do not believe the text provides evidence with which to reach a more precise date.

The vision involves four examples of one symbol: a tree. Each tree represents a different kingdom. Several other actors appear in the text including deities, angels, and humans. It is unclear, however, how many of these actors are actually part of the vision and how many are part of the literary context of the vision. Since the number of actors is so small, I discuss all of them below. The reader is cautioned that only the trees can be placed definitively within the vision itself.

The text must be categorized somewhere between symbolic and non-symbolic. The visionary requires interpretation for the individual symbols, but in an unusual twist the symbols provide their own interpretation. In other words, the visionary carries on a conversation with the trees in precisely the same way that, for example, Nabonidus carries on a conversation with God or Samuel carries on a conversation with YHWH in the dream

---

[73] Puech treats the script as a Late Hasmonean or early Herodian script (cf. 4QSam^a) and dates it to the third quarter of the first century B.C.E. See Puech, *Qumrân Grotte 4 XXVII*, 59–60.

[74] For 4Q553, Puech and I are far closer to agreement. He also categorizes it as a Hasmonean semi-cursive script likely produced in the second half of the first century B.C.E. Puech, *Qumrân Grotte 4 XXVII*, 73–74.

[75] See the examples of ש in Frank Moore Cross, "Paleography and the Dead Sea Scrolls," in *The Dead Sea Scrolls after Fifty Years: A Comprehensive Assessment* (ed. Peter Flint and James VanderKam; Leiden Brill, 1998–9), pl. 12.

visions described above in chapter one. We have already seen a precedent for an apocalyptic vision whose representation techniques place it between symbolism and realism above in chapter two. For example, in Daniel chapter 7 the visionary experiences both a symbolic dream as well as an explicit revelation/interpretation in the same vision. Nevertheless, the mixture of symbolic/non-symbolic elements found in 4QFour Kingdoms[a–b] ar is different than Dan 7 in that the symbols interpret themselves (i.e., Daniel does not converse with the beasts in his visions).

Descriptions of Deities, Angels, and Demons
There is only one unambiguous reference to a deity in the text. It is unclear whether the deity is mentioned as part of the vision report, part of a conversation with an angel, or part of an introduction or other editorial comments. The description of the deity in 4Q552 3 10 is אל עליון "God Most High." No other complete words are extant on the same line. Even though the fragment is poorly preserved, the few words extant in the two following lines provide important context for the "God Most High." Two full words are preserved in 4Q552 3 11 and four full words in 4Q552 3 12. Line eleven reads די עליהון "who/which is upon them" and line twelve reads די כול מותבה דינין "of all his seat, judges." Lines eleven and twelve appear to indicate a judgment scene. Parallels can be found in judgment scenes from Dan 7, *1 En.* 14 and the *Book of Giants* where judges are seated for a final reckoning.[76] One should also note that in art from the ancient Neast East, those depicted as sitting are deities and kings.[77]

Numerous studies have been devoted to the divine name/epithet עליון.[78] It or its cognate forms are attested early in West Semitic sources. It appears

---

[76] On the tradition-historical relationships between these texts, see Loren Stuckenbruck, "Daniel and Early Enoch Traditions in the Dead Sea Scrolls," in *The Book of Daniel: Composition and Reception* (ed. John J. Collins and Peter Flint; Leiden: Brill, 2001), 368–86. See also Loren Stuckenbruck, "The Book of Daniel and the Dead Sea Scrolls: The Making and Remaking of the Biblical Tradition," in *The Hebrew Bible and Qumran* (ed. James Charlesworth; N. Richland Hills, TX: BIBAL, 2000), 135–71. Stuckenbruck argues that the version of the judgment scene found in the *Book of Giants* preserves the oldest tradition (even if the text itself is not the oldest).

[77] This tradition may be especially important for Israelite religion since YHWH's physical presence was apparently signified by the cherubim throne. See Tryggve Mettinger, "Israelite Aniconism: Developments and Origins," in *The Image and the Book: Iconic Cults, Aniconism, and the Rise of Book Religion in Israel and the Ancient Near East* (ed. K. van der Toorn; Leuven: Peeters, 1997), 172–203. Several of the essays in this volume address the question of YHWH's throne to greater or lesser extents.

[78] O. Eissfeldt, "El and Yahweh," *JSS* 1 (1956): 25–37. R. Rendtorff, "El, Ba'al und Jahweh," *ZAW* 78 (1966): 277–91. B. Uffenheimer, "*El Elyon*, Creator of Heaven and Earth," *Shnaton* 2 (1977): 20–6. Cross, *Canaanite Myth*, 45–75. Zobel, "עֶלְיוֹן," in *TDOT* (ed. G. J. Botterweck, et al.; Grand Rapids: Eerdmans, 2001), XI: 121–39.

consistently though modestly in the literary and epigraphic records of West Semitic (Ugaritic, Aramaic, and Hebrew) from the Late Bronze Age until the Persian Period. The range of meanings of for the expression over the approximate millennium between the Late Bronze Age and the beginning of the Hellenistic period is not large, but there is variation. During the late Persian Period and especially in the Hellenistic Period use of the expression increases considerably. It is a common designation for the God of Israel in Jewish writings from the Hellenistic Period – indeed, by some accounts, it is *the* standard designation.[79] But studies on the semantic range of עליון in the Hellenistic period have not been nearly as prolific as those for earlier periods. In what follows I attempt to situate the use of אל עליון in *Four Kingdoms* within the semantic range mapped out by other texts.

The earliest evidence for the epithet עליון is found at Ugarit, where – notably – it is used in parallelism with Baal, not El. Here the form is ʻly.[80] In both instances, it is specifically related to Baal's role as bringer of the rain:

ʻn l'arṣ . mṭr . bʻl

w l šd . mṭr . ʻly

Look to the earth (for) the rain of Baʻlu,

And to the field(s), (for) the rain of the most high[81]

According to Rahmouni, the epithet probably refers to Baal's role as acting king of the gods.[82] There is no evidence that ʻly ever represents a deity distinct from Baal in the Ugaritic texts. But there is evidence for such a meaning in one of the Aramaic Sefire inscriptions.

The first Sefire Inscription begins by listing the parties to the treaty executed in the text. It then lists the deities who witness the treaty. Among those in the list are אל ועליןן "El and Elyān."[83] It is possible that the text understands El and Elyān to represent a kind of dual-named deity *a la* ktr

---

[79] Zobel, "עֶלְיוֹן," XI: 139. G. Wehmeier, "עלה," in *TLOT* (ed. E. Jenni and C. Westermann; Peabody, MA: Hendrickson, 2006), 895–6.

[80] This name is not related to the phonetically similar epithet of Baal, ʼalʼiyn bʻl "Baʻlu the mighty one." Cf. the discussion in Rahmouni, *Divine Epithets in the Ugaritic Alphabetic Texts*, 53–63.

[81] KTU 1.16:III:6, transcription and translation (with some small adjustments) by Rahmouni, *Divine Epithets in the Ugaritic Alphabetic Texts*.

[82] Rahmouni, *Divine Epithets in the Ugaritic Alphabetic Texts*, 259.

[83] Sefire I.II.11,cf. Joseph Fitzmyer, *The Aramaic Inscriptions of Sefire* (BO 19/A; Rome: Editrice Pontifico Instituto Biblico, 1995), 42–3. On the orthography of the Aramaic form, note that unlike the Canaanite branch of the Semitic languages, Aramaic did not undergo the so-called "Canaanite shift" in which long-a vowels became long-o vowels. The most obvious expression of this distinction can be found in the masculine singular versions of the Qal (Hebrew) and Pᵉʻal (Aramaic) participles, i.e., קָטֵל vs. קָטֵל.

wḫss from Ugarit.[84] But I doubt this possibility because several other pairs of deities are listed in Sefire I.II.6–14 and the others are demonstrably not double-name deities. Indeed, they often name deity-consort pairs, e.g., Marduk and Zarpanit, Shamash and Nur, etc.[85]

The evidence for עליון in the Hebrew Bible is considerably more diverse. Fitzmyer nicely summarizes the use of עליון and especially its interaction with other divine names:

> עליון is a name familiar in the OT, as an epithet of אל (Gen 14:18–22; Ps 78:35), of יהוה (Ps 7:18; 47:3), of אלהים (Ps 57:3; 78:56); it is also used in parallelism with אל (Num 24:16; Ps 73:11; 107:11), with יהוה (Deut 32:8–9; 2 Sam 22:14 [=Ps 18:14]; Ps 91:9), with אלהים (Ps 46:5; 50:14), with שדי (Num 24:16; Ps 91:1). It is also used alone (Ps 9:3; 77:11; 82:6; Isa 14:14). In these cases, עליון designates the monotheistic God of Israel.[86]

I have one disagreement with Fitzmyer's summary. He invokes monotheism for some texts that may indicate at best monolatry or henotheism. I take issue specifically with Fitzmyer over Deut 32:8–9, which I believe presents an important exception to his overall conclusion that עליון designates the (monotheistic) God of Israel. "When Elyon apportioned the nations, when he divided humankind, he fixed the boundaries of the peoples according to the number of the gods[87] YHWH's own portion was his people, Jacob his allotted share." In this passage YHWH is of lower status than Elyon.[88] YHWH is one of several lesser gods to whom geographic regions of dominion are assigned. This same concept is reflected elsewhere in the Deuteronomistic History. For example, it is found in 2 Kgs 5:17 where the Syrian Naaman requests of Elisha that he might take Israelite soil back with him to Syria in order to worship YHWH. "Then Naaman said, 'If not, please let two mule-loads of earth be given to your servant; for your servant will no longer offer burnt offering or sacrifice to any god except YHWH.'" The basic idea is that different gods rule over distinct geographical areas (cf. also 1 Sam 26:19, 1 Kgs 20:23, 2 Kgs 17:26). Thus עליון in Deut 32:8–9 is distinct from the God of Israel.

As Fitzmyer points out, the specific combination of the divine name אל "God" and the epithet עליון "Most High" is used in the books of Genesis and Psalms. Four of the five instances occur in the account of Abraham's meet-

---

[84] Cf. 51.V.109 where the double name occurs with a singular verb.
[85] Fitzmyer, *The Aramaic Inscriptions of Sefire*, 42–3. Cross, *Canaanite Myth*, 51–2.
[86] Fitzmyer, *The Aramaic Inscriptions of Sefire*, 75.
[87] Reading with 4QDeut^j and LXX vs. MT and SP.
[88] Jan Joosten, "A Note on the Text of Deuteronomy xxxii 8*," *VT* 57 (2007): 548–55. Smith, *The Early History of God: Yahweh and Other Deities in Ancient Israel*, 32–43. Georg Braulik, "Das Deuteronomium und die Geburt des Monotheismus," in *Gott, der einzige: zur Entstehung des Monotheismus in Israel* (ed. Ernst Haag; Freiburg im Breisgau: Herder, 1985), 115–59.

ing with Melchizedek in Gen 14. The narrator describes Melchizedek as "king of Salem" and כֹהֵן לְאֵל עֶלְיוֹן "priest of God Most High" (Gen 14:18). Melchizedek blesses Abraham by "God Most High" and then blesses "God Most High" himself (Gen 14:19). Finally, after Melchizedek makes an offer of material goods to Abraham, the patriarch refuses based on a pledge he claims to have made to "God Most High": "I have sworn to YWHW, God Most High (El Elyon), maker of heaven and earth, that I would not take a thread or a sandal-thong or anything that is yours, so that you might not say, 'I have made Abram rich'" (Gen 14:22–23). This passage is significant for at least two reasons. First, Abraham explicitly connects YHWH with the highest indigenous Canaanite deity, "God Most High." Both Abraham's invocation of YHWH and the syncretism he implies contradicts Exod 6:2–3: "Elohim also spoke to Moses and said to him: 'I am YHWH. I appeared to Abraham, Isaac, and Jacob as El Shaddai, but my name, YHWH, I did not reveal to them.'" Second, the syncretism implied by Abraham's statements directly contradicts the descriptions of עליון and יהוה in Deut 32:8–9 where YHWH is a minor God in the pantheon of "Most High" (see above). It is precisely the syncretism invoked by Abraham that is standard throughout the Hebrew Bible. But I think the effort involved in joining YHWH with "Most High" vindicates my interpretation of Deut 32 above. In other words, the rhetoric of the Gen 14 passage implicitly recognizes "Most High" as a separate (and perhaps more significant) deity than YHWH in its attempt to remedy to problem. It attempts to take a god that is not connected to Israelite/Jewish tradition and invest it with Israelite/Jewish tradition.

The most prolific use of the expression "Most High" is unquestionably found in the Hellenistic Period. Sirach and 4 Ezra alone use the term many more times than the entire Hebrew Bible. It is also used in *Serek haYahad*, the *Damascus Document*, the *War Scroll*, 4QAramaic Apocalypse (4Q246), the *Genesis Apocryphon*, *Jubilees*, *1 Enoch*, the *Prayer of Nabonidus*, *Proto-Esther*, *Apocryphal Pslams*, the *Hodayot*, and several other smaller texts. The largest concentrations in Aramaic are found in the Book of Daniel and the *Genesis Apocryphon* (including the *Book of the Words of Noah*). These texts highlight a nuance in the semantic range of "God Most High" not seen in most pre-exilic texts Israelite and non-Israelite texts.

I discussed the expression קַדִּישֵׁי עֶלְיוֹנִין "holy ones of the Most High" from Dan 7 in chapter two above. Besides these four instances, "Most High" is used nine times in chapters 3–5.[89] It is intriguing that the name is used in chapters 3–7 in the same way that the name אֱלָהּ שְׁמַיָּא "God of

---

[89] 3:26, 3:32[4:2], 4:14[17], 4:21[24], 4:22[25], 4:29[32], 4:31[34], 5:18, 5:21 (English verses in brackets).

Heaven" is used in Dan 2.⁹⁰ This association is intriguing because, as we have seen, many of the earliest uses of "God Most High" describe the deity's height in terms of his place in the hierarchy of the pantheon, i.e., he is the high god. In the Book of Daniel, however, the height of the deity seems to be more of a spatial reference, i.e., the deity who is in heaven. Precisely the same connection between the "God of Heaven" and the "God Most High" is made in the *Genesis Apocryphon* (*Book of the Words of Noah*). After Noah disembarks the ark and plants a vineyard, he builds an altar and blesses למרא שמיא לאל עליון "The Lord of Heaven, God Most High" in 1QapGen 12 17.⁹¹ Based on usage in the Book of Daniel and 1QapGen, I suspect that the expression "God Most High" in 4QFourKingdoms^(a–b) ar must also be synonymous with the divine name "God of Heaven."

A second description of a deity may be found in the expression רב איל]ניא "ruler of the trees" (4Q553 10 2).⁹² We shall see below that trees are primarily used to symbolize kingdoms. But the use of the four kingdoms motif makes it unlikely that the "ruler of the trees" should be construed as one of the four trees. In virtually every expression of the four kingdoms motif one kingdom is replaced by another in chronological succession. The kingdoms do not co-exist and one kingdom never rules over all the others. Therefore it is unlikely that the "ruler of the trees" should be construed as one of the trees. A precedent for the description "ruler of the trees" may be found in the description of God as מ̊רא] ענא "Lord of the Sheep" in the *Animal Apocalypse* (4Q206 4ii 21, ዕጊየ አባግዕ 'ᵉgzi' 'abāgᵉ'). It is clear in the *Animal Apocalypse* that the Lord of the Sheep cannot be one of the sheep – nor can it be a shepherd. Shepherds do appear in the text but as we saw above, "shepherds" is the description used for wicked angels. Perhaps in the same way that the Lord of the Sheep is a description for the God of Israel in the Animal Apocalypse, the Ruler of the Trees should be considered a description of the God of Israel in *Four Kingdoms*.

Angels appear several times in the short text, but in most cases there is so little context that nothing useful can be said about them. No angels are addressed with personal names, but neither are any angels described with the conventional symbolic techniques. In other words, angels are not depicted as humans or stars. In all cases the word מלאך is used. The first instance does not seem to be located within the vision report itself. 4Q552 2i 5 mentions מלאביא די הוו "angels that were." Three lines later the visionary reports, ואמר לי מלכא "and the king said to me." It is possible that the

---

⁹⁰ Cf. 2:18, 19, 28, 37, 44.

⁹¹ Cf. Also 1QapGen 22 16, 21. Like all examples from Qumran, 1QapGen uses Hebrew orthography/vocalization. A similar situation obtains in 4Q457b 2 3 (part of an eschatological hymn edited by E. Chazon in DJD XXIX).

⁹² Puech would recategorize this fragment as 4Q553a 7. Puech, *Qumrân Grotte 4 XXVII*, 88.

text functions similarly to Dan 2 or 4 where a Jewish diviner interprets a dream for a foreign king. In such a case, the angels could be elements of the king's dream or could provide an interpretation for the vision.

The other two mentions of angels come in lines 1–2 of 4Q553 2ii: מלאביא לי מלאכא . . . קד[שיא "ho[ly] angels . . . to me the angel." Very little context exists to help the reader understand these references to angels. What is clear is that the language used to describe angels is, like that used to describe deities in this text, non-symbolic.

Descriptions of Persons

Several individuals appear in 4QFour Kingdoms[a–b] ar, but only one is described with a personal name. Moses (מושה) appears in 4Q553 8i 2. Unfortunately the fragment gives no indication about Moses' function in the text. There is little obvious indication from what is preserved in the text that contains, refers to, or claims to be a Mosaic discourse.[93] The only clue to Moses function is that the name is preceded by the preposition מן "from." Does the text present its symbolic revelation as having come "from Moses"? Is Moses the visionary? The text could also be describing a series of events "from (the time) of Moses." [94] Unfortunately, there is insufficient evidence to know. It is important for the purposes of this study to note that whatever Moses' function in the text, his description is non-symbolic. In other words, unlike the *Animal Apocalypse* above, this human is not described with animal terminology.

Other, unnamed humans are also described with titles in 4QFour Kingdoms[a–b] ar. A king (מלכא) is mentioned in 4Q552 2i 8 and 4Q553 5 1. The only information one may derive from these references is that the king almost certainly has a direct conversation with the visionary in the text: "and the king said to me, because of this" (4Q552 2i 8). Other humans may be described with a similar title in 4Q553 3ii 2: שלי[ט "ruler." It is not entirely clear, however, that the ruler is a human since context provides the reader with no clues. The text says only that טמרו כול שלי[ט "they hid every ruler."

---

[93] On the concept of Mosaic discourse, see Hindy Najman, *Seconding Sinai: The Development of Mosaic Discourse in Second Temple Judaism* (JSJSup 77; Leiden Brill, 2002). Particularly relevant for this study is Najman's second chapter. Therein she takes up *Jub.*, which claims to have been dictated to Moses by an angel. Unfortunately, the function of Moses and the angels in this symbolic apocalypse are entirely unclear.

[94] Thanks to Armin Lange for this suggestion.

Descriptions of Ethno-Political Groups

The final category of historical actors in 4QFour Kingdoms[a–b] ar is the only one described with symbolic language: ethno-political groups. It is these techniques that dominate the text. Four nations are described as trees. Unlike most other apocalypses, the visionary actually interacts with the symbols. I noted examples of dream reports in chapter one where the dreamer converses with a deity, but I am not aware of any cases in which a dreamer/visionary has verbal interaction with the symbols in their dreams – apart from an angelic interpreter.

The number of total trees included in the vision is clear: ארבעה "four" (4Q552 2ii 1, cf. 4Q553 6ii 2). The beginning of the vision report is not preserved, but the beginning of what is preserved depicts the visionary in conversation with someone or something. It is possible that the opening conversation is held with an angel, but the latter conversation is clearly with the individual trees. It is also possible that the entire conversation is between the visionary and the trees, but I find this interpretation less likely since the visionary appears to introduce himself to each tree in turn. During the initial conversation in the vision, he refers to them as a collective group, "four trees."

Part of the meaning of the vision is expressed in terms of the visionary's question (perhaps addressed to an angel): אן אחזה ואתבונן בה "Where should I look that I may understand it?" (4Q553 6ii 3–4, cf. 4Q552 2ii 3–4). While the reader does not know exactly what the visionary desires to understand, the text signals that the answer lies among the trees. After asking אן אחזה "Where should I look?" the visionary finds his answer when he says, וחזית אלנא "And I saw the tree."[95] The verb חזה is used twice – once to ask a question and once to answer it. This question and its solution give the impression that the vision was not a simple example of intuitive divination, such as a dream, but that it is part of a larger revelatory scenario.

The visionary asks the first tree for its name and it replies בבל "Babylon" (4Q553 6ii 4, cf. 4Q552 2ii 5). It is notable that Babylon is also the first kingdom listed among those found in the four kingdom motifs in Dan 2, 7, and 8. In possession of the first tree's name, the visionary replies, ואמרת לה אנתה הוא די שליט בפרס "You are the one who rules over Persia."[96] It is odd that the visionary would describe the tree as "the one who rules over Persia." It was Persia that conquered Babylon in 539 B.C.E.. Moreover, there is little evidence that the Neo-Babylonian empire ever had large holdings in Persia. Its borders seem to have extended only modestly to the east of the

---

[95] Here I combine the readings from 4Q552 2ii 3–4 and 4Q553 6ii 4.
[96] Here I combine the readings from from 4Q552 2ii 6 and 4Q553 6ii 4–5.

Tigris – never beyond the Zagros mountains.[97] On the other hand, Media did rule over Persia and it figures prominently in the histories in Book of Daniel. I suggest that if 4QFour Kingdoms[a–b] ar is reframing or reshaping the traditional four kingdoms motif to include Ptolemaic Egypt or Seleucid Syria or both, the description that the visionary gives to the first tree helps to advance that strategy. Based on other expressions of the motif – particularly Jewish ones – neither Babylon nor Persia nor Media can be ignored. Both Babylon and Persia and perhaps Media are subsumed in one tree and this makes room to include more/later ethno-political groups in the framework of the motif.

Immediately the visionary sees another tree and asks for its name. The tree's response is not preserved, but two clues provide strong evidence for the identification of the tree. First, when the visionary looks at the second tree he claims חזית למערבא "I looked to the west." At the very least one must construe "west" to be west of Babylon. But "west" probably indicates a direction from the perspective of Judea. A second piece of evidence increases the likelihood of a location west of Judea for the tree (i.e., the Mediterranean). The visionary replies to the second tree's (missing) self-identification in the same way that he replied to the first tree's self-identification – by adding precision to the ethno-political term used by the tree: אנתה הוא ד[י] שליט [ועל] תקפי ימא ועל מחוזא "You are he w[ho rules and over the harbors and over the strongholds of the sea" (4Q552 2ii 9–10). Based on the visionary's location of the second tree in the "west" and his attribution to the tree of dominion of "harbors" and "strongholds of the sea," one should probably identify the second tree as Greece.[98] Like the Book of Daniel, "Greece" here could refer to the Macedonian kingdom of Philip and/or Alexander. The tree seems less likely a reference to Phoenicia since the inhabitants of Tyre, Sidon, and Byblos hardly played as significant a role in the geo-politics of the ancient Near East/Mediterranean as Babylon and Persia. Greece did.

The third tree is mentioned, but none of the dialogue between the tree and the visionary is preserved. Nothing about the fourth tree is preserved. One only knows of its existence because of earlier declarations about "four trees." If the second tree represents Greece, then I speculate that the third and fourth kingdoms should be identified as Ptolemaic Egypt and Seleucid

---

[97] Amélie Kuhrt, *The Ancient Near East c. 3000–330 BC.* (vol. 2; London: Routledge, 1995), 589–622. Marc Van De Mieroop, *A History of the Ancient Near East ca. 3000–323 BC* (Padstow, Cornwall: Blackwell, 2004), 253–66.

[98] Puech prefers to read the second kingdom as Media (Persia) and the third as Greece. Given the fragmentary state of the manuscripts, there are several possibilities and this is one. The problem I have is that I am unsure how we should understand Media (Persia) to be west of either Babylon or Judea. Cf. Puech, *Qumrân Grotte 4 XXVII*, 67.

Syria. In the examples of the four kingdoms motif surveyed in chapter one, the kingdoms always appear in historical succession. This general pattern in confirmed by the movement from Babylon to Greece with the first two trees. One should expect, then, that the last two trees should not be contemporaries of Babylon or Greece. Given the date of the text, it is possible that the fourth tree could be Rome. In this case, the third kingdom would need to represent both Ptolemaic Egypt and Seleucid Syria. There is precedent for such a combined description in Dan 2 where the successors of Alexander are described as brittle clay.

Like all symbolic apocalypses, there is a highly structured symbolic framework in *Four Kingdoms*. Many elements of these frameworks can be found across the genre, i.e., Dan 7, 8, and the *Animal Apocalypse* all use humans to represent angels. For other apocalypses, the symbol system is limited to just one text. The symbolic framework of *Four Kingdoms* is dominated by just one symbol-type: the tree. Other ancient Jewish apocalypses make use of the trees as their primary symbol – though the categorical associations they create do not all cut across the genre. For example, in *Four Kingdoms*, trees are used to symbolize kingdoms. On the other hand, a tree is used to symbolize an individual king in Dan 2. What is especially interesting about the use of tree-type symbols in apocalypses is that they function differently than most other uses of trees in ancient Israelite/Jewish literature and material culture. Since the last text in this chapter (*Book of the Words of Noah*) also uses trees as its primary symbol-type, it is useful to survey briefly the most common uses of trees in the literature and material culture of ancient Israel. The tree has a long history in the iconography of the ancient Near East and the literature of ancient Israel, but the use of trees in apocalyptic visions differs from the vast majority of other uses in ancient Judaism.

One may observe the prominence of trees as cultural icons in the ancient Near East from the Early Bronze Age through the Hellenistic period. One of the most recent surveys of this evidence is Othmar Keel's 1998 monograph *Goddesses and Trees, New Moon and Yahweh*.[99] Keel investigates the use of trees as symbols for goddesses in the art of the ancient Near East and the literature of ancient Israel. Keel uses a wide spectrum of evidence – both in terms of chronology and geography – to connect tree images with goddesses.[100] Evidence for the use of trees in connection with goddesses in Israel (*qua* Israel) goes back perhaps to the Late Bronze Age paintings of

---

[99] Othmar Keel, *Goddesses and Trees, New Moon and Yahweh* (JSOTSup 261; Sheffield: Sheffield Academic Press, 1998).

[100] Keel, *Goddesses and Trees*, 20–48.

stylized trees from Tel Qashish, Lachish, and Megiddo.[101] The use of astral symbols in examples from Megiddo lends credence to Keel's claim that the paintings are not merely art, but reflect a cult-based *Sitz im Leben* (similar artistic expressions during the time of the Neo-Assyrian empire are unquestionable).[102]

If the Late Bronze Age evidence is not Israelite, then the Iron Age material certainly is. An important example that underscores Keel's thesis that trees are connected to a goddess (or several goddesses) was mentioned in chapter two: the Ta'anach cult stand (Iron Age II A). In the third register of the cult stand is a stylized tree guarded by lions and flanked by caprids.[103] According to Keel this and other examples of stylized trees from Iron Age Israel stress "the age old Near Eastern concept of the tree as a symbol and signal of the presence of a divine power, namely of prosperity and blessing, which ultimately resides in the earth."[104] A crucial nuance to Keel's argument is that he does not perceive the concept of "tree-goddess" to be appropriate for the ancient Near East or ancient Israel. Rather, Keel argues, "Here we deal more with a goddess of the Earth, of Plant Life, of Sexuality and Prosperity. She does not reveal herself in the tree, which has its own prior existence. The tree is rather the 'most eminent case,' a symbol of vegetation, her most important achievement. The earth goddess existed before the tree, which was brought forth by her."[105]

The literary (i.e., biblical) evidence for trees used as symbols is both larger and more diverse than the evidence that survives in material culture. For example, in several cases there is a connection between a male deity and a tree in the Hebrew Bible. YHWH appears to Moses in הַסְּנֶה "the bush" or "the tree" in Exod 3:1–5. YHWH appears to Abraham בְּאֵלֹנֵי מַמְרֵא "by the oaks at Mamre" in Gen 18:1. Nevertheless the association of tree and goddess found in the material culture of Israel not only survives in, but dominates the literature of ancient Israel. A large number of texts that associate tree and goddess explicitly attack them. A chief example is Hosea 4:13. "They sacrifice on the tops of mountains, and make offerings upon the hills, under oak (אַלּוֹן), poplar (לִבְנֶה), terebinth (אֵלָה), because their (lit. "her") shade (צִלָּה) is good. Because your daughters are promiscuous and your daughters-in-law commit adultery." The verse is part of Hosea's at-

---

[101] Keel, *Goddesses and Trees*, 30, figs. 37–8.
[102] For the iconography of Palestine during the time of the Neo-Assyrian period, see Keel and Uehlinger, *Gods*, 283–372.
[103] Cf. Keel and Uehlinger, *Gods*, 154–60.
[104] Keel, *Goddesses and Trees*, 46.
[105] Keel, *Goddesses and Trees*, 48.

tack on a chief priest and his children.¹⁰⁶ Another, even more obvious connection between a tree and a goddess is found in the description of the reign of Asa in 1 Kgs 15:13. "He also removed Maacah his mother from being queen because she had made an abominable image for Asherah (מִפְלֶצֶת לָאֲשֵׁרָה), Asa cut down her image and burned it at the Wadi Kidron." The verb כרת "cut" is of primary importance. In terms of cult images known from ancient Israel, a stylized tree or pole is what one would "cut down."¹⁰⁷ The association of the goddess Asherah with the cult-tree of Maacah is clear.¹⁰⁸

Despite strident criticisms such as the ones leveled by Hosea and the Deuteronomistic Historian, the connection between trees and goddesses seems to have survived – even if mitigated or transformed – in Hellenistic period. For example, Sir 24:12–19 uses a variety of tree images to describe חכמה – "Lady Wisdom." Moreover, Carol Meyers has drawn attention to the similarity of the seven-branched lampstand in the priestly tradition (i.e., the menorah) and the older stylized tree:

> Not only does the opposite verticillate arrangement of the branches of the tabernacle menorah find extensive analogy among plant representations of the ancient Near East, but the very number of branches, six-plus-one, turns out to be the preferred arrangement of its parallels.¹⁰⁹

While there is some continuity between the Iron Age and the Hellenistic Period, different and diverse uses of tree symbolism also begin to develop in the Hellenistic period. Nowhere is this truer than in apocalyptic visions. Several apocalypses/apocalyptic visions use trees as symbols – but never for a goddess. Instead, trees are used to represent ethno-political groups (kingdoms) and individual humans (sometimes kings and sometimes notable Jewish figures).

The most conspicuous use of a tree in the context of a vision in the Hebrew Bible is Dan 4. Dan 4 is not an apocalypse according to the strictest definitions. It does stand in very close proximity to apocalypses in terms of its 1) literary form and its 2) inclusion in the Maccabean Daniel-collection. The latter is probably the most important association for the present purposes. Dan 4 might not be a product of the Hellenistic period, but the Book

---

¹⁰⁶ This passage has often been read as a reference to cult prostitution. See Francis Anderson and David Noel Freedman, *Hosea* (AB 24; New York: Doubleday, 1980), 368. More recent work calls any such practice into doubt. See most recently Stephanie Lynn Budin, *The Myth of Sacred Prostitution in Antiquity* (Cambridge: Cambridge University Press, 2008).

¹⁰⁷ Other types of objects were made for Asherah. For example, 2 Kings 23:7 claims that certain women "did weaving" (אֹרְגוֹת) for Asherah. The act of cutting or chopping is more likely relevant to a tree or pole.

¹⁰⁸ Cf. also Deut 16:21, 2 Kgs 21:3, 23:15.

¹⁰⁹ Meyers, *The Tabernacle Menorah*, 95–122.

of Daniel certainly is and it is only reasonable to expect that the overall shape of Daniel affected how chapter 4 was interpreted both in the Hellenistic period and in later times. In the text King Nebuchadnezzar has a dream about a great tree and only Daniel is able to interpret it for him. Unlike Dan 2, the king is willing to give a description of his vision to any diviner who will attempt to interpret it.

> Upon my bed this is what I saw, there was a tree at the center of the earth, and its height was great. The tree grew great and strong, its top reached to heaven, and it was visible to the ends of the whole earth. Its foliage was beautiful, its fruit abundant, and it provided food for all. The animals of the field found shade under it, the birds of the air nested in its branches, and from it all living beings were fed (Dan 4:7–9[10–12]).

After a brief interlude, Nebuchadnezzar's dream continues and an angel descends from heaven to pronounce judgment on the tree:

> Cut down the tree and chop off its branches, strip off its foliage and scatter its fruit. Let the animals flee from beneath it, and the birds from its branches. But leave its stump and roots in the ground, with a band of iron and bronze, in the tender grass of the field. Let him be bathed with the dew of heaven, and let his lot be with the animals of the field in the grass of the earth. Let his mind be changed from that of a human, and let the mind of an animal be given to him. And let seven times pass over him. (Dan 4:10–13[13–16])

Daniel tells Nebuchadnezzar that he is the tree. But this tree symbolism is not as different from that of 4QFour Kingdoms^{a–b} ar as it might first appear. The tree represents not only Nebuchadnezzar as an individual, but the entirety of Babylon to the extent that Babylon is an extension of the king himself. Reading the tree as a symbol of "king" and "kingship" is reinforced by Daniel's interpretation of the tree, "It is you, O King! You have grown great and strong. Your greatness has increased and reaches to heaven, and your sovereignty (שָׁלְטָנָךְ) to the ends of the earth" (Dan 4:19[22]). In other words, the greatness of the king is not related to morality or piety. The size of the tree is related to the size of the kingdom – not the significance of Nebuchadnezzar's character. Moreover, Daniel's interpretation of the stump makes the connection even more emphatic. "As it was commanded to leave the stump and roots of the tree, your kingdom shall be reestablished for you from the time that you learn that Heaven is sovereign" (Dan 4:23[26]). Enough of the tree will be left to reconstitute the kingdom of Nebuchadnezzar – not just the man.

Additional evidence from the account of the events presaged by Nebuchadnezzar's dream associates the tree not only with the person of Nebuchadnezzar, but also his kingdom. In a final, defiant, albeit unwitting act of hubris, the king declares, "Is this not magnificent (רַבְּתָא) Babylon, which I have built as a royal capital by my mighty power (בִּתְקָף חִסְנִי) and for my glorious majesty (לִיקָר הַדְרִי)?" (Dan 4:27[30]). Some of the same words used to describe Babylon in 4:27[30] are used to describe the tree in the vision and in the interpretation: "The tree grew great (רְבָה) and strong (וּתְקֵף)" (Dan 4:8[11]). Thus while there is a difference in the meaning of the trees used in 4QFour Kingdoms[a–b] ar and Dan 4, it is not as significant as it first appears. *Four Kingdoms* uses trees to symbolize kingdoms and Dan 4 uses a tree to symbolize a king – with specific associations to his kingdom. In both cases trees are used as symbols for humans (i.e., both individuals and groups).

Trees are also used in two apocalyptic visions unknown before the discovery of the Dead Sea Scrolls. These visions are embedded in *The Book of the Words of Noah* (1QapGen 5–18) and *The Book of Giants* respectively. I deal with these texts below, but I mention for now that at least one of the trees in the *Book of the Words of Noah* represents Noah and another perhaps represents Adam. It also appears as if one of the trees in a dream from the *Book of Giants* might be Noah. What one can conclude at this point, however, is that the use of trees as symbols in 4QFourKingdoms[a–b] ar is consistent with other uses in apocalyptic visions from the Hellenistic Period. It is considerably different, however, than the vast majority of tree-imagery known from Israelite literature and material culture.

Raw Data from 4QFour Kingdoms[a–b] ar

4Q552 3 10	אל עליון	God Most High	Explicit: Divine Name + Epithet
4Q552 2i 5	מלאכיא	The angels	Explicit: title
4Q553 2ii 1	מלאכיא קד[ישיא	The holy angels	Explicit: title + adjective
4Q553 2ii 2	מלאכא	The angel	Explicit: title

4Q553 8i 2	מושה	Moses	Explicit: Personal Name
4Q552 2i 8	מלכא	The king	Explicit: title
4Q553 5 1	מֹלכֹּא	The king	Explicit: title
4Q553 3ii 2	שלי]ט	Ruler	Explicit: title
4Q552 2ii 1=4Q553 6ii 2	ארבעה איליניא	Four trees (Babylon, Greece, Ptolemaic Egypt?, Seleucid Syria?)	Symbolic: tree
4Q552 2ii 4=4Q553 6ii 4	אילנא	Tree (Babylon)	Symbolic: tree
4Q552 2ii 6=4Q553 6ii 5	אילנא	Tree (Greece?)	Symbolic: tree
4Q552 2ii 11	אילנא תליֹתי]א	The third tree (Ptolemaic Egypt?)	Symbolic: tree
4Q553 10 2	רב איל]ניא	Ruler of the tre[es	Symbolic: tree
4Q553 10 3	איל]ניא	The trees	Symbolic: tree

Book of the Words of Noah (1QapGen 5 29–18 ?)
There are at least five dream visions in the *Genesis Apocryphon*. Three of the dreams are visions experienced by Abraham. One is a symbolic dream (1QapGen 19 14–18) and the other two are non-symbolic (message) dreams (1QapGen 21 8–10, 22 27ff). None of the dreams attributed to Abraham exhibit an imminent eschatology. While it is possible to overstate the importance of imminent eschatology in apocalypses, it is probably fair to say that there is no eschatology involved in Abraham's visions. The dreams of Noah are another matter.[110]

Two dream visions are associated with Noah. One is symbolic (1QapGen 12?–15) and the other non-symbolic (1QapGen 6). The portions of the text containing the dreams are poorly preserved, but enough evidence exists to characterize the language used therein. The symbolic dream is of primary interest for this chapter, though the raw data for the non-symbolic vision is also included below. Some preliminary remarks about the literary context of the dream (1QapGen 5 29–18 ?) are necessary before discussing the language of Noah's symbolic vision.

The *Book of the Words of Noah* perhaps exists, though not necessarily in a pristine or original form, in 1QapGen (5 29–18 ?). That there once existed a *Book of Noah* was suspected long before the discovery of the *Genesis Apocryphon*. Twice the book of *Jubilees* appears to allude to a book of Noah:

> Noah wrote down in a book everything (just) as we had taught him regarding all the kinds of medicine, and the evil spirits were precluded from pursuing Noah's children. He gave all the books that he had written to his oldest son Shem because he loved him much more than all his sons. (*Jub.* 10:13–14)

> Eat its meat during that day and on the next day; but the sun is not to set on it on the next day until it is eaten. It is not to be left over for the third day because it is not acceptable to him. For it was not pleasing and is not therefore commanded. All who eat it will bring guilt on themselves because this is the way I found (it) written in the book of my ancestors, in the words of Enoch and the words of Noah. (*Jub.* 21:10)[111]

Another allusion is found in the *Aramaic Levi Document*.[112] The relevant passage is not extant in Aramaic from Qumran, but can be found in a Greek translation (a variant Greek manuscript of *The Testament of the Twelve*

---

[110] On reading the *Genesis Apocryphon* as an apocalypse, see Daniel A. Machiela, "Genesis Revealed: The Apocalyptic Apocryphon from Qumran Cave 1," in *Qumran Cave 1 Revisited. Texts from Cave 1 Sixty Years after Their Discovery: Proceedings of the Sixth Meeting of the IOQS in Ljubljana* (eds., Daniel K. Falk et al; STDJ 91; Leiden: Brill, 2010), 205–21.

[111] Trans. VanderKam, *The Book of Jubilees*, 60, 123.

[112] The definitive study of this text is Greenfield et al., *The Aramaic Levi Document: Edition, Translation, Commentary*.

Patriarchs (*Testament of Levi*). There it is reported that several commandments given by Isaac to Levi were τῆς βιβλίου τοῦ Νῶε περὶ τοῦ αἵματος "of the Book of Noah concerning the blood" (*Aramaic Levi Document* 10 10).[113]

F. García-Martínez made a major step forward when he argued that these passages present more than passing mentions of a hypothetical *Book of Noah*.[114] According to him, the passages summarize the contents of the putative book. By comparing the content summarized in *Jubilees* with the Noachic materials in *1 Enoch* and *Jubilees*, he concluded that a *Book of Noah* must have existed and suggested that it is probably summarized by the *Genesis Apocryphon*.[115] As more advances were made in deciphering and organizing the text of the *Genesis Apocryphon*, a major discovery gave support to his view.

Richard Steiner published an article in 1995 in which he argued that three newly deciphered words in 1QapGen 5 29 (כתב מלי נח) should be understood as a title, "Book of the Words of Noah."[116] By comparing the title with other similar formulae from biblical and post-biblical Jewish writings, Steiner lent credence to the original instincts of Avigad and Yadin that 1QapGen should not be understood as a single work, but an anthology: "The work is evidently a literary unit in style and structure, though for the reasons referred to above, it may perhaps be divisible into books – a Book of Lamech, a Book of Enoch, Book of Noah, a Book of Abraham."[117]

The particular source-divisions made by Avigad and Yadin have not all been retained as such. In A. Lange's more recent assessment, he divides

---

[113] Neither grammar nor syntax can resolve the ambiguity in the text presented by περὶ τοῦ αἵματος. On the two (equally) possible readings, see Greenfield et al., *The Aramaic Levi Document: Edition, Translation, Commentary*, 180.

[114] Florentino García Martínez, *Qumran and Apocalyptic. Studies on the Aramaic Texts from Qumran* (Leiden Brill, 1992), 24–6. It must be noted, as García-Martínez himself points out, that such a work is not found in any of the old catalogues of apocryphal books. Cf. A.-M. Denis, *Introduction aux Pseudépigraphes grecs d'Ancien Testament* (SVTP 1; Leiden Brill, 1970), XIV–XV. Moreover, he is skeptical of the evidence from medieval texts.

[115] I must leave aside for now the contentious issue of influence between *Jub.*, *1 En.*, and *Genesis Apocryphon*. Most recently, see James Kugel, "Which is Older, Jubilees or the Genesis Apocryphon? Some Exegetical Considerations" (paper presented at the conference The Dead Sea Scrolls and Contemporary Culture, Hebrew University, Jerusalem, July 6–8, 2008 2008). Hanneken, "The Book of Jubilees among the Apocalypses" 146–7. Machiela, "Each to His Own Inheritance: Geography as an Evaluative Tool in the Genesis Apocryphon," 50–66. Michael Segal, *The Book of Jubilees: Rewritten Bible, Redaction, Ideology and Theology* (JSJSup 117; Leiden Brill, 2007).

[116] Richard Steiner, "The Heading of the *Book of the Words of Noah* on a Fragment of the Genesis Apocryphon: New Light on a "Lost" Work," *DSD* 2 (1995): 66–71.

[117] N. Avigad and Y. Yadin, *A Genesis Apocryphon: A Scroll from the Desert of Judah: Description and Contents of the Scroll, Facsimiles, Transcription and Translation of Columns II, XIX–XXII* (Jerusalem: Magnes Press, 1956), 38.

the scroll into three major sections: 1) a narrative on the birth of Noah (I–V), 2) the *Book of the Words of Noah* (V–XVIII), and 3) a rewritten Bible version of the Abraham cycle (XVIII–XXII).[118] Lange characterizes the *Book of the Words of Noah* as, "A renarration of Gen 6–9, which enlarges the Biblical story with two apocalyptic dreams of Noah and a detailed description of the apportionment of the earth to Noah's sons."[119] Not all scholars accept the hypothesis of a *Book of Noah*, though their rejection of the concept of an original, independent book would not alter Lange's basic characterization of the narrative structure of 1QapGen V–XVIII.

The most prominent voices who reject the concept of a *Book of Noah* are Cana Werman, Moshe Bernstein, and Devorah Dimant.[120] Werman argues (contra García-Martínez) that the material attributed to a *Book of Noah* by several of the texts that ostensibly paraphrase or quote from it is far too diverse to reflect a single parent-text. Werman is no doubt correct that a range of material is attributed to the *Book of Noah*. But this diversity does not demand that a *Book of Noah* could not have existed (one might consider the variety of literary forms and context in the Book of Numbers). Moreover, some of the ancient witnesses appear to agree on the content of the book. For example, the accounts of Noah planting a vineyard in the 1QapGen (XII) and *Jub.* (7) are quite similar. Werman acknowledges these agreements, but prefers to explain them by positing that *Jubilees* used both the *Genesis Apocryphon* and *1 Enoch* as sources.[121] Another point that must be raised against Werman's argument is that some of the evidence she uses to impeach the contents of the *Book of Noah* is far from certain itself. For example, whether or not *Jubilees* was influenced by a precursor to the me-

---

[118] Armin Lange, "The Parabiblical Literature of the Qumran Library and the Canonical History of the Hebrew Bible," in *Emanuel: Studies in the Hebrew Bible, Septuagint, and Dead Sea Scrolls in Honor of Emanuel Tov* (ed. S. Paul, et al.; vol. XCIV of *VTsup*; Leiden: Brill, 2003), 312. Cf. also Sidnie White Crawford, *Rewriting Scriptures in Second Temple Times* (Grand Rapids: Eerdmans, 2008), 105–29.

[119] Lange, "The Parabiblical Literature," 312. VanderKam has shown that in its renarration of Gen, 1QapGen presupposes a pre-Samaritan (Pentateuch) text-type. VanderKam labels this Old Palestinian. James VanderKam, "The Textual Affinities of the Biblical Citations in the Genesis Apocryphon," 97 (1978): 45–55.

[120] Cana Werman, "Qumran and the Book of Noah," in *Pseudepigraphical Perspectives: Proceedings of the Second International Symposium of the Orion Center for the Study of the Dead Sea Scrolls and Associated Literature, 12–14 January, 1997* (ed. E. Chazon and M. Stone; vol. 31 of STDJ; Leiden: Brill, 1999), 91–120. Moshe Bernstein, "Noah and the Flood at Qumran," in *The Provo International Conference on the Dead Sea Scrolls. Technological Innovations, New Texts, & Reformulated Issues* (ed. D. Parry and E. Ulrich; vol. 30 of STDJ; Leiden Brill, 1999), 199–231. Devorah Dimant, "Two 'Scientific' Fictions: The So-called Book of Noah and the Alleged Quotation of Jubilees in CD 16:3–4," in *Studies in the Hebrew Bible, Qumran, and Septuagint Presented to Eugene Ulrich* (ed. P. Flint, et al.; vol. 101 of VTsup; Leiden: Brill, 2006), 230–49.

[121] Werman, "Qumran and the Book of Noah," 181.

dieval composition, *Book of Asaph*, is at least as questionable as whether or not there existed a *Book of Noah*.[122]

M. Bernstein deals with the question of the *Book of Noah* in an essay published in the same year as Werman's essay. Bernstein takes a more measured view to the extent that he only opposes the concept of a *Book of Noah* as a broad, large-scale document. Indeed he attempts to reframe the question away from "was there or was there not a *Book of Noah*" and asks if there might not have been several small-scale "books of Noah" that would have been expansions and reworkings of various aspects of Gen 6–9. He suggests that, "The 'book of the words of Noah' apparently cited in 1QapGen 5:29 might very well be an expanded first-person narrative of the flood story, including the events leading to it and its aftermath."[123] Thus, Bernstein does not reject the evidence for a *Book of Noah* (*a la* Werman and Dimant) as much as he urges a minimalist interpretation of the evidence. While I am less concerned about the apparent variety of material that must have been included in a large scale *Book of Noah* if one existed, I find nothing objectionable in the logic of Bernstein's analysis. He may be correct.

Devorah Dimant has dealt with the question of the *Book of Noah* in three different essays.[124] For issues of space and fairness to Dimant, I comment only on her last essay. Dimant attacks the concept of a *Book of Noah* as a "scientific fiction" in her latest contribution to the ongoing debate. She approaches the question from two angles. She first considers theories about the *Book of Noah* from before the discovery of the Dead Sea Scrolls and then considers theories developed after the discovery of the scrolls. She attempts to show that some of the first theories about a *Book of Noah* were uncritically accepted and that, in light of the data from the scrolls, these theories grew into accepted facts. One must agree with Dimant that the existence of the *Book of Noah* is hardly a scientific fact and she raises some important concerns – especially, to my mind, the association of 4Q534, 4Q535, and 4Q536 (*Birth of Noah*$^{a\text{-}c}$) with Noah.[125] But I am not persuaded that she has falsified any of the arguments made for a *Book of Noah* – whether before or after the discovery of the scrolls. For example, while the allusions to books of Noah in the *Book of Jubilees* are hardly definitive

---

[122] Werman, "Qumran and the Book of Noah," 171–3.

[123] Bernstein, "Noah and the Flood at Qumran," 229.

[124] Devorah Dimant, "The Fallen Angels in the Dead Sea Scrolls and in the Apocryphal and Pseudepigraphical Books Related to Them [Hebrew]" (Unpublished Ph.D. dissertation, Hebrew University of Jerusalem, 1974) 122–40. Devorah Dimant, "Noah in Early Jewish Literature; Appendix: The So-Called Book of Noah," in *Biblical Figures Outside the Bible* (ed. M. Stone and T. Bergren; Harrisburg, PA: Trinity Press, 1998). Dimant, "Two 'Scientific' Fictions," 230–49.

[125] Dimant, "Two 'Scientific' Fictions," 239–40.

evidence, neither can they be dismissed since *Jubilees'* allusion to a Book of Enoch (21:10) is demonstrably correct.[126] Similarly, Dimant treats the heading כתב מלי נח from 1QapGen 5 29 as no different from the allusions cited from *Jubilees* above. She is correct that appealing to a fictitious book is a known literary device from antiquity, but this does not make the heading irrelevant as evidence (one would not want to claim that *every* use of a heading in antiquity is an appeal to a fictitious book).[127] Steiner marshals not a small amount of comparative data for the title *Book of the Words of Noah* (*qua* title), but Dimant dismisses it out of hand.[128] Therefore, while Dimant's essay clearly intends to urge caution (a welcome sentiment), its ultimate claim that all arguments for a *Book of Noah* are faulty and unsupported by available evidence significantly underestimates the positive arguments.[129]

In the most recent publications that address the question, it is safe to say that a majority of scholars adopt a cautiously optimistic position that the book existed and is in some way present in 1QapGen.[130] The most recent of these voices to argue about the subject in detail is Michael Stone.[131] His presentation of the evidence is the most sophisticated to date. Nevertheless, he calls for a fresh analysis of all materials mentioning Noah, especially the birth narratives.[132] He makes this call because while he is convinced that there was a *Book of Noah*, he thinks is possible that there might have existed more than one.[133] His position is, therefore, not entirely different than Bernstein even if he presents a less minimalist interpretation of the evidence.

---

[126] The declarative statement of Torrey, quoted by Dimant, is no argument at all: "The allusions to Noah's written wisdom in *Jub* 10:10–14 and 21:10 are no evidence of a lost book!" Cf. Dimant, "Two 'Scientific' Fictions," 232.

[127] Dimant, "Two 'Scientific' Fictions," 241.

[128] Steiner, "The Heading of the *Book of the Words of Noah* on a Fragment of the Genesis Apocryphon: New Light on a "Lost" Work," 66–9.

[129] Dimant, "Two 'Scientific' Fictions," 242.

[130] Crawford, Rewriting Scriptures in Second Temple Times, 110–1. Daniel Falk, *The Parabiblical Texts: Strategies for Extending the Scriptures in the Dead Sea Scrolls* (63; London: T&T Clark, 2007), 100–1. Joseph Fitzmyer, *The Genesis Apocryphon of Qumran Cave 1 (1Q20): A Commentary* (BO 18B; Rome: Editrice Pontificio Instituto Biblico, 2004), 144. The same position has been argued in several conference papers as well as personel communication to me by University of Vienna Ph.D. candidate Matthias Weigold.

[131] Michael Stone, "The Book(s) Attributed to Noah," *DSD* 13 (2006): 4–23. See also the new collection of essays: Michael Stone, Aryeh Amihay, Vered Hillel, eds., *Noah and His Book(s)* (EJS 28; Atlanta: SBL, 2010). Stone's collected volume appeared too late to be incorporated into this study.

[132] Several recent and forthcoming studies address this problem. See Dorothy Peters, *Noah Traditions in the Dead Sea Scrolls: Conversations and Controversies of Antiquity* (SBLEJL 26; Atlanta: SBL, 2008).

[133] Stone, "The Book(s) Attributed to Noah," 18.

Dating the *Book of the Words of Noah* is difficult, but one can establish a *terminus ante quem* with the date of composition for the *Genesis Apocryphon*. It is impossible to be precise in dating the *Genesis Apocryphon*, but as A. Lange points out, the text's language and its reception point to a date in the third century B.C.E.:

> To date the *Book of the Words of Noah* to the third century B.C.E. is recommended by its reception in *Jub.* 8–9, in the 3rd book of the *Sib. Or.* (110–61), and in 1QM I–II. According to Morgenstern, Qimron, and Sivan, this date is confirmed by the Aramaic peculiarities of the *Book of the Words of Noah*.[134]

Lange has addressed the date of the text more recently and raised the possiblility that the *Book of Tobit* is influenced by Noah's endogamy in the *Book of the Words of Noah*. Such a reception would certainly point towards an origin no later than the third century B.C.E..[135] Others take a different tack and prefer to date the *Genesis Apocryphon* later. Sidnie White Crawford argues for a first century date by arguing that the text is dependant upon the books of *1 Enoch* and *Jubilees*.[136] Fitzmyer argues that the Aramaic of the text indicates a date between the first century B.C.E. and the first century CE.[137] As mentioned above, however, Morgenstern, Qimron, and Sivan believe that the Aramaic indicates a third century date.

Within the *Book of the Words of Noah*, only a portion of the text is immediately relevant for this study. As mentioned earlier, the book contains two apocalyptic dreams of Noah. The first is found in column six and the second in columns twelve(?)–fifteen. There are actually two allusions to visions in column 6 (11, 14). It is not necessary, however, that these allusions indicate two separate visions. I agree with M. Bernstein that it is possible that, "The 'first' is a general statement which is then expanded and explained in the 'second.'"[138] In other words, the first allusion is made as

---

[134] Lange, "The Parabiblical Literature," 313. On the reception of the *Book of the Words of Noah*, see James Scott, "The Division of the Earth in *Jubilees* 8:11–9:15 and Early Christian Chronography," in *Studies in the Book of Jubilees* (ed. M. Albani, et al.; vol. 65 of *TSAJ*; Tübingen: Mohr Siebeck, 1997), 295–323. On the Aramaic of the text, see M. Morgenstern et al., "The Hitherto Unpublished Columns of the Genesis Apocryphon," *AbrN* 33 (1995): 30–54.

[135] Armin Lange, "Your Daughters Do Not Give to Their Sons and Their Daughters Do Not Take for Your Sons: Intermarriage in Ezra 9–10 and in the Pre-Maccabean Dead Sea Scrolls. Teil 1," *BN* 137 (2008): 34. See also Armin Lange, "Your Daughters Do Not Give to Their Sons and Their Daughters Do Not Take for Your Sons: Intermarriage in Ezra 9–10 and in the Pre-Maccabean Dead Sea Scrolls. Teil 2," *BN* 139 (2008): 79–98.

[136] Crawford, *Rewriting Scriptures in Second Temple Times*, 106.

[137] Fitzmyer, *The Genesis Apocryphon*, 29–37.

[138] Moshe Bernstein, "From the Watchers to the Flood: Story and Exegesis in the Early Columns of the Genesis Apocryphon," in *Reworking the Bible: Apocryphal and Related Texts at Qumran. Proceedings of a Joint Symposium by the Orion Center for the Study of the Dead Sea Scrolls and Associated Literature and the Hebrew University Institute for Advanced Studies*

an introduction which summarizes the contexts of the vision and the second allusion is part of the formula that bounds the report of the actual vision. Noah's own brief characterization of the vision (i.e., the first allusion) states that he was, "shown and informed about the conduct of the sons of heaven" (1QapGen 6 11).[139] With the second allusion, the reader is informed of the means of revelation: an angel. "In a vision he spoke with me; he was standing before me" (וקובלי קם 1QapGen 6 14). One should note that we have already seen that it is characteristic of non-symbolic dream visions (and many apocalypses) to describe a deity or angel as "standing" before the dreamer or visionary.

The content found in lines nineteen and twenty agrees with the introductory summary found in line eleven. Line 19 of the angelic interpretation mentions "the blood that the Nephilim shed" and line 20 mentions "holy ones who were with the daughters of m[en]." Thus, as Bernstein points out, the sins of the fallen angels in the dream vision of 1QapGen 6, "involve both murder and immorality."[140] It is not clear exactly when the dream vision ends in column six, though it must end before line twenty-six where cattle, animals, and birds are used *not* symbolically, but explicitly to refer to the wildlife that Noah took on the ark with him.

The second vision located in columns 12(?)–15 unquestionably contains both a symbolic vision and an angelic interpretation. A variety of representation techniques are used, but the primary symbol is the tree. Metals, stars, and humans are also used. These symbol types align with those seen in other symbolic apocalypses. Indeed, in light of the Daniel apocalypses, the *Animal Apocalypse*, and 4QFourKingdoms$^{a–b}$ ar, there appears to have been a relatively limited and stable repertoire of symbol types used by those who crafted apocalypses/apocalyptic visions during the Hellenistic period.

The content of the second vision shares some similarities with other well known apocalyptic visions such as Enoch's *Vision of Earth's Destruction* (*1 En*. 83–84, i.e. the first vision in the *Book of Dreams*) and Balaam's Vision of the Deluge in the *Deir Alla Inscription*.[141] These similarities are interesting because in the biblical account of the Flood, God speaks directly to Noah and informs him, "I have determined to make an end of all flesh, for the earth is filled with violence because of them; now I am going to destroy

---

Research Group on Qumran, 15–17 January, 2002 (ed. E. Chazon, et al.; vol. LVIII of STDJ; Leiden: Brill, 2005), 55.

[139] Unless otherwise noted, translations of 1QapGen are taken from Fitzmyer, *The Genesis Apocryphon*. In some cases I have made minor adjustments to Fitzmyer's translations without providing special notice.

[140] Bernstein, "From the Watchers to the Flood," 55.

[141] Nickelsburg, *1 Enoch 1*, 347–8. For the *Deir Alla Inscription*, see Jo Ann Hackett, *The Balaam Text from Deir Alla* (31; Chico: Scholars Press, 1984).

them along with the earth" (Gen 6:13, *P* account). God then gives Noah instructions for constructing and filling the ark. In the *Genesis Apocryphon*, however, Noah is apparently warned through a symbolic vision that must be interpreted by an angel.

One problem with this interpretation of the vision is that the flood has apparently taken place in the text before it is predicted in the dream vision. For example, the ark comes to rest "on of the mountains of Ararat" in 10 12. The fragmentary nature of the text makes this problem especially pronounced since various kinds of transitions and other structural elements that might clarify the narrative flow of the text could be missing. One must for now live with the possibility that the discovery of a more intact copy of the text would falsify or confirm my reading.

Descriptions of Persons
The most obvious description of a person in the symbolic vision of the *Book of the Words of Noah* is Noah himself, who appears as a tree. The vision involves several trees, some of which are designated as particular species. Cedar (14 9, 11, 27) and olive (13 13, 15–16) are explicitly mentioned. The angelic interpreter tells Noah, אנתה הוא ארזא רב[א "You are the great cedar" (14 9). Unfortunately, the actual description of the great cedar from the symbolic vision is not extant. There is, however, a lengthy description of an olive tree in the vision and one expects that the same kind of description was also used for the great cedar in the vision (the schematic use of the trees indicates that the narrative pattern probably repeats for each tree).

We saw above that trees are also used to describe kingdoms (4QFour Kingdoms[a–b] ar) and individual humans (Dan 4, *Book of Giants*). The use of trees in this text agrees with the pattern of usage found in these texts. Trees were used to represent humans (both individuals and groups) in ancient Jewish historical apocalypses. Evidence from the *Book of the Words of Noah* helps to indicate that a preliminary conclusion made above is accurate: a stable and limited repertoire of symbol-types is used in ancient Jewish apocalypses. Moreover, these symbol types often reflect categorical relationships that are manifest across the genre. For example, stars and humans are always used to represent angels. Now we see that trees are always used to represent humans (both individuals and ethno-political groups).

Noah's son's Ham, Shem, and Yaphet are also described in the vision as tree branches: "[and h]igh grew a scion (חלפא) that comes forth from it and rises to its height (as) three s[on]s (10 14) "(תלתת ב[ני]ן). The text becomes highly fragmentary after this, but seems to give descriptions of individual scions and designates one scion as the "true" heir of Noah, the one, "who will part from you all his days, and among his descendants your n[am]e will be called" (14 12). This scion is undoubtedly Shem. At least one other scion is described individually, but there is virtually nothing left in the text to help interpret it (14 15).

The descendents of Noah's sons are described as קצת "branch(es)." Intermarriage is specifically implied and implicitly condemned when the dream reports describes, "some of their branches entering into the branches of the first one" (14 16, 17).[142] In other words, there takes place an inappropriate mixing of tree branches (descendents). This meaning would agree with the more general way in which the *Book of the Words of Noah* champions endogamy.[143] It is unclear if the text envisions any specific instance of intermarriage, but if so the candidates are few. The most likely possibility would appear to be Abraham's relationship with Hagar and the resulting birth of Ishmael (Gen 16). The union of Abraham and Hagar represented a union between the lines of Shem (Abraham) and Ham (Hagar).

A parallel for this vision of trees can be found in the *Book of Giants*. Therein two giants, *Hahyah* and *Ohya,* each have a dream. *Hahyah* dreams of a garden in which there are trees. One of the trees has three shoots (6Q8 2 1).[144] It is possible that these three shoots (תלתת שרשוהי) could represent the three sons of Noah. Other copies of the same text allude to a time when the garden was "covered with all the water" (4Q530 2ii + 6 + 7i + 8–11 + 12 10). Thus *Hahyah*'s dream may involve Noah, his three sons, and the great deluge.

The *Book of Giants* may be dated between 250 and 164 B.C.E..[145] The main criteria used to arrive at this date are 1) dependence on the *Book of Watchers* (*1 En.* 1–36) and 2) its influence on Dan 7. It may provide additional evidence for the use of trees to symbolize humans in apocalyptic/visionary literature of the Hellenistic Period.

Other Symbols
Several symbols are used in addition to the ones discussed above, but there is very little context with which to interpret them. Therefore I treat them all together here. Several trees other than the great cedar and its descendents function in the text. The most notable is an olive tree (זיתא) in 13 13–17.

---

[142] Line 17 may be a case of dittography.

[143] Lange, "Your Daughters Do Not Give to Their Sons," 34–36.

[144] There are differing opinions on which dream these three shoots of a tree fit. See Loren Stuckenbruck, *The Book of Giants from Qumran: Texts, Translation, and Commentary* (TSAJ 63; Tübingen: Mohr Siebeck, 1997), 201–3.

[145] Lange, "The Parabiblical Literature," 311. Stuckenbruck, *The Book of Giants from Qumran: Texts, Translation, and Commentary*, 28–31.

The olive tree seems to precede the appearance of the oak tree in the dream vision, but this is unclear since at least six lines of columns fourteen and fifteen are missing. Thus, we have only the interpretation of the oak tree (but not its description in the vision) and only the description of the olive tree (but not its angelic interpretation). Noah reports that he is amazed at the rapid growth of the olive tree. Its height as well as its abundant foliage and fruit are emphasized. It lasts only a brief time though. The olive tree becomes a victim of [ארבע] [רוחי שמיא] "the [four] winds of heaven" (13 16). The tree is limbed and broken into pieces. Descriptions for the damages inflicted by each individual wind are apparently included in the text, but only the damage wrought by the west wind is preserved (13 16–17). The west wind strips the tree of its fruit and leaves. The angelic interpretation for the olive tree is not preserved, but the literary conventions of symbolic apocalypses offer some help.[146] While not every apocalypse uses every symbol in precisely the same way, we have seen that the symbols used in each apocalypse function in a limited, categorical relationship with particular classes of referents. In other words, since one can know with certainty that a cedar tree is used to describe Noah and that an oak tree refers to Abraham in a vision later in the *Apocryphon of Jeremiah*, one can reasonably deduce the relationship *tree=human* in Noah's symbolic dream vision. Based on this educated assumption as well as the possibility that the olive tree appears before the cedar tree, it would make most sense to identify the olive tree as Adam.[147] All of Adam's offspring and their descendents (with the exception of Noah and family) are destroyed in the flood. It is unclear to me who else would even be a candidate as long as one presumes that the olive tree precedes the cedar tree in the vision. If the olive tree does not precede the cedar tree (historically) in the vision itself, however, the referent of the olive tree is unclear.

In addition to the specific description of an olive tree, other arbors are described merely as אילניא "trees" (13 10). This is the same tree terminology used by 4QFour Kingdoms[a–b] ar. In column thirteen Noah sees multiple trees cut down. Within the same portion of the dream Noah also sees some items comprised of gold, silver, and iron as well as the sun, moon, and stars:

They were breaking stones and ceramic pots and taking from it for themselves. (As) I was watching those of gold and silver (דהבא ולכס[פי]א), the [of] iron (פרזלא); and they were chopping all the trees and taking for themselves from it. I (also) was watching the sun, the moon, and the stars (לשמשא ולשהרא ולכוכביא); they were chopping and taking from it for themselves. (1QapGen 13 9–11a, trans. Fitzmyer)

---

[146] Uses of an olive tree in prophetic visions such as Zech 4:3–14 are of no help here.
[147] Crawford, *Rewriting Scriptures in Second Temple Times*, 114.

Apparently "those of gold and silver" as well as of those of "iron" chop down trees, but this activity is highly unusual and a fully extant text could present a considerably different picture of the action. It is also possible that the text describes the sun, moon, and stars as chopping down trees. The meaning of these actions is unclear, but it seems reasonable to infer that the action of chopping down trees does not find a parallel in biblical descriptions where chopping down trees/poles has a specific religious connotation, i.e., the rejection of the Asherah cult. The religious reforms of Josiah attempted not only attempted to centralize the cult in Jerusalem, but to limit the scope of the cult. According to the Deuteronomistic Historian, he "broke the pillars, cut down the *Asherim*, and filled their places with human bones" (2 Kgs 23:14). We saw similar sentiments in the discussion of texts from Hos 4 and 1 Kgs 15 above. But those pre-exilic/exilic literary contexts are hardly plausible for this vision of Noah.

The use of metals, (non species specific) trees, and heavenly bodies as symbols in this dream vision is confusing and any attempt to identify them is nothing more than a guess in light of their lack of context. The best one can do is to posit associations based on the general symbol-referent patterns seen in other symbolic apocalypses. For example, one assumes that the heavenly bodies, i.e., the sun, moon, and stars, represent angels. We saw in chapter two and in the analysis of the *Animal Apocalypse* above the use of heavenly bodies – especially stars – to represent angels is widespread both in apocalypses and in other ancient Jewish writings. There is also significant precedent for trees to be used as descriptions of both kingdoms and individual humans during the Hellenistic Period. Finally, we saw that different types of metals are used to represent kingdoms in Dan 2 and that parallels for this type of symbolism are widespread in the ancient Mediterranean world. The image of breaking stone and clay (or ceramics) in the *Book of the Words of Noah* finds some parallel in Dan 2:34 where the iron/clay feet of the statue are smashed. "As you looked on, a stone was cut out, not by human hands, and it struck the statue on its feet of iron and clay and broke them in pieces." Another parallel with Dan 2 is found in the description חיות ברא "beasts of the field" from 1QapGen 13 8. Dan 2 uses the same expression in its description of the gold head of the statue about which Nebuchadnezzar dreamed, "O king . . . into whose hand he has given human beings, wherever they live, the beasts of the field (חֵיוַת בָּרָא), and the birds of the air, and whom he has established as ruler over them all – you are the head of gold."

What is truly intriguing about Noah's dream vision in 1QapGen 12(?)–15 is that within only a few lines of column thirteen, the *Genesis Apocryphon* virtually exhausts every symbol-type encountered in every Jewish apocalypse (combined): stars, trees, humans, and metals. I am of the opinion that the "beasts of the field" (חֵיוָת ברא) in 13 8 are part of the vision, but may not function as symbols. If they are symbols, one could add animals to this list and 1QapGen would have used every known symbol type in the space of just four lines.

The use of the many symbols occurs in the text just before the appearance of the olive tree. If I am correct that the olive tree represents Adam, then the scene in which the metals, trees, and heavenly bodies appear may depict the creation of the earth. Indeed, lines eleven and twelve of column thirteen seem to hint at this: "They were releasing the land and releasing the waters; and the water stopped, and it came to an end" (1QapGen 13 11–12). These lines might also be appropriate for the Flood, but if that is the case, then the olive tree cannot precede the cedar tree in the vision. In either case, one imagines that the sun, moon, and stars (i.e., angels) must be the subject of שרון "they were releasing" in 1QapGen 13 11. It is hardly imaginable that a human could do such a thing.

The most important words in this section of the vision must be ונסבין להון מנה "And they were taking from it for themselves" because they are repeated at least three times (13 9, 10, 11). The accusation is perhaps one of greed and could thus refer to the fallen angels who slept with human women. The use of להון emphasizes that the act is one of greed as it specifically implies that what is taken belongs to someone else. It is interesting that while several trees are chopped down, the object from which the unnamed assailants "take" is in every case singular (מנה "from it"). Perhaps the object is the earth, perhaps it is the tree of life.

Raw Data from the Book of the Words of Noah

Dream Vision 1	(non-symbolic)		
1Q20 6 15	נוֹח	Noah	Explicit
1Q20 6 16	בני ארעא	Children of the earth	Explicit
1Q20 6 19	נפיליא	Nephilim	Explicit

Other Symbolic Apocalyptic Visions

1Q20 6 20	קדישין	Holy Ones	Explicit
1Q20 6 20	בנות אנו[ש	Daughters of me[n]	Explicit
Dream Vision 2	(symbolic)		
1Q20 13 9	לדהבא ולכס[פ]א	"those of gold and silver"	Symbolic: metals
1Q20 13 10	פרזלא	Iron	Symbolic: metal
1Q20 13 10	אילניא	The trees	Symbolic: trees
1Q20 13 10–11	לשמשא ולשהרא ולכוכביא	The sun, the moon, and the stars	Symbolic: heavenly bodies
1Q20 13 13, 14	זיתא (x3)	Olive tree	Symbolic: tree
1Q20 14 9 (+27)	ארזא ר[ב]א	The great cedar	Symbolic: tree
1Q20 14 10, 11	חלפא	The scion	Symbolic: tree
1Q20 14 13	נצבת קושט	Upright planting	Symbolic: tree
1Q20 14 15	חלפתא אחר[ית]א	Other scion	Symbolic: tree

1Q20 15 10	גֻּבְרָא	The man (coming from the south of the land)	Symbolic: human
1Q20 15 14	ארבעא מלאכין	Four angels	Explicit: title

Findings From Chapter Three

The language found in the *Animal Apocalypse*, 4QFourKingdoms[a–b] ar, and the *Book of the Words of Noah* is closely related to the language found in the Daniel apocalypses. For virtually every *dramatis persona* in each text's historical review – at least the actors that can be confidently placed within the visions themselves and not in a prologue or epilogue – each text uses language that points beyond itself. The actors that appear in each history must be interpreted in order for the visionary (and the reader) to understand their meaning. This situation obtains whether or not the actor is a deity, angel, demon, human, or ethno-political group. The only nuance to this phenomenon is that the symbols in 4QFourKingdoms[a–b] ar actually provide their own interpretation for the visionary, i.e., the visionary corresponds with the trees themselves. Like the Daniel apocalypses, the kind of language used in the *Animal Apocalypse*, 4QFourKingdoms[a–b] ar, and *Book of the Words of Noah* fits into the basic language typology derived from Artemidorus/Oppenheim under the rubric "symbolic."

It is noteworthy that none of the three texts surveyed in this chapter present even one symbol type that is not already found in one or more of the symbolic apocalypses from the Book of Daniel. One can only conclude that despite the variation and nuance within the symbolic categories themselves (i.e., the use of various species of animals or trees), writers of ancient Jewish apocalypses used a limited and stable repertoire of symbols to construct their texts: animals, metals, trees, humans, stars. But the symbolic apocalypses from this chapter do not simply agree with the Daniel apocalypses in terms of the basic repertoire of symbol types. In most cases, the symbols types encountered in this chapter are used to describe the same categorical relationships (i.e., conventional pairs) seen in the Daniel apocalypses. For example, stars and humans are consistently used to represent angels. Animals are used to represent both individual humans and collections of humans (including political organizations). Trees are also used to represent humans. In this way the symbolic language of these apocalypses is also illuminated by the concept of symbol derived from Structuralist poetics/semiotics, i.e., the symbol as a conventional sign or signifier of an arbitrary relationship. The ways in which de Saussure thought about language (writ large) or Peirce thought about mathematics can also illuminate the language of literary texts.

The apocalypses encountered in this chapter often agree with the type of allegory found in the Daniel apocalypses. Each text in this chapter contains an allegory in the strictest sense, i.e., a story with two levels of meaning.[148] But at least two of the apocalypses surveyed in this chapter specifically reframe older literary traditions in symbolic language. In other words, in the same way that Dan 7 allegorizes the Canaanite Combat Myth or Dan 8 allegorizes the Canaanite myth of "Daystar, Son of Dawn," both the *Animal Apocalypse* and the *Book of the Words of Noah* appear to retell an older story in different and symbolic language. It is interesting that both of these apocalypses appear to allegorize Jewish scripture rather than Canaanite myth. The *Animal Apocalypse* retells parts of the history of Israel from books such as Genesis, Exodus, and 1–2 Kings, while the *Book of the Words of Noah* seems to be limited to the Book of Genesis. The consistency of the symbol-types as well as the conventional referents in each allegory is particularly striking when read against, for example, the language used in the various versions Gnostic *Apocryphon of John*. Just one of the *dramatic personae*, "first God," is described variously as father, monarch, pure light, pneuma, living water, self-searching (*sunaisthêsis*), and maker.[149]

Both the individual symbols as well as the literary motifs in which they were framed in the Book of Daniel found significant antecedents in ancient Israelite/Jewish literature and often times more broadly in the ancient Near East. Some of the same motifs are found in the apocalypses in this chapter. The four kingdoms motif in 4QFourKingdoms^{a-b} ar no doubt fits the normal pattern. In other cases, however, the symbols used in this chapter break with earlier traditions. Specifically, the use of trees as symbols for humans (and human kingdoms) is different than the normal role for trees in representing the divine – particularly a goddess. The use of the symbol

---

[148] Cuddon, ed., *Dictionary of Literary Terms and Literary Theory*, 120–22. Fletcher, *Allegory: The Theory of a Symbolic Mode*.

[149] See Zlatko Pleše, *Poetics of the Gnostic Universe: Narrative Cosmology in the Apocryphon of John* (NHMS 52; Leiden: Brill, 2006), 134. As Pleše shows, the language used to describe *dramatis personae* (deities) in the *Apocryphon of John* does fit into categories that appear to obtain for the First God, Barbelo, Christ, Sophia, and Ialdabaoth. These categories reflect, for example, reproduction, kingship, water, epistemology, etc., and are sometimes at odds with each other. But both the categories and the descriptions found in each are considerably more diverse than one what finds in either symbolic or non-symbolic Jewish apocalypses of the historical type.

across the genre apocalypse is, however, remarkably consistent. It thus represents a more limited and specific snapshot of the ancient Jewish cultural encyclopedia, a snapshot that is almost certainly peculiar to the Hellenistic period.

Part 2: Non-Symbolic Apocalypses

Every apocalypse examined in part one of this study shares at least one common element. Each text uses language that points beyond itself to describe the actors in its history. In each case the visionary requires an interpretation to understand the identities of the actors present in the historical reviews. The major difference between symbolic apocalypses and symbolic dream reports is that symbolic apocalypses often include an interpretation as (a second) part of the vision. But the significance of the symbolic apocalypses reaches much farther than their typological similarity to dream reports. Indeed, the ultimate value of the symbolic/non-symbolic typology borrowed from Artemidorus/Oppenheim was primarily heuristic. The grouping of symbolic apocalypses provided the occasion to see much deeper linguistic patterns in the genre. I observed a limited and stable set of symbol categories and a series of conventional relationships that sometimes obtain across the genre.

One finds a significantly different type of language in the three texts considered in this section. Symbolic language is virtually never used. Obtuse, cryptic, or as I argue, "group-specific" language is sometimes used. In other words, non-symbolic apocalypses do not use language that point beyond themselves. In some cases, however, the texts appear to use explicit language in a way that requires a reader/hearer to possess privileged information in order to understand it correctly. Unlike much of the symbolic language encountered in chapter one, neither these group specific terms nor the motifs in which they appear contain within themselves tools for interpretation. Privileged, "insider" information is required. This type of group specific language is hardly limited to apocalypses, but its consistent presence in non-symbolic apocalypse highlights an irony. It appears that the symbolic language encountered in chapter one must have been intended for large audiences, while the non-symbolic apocalypses analyzed in part two appear to presume a more limited social context.

The texts I analyze in part two are Dan 10–12, the *Apocryphon of Jeremiah C*, and *Pseudo-Daniel^{a-b} ar*. I proceed with the same basic methodology used in section one. I examine the language used to depict deities, demons/angels, and humans (both individuals and groups) by means of linguistic- and motif-historical investigation.

Chapter 4

Daniel 10–12

Daniel 10–12 does not use symbolic ciphers to describe earthly or heavenly realities. Instead, the text employs explicit, realistic terminology. Some of the language might be described as esoteric, but opaque language is significantly different from symbolic, metaphorical, or allegorical language. An example helps to introduce the differences that are highlighted in this chapter. Below I compare depictions of the kingdom of Greece (i.e., Alexander's Empire and its continued manifestations under the *diadochoi* from Dan 2, 7, 8, the *Animal Apocalypse*, and 4QFour Kingdoms[a–b] with an example from Dan 10–12 on the other.

Daniel 2	שָׁקוֹהִי דִּי פַרְזֶל (2:33, 35, 40, 45)	"legs of iron"
Daniel 7	... חֵיוָה רְבִיעָיָה ... שִׁנַּיִן דִּי־פַרְזֶל לַהּ רַבְרְבָן קַרְנַיִן עֲשַׂר לַהּ (7:7)	"A fourth beast . . . with great iron teeth . . . (and) with ten horns"

Daniel 8	צָפִיר (8:5, 21)	Male Goat
Animal Apocalypse	አንስርት 'ansert (90:2)	eagles
4QFour Kingdoms[a–b] ar	אלנא	tree
Daniel 10–12	מַלְכוּת יָוָן (11:2)	"Kingdom of Greece"

In the first five examples charted above, Greece is depicted symbolically. There are several different symbolic systems employed, but one is most common. In Dan 7 and 8 as well as in the *Animal Apocalypse*, animals are used to symbolize humans (i.e., ethno-political groups). No particular animal has a conventional association with Greece. Three completely different animals are used. When one considers the attributes of each beast it is not difficult to see why each beast might have been used to depict the powerful empire of Alexander (i.e., note that mice or moles or sparrows are not used). Still, without helpful context, the various animals could reasonably be assumed to represent any one of five or six different kingdoms from the period. The main characteristics are power and speed. In Dan 7, the beast is a hybrid creature. In Dan 8, it is a male goat. Finally, in the *Animal Apocalypse*, Greece is depicted as eagles. The symbolic system in Dan 2 describes earthly kingdoms not in terms of beasts, but in terms of different metals. The system in 4QFour Kindoms[a–b] describes earthly kingdoms as trees (as we saw in chapter three, this is a symbolic system also found in Dan 4, the *Book of the Words of Noah*, and the *Book of Giants*). These types of symbolic descriptions are markedly different than what one finds in Dan 10–12. In Dan 11:2, Greece is described as מַלְכוּת יָוָן "The Kingdom of Greece." One cannot find a more explicit description in the Hebrew language.

It is important to note that the description "Kingdom of Greece" does not occur outside the dream vision as an explanatory feature (e.g., Dan 8:21). It is part of the vision itself and Daniel does not require that an angel interpret the meaning of the expression for him. This type of realistic language is characteristic of the whole of Dan 10–12. While the meaning of every phrase used to describe an animate object in Dan 10–12 might not be immediately obvious to a twenty-first century reader and while some might not have been obvious to all second century Jews living in Judea, the language is nonetheless explicit and realistic. Uncovering and describing this explicit language is in itself an important task, but in the same way that I attempted to go beyond merely labeling language as "symbolic" in section one above, I hope to push beyond merely labeling language "non-symbolic" in part two. I hope to point out, in what is perhaps the most significant irony uncovered by this study, that the non-symbolic apocalypses might have been more difficult to interpret for their contemporary audiences than the symbolic ones. Numerous expressions in this chapter and throughout part two of this study appear to function as group-specific terminology and may have been produced for (and/or helped to produce) limited or specialized audiences.

Language in Daniel 10–12

While nearly all the descriptions used in Dan 10–12 utilize explicit language, not all are as transparent as מַלְכוּת יָוֶן "The Kingdom of Greece." Several kinds of descriptions are used. In some cases personal names are used. In other cases only titles such as "king of the south" are used. Yet other cases name figures or groups with adjectival descriptions such as "those who lead to righteousness" or "the wise among the people." These kinds of descriptions are not mutually exclusive. In some cases two different kinds of descriptions are combined, i.e., a name plus a title or a title plus an adjectival description. Thus there are three basic techniques used (sometimes in combination) by Dan 10–12 to depict animate objects: explicit, titular, and adjectival descriptions.

Descriptions of Deities, Angels, and Demons

Deities are only mentioned in passive circumstances in Dan 10–12. For example, a group of Jews is described in 11:32 as עַם יֹדְעֵי אֱלֹהָיו "the people who know their God." The reference is clearly YHWH. The God of Israel is mentioned again when the text narrates the installation of the abomination of desolation in the Jerusalem temple. Dan 11:36 claims that Antiochus, "shall speak horrendous things against the God of gods" (אֵל אֵלִים). The same description of the god of Israel is found several times in the Hebrew Bible (with varying orthography): Deut 10:17, Josh 22:22, Pss 84:8 (7), 136:2, and Dan 2:47. The description in Dan 2 is especially important since in it Nebuchadnezzar tells Daniel, "Truly your God is God of gods."[1]

Antiochus' abomination is derided by the text not only as an injury to Jews, but to his own native pantheon and beyond: "He shall pay no respect to the gods of his ancestors (אֱלֹהֵי אֲבֹתָיו) or to the one loved by women (חֶמְדַּת נָשִׁים), nor to any other god (כָּל־אֱלוֹהַּ) shall he pay respect." The first and last descriptions are common and explicit. The second one is more difficult. It may be a reference to Tammuz (cf. Ezek 8:14, "women were sitting there weeping for Tammuz").[2]

Finally, the text describes the deity installed by Antiochus in Jerusalem as אֱלוֹהַּ מָעֻזִּים "the god of strongholds." 2 Macc 6:1–2 designates this god as Zeus Olympias: "Not long after this the king sent an Athenian senator to compel the Jews to forsake the laws of the ancestors and no longer to live by the laws of God; also to pollute the temple in Jerusalem and to call it the temple of Olympian Zeus (Διὸς Ὀλυμπίου, NRSV). It is unclear whether "strongholds" is in any sense an approximation of Olympus. Collins associates the title with the Akra, the garrison Antiochus established in the City of David.[3] While deities are only described in passive roles in the text, several angels play very active roles.

Several different techniques are used to depict angels. One angel is described explicitly with a personal name. 10:13, 21 and 12:1 each mention the angel Michael (מִיכָאֵל) by name. In each case, Michael is also given a title or epithet. In 10:13 Michael is referred to as אַחַד הַשָּׂרִים הָרִאשֹׁנִים "one of the chief princes." In 10:21 he is described as שַׂרְכֶם "your prince" and in 12:1 he is described as הַשַּׂר הַגָּדוֹל "the great prince." He is not mentioned elsewhere in the Hebrew Bible, but he does figure in other Jewish literature from the Hellenistic period: *1 En.*, the *War Scroll*, and several fragmentary texts from Qumran.[4] These texts help to contextualize the explicit description of Michael in Dan 10–12.

In his *The Apocalyptic Vision of the Book of Daniel*, Collins argues that the epithets used to describe Michael (e.g., prince) in Dan 10–12 are based on the same kind of mythological framework that one finds in Dan 7–8 (i.e., the Canaanite Combat Myth and the Canaanite myth "Daystar Son of

---

[1] The title is also found within the danielic corpus in Pr Azar 1:18.
[2] See Collins, *Daniel*, 387.
[3] Collins, *Daniel*, 388.
[4] The figure is also mentioned in the NT in Rev 12:7 and in numerous places in Rabbinic literature (e.g., *Midrash Genesis Rabbah* xliv, 16; *Talmud B.M.* 86b; *Midrash Exodus Rabbah* xviii, 5)

Dawn" respectively). "In chs. 10–12, we meet again familiar mythic motifs. Each people on earth is represented by an angelic prince in heaven . . . this mythic system is a Jewish adaptation of the common world-view of the ancient Near East. Each people has its own patron deity."[5] That each people in the ancient Near East had their own national deity is unquestionable and certainly that may influence the concept of national or "patron" angels in Daniel and elsewhere in Hellenistic Jewish literature. But I am unsure if one can really explain the language of, e.g., Dan 7 and Dan 10–12 with reference to mythology. The combat myth contains several components and it found in multiple iterations. The use of patron angels can be described, at best, as a motif.

Collins is correct that "the relation between the heavenly battle of Michael and the "princes" of Persia and Greece in ch. 10 and the historical battles of the kings of Persia and Greece in ch. 11 is clearly analogous to the relation between the beasts which arise out of the sea and the kings which arise out of the earth in ch. 7."[6] In terms of language, however, the accounts are very different. Expressions like "Michael your prince" do not point beyond themselves. Daniel does not require interpretation for these expressions and one cannot describe them as symbolic in terms of the definition used by Oppenheim/Artemidorus. Moreover, unlike Dan 7 and 8, Dan 10–12 is not based on the narrative framework of an ancient myth. In what follows I examine how Michael functions in other Hellenistic Jewish texts to better understand how the language of Dan 10–12 functions. I hope to show that it is unlikely that an ancient reader might have relied on a particular mythological meta-narrative to interpret descriptions like "Michael your prince."

Michael figures prominently in both the *Book of the Watchers* (*1 En.* 1–36) and the *Similitudes* (*1 En.* 37–70).[7] He first appears in the *Book of Watchers* after the angels procreate with human women and begin to instruct the people in the abominations of warfare, cosmetics, etc (*1 En.* 8:1–3). In the wake of these events Michael, Surafel, and Gabriel bring the plight of earth's people before God (9:1–11). Subsequently, God commands Michael to "bind Shemihazah and the others with him, who have mated with the daughters of men, so that they were defiled by them in their uncleanness" (10:11).[8] One of the earliest depictions of Michael places him in a marshal-role. After binding the fallen angels and destroying their

---

[5] Collins, *The Apocalyptic Vision*, 108.

[6] Collins, *The Apocalyptic Vision*, 115.

[7] In dealing with texts from *1 Enoch*, I use the Aramaic if it is available. If it is not extant I use the Greek and if neither Aramaic nor Greek is extant I use the Ethiopic. I take the Ethiopic and Greek readings from Knibb, *The Ethiopic Book of Enoch*.

[8] Trans. Nickelsburg, *1 Enoch 1*, 215.

offspring, Michael is charged with the restoration of the earth (10:16–11:2). Later in the text, during Enoch's second journey, Michael appears before Enoch in his vision of the tree of life and warns Enoch not to touch it. It is reserved for the elect at the time of the great judgment. In this scene Michael is described not only as "one of the holy and revered angels" (፩እምነ መላእክት ቅዲሳን ወክቡራን, *1 'emenna malā'eket qedīsān wakeburān*), but also "their chief" (ዘዲቤሆሙ, *zadībēhōmu*).[9] While comparative linguistic analysis is less useful for the Ethiopic since it was translated from Greek, one should note the fact that an epithet such as שׂר "commander" or "prince" is already entirely appropriate here (cf. ዘዲቤሆሙ, *zadībēhōmu*) without any mythological meta-narrative. The title is based on Michael's specific actions in the text – not on outside-narrative factors. Dan 10–12 would not need a mythological meta-narrative to generate its description of Michael.

Michael is described with epithets in one other passage in the *Book of Watchers*. Chapter 20 breaks from the narrative flow of the book. It is comprised of a list of archangels. Seven angels are named and Michael is given two epithets. The first one is the same one used for Michael in 24:6 and is applied to other angels in chapter 20:2–8, "one of the holy angels." The second and most important epithet for our purposes, however, describes him as one, "who is in charge of the good ones of the people" (ὁ ἐπὶ τῶν τοῦ Λαοῦ ἀγαθῶν τεταγμένος, 20:5).[10] H. Stratham has argued that the term Λαός "people" often functions as a technical term for the people of Israel in the Greek of the LXX and the New Testament.[11] I would add that the expression "good ones" is used in Widsom of Solomon to describe the children of Israel participating in the first Passover feast in Egypt: "For in secret the holy children of good people (ἀγαθῶν), and with one accord agreed to the divine law . . ." (Wisdom 18:9, NRSV). But whether or not the epithet used for Michael in *1 En.* 20:5 places all of Israel or only the righteous ones in his purview, it almost certainly anticipates Michael's role as patron of Israel in Dan 10:13, 21, and 12:1. I emphasize here that the descriptions found in *1 Enoch* entirely provide for the epithets given to Michael in the Book of Daniel without the need for a mythological meta-narrative about patron angels. The similarity is not only in general terms.

---

[9] *1 Enoch* 24:6.

[10] The text is corrupt here and I follow Nickelsburg's reading. While both the Greek and Ethiopic witnesses attribute two (different) objects to Michael's purview, I agree with Nickelsburg that, "The lack of a copula in G suggests that these objects are double readings of an original single text (G^{a'} has smoothed over the text by inserting the copula καί, "and"). Nickelsburg, *1 Enoch 1*, 294.

[11] H. Strathmann, "Λαος," in *TDNT 4* (Grand Rapids: Eerdmans, 1967), 34–5, 52–4.

Nickelsburg argues that the descriptions of Daniel in 12:1 as שַׂר "prince" and עָמֵל עַל "(he who) stands over (Israel)" indicate not that Michael is "leader" of the people, but that he is "protector" or "defender" of the people in military terms and in judicial terms (i.e., the same way he is described in the *Book of Watchers*).[12] The military aspect is obvious from the normal semantic range of the noun שַׂר "commander" or "prince." A representative example of this common usage is the description of the Egyptian official Potiphar in the Joseph Novella: שַׂר הַטַּבָּחִים "commander of the guards" (Gen 39:1). The judicial aspect is slightly more obscured. Nickelsburg points to scenarios in Zechariah, *Jubilees*, the *Testaments of the Twelve Patriarchs*, and the *Animal Apocalypse* in which one angel defends an individual against an accusing angel. In the latter two texts, "Israel's patron angel emerges unambiguously as the defender of the righteous before the throne of God and against the powers of Evil."[13] This is how Nickelsburg reads *1 En.* 20:5 where Enoch is depicted as, "one of the holy angels, who has been put in charge of the good ones of the people."[14] He presumes that the same role is reflected in the epithet שַׂר in Dan 10–12. I find this reading convincing in part because it is reflected in most every other text mentioning Michael that post-dates the *Book of Watchers*.

The descriptions of Michael found in the *Similitudes* (*1 En.* 37–71), where he interprets visions for Enoch (e.g., *1 En.* 60, 67–68), are similar to those found in the *Book of Watchers*.[15] Together with Gabriel, Raphael, and Phanuel, Michael casts the hosts of Azazel into the burning furnace so that God can execute vengeance on them (*1 En.* 54:6).[16] Michael serves alongside Gabriel, Raphael, and Phanuel as an escort for God whenever he leaves his throne (*1 En.* 70:9–17). Like *1 En.* 20 (*Book of Watchers*), Michael is included in a list of angels to whom various epithets are attributed in *1 En.* 40:9. Like the other passages referenced above, Michael is included together with three other angels: Gabriel, Raphael, and Phanuel. Michael is described as, "merciful and longsuffering" (መሐሪ ወርኁቅ መዓት, maḥara wareḥuqa ma'āt).

Michael is mentioned five times in the *War Scroll*. The first two examples are found in the context of instructions for inscriptions on the shields

---

[12] George Nickelsburg, *Resurrection, Immortality, and Eternal Life in Intertestamental Judaism and Early Christianity* (HTS 26; Cambridge: Harvard University Press, 2006), 23–30.

[13] Nickelsburg, *Resurrection*, 26.

[14] Trans. Nickelsburg and VanderKam, *1 Enoch: A New Translation*, 40. Nickelsburg notes that the text is corrupt here and that the original may have placed Michael in charge of all of Israel and not just the righteous. Cf. Nickelsburg, *1 Enoch 1*, 294–6.

[15] These chapter numbers for the *Similitudes* are based on the text found in Nickelsburg and VanderKam, *1 Enoch: A New Translation*.

[16] This role is also reflected in 1QM XVII (see below).

of tower soldiers (1QM IX 15–16). Michael's name is inscribed along with at least three other names of angels familiar from the archangel list in *1 En.* 20: Sariel, Raphael, and Gabriel.[17] In the context of the eschatological battle, at the appointed time for the binding of the "prince of the realm of wickedness," God sends support to the faithful in the person of Michael. He plays a major role in the defeat of Belial. This role reflects precisely the same one seen in the *Book of Watchers* when he is dispatched by God to punish the wicked angels. He is described in terms of his majesty אדיר and authority משרת (1QM 17 6). Indeed, Michael's authority is described as exalted "among the gods" באלים (1QM 17 7).[18] Yadin argued that the "prince of light" (שר מאור) from 1QM 13 10 should also be identified as Michael.[19] He bases this connection on the titles such as "prince" used in the book of Daniel as well as the claim from the *War Scroll* that "by eternal light" (באור עולמים) Michael will "light up" (להאיר) the covenant of Israel" (1QM 17 6–7). The title "prince of light" is then one more (explicit) example of a description of Michael as "prince" that does not depend on a mythical meta-narrative, but on the specific actions of the angel in the text – actions that are very similar to the ones found in the *Book of Watchers*. In other words, the description of Michael cannot be construed as somehow symbolic or as allegorizing an older myth. It perhaps appropriates specific and explicit ideas from the *Book of Watchers*, but even that would not be necessary.

1QM is not the only text from Qumran in which Michael plays a role. 4QText Mentioning Zedekiah (4Q470) is a text that likely describes a covenant struck between God and the Judahite king Zedekiah (597–586 B.C.E.) through the agency of the angel Michael:

---

[17] The same list of angels is also found in 4Q285 1 3. Though the fragment is poorly preserved, it is clear that the context is not the same as the one found in 1QM IX.

[18] Michael may also play a role in other texts (at least one of which is related to the war-texts) in which he is not explicitly named: 4Q491, 4Q471b, and 11QMelchizedek. For 4Q491 see Maurice Baillet, *Qumrân grotte 4.III (4Q482–4Q520)* (DJD VII; Oxford: Clarendon, 1982), 26–30. See also the pointed response of Morton Smith, "Ascent to Heaven and Deification in 4QM^a," in *Archaeology and History in the Dead Sea Scrolls* (ed. Lawrence Schiffman; vol. JPS 8 / ASOR 2 of; Sheffield Sheffield Academic Press, 1990), 187. For 4Q471b see Esther Eshel, "471b. 4QSelf-Glorification Hymn (=4QH^e frg. 1?)," in *Qumran Cave 4.XX* (ed. E. Chazon; vol. XXIX of DJD; Oxford Clarendon, 1999), 421–32. For 11QMelchizedek, see Paul Kobelski, *Melchizedek and Melchireša'* (CBQMS 10; Washinton: Catholic Biblical Association of America, 1981), esp. 72.

[19] Yigael Yadin, *The Scroll of the War of The Sons of Light Against the Sons of Darkness* (Oxford: Oxford University Press, 1962), 235–6.

2] . . . Michael[

3] . . . Zedekiah [shall en]ter, on [th]at day, into a/the co[ven]ant

4] . . . to perform and to cause the performance of all the law

5 At] that time M[ich]ael shall say to Zedekiah

6]I will make with you [a cove]na[nt] before the congregation[20]

In this text Michael serves as God's representative on earth. Indeed, at least in the imagination of the writer, the covenant struck through the agency of Michael will be enacted before all the congregation – not only with the person Zedekiah. The text indicates, at least in the imagination of the writer, that the whole of Judah viewed Michael as the angelic *liaison* between themselves and YHWH.

In 4QWords of Michael ar (4Q529) Michael mediates a divine revelation. In this case, however, the revelation is presented not to a human but to other angels. Michael seems to give a report to some angels about visions that he has already imparted to other angels, including one to the angel Gabriel (cf. 4Q529 1 4–5). The impression is thus given that Michael is the highest of the angels. In other words, not only humans, but even other angels – including Gabriel – need Michael to mediate revelations from God. The work purports to be or to excerpt from a "Book of Michael." It begins with the formula "Words of the book that Michael spoke to the angels" מלי כתבא די אמר מיכאל למלאכיא (4Q529 1 1).

One last text is relevant, but it is only necessary to examine its preface. The Greek text of *The Life of Adam and Eve* (*Apocalypse of Moses*) is similar to the *Book of Watchers* and the Book of Daniel in that Michael delivers a message/ imparts a vision to a human recipient. The preface to the text reads, "The narrative and life of Adam and Eve the first-made, revealed by God to Moses his servant when he received the tablets of the law of the covenant from the hand of the LORD, after he had been taught by the archangel Michael."[21] This text assigns Michael his role with Moses before Israel even existed. Despite the late dates of the surviving manuscripts, the text probably dates between 100 B.C.E. and 200 CE.[22]

---

[20] Trans. Erik Larson, "4Q470 and the Angelic Rehabilitation of King Zedekiah," *DSD* 1 (1994): 211.

[21] Trans. M. D. Johnson, "Life of Adam and Eve," in *OTP* 2 (ed. J. H. Charlesworth; New York: Doubleday, 1985), 259. For the most recent critical edition, see Johannes Tromp, *The Life of Adam and Eve in Greek: A Critical Edition* (Leiden: Brill, 2005).

[22] Cf. Michael Eldridge, *Dying Adam with his Multiethnic Family: Understanding the Greek Life of Adam and Eve* (SVTP 16; Leiden: Brill, 2001), 20–30. But see De Jonge who argues that a pre-Chistian date is out of the question. Marinus de Jonge, *Pseudepigrapha of the Old Testament*

It is unlikely, according to M. D. Johnson, that the preface to the Greek text is original.²³ But it seems equally unlikely to me that the text would begin *in media res* in the way attested by the Latin text tradition. Moreover, the preface is attested in all four Greek text forms isolated by Levison.²⁴ One would not expect the preface to be as widely attested in the Greek manuscript tradition if it came in very late (i.e., after other text traditions such as Latin and Armenian had already moved forward without it). Text forms I, IA, and II explicitly mention Michael while text form III describes him only as τοῦ ἀρχαγγέλ[ου] "the archangel."²⁵ While the Armenian and Georgian versions go back to a common Greek ancestor, it is important to note that they do not simply omit the preface and keep everything else intact. As de Jonge and Tromp note, "They begin with the stories of (a) Adam and Even looking for food; (b) the penitence of Adam and Eve; (c) the fall of the devil; (d) the separation of Adam and Eve, and Cain's birth – as the Latin *Life of Adam and Eve*."²⁶ Only afterwards do these versions adapt a version of the text known from chapters 1–4 in the Greek. It is hardly surprising that the preface would have fallen out in these cases.

The preceding look at Michael in Hellenistic Jewish literature helps to clarify the descriptions found in Dan 10–12 such as, "Michael, your prince." Especially important is the image of Michael in the *Book of Watchers* and similar reflexes
like the *War Scroll*. *1 En.* 1–36 undoubtedly predates Dan 10–12 and paints a picture of Michael in which he is not merely an angel or even an archangel, but the patron angel of Israel. This role is not based on a mythic meta-narrative from a much older myth but on specific actions in the texts. Moreover, the same role is reflected in numerous later texts. Collins might be correct that the basic assignment of one patron angel per nation in some way appropriates the concept ancient Near Eastern concept of national deities.²⁷ But the language used to describe Michael is not based on a par-

---

as part of Christian Literature: the Case of the Testament of the Twelve Patriarchs and the Greek Life of Adam and Eve (Leiden: Brill, 2003), 181–200. Cf. also Marinus de Jonge and Johannes Tromp, *The Life of Adam and Eve and Related Literature* (Sheffield: Sheffield Academic Press, 1997), 65–78.

²³ Johnson, "Life of Adam and Eve," 259. For a synopsis of the readings in all versions, see Gary Anderson and Michael Stone, *A Synopsis of the Books of Adam and Eve* (SBLEJL 17; Atlanta: Society of Biblical Literature, 1999).

²⁴ John R. Levison, *Texts in Transition: The Greek Life of Adam and Eve* (EJL 16; Altanta: Society of Biblical Literature, 2001), 49.

²⁵ Levison, *Texts in Transition*, 49.

²⁶ Jonge and Tromp, *The Life of Adam and Eve and Related Literature*, 35. On the relationship between the Armenian, Georgian, and Greek versions, see Michael Stone, *A History of the Literature of Adam and Eve* (SBLEJL 3; Atlanta: Scholars Press, 1992), 36–9, 69.

²⁷ Cf. the story of Naaman the Syrian in 2 Kings 5. After being healed, Naaman is discouraged that he cannot worship YHWH in his home territory since that nation is under the auspices of

ticular myth that was passed down with a narrative framework. Finally, while the system of patron angels seems similar to the concept of national deities expressed in Deut 32:8–9, one might note that Deuteronomy reflects a pre-exilic polytheism that is not present in Daniel. In Dan, the gods of old are replaced by angels.[28]

Two other techniques are used to describe angels in Dan 10–12. The first is an honorific title. The second is a symbolic description. On four occasions Daniel addresses angels as אֲדֹנִי "my lord."[29] This description occurs hundreds of times in the Hebrew Bible and is a standard designation for one of higher status or power. It has significant semantic overlap with בעל "lord."[30] It is most often used as a title for the God of Israel, but is also used as a description for angels on several occasions.[31] For example, when the three angels appear to Abraham at the oaks of Mamre, he entreats them, "My Lord (אֲדֹנָי), if I have found favor in your eyes, do not pass by your servant" (Gen 18:3). Similarly, after Zechariah sees the vision of the man riding a horse, he inquires, "What are these, my Lord (אֲדֹנִי)? (Zechariah 1:9)." The text explicitly designates the one from whom Zechariah seeks counsel as an angel. "The angel who talked with me said to me, 'I will show you what they are'" (Zechariah 1:9).[32] But אדני is never used as a technical term for angels. Its use in Daniel is, like in Genesis and Zechariah, merely an honorific title. The language is clear and non-symbolic. The title does not point beyond itself.

As indicated above, there is one exception to the otherwise non-symbolic language of Dan 10–12. Indeed, this is the only exception that we encounter in all of part two of this study. It is the exception that proves the rule. There is, in Dan 10–21, an occasional depiction of angels in terms of human beings. At the beginning of Daniel's vision in 10:5, he sees an angel that he describes as אִישׁ־אֶחָד לָבוּשׁ בַּדִּים "a man clothed in linen." 10:16 and 10:18 describe angels as כִּדְמוּת בְּנֵי אָדָם "one like the form(s) of a human being," and כְּמַרְאֵה אָדָם "one with the appearance of a human." Finally, 12:6–7 uses the same language as 10:5 to describe an angel: אִישׁ לְבוּשׁ הַבַּדִּים "a man clothed in linen." These descriptions reflect one of the major symbolic representation techniques encountered in part one of this study. In

---

another deity. Elisha instructs him to return to Syria with two loads of dirt from Israel in order that he might offer sacrifices to YHWH.

[28] A similar demotion of deities to the realm of angels and demons can be seen in *4QPseudo-Daniel*[a–b] *ar*. Cf. Bennie H. Reynolds III, "What Are Demons of Error? The Meaning of שידי טעותא and Israelite Child Sacrifices," *RevQ* 88 (2006): 593–613.

[29] 10:17 (x2), 19, 12:8.

[30] Bennie H. Reynolds III, "בעל," in *Theologisches Wörterbuch zu den Qumrantexten* (ed. H. J. Fabry and U. Dahmen; Stuttgart: Kohlhammer-Verlag, 2011), forthcoming.

[31] It is used sparingly to describe other subjects, e.g., the king of Judah in Jer 38:9.

[32] The same expression is used in the same way in Zech 4:4, 5, 13, 6:4.

both the Book of Daniel and the *Animal Apocalypse* angels are described as humans. The most notable example is the כְּבַר אֱנָשׁ "one like a human being" from Dan 7:13, but equally important are the descriptions of figures like Moses in the *Animal Apocalypse*: "And that sheep that had led them, that had become a man, was separated from them and fell asleep" (*1 En.* 89:38).[33] Not only in one text, but widely across the genre, humans are used as conventional symbols for angels. The two form a structure of conventional association. The same conventional association observed in symbolic apocalypses obtains in Dan 10:5, 16, 18, and 12:6–7. In this case the language does point beyond itself. The category humans points the reader to the identity, "angel." What separates the angel terminology of Dan 10–12 from Dan 7 and 8 is that Dan 7 and 8 use exclusively symbolic language to describe angels. In Dan 10–12 only a few cases do so. The majority of the descriptions of angels are explicit and non-symbolic.

Descriptions of Persons
Most, but not all, of the individuals described in Dan 10–12 are kings. The revelation in chapter 11 describes a period from the middle of the Persian Empire to the reign of Antiochus IV in the ancient Near East. The history is surprising both in its detail and its accuracy. Much of it appears to be corroborated by other ancient and independent accounts of the same events.

One individual is explicitly described with a personal name (Darius the Mede דָּֽרְיָוֶשׁ הַמָּדִי) though the description does not occur within the main-body of the revelation itself. The (*ex-eventu*) history recounted to Daniel by Michael technically begins in 11:2 with a description of the fate of the Persian Empire, "Three more kings shall arise in Persia, and a fourth shall be richer than all of them, and when he has become strong through his riches, he shall stir up all against the kingdom of Greece" (Dan 11:2 NRSV). Michael's first-person narration of the future-history of the ancient Near East in chapter 11 is preceded, however, by a formulaic preface that sets the time frame for the vision. The chronological marker used by the writer follows a common practice in writing from across the ancient Near East. Dates are given in terms of the regnal years of a king: "And I, in the first year of Darius the Mede (דָּֽרְיָוֶשׁ הַמָּדִי), stood up to strengthen and aid him" (Dan 11:1).

It is unclear whether the text misrepresents the native land of Darius (Darius was a Persian king) intentionally or unintentionally. The description is nevertheless explicit and precise (even if incorrect): a personal name and a ethno-political qualifier. It is true that explicit descriptions are also used for

---

[33] Trans. Nickelsburg and VanderKam, *1 Enoch: A New Translation*, 127.

gentile kings in the prefaces to symbolic apocalypses such as Dan 7 and 8. But there is a significant difference between those apocalypses and Dan 11. In Dan 7–8, the preface is presented by an anonymous third-person narrator. The main revelation is then presented by Daniel himself in the first-person. The preface in Dan 11 is part of a conversation between Michael and Daniel that precedes the historical review. In other words, it too is part of the revelation from Michael to Daniel.

In addition to the description of Darius, four Persian kings are explicitly described – though not with personal names. Dan 11:2 narrates a history that appears to include the last four kings of Persia. The first three are described simply as מְלָכִים עֹמְדִים לְפָרַס "kings standing over Persia." The fourth king of Persia is described in terms of riches (יַעֲשִׁיר), but also in terms of hubris because it is with strength bought by riches that the final king "shall rouse all the kingdom of Greece" (יָעִיר הַכֹּל אֵת מַלְכוּת יָוָן). The four kings of Persia are noteworthy in light of the fact that Dan 7:6 depicts Persia as a leopard with four wings and that only four Persian kings are named in the Bible: Cyrus, Darius, Xerxes, and Artaxerxes. Collins rightly cautions that "there was more than one king named Darius and more than one king named Artaxerxes."[34] Moreover, it is clear that the rousing of Greece refers to Alexander the Great. The last Persian king before Alexander was Darius III Codomannus (335–330 B.C.E.).[35] He was preceded by Artaxerxes IV (338–336 B.C.E.) Artaxerxes III (359/8–338 B.C.E.), Artaxerxes II (405/4–359/8 B.C.E.), and Darius II (425/4–405/4 B.C.E.).[36] It is not clear, however, whether any of the four kings in Dan 11:2 represent specific persons in the way that the description of the next king in Dan 11:3–4 does.

After stating that the last king of Persia would "stir up all against the kingdom of Greece," the writer introduces מֶלֶךְ גִּבּוֹר "a warrior king." There is little doubt that the warrior king is Alexander the Great.

[He] shall rule with great dominion and take action as he pleases. And while still rising in power, his kingdom shall be broken and divided toward the four winds of heaven, but not to his posterity, nor according to the dominion with which he ruled; for his kingdom shall be uprooted and go to others besides these (11:3–4, NRSV).

If this description leaves any doubt that the warrior king is Alexander, the manner in which the text describes the political aftermath of the king's demise leaves no question. The Ptolemaic and Seleucid kings who rule over his defunct empire are described respectively as מֶלֶךְ הַנֶּגֶב "King of the

---

[34] Collins, *Daniel*, 377, n. 70.

[35] For a detailed account, see Pierre Briant, *From Cyrus to Alexander. A History of the Persian Empire* (Winona Lake: Eisenbrauns, 2002), 817–71.

[36] Briant, *From Cyrus to Alexander*, 588–91, 612–90.

South," and מֶלֶךְ הַצָּפוֹן "King of the North." This type of titular description is the dominant one used in the revelation in Dan 11.

Ptolemy I Soter (11:5), Ptolemy II Philadelphus (11:6) Ptolemy III Euergetes (11:9) Ptolemy IV Philopator (11:11), Ptolemy V Epiphanes (11:14) Ptolemy VI Philometor (11:25) are each described as מֶלֶךְ־הַנֶּגֶב "king of the south."[37] Seleucus II (11:6, 7, 8), Antiochus III (11:11, 13, 15), and Antiochus IV (11:40) are each described as מֶלֶךְ הַצָּפוֹן "the king of the north." These descriptions, while they do not use personal names, are nonetheless explicit and non-symbolic.

The first "king of the south" to appear on the scene in 11:5 is Ptolemy I Soter, who took control of Egypt first as satrap (323–305 B.C.E.) and then as king (305–282 B.C.E.) after Alexander's death.[38] The identification of Ptolemy I is confirmed by the text's claim that, "One of his officers (מִן־שָׂרָיו) shall grow stronger than he and shall rule a realm greater than his own realm" (Dan 11:5 NRSV). The officer in question is Seleucus I Nicator.[39] After the death of Alexander Seleucus I was appointed to Babylonia, but he was soon expelled by Antigonus. Seleucus fled to Ptolemy but returned in 312 (with the help of Ptolemy), defeated Antigonus in Babylonia in 308, and continued to defeat other local rulers put in place by Antigonus.[40] Seleucus then added the territories that Alexander conquered in Persia as well as Syria and Phoenicia by means of a treaty.[41] According to Graham Shipley, by the beginning of the third century B.C.E., "He was now master of virtually all Alexander's conquests outside Greece, apart from Egypt and parts of Asia-Minor – in effect, the former Persian Empire with all its tribute-bearing lands."[42] Thus, Daniel's description of the officer (Seleucus I) as growing stronger and ruling a realm greater than Ptolemy I is hardly an exaggeration. The same sentiments about Nicator are expressed by Arrian in his *Anabasis Alexandri*, "Seleucus was the greatest king of those who succeeded Alexander, and of the most royal mind, and ruled over the greatest extent of territory."[43]

---

[37] The reference to king of the south in 11:40 part of a genuine prophecy, but one presumes that Ptolemy VI Philometor is still the subject.

[38] Cf. Hölbl, *A History of the Ptolemaic Empire*, 9–34.

[39] I prefer the NRSV translation of שר as "officer" to Collins's translation of prince since the English term prince implies a blood relationship with the king. A rigid understanding of שר is almost certainly what led Jerome to erroneously identify the figure with Ptolemy II Philadelphus. Cf. *Jerome's Commentary on Daniel* (trans. Gleason Archer; Grand Rapids: Baker Book House, 1956), 122.

[40] Cf. Graham Shipley, *The Greek World After Alexander: 323–30 BC* (London: Routledge, 2000), 286.

[41] Shipley, *The Greek World After Alexander: 323–30 BC*, 286–7.

[42] Shipley, *The Greek World After Alexander: 323–30 BC*, 287.

[43] E. Iliff Robson, *Arrian* (LCL 269; vol. 2; London: William Heinemann LTD, 1933), 283 (7.22).

The "king of the south" described in 11:6 must be Ptolemy II Philadelphus. The text does not explicitly describe a succession event, but it does claim that, "After some years they shall make an alliance, and the daughter of the king of the south shall come to the king of the north." The daughter of Ptolemy II (Berenice) was married to the grandson of Seleucus, Antiochus III Theos.[44] There are several witnesses to this event apart from Daniel. Indeed, there is an eyewitness account in the *Zenon Papyri* (one Artemidorus to Zenon): "We have just arrived in Sidon after accompanying the queen as far as the border, and I expect to be with you soon."[45] Berenice ultimately met an abrupt and ignominious end, but not before she and her brother (Ptolemy III Euergetes, succeeded Ptolemy II in 246 B.C.E.) nearly claimed all of the Eastern Mediterranean seaboard and Mesopotamia.

It is Ptolemy III Euergetes that is described as "a branch (נֵצֶר) from her roots" in 11:7 and "the king of the south:" in 11:9. The "branch" terminology does not connote, as do other biblical passages (e.g., Isa 11:1), the concept of a messianic scion. Instead, the image invoked is more precisely that of the "family tree." The branch functions as a metaphor in the restricted sense, i.e., transference by analogy.

The description מֶלֶךְ הַצָּפוֹן "king of the north" appears for the first time in 11:9 in the context of a short-lived invasion by the king of the south. The king of the north must be Seleucus II Callinicus. Callinicus invaded Egypt ca. 242/1 B.C.E., but Ptolemy III Euergetes quickly regained control over the land that Callinicus claimed. The Roman historian Marcus Junianius Justinus (Justin) makes a similar claim: "He [Seleucus] thought himself now in a condition to make war upon Ptolemy. But as he had been only born to make sport for fortune, and had recovered his kingdoms only to lose them again, he lost the battle."[46] It is notable, as Collins points out, that, "Daniel implies that he [Callinicus] attempted an unsuccessful invasion of Egypt, a motif that will reappear in the career of Antiochus Epiphanes."[47] In other words, in spite of the general accuracy of the historical details found in Daniel, it is clear that the history is not being told from a detached, disinterested point of view. There is both a literary artistry and a theological agenda at work even in the most banal details of the history. Indeed, Daniel

---

[44] Hölbl, *A History of the Ptolemaic Empire*, 44–5.

[45] P.Cair.Zen. II 59351 translated in R. S. Bagnall and P.S. Derow, *The Hellenistic Period. Historical Sources in Translation.* (Oxford Oxford University Press, 2003), 48–9. Artemidorus includes a precise date in the closing formulas of the document.

[46] Just. XXVII.2 The translation with some slight alterations is taken from, T. Brown, *Justin's history of the world from the Assyrian monarchy down to the time of Augustus Cæsar; being an abridgment of Trogus Pompeius's Philippic history, with critical remarks upon Justin* (London: D. Midwinter and H. Clements, 1719), 271.

[47] Collins, *Daniel*, 378.

omits several details that might otherwise significantly alter the tone that is struck with the narration of 11:9. For example, Seleucus II was hardly the aggressor in the third Syrian War (246–241 B.C.E.). Ptolemy III mounted major attacks against Syrian territories in support of a rival heir to the throne of Seleucid Syria (a son of Berenike, herself the daughter of Ptolemy II). After initiating a major military operation in the north, however, his plans were foiled by the murder of Berenike and her son before the conflict could be settled.[48] Despite claims in the Adulis Inscription, Ptolemy found little support for a regime change among the local populations in Syria once Berenike and her son where out of the picture.[49] He was forced to abandon hopes of Ptolemaic control of Syria. It is in this context, i.e., a quasi-retreat on the part of Ptolemy III, that Callinicus invaded Egypt.

Antiochus III the Great is first described as one of the "sons" of Callinicus (וּבָנָיו)[50] in 11:10, but as "king of the north" in 11:11 without specific description of a succession.[51] Seleucus III Ceraunus is mentioned only to the extent that one infers he is one of the "sons" (וּבָנָיו) of Callinicus described in 11:10. He is never described as a "king of the north" even though he did rule briefly (227–223 B.C.E.).

Dan 11:11[52] describes the battle of Raphia in 217 B.C.E. when Ptolemy IV Philopator defeated Antiochus III the Great: "Then the king of the south (מֶלֶךְ הַנֶּגֶב) will become furious with the king of the north (מֶלֶךְ הַצָּפוֹן), and the army shall be given into his hand."[53] Verse 13 describes Antiochus' renewed challenge to Egypt in the wake of the accession of the six year old king Ptolemy V Epiphanes. Antiochus had already regained much of the Eastern part of the kingdom between 212–205 B.C.E. – even assuming the title μέγας βασιλεύς "Great King."[54] Antiochus struggled against the Egyptian general Scopas, but won a decisive victory at Paneas in 200 B.C.E. (cf. Polybius 16.8–19, 22a, 19). The battle of Paneas set in motion numerous

---

[48] Hölbl, *A History of the Ptolemaic Empire*, 48–51.

[49] For the Adulis Inscription, see Stanley Burstein, *The Hellenistic Age from the Battle of Ipsos to the Death of Kleopatra VII* (Cambridge: Cambridge University Press, 1985), 125–6.

[50] Reading with the *Qere, et al*, against the MT וּבְנוֹ.

[51] A description of the succession as well as the revolt of Molon (223–220) is found in Polybius V. 40–4. For a recent translation, see Michael Austin, *The Hellenistic World From Alexander to the Roman Conquest. A Selection of Ancient Sources in Translation*. (Cambridge: Cambridge University Press, 2006), 329–31.

[52] This verse is significantly longer in MT and θ, but I agree with Collins that Papyrus 967 provides the more likely reading. See Collins, *Daniel*, 364. The explanatory force of the pluses as well as the evidence from Ms. 88 and Syh indicate that MT is secondary here.

[53] The antecedent of "hand" here is Ptolemy IV. The battle is described in considerably more detail by Polybius (5.79). He numbers the forces of Antiochus as sixty-two thousand foot soldiers, six thousand horses, and one hundred and two elephants. He also describes the national origin and military specialization of all of the troops.

[54] Hölbl, *A History of the Ptolemaic Empire*, 132.

challenges – not least of which internal ones – for the young Ptolemy V, described in 11:14 as king of the south: "In those times many shall rise against the king of the south." Polybius and Diodorus each tell a similar tale.[55] One imagines the "many" described by Daniel to include, for example, figures such as Aristomenes who was at one time a leading advisor of the young Ptolemy V but was ultimately forced to take poison (cf. Diodorus 28.14).[56] It is in this time frame that Dan 11:15 gives an enigmatic description of a group of people: בְּנֵי פָּרִיצֵי עַמְּךָ "the violent ones of your people." Considerable ink has been spilled over the identity of this group – virtually all to no avail. The same historical events are narrated by Josephus, but the "violent ones" do not figure in his narrative (cf. *Antiquities* 12.3.3–4). One may draw three positive conclusions about the description: 1) the "violent ones" are Jews, 2) the writer holds a negative opinion of the group and 3) they (the party of violence) claimed visionary support for their program.[57] To read the "violent" ones as a pro-Seleucid party along with Meyer and Hartmann and DiLella is perhaps the most reasonable interpretation. According to this line of thinking, the group was stymied when Scopas regained control of Jerusalem,[58] and Daniel's negative attitude is a retrojection onto the text based on knowledge of what the Seleucids would eventually do during the reign of Antiochus IV.[59]

The description פָּרִיצֵי "violent, lawless ones" is different than the explicit and titular descriptions encountered thus far. It is an adjectival description. While the language is explicit, it is nonetheless opaque. It accords with U. Eco's definition of the symbolic mode encountered in chapter one and it is, at least potentially, a group-specific locution (i.e., an insider-sobriquet). The fact that neither Josephus nor Polybius mentions any such group lends credibility to the notion that the "violent ones of your people" was a term with limited currency. The description does not point beyond itself even if privileged information is required in order to understand it. A possible clue is found in a discrepancy between Daniel and Josephus in the events that follow.

The description "king of the north" in 11:15 must continue to describe Antiochus III. The text is aware that after the battle of Paneas, Scopas retreats to Sidon, "a well-fortified city," to which Antiochus lays siege. It is worth noting that while Dan 11:16–19 describes Antiochus III's capture of Israel, Josephus claims that many Jews chose to fight with Seleucid forces against Ptolemy/Scopas:

---

[55] Hölbl, *A History of the Ptolemaic Empire*, 138–40.
[56] Hölbl, *A History of the Ptolemaic Empire*, 139.
[57] Collins, *Daniel*, 379.
[58] Eduard Meyer, *Ursprung und Anfänge des Chistentums* (Stuttgart: Cotta, 1924), 2.127.
[59] Hartman and DiLella, *The Book of Daniel*, 292.

When Antiochus [III] took possession of the cities in Coele-Syria which Scopas had held, and Samaria, the Jews of their own will went over to him and admitted him to their city and made abundant provision for his entire army and his elephants; and they readily joined his forces in besieging the garrison which had been left by Scopas in the citadel of Jerusalem. (*Antiquities* 12.3.3)[60]

The difference between the accounts of Josephus and Daniel indicates that interpreting the "violent ones" in 11:14 as a pro-Seleucid group is perhaps correct. In other words, because Daniel ignores the Jewish support for Antiochus III he is more likely not to see such Jews in a positive way.

Seleucus IV Philopator (187–175 B.C.E.) appears in 11:20, but he is not described as a "king of the north." Indication of a royal succession is given, however, as well as information about specific action undertaken by the king: "Then shall arise in his place one who shall send a "tyrant of splendor" (נוֹגֵשׂ הֶדֶר) for the glory of the kingdom." Most read this verse as a reference to the attempt of Heliodorus to despoil the Jerusalem temple. The episode is recounted fancifully in 2 Maccabees 3 where Heliodorus is prevented from entering the temple by divine intervention in response to the prayers of the citizens of Jerusalem:

For there appeared to them a magnificently caparisoned horse, with a rider of frightening mien; it rushed furiously at Heliodorus and struck him with its front hoofs. Its rider was seen to have armor and weapons of god. Two young men also appeared to him, remarkably strong, gloriously beautiful and splendidly dressed, who stood on either side of him and flogged him continuously, inflicting many blows on him.[61]

11:21 indicates the accession of Antiochus the IV over Seleucus IV and names him with the first of several descriptions: נִבְזֶה "a contemptible person." The text accuses Antiochus IV of assuming the throne by means of intrigue. This accusation could name any one of several events surrounding the accession of Antiochus IV. For example, a young son of Seleucus IV may have been co-regent with Antiochus for five years until he was murdered in unusual circumstances.[62] Antiochus IV is also referred to as הַמֶּלֶךְ "the king" in 11:36 and מֶלֶךְ הַצָּפוֹן "the king of the north" in 11:40. Narration about Antiochus IV continues through the end of chapter 11 (11:45).

It is clear to the reader based on the amount of narrative devoted to Antiochus IV as well as the tone taken by the narrative that s/he has arrived at the climax of the text. Despite belittling Antiochus IV numerous times, the text attributes great strength to him and even claims that he defeated נְגִיד בְּרִית "the prince of the covenant" (11:22, see more below on this descrip-

---

[60] Peter Schäfer, *The History of the Jews in the Greco-Roman World* (London: Routledge, 2003), 23–4.
[61] 2 Macc 3:25–26, NRSV.
[62] Collins, *Daniel*, 382.

tion). It is notable that the wars with Ptolemaic Egypt described beginning in 11:25 are accomplished in part based on an alliance with a group of Jews, "And after an alliance is made with him, he shall act deceitfully and become strong with a small party (מְעַט־גּוֹי)" (Dan 11:23, NRSV). Collins prefers to see the group as a small mercenary army derived from an alliance with Pergamum.[63] But the action undertaken by Antiochus immediately after rousing this small group is not a military campaign, but a public relations campaign: "Without warning he shall come into the richest parts of the province and do what none of his predecessors had ever done, lavishing plunder, spoil, and wealth on them" (11:24, NRSV). At least according to the writer of Daniel, Antiochus' activities in 11:23–24 lay the groundwork for strike-capabilities against Egypt. The description מְעַט־גּוֹי "a small party" is not clear but it is not symbolic. In other words, it is clear to Daniel – he requires no assistance to understand it.

The description "king of the south" reappears in 11:25, this time naming Ptolemy VI Philomator. He is described again in 11:27 along with Antiochus IV Epiphanes as one of the "two kings" (שְׁנֵיהֶם הַמְּלָכִים). At this point in the history one encounters significant variations in the course of events narrated by different ancient authors. Antiochus successfully campaigned against Egypt in 170, but was turned back during another campaign in 168 (cf. the discussion of *Kittim* below). Shortly after the second campaign he sets in place oppressive religious policies over Judea (the relevant passages from 1 and 2 Maccabees have already been quoted in chapter 2). Dan 11:29–39 implies not only a new civic religious policy, but military operations in Jerusalem and the despoiling of the temple.

It is in this context, i.e., the Hellenistic religious reforms, that one encounters two explicit, but nevertheless esoteric references to a group of Jews: עֹזְבֵי בְּרִית קֹדֶשׁ "those who forsake the holy covenant" and מַרְשִׁיעֵי בְרִית "those who violate the covenant" (Dan 11:30, 32). The terms are synonymous. The descriptions do not point beyond themselves, but a decisive interpretation for either would require privileged information. In other words, it does not fit with the definitions of symbolism offered up by Oppenheim/Artemidorus or Peirce/Culler. It should, however, be treated as a potential case of group-specific language. The same expression is found in two other texts: *The War Scroll* and *Apocryphon of Jeremiah C*. It is noteworthy that both texts show clear signs of using Dan 11 as a source text. In other words, the modest attestation of the expression in ancient Jewish literature does not necessarily point to the conclusion that it would or could have been easily understood by all Jews in the late Hellenistic period. It was not used outside the specific influence of the Book of Daniel.

---

[63] Collins, *Daniel*, 382.

In 1QM the expression "violators of the covenant" is used to describe Jews who collaborate with foreign powers against the faithful:

The first attack of the Sons of Light shall be undertaken against the forces of the Sons of Darkness, the army of Belial the troops of Edom, Moab, the sons of Ammon, and [ ] Philistia and the troops of the Kittim of Asshur. Supporting them are those who have violated the covenant (מרשיעי ברית).[64]

David Flusser has shown that Dan 11:29–39 and the specific term מרשיעי ברית was taken up by the writer of 1QM and used to describe those who collaborate with Greek imperialists – though in a later historical setting than Daniel. Flusser finds that 1QM appropriates the term to name Seleucid sympathizers in the time of Alexander Jannaeus – preferring to see in the "violators of the covenant" a reflection of the invasion of Demetrius II (Eucaerus) in 89 B.C.E. with Jewish help.[65]

The expression "violators of the covenant" also appears in the *Apocryphon of Jeremiah C* with a variant orthography: מרישיעי ברית. I argue in chapter five that like the writer of the *War Scroll*, the author of *Apocryphon of Jeremiah C* adopts language directly from Dan 11. I suggest that the writer of the *Apocryphon* recognized that Daniel's prophecy failed and reinterpreted (or, updated) it for a new time. The *Apocryphon* describes the downfall of the "violators of the covenant" during the reigns of the Hasmoneans Jonathan, Simon, and John Hyrcanus: "] three priests <u>who will not walk in the ways</u> [of the] first/former [priests] (who) by the name of the God of <u>Israel were called</u>. And in their days will be brought down the pride of those who act wickedly (against the) <u>covenant as well as servants of the foreigner</u>."[66] The three priests "who will not walk in the ways" are Jonathan, Simon, and John Hyrcanus and "those who act wickedly are Seleucid sympathizers (see more in chapter 5).

In both texts that adopt Daniel's language the expression "violators of the covenant" is used to describe Hellenizing Jews who collaborate with foreign powers, namely the Seleucids. I argue in chapter 5 that it makes best sense to read the "violators of the covenant" in Dan 11 along the same lines. Specifically, they should be identified as the party of Menelaus. According to 2 Maccabees 5:15, Menelaus not only allowed Antiochus' desecration of the temple, but personally guided Antiochus through the temple. He is described as καὶ τῶν νόμων καὶ τῆς πατρίδος προδότην

---

[64] Trans. By M. Wise, M. Abegg, and E. Cook in Donald Parry and Emanuel Tov, eds., *Texts Concerned with Religious Law* (*DSSR 1*; Leiden: Brill, 2004), 209.

[65] David Flusser, *Judaism of the Second Temple Period: Qumran and Apocalypticism* (vol. 1; Grand Rapids: Eerdmans, 2007), 154–5.

[66] 4Q385a 5a–b 6–8 = 4Q387 3 4–6 = CE 74–6. *CE refers to the combined edition of the text I provide below.

γεγονότα "a traitor both to the laws and to his country." Moreover, since the legitimate high priest is described as "prince of the covenant" (11:22), it may be that a description such as "violator of the covenant" specifically invokes the priesthood. But even though the term "violators of the covenant" is explicit, i.e., it is not a figure of speech, it may have only been intelligible in a particular community of readers. The way in which it invokes a certain dualism as well as its absence from other Jewish texts that describe the same events indicates that it might be a group-specific term.[67] In other words, the expression "violators of the covenant" implies a second and opposite group, i.e. "those who are faithful to the covenant." One apparently finds a description of this opposite group in the term "the people who know their God" (11:32b). An expression like "violators of the covenant" provides a platform that is divorced from the kinds of markers that could help a reader interpret its meaning. The expression could have taken on different meanings among different groups more easily than expressions such as "Pharisee" or "Sadducee" could not have. In spite of the fact that the language does not point beyond itself to some other reality, it may have proven considerably more difficult to interpret than the symbolic language found in apocalypses such as Dan 7 and 8 because it is not embedded in linguistic structures that reflect conventional associations or recurrent motifs that function as interpretative tools.

Three more explicit, adjectival descriptions of Jews are found in the narration of the Hellenistic religious reforms. After the abomination of desolation is erected in the holy of holies of the Jerusalem temple, a group of people arises that is contrasted with "those who violate the covenant." "But the people who know their God (עַם יֹדְעֵי אֱלֹהָיו) shall stand firm and take action" (11:32b).[68] The text gives even more information about the subset of Jews loyal to YHWH, "The wise among the people (מַשְׂכִּילֵי עָם) shall give understanding to many" (11:33a). The הַמַּשְׂכִּילִים "wise ones" appear again in 11:35 where they apparently take significant losses during the early period of the resistance movement and in 12:3 where the reward for their faithfulness in given to them in the *eschaton*. The text claims that they will "shine like the brightness of the sky" (12:3). The verse also provides another parallel, adjectival description of the wise: "those who lead many to righteousness" (מַצְדִּיקֵי הָרַבִּים). The reward for those who lead to righteous-

---

[67] The use of language that divides Jews into groups such as "the faithful" and "the unfaithful" – especially when only "the faithful" may understand this language – perhaps reflects the sort of "tension" characteristic of sectarianism and described in W. S. Bainbridge, *A Sociology of Religious Movements* (New York: Routledge, 1997), 21–25, 38–42.

[68] Dan 1:17 claims that God gave knowledge (מַדָּע) to Daniel and his three friends. Knowledge of God is a recurrent concept in the Book of Hosea. The prophetic predicts judgment because there is no knowledge of God (דַּעַת אֱלֹהִים) in the land (cf. 4:1, 4:6, 6:6).

ness is the same as that of the wise: "[they shall shine] like the stars forever and ever." Based on the symbolic meaning of stars encountered earlier in this project (i.e., star is used as a conventional symbol for angel), it appears safe to assume that the text claims that the wise/those who lead to righteousness will become angels. We saw in chapter two above that the writer of 4QInstruction^d 81 4–5 encourages the students to yearn for fellowship among the angels.

The most famous and successful resistance party during the Hellenistic religious reforms was the Maccabees. But "the wise" and "those who lead many to righteousness" should not be construed as Maccabees. Why? It is clear that "the wise" were not successful in their resistance and look forward to a reward not in the present age, but in the age to come. The Maccabees are probably referred to in 11:34 as עֵזֶר מְעָט "a little help." Porphyry, one of Daniel's earliest interpreters, held this opinion. An account of his interpretation is preserved in Jerome's commentary on Daniel: "Porphyry thinks that the 'little help' was Mattathias of the village of (variant: mountain of) Modin, for he rebelled against the generals of Antiochus and attempted to preserve the worship of the true God."[69] According to Jerome, Porphyry arrives at this identification because, "Mattathias was slain in battle; and later on his son Judas, who was called Maccabaeus, also fell in the struggle."[70] The writer of Daniel could not have foreseen the great success of the Maccabees since the book was finished before Antiochus IV was dead. "The wise" names a group that looks past the Maccabees – not one that trusts in them. Collins is surely correct that the author of Daniel belonged to "the wise ones" and that the instruction they impart corresponds to the apocalyptic wisdom of the book."[71]

The expression מַשְׂכִּילִים may be adapted from a description of the suffering servant in Isa. Therein the roots שכל and צדק are used in close proximity to describe the servant. YHWH announces through the prophet in Isa 52:13, הִנֵּה יַשְׂכִּיל עַבְדִּי "See my servant shall prosper." In Isaiah the servant is also described as יַצְדִּיק צַדִּיק עַבְדִּי לָרַבִּים "the righteous one, my servant, who will lead many to righteousness (Isa 53:11)."[72] We have already seen that in Dan 12:3, the מַשְׂכִּלִים are synonymous with מַצְדִּיקֵי הָרַבִּים "those who lead many to righteousness." The parallelism thus connects Dan 11 with Isa 52–3. H. L. Ginsberg has argued that the writer of Daniel had a keen interest in Israelite prophecies about Assyria and the suffering servant

---

[69] *Jerome's Commentary on Daniel*, 155.
[70] *Jerome's Commentary on Daniel*, 155.
[71] Collins, *Daniel*, 385.
[72] Cf. H. L. Ginsberg, "The Oldest Interpretation of the Suffering Servant," *VT* 3 (1953). Collins accepts Ginsberg's suggestion to excise צַדִּיק as a dittography. He also amends יַצְדִּיק to מַצְדִּיק even though there is no textual evidence for this reading. Cf. Collins, *Daniel*, 385.

and even appropriated their language towards a new end.[73] This may be so but the specific uses of the roots שכל and צדק are considerably removed from their Isaian context and would hardly have been recognized as such without privileged information (i.e., access to in-group exegesis, rhetoric, etc.). The expressions themselves are group specific terms whose context is too weak to support a definitive interpretation. In other words, only "those who lead many to righteousness" would know how to identify "those who lead many to righteousness." This cryptic use of Isaiah to develop community terminology may be exactly the same phenomenon that Maxine Grossman highlights in CD 1 1–2 1. The opening lines of the Damascus Document offer several nuanced reflections on Jewish scripture (Hos 4:16, 10:11, Exod 32:8, 10, Deut 9:12, Ps 106:40). Grossman claims:

> For a reader or hearer who makes these connections, picking up on direct and indirect scriptural references *and* the thematic ribbon that runs through them all, the primary message of the text is now enlivened and exemplified by a secondary level of communication. With cleverness, subteltly, and a fair degree of scriptural "play," this audience might link the congregation of traitors – or any other opposition force – to the many cattle of Hosea and beyond. From this perspective, outsiders become the original rebellious Israelites, makers of the golden calf, and the transgressive idolators alive in the literary or mythic time of Hosea's prophecies.[74]

Grossman goes on to claim, "The insider who recognizes these references and links them together has demonstrated both technical skill and an understanding of how the game is played . . . Sectarians become sectarians by learning to think and reason like insiders."[75]

The high priest Onias III appears in the text at 11:22. He is described as נְגִיד בְּרִית "the prince of the covenant" and the text claims that he "will be swept away" (יִשָּׁטֵפוּ) along with some troops (זְרֹעוֹת, i.e., resistance fighters). A similar description is found of David in 11QPs^a XXVIII 11–12. Therein David claims that YHWH "made me leader of his people" (וישימנו לעמו נגיד), and ruler "over the sons of his covenant" (בבני בריתו). David is described as נגיד in 4Q504 and numerous times in Hebrew Bible. But the expression נגיד is also used to describe high priests in the Hebrew Bible – specifically in Late Hebrew (Chron). For example, in the genealogical lists of the first people to return and live in Jerusalem after the Babylonian Exile, the list of priests includes עֲזַרְיָה בֶן־חִלְקִיָּה בֶּן־מְשֻׁלָּם בֶּן־צָדוֹק בֶּן־מְרָיוֹת בֶּן־אֲחִיטוּב נְגִיד בֵּית הָאֱלֹהִים "Azariah, son of Hilqiah, son of Meshullam, son

---

[73] Ginsberg actually argues that a source of the Book of Daniel (his "apoc. III" source) does this. It is not necessary to reach the same source-critical conclusion as Ginsberg (I do not) in order to accept his conception of the hermeneutic at work in the text.

[74] Grossman, "Cultivating Identity: Textual Virtuosity and "Insider" Status," 7.

[75] Grossman, "Cultivating Identity: Textual Virtuosity and "Insider" Status," 8.

of Zadok, son of Meraiot, son of Achitub, prince of the house of God." The high priest is described again in 2 Chron 31:13 as נְגִיד בֵּית הָאֱלֹהִים "prince of the house of God." Thus it appears that נְגִיד בְּרִית is an explicit description. It is true that the writer could have perhaps been even more specific by using a title such as הַכֹּהֵן הַגָּדוֹל "the high priest." But if the title given to Jonathan the Maccabee by Antiochus Epiphanes, i.e., ἀρχιερέα τοῦ ἔθνους σου "high priest of your nation," was also taken by figures such as Jason and Menelaus, the writer of Daniel could be making a point of emphasizing the religious versus political nature of the true high-priesthood as he understands it.

Descriptions of Ethno-Political Groups
The first ethno-political designation not bound in the title of an angel or king (e.g., "Prince of Persia" or "Kingdom of Greece") is *Kittim* (כִּתִּים). Context leaves little doubt about the identification of the *Kittim* as Romans in Dan 11:30: "For ships of *Kittim* shall come against him, and he shall lose heart and withdraw."[76] The verse refers to the famous incident now referred to as the "Day of Eleusis" where an advancing Antiochus IV was confronted by the Roman consul Popilius Laenas in Eleusis (a suburb of Alexandria) in July of 168 B.C.E..[77] According to Polybius, Popilius presented Antiochus with an ultimatum and then, in the face of Antiochus' indecision, used a stick to draw a circle around him in the dirt. He then told the Greek king that a decision had to be made before stepping out of the circle (Polybius 29.27.5). While the specific meaning of the term *Kittim* is clear in this verse, the nature of the expression is not clear. Should it be read as an explicit description of Rome? A gentilic? Is the description adjectival or even metaphorical? I suggest it should be read as a proper noun – not an adjectival description or an epithet of some sort. In order to demonstrate this it will be necessary to consider how the expression is used in other sources.

Not all uses of the term *Kittim* carry the same meaning in ancient Jewish literature. It is used five times in the Hebrew Bible outside of the Book of Daniel. It is also found in numerous inscriptions as well as in the Apocrypha, the Dead Sea Scrolls, and Josephus.[78] In what follows I consider these

---

[76] Cf. Henri del Medico, "L'identification des Kittim avec les Romains," *VT* 10 (1960).

[77] Hölbl, *A History of the Ptolemaic Empire*, 147.

[78] One example may also be found in Ugaritic and another in Punic. The evidence is not entirely clear in these examples. For the Ugaritic example, see Lete and Sanmartín, *A Dictionary of the Ugaritic Language*, 468. Cyrus Gordon, *Ugaritic Textbook : Grammar, Texts in Transliteration, Cuneiform Selections, Glossary, Indices* (Rome: Pontifical Biblical Institute, 1998), 19: 1319. While both *kt* and *rt* are possible readings in the inscription, I agree with Gordon that given the

uses. The precise identification of *Kittim* in each example is not as important as the way in which the term is contextualized. In chapter 5 a more significant weight will be placed on the *precise* meaning of *Kittim* in the *War Scroll*. For now I am most interested in whether the term is used as an adjective, a place-name, a gentilic, etc., in ancient Jewish literature.

In the Table of Nations (i.e., the descendents of Noah in Gen 10), *Kittim* (כִּתִּים) is mentioned alongside Elishah, Tarshish, and Rodanim as descendents of *Yawan* (יָוָן), one of the sons of *Yaphet* (Gen 10:4). Thus, in Genesis *Kittim* is a gentilic ("demonym" or "ethnonym") based on the eponymous ancestor *Kittim* (a descendant of Noah). 1 Chron 1:7 presents precisely the same genealogy and almost certainly borrows it from Gen.[79]

At the end of the last oracle found in the Balaam legends, the prophet names *Kittim* as an agent of divine retribution: "Who shall live when God does this? But ships shall come from *Kittim* (כִּתִּים) and shall humble *Assur* and *Eber*; and he too shall perish forever" (Num 24:24). The use of *Kittim* in Numbers presumes that the term is associated with a particular geographic region. A specific geography is also presumed by the use of *Kittim* in the lamentation over Tyre in Ezek 27. The poem in 27:3–11 depicts the great adornments of Tyre. One of its attributes is that, "they made your deck of pines from the coasts of כִּתִּים "Kittim."[80] The Book of Jeremiah also uses the term *Kittim* with a specific geography in mind. In an oracle that pleads with the residents of Jerusalem to repent, the prophet exclaims: "Therefore, again I accuse you – oracle of YHWH! – and I accuse your children's children. Cross to the coasts of כִּתִּיִּים "Kittim" and look!" (Jer 2:9–10). Finally an oracle concerning Tyre from the so-called "Isaianic Apocalypse" in Third Isaiah promises that Sidon will find not rest even if they "cross over to כִּתִּים "Kittim."[81] This passage also presumes a specific geography. Most biblical texts imply that that the location of *Kittim* requires its people to arrive in Israel by ship from the West (this is also implied in Genesis and 1 Chronicles to the extent that the father of *Kittim* is *Yawan*).[82]

Josephus explicitly combines notions of ethnicity (Genesis, 1 Chronicles) and geography (Numbers, Ezekiel, Jeremiah, Isaiah) in his own appropriation and commentary on the Table of Nations:

---

context (*bn.amht.kt* "among handmaids of the *Kittim*"), the original reading (*kt*) is correct. Cf. C. Virolleaud, *Syria* 30 (1954): 193. The Punic example is less certain. See Hoftijzer and Jongeling, *DNWSI*, 540.

[79] Knoppers, *1 Chronicles, 1–9*, 247–8.

[80] Reading with the *Qere* vs. כִּתִּיִּים in light of the standard orthography (כתים) in the inscriptions found at Arad. See more below on Arad.

[81] Ibid.

[82] Cf. Brian Schultz, "The Kittim of Assyria," *RevQ* 23 (2007): 63–77.

Chetimos held the island of Chetima – the modern Cyprus – whence the name Chetim (Χεθίμ) given by the Hebrews to all islands and to most maritime countries; here I call to witness one of the cities of Cyprus which has succeeded in preserving the old appellation, for even in its Hellenized form Cition is not far removed from the name of Chetimos (*Antiquities* 1.128.)[83]

A similar combination of meaning is found in the use of the term in 1 Maccabees 1:1 where Alexander the Great is described as coming from γῆς Χεττιιμ "the land of *Kittim*." That Alexander "comes from" the land of *Kittim* does not imply only a location. It also names an ethnic identity. That the term *Kittim* was not a purely geographic designation is made clear by several inscriptions from Arad.[84] The Arad inscriptions describe deliveries of staple supplies to the *Kittim* (כתים) who are in the city. Y. Aharoni argues that the expression was used to describe the kind of Aegean mercenaries one also finds evidence of at Meṣad Ḥashavyahu and Tell el-Milḥ.[85] It may have been a term used for any or all inhabitants of the Western Mediterranean at certain points.[86] A more specific geographical connection with Cyprus might have also obtained. Whatever meanings might have been originally attached to the word, Hanan Eshel is certainly correct that its meaning was in dispute by the end of the second century B.C.E..[87] Following Sukenik and Flusser, Eshel shows that *Kittim* refers to the Romans in most of the *Pesharim*, but to the Seleucids in the *War Scroll*.[88] For example, the *Pesher Nahum* describes not only the Seleucid ruler Demetrius as מלך יון "king of Greece," but declares "[God did not deliver Jerusalem] into the hand of the kings of Greece (מלכי יון) from Antiochus up to the appearance of the chiefs of the *Kittim*" מושלי כתיים (4Q169 3–4i 2–3). It is impossible for *Kittim* to refer to the Seleucids in this context. In the *Pesher Nahum*, *Kittim* refers to Romans while "kings of Greece" refers to Seleucids. In other words, "kings of Greece" has the same meaning that *Kittim* does in the *War Scroll*.[89] Both the *Pesharim* and the *War Scroll* presume not merely a geographical location, but a specific ethnos (even if it is not the same one). Thus the use of *Kittim* in Daniel is not symbolic,

---

[83] Josephus, *Jewish Antiquities, Books I–IV* (trans. H. St. J. Thackaray; Cambridge: Harvard University Press, 1926), 63.

[84] Cf. Yohanan Aharoni, *Arad Inscriptions* (Jerusalem: Israel Exploration Society, 1981). One can find a convenient collection of transcriptions and translations for these inscriptions in Sandra Landis Gogel, *A Grammar of Epigraphic Hebrew* (SBLRBS 23; Atlanta: Scholars Press, 1998), cf. Arad #s 1, 2, 4, 5, 7, 8, 10, 11, 14, 17.

[85] Yohanan Aharoni, "Arad: Its Inscriptions and Temple," *BA* 13 (1968): 14.

[86] The reference to Kittim of Ashur may indicate that the writer of 1QM used the term to refer to Seleucids. See Collins, *Daniel*, 73–4.

[87] Eshel, "The Kittim in the War Scroll and in the Pesharim," 29.

[88] The Pesher on Isaiah is probably an exception.

[89] Eshel, "The Kittim in the War Scroll and in the Pesharim," 29–44.

cryptic, or even adjectival. It fits well with other uses in ancient Judaism and had significant currency in the socio-cultural encyclopedia of ancient Israel.

The proper names of several ethno-political groups are clustered together in the final stages of the historical review in Dan 11. While it is clear that the writer erroneously predicts that Antiochus would die, "between the sea and the beautiful holy mountain,' i.e., in the *shefelah*, in 11:45, it is unclear if the references to battles with these ethno-political groups is part of the *ex eventu* revelation or is actual prophecy. Multiple other accounts of Antiochus' death place it in Persia (though they disagree on some of the circumstances).[90] No such clear evidence exists in the cases of the literary map used to describe Antiochus' military exploits. The ethno-political groups (nations) named in 11:41–3 are: Edom (אֱדוֹם), Moab (בְּנֵי עַמּוֹן), Amon (עַמּוֹן), Egypt (מִצְרַיִם), Libians (לֻבִים), and Ethiopians (כֻּשִׁים). These descriptions are significantly different than the descriptions typically used for ethno-political groups in symbolic apocalypses such as Dan 7 and 8 or the *Animal Apocalypse*. These descriptions do not point beyond themselves. Neither do they require any kind of privileged information for interpretation (either for the purported recipient of the vision or the ancient or modern reader). Two elements are especially noteworthy about this literary map. First, each term implies an ethno-political group, but they also imply a specific geographical locale. So Dan 11 not only depicts different ethno-political groups, but depicts them in a context that places each one in its own homeland. The text forms a literary map that makes explicit not only with *whom* but *where* the battles that culminate in the end of time will take place.

Second, as Collins points out, the particular nations found in Daniel's literary map are somewhat surprising.

> Edom, Moab, and Ammon were traditional enemies of Israel. They are aligned with Belial and the Sons of Darkness in 1QM 1:1. Judas Maccabee attacked the Edomites and Ammonites (1 Macc 5:1–8). In light of this we would not expect Antiochus to attack them. What is surprising is that they are not listed as his allies.[91]

One potential explanation is that the literary map that appears in Dan 11 encompasses all of the Seleucid and Ptolemaic territories. In other words, the entire political world of Judea would be engulfed in a war.

---

[90] The relevant texts are Polybius 31.9, Appian *Syr* 11.66, 1 Macc 6:1–17, 1 Macc 1:14–16, 9:1–29. See the discussion in Collins, *Daniel*, 389–90.

[91] Collins, *Daniel*, 389.

Raw Data from Daniel 10–12

Citation		Description	Identity
10:1	כּוֹרֶשׁ מֶלֶךְ פָּרַס	Cyrus, King of Persia	Cyrus
10:1	דָּנִיֵּאל	Daniel	Daniel
10:1	בֵּלְטְשַׁאצַּר	Belteshazzar	Daniel
10:2	דָּנִיֵּאל	Daniel	Daniel
10:5	אִישׁ	A man	An angel
10:7	דָּנִיֵּאל	Daniel	Daniel
10:10	דָּנִיֵּאל	Daniel	Daniel
10:12	דָּנִיֵּאל	Daniel	Daniel
10:13	שַׂר מַלְכוּת פָּרַס	The prince of the kingdom of Persia (x2)	Patron angel of Persia

10:13	מִיכָאֵל אַחַד הַשָּׂרִים הָרִאשֹׁנִים	Michael, one of the chief princes	Michael, patron angel of Israel
10:16	כִּדְמוּת בְּנֵי אָדָם	One like the form(s) of a human being	Angel
10:17	אֲדֹנִי	My lord (x2)	Angel
10:18	כְּמַרְאֵה אָדָם	one with the appearance of a human	Angel
10:19	אִישׁ־חֲמֻדוֹת	treasured man	Daniel
10:19	אֲדֹנִי	my lord	angel
10:20	שַׂר פָּרַס	prince of Persia	Patron angel of Persia
10:20	שַׂר־יָוָן	Prince of Greece	Patron angel of Greece
10:21	מִיכָאֵל שַׂרְכֶם	Michael, your prince	Patron angel of Israel

11:1	דָּרְיָוֶשׁ הַמָּדִי	Darius the Mede (sic)	Darius of Persia
11:2	שְׁלֹשָׁה מְלָכִים עֹמְדִים לְפָרַס	Three Kings of Persia	Three Persian Kings
11:2	הָרְבִיעִי	Fourth King of Persia	Either Xerxes or Darius III Codomannus
11:2	מַלְכוּת יָוָן	Kingdom of Greece	
11:3	מֶלֶךְ גִּבּוֹר	Mighty King	Alexander the Great
11:4	מַלְכוּתוֹ וְתֵחָץ לְאַרְבַּע רוּחוֹת הַשָּׁמָיִם	Kingdom divided to the four winds of heaven	Alexander's kingdom after his death
11:5	מֶלֶךְ־הַנֶּגֶב	King of the South	Ptolemy I
11:5	מִן־שָׂרָיו	One of his princes	Seleucus I Nicator
11:6	בַת מֶלֶךְ־הַנֶּגֶב	Daughter of King of the South	Berenice (daughter of Ptolemy I)

11:7	נֵ֫צֶר	A shoot	Ptolemy III Euergetes (Berenice's brother)
11:7	מֶ֫לֶךְ הַצָּפוֹן	King of the North	Seleucus II Callinicus, son of Laodice
11:8	מִצְרַיִם	Egypt	Egypt
11:8	מֶ֫לֶךְ הַצָּפוֹן	King of the North	Seleucus II Callinicus, son of Laodice
11:9	מַלְכוּת מֶ֫לֶךְ־הַנֶּ֫גֶב	Kingdom of the king of the South	Ptolemaic Egypt
11:10	בָּנָיו (Qere)	His sons	Seleucus III Ceraunus and Antiochus III the Great
11:11	מֶ֫לֶךְ־הַנֶּ֫גֶב	King of the South	Ptolemy IV Philopater
11:11	מֶ֫לֶךְ הַצָּפוֹן	King of the North	Antiochus III the Great
11:13	מֶ֫לֶךְ הַצָּפוֹן	The king of the North	Antiochus III the Great

11:14	מֶלֶךְ־הַנֶּגֶב	The king of the South	Ptolemy V Epiphanes
11:14	בְּנֵי פָּרִיצֵי עַמְּךָ[92]	The sons of violence among your people	unknown
11:15	מֶלֶךְ הַצָּפוֹן	The king of the North	Antiochus III the Great
11:15	זְרֹעוֹת הַנֶּגֶב	The forces of the south	Ptolemaic troops
11:15	מִבְחָרָיו	His "special forces"	Scopas' Aetolian mercenaries
11:16	הַבָּא אֵלָיו	The one who comes against him	(i.e., the king of the South)
11:17	כָל־מַלְכוּתוֹ	His whole kingdom	
11:17	בַּת הַנָּשִׁים	A daughter of wives	Cleopatra
11:18	קָצִין	A leader	Lucius Cornelius Scipio (victor at Magnesia)

---

[92] In the MT this form is preceded by a *waw* and so it is spirantized. I have not added a *dagesh* to the *bet* in this chart order to avoid misrepresenting the MT. I follow the same procedure throughout this chart.

11:20	עָמַד עַל־כַּנּוֹ	One (who will stand in his place)	Seleucus IV Philopater
11:20	נוֹגֵשׂ הֶדֶר	A tyrant of splendor	Heliodorus
11:21	עָמַד עַל־כַּנּוֹ	One who will stand in his place ([who will] be despised, will not be given the majesty of the kingdom, will come in secrecy, will seize the kingdom with deceit)	Antiochus IV Epiphanes
11:22	נְגִיד בְּרִית	The prince of the covenant	Onias III
11:23	מְעַט־גּוֹי	A small nation	Pergamum (?)
11:24	אֲבֹתָיו וַאֲבוֹת	His father, his father's fathers	Previous Seleucid Kings
11:25	מֶלֶךְ־הַנֶּגֶב	The king of the South (x2)	Ptolemy VI Philometor
11:26	אֹכְלֵי פַת־בָּגוֹ	Those devouring his royal food	Egyptian advisors to Ptolemy VI

11:27	שְׁנֵיהֶם הַמְּלָכִים	Two Kings	Antiochus IV Epiphanes and Ptolemy VI Philometor
11:29	הַנֶּגֶב[93]	The south	Ptolemaic Egypt
11:30	כִּתִּים	Kittim	Romans
11:32	מַרְשִׁיעֵי בְרִית	The violators of the covenant	Hellenistic Sympathizers
11:32	עַם יֹדְעֵי אֱלֹהָיו	The people who know their God	Jewish resistance
11:33	מַשְׂכִּילֵי	The wise among the people	Jewish resistance
11:34	עֵזֶר מְעָט	A little help	The Maccabees
11:35	הַמַּשְׂכִּילִים	The wise	Jewish resistance
11:36	הַמֶּלֶךְ	The king	Antiochus IV Epiphanes
11:40	מֶלֶךְ־הַנֶּגֶב	The king of the South	Ptolemy VI Philometor

---

[93] The definite article has disappeared in the MT because of a preposition.

11:40	מֶלֶךְ הַצָּפוֹן	The king of the North	Antiochus IV Epiphanes
11:41	אֱדוֹם	Edom	Edom
11:41	מוֹאָב	Moab	Moab
11:41	רֵאשִׁית בְּנֵי עַמּוֹן	Remainder of Amon	Amon
11:42	מִצְרַיִם	Egypt	Egypt
11:43	מִצְרַיִם	Egypt	Egypt
11:43	לֻבִים	Libians	Libians
11:43	כֻּשִׁים	Ethiopians	Ethiopians
12:1	מִיכָאֵל הַשַּׂר הַגָּדוֹל	Michael, the great prince	Michael (patron angel of Israel)
12:1	כָּל־הַנִּמְצָא כָּתוּב בַּסֵּפֶר	Everyone found written in the book	Those whose ideology comports with the author

12:2	רַבִּים מִיְּשֵׁנֵי אַדְמַת עָפָר	Many sleeping in the Earth	The dead
12:3	הַמַּשְׂכִּלִים	The wise	Jewish resistance
12:4	דָּנִיֵּאל	Daniel	Daniel
12:5	דָּנִיֵּאל	Daniel	Daniel
12:5	שְׁנַיִם אֲחֵרִים	Two others	Angels
12:6	אִישׁ לְבוּשׁ הַבַּדִּים	The man clothed in linen	Angel
12:7	אִישׁ לְבוּשׁ הַבַּדִּים	The man clothed in linen	Angel
12:7	עַם־קֹדֶשׁ	The holy people	Israel
12:8	אֲדֹנִי	My lord	Angel
12:9	דָּנִיֵּאל	Daniel	Daniel

12:10	רְשָׁעִים	Evil ones (x2)	
12:10	הַמַּשְׂכִּלִים	The wise	

Findings From Chapter Four

One
A linguistic- and motif-historical analysis of the language in Dan 10–12 reveals that, contrary to the opinion of nearly every scholar we encountered in the history of research, not all apocalypses are characterized (coined!) by symbolic language. Dan 10–12 is a non-symbolic apocalypse. Daniel does not require the angel Michael to provide him an interpretation of the vision he experiences. The meaning is clear. The text matches more closely with the non-symbolic (or "message") dream type. In this type a human has a plain conversation with a heavenly being and understands the contents of the message imparted by the deity or angel. The language used in Dan 10–12 to describe deities, angels/demons, and humans (both individuals and groups) does not point beyond itself. There are different kinds of explicit descriptions attested (e.g., personal names, titles, and even adjectival descriptions), but none is symbolic. The systems of conventional pairs familiar from the symbolic apocalypse are largely missing from Dan 10–12 and the descriptions used in Dan 10–12 are not pregnant with the type of interpretative tools we observed in the apocalypses in chapters two and three.

Two
While with one or two exceptions there is no symbolic language in Dan 10–12, there are several instances of expressions that are esoteric. This type of language has probably led scholars to label it "symbolic," but it is important to distinguish between language comprised of tropes such as metaphors and language that is occluded by other means. The language used in these types of descriptions (e.g., "the wise ones" or "those who lead to righteousness") is explicit, but it nevertheless requires privileged information for a definitive interpretation. I suggest this language functions to create what M. Barkun calls the "microcosm" of apocalypticism. In chapter one we saw

examples of how both ancient Jews and a variety of modern apocalypticists use language to construct and maintain their linguistic universe. This language often sets up binary relationships in order to make the boundaries of the microcosm obvious to those that are in it. For example, the expression "the wise ones" (משכלים) in Daniel hardly has the same function that חֲכָמִים "the wise ones" does in the Book of Proverbs, much less מַשְׂכִּיל/מַשְׂכִּלִים in Psalms and Proverbs (which has at least three distinct meanings). Instead, this is an "us and them" expression. The expression lets the reader/hearer know that they are on the inside (only the "wise ones" could understand the expression "wise ones"). This feature of the language is to me a potential indication of the group-specific dynamics present in some quarters of Hellenistic Jewish apocalypticism. In other words, without the help of insider-information, no one interpretation can take precedence over the other. It has been clear for some time that the Qumran sectarians/Essenes made use of such linguistic tools. It is now possible to venture outside of that limited body and data and explore the phenomenon in a wider swath of Judaism. Daniel 10–12 provides evidence that can be compared with the evidence in chapters five and six. More work needs to be done to further develop and refine criteria for isolating group-specific language, but I hope to have provided a survey that maps out the landscape in Dan 10–12.

Three

Daniel 10–12 reveals far more detailed, precise information than the apocalypses in Dan 7 and 8. While it might seem at first that a non-symbolic apocalypse would be, *de facto*, more detailed than symbolic apocalypses, the examination of the *Animal Apocalypse* above illustrated how a symbolic apocalypse can be quite detailed. Thus, the relative level of precision in the description of historical events seems not to be a significant distinction between symbolic and non-symbolic apocalypses. Nevertheless, it is possible – at least in the Book of Daniel – that a non-symbolic apocalypse is used to interpret or perhaps "demythologize" a symbolic apocalypse *a la* Dan 7 or 8. A similar situation could obtain in the *Book of Dreams* from *1 En.* (83–90) where both a symbolic and non-symbolic apocalypse are presented together.

Chapter 5

Apocryphon of Jeremiah C

The *Apocryphon of Jeremiah C* opened the door for this study. A comparison of *The Apocryphon of Jeremiah A–C* with the Book of Daniel led A. Lange and U. Mittman-Richert to propose the categories "symbolic" and "non-symbolic" for apocalypses in DJD 39.[1] In this chapter I analyze the language used in the *Apocryphon of Jeremiah C*. Before performing an analysis of the text, two *Prolegomena* must be addressed. There is still disagreement over 1) what constitutes *The Apocryphon of Jeremiah* and 2) whether or not it is an apocalypse.

Do 4Q383–391 Constitute One Text?

John Strugnell first grouped the manuscripts 4Q383–4Q391 and described them as *"un écrit pseudo-jérémien."*[2] He later remarked that the work contained "a notable pseudo-Ezekiel section."[3] Devorah Dimant, the editor of the *editio princeps*, initially argued for the existence of a third literary work within 4Q383–4Q391, which she characterized as "pseudo-Moses" (4Q390).[4] She has since abandoned that thesis and essentially settled on the two works that Strugnell initially indicated.[5] Dimant establishes the two

---

[1] Lange and Mittmann-Richert, "Annotated List of the Texts from the Judean Desert Classified by Genre and Content," 120–1.

[2] J. T. Milik, "Le travail d'édition des fragments manuscrits de Qumrân," *RB* 63 (1956): 65. Cf. J. T. Milik, *Ten Years of Discovery in the Wilderness of Judea* (SBT; trans. John Strugnell; London: SCM Press, 1959), 36.

[3] John Strugnell, "The Angelic Liturgy at Qumran – 4QSerek Šîrôt 'Ôlat Haššabat," in *Congress Volume* (VTSup 7; Leiden: Brill, 1960), 344.

[4] Devorah Dimant, "New Light from Qumran on the Jewish Pseudepigrapha – 4Q390," in *The Madrid Qumran Congress: Proceedings of the International Congress on the Dead Sea Scrolls* (eds., J.T. Trebolle Barrera and L.V. Montaner; STDJ 11:2; Leiden: Brill, 1992), 405–448.

[5] Devorah Dimant, "Pseudo-Ezekiel" and "Apocryphon of Jeremiah C" in *Qumran Cave 4 XXI* (vol. 30 of DJD; Oxford: Clarendon, 2001), 7–88; 91–260. Eventually Strugnell came to believe that all manuscripts belonged to one work, "An Apocryphon of Ezekiel, first designated as *Pseudo-Ezekiel* and later as *Second-Ezekiel*." Devorah Dimant, "New Light from Qumran on the

text groups based on differences in style, vocabulary, and form discovered between 4Q390 and 4Q386. Dimant uses the 4Q390 and 4Q386 as exemplars of the groups into which she sorts the other manuscript fragments. Her approach is a logical one and it is executed carefully, though it is perhaps unfortunate that she did not at some point choose to replace 4Q390 as exemplar of the *Apocryphon of Jeremiah C* with one of the long overlapping sections of 4Q385a, 4Q387, 4Q388a, and 3Q389 once she collapsed so-called *Pseudo Moses* into the *Apocryphon*. Doing so could have shielded her against criticism that she is manipulating the evidence since in earlier remarks she referred to the majority of what is now the *Apocryphon of Jeremiah C* as, "very different in character and style from both *PsEz* and *PsMos*[4Q390]."[6]

More recently Monica Brady has argued that the manuscripts 3Q383–391 form a single literary work and Cana Werman has defended Dimant's original tripartite division of the manuscripts.[7] Armin Lange and Ulrike Mittmann-Richert have argued that 4Q383 (4QapocrJer A) and 4Q384 (4Qpap apocrJer B?) should be grouped with the Apocryphon of Jeremiah C manuscripts (4Q385a, 387, 388a, 389–90, 387a).[8] Hanan Eshel has argued that 4Q390 should not be read as part of the larger work – though he does not agree with Werman's characterization of it as "pseudo-Moses."[9] These arguments represent three basic problems: 1) the relationship of *Pseudo-Ezekiel* (4Q385, 386, 385b, 388, and 391) to *Apocryphon of Jeremiah C* (4Q385a, 387, 388a, 389–90, 387a), the relationship of *Apocryphon*

Jewish Pseudepigrapha - 4Q390," in *The Madrid Qumran Congress: Proceedings of the International Congress on the Dead Sea Scrolls* (ed. J.T. Trebolle Barrera and L.V. Montaner*STDJ*; Leiden: Brill, 1992), 406.

[6] Dimant, "New Light from Qumran on the Jewish Pseudepigrapha - 4Q390," 412.

[7] Monica Brady, "Prophetic Traditions at Qumran: A Study of 4Q383–391." (Ph.D. Diss., University of Notre Dame, 2000). In a more recent article, Brady pushes further by arguing that the manuscripts 3Q383–391 all make use of the same type of biblical interpretation. Monica Brady, "Biblical Interpretation in the "Pseudo-Ezekiel" Fragments (4Q383–391) from Cave Four," in *Biblical Interpretation at Qumran* (ed. M. Henze; Grand Rapids: Eerdmans, 2005), 88–109. Cana Werman, "Epochs and End-Time: The 490-Year Scheme in Second Temple Literature," *DSD* 13 (2006): 229–55.

[8] In 4Q383 Jeremiah speaks in the first person and this is different from the other manuscripts. But Lange and Mittmann-Richert argue that the use of both first and third person narrative should be expected: "4Q383's use of the first person can also be explained in the context of Jeremiah's letter from Egypt to the exiles in Babylon which is mentioned in 4Q389 1." Lange and Mittmann-Richert, "Annotated List of the Texts from the Judean Desert Classified by Genre and Content," 127.

[9] Hanan Eshel, "4Q390, the 490-Year Prophecy, and the Calendrical History of the Second Temple Period," in *Enoch and Qumran Origins: New Light on a Forgotten Connection* (ed. Gabriele Boccaccini; Grand Rapids: Eerdmans, 2005), 102–10. Eshel, *The Dead Sea Scrolls and the Hasmonean State* 22–7, 131.

of Jeremiah A–B (4Q383–384) to *Apocryphon of Jeremiah C*, and the relationship of 4Q390 to *Apocryphon of Jeremiah C*.

I take a conservative approach and treat only the overlapping manuscripts of *Apocryphon of Jeremiah C* (4Q385a, 387, 388a, 389, 387a). In what follows I justify this position *vis a vis* the three basic problems raised above. Brady has argued convincingly that none of Dimant's criteria *demand* two distinct texts, however, as Brady herself recognizes, Dimant's criteria probably do demand that *Apocryphon of Jeremiah C* and *Pseudo-Ezekiel* be treated as separate chapters or sections of the same literary work.[10] Brady uses the diversity of material in the Book of Jeremiah to argue that a single literary work could contain, for example, both first and third person speech, poetry, dialogue, and annalistic history.[11] This diversity of material is undeniable, but more must be said about the reason for the diversity. While the final form of the Book of Jeremiah does contain all the elements that Brady presents, it is not because a single writer produced them all in one integral whole. Many of the seemingly discordant features of the Book of Jeremiah exist precisely because of its complex literary and textual history. The final, canonical shape of the book lends a sense of unity, but Jeremiah is hardly a single, continuous work produced by a lone writer. The most glaring evidence of this confronts the exegete when s/he examines Jeremiah's Greek text tradition. One seventh of the MT text is missing and a significantly different textual shape (i.e., chapter order) is found.[12] In order to explain the problems with the content of the Book of Jeremiah, William McKane proposed the notion of the "rolling corpus."[13] One of the stages in this corpus has recently been highlighted by Armin Lange. His study of the Deuteronomistic Jeremiah Redaction shows that the redaction probably occurred ca. 520–15 B.C.E. and functioned as a response to figures such as Haggai and Zechariah.[14] The canonical shape of

---

[10] Monica Brady, *Prophetic Traditions at Qumran: A Study of 4Q393–391* (Ph.D. Diss.: University of Notre Dame, 2000), 561.

[11] Brady, "Prophetic Traditions at Qumran: A Study of 4Q393–391," 11–12.

[12] J. Gerald Janzen, *Studies in the Text of Jeremiah* (HSM 6; Cambridge: Harvard University Press, 1973). See Emanuel Tov, *The Septuagint Translation of Jeremiah and Baruch: A Discussion of Early Revisions of the LXX of Jeremiah 29–52 and Baruch 1:1–3:8* (HSM 8; Missoula: Scholars Press, 1976).

[13] William McKane, *A Critical and Exegetical Commentary on Jeremiah I. Introduction and Commentary on Jeremiah I–XXV* (ICC; Edinburgh: T&T Clark, 1986).

[14] Armin Lange, *Vom prophetischen Wort zur prophetischen Tradition: Studien zur Traditions- und Redaktionsgeschichte innerprophetischer Konflikte in der Hebräischen Bibel* (FAT 34; Tübingen: Mohr Siebeck, 2002), 313–15. For more on the Deuteronomistic Jeremiah Redaction, see J.P. Hyatt, "The Deuteronomic Edition of Jeremiah," in *Vanderbilt Studies in the Humanities 1* (ed. Richmond Beatty, et al.; Nashville: Vanderbilt University Press, 1951), 71–95. It is more recently published in Leo Perdue and Brian Kovaks, eds., *A Prophet to the Nations: Essays in*

Jeremiah obscures the socio-historical location of this part of the book. In light of the Book of Jeremiah, I suggest that even if *Apocryphon of Jeremiah* and *Pseudo-Ezekiel* are part of the same text, Dimant's concerns about form and content indicate that they do not form a single, seamless narrative.[15] I do not attempt to force them into one below. *Pseudo-Ezekiel* must be treated as separate from the *Apocryphon of Jeremiah* – even if they do derive from the same overall text.

While Lange and Mittmann-Richert agree with Dimant's formal distinction between *Pseudo-Ezekiel* and *Apocryphon of Jeremiah*, they disagree that *Apocryphon of Jeremiah A–B* should be separated from *Apocryphon of Jeremiah C*.[16] In particular, they object to the notion that the first person speech of Jeremiah in *Apocryphon of Jeremiah A* (4Q383) would be out of place in *Apocryphon of Jeremiah C*. They argue that this feature of the text "can be explained in the context of Jeremiah's letter from Egypt to the exiles in Babylon which is mentioned in 4Q389 1."[17] Regarding *Apocryphon of Jeremiah B* they argue, "There is a correspondence between the reference to the *Book of Jubilees* in 4Q384 9 2 and the ten jubilees mentioned in 4Q387 2ii 3–4. The concern with Jubilees in two manuscripts, attesting a Jeremiah Apocryphon, suggests that we should understand them as two witnesses of the same literary work."[18] I find nothing objectionable in these arguments but I do not include *Apocryphon of Jeremiah A–B* in my text-edition for practical reasons. Each manuscript preserves only a few isolated words and it would be a mere guessing game to place them among the fragments of *Apocryphon of Jeremiah C*.

The final concern is the placement of 4Q390 within *Apocryphon of Jeremiah C*. Dimant treated the text manuscript separately from other *Apocryphon of Jeremiah C* manuscripts for a time and Werman and Eshel continue to do so.[19] There is at least one compelling argument to treat 4Q390 and *Apocryphon of Jeremiah C* as part of the same text though. Dimant notes that 4Q390 and 4Q387 both use a locution that is not found in any

---

Jeremiah Studies (Winona Lake: Eisenbrauns, 1984), 247–67. See also Winfried Thiel, *Die deuteronomitische Redaktion vom Jer 1–25* (WMANT 41; Neukirchen: Neukirchener, 1973).

[15] Dimant, "New Light from Qumran on the Jewish Pseudepigrapha - 4Q390" 405–48.

[16] Lange and Mittmann-Richert, "Annotated List of the Texts from the Judean Desert Classified by Genre and Content," 126–7.

[17] Lange and Mittmann-Richert, "Annotated List of the Texts from the Judean Desert Classified by Genre and Content," 127.

[18] Lange and Mittmann-Richert, "Annotated List of the Texts from the Judean Desert Classified by Genre and Content," 127.

[19] For Dimant's account of her own history of research, see Dimant, *Qumran Cave 4 Parabiblical Texts, Part 4: Pseudo-Prophetic Texts*, 1–3.

other ancient Jewish text: מלאכי משטמות "Angels of Mastemot."[20] The singular form מַשְׂטֵמָה "Mastemah" is well attested. It appears twice in the Hebrew Bible (Hosea 9:7–8) as an abstract concept: "hostility, persecution." By the time *Jubilees* was written, Mastemah had become personified as a satan figure (cf. *Jub.* 17:15–16). The expression is used 18 times in the Dead Sea Scrolls, but only 4Q390 and 4Q387 use the peculiar plural form משטמות (see the analysis below).[21] The sharing of such an idiosyncratic expression is one of the key connections used by Dimant to argue that both manuscripts belong to the same text. On this point I agree with her. But even if they belong to the same text, there are indications that they belong to distinct chapters or sections within that text – sections that cannot be interwoven narratively.

Werman notes several reasons to separate 4Q390 from the *Apocryphon of Jeremiah C*. Here I note only her best arguments. Werman seems to be correct that the texts differ in how they understand the end of the 490 years that each text predicts:

Whereas *Pseudo-Moses* [4Q390] shares the expectation that 490 years will pass from the late First Temple period to the coming of the longed-for change, it does not link this desired change with Antiochus' decrees, which are mentioned in the beginning of fragment B [4Q390 2]. The rule of Belial which "deliver[s] them to the sword" for a "week of years" is that of Antiochus. Yet the decrees do not mark the end of the process. They are followed by another seventy years of sin.[22]

Werman's position is strengthened by the fact that the texts disagree over the terms of the dissension that follow Antiochus' decrees: "According to the *Apocryphon* the dispute concerns the interpretation of God's word; in *Pseudo-Moses* [4Q390] the entire people, 'will have done what is evil in my eyes, and what I did not want they will have chosen.'"[23] 4Q390 names the evil in the eyes of YHWH as the pursuit of wealth and gain, theft, oppression, defiling the temple, forgetting festivals, and (perhaps) marrying non-Jews (4Q390 2 8–10).

There is, in my judgment, an even more compelling reason to treat 4Q390 and *Apocryphon of Jeremiah C* as distinct pieces of the same overall text. Their chronologies appear to be in conflict. Dimant believes that the group described as העולים רישונה מארץ שבים "the ones going up first from the land of their captivity" can be used to deduce that that the fragment in

---

[20] Dimant, *Qumran Cave 4 Parabiblical Texts, Part 4: Pseudo-Prophetic Texts*, 104. Cf. 4Q387 2iii 4, 4Q390 1 11, 2i 7.

[21] For the uses of the singular form among non-biblical scrolls, see Martin Abegg, ed., *The Dead Sea Scrolls Concordance. Volume One: The Non-Biblical Texts from Qumran* (Leiden: Brill, 2003), 489. See also the analysis below.

[22] Werman, "Epochs and End-Time," 245.

[23] Werman, "Epochs and End-Time," 246.

which they appear (4Q390 1 5) is about the early post exilic period.[24] But "the ones going up first" is not the subject of the fragment. They are foils against which individuals much later in history are compared. The generation that the fragment addresses lives in the seventh jubilee of the devastation of the land (cf. 4Q390 1 7-8). The calculation of this jubilee cannot be precise since one does not know if the 10 jubilees of devastation commence in 597 or 586 B.C.E. (or perhaps even the ascension of Nebuchadnezzar). But one can arrive at a close approximation of the date. If 586 is used, one may arrive at a date between approximately 292 and 243 B.C.E.. This date is considerably later than Dimant places it in the relative historical progression of the *Apocryphon*.[25] Indeed, because of the overlaps in other manuscripts of the *Apocryphon of Jeremiah C*, it would be impossible to insert 4Q390 1 into the narration of the third century B.C.E. (cf. the overlaps in lines 41–67 in the combined edition below).

Texts like Daniel include multiple and slightly different accounts of the same events. They are all part of the same text, but one could not intergrate the histories of Dan 7 with Dan 10–12. I suggest that the same situation obtains in the *Apocryphon of Jeremiah C*. 4Q390 is part of the same text, but reflects a section of the text whose narrative is unrelated to (i.e., not integrated with) the rest of the *Apocryphon of Jeremiah C*.

One final note is worthwhile before moving forward. None of the manuscripts in the group 4Q383–391 use symbolic ciphers. Therefore, if I am wrong the worst consequence is that I have performed a representative rather than a comprehensive analysis of the language found in the text. By taking a conservative approach and using only those manuscripts that are joined to each other explicitly by overlaps I reduce considerably the possibility of invalid data.

Is Apocryphon of Jeremiah C an Apocalypse?

I take it as self-evident that the *Apocryphon of Jeremiah C* is a revelatory text with a narrative framework. No scholar has doubted that the text constitutes a Hellenistic narration of a lengthy ex-eventu prophecy in the name of a famous Judahite prophet. I focus here on the more nuanced aspects of the generic form. The Collins/*Semeia* 14 definition of apocalypse discussed in chapter one addresses three basic elements of revelatory texts with narrative frameworks: 1) mode of revelation, 2) space, and 3) time. *Apocryphon of Jeremiah C* clearly follows the *Semeia* 14 definition for the last two

---

[24] Dimant, "4QApocryphon of Jeremiah," 235–6. Werman, "Epochs and End-Time," 244.
[25] See Dimant, "4QApocryphon of Jeremiah," 99–100.

elements. Not enough of the text is preserved to completely understand the mode of revelation, but there are some reasons to think it also meets the first criterion set out in the *Semeia* definition.

According to *Semeia* 14, the spatial aspect of apocalypses concerns the revealing of information that indicates the presence of another, supernatural world. This supernatural world is most clearly indicated in *Apocryphon of Jeremiah C* by the presence of a feature common to most apocalypses: a developed angel-/demonology.[26] The appearance of the literary genre apocalypse in ancient Judaism corresponded, in large part, to the appearance of a robust angel-/demonology.[27] In more than one of the Daniel apocalypses, an angel presents and/or interprets a revelation for the visionary – though apocalyptic interest in angels goes far beyond the handful of angelic vision-interpreters. The robust role of angels in apocalypses (not limited to the act of revelation itself) is another feature that distinguishes apocalypses from prophetic oracles.

Apocryphon of Jeremiah C focuses considerably more on demons than angels, but when it comes to Jewish tradition about heavenly/liminal beings, it is unwise to bifurcate angelology and demonology. One need only consider motifs such as the fallen angels in Gen 6 and its reflexes in works such as the *Book of Watchers* to see that angels and demons are two sides of the same coin. Precisely this point is illustrated in an expression used to designate demons in *Apocryphon of Jeremiah C*: מלאכי המשטמות "Angels of Mastemot." מלאך can be used to designate both angels and demons. Also mentioned in *Apocryphon of Jeremiah C* are שעירים "goat demons." These terms are discussed in the analysis below, so I will limit my discussion in this section to the following comment: the *Apocryphon* sets itself apart from the prophetic books of the Hebrew Bible, in part, because of its robust demonology. In other words, while foreign military powers exist in the *Apocryphon's* metaphysics, they provide a mirror image or reflection of a reality from another realm: otherworldly forces of evil. While prophetic

---

[26] Frey, "Die Bedeutung der Qumrantexte für das Verständnis der Apokalyptik im Frühjudentum und im Urchristentum," 30. See also Jörg Frey, "Different Patterns of Dualism in the Qumran Library," in *Legal Texts and Legal Issues. Proceedings of the Second Meeting of the International Organization of Qumran Studies, Cambridge 1995, Published in Honor of J. M. Baumgarten* (ed. Moshe Bernstein, et al.; vol. 25 of *STDJ*; Leiden: Brill, 1997), 325.

[27] For a brief, but concise and comprehensive statement on the angelology of ancient Israel and Second Temple Judaism, see Carol Newsom, "Angels (Old Testament)," in *ABD* (ed. David Noel Freedman; New York: Doubleday, 1992), 248–53. The most comprehensive statement on Jewish demonology in Second Temple times remains: Esther Eshel, "Demonology in the Land of Israel in the Second Temple Period (Hebrew)" (Hebrew University, 1999). The best English language survey is found in Philip Alexander, "The Demonology of the Dead Sea Scrolls," in *The Dead Sea Scrolls after Fifty Years: A Comprehensive Assessment* (ed. Peter Flint and James VanderKam; Leiden: Brill, 1999), II: 331–53.

books such as Jeremiah and Ezekiel castigate Judah for worshipping heavenly beings other than YHWH, they never presume that the figures take a real and active role in the unfolding drama of history and in the everyday lives of Jews.[28] They are "wood and stone" (Ezek 20:32). *Apocryphon of Jeremiah C* presumes a different metaphysics than one finds in the prophetic books in the Hebrew Bible. 4Q390 follows suit; mentioning the "angels of Mastemot" as well as Belial. For both the *Apocryphon* and 4Q390, demons take an active role in and among humans in the earthly realm – not unlike the concept of demons found in the *Book of Tobit* or even in some Akkadian texts from millennia before.[29] So to assume that the *Apocryphon* is essentially a collection of apocryphal extras, i.e., a text intended to mimic biblical prophecy (Jeremiah), does not work. The metaphysics of the world have changed and so has the genre.

The temporal aspect of the *Semeia* 14 definition indicates that the text envisages eschatological salvation. While one cannot fully reconstruct the picture of the eschaton envisioned by the text, the reader is left with some important clues. 4Q385a 17ii 2–3 provides a few enticing details: "]the days of their lives[. . . in the foliage of the tree of life (עֵץ הַחַיִּים)."

There are three references to the tree of life in the *Yahwist's* account of creation. When YHWH created the garden he planted trees of every type, but also עֵץ הַחַיִּים "the tree of life" and עֵץ הַדַּעַת טוֹב וָרָע "the tree of the knowledge of good and evil" (2:9). The properties of the tree of life are revealed in 3:22 after the man and woman eat fruit from the tree of the knowledge of good and evil: "Then YHWH Elohim said, 'See, the man has become just like one of us . . . and now, he might also reach out his hand and take from the tree of life, and eat, and live forever!" YHWH's fear of the first humans leads the deity to block access to the tree of life with *kerubim* and a flaming sword (3:24). The tree of life represents and provides eternal life.

Another text provides a link between the tree of life in Genesis and the one in *Apocryphon of Jeremiah C*: *1 En.* 24–5.[30] During his heavenly journey, Enoch is shown a range of seven mountains. A tree on the seventh mountain, and especially its fragrance, intrigues him. The angel Michael responds to his curiosity: "As for this fragrant tree, not a single human

---

[28] Representative examples from Jeremiah include Baal (7:9) and the Queen of Heaven (7:18). In Ezek one finds Tammuz (8:14). Many more vague references to deities can be found.

[29] See Reynolds, "What Are Demons of Error?," 610–13.

[30] See Dimant, "4QApocryphon of Jeremiah," 157. While I agree with Dimant that the metaphorical uses of עֵץ הַחַיִּים in Prov 3:18, 11:30, and 15:4 are less useful for understanding the expression in the *Apocryphon*, I must disagree that the Gen passages (2:9, 3:22, 24) are not relevant for understanding the usage here. The tree is unambiguously associated with eternal life (denied to humans).

being has the authority to touch it until the great judgment, when he shall take vengeance on all and conclude (everything) forever. This is for the righteous and the pious. And the elect will be presented with its fruit for life."[31]

According to the *Book of Watchers* the righteous will eat from the fruit of life at the end of days. Dimant points out that *1 En.* 24:5, "provides a suitable meaning also for the mention of 'their days of life' in col. ii 2."[32] She adds, "Incidentally, according to *1 En.* 24–25, the Tree of Life is not located in the Garden of Eden, but the top of one of seven mountains situated at 'the west, at the ends of the Earth' (*1 En.* 23:1), and this may tie it with the mention of בתר in col. ii 1."[33] Thus the *Apocryphon* picks up on a motif that hints at both resurrection and eternal life.

In the final judgment, those judged righteous and holy will partake of the fruit of the tree and live forever. This meaning is supported by the use of the term ξυλον ζωης "tree of life" in 4 Macc 18:16 where after the torture and murder of seven faithful Jews, their mother recounts the teaching of the boys's father. Among his admonitions, "He recounted to you Solomon's proverb, 'There is a tree of life for those who do his will'".[34] After the mother's speech, the narrator tell the reader, "But the sons of Abraham with their victorious mother are gathered together into the chorus of the fathers, and have received pure and immortal souls from God" (18:23).

The tree of life also points to eternal life in 5 Ezra (2 Esd 1–2). The text is probably of Christian provenance (or heavy redaction), but it is relevant since the language is hardly innovative in terms of the tree of life motif: "And I will reclaim for myself their glory and give them the eternal tabernacles which I had prepared for them.[35] The tree of life will become an aromatic perfume for them; they will neither toil not be fatigued . . . the kingdom is already prepared for you. Watch [for it]!"[36]

This brief motif-historical glance at the Tree of Life indicates that both resurrection and eternal life are almost certainly indicated by the use of the

---

[31] *1 Enoch* 25:4–5, trans. E. Isaac, "1 Enoch," in *OTP I: Apocalyptic Literture and Testament* (ed. J. H. Charlesworth; New York Doubleday, 1983), 26.

[32] Dimant, "4QApocryphon of Jeremiah," 157.

[33] Dimant, "4QApocryphon of Jeremiah," 157.

[34] Trans. of 4 Macc are from the NRSV.

[35] On the issue of provenance, see Jacob Myers, *I and II Esdras* (AB 42; Garden City: Doubleday, 1974), 148–58. See also Theodore Bergen, *Fifth Ezra: The Text, Origin, and Early History* (SBLSCSS 25; Atlanta: Scholars Press, 1990), 313–33.

[36] Trans. Myers, *I and II Esdras*, 144. The language of this passage in 5 Ezra perhaps borrows from Matt 25:34 and Luke 12:32. A different meaning is found in 1QH 8:5 where the psalmist uses the plural "trees of life" in a description of the spiritual state of bliss the he encounters. Even in the case of 1QH, however, it is reasonable to assume that the concept of eternal life influenced the psalmist's ethereal descriptions of the worship of God.

term in *Apocryphon of Jeremiah C*. This feature once again sets the *Apocryphon* apart from almost all prophetic texts that do not conceive of a full-blown eschatological end and its aftermath. It is likewise set apart from some "apocalyptic" texts that appear to presume resurrection and eternal life (i.e., 1QS 4:11–14), but which do not actually narrate the eschaton as part of a heavenly revelation.

The mode of revelation found in *Apocryphon of Jeremiah C* is more difficult to ascertain. The text undoubtedly presents an *ex eventu* prophecy that details a history extending from at least the Babylonian Exile through the eschaton. It is not clear if Jeremiah's prophecy is based on a vision, dream, audition, etc. A noteworthy feature of the revelation is that its authority is apparently vested in the figure of Jeremiah. This feature sets *Apocryphon of Jeremiah C* apart from other so-called "apocalyptic" texts (not literary apocalypses) found at Qumran. Texts like Dan, *1 En.*, and *Apocryphon of Jeremiah C* gain their authority based on the ostensible visionary experience of famous Jews, reputed for their close relationships with God. One finds a different situation in many of the "apocalyptic" texts from Qumran. Collins writes, "In the Dead Sea sect, authority was vested in the Teacher of Righteousness and his successors. He is the one in whose heart God has put the source of wisdom for all those who understand (1QH 10:18 = 2:18). To him, 'God has disclosed all the mysteries of the words of his servants the prophets' (1QpHab 7:4)."[37] In other words, the apocalyptic community at Qumran (and ostensibly all Essenes) had no need to employ the authority of a venerable sage or prophet in their literature when they had the Teacher of Righteousness. Indeed the *Pesharim* testify that the authority of the Teacher was greater than prophets such as Habakkuk, Nahum, and even Isaiah because he, unlike them, fully undertood the words with which YHWH had entrusted them. In Collins's words, "The Teacher had superseded the prophets of old. Consequently, revelation at Qumran is found, indirectly, in the rule books that regulate the life of the community, present and future, and piecemeal in the biblical commentaries (pesharim) and midrashic texts."[38] It is no small matter that *Apocryphon of Jeremiah C* phrases its message in terms of a divine revelation given to the prophet Jeremiah in the wake of the Babylonian destruction of Jerusalem in 586 B.C.E.. The authority of the text as a revelation is vested in the name of the prophet to whom the message is entrusted.

Not enough of the text of *Apocryphon of Jeremiah C* is preserved to make a definitive statement about its genre. I hope the foregoing analysis has shown that it is most reasonably read together with other apocalypses.

---

[37] Collins, *Apocalypticism in the Dead Sea Scrolls*, 153.
[38] Collins, *Apocalypticism in the Dead Sea Scrolls*, 153.

The Text of Apocryphon of Jeremiah C

One of the most important factors leading to the determination of the overall shape of the text of 4QApocryphon of Jeremiah C is the overlaps among the manuscripts. In her DJD volume, Devorah Dimant rightly treats each manuscript and fragment individually regardless of their potential/obvious relationship with others. She does not, however, provide a final combined reconstruction and translation of the entire text. She does give an opinion about the order of the fragments. Dimant also mentions some of the text-critical problems that arise with a combined edition of the text. In order to do an analysis of the language in the *Apocryphon*, I needed a fully combined, running-edition of the text. My new text and translation are presented below before the linguistic analysis.

The transcription, translation, and fragment placement below is very much influenced by Dimant's work. No aspect of my edition, however, is a reproduction of hers. For the transcription, I first consulted the manuscript photographs alone. While I disagree with her on some issues, Dimant's transcriptions are – in my opinion – extremely accurate and in some cases helped to correct errors in my initial transcription. More frequently, my English translation differs from hers – less as a matter of correction than of stylistic preference. My collation of overlapping manuscripts and text-critical work was produced independently – only later checking my results with those of Dimant, Brady, and others. Discussion of critical issues can be found in the footnotes. In several cases I have adopted Dimant's reconstructions, which are generally conservative. I have attempted to use the standard (DJD) sigla for full and partial reconstructions of the text, however, such sigla are not always possible in some cases of overlapping text in a combined edition. In several cases where as many as three fragments preserve the same line of text – each to a different extent – it is impossible to economically mark a word or letter simultaneously as a full reconstruction, a partial reconstruction, and a fully-preserved character in a combined edition. Thus, for readings only extant in one manuscript, normal sigla are used. For cases of overlapping lines, however, no notations are made on the letters themselves. Explanations are provided in the footnotes. Those with special interests in the readings of particular letters on the overlapping lines should consult either the photographs or Dimant's edition. Another related issue concerns the indication of overlaps. Explicit overlaps are identified by an underline. In some cases, however, as many as three manuscripts overlap in a given line. Each letter of each word is not necessarily extant in each manuscript of the overlap. Rather than resorting to acrobatic sigla, I have underlined words as overlapping as long as at least two manuscripts contain at least one letter of a given word. The reader is referred to the footnotes of the transcription to see precisely which letters are preserved in each overlapping manuscript.

I have not attempted to provide "to-scale" reconstructions of line length and word spacing within fragments since the overlaps make this impossible. I have also omitted several sections of Dimant's reconstructed narrative frame based on lack of context. For example, Dimant places 4Q389 4 just before 4Q389 5 2–3 in her reconstruction of the *ex eventu* prophecy. But the only legible word on the fragment (4Q389 4) is הארץ. She proposes the fragment concerns the children of Israel entering of the land of Canaan. Her reconstruction is possible, but since there is hardly a period of Israel's history when הארץ could/would not have functioned as an important term, I cannot include the fragment in my reconstruction. Omissions such as this one are detailed in the footnotes.

I have excluded manuscript lines that do not contain legible text rather than including them as "ghost lines" in the combined edition (in some cases, the missing text from, for example, the damaged top-line of a fragment is provided in an overlapping manuscript anyway). An example of this is found in the overlapping fragments 4Q388a 3 1–2 (Combined Edition 27–28) and 4Q385a 3 2–10 (CE 28–35). In this case there are no extant letters on the first line of 4Q385a 3. I start the numbers with line two rather than leaving a blank line one since 4Q388a 3 2 preserves some material missing from what would be 4Q388a 3 1. In other words, anytime a line is omitted for not preserving any text, it is accounted for in the numbering scheme that precedes each fragment. I never re-assign or change original numbers of fragment lines. Finally, the reader is reminded that this combined edition does not present a truly continuous text. The continuous line numbers can be misleading but I know of no other way to number the lines in a way that both highlights the extensive overlaps and does not lead to even greater confusion.

Prologue

4Q389 1 2–7 = CE 1–6

[ ] ̊ה בארץ י[הודה	1
[ ] ו[בקשו על כ]ל	2
[ ] ו[כ̊ל הנשאר בארץ מצ̊]רים	3
[ ] י[רמיה בן חלקיה מארץ מצר]ים	4

[שלו]שים ושש שנה לגלות ישראל קראׄוׄ הדברים] האלה לפני[5
בׄ]ל בני יׄ[שראל על נהר סור   במעמד ד 6

Review of History[39]

4Q389 2 1–8 = CE 7–14
4Q388a 2 1–5 = CE 12–16

[   ]ות[דרשני הייתי] 7
[   ]וא[ב]ׄים ראשיכם בהוציאיׄ אׄ[תכם מארץ מצרים 8
[40][   ] להם ואת אשר גמלוני ואשאׄם[כאשר ישא איש את בנו עד] 9
[בואם אל [קׄדש ברנע ואמרה להם [ ] לׄ] 10
[   ]תם עליהם ואשבעה בׄ]ׄ[11
[   ]ׄ[להם ואת בניהם הבאתי אל ה]ארץ 12
[תׄם ואתהלכה עמהם בׄ]ׄ וצותי אתם לעשות אהל[בירייעות עזי]ם 13
[   ]ארבעים שנה ויהי [14
וי[פנו אחרי יׄ] 15
[ה]ׄ אתם 16

4Q389 5 2–3 = CE 17–18[41]

[אׄ]מרו תנה לנו מלך אשר 17
שמוא[ל] בן א[לקנה לדׄ] 18

4Q385a 1ii 1–7 = CE 19–25

---

[39] Dimant begins the *vaticinium ex eventu* with 4Q388a 1, which she proposes concerns the revelation to Moses at Sinai. But the only word completely extant in the fragment is שמים "heavens" and I do not believe it provides enough evidence to be incorporated meaningfully into the text of 4QApocryphon of Jeremiah C. She bases her identification of the Sinai tradition based on biblical descriptions of the event as divine speech from heaven (cf. Exod 20:22, Deut 4:36, Neh 9:13). Dimant's connection is within the realm of possibility, but it is guesswork. Within the context of the fragment, the word heavens is preceded by either a masculine plural noun (or participle) or a dual noun. This combination occurs only once in the Hebrew Bible (Ps 115:16): הַשָּׁמַיִם שָׁמַיִם לַיהוָה "The heavens are YHWH's heavens." The psalm is demonstrably not being quoted within 4Q388a 1.

[40] Dimant's connection of this fragment with themes and language in Deut 1:31 makes her reconstruction כאשר ישא איש את בנו עד plausible. Kadesh Barnea is mentioned in Deut 1:2, 19, 2;14, 9:3.

[41] Dimant places 4Q389 4 just before 4Q389 5 2–3 in her reconstruction of the *ex eventu* prophecy. The only readable word on the fragment is הארץ and she proposes the fragment concerns the entering of the land of Canaan. Her theory is possible, but since there is hardly a period of Israel's history when הארץ could/would not have functioned as an important term, I cannot include the fragment in my reconsruction.

19 וא[קימה לב̇]
20 [את איבו]
21 [א̊ איבו ואסי]רה
22 בשחרו פני ולא רם לבבו ממני ש̇[
23 וישלמו ימיו וישב שלמה]○○○
24 ואתנה נפש איביו בכפ̇ו[
25 ע○[ואקחה מידו עול]ה

4Q385a 2 2 = CE 26

26 [○בׄים וישכ֯חו[42]

4Q388a 3 1–2 = CE 27–28
4Q385a 3 2–10 = CE 28–35
4Q387 1 1–10 = CE 30–39
4Q388a 5 1 = CE 31
4Q389 6 1–2 = CE 36–37
4Q389 7 2–3 = CE 39–40

27 ב[ע̇ת ה]היא
28 בהתהלככם בשגגה מלפני[43]
29 ק[ר]יאי השם ○
30 [ר̇ת̇]כ[ס כאשר אמרתי ליעקוב[44]
31 [א̊ ותאמרו עזבתנ̇ו̇] אלהינו ותמאסו[את חקותי[45]
32 [ותשכחו את]מועדי בריתי ותחללו את [שמי ואת קדשי][46]
33 [ותטמאו את] מקדשי ותזבחו [את זבחיכ]ם לשעירים ות[47]

---

[42] Dimant transcribes וישבחו "and they praised," but notes that the reading וישכחו is also possible. I have chosen the latter because of it frequency within the Deuteronomistic History and Jeremiah/Dtr Jeremiah, i.e., the literature that this text appears to resemble and after which it may model itself. See Deut 8:14, 19, Judg 3:7, 1 Sam 12:9, Jer 3:21.

[43] 4Q385a preserves only לככם ב whereas 4Q388a preserves all three words in line 28. It is noteworthy, however, that בשגגה is written in superscript text in 4Q388a – most likely an omission and correction by a scribe.

[44] The readings provided by each manuscript are: 4Q385a כאשר אמרתי ליע, 4Q387 כ ס[ת̇ר̇, 4Q388a כאשר אמרתי ליעק. Precise column widths are uncertain, but it appears that 4Q388a has omitted as much as a line of text.

[45] The readings provided by each manuscript are: 4Q385a 3a–c [עזבנו] and [את חקותי], 4Q388a 3 את חקותי, and 4Q387 1 [מרו עזב]תנו] [ותא. See Dimant, "4QApocryphon of Jeremiah," 136–8.

[46] The readings provided by each manuscript are: 4Q385a 3a–c [ללו בריתי ותח̇], 4Q388a 3 [ו.תחללו], and 4Q387 1 [את] [ברי]תי ותחל[לו].

[47] Explicit parallels for ם לשעירים ות are found in all three witnesses. One may presume with a high degree of probability that the words מקדשי ותזבחו, now only extant in 4Q385a, must have been present in all three witnesses. Suggestions for the lacunae are a different matter but given parallels in texts like 4QpsDan[a–b] ar (4Q243 13 2, 4Q244 12 2), they hardly stretch the evidence.

4QApocryphon of Jeremiah C

34 ר ותפר הכל ביד ר[מה]⁴⁸
35 ואבקש אמונה ולא מצאתי⁴⁹
36 ואתנ[כ]ם ביד איביכם ואשמה את] ארצכם[⁵⁰
37 והארץ] רצתה שבתותיה בהשמה]⁵¹
38 [ם בארצ[ות] איבי[כ]ם [עד שנת]
39 א]ל אדמתכם [   ]לפ[קוד]°
40 ר]שו בו

4Q387 2ii 1–12 = CE 41–52
4Q385a 4 1–9 = CE 44–51
4Q389 8i–ii 1–11 = CE 49–59
4Q387 2iii 1–7 = CE 58–64
4Q388a 7 1–10 = CE 55–67

41 [יע]   [   ]°[   ]כ̇ם] ו̇תחזקו לעבדנו בכל לבבכם
42 ובכ̇]ל נפשכם ובק[ש]ו̇] פ̇]נ̇]י̇ בצר להם ולא אדרש להם
43 בעבור מעלם [א]ש̇ר מעלו] ב̇]י̇ [עד שלמות עשרה
44 יבלי שנים והתהל̇]כתם בש̇]געון [ובעורון ותמהן̇⁵²
45 הלבב ומתם הדור̇] ההוא א̇]קרע [את הממלכה מיד המחזיקים⁵³
46 אתה והקימותי עליה אחרים מעם אחר ומשל̇⁵⁴
47 הזדון בכל] הא[ר]ץ וממלכת ישראל תאבד בימים⁵⁵
48 ההמה י̇]ה̇]יה מלך וה̇]וא גדפן ועשה תעבות וקרעתי⁵⁶
49 את ממלכ̇]תו והמלך] ההוא למכלים ופני מסתרים מישראל⁵⁷

---

⁴⁸ Uncertain column lengths make precise judgments impossible, but it appears that 4Q385a may preserve up to one additional line of text. רמה would need to begin in 4Q385a 3 10. The readings provided by each manuscript are: 4Q385a 3a–c ותפרו הכל ביד, 4Q388a 3 ביד ל, and 4Q387 1 ד ב̇]י̇]ל הכל ותפר ר.

⁴⁹ 4Q385a preserves לא whereas 4Q387 preserves מצאתי ואב]קש אמונה ו]לא מצאתי. מצאתי would need to begin line 11 of 4Q385a 3.

⁵⁰ There is a textual variant with "their enemies." 4Q389 6 1 reads איביכם while the overlapping text in 4Q387 1 7 reads איבכם (missing the second yod). Since 4Q387 1 9 uses the same orthography as 4Q389 (איביכם) it is most likely that the defective reading (minus) in 4Q387 1 7 is an inadvertent scribal error.

⁵¹ I accept Dimant's proposed reading of והארץ on the following grounds: 1) the verb that follows must be a Qal perfect 3ʳᵈ person feminine singular, 2) the root of the verb must be a III-ה root, and 3) the middle radical of the verb must be צ. Within the context of this text, that provides a limited number of potential reconstructions and Dimant's seems the least risky.

⁵² 4Q385a 4 preserves התה whereas 4Q387 2ii preserves והתה̇]ל̇]כתם.

⁵³ In 4Q387 2ii 5, the last four characters in המחזיקים are written below the line.

⁵⁴ 4Q385a 4 3 attests the expected *plene* spelling אותה rather than the אתה spelling in 4Q387 2ii 6.

⁵⁵ Each underlined word is fully extant in 4Q387 2ii, but 4Q385a 4 provides מל̇]מ̇]לכת ישרא]ל תא]בד.

⁵⁶ The overlapping words are fully extant in 4Q387 2ii.

⁵⁷ מישראל occurs only in 4Q387 2ii 9 where the last two characters appear below the line.

50 תשוב לגוים רבים ובני ישראל זעקים[⁵⁸]
51 מפני על כבד ב<u>ארצות שבים ו</u>אין משיע להם
52 יען ביען חקתי מאסו ותרתי געלה נפשם <u>על</u> כן הסתרתי
53 פני מ[הם עד] אשר ישלימו עונם   וזה להם האות בשלם
54 עונם [כי] עזבתי את הארץ ברום לבבם ממני ולא ידעו
55 כ[י] מאסתים <u>וישבו ועשו רעה ר</u>[ב]ה̊ <u>מן</u> ה<u>רעה</u> הראשנה
56 [והפרו את] הברית אשר כרתי <u>עם אברהם ועם יצחק</u> ועם
57 [יעקוב בימים] ההמה יקום מלך <u>לגוים גדפן ועשה רעות ו</u>[⁵⁹
58 וב<u>ימו</u>[אעביר] את ישראל <u>מעם בימו אשבור את ממלכת</u>
59 מצרים]   [ו<u>את מצרים ואת ישראל אשבור ונתתו לחרב</u>[⁶⁰
60 [והש<u>מ</u>ותי א[ת ה̊]ה̊[א]ר̊ץ <u>ורחקתי את האדם</u> ועזבתי
61 <u>את הארץ</u> ביד מלאכי המשטמות והסתרתי [פני][⁶¹
62 [מיש[ר]אל וזה להם האות ביום עזבי את הארץ <u>בה</u>]שמה
63 [וישב]ו̊ כהני ירושלים <u>לעבוד אלהים אחרים</u> [ולעשו]ת̊
64 כתעבות ה[גוים]
65 שלשה אשר ימלכ[ו]
66 [ו]ק̊[ד]ש הקדשי[ם]
67 [ ]ר והמצדקי[ם]

4Q385a 5a–b 1–9[⁶²] = CE 68–77
4Q387 3 1–9 = CE 71–79

68 [   ] [אלהים]
69 [   ] [מנין כהנים]
70 [   ] [א]ו̊ אחרים
71 [   ] [המזבח]
72 [   ] הנופלים בחרב[⁶³]

[⁵⁸] 4Q387 2ii preserves all but תשוב in the overlapping material. 4Q385a 4 preserves לגוים תשוב and 4Q389 8ii preserves ובני ישר] לגוים רבים ו.

[⁵⁹] In 4Q387 2iii, אשבור appears in the defective spelling (אשבר) and is written as a superscription. Perhaps the orthography was shortened to help fit the nearly omitted word back into the manuscript. Only [מ]ל̊[כת א]ת̊ אשבור [בימו]ל מעם̊[is preserved in 4Q389 8. 4Q388a 7ii preserves everything but אעביר, and 4Q387 2ii preserves everything beginning with the *lamed* of ישראל.

[⁶⁰] The photograph of 4Q388a 7 5 shows that ונתתו is the correct reading even though, grammatically speaking, the form should be ונתתי. The final letter clearly connects to the ת on its vertical stroke. The ו can be explained as a slip of the hand, spreading of ink, or an error on the part of the scribe. 4Q388a 7ii preserves the entire line. 4Q387 8 preserves only the *lamed* of ישראל, and 4Q387 2iii preserves [אשבור ישראל ואת ם.

[⁶¹] The text in 4Q388a 7 is skips almost two full lines of text due to parablepsis. It skips straight from את הארץ to בהשמה (in the following line) since בהשמה appears again eleven words later directly after another example of the collocation את הארץ.

[⁶²] Strugnell joined fragments a–b of 3Q385 5 on the basis of the overlaps they share with 4Q387 3. See Dimant, "4QApocryphon of Jeremiah," 140.

4QApocryphon of Jeremiah C

73 [ ]וֹב[ ] [חנפֿה את]°ׄ
74 [ ]יׄם כהנׄים שלושה אשר לא יתהלכו בדרכֿיׄ
75 [הכהנים ה]רׄאשנים על שם אלהי ישראל יקראוׄ
76 והורד בׄימיהם גאון מרישיעי ברית ועבדי נאכרׄ[64]
77 וׄיתקרע ישראל בדור ההׄ[וא] להלחם אׄ[י]ׄש ברעהו
78 על התורה וׄעל הברית וֹשׄלחׄתי רעב בֹ[אר]ֿץ ולא
79 לֹלׄ[ח]ֿםׄ ומצא וֹלֿ[א] לֿמֿ[ים] כי [אם ל]שמוע את דברי[65]

4Q387 4 1–4 = CE 80–83

80 [א בגורׄל למטוׄתיה]ׄם
81 [לׄ] [מֿלכי הצפון שניםֿ]
82 [ה וֿ]זׄ[עֿ]קׄוןׄ] [בֿנׄי ישראל לאלהים
83 וגשם שוטף וא[בנׄ]י אׄ[לׄ]ֿ[גב]יׄש אש וגפרית [[66]

4Q385a 16a–b 1–8 = CE 84–91

84 [ה יתרׄ]
85 [בֹר עם לעדרי עֿ]
86 [עֿם וזרע ויסב ∘ עמו וֹי]
87 [וה]ורשתי את יוןֿ]
88 והשלחתׄ[י]ֿ החיה בכן הׄ°°]
89 ההׄ]רׄ והלבנון ירשוֿ]
90 ידר]וֿשון ליהוה לאמרֿ]
91 [יׄקוב ולֿ]

4Q385a 17i 4–5 = CE 91–93

92 [מת נהרי
93 [תֿכבש

4Q385 17ii 1–9 = CE 94–102

---

[63] 4Q385a 5a–b 5 preserves only a לֿ, but the lines before and after guarantee that the reading הנופלֿיםׄ בחרב is correct.

[64] The traditional orthography for נכר is found in 4Q385a. For the use of the א in 4Q387, see Dimant, "4QApocryphon of Jeremiah," 194.

[65] This line quotes Amos 8:11 and Dimant's reconstruction is entirely appropriate in light of the quotation. Dimant, "4QApocryphon of Jeremiah," 194.

[66] Dimant restores this line based on Ezek 38:22. Given the explicit mention of fire and brimstone as well as the partial reconstruction of hail stones, Dimant's reconstruction seems reasonable.

94	[הבתר וא]
95	[֯◦ ֯◦ ימי חייהם]
96	בֹּעֳפִׄיׄ עֵׂץ החיים
97	היכן חלקך אמון ה[ש]בׄנה ביארי[ם]
98	מים סביב לך חׄ[ייל]ׄך ים ומים חמ[תד]
99	כוש מצרי[ם עצמה ו]אין קץ לבריח[יד]
100	לוב בסעדך והיא בגולה תלך בשׁׄ[בי]
101	[וׄ]עׄלליה יׄ[רטש]וֹׁ[ ] בראשׁׄ הרׄ[ים ועל]
102	נכבדיה ידו [גורל וכל [גדול]יׄה בזקׄ[ים]

Epilogue

4Q385a 18i 2–11 = CE 103–112

103	[ויצא]יׂרמיה הנביא מלפני יהוה
104	[וילך עם ה]שבאים אשר נשבו מארץ ירושלים ויבאו
105	[לרבלה אל]מלך בבל[ ]בׄהכות נבוזרדן רב הטבחים
106	[ ]עׄים ויקח את כלי בית אלהים את הכהנים
107	[החרים]וׄבני ישראל ויביאם בבל וילך ירמיה הנביא
108	[עמהם עד]הנהר ויצום את אשר יעשו בארץ שביא[ם]
109	[וישמעו] בקול ירמיה לדברים אשר צוהו אלהי
110	[לעשות]וׄשמרו את ברית אלהי אבותיהם בארׄץ
111	[בבל ולא יעשו]כׄאשר עשו הם ומלכיהם כהניהם
112	[ושריהם]◦◦◦[ ]וׄ[ ]חׄללוׁ֯ שׁ[ם֯ אלהים ל]ׄ[טמא]

4Q385a 18ii 1–10 = CE 113–122

113	בתחפנס א[שר בארץ מצרים
114	ויאמרו לו דרוש[נא בעדנו לאל]הֹׄים[ולא שמע]
115	להם ירמיׁ[ה ל]בׄלתי דרוש להם לאלה[ים ושאת בעדם]
116	רנה ותפלה ויהי ירמיה מקונן]◦[קינות]
117	[ע]ׄל ירושלים [ ] ויהי דבר יהוה אל[
118	ירמיה בארץ תחפנס אשר בארץ מצׄרים לאמר דבר אל
119	בני ישראל ואל בני יהודה ובנימים ◦[כה תאמר אליהם]
120	יום יום דרשו את חקותי ואת מצותי שמׄ[רו ואל תלכו]
121	אחרי פׄ[ס]ׄילי הגוים אשר הלׁ[ ]כׄו אחריהם אבותיכם כי
122	לא יושׁי[עו] לׄ[כם]◦ לא ◦[

Prologue

4Q389 1 2–7 = CE 1–6

1 in the land of J]erusalem/Judah
2 And they inquired concerning a]ll
3 And] all those remaining in the land of Eg[ypt
4 J]eremiah, son of Hilqiah from the land of Egp[pt
5 [the thi]rty sixth year of the exile of Israel and they read [these] words [before]
6 a[ll the children of I]srael upon (at) the river Sur   in the presence of

Review of History

Biblical Period

4Q389 2 1–8 = CE 7–14
4Q388a 2 1–5 = CE 12–16

7 And yo]u inquired of me. I am/was[
8 And I] lifted up your heads when I delivered y[ou from the land of Egypt
9 to them and what they repaid me, and I carried them[just as a man carries his son until
10 [they come to] Qadesh Barnea and I said to them
11 upon them and I swore
12 to them and their children I brought to the [land
13 [and I commanded them to make a tent] with goa[t]-hair flaps   ] so that I might   walk with them in
14 forty years and it was
15 and they turned after
16 them

4Q389 5 2–3 = CE 17–18

17 And they said, "Give us a king who

| 18 | Samuel, son of Elqanah to |

4Q385a 1ii 1–7 = CE 19–25

19	And I] will raise up for [
20	his enemy
21	his enemy and I remo[ved
22	when he sought my face and his heart did not exalt (itself) before me
23	Then his days were complete and Solomon sat
24	And I delivered the life of his enemies into his hand
25	And I took from his hand a burnt offering

4Q385a 2 2 = CE 26

| 26 | And they forgot |

4Q388a 3 1–2 = CE 27–28
4Q385a 3 2–10 = CE 28–35
4Q387 1 1–10 = CE 30–39
4Q388a 5 1 = CE 31
4Q389 6 1–2 = CE 36–37
4Q389 7 2–3 = CE 39–40

27	at tha]t time[
28	<u>When you were walking in error</u> before me
29	Those called by name
30	<u>Just as I said to Jacob</u>
31	And you said, "You have abandoned u[s our God," but you have rejected my statutes
32	[and you have forgotten] the festivals of my <u>covenant and you have profaned</u> [my name and my holy things]
33	[and you have defiled] my temple and you have <u>sacrificed [your sacrifi]ces to goat demons</u> and you (have)
34	<u>and you have broken all (aspects of the covenant)</u>[67] <u>arrogantly</u>
35	<u>And I sought faithfulness but I did not find (it)</u>
36	So I ga]ve you <u>into the hand of your enemy and I desolated</u> [your land]
37	And the land] restored its Sabbaths <u>in desolation</u>

---

[67] In the Hebrew Bible, the root פרר is used to describe violations of the covenant.

38	in the land[s] of [you]r enemies until the year of
39	t]o your land [to (re)v]isit
40	in it

> 4Q387 2ii 1–12 = CE 41–52
> 4Q385a 4 1–9 = CE 44–51
> 4Q389 8i–ii 1–11 = CE 49–59
> 4Q387 2iii 1–7 = CE 58–64
> 4Q388a 7 1–10 = CE 55–67

41	[ ] [ ]your[ ] and commit yourselves to serve me with all of your heart
42	[and with a]ll of your soul. And they will s[ee]k my f[ac]e in their affliction, but I will not pay attention to them
43	because of the transgressions [w]hich [they] have perpetrated against [me], until the completion of ten
44	jubilees of years, <u>and they will wa[l]k</u> in ma[dness] and in blindness and in confusion
45	of heart. And after the completion of that <u>generation,</u> I will [tear away] the kingdom from the hand of <u>those who (have) seized</u>
46	<u>it.</u> And I will raise up over it others, from <u>another</u> people, <u>and arrogance will rule</u>
47	over all [the l]and, and the kingdom of Israel will perish. In those days
48	there wi[ll b]e [a king and h]e (will) be <u>a blasphemer and he will Commit</u> abominations, but I will tear away
49	[his] kingdom, [and] that [king] <u>(shall) belong to the lot of destruction and my face</u> will be hidden from Israel
50	<u>will return to many nations and the children of Israel will cry out</u>
51	because of the heavy burden <u>in the lands of captivity and there will not be a deliverer for them.</u>
52	because they have rejected my statutes and they (lit. their soul) have loathed my teaching, <u>therefore</u> I will hide
53	my face from [them until] the time that they complete their iniquity. And this will be for them the sign of the completion
54	of their iniquity: That I will abandon the land on account of their pride-of-heart before me. And they will not know
55	[th]at I have rejected them so they will continue doing evil – evil greater than <u>the former evil.</u>
56	[And they will invalidate] the covenant that I established <u>with Abraham and with Isaac</u> and with

57	[Jacob. In] those[days] <u>will arise a king of the nations, a blasphemer, and a doer of evils</u> and [
58	<u>And in his days</u> [I will invalidate (i.e., remove)] Israel from <u>(being) a people. In his days I will break the kingdom of</u>
59	Egypt [ ] and Egypt <u>and Israel I will break and hand over</u> to the sword
60	And I will [dev]astate the [la]nd and (from it) will <u>I remove humanity</u> and I will abandon
61	the land into the hands of the angels of Mastemot, and I will hide [my face]
62	[from Is]rael. And this will be a sign for them: On the day that I abandon the land <u>in d[esolation]</u>,
63	then the priests of Jerusalem will [return] <u>to serving other gods and [to ac]t</u>
64	according to the abominations of the [nations].
65	three who will rul[e
66	[and] the holy of holie[s]
67	and th[ose] who lead to righteousness

$$\text{4Q385a 5a–b }_{1-9}{}^{68} = \text{CE 68–77}$$
$$\text{4Q387 3 }_{1-9} = \text{CE 71–79}$$

68	] God[
69	]a number of priests[
70	] others [
71	]the altar[
72	those felled by the sword
73	] <u>it defiled</u> [
74	] three priests <u>who will not walk in the ways</u>
75	[of the] first/former [priests] (who) by the name of the God of <u>Israel were called</u>.
76	And in their days will be brought down the pride of those who act wickedly (against the) <u>covenant as well as servants of the foreigner</u>.
77	And in th[at] generation, Israel will be rent asunder, each m[a]n warring with his neighbor
78	over the Torah (or, "teaching") and over the covenant and I will cast a hunger over the l[an]d, but not

---

[68] Strugnell joined fragments a–b of 3Q385 5 on the basis of the overlaps they share with 4Q387 3. See Dimant, "4QApocryphon of Jeremiah," 140.

79	for bread, and a thirst, but n[ot] for water, [ra]ther, to [hear my word]

$$4Q387\ 4\ \text{1--4} = \text{CE } 80\text{--}83$$

80	] by lot according to their tribe]s
81	] the kings of the north (for) years[
82	] and the children of Israel will [c]all out to God
83	[and torrential rain and h]a[i]l st[on]es, fire, and brimstone

$$4Q385a\ 16a\text{--}b\ \text{1--8} = \text{CE } 84\text{--}91$$

84	] a remnant[
85	] people to the flocks of [
86	]a people and a seed and he will surround his people and [
87	and]I wi[ll] dispossess Greece[
88	and]I wi[ll loose] wild beasts upon you
89	the mou]ntain and the Lebanon shall be his possession[
90	th[ey] shall [se]ek YHWH, saying, "
91	]Jacob [

$$4Q385a\ 17i\ \text{4--5} = \text{CE } 92\text{--}93$$

92	] the rivers of
93	shall be subdued

$$4Q385a\ 17ii\ \text{1--9} = \text{CE } 94\text{--}100$$

94	]the cleft and [
95	] the days of their lives[
96	in the foliage of the tree of life
97	Where is your portion, O Amon, who dwells on the rive[r][69]
98	waters surround you, [your rampa]rt is the sea, and waters are [your w]all
99	Cush, Egyp[t is your might and] there is not end to [your] bar[s]
100	Libya is your strength (or, ally), but she will go into exile, into cap[tivity]

---

[69] Here Amon does not refer to the Trans-Jordanian city-state. The reference to יאר as well as the context of this passage in Nah 3 indicate that it refers to Thebes, i.e., מנו אמון. As Dimant notes, however, the name אמן could be a cryptogram for Alexandria.   See Dimant, "4QApocryphon of Jeremiah," 157. (See more in the analysis below).

101   And her babes shall be [dashed] at the head[of the mou]ntains. And concerning
102   [(for) her honored ones,] lots [will be cast] and all of her [great one]s in chain[s]

4Q385a 18i 2–11 = CE 103–112

103   And Jeremiah the prophet [went out] from before YHWH
104   [And he went with the] captives who were led captive from the land of Jerusalem and came
105   [to Riblah, to] the king of Babylon, when Nebuzaradan, the commander of the guards, smote[70]
106   [   ] and he took the vessels of the House of God, the priests
107   [the nobles] and the children of Israel, and he brought them to Babylon and Jeremiah the prophet went
108   [with them unto] the river. And he instructed (them about) what they should do in the land of [their] captivity.
109   [And they listened] to the voice of Jeremiah, to the things that God commanded him
110   [to do   ] That they should keep the covenant of the God of their fathers in the land
111   [of Babylon and that they should not do] just as they had formerly done, they and their kings and their priests
112   [and their princes   ]   (i.e.,) [they] profaned [the n]ame of God to [desecrate]

4Q385a 18ii 1–10 = CE 113–122

113   In Tahpanes, wh[ich is in the land of Egypt]
114   And they said to him, "Inquire [of G]od [on our behalf   but] Jeremi[ah did not listen]
115   to them, [n]ot beseeching Go[d] for them, [not offering up on their behalf]
116   lamentation or prayer. But Jeremiah did lament [laments]
117   [ov]er Jerusalem. [Then the work of YHWH came to]
118   Jeremiah in the land of Tahpanes, which is in the land of Eg[ypt, saying, "Speak to
119   the children of Israel and to the children of Judah and Benjamin: [Thus says God:]

---

[70] טבחים are bodyguards and executioners. See Koehler and Baumgartner, eds., *The Hebrew and Aramaic Lexicon of the Old Testament*, 1: 368.

120	'Day by day shall you seek my statutes and my commandments shall [you k]eep. [You shall not go]	
121	after the i[d]ols of the nations [after] which [your fathers] we[nt, for]	
122	Th[ey] cannot sav[e] y[ou]	not

Language in Apocryphon of Jeremiah C

The language used in the *Apocryphon of Jeremiah C* is similar to what is found in Dan 10–12 and may be contrasted with what is found in Dan 2, 7, 8, and the *Animal Apocalypse*. More specifically, the *Apocryphon* never uses language that points beyond itself to another reality in the way that, for example, humans are used to represent angels in symbolic apocalypses. As we saw in chapter four, however, non-symbolic language takes on a variety of forms and is hardly limited to apocalypses.

There are two basic kinds of non-symbolic descriptions: 1) Explicit and 2) Adjectival. The first group may be further divided into two groups: 1) descriptions that employ proper names (e.g., אברהם Abraham, 4Q389 8ii 8=4Q388a 7 2) and 2) descriptions that employ titles (e.g., מלכי הצפון the kings of the north, 4Q387 4 2). In some cases, both kinds of descriptions are used simultaneously (e.g., ירמיה הנביא Jeremiah the prophet, 4Q385a 18i 2). The second kind of non-symbolic description, the adjectival type, is used to describe figures or ethno-political groups, etc., based on characteristics or actions (e.g., מרישיעי ברית "Those who act wickedly against the covenant," 4Q387 3 6). The adjectival descriptions are especially difficult because while they do not point beyond themselves, they are often opaque. In many cases they appear to have functioned as group-specific terms in the way that מורה הצדק "the teacher of righteousness" seems to have for the Essenes. An expression like "teacher of righteousness" could have probably been interpreted in virtually unlimited ways by most in Hellenistic times. The words themselves cannot demand one connotation and not others unless an individual is privy to insider-information. For the Essenes, however, the term had a very specific meaning. But it is unlikely that non-Essenes would have readily understood the term in the same way Essenes did. Only membership in the group could have provided sufficient/correct context to understand the term in the way the Essenes intended. The presence of such non-symbolic expressions in the *Apocryphon of Jeremiah C*, like Dan 10–12, suggests an underlying social reality: an exclusive religious/political organization – if not in reality than at least in rhetoric.

In the analysis that follows I have grouped the terminology according to the model found in chapter four. In other words, I treat descriptions of deities/liminal beings together, descriptions of individual humans together, and descriptions of human groups (i.e., ethno-political groups) together. This organization most clearly shows the range of descriptions used for any single subject-type in the text and helps to facilitate comparisons with descriptions of the same subject-type in the symbolic apocalypses. Following the analysis one finds a chart of the raw data presented in the order of appearance in the text. One will notice that a few terms in the chart are not subjected to analysis. In these cases, insufficient context has ruled out a meaningful analysis. A final note is useful before beginning the analysis. I have already indicated that non-symbolic and even group-specific language is not only characteristic of non-symbolic apocalypses. Despite the fact that they appear to target limited audiences, non-symbolic apocalypses participate in larger rhetorical practices that were apparently common to Hellenistic Judaism.[71]

Descriptions of Deities, Angels, and Demons
Several deities and/or liminal figures are given explicit description in the *Apocryphon*. In most cases a proper name is used. In some cases an epithet or other adjective is added. The God of Israel is named with four different locutions: אליהם 4Q385a 5a–b 1, 18i 8, 11, 18ii 2, 3 4Q387 4 3; ישראל אלהי 4Q387 3 5=4Q385a 5a–b 8; יהוה 4Q385a 16a–b 7, 18i 2; and אלהי אבותיהם 4Q385a 18i 9. The first three descriptions are found throughout the Hebrew Bible, while the last one is mentioned elsewhere only in the Book of Chronicles.[72]

The use of the tetragrammaton (יהוה) is significant for two reasons. First, it contrasts with a kind of symbolic presentation of the divine name known from Essene documents: the use of four dots of ink. This kind of symbolism is different from what we have seen in the symbolic apocalypses in that it works on the level of orthography. Among the Essene/sectarian documents that are more or less undisputed, the proper name of the God of

---

[71] One can see similar patterns in the language used by groups such as the Fundamentalist Church of Jesus Christ of Latter Day Saints. They use a expressions familiar from other LDS groups and conservative American Christians more generally. But they often use familiar terms with highly specialized meanings. A prime example is their use of the expression "prophet." For FLDS members, "prophet" refers exclusively to Warren Jeffs.

[72] The passages, which always include the lene spelling for *Elohē* (אלהי אבותיהם), are 1 Chron 5:25, 2 Chron 11:16, 13:14, 14:3, 15:12, 19:14, 24:18, 24:24, 30:7, 30:22, 34:32, 34:33, 36:15. The slightly different orthography אלהי אבותם also appears in Judg 2:12 and 2 Chron 28:6.

Israel is not normally written.[73] Essenes avoided writing the name (except in scripture) by using several techniques. According to the *Serek haYaḥad*, even an inadvertent pronunciation of the name while reading a text was an offense so serious that the offender had to be excluded from the council of the community:

> He has taken the law into his own hands; he will be punished for a year [. . .] Whoever enunciates the Name (which is) honoured above all [. . .] whether blaspheming, or overwhelmed by misfortune or for any other reason, . . . or reading a book, or blessing, will be excluded and shall not go back to the Community Council. (1QS 5 27–6 2)[74]

In an apparent effort to prevent such inadvertent sins, the scribe of 1QS represented the four letters of the divine name with four dots of ink. That the *Apocryphon of Jeremiah C* freely uses the tetragrammaton is a strong indication that the text is not Essene/sectarian. While some of its language (see below) appears to reveal an underlying, exclusive religious group – that group is almost certainly not the Essenes.[75] The use of the tetragrammaton is also significant for the date of the text. The free use of the divine name outside of scripture becomes rare in the Maccabean Period.[76]

In one instance the term אלהים is applied to a subject other than the God of Israel: אלהים אחרים "other gods" (4Q387 2iii 6=4Q388a 7 7). The expression is used sixty-eight times in the Hebrew Bible – most often in Deuteronomy (20x) and Jeremiah (18x) – and is probably most well known from its usage in the Decalogue: "You shall have no other gods before me."[77] The context in the *Apocryphon* indicates that the expression is used to describe events in the Hellenistic period. For example, in the combined edition above (CE) one finds a description of the Babylonian exile in lines 42–44, the transition to Persian rule in line 45, the reign of Darius in lines 48–56, and the conquest of Alexander the Great in lines 57–60. Thus, when the text says in lines 63–64, "The priests of Jerusalem shall [return] to serve

---

[73] See Lange, "Kriterien essinischer Texte," 59–69. Carol Newsom, "Sectually Explicit Literature from Qumran," in *The Hebrew Bible and Its Interpreters* (ed. Baruch Halpern and David N. Freedman; Winona Lake: Eisenbrauns, 1990), 167–87. Devorah Dimant, "Qumran Sectarian Literature," in *Jewish Writings of the Second Temple Period* (ed. Michael Stone*CRINT*; Philadelphia: Assen), 483–550.

[74] Florentino García Martínez, *The Dea Sea Scrolls Translated: The Qumran Texts in English* (Grand Rapids: Eerdmans, 1996).

[75] It is true that the *Apocryphon* appears to share the Essene view of the Jerusalem temple priests. Perhaps it is this shared attitude that led to the text being brought to Qumran. It is clear from Josephus that other Jewish groups such as the Pharisees regarded (Hasmonean) priests as illegitimate.

[76] The tetragrammaton is not used in Song, Qoh, or Esth. It is used only seven times in Dan – and there only in chapter 9. Lange, "The Parabiblical Literature," 310.

[77] Exod 20:3, Deut 5:7.

other gods and [to ac]t according to the abominations of the [nations]" (4Q388a 7 6–7=4Q387 2iii 6), it is likely that the text is referring to the Hellenistic religious reforms. The text does not specifically name Antiochus IV, but in terms of accusing the Jerusalem priests of worshipping foreign gods, the Hellenistic religious reforms of Antiochus IV probably provide the correct context for this accusation. There is little doubt that Menelaus and those who supported him accepted the religious reforms, which included the worship of Zeus Olympias in the Jerusalem temple. If the text is taken literally, it is hard to imagine another incident in the Hellenistic period concerning which the Jerusalem priests might have been accused of worshipping other gods.

Apocryphon of Jeremiah C also contains descriptions of figures from the angelic/demonic realm. The Angels of Mastemot (מלאכי משטמות) represent an intriguing variant of traditions about Mastema, a figure sometimes linked to Belial (the Angels of Mastemot are explicitly linked to Belial 4Q390).[78] The expression could at first appear to be an adjectival description for humans, i.e., a pejorative term. The expression is not, however, a derogatory or euphemistic reference to a group of humans.

מַשְׂטֵמָה appears twice in the Hebrew Bible (Hos 9:7–8) as an abstract concept: "hostility, persecution." Centuries later and much closer to the time of the *Apocryphon of Jeremiah C*, the *Book of Jubilees* treats מַשְׂטֵמָה as a personified satan figure – not in the New Testament sense, but as God's appointed (if not entirely loyal) lead-prosecutor.[79] Mastema's identity as a satan figure is similar to the satan figure that appears in the Book of Job.[80] For example, in *Jub.* 17:15–16 after YHWH receives a report of Abraham's great faithfulness, Mastema comes before YHWH and counsels him to test Abraham by instructing him to sacrifice Isaac. The test is designed to validate Abraham's faith.[81]

---

[78] The most recent treatment of Mastema and Belial is found in Devorah Dimant, "Between Sectarian and Non-Sectarian Texts: Belial and Mastema" (paper presented at the conference The Dead Sea Scrolls and Contemporary Culture, Hebrew University, Jerusalem, July 6–8, 2008). Dimant highlights the unique character of the *Damascus Document* in that unlike other sectarian documents, it favors the designation Mastema over Belial.

[79] Saul Olyan, *A Thousand Thousands Served Him: Exegesis in the Naming of Angels in Ancient Judaism* (TSAJ 36; Tübingen: Mohr Siebeck, 1993), 25–7, 66–7. Moshe Bernstein, "Angels at the Aqedah: A Study in the Development of a Midrashic Motif," *DSD* 7 (2000): 263–91. cf. also Esther Eshel, "Mastema's Attempt on Moses' Life in the "Pseudo-Jubilees" Text from Masada," *DSD* 10 (2003): 359–64.

[80] The term שטן "satan" is likely derived from a bi-form of the root of שטם: מַשְׂטֵמָה. See Koehler and Baumgartner, eds., *The Hebrew and Aramaic Lexicon of the Old Testament*, 2: 1316–7.

[81] See the slightly different nuance of Mastema's identity in 48:9–19.

In the 18 examples of משטמה found in the Dead Sea Scrolls, both the abstraction and the personification described above are attested.[82] In some cases (e.g., CD XVI 5, 1QM XIII 11), Mastema is explicitly described as an angel (מלאך). As indicated above, the examples from *Apocryphon of Jeremiah C* are unique among ancient Jewish texts in that they present Mastema in the plural: מלאכי משטמות. The plural form משטמות might at first appear to indicate an abstract translation, but the position of the word (as genitive) in construct with מלאכי indicates otherwise.

The Mastemot Angels appear to arrive on the scene simultaneously with Antiochus IV or perhaps Alexander the Great. It is important to note that while the Greek ruler brings destruction/loss of self-determination, the text does not describe him as being in control of the land. Instead, both the land and its inhabitants are handed over to the Angels of Mastemot. These angels do not function as a cipher for Greeks, nor are they in any way related. The importance of this observation is that the upheaval and turmoil experienced in Israel is explained as a direct action of YHWH on account of sin – not the guile of other nations. "And I shall [dev]astate the [la]nd and (from it) shall I remove humanity and I shall abandon the land into the hands of the angels of Mastemot, and I shall hide [my face from Is]rael" (4Q387 2iii 3–4). As noted in chapter three, Dimant and Tiller have observed that the Angels of Mastemot appear to serve the same function as the demons described as seventy shepherds in the *Animal Apocalypse*.[83] The difference between the demonic forces in *Apocryphon of Jeremiah C* and the *Animal Apocalypse* is that the demons appear after the arrival of Alexander the Great in the former (cf. lines 57–64 in the combined edition below) and before the Babylonian Exile in the latter (cf. *1 En.* 89:65–72a). The use of the Angels of Mastemot highlights a difference between the apocalyptic visions in *Apocryphon of Jeremiah C* and Dan 7–8. In apocalypses like Dan 7 and 8, the enemies of God's people are humans (nations). These nations are couched in cosmic terminology, but the terminology always points beyond itself – the angelic interpretations make this clear. In the *Apocryphon of Jeremiah C* the opponents of the people of God do not function as a cosmic parallel to earthly powers. Instead, the earthly powers function as an adjunct threat.

The *real* enemies of God's people are found in the realm of angels/demons – a realm that has merged with the realm of humans in the *Apocryphon*. This text does not envision parallel worlds, but a world into which the cosmic forces of darkness have really and fully penetrated and

---

[82] CD XVI 5, 1QS III 23, 1QM XIII 4, 11, 4Q177 9 5, 4Q225 2i 9, 2ii 6, 2ii 13–14, 4Q270 6ii 18, 4Q271 4ii 6, 4Q286 7ii 2, 4Q387 2iii 4, 4Q390 1 11, 2i 7, 4Q525 19 4, 6Q18 9 1, 11Q11 II 4.

[83] Tiller, *A Commentary on the Animal Apocalypse*, 53.

become integrated. So while the *Apocryphon* involves the heavenly/angelic realm in a way that, for example, the Deuteronomistic History does not, its use of the מלאכי משטמות indicates that Deuteronomic (retributive) theology is nevertheless strong in the text.

Another group of liminal beings given explicit description are the שעירים "goat demons" (4Q385a 3 7=4Q388a 3 6=4Q387 1 4).[84] Goat demons are attested in the Hebrew Bible: "And they shall no longer offer their sacrifices to the goat-demons לַשְּׂעִירָם, to whom they prostitute זֹנִים themselves" (Lev 17:7). This passage is part of a polemic against P (specifically 16:8) by the Holiness Code Redactor (H_R).[85] The biblical passage is set in the time of Moses and is part of a directive YHWH gives to Moses for the people – specifically Aaron and his sons (i.e., the priests). It primarily addresses the interdiction of offerings not brought, "to the door of the tent of meeting," and made, "before the tabernacle of YHWH" (Lev 17:4). H_R is likely post-exilic, however, and the passage probably reflects priestly attempts to centralize religious (and economic) activity around the Jerusalem temple. *Apocryphon of Jeremiah C* places sacrifices to goat demons in a list of sins that resulted in the Babylonian Exile.

A crucial aspect of context for the goat demons in the *Apocryphon* is that the list of sins in which worship of goat demons is included contains sins that are exclusively cultic in nature: "You have rejected my statutes [and you have forgotten] the festivals of my covenant and you have profaned [my name and my holy things and you have defiled] my temple and you have sacrificed [your sacrifi]ces to goat demons and you (have) . . . and you have broken all (aspects of the covenant)" (4Q385a 3 5–9=4Q388a 3 4–7=4Q387 1 2–5).

The goat demons play a different role in the text than the last demons we encountered (Angels of Mastemot). Goat demons are an object of veneration – not an evil force that has broken into the human realm to rule over and chastise humans. The meaning of goat demons is similar to another group of demons found in a different *ex eventu* prophecy that frames the Babylonian exile with an indictment over sacrifice to demons. In 4QPsDan$^{a–b}$ ar, Judah is given into the hand of Nebuchadnezzar after "the

---

[84] Cf. also 2Q23 1 7, 4Q270 2i 10.

[85] I agree with Milgrom's assessment that 17 is a polemic against P by H_R. One need not agree with his pre-exilic dating of H in order to accept this position. There seems little doubt that portions of both P and H are pre-exilic, though I do not prefer to see either as finished before at least the early post-exilic period. In defense of my dating, I would offer the transition from the temple tax of one-third a shekel in Nehemiah's time (10:32) to one-half a shekel sometime thereafter (Exod 30:13–15). In any case, the explicit polemic against P in 17:7 seems to indicate that the verse is not an original part of H, but part of the H redaction (surely post-exilic). See Jacob Milgrom, *Leviticus 17–22* (AB; vol. 3a; New York Doubleday, 2000), 1462.

children of Israel [ch]ose their presence [rather than they presence of God . . . sacri]ficing their sons to the demons of error so that God became angry with them."[86] In *Pseudo-Daniel*$^{a-b}$ *ar*, demons of error are a cipher for the deities in the pre-exilic Israelite pantheon.[87] I suggest that the goat demons of *Apocryphon of Jeremiah C* essentially represent the same deities, but are framed in a specifically priestly terminology borrowed from the Holiness Code in Lev 17. After YHWH communicates the prohibition of sacrifices for goat-demons to Moses, he says, "This shall be a statute to them throughout their generations" (Lev 17:7). The writer of *Apocryphon of Jeremiah C* uses Lev 17:7 as a legal precedent for condemning Israelite sacrifices to other deities in pre-exilic times. Support for my reading is provided in 4Q387 2iii 6: [ושב]ו כהני ירושלים לעבוד אלהים אחרים "[Then] the priests of Jerusalem shall [return] to serving other gods." This passage perhaps indicates a reversion back to the kind of pre-exilic sinfulness characterized by 4Q385a 3 5–9=4Q388a 3 4–7=4Q387 1 2–5.

Descriptions of Persons

Apocryphon of Jeremiah C's *ex eventu* review of history mentions many figures by name – a feature absent from apocalypses like Dan 2, 7, and 8. Like Dan 10–12, but unlike 4QpsDan^{a-b} ar, the history does not appear to include pre-Israelite people or events (e.g., antediluvian figures such as Noah). The earliest portion of the historical review describes the early Iron Age. More specifically, it details the transition point from the period of the Judges to the monarchy in Ancient Israel. Samuel is the earliest figure explicitly named in the history. Additional precision is added to his name with the familial title בן אלקנה "son of Elqanah" (4Q389 5 3). The text also mentions Solomon and gives clear indication that the name of David was originally present in the text (4Q385a 1ii 5). Jacob is named once in a flashback (4Q385a 3 4, 4Q387 1 1, 3Q388 3 3), once with Abraham and Isaac among the patriarchal trio (4Q388a 7 1–2, 4Q389 8i–ii 9), and once with no context at all (4Q385a 16a–b 8). A Babylonian military official named Nebuzaradan appears in the epilogue with the title רב הטבחים "commander of the guards."

The most frequently attested personal name is Jeremiah, sometimes appearing alone, sometimes with the title הנביא "the prophet" (4Q385a 18i 2, 6 ,8, 18ii 2, 4, 6), and once with the familial title בן חלקיה "son of Hilqiah" (4Q389 1 5). All explicit mentions of Jeremiah, however, occur in the prologue and epilogue of the vision – not in the revelation itself. This pattern

---

[86] 4Q243 13 + 4Q244 12 1–2. See more on this text in the next chapter.
[87] Reynolds, "What Are Demons of Error?," 593–613.

of usage is not abnormal. Prophets in the Hebrew Bible are rarely addressed by name in the main body of the oracles they receive. Their names are more often indicated in set formulas (e.g., the Messenger Formula) that frame the main body of the oracles.

Not all figures are described by name. In some cases a title is used to identify these figures. The description is not symbolic. It does not point beyond itself to another reality or category of subject. One of the most common titular descriptions for individual humans is "king." The title מלך "king" is used in several different ways in the revelation. In the first instance it functions as a common noun to describe the sort of political leadership that the tribes of Israel demand from Samuel: אמרו תנה לנו מלך אשר "They said give us a king who . . ." (4Q389 5 2, CE 17).[88] The polemics against Jerusalem priests are obvious in the *Apocryphon* (cf. 4Q387 2iii 6–7, CE 63–4), but including the account of the demand for a king in the *ex eventu* history could also reflect a negative attitude toward Hasmoneans such as Jonathan, Simon, and John Hyrcanus.[89]

The second instance has more significance for this study. It occurs in the eschatological section of the revelation and probably describes the Seleucid kings as a group: מלכי הצפון "the kings of the North." In the Hebrew Bible this expression can be used as a general designation for a threatening political power as in Jer 25:26 (most military threats to Ancient Israel came from the north regardless of their actual location because of the geography of the Levant).[90] There is good reason to think that *Apocryphon of Jeremiah C* intends a far more specific meaning though.

The non-symbolic apocalypse in the Book of Daniel (chapters 10–12) uses the term "king of the north" seven times. Seleucus II (11:6, 7, 8), Antiochus III (11:11, 13, 15), and Antiochus IV (11:40) are each described as מלך הצפון "the king of the north" in a detailed *ex eventu* prophecy. The meaning of "king of the north" in Dan 11 is made plain by its interaction with the expression "king of the south." Ptolemy I Soter (11:5), Ptolemy II Philadelphus (11:6) Ptolemy III Euergetes (11:9) Ptolemy IV Philopator (11:11), Ptolemy VI Philometor (11:25) are each described as מלך הנגב.[91] The many points of linguistic similarity between *Apocryphon of Jeremiah C*

---

[88] This line is clearly quoting a portion of 1 Sam 8:6. In the MT the word "king" is followed by לְשָׁפְטֵנוּ "to rule over us." The OG reflects the MT reading by using an infinitive form of the verb δικάζω followed by a first-person, plural pronoun: εἶπαν δὸς ἡμῖν βασιλέα δικάζειν ἡμᾶς. The *Apocryphon* continues instead with אשר "who (will)."

[89] This list could theoretically include Alexander Jannaeus, Hyrcanus II, and Aristobulus II, but I argue below that the text must have been written during the reign of John Hyrcanus.

[90] Robert Engberg, "Megiddo: Guardian of the Carmel Pass," *BA* 3 (1940): 41–51.

[91] The reference to king of the south in 11:40 part of a genuine prophecy, but one presumes that Ptolemy VI Philometor is still the subject.

and Daniel indicate that the term "kings of the north" should be read as a reference to Seleucid kings. Contextual evidence from within the *Apocryphon* strengthens this reading: 1) the expression comes in the context of the eschatological battle, 2) the texts shows no knowledge of a Roman presence in Palestine, and 3) Ptolemaic Egypt is mentioned separately in the account of the eschatological battle (4Q385a 17ii 4–9).[92]

Two other figures in *Apocryphon of Jeremiah C* are described with title מלך. These two figures are described with similar epithets though they are not the same person. The first figure is found in 4Q388a 7 3=4Q389 8ii 8: מלך לגוים "a king for the nations." He is also described as גדפן ועשה רעות "a blasphemer, and a doer of evils." A different figure is described as a king who will be גדפן ועשה תעבות "a blasphemer and will commit abominations" (4Q385a 4 6=4Q387 2ii 8). Before parsing the individual elements of these descriptions it is helpful to use the surrounding context to determine their likely identities.

Dimant proposes that the two blaspheming kings be identified as Nebuchadnezzar II and Antiochus IV. I agree that the second king is probably Antiochus IV, but the first king cannot be Nebuchadnezzar II. The first king appears after the Babylonian exile when God will tear away, "the kingdom from the hand of those who (have) seized it," and then "raise up over it others, from another people" (4Q387 2ii 5–6 = 4Q385a 4 2–4). The transition occurs after the first generation of those living under the ten jubilees of years of the destruction of the land. Since "those who (have) seized it" are unambiguously the Babylonians, the text makes the point that the exile/punishment does not end in 539 B.C.E. with the fall of Babylon. The period of punishment is merely transferred under the auspices of another overlord. The "others from another people" who take over the land from "those who (have) seized it" (i.e., Babylonians) must be the Persians.

Cyrus conquered Babylonia in 539 B.C.E.. Some Jewish traditions about Persian kings might appear to make a description such as "blasphemer" unlikely for him. For example, according to Deutero-Isa, YHWH describes Cyrus of Anshan as משיחו "his messiah:" "Thus says YHWH to his messiah (or, anointed), to Cyrus whose right hand I have grasped to subdue the nations before him" (Isa 45:1). But a less flattering picture is drawn of Xerxes in the Book of Esther where the Persian king is far more mercurial. Morevoer, in Dan 6:6–9 Darius commits blasphemy by signing an edict that

---

[92] A plural "kings of the north" is also found in 1QM. While Flusser has shown that the Book of Daniel (especially chapter 11) has exerted influence on the *War Scroll*, he is correct that in this instance, the influence can only be a linguistic one. In 1QM, the king of the *Kittim*, "will go out with great rage to wage war against the kings of the North" (1 4). In this case the kings of the north cannot be the Seleucids, but their northern enemies (i.e., rulers of Parthia and Media). Flusser, *Judaism of the Second Temple Period: Qumran and Apocalypticism*, 148.

all persons must pray to him alone. The first blaspheming king in the *Apocryphon of Jeremiah C* is must be a Persian king since he must rise after the Babylonian Exile. The specific Persian king is more difficult to ascertain. I argue below that there may be some points of contact between the *Apocryphon* and Deutero-Isaiah. It is possible that the *Apocryphon* might reject or rewrite some ideas from Deutero-Isaiah. In this case, the figure in question could be Cyrus. Cyrus is no doubt lionized by Deutero-Isaiah, but that esteem might have faded over time. Given the multiple points of contact between the Book of Daniel and *Apocryphon of Jeremiah C*, he might also be Darius I – a figure for whom the title "blasphemer" undoubtedly fits in ancient Jewish eyes.

While I think that Dimant incorrectly identifies the first blaspheming king as Nebuchadnezzar II, she is probably right that the second king is Antiochus IV, although it is possible that the figure could be Alexander the Great. There seems little doubt that the king is Greek. According to the text, YHWH claims that during the reign of the second blaspheming king, "I shall break the kingdom of Egypt [   ] and Egypt and Israel I shall break and hand over to the sword" (4Q387 2iii 1–2 = 4Q388a 7 4–5 = 4Q389 8ii 10–11). This line could refer to Alexander's conquest of the Near East in 333 B.C.E., to Antiochus III's defeat of Scopas at the Battle of Panium in 198 B.C.E., or to Antiochus IV's campaign against Egypt in 170 B.C.E.. Antiochus IV did conquer Egypt in 170 – capturing all but Alexandria.[93] The lines of text that follow, however, indicate an identification with Antiochus IV. The reader is told that during the reign of this blaspheming king, God will abandon, "the land into the hands of the Angels of Mastemot" (4Q387 2iii 5 = 4Q388a 7 6). In the Book of Ezekiel, YHWH abandons not only the temple, but the land before the Babylonians arrive and desecrate the temple.[94] The *Apocryphon* could depict YHWH as making a similar move ahead of Antiochus IV's desecration of the temple.

This possibility seems probable since two lines later it is claimed that during the reign of this blaspheming king, "The priests of Jerusalem shall [return] to serving other gods and [to acti]ng according to the abominations of the [nations]" (4Q387 2iii 6–7 = 4Q388a 7 6–7).[95] If the *Apocryphon's* accusations are based on real or imagined acts committed in the Jerusalem temple, the most reasonable candidates would be the priests who collaborate with Antiochus IV's vision for a pantheistic Greek-style cult in the Jerusalem temple. The adjectival descriptions of these kings may shed even more light on their identities.

---

[93] Hölbl, *A History of the Ptolemaic Empire*, 143–8.
[94] Cf. Ezek 9:3, 10:4, 11:22–3.
[95] Cf. Ezek 8:5–18.

The term גדפן "blasphemer" is unique to *Apocryphon of Jeremiah C*, though the verbal root גדף is attested several times in the Hebrew Bible and the Dead Sea Scrolls.[96] The most pertinent uses in the Hebrew Bible are 2 Kgs 19:22=Isa 37:23.[97] Therein, the commander of the Assyrian army hurls insults and blasphemous words against the God of Israel while laying siege to Israel. This description is interesting because it frames the evil character of the kings in specifically religious language. In other words, it frames the primary offense as one against God, not God's people.

Besides being described as blasphemers, each of the two kings in the *Apocryphon* are given a second negative description. The respective descriptions are similar but not verbatim. Concerning the first blaspheming king (a Persian King – Cyrus, Darius I?), *Apocryphon of Jeremiah C* claims ועשה תעבות "And he will commit abominations" (4Q385a 4 6=4Q387 2ii 8). The second king (Antiochus IV) is described as עשה רעות "a doer of evil" (4Q389 8ii 9=4Q388a 7 3). The same verbal root is used both times: עשה. In the first case it is a Qal perfect 3ms with a waw-relative (waw-consecutive).[98] In the second case it should be parsed as a masculine singular active participle. The text appears to treat רעות and תעבות as synonyms. These terms continue to highlight a point made above about the description גדפן. Blasphemy names an offense against God, not humans. The term תעבות carries the same, cult-primary connotations. For example, after detailing a series of purity violations in Lev 18:6–23, Moses admonishes, "You shall keep my statutes and my ordinances and commit none of these abominations (התועבת)" (18:26).[99] Similar connotations are found in the eleven uses in the *Temple Scroll* as well as other texts from Qumran such as the *Damascus Document*.[100] For example, the *Temple Scroll* demands,

---

[96] Cf. CD XII 8, 1QpHab X 13, 4Q271 5ii 2, 4Q371 1a–b 12, 4Q372 1 13, 4Q396 1–2iii 10, 4Q397 6–13 9.

[97] The scrolls mentioned above are all Essene texts and use the verb גדף in specifically sectarian contexts. Their specialized use of the verb does not appear to be reflected in the noun used by *Apocryphon of Jeremiah C*.

[98] I object to the notion of "inversion" or "conversion" of verb "tenses" in ancient Hebrew. For the term waw-relative, see Bruce Waltke and M. O'Connor, *An Introduction to Biblical Hebrew Syntax* (Winona Lake, IN: Eisenbrauns, 1990), 519ff. The most sophisticated study of the concept of the so-called "waw-consecutive" forms is Mark Smith, *The Origins and Development of the Waw-Consecutive* (HSS 39; Atlanta: Scholars Press, 1991). Smith successfully puts to rest the conceptions of "inversion" or "conversion" by showing how the peculiar and widespread waw-forms in the prefix and suffix conjugations began and developed separately. Thus, he shows that neither the perfect nor imperfect aspects need any "conversion" to express the full range of meanings that they take in the Hebrew Bible.

[99] Cf. Lev 18:27, 29–30. Nearly 100 other usages in the Hebrew Bible attest the same meaning.

[100] For the *Temple Scroll*, see 11Q19 XLVIII 6, LII 4–5, LV 5–6, 20, LX 17, 19–20, LXII 16, LXVI 14, 17. See also CD V 12, XI 21. Most of the Hebrew examples of the fifty-four תעבה from Qumran contain cult-specific connotations. Cf. Abegg, ed., *The Dead Sea Scrolls Concordance*.

"You shall not sacrifice to me a bull or a sheep that has in it any serious blemish, for they are an abomination (תועבה) to me. And you shall not sacrifice to me a cow, or ewe, or goat that is pregnant, for they are an abomination (תועבה) to me" (11Q19 LII 4–5). The highly formulaic nature of these two descriptions of foreign kings indicates that other rulers may have been described similarly in sections of the text that are now lost.

As well as being described as a one who "will commit abominations" (4Q385a 4 6=4Q387 2ii 8), the first blaspheming king (Cyrus, Darius I?) is described as belonging to the מכלים "lot of destruction." Like מלך גדפן, this locution is peculiar to *Apocryphon of Jeremiah C*.[101] The form is a masculine plural piel active participle from כלה. The descriptions of the abominating kings in the *Apocryphon of Jeremiah C* are considerably different than they way kings (or for that matter humans) are depicted in Dan 2, 7, 8, the *Animal Apocalypse*, 4QFourKingdoms[a–b] ar, and the *Book of the Words of Noah*. In other words, the descriptions used in *Apocryphon of Jeremiah C* do not point beyond themselves to a deeper reality. Despite their non-symbolic language, the descriptions are cryptic and apparently unique to the *Apocryphon of Jeremiah*. They presume a certain linguistic competence that only a reader/hearer with privileged status/information can correctly understand. While perhaps not created with the specific purpose to exclude some hearers/readers, one imagines they had the practical effect of organizing a tighly-knit community whose members knew they belonged because of their ability to demonstrate linguistic competence.

The term כהן "priest" is used several times generically and in some cases there is little context surrounding the term and little one can say about its usage. One instance, however, is especially significant for the overall interpretation of the text: "Three priests who will not walk in the ways [of the] former [priests] (who) by the name of the God of Israel were called" (4Q385a 5a–b 7–8=4Q387 3 4–5). Before the three priests arise, the action of the highly fragmentary text is characterized by mentions of 1) the altar, 2) those felled by the sword and 3) an act of defiling. During the time of the three priests the text describes 1) the downfall of those who have colluded with foreigners, and 2) severe internal strife over religious issues in the Jewish community. For Dimant there are two possible interpretations of the three priests. "The priests referred to here could be High Priests (Jason [174–171 B.C.E.], Menelaus [171–167 B.C.E.], Alcimus [162–161 B.C.E.]), or the Hasmonean priestly kings (Simeon [142–134 B.C.E.], John Hyrcanus

---

Volume One: The Non-Biblical Texts from Qumran, II: 758–9. Some, however, such as 1QS IV 10 use the term in an explicitly sectarian way. This meaning is obviously not intended in *Apocryphon of Jeremiah C*.

[101] Dimant, "4QApocryphon of Jeremiah," 103–4.

[134–104 B.C.E.], Alexander Jannaeus [103–76 B.C.E.]).[102] Dimant's second possibility is considerably more attractive than the first. I think she is correct that the three priests under discussion are probably Hasmoneans, but I propose a slightly different combination than Dimant: Jonathan, Simon, and John Hyrcanus. Why these three? First I shall indicate why the possibility of Hellenizing high priests (Jason, Menelaus, Alcimus) is unlikely and then I argue for my combination of Maccabean/Hasmonean high priests.[103]

While one imagines that Jason, Menelaus, and Alcimus would, in a certain sense, fit into the category of those "who will not walk in the ways of the former priests of Israel," there are problems with such an association. First and most importantly the three priests in the *Apocryphon* arise after the desecration of the Jerusalem temple. Jason and Menelaus were both active before and during the time of the Hellenistic religious reforms.[104] Second, unlike the Maccabean high priests who were criticized by prominent Jewish groups for being illegitimate holders of the office, Jason had the correct priestly credentials – even if he acquired the office through intrigue.[105] He was the brother of the high priest Onias III. If the phrase, "will not walk in the ways of the former priests of Israel," has anything to do with correct family lineage it cannot be applied to a group that includes Jason. Third, the text reports that, "in their days will be brought down the pride of those who violate the covenant as well as the servants of the foreigner" (4Q385a 5a–b 8–9=4Q387 3 6). Such a scenario is hardly characteristic of the terms of Jason, Menelaus, and Alcimus. Indeed *they* are the leaders of those who "violate the covenant" and are "servants of the foreigner." Below I argue that "those who violate the covenant" (מרישיעי ברית) must be understood as Seleucid sympathizers. What second century Jew could be described as more sympathetic to Seleucid concerns than Menelaus? The three priests in *Apocryphon of Jeremiah C* appear after the Hellenistic religious reforms and it is during their time that Hellenizing Jews are repeatedly dealt strong political blows.

The three priests "who will not walk in the way" are better identified as Maccabeans/Hasmoneans, but I offer a list slightly different than Dimant's

---

[102] Dimant, "4QApocryphon of Jeremiah," 193.

[103] Cf. my use of this argument for different purposes in Bennie H. Reynolds III, "Adjusting the Apocalypse: How 4QApocryphon of Jeremiah C updates the Book of Daniel," in *The Dead Sea Scrolls in Context: Integrating the Dead Sea Scrolls in the Study of Ancient Texts, Languages, and Cultures* vol. 1, (eds. Emanuel Tov, Armin Lange, Matthias Weigold, and Bennie H. Reynolds III; Leiden: Brill, 2011), 279–94.

[104] Cf. 2 Macc 4:7–5:20

[105] See for example the story about John Hyrcanus and the Pharisees related by Josephus in *Antiquities of the Jews* 13.288–300. Cf. James VanderKam, *An Introduction to Early Judaism* (Grand Rapids: Eerdmans, 2001), 27–30.

group of Hasmoneans (Simon, John Hyrcanus, Alexander Jannaeus). Why? Most importantly, *Apocryphon of Jeremiah C* describes three priests, not five. There is no doubt that Jonathan held the office of high priest and that he was the first Maccabee to do so. According to 1 Maccabees 10:21, "Jonathan put on the sacred vestments in the seventh month of the one hundred sixtieth year, at the festival of booths" (NRSV). Jonathan (164–43 B.C.E.) was followed by Simon (142–35 B.C.E.), John Hyrcanus (134–04 B.C.E.), and Aristobulus I (104–03 B.C.E.). Alexander Jannaeus would be the fifth Maccabean high priest – two too many. In order for Dimant's list to work one would need to explain why two Hasmoneans are ignored.

The text is an *ex eventu* prophecy and since it only knows of three Maccabean high priests, it makes the most sense to identify them with the *first* three Maccabean high priests (Jonathan, Simon, John Hyrcanus). If my thesis about the three priests is correct, then the text must have been written after 134 but before 104 B.C.E., i.e., during the reign of Hyrcanus. This adjectival description does not only tell us about the date of the text, however, but bears witness to a specific view of the priesthood. The adjectival description is probably another instance of language that carried specific connotations with a narrow group of Jews, but that could have easily been interpreted in a multitude of ways by other Jews. The text may indicate that family lineage is important to the proper/legitimate functioning of the priesthood. At least one group known to have espoused this view is the Pharisees. We know from Josephus that some Pharisees apparently asked John Hyrcanus to give up the priesthood on account of his pedigree.[106]

A group in existence just before the Babylonian exile is given an enigmatic adjectival description in 4Q385 3 2: ק[ריאי השם "those called by name." Dimant reads this expression as an abbreviated version of the biblical formula קראי מועד אנשי שם "those chosen from the assembly, men of repute" from Num 16:2b.[107] While *Apocryphon of Jeremiah C* does not replicate the narrative context of Num 16:2, it may carry over the major concern. Num 16–17 interweaves two separate stories of rebellion.[108] The JE story (16:1b–2a, 12–15, 25–26, 27b–32a, 33–34) revolves around two figures: Dathan and Abiram. They complain about Moses's leadership so Moses devises a test of his legitimacy by declaring that if the men die natural deaths they were correct, but if YHWH intervenes to take their lives in a

---

[106] *Antiquities of the Jews* 13.288–300.

[107] This expression is also found fully or in part in 1QM II 7, 1QSa II 2, CD II 11, IV 4, and 4Q275 4.

[108] Thanks to Moshe Bernstein for helping me avoid an error with the Korah material. On the source criticism of this passage, see Baruch Levine, *Numbers 1–10* (AB 4a; New York: London, 1993), 405–32. For a very creative reading of the Korah incident, see J. Duncan Derrett, "The Case of Korah Versus Moses Reviewed," *JSJ* XXIV (1993).

spectacular way, he is correct. A definitive judgment comes when ground opens and swallows the men and their households.

The P story (16:1a, 2b, 3–11, 16–24, 27a, 35, chap. 17) revolves around a Levite named Korah and a group of two hundred and fifty Israelites described as נְשִׂיאֵי עֵדָה קְרִאֵי מוֹעֵד אַנְשֵׁי־שֵׁם "chiefs of the congregation, those called (in the) assembly, men of renown." It is the Korah incident that is most germane to the expression found in the *Apocryphon*, although presumably any influence from the Book of Numbers would have been derived from a text in which the stories were already fully integrated since the *Apocryphon of Jeremiah C* was written in the late second century B.C.E..[109] Korah and his party apparently demand that the Korahites (another member of the Kohathite clan) be allowed to function as priests.[110] Moses rebukes them in 16:9–10:

Is it too little for you that the God of Israel has separated you from the congregation of Israel, to allow you to approach him in order to perform the duties of YHWH's tabernacle, and to stand before the congregation and serve them? He has allowed you to approach him, and all your brother Levites with you; yet you seek the priesthood as well!

B. Levine suggests that the P (Korah) story is post-exilic and perhaps reflects a rivalry in the priesthood of the second temple.[111] If Levine is correct, the passage could shed more light on the *Apocryphon* than has yet been realized. At several junctures, *Apocryphon of Jeremiah C* condemns corrupt priestly behavior; sometimes contrasting such behavior with other priests who have performed correctly or legitimately (e.g., 4Q385a 5a–b 7–8=4Q387 3 4–5). Since the Korah incident in Num 16–17 highlights an attempt to usurp legitimate priestly power, the expression ק[ריאי השם could be adapted to describe some priests or some other (fictitious) group before the Babylonian conquest in 586 B.C.E. in a way that foreshadows the usurpation of the priesthood by Jason and Menelaus several hundred years later.

There is, however, another possible interpretation for "those called by name." Two points are clear about ק[ריאי השם based on context in the *Apocryphon*. First, the group is active right before the Babylonian exile (4Q387 1 7–9=4Q389 6 1–2; CE 36–8). Second, in the line of text that follows "those called by name," one reads, "Just as I said to Jacob" (4Q385a 3 5=4Q387 1 1=CE 30). It is possible that the name Jacob refers to the patriarch, but it is more likely that by "Jacob," the text indicates Israel as a collective group because in the next line YHWH says, "And you said, 'You

---

[109] There is no textual evidence from Qumran or elsewhere in which these stories are unincorporated.
[110] Levine, *Numbers 1–10*, 430.
[111] Levine, *Numbers 1–10*, 430.

have abandoned u[s." In other words, since a second-person plural subject addresses YHWH, it is unlikely that "Jacob" could be construed as a single individual. If Jacob is treated as a collective, then one might locate a scriptural context for this section of the *Apocryphon* in Deutero-Isaiah, where YHWH says: "But hear now, O Jacob my servant, Israel whom I have chosen . . . This one will say, 'I am the LORD's,' another will be called by the name of Jacob (יִקְרָא בְשֵׁם־יַעֲקֹב), yet another will write on the hand, 'The LORD's,' and adopt the name of Israel" (Isa 44:1, 5; NRSV). Understanding this passage as the background for ק[ריאי השם "those called by name" is an attractive option given how closely the text of the *Apocryphon* parallels Deutero-Isaiah just two lines later:

And you said, "You have abandoned u]s ". . . (עזב[תנו] 4Q387 1 2 = CE 31)

But Zion said, "YHWH has abandoned me (עֲזָבַנִי), my Lord has forgotten me." (Isa 49:14)

If this association is correct then the *Apocryphon* could be using Deutero-Isaiah's retrospective on the Babylonian exile in order to construct an *ex eventu* prophecy that predicts the Babylonian exile. Since the period addressed by Deutero-Isaiah is precisely the time frame that the *Apocryphon* addresses, it perhaps provides more persuasive context since the Korah incident in Num 16–17 addresses a wilderness setting.

A much more familiar adjectival description is found in the depiction of the transition from Babylonian to Persian control in Palestine: משיע "Deliverer." After the text appears to indicate that many will return to their homeland, but that many will remain in the land of their captivity, it reports, "The children of Israel shall cry out because of the heavy burden in the lands of captivity and there shall not be a deliverer for them" (4Q387 2ii 11=4Q389 8ii 3). The term is used modestly in the Hebrew Bible – normally with full orthography (i.e., מושיע). It is not used in the non-biblical scrolls from Qumran. The usage in *Apocryphon of Jeremiah C* is close to its usage in the Deuteronomistic History (Deut 22:27, 28:29, 31, Judg 12:3, 2 Sam 22:42, 2 Kgs 13:5). A particularly close example is Deut 28:29: "You shall grope about at noon as blind people grope in darkness, but you shall be unable to find your way; and you shall be continually abused and robbed, without anyone to help (אין מושיע)." Thus, while *Apocryphon of Jeremiah C* shows strong concern for priestly affairs, it also reflects deuteronomic theology – not in the sense that covenant faithfulness is rewarded or punished within one's lifetime, but in the cyclical model of apostasy, retribution, outcry, and deliverance. In *Apocryphon of Jeremiah C*, however, deliverance is missing from the cycles until the *eschaton* at which point it is decisive.

Another possible reading of this adjectival description, however, would be to see it as a play on Isa 45:1. We have already seen above the possibility that the *Apocryphon of Jeremiah* uses Deutero-Isa to frame its description of the Babylonian exile. But it does not appear to share Deutero-Isa's positive view of Cyrus and Persia. For example, we have seen that *Apocryphon of Jeremiah* appears to have a negative view of Persian kings – apparently describing Cyrus or Darius I as a "blasphemer" (גדפן). Isa 45:1 describes Cyrus of Persia as YHWH's anointed (כֹּה־אָמַר יְהוָה לִמְשִׁיחוֹ לְכוֹרֶשׁ). The *Apocryphon*'s claim אין משיע להם "There shall not be a deliverer for them," could be a pun. It may take Deutero-Isaiah's claim that Cyrus is God's anointed (משיחו) and reverse it to claim that there will be no savior (אין משיע) during the transition from Babylonian to Persian rule. In other words, the text claims that the exile did not end with the rise of Persia. Instead, the chronology of the text describes ten jubilees, or 490 years of destruction (cf. lines 43–44 of the combined edition).

Four adjectival descriptions from *Apocryphon of Jeremiah C* have significant parallels in Dan 10–12.[112] Three of the expressions are found in the overlapping fragments 4Q385a 5a–b and 4Q387 3 and parallel terms used in Dan 11: הנופלים בחרב ("those felled by the sword"), מרישיעי ברית ("violators of the covenant"), and עבדי נאכר ("servants of the foreigner"). A fourth expression, from 4Q388a 7 9, has a parallel in Dan 12: [המצדקי]ם ("those who lead to righteousness"). We have already seen several points of contact between the *Apocryphon* and Dan 9–12 and others will be encountered in the section below on ethno-political groups. In table below I gather all the connections.

The cluster of adjectival descriptions in 4Q385a 5a–b=4Q387 3 functions within the context of a narrative that "predicts" the Hellenistic relgious reforms, the Maccabean revolt, and the advent of the Hasmonean state. The first few lines preserve only one or two words each. The first important expression is found in 4Q385a 5a–b 5=4Q387 3 2: נופלים בחרב "those felled by the sword." The time frame in which the individuals fall by the sword is not the final apocalyptic battle, but apparently the time of Antiochus' religious reforms and the Maccabean revolt. This scenario finds a parallel in the Book of Daniel.

Within the very same historical context, i.e., the Hellenistic religious reforms and the Maccabean revolt, the Book of Daniel reports that the משכילים will "fall by the sword" (ונכשלו בחרב): "The wise among the people will give understanding to many; for some days, however, they shall fall by the sword and flame, and suffer captivity and plunder" (Dan 11:33).

---

[112] I have adapted my argument about these four descriptions for a different purpose in Reynolds, "Adjusting the Apocalypse," 287–94.

Alone this expression might tell an interpreter very little, but when coupled with the expressions מרישיעי ברית and עבדי נאכר, which find even more compelling parallels in Dan 11:32, the Book of Daniel emerges as a likely source of this portion of the *Apocryphon*.

מרישיעי ברית "Those who act wickedly (against the) covenant" and עבדי נאכר "servants of the foreigner" (4Q385a 5a–b 9=4Q387 3 6) appear to be synonymous. Both adjectival descriptions portray Jews by characteristic actions. The expression מרישיעי ברית,[113] is used in at least two other roughly contemporary texts: Daniel and 1QM.[114] Dan 11:30–35 details Antiochus' failed attack on Egypt (foiled by the Romans) and his subsequent campaign into Jerusalem. The brief passage is worth quoting in its entirety:

> The ships of the *Kittim* shall come against him and he shall lose heart and retreat. He shall rage against the holy covenant (וזעם על־ברית־קודש) and he shall take action and returning he shall pay heed to those who forsake the holy covenant (עזבי ברית קודש). His forces shall occupy and profane the temple and the fortress. They shall do away with the regular offering and set up the abomination of desolation. Now those who have violated the covenant (מרשיעי ברית) he shall seduce with flattery, but the people who know their God shall stand strong and take action. The wise among the people shall give understanding to many. They shall fall by sword (ונכשלו בחרב) and flame and (shall suffer) captivity and plunder for some days. When they stumble, they shall receive a little help, but many shall join them insincerely. Some of the wise shall stumble, so that they might be refined, and purified, and whitened until the time of the end, for it is yet the appointed time.

In Dan 11, עזבי ברית "those who forsake the holy covenant" and מרשיעי ברית "those who have violated the covenant" are synonymous. In both cases they refer to Jewish officials who were hellenizers. In other words, these figures are sympathetic to the vision of *oikumene* pursued by Alexander the Great and developed in Syro-Palestine by Antiochus IV. "Those who have violated the covenant" (מרשיעי ברית) is almost certainly a reference to the high priest Menelaus and his party (though it could probably be as well applied to the former high priest Jason). According to 2 Maccabees 5:15, Menelaus not only allowed Antiochus' desecration of the temple, but personally guided Antiochus through the temple. He is described as καὶ τῶν νόμων καὶ τῆς πατρίδος προδότην γεγονότα "a traitor both to the laws and to his country." Martin Hengel points to an account in the *Tosefta*, that while legendary, nevertheless expresses how in his words, "The extreme

---

[113] Cf. also עזבי ברית in Dan 11:30.

[114] The orthography in *Apocryphon of Jeremiah* is unusual. The first *yod* is unanticipated. Dimant offers the following speculation: The first *yod* placed after the *reš* may stand for the *i*-sound of *reš* which was pronounced as the *i*-sound of the following *šin*. Based on extant vocalizations of III-guttural hiphil participles, however, I suggest that it is more likely a scribal error.

Hellenists under Menelaus had lost any interest in sacrifice according to the law:"[115]

> And when the gentiles went into the sanctuary, she came along and stamped on the altar, screaming at it, "Wolf, wolf! You have wiped out [devoured] the fortune of Israel and did not then stand up for them in the time of their trouble."[116] (*T. Sukk* 4, 28)

Hengel comments about the passage, "The uselessness of the *tamid* offering could not be expressed more vividly. The age of this legend is shown by the fact that it was later transferred to Titus."[117] Indeed, the thesis of Hengel's famous dissertation is that Menelaus and his Tobias supporters were the authors of the edict of persecution. While I disagree with Hengel that, "One cannot speak of a deliberate policy of Hellenization on the part of the Seleucids or Antiochus IV," there seems little doubt that the political ambitions of Jews such as Menelaus played a major role in the development and implementation of the Hellenistic religious reforms. Regardless of who was the driving force (and there was surely more than one) behind the Hellenistic religious reforms, Menelaus' role would have easily won him and his supporters the title מרישיעי ברית "violators of the covenant." Other, more indirect linguistic evidence points in the same direction.

In 1QM I 2 the expression מרשיעי ברית is used to describe Jews who collaborate with foreign powers against the faithful:

> The first attack of the Sons of Light shall be undertaken against the forces of the Sons of Darkness, the army of Belial the troops of Edom, Moab, the sons of Ammon, and [ ] Philistia and the troops of the Kittim of Asshur. Supporting them are those who have violated the covenant (מרשיעי ברית).[118]

David Flusser has shown that Dan 11:29–39 and this specific term was taken up by the writer of 1QM and used to describe those who collaborate with Greek imperialists – though in a later historical setting. Flusser finds that 1QM appropriates the term to name Seleucid sympathizers in the time of Alexander Jannaeus – preferring to see in the "violators of the covenant" a reflection of the invasion of Demetrius II (Eucaerus) in 89 B.C.E. with Jewish help. In any case, he holds that the historical situation must be in Hasmonean times and must predate the fall of Seleucid Syria in 83 B.C.E.,

---

[115] Martin Hengel, *Judaism and Hellenism: Studies in their Encounter in Palestine during the Early Hellenistic Period* (Philadelphia: Fortress Press, 1981), 283.

[116] Trans. Jacob Neusner, *The Tosefta: Second Division, Moed (The Order of the Appointed Times)* (New York: Ktav Publishing House, 1981).

[117] Hengel, *Judaism and Hellenism*, 283.

[118] Trans. By M. Wise, M. Abegg, and E. Cook in Parry and Tov, eds., *Texts Concerned with Religious Law*, 209.

since the text include the Kittim of Ashur in the battle.[119] I contend, like Flusser did about 1QM, that *Apocryphon of Jeremiah C* attempts to update the eschatological prophecy from Dan 11 (as well as the 490 year prophecy).[120] I suggest a later date for the update in *Apocryphon of Jeremiah* though.[121]

A final expression that finds an important parallel in the Book of Daniel is located in 4Q388a 7 9 (two lines below the [ימלכו] אשר שלשה["three who will rule") a group is described as [המצדקי]ם["th[ose] who lead to righteousness." Like the "three who will rule," the description [המצדקי]ם[comprises the only extant word of the line – leaving no immediate context within which to understand the expression. Between the description of the "three who will rule" and "those who lead to righteousness," however, is a mention of the innersanctum of the temple: [הקדשי]ם קדש["the holy of holies." Dimant suggests a parallel with Dan 12:3: "Those who are wise shall shine like the brightness of the sky, and those who lead many to righteousness (מצדיקי הרבים), like the stars forever and ever." In Dan 12:3, the משכלים and the מצדיקי הרבים are probably synonyms. Both expressions describe groups present during the Hellenistic religious reforms who will be rewarded for their faithfulness at the end of days. They are not groups that emerge after the death of Antiochus IV and the advent of the eschaton. The eschaton is merely the time of their reward. Since the context of 4Q388a 7 10 appears to be the reign of Antiochus IV and his religious reforms, this fragment provides a group-specific term shared by the *Apocryphon* and Dan 12.

It is not obvious that the similar expression would have been understood in the same way by the writer of Daniel and the writer of the *Apocryphon*. It seems clear, however, that a person would not have known who the "wise" or "those who lead many to righteousness" were unless that person was one of them already. The contexts in which the expressions are used are otherwise too weak to support a definitive interpretation. Dan 10–12 is important for illustrating the point that opaque meanings are simply products of a fragmentary text when it comes to the *Apocryphon*. In other words, even with the full text of Dan 10–12, one is no better equipped to identify the "wise" or the "those who lead to righteousness."

An interesting aspect of the identity of the group from which the *Apocryphon* emerged is that they seem, like Daniel, not to have been supporters of the Maccabees. In Daniel, they are referred to as a "little help" in 11:34.

---

[119] Flusser, *Judaism of the Second Temple Period: Qumran and Apocalypticism*, 154–5.

[120] Another related expression is found in CD XX 26–7: Cf also CD IV–V, Pss. Sol. 2:8–13, 8:9–13.

[121] See my arguments above about the "three priests" as well as in Reynolds, "Adjusting the Apocalypse," 281–84.

There are no explicit references to the Macabees in *Apocryphon of Jeremiah C* and if I am correct that the text should be dated to approximately the time of John Hyrcanus (end of the 2nd century), it is hardly possible that they were viewed in high esteem by the writer. Indeed, several Maccabees may be described as illegitimate holders of the high priesthood (see discussion on the "three priests who will not walk" above). We have also seen that it is unlikely that the *Apocryphon* could have been produced by Essenes because of its free use of the tetragrammaton among other reasons. It seems equally unlikely that the text was a product of Sadducees in light of their rejection of the concept of resurrection (cf. Luke 22:29–32, Acts 23:8). One intriguing possibility – though it is mere speculation – is that the group-specific language of the *Apocryphon* may point towards the Pharisees.[122] I indicated above that the writer of Apocryphon of Jeremiah C shares some common ground with the Pharisees in that they both critique John Hyrcanus' role as high priest (cf. *Antiquities of the Jews* 13.288–300 and 4Q385a 5a–b 7–8=4Q387 3 4–5).

Descriptions of Ethno-Political Groups
Among political/people groups explicitly named in the *Apocryphon of Jeremiah C*, Israel is mentioned most. ממלכות ישראל, ישראל, and בני ישראל are used a combined nine times in the revelation. The term is never used as designation for the historical, northern kingdom of Israel. Instead, it refers to the kingdom of Judah as well as its land and people after the nation became a Babylonian and later Persian vassal state. As we have seen, the mention of Jacob (יעק[וב]) in 4Q385a 3 4 is probably also a reference to Israel, not the patriarch.

מצרים "Egypt" is mentioned in two different contexts. The first is a passage that predicts the destruction of both Egypt and Israel: "Egypt and Israel I shall break and hand over to the sword. And I shall [dev]astate the [la]nd and (from it) shall I remove humanity" (4Q388a 7 5=4Q387 2iii 2–3=4Q389 8ii 11). The second reference is found within the context of a literary-map in 4Q385a 17i–ii. Therein, four explicit descriptions are given for geo-political entities at the advent of the apocalypse: מצרים "Egypt," אמון "Thebes," כוש "Cush," and לוב "Libya." These designations are part of a reworked portion of Nahum 3:8–10, but they hardly address the same setting presumed in Nahum (i.e., a comparison of Thebes and Nineveh in anticipation of the divine destruction of Nineveh). Instead, the map seems to indicate Ptolemaitc Egpyt.[123]

---

[122] This suggestion was made to me by Armin Lange.
[123] Dimant speculates about this possibility. Dimant, "4QApocryphon of Jeremiah," 158–9.

יון "Greece" and הלבנון "The Lebanon" are both mentioned in 4Q385a 16a–b. הלבנון is used purely as a geographic designation. The use of יון is more complicated. יון could potentially refer to the Aegean City-States, to Alexander's kingdom, or to the *diadochoi* more generally. In the present context, however, it refers to Seleucid Syria. 4Q385a 16a–b, which mentions יון, precedes the fragment forecasting the downfall of Ptolemaic Egypt (see above). The roots of the Ptolemies were just as Greek (Macedonian) as the Seleucids, but there is precedent for describing only Seleucid Syria as יון. The *Pesher Nahum* describes not only the Seleucid ruler Demetrius as מלך יון "king of Greece," but declares "[God did not deliver Jerusalem] into the hand of the kings of Greece (מלכי יון) from Antiochus up to the appearance of the chiefs of the *Kittim*" (4QpNah 3–4i 2-3). In the *Pesher Nahum*, Kittim refers to Romans while "kings of Greece" refers to Seleucids. In other words, "kings of Greece" has the same meaning that *Kittim* does in the *War Scroll*.[124] The language used to describe nations and other political groups in *Apocryphon of Jeremiah C* is striking when read against texts like Dan 7 and 8. Nations are entirely disintegrated from the cosmic sphere.[125] In *Apocryphon of Jeremiah C* nations are nations and cosmic powers are cosmic powers but one is not a mirror of the other. Entirely missing is any attempt to incorporate nations into an allegorical scheme. *Apocryphon of Jeremiah C* does not employ a mythological meta-narrative into which the powers of earth are incorporated. Rather than reflecting the heavenly realm, the earthly realm is infiltrated by the heavenly realm.

Raw Data from 4QApocryphon of Jeremiah C

Citation		Description	Description-Type
4Q389 2 6	בניהם	children	Explicit: title
4Q389 5 2	מלך	King	Explicit: title

---

[124] Eshel, "The Kittim in the War Scroll and in the Pesharim," 29–44.
[125] Cf. Werman, "Epochs and End-Time," 242.

4Q389 5 3	שמואל בן אלקנה	Samuel, Son of Elqanah	Explicit: name + title
4Q385a 1ii 2	איבו	His enemy	Explicit: title
4Q385a 1ii 3	איבו	His enemy	Explicit: title
4Q385a 1ii 5	שלמה	Solomon	Explicit: name
4Q385a 1ii 6	איביו	His enemies	Explicit: Title
4Q385a 3 3 4Q388a 3 2–3	קריאי השם	Those called by name	Adjectival
4Q385a 3 4 4Q388a 3 3 4Q387 1 1	יעקוב	Jacob	Explicit: name
4Q385a 3 7 4Q387 1 4 4Q388a 3 6	שעירים	Goat demons	Explicit

4Q389 6 1 4Q387 1 7	איביכם	Your enemies	Explicit: Title
4Q387 1 9	איביכם	Your enemies	Explicit: Title
4Q387 2ii 5	הממלכה	The kingdom	Explicit: Title
4Q385a 4 4 4Q387 2ii 6	אחרים מעם אחר	Others, from another people	Adjectival
4Q385a 4 5 4Q387 2ii 7	ממלכת ישראל	The kingdom of Israel	Explicit: name + title
4Q385a 4 6 4Q387 2ii 8	גדפן	Blasphemer	Adjectival
4Q387 2ii 9 4Q389 8ii 1	ממלכתו	His Kingdom	Explicit: Title
4Q387 2ii 9 4Q385a 4 7	מכלים	The lot of destruction	Adjectival

4Q387 2ii 9	ישראל	Israel	Explicit: name
4Q387 2ii 10 4Q489 8ii 2 4Q385a 4 8	גוים רבים	Many nations	Explicit: Title
4Q387 2ii 9 4Q389 8ii 2	בני ישראל	The children of Israel	Explicit: name
4Q387 2ii 11 4Q389 8ii 3	משיע	Deliverer	Adjectival
4Q389 8ii 8 4Q388a 7 2	אברהם	Abraham	Explicit: name
4Q389 8ii 8 4Q388a 7 2	יצחק	Isaac	Explicit: name
4Q389 8ii 9 4Q388a 7 2	[יעקוב]	Jacob	Explicit: name

4Q389 8ii 9 4Q388a 7 3	מלך לגוים	A king of the nations	Explicit: Title
4Q389 8ii 9 4Q388a 7 3	גדפן	A blasphemer	Adjectival
4Q389 8ii 9 4Q388a 7 3	עשה רעות	A doer of evils	Adjectival
4Q389 8ii 10 4Q388a 7 4 4Q387 2iii 1	ישראל	Israel	Explicit: name
4Q389 8ii 10 4Q388a 7 4 4Q387 2iii 1	עם	A people	Explicit: Title
4Q389 8ii 10–11 4Q388a 7 4 4Q387 2iii 1	מלכת מצרים	The Kingdom of Egypt	Explicit: name + title

4Q388a 7 5 4Q387 2iii 2	מצרים	Egypt	Explicit: name
4Q388a 7 5 4Q387 2iii 2 4Q389 8ii 11	ישראל	Israel	Explicit: name
4Q388a 7 6 4Q387 2iii 3	האדם	Humanity	Explicit: name
4Q387 2iii 4	מלאכי המשטמות	The Angels of Mastemot	Explicit: name
4Q387 2iii 5	ישראל	Israel	Explicit: name
4Q387 2iii 6	כהני ירושלים	The priests of Jerusalem	Explicit: title
4Q387 2iii 6 4Q388a 7 7	אלהים אחרים	Other Gods	Explicit: title
4Q388a 7 8	שלשה אשר ימלכו	Three who will rule	Adjectival

4Q388a 7 10	המצדקים	Those who lead to righteousness	Adjectival
4Q385a 5a–b 1	אלהים	God	Explicit: name
4Q385a 5a–b 2	כהנים	Priests	Explicit: Title
4Q385a 5a–b 5 4Q387 3 2	הנופלים בחרב	Those felled by the sword	Adjectival
4Q385a 5a–b 7 4Q387 3 4	כהנים שלושה אשר לא יתהלכו בדרכי	Three priests who will not walk in the ways	Explicit: title + adjective
4Q385a 5a–b 2	מנין כהנים	A number of priests	
4Q387 3 4	[הכהנים ה[ראשים	[the] first/former [priests]	Explicit: title + adjective
4Q387 3 5 4Q385a 5a–b 8	אלהי ישראל	The God of Israel	Explicit: name
4Q387 3 6	מרישיעי ברית	Those who act wickedly against the covenant	Adjectival

4Q387 3 6 4Q385a 5a–b 9	עבדי נאכר	Servants of the foreigner	Adjectival
4Q387 3 7	ישראל	Israel	Explicit: name
4Q387 3 7	איש	Each man	Explicit: name
4Q387 3 7	רעהו	His neighbor	Explicit: title
4Q387 4 2	מלכי הצפון	The kings of the North	Explicit: title
4Q387 4 3	בני ישראל	The Children of Israel	Explicit: name
4Q387 4 3	אלהים	God	Explicit: name
4Q385a 16a–b 1	יתר	A Remnant	Adjectival
4Q385a 16a–b 2	עם	People	Explicit: title
4Q385a 16a–b 2	עדרי	The flocks of	Explicit or Adjectival?
4Q385a 16a–b 3	עם	People	Explicit: title

4Q385a 16a–b 3	זרע	A seed	Adjectival
4Q385a 16a–b 3	עמו	His people	Explicit: title
4Q385a 16a–b 4	יון	Greece	Explicit: name
4Q385a 16a–b 5	החיה	Wild beasts	Adjectival
4Q385a 16a–b 7	יהוה	YHWH	Explicit: name
4Q385a 16a–b 8	יקוב	Jacob	Explicit: name
4Q385a 17ii 4	אמון	Amon (Thebes, i.e., מנו אמון)	Explicit: name
4Q385a 17ii 6	כוש	Cush	Explicit: name
4Q385a 17ii 6	מצרים	Egypt	Explicit: name
4Q385a 17ii 7	לוב	Libya	Explicit: name
4Q385a 17ii 8	עלליה	Her babes	Adjectival
4Q385a 18i 2	ירמיה הנביא	Jeremiah the prophet	Explicit: name + title

4Q385a 18i 2	יהוה	YHWH	Explicit: name
4Q385a 18i 3	השבאים	The captives	Explicit: title
4Q385a 18i 4	מלך בבל	The King of Babylon	Explicit: title
4Q385a 18i 4	נבוזרדן רב הטבחים	Nebuzaradan, commander of the special forces	Explicit: name + title
4Q385a 18i 5	הכהנים	The priests	Explicit: Title
4Q385a 18i 6	בני ישראל	Children of Israel	Explicit: name
4Q385a 18i 6	ירמיה הנביא	Jeremiah the prophet	Explicit: name + title
4Q385a 18i 8	ירמיה	Jeremiah	Explicit: name
4Q385a 18i 8	אלהים	God	Explicit: name
4Q385a 18i 9	אלהי אבותיהם	The God of their fathers	Explicit: name
4Q385a 18i 10	מלכיהם	Their kings	Explicit: title

4Q385a 18i 10	כהניהם	Their priests	Explicit: title
4Q385a 18i 11	אלהים	God	Explicit: name
4Q385a 18ii 2	אלהים	God	Explicit: name
4Q385a 18ii 2	ירמיה	Jeremiah	Explicit: name
4Q385a 18ii 3	אלהים	God	Explicit: name
4Q385a 18ii 4	ירמיה	Jeremiah	Explicit: name
4Q385a 18ii 6	ירמיה	Jeremiah	Explicit: name
4Q385a 18ii 7	בני ישראל	The children of Israel	Explicit: name
4Q385a 18ii 7	בני יהודה ובנימין	The children of Judah and Benjamin	Explicit: names
4Q385a 18ii 9	פסילי הגוים	The idols of the nations	Explicit: title

Raw Data from 4Q390

4Q390 1 2	בני אהרון	Sons of Aaron	Explicit: title
4Q390 1 4	ישראל	Israel	Explicit: name
4Q390 1 5	מלכתו הרישונים	their (Israel's) former kingdom	Explicit: title + adjective
4Q390 1 7	אבותיהם	their fathers	Explicit: title
4Q390 1 7	הדור ההוא	that generation	Explicit: title
4Q390 1 9	איביהם	their enemies	Explicit: title
4Q390 1 10	פליטים	Survivors	Explicit: title
4Q390 1 11	מלאכי המשטמות	The angels of Mastemot	Explicit: name
4Q390 2i 4	בליעל	Belial	Explicit: name
4Q390 2i 5	עבדי הנביאים	My servants the prophets	Explicit: title + adjective
4Q390 2i 7	מלאכי המשטמות	The angels of Mastemot	Explicit: name
4Q390 2i 9	רעהו x2	His neighbor	Explicit: title

4Q390 2i 9	איש	Each man	Explicit: title
4Q390 2i 10	בני	The sons of	?
4Q390 2i 10	כוהניהם	Their priests	Explicit: title
4Q390 2i 12	בניהם	Their children	Explicit: title

Findings From Chapter Five

One

The primary model I used in chapter one for understanding the language of apocalypses is the typology of dream reports devised by Artemidorus/Leo Oppenheim. The primary distinction in their typology differentiates dreams that require interpretation and those whose meanings are immediately obvious to the dreamer. In other words, some dreams use language that points beyond itself and others use language that is explicit (or, at least intelligible to the dreamer). The symbolic apocalypses in chapters two and three used language that primarily fits the symbolic type. The expressions point beyond themselves – both in terms of the underlying linguistic structures and the specific, historical referents for each description. Like Dan 10–12,[126] however, the *Apocryphon of Jeremiah C* does not make use of language that points beyond itself. None of the expressions appear to reflect the system of conventional pairs uncovered in the symbolic apocalypses (i.e., humans or stars always used to describe angels). But the language found in *Apocryphon of Jeremiah C* is not uncomplicated. In light of the analysis above I can conclude that at least one source for the language of *Apocryphon of Jeremiah C* is clear: Jewish scripture.

---

[126] Occasionally the description of angels departed from this model in Dan 10–12.

Two

In the analysis above, I highlighted several connections between the language of *Apocryphon of Jeremiah C* and Jewish scripture. The most significant connections appear to be with the Jeremiah, Deutero-Isaiah, Daniel, and the Nahum. The Book of Jeremiah appears to have provided a narrative framework by supplying an incident in which *Apocryphon of Jeremiah C*'s revelation could take place. Two incidents from the Book of Jeremiah are referenced: 1) the execution of the royal family and Judean officials after the siege of Babylon in 586 B.C.E. found in Jer 52 and 2) the abduction of Jeremiah and his conduction to Egypt in Jer 43 (cf. lines 103–122 in the combined edition). Nah 3:8–10 is almost certainly the source of the literary map found in 4Q385a 17i–ii, though Dan 11:41–2 seems to have also played a part. Two expressions, קריא השם "those called by name" (4Q385a 3 2) and משיע "savior" (4Q387 2ii 11=4Q389 8ii 3) may be taken from Deutero-Isa 44:5 and 45:1 – the latter as a polemical pun. Finally, a significant number of expressions are taken from Daniel and the narrative framework of Dan 11:29–39 might be appropriated as well. I summarize the points of contact with Daniel in the table below.

	Book of Daniel	*Apocryphon of Jeremiah C*
Motif-Historical Connections		
	490 year scheme (9:24)	490 year scheme (4Q387 2i–ii 1–5)
Linguistic Connections		

	מצדיקי הרבים those who lead many to righteousness (12:3)	[המצדקי]ם th[ose] who lead to righteousness (4Q388a 7 10)
	ונכשלו בחרב And they will fall by the sword (11:34)	הנופלים בחרב those felled by the sword (4Q385a 5a–b 5=4Q387 3 2)
	מרשיעי ברית those who have violated the covenant (11:32) Cf. עזבי ברית קודש who forsake the holy covenant (11:30)	מרישיעי ברית those who have violated covenant (4Q385a 5a–b 9=4Q387 3 6)
	King of the North (11:6, 7, 8, 11, 13, 15, 40)	Kings of the North
	Greece (10:20, 11:2)	Greece (4Q385a 16a–b)
Literary Map		

	Egypt (11:42–3)	Egypt 4Q388a 7 5=4Q387 2iii 2–3=4Q389 8ii 11, 4Q385a 17i–ii
	Amon (11:41)	Amon [Thebes] (4Q385a 17i–ii)
	Cushites (11:43)	Cush (4Q385a 17i–ii)
	Libians (11:43)	Libya (4Q385a 17i–ii)

Three

The use of scripture in *Apocryphon of Jeremiah* is complicated. The language borrowed from scripture seems to have been appropriated as in-group language in some cases. In other words, merely knowing Jewish scripture would not have necessarily permitted an ancient reader entrance into the world of this text. There are two indications of this. First, the only case in which the text appears to explicitly quote or allude to scripture is the Jeremiah framework passages. The text sometimes pulls only one or two words at a time from Daniel and Deutero-Isaiah. In one of these cases, it is possible that the text refers obliquely to Deutero-Isaiah by creating a pun on Cyrus' description as משיח (cf. אין משיע in 4Q387 2ii 11=4Q389 8ii 3).[127] In other words, understanding the *Apocryphon of Jeremiah C* presumes not only a high level knowledge and interaction with Jewish scriptures, but it also presumes a particular hermeneutics. As noted in chapters one and four, Maxine Grossman has called attention to this type of hermeneutical in-group identity-construction in the *Damascus Document*. She highlights a

---

[127] Cf. Newsom's look at how some texts from Qumran construct identity with a discourse that makes subtle changes to other works. Newsom, "Constructing 'We, You, and Others" through Non-Polemical Discourse," 13–21. She shows, for example, how 1QH[a] makes small changes to the language of Sir 15:14–16 that result in significant changes in meaning.

string of references to Hos 4:16, 10:11, Exod 32:8, 10, Deut 9:12, and Ps 106:40 in CD 1 12–2 1 and comments:

> The insider who recognizes these references and links them together has demonstrated both technical skill and an understanding of how the game is played. This success brings with it a sense of mastery and also of connection: to the teachers who showed the sectarian how to interpret, to the text itself, and to shared experiences within the community.[128]

In other words, Grossman describes how a text can presume a certain exegetical sophistication and how that "textual virtuosity" may point towards an in-group.[129] The explicit terminology serves to construct what Barkun refers to as the apocalyptic "microcosm." It is not symbolic language and it is not even secretive language, although its function in affirming and constructing member-identities would have had the effect of confusing or alienating those outside the immediate interpretative community. This alienation would function similarly to the way that Catholics or Mormons are alienated by the specialized Protestant language of the *Left Behind* books, which I highlighted in chapter one. Second, several of the terms borrowed from scripture (and this applies to other terms found in the *Apocryphon of Jeremiah C*) are polemical terms. Terms like מרישיעי ברית "violators of the covenant" (4Q385a 5a–b 9=4Q387 3 6, cf. Dan 11:32) are not neutral. Those who know the meaning of such terms demonstrate their competence in the language used by the in-group (and demonstrate that the competent reader is *not* a violator of the covenant). Moreover, like in the Book of Daniel, the "violators of the covenant" are contrasted with an opposite group: המצדקים "those who lead to righteousness" (4Q388a 7 9).[130] This type of identity-constructing contrast is evident in many of the Essene texts from Qumran. For example, CD 2 13–16 contrasts those who "stray" (התעה) with those who walk "perfectly on all his paths" (להתהלך תמים כל

---

[128] Grossman, "Cultivating Identity: Textual Virtuosity and 'Insider' Status," 7.

[129] Others have made similar points. Cf. for example Jonathan Campbell, *The Use of Scripture in the Damascus Document 1–8, 19–20* (BZAW 228; Berlin: de Gruyter, 1995), 43–4.

[130] See most recently George Nickelsburg, "Polarized Self-Identification in the Qumran Texts," in *Defining Identities: We, You, and the Other in the Dead Sea Scrolls. Proceedings of the Fifth Meeting of the IOQS in Groningen* (ed. Florentino García Martínez and Mladen Popović; vol. 70 of *STDJ*; Leiden: Brill, 2008), 23–31. This piece builds on previous work in George Nickelsburg, "Religious Exclusivism: A World View Governing Some Texts Found at Qumran," in *Das Ende der Tage und die Gegenwart des Heils: Begegnungen mit dem Neuen Testament und siener Umwelt: Festschrift für Heinz-Wolfgang Kuhn zum 65. Geburtstag* (ed. M. Becker and W. Fenske; vol. 44 of *AGJU*; Leiden: Brill, 1999), 45–67. Cf. the reprint with response by Carol Newsom in George Nickelsburg, "Religous Exclusivism: A World View Governing Some Texts Found at Qumran," in *George W.E. Nickelsburg in Perspective: An Ongoing Dialogue of Learning* (ed. A. J. Avery-Peck and J. Neusner; vol. 80 of *JSJSup*; Leiden: Brill, 2003), I: 139–68.

(דרכיו).¹³¹ An intriguing aspect of the group-specific language in the *Apocryphon of Jeremiah C* is that it provides non-sectarian/Essene evidence for this practice and indicates that while apocalypticism might need a microcosm, it does not have to be a literal microcosm – it can be a rhetorical one.¹³²

A paradox is raised by the possibility that the *Apocryphon of Jeremiah C* makes frequent use of group-specific language. I argued above that symbolic apocalypses all make use of language, linguistic structures, motifs, and meta-narratives that are widely attested in the cultural memory of the ancient Near East and ancient Judaism. The *Apocryphon of Jeremiah C*, on the other hand, uses no symbolic language but appears to have been intended for a much more limited audience. It is especially interesting that some of the group-specific terms are borrowed from a larger Hellenistic discourse but used in highly specialized ways. The *Apocryphon of Jeremiah C* appears to use plain, explicit terminology to construct a message that is intended for a limited audience. It may be precisely the explicit nature of the language that makes it oblique. In other words, what are the chances that a term like "violators of the covenant" would have been as obvious as "Pharisees" to a Hellenistic audience?¹³³ The evidence continues to point to the intriguing conclusion that symbolic apocalypses were intended for the largest possible audience while non-symbolic apocalypses were read by more limited audiences.

---

[131] Nickelsburg, "Polarized Self-Identification in the Qumran Texts," 24.
[132] Nickelsburg, "Polarized Self-Identification in the Qumran Texts," 27–8.
[133] I do not imply that the Pharisees are the violators of the covenant.

Chapter Six

4QPseudo-Daniel^{a–b} ar

4QPseudo-Daniel^{a–b} ar is a non-symbolic apocalypse found in two manuscripts (4Q243–244) from Cave 4 at Qumran.[1] In it Daniel appears to recount a history of the world in the court of the Babylonian king Belshazzar.[2] Unlike the historical reviews in Dan 7 or 8, the history in 4QPseudo-Daniel^{a–b} ar tilts heavily in favor of persons, places, and events of primarily Jewish concern. There is no evidence that the historical review is divided into distinct periods, but neither is there evidence to disprove such an organization. Daniel's recitation of history seems to be a result of the interpretation of a scroll or tablet.[3]

The history begins in primeval times. A mention of the prediluvian figure Enoch (חנוך) marks the earliest point in history that is preserved in the text (4Q243 9 1). It is unclear if the text deals with creation and/or the origins of evil. The presence of the Greek name Balakros in 4Q243 21 2 indicates that the survey of history extends into the Hellenistic period. Precisely how far into the Hellenistic period the name Balakros takes the text is a matter of debate as Balakros was not an uncommon Hellenistic name. (See more on Balakros below). In any case, the text appears to end

---

[1] One other manuscript from Qumran is labeled "Pseudo-Daniel" (4QpsDan^c ar or 4Q245). This manuscript is probably not a copy of the same text represented by manuscripts a and b. See more below.

[2] Belshazzar is also referred to as "king of Babylon" in Dan 5 and 8. On the historical problems associated with calling Belshazzar "king," see Collins, *Daniel*, 30. The notion that Daniel is the one who recounts the history is based on the clear descriptions of a conversation between Daniel and Belshazzar (see combined edition lines 3–22 below) and the fact that the history recounted focuses on Jewish history.

[3] For example, 4Q243 6 2–4 reads, "[ובה כתיב] . . . [דניאל די י] . . . ויש[תכח כתי]ב בה]" "]And upon it was written[. . .]Daniel who wi[ll . . . And it was f]ound writt[en in (or, on) it. It seems less likely that there is in this text (as in some other Danielic texts) an *angelus interpres*. See John J. Collins and Peter Flint, "4Qpseudo-Daniel^a ar" in *Qumran Cave 4 XVII: Parabiblical Texts*, Part 3 (DJD 22; ed. J. VanderKam; Oxford: Clarendon Press, 1996), 135, 149. More recently, Lorenzo DiTommaso, "4QPseudo-Daniel^{a–b} (4Q243–4Q244)," *DSD* 12 (2005): 128–30.

not with the Hellenistic period, but with an eschatological period that breaks out at some point during Greek hegemony.[4]

The manuscripts of 4QpsDan^{a-b} ar can be dated paleographically to the first half of the first century CE.[5] The text itself is almost certainly older. The most conservative estimates would place it around a century earlier. J.T. Milik dated the text to around 100 B.C.E..[6] Gabrielle Boccaccini has concurred with Milik that the text is a product of the Qumran community and consequently a product of the 1st century B.C.E..[7] One cannot rule out the possibility that text was written in the 1st century B.C.E., but I disagree with Milik and Boccaccini that it is a product of the Qumran community or any other group of Essenes. While its fragmentary nature makes decisive judgment impossible, it does not appear to comport well with some of the more recognized criteria for determining Essene texts.[8] For example, 4QpsDan^{a-b} ar is written in Aramaic. While Essenes certainly owned texts written in Aramaic, what is preserved of the Essene literature was written in Hebrew only.[9] The text appears to use some in-group language, but it lacks any of the terminology normally associated with the Qumran community, i.e., אנשי היחד "men of the community," עדת היחד "assembly of the community," or מורה הצדק "Teacher of Righteousness." The text also lacks any of the characteristically Essene Halakhah.[10] Temple/priest issues do seem to be important to the text, but as we have seen in *Apocryphon of Jeremiah C* and Dan 10–12, the Essenes hardly had an exclusive purchase on those themes in Second Temple literature. Finally, unlike Essene texts, religious

---

[4] See, for example, 4Q243 16, 25, 24. One other presumably Greek name occurs in 4Q243 19, but it is only partially preserved. Milik renders רהוס as "Demetrius." Collins and Flint note, however, that Demetrius is never spelled with an ה in Aramaic. They offer Pyrrus of Epirus (319–272 B.C.E.) as a conjecture. The partial name cannot be used to date the text. See Collins and Flint, "4Qpseudo-Daniel^a," 111, 150.

[5] The script is "Late Herodian Formal Script" and is also characteristic of 4QDeut^j. See Collins and Flint, "4Qpseudo-Daniel^a ar," 97–98. On the various scripts found at Qumran and their relative dates, see Cross, "Paleography and the Dead Sea Scrolls," plates 11–14.

[6] See J.T. Milik, "Prière de Nabonide et autres écrits d'un cycle de Daniel," *RB* 63 (1956): 407–15.

[7] Boccaccini, Beyond the Essene Hypothesis, 16.

[8] For these criteria, see Lange, "Kriterien essinischer Texte," 59–69. In the same volume, see Charlotte Hempel, "Kriterien zur Bestimmung 'essinischer Verfasserschaft' von Qumrantexten," 71–85. See also Newsom, "Sectually Explicit Literature from Qumran," 167–87. Devorah Dimant, "Qumran Sectarian Literature," in *Jewish Writings of the Second Temple Period: Apocrypha, Pseudepigrapha, Qumran Sectarian Writings, Philo, Josephus* (ed. M. E. Stone; Philadelphia: Assen, 1984), 483–550.

[9] Lange, "Kriterien essinischer Texte," 64. See also Stanislav Segert, "Die Sprachenfrage in der Qumrangemeinschaft," in *Qumran-Probleme: Deutsche Akademie der Wissenschaften zu Berlin* (ed. H. Bardtke; vol. 42 of *Schriften der Sektion für Altertumswissenschaft* Berlin, 1963), 315–39, esp. 22.

[10] Lange, "Kriterien essinischer Texte," 65, 67.

authority is vested in a figure outside of the community. Collins and Flint suggest that the text's relation to the Dead Sea sect, "may be analogous to that of *Jubilees* or the Enoch literature."[11]

Most recently Lorenzo DiTommaso has put forward a provocative proposal that 4QpsDan^{a-b} ar must have been written after the collection of Dan 1/2–6 but before Dan 7–12 and that Dan 9 was written in response to it.[12] DiTommaso forms this proposal in four basic steps. First, based on two similarities between 4Q243/244 and Dan 5 he concludes that 4QpsDan^{a-b} ar presumes the existence of Dan 5. Both Dan 5 and 4Q243/244 have setting in the court of the Babylonian king Belshazzar and both texts center around Daniel's ability to interpret an undecipherable text.[13] Second, DiTommaso argues that the royal figure Belshazzar must have been chosen as an antagonist in light of the standing connections between king Nebuchadnezzar and dream visions.[14] Third, the presence of Deuteronomic theology and the apparent lack of any discussion of the Hellenistic religious reforms indicates that the text predates the period of 167–164 B.C.E..[15] Fourth, because the way that the theology of history presented Dan 9:24–7 contradicts the Deuteronomic theology of the prayer in 9:3–19, DiTommaso avers that Dan 9 was written in response to and in contradiction of *Pseudo-Daniel*.[16]

I agree that 4Q243/244 appears to have been influenced by the setting found in Dan 5. It is also plausible, according to DiTommaso's reasoning, that 4Q243/244 postdates the early Aramaic Daniel book consisting of chapters 2–6.[17] DiTommaso is correct that there are no signs that the text was written after the Hellenistic religious reforms or any part of Dan 7–8 and 10–12 – though the highly fragmentary nature of the text should caution us against being too certain of this. One can hardly doubt that the Deuteronomic theology present in 4QpsDan^{a-b} ar is cut from the same cloth as the theology of the prayer in Dan 9:3–19. But I am not sure this necessitates contact between the texts. There are other texts from which 4QpsDan^{a-b} ar could have derived its Deuteronomic thought (e.g., any of

---

[11] Collins and Flint, "4Qpseudo-Daniel^a ar," 137.
[12] DiTommaso, "4QPseudo-Daniel^{a-b} (4Q243–4Q244)," 101–33.
[13] DiTommaso, "4QPseudo-Daniel^{a-b} (4Q243–4Q244)," 112–3, 28.
[14] DiTommaso, "4QPseudo-Daniel^{a-b} (4Q243–4Q244)," 108.
[15] DiTommaso, "4QPseudo-Daniel^{a-b} (4Q243–4Q244)," 127.
[16] DiTommaso, "4QPseudo-Daniel^{a-b} (4Q243–4Q244)," 125–7.

[17] The earliest Aramaic Daniel book probably consisted of chapters 4–6, though those chapters could have also circulated independently before being joined. Narrative discrepancies between chapters 4–6 indicate that they are not the product of one writer. See Albertz, *Der Gott des Daniel*. On narrative discrepancies between chapters 4–6, see Bennie H. Reynolds III, "Identity Crisis: Mapping Daniel Figures and Traditions in Second Temple Judaism," in *The Reception of Biblical Protagonists in Early Judaism* (ed. Matthias Weigold and Bennie H. Reynolds III, 2012), submitted to Peeters Press for peer review. An earlier form of this paper was presented at the International Meeting of the Society of Biblical Literature, Vienna, Austria, July 26, 2007.

the Deuteronomistic History, the Deuteronomistic Jeremiah Redaction, etc.). Even if there is contact, however, the fragmentary nature of 4QpsDan^{a-b} ar casts doubt over which direction the influenced flowed (i.e., one does not know for sure that 4QpsDan^{a-b} ar does not mention the Hellenistic religious reforms). There is nothing in either text that demands we find contact between the two texts, but it is an intriguing proposal that should be kept on the table as further research is done.

Is 4QPseudo-Daniel^{a-b} ar an Apocalypse?

It is perhaps worth reiterating at the beginning of this section that the genre apocalypse is a modern construct. A careful comparison of form can demonstrate the relative inner coherence of the texts most scholars label "apocalypses." Consideration of features such as language, motifs, traditions, themes, reception, etc., can add even greater precision to our descriptions. But the ancient writers hardly felt constrained by an official mold and the evidence shows no insignificant amount of deviation and innovation from the literary model that most modern scholars imagine was operative among Jewish writers in the Hellenistic period. The significance of the modern category "apocalypse" is that it, like other generic categories, teaches us how to read texts by knowing which texts are best read together.[18] An example might be taken from the newspaper. Newspapers contain multiple literary genres. Categories such as "op/ed," "sports," and "obituaries" are significant to the extent that they help individuals understand how a certain text should be read by knowing which texts with which it should be read. One would not read an obituary with the same set of assumptions that one brings to the sports column. It is of course possible that innovation can blur the lines between newspaper genres. One imagines that if a famous sports figure or sports writer died that their obituary might synthesize elements of both a sports column and an obituary. In other words, the obituary might be written in the form of a sports column. But this type of innovation does not make the categories "obituary" and "sports column" useless. The text simply requires a larger pool of generic partners in order to be intelligible (i.e., it must be read in light of *both* obituaries and sports columns). In the

---

[18] "In one sense genre theory may be seen as an attempt to apply a certain scientific method to dividing works of literature along lines much in the same way as biological classification of species. The only problem is that literary works defy such scientific rigidity. Therefore, in a truer sense genre theory is more of an etymological exercise in which specific conventions in a piece of writing are exercised so as to conform to reader expectations." Timothy Sexton, "Genre Theory," *American Chronicle*, April 22 2009, electronic access: http://www.americanchronicle.com/articles/view/24975.

discussion below I argue that *Pseudo-Daniel*$^{a-b}$ *ar* is most profitably read against other Jewish historical apocalypses. It does not match the *Semeia* 14 definition perfectly. Where 4QpsDan^{a-b} ar differs it is not because of a blatant disagreement, but because of silence.

One presumes that the frequent use of the name Daniel in both 4QpsDan^a ar and 4QpsDan^b ar was enough to cause its first translators to assume that it was at least related to apocalyptic literature if it was not itself an apocalypse (those early interpreters would have used the pseudo-noun "apocalyptic"). John Collins has written most prolifically on the question and he has expressed variations on the same theme: we cannot know. In one of his articles in *Semeia* 14, he writes, "Because of the fragmentary nature of the text we cannot be sure that the revelation was not mediated. Insofar as it is known, however, 4QpsDaniel is a prophecy with apocalyptic eschatology, not an apocalypse."[19] In the *editio princeps*, he and Flint characterize it as having literary affinities with each of the following categories: "1. literature set in a royal court; 2. apocalyptic and prophetic reviews of Israel's history; 3. the biblical book of Daniel; and 4. the sectarian literature of Qumran."[20] This characterization is especially helpful since it helps to dampen the kind of generic realism that assumes all texts belong to one and only one genre. In an article in the *Dead Sea Scrolls after Fifty Years* collection, Collins considers it doubtful that 4Q243/244 is an apocalypse unless the writing interpreted therein is a heavenly book revealed by an angel.[21] In the discussion below I argue that the text does present clues that Daniel interprets heavenly tablets. It is noteworthy that Collins and others locate *Pseudo-Daniel*'s closest literary relatives in 1 Enoch and the Book of Daniel to the extent that they contain reviews of history with an eschatological bent. In his *Apocalypticism in the Dead Sea Scrolls*, Collins suggests that the document be considered "apocalyptic," "at least in the broad sense of the term."[22] In other words, the text shares many of the features/themes of apocalypses without necessarily bearing witness to the literary form of an apocalypse. But this categorization would seem to indicate that its closest literary relatives might be something along the lines of 1QM or the *Pesharim*. From my perspective, the problem with labeling the text with the adjective "apocalyptic" obscures the fact that it presents a divine revelation of past, present, and eschatological history. 1QM can be described as "apo-

---

[19] John J. Collins, "The Jewish Apocalypses," in *Semeia 14* (ed. John J. Collins; Missoula: Scholars Press, 1979), 48.

[20] Collins and Flint, "4Qpseudo-Daniel^a ar," 134–7.

[21] John J. Collins, "Apocalypticism and Literary Genre in the Dead Sea Scrolls," in *The Dead Sea Scrolls After Fifty Years: A Comprehensive Assessment* (ed. Peter Flint and James VanderKam; Leiden: Brill, 1998), 410–13.

[22] Collins, *Apocalypticism in the Dead Sea Scrolls*, 15.

calyptic," but 4QpsDan^{a-b} ar is far closer to texts like Daniel and *1 Enoch* than to 1QM.

In chapter five I indicated that the *Semeia* 14 definition of apocalypse has three basic elements and argued that *Apocryphon of Jeremiah C* meets at least two of them: the spatial and temporal aspects characteristic of apocalypse. In what follows I argue that 4QpsDan^{a-b} ar also meets two (and probably all three) of the basic elements of *Semeia* 14 definition. I begin by considering the mode of revelation.

4QpsDan^{a-b} *ar* is certainly a piece of revelatory literature since its Daniel figure purports to recount information that a sixth century figure could not possibly have known. Both the beginning and the end of the historical review make this point. In the beginning the figure recounts information from the prediluvian period – a history only accessible through divine revelation.[23] At the end of the text Daniel recounts events that are unambiguously from the Hellenistic period and he appears to narrate the eschatological end of history – even if that history does not necessarily involve the threat of Antiochus IV or the problems associated with the Hasmonean priesthood.[24] So it seems unlikely that Daniel is depicted merely as some sort of emissary or diplomat who, during the reign of Belshazzar, gives a banal report of the history of the world or even of the history of the Jewish people as a sort of apologetic account of Judaism without an implicit judgment on both the putative and actual imperial power of the day. Such a depiction would be a drastic departure from other literature that places Daniel in Mesopotamian courts as a diviner/visionary.

The mode of Daniel's revelation is crucial. Collins describes it as a "prophecy with apocalyptic eschatology."[25] Even if Collins is correct that 4QpsDan^{a-b} ar was not based on the canonical Book of Daniel (and at least concerning chapters 7–12 I think he must be correct), one should not be surprised if its court-diviner motif functioned in the same way since many chapters of the Book of Daniel were written at different times by different people and still attest to the basic motif. Thus, if 4QpsDan^{a-b} ar is even marginally consonant with the other uses of Daniel-in-court scenarios, how would one understand the text as an example of prophecy (if by prophecy we mean in particular the practice well attested in Iron Age Levant and Mesopotamia and characterized by literature such as the Book of Amos or the oracles from the Assurbanipal library at Nineveh). Are those really the

---

[23] For the use of Enoch as well as descriptions of the flood and its aftermath, see CE 23–9 below (4Q243 9, 23, 4Q244 8).

[24] The use of Greek names (e.g., Balakros) makes clear that the text narrates events from the Hellenistic period (cf. CE 52–7=4Q243 21 1–2, 19 1–4). For a possible description of eschatological events see CE 72–6 (4Q243 24 1–5).

[25] Collins, "The Jewish Apocalypses," 48.

most useful documents with which to make formal comparisons? 4QpsDan^{a-b} ar perhaps reflects a revelation by means of divination, but it is not clear that the form of divination used is prophecy. One would need to provide a definition of prophecy different than the ones developed to describe both ancient Israelite and ancient Mesopotamian prophecy. As I pointed out above, Alex Jassen has demonstrated that the concept of prophecy found in the writings at Qumran is significantly evolved from the concept as we imagine it was understood during the time that, for example, most of the prophetic books of the Hebrew Bible were produced.[26] The prophetic books themselves likely reflect only a partial snapshot of the phenomenon – it is clear from the Hebrew Bible that there were many prophets in ancient Israel whose roles were not entirely the same as the figures for whom books were eventually named. According to at least one text found at Qumran, the Book of Daniel is itself an example of prophecy. 4QMidrEschat^a II 3 prefaces a quote from Daniel with the following formula: "that wh[ich] is written in the book of Daniel, the prophet" (אשר כתוב בספר דניאל הנביא). But in what sense would *modern scholars* want describe the Book of Daniel as prophecy? It is not a methodological problem to apply categories to peoples and texts that they might not have used themselves because modern scholars have the benefit of history. In other words, we can see that they use an expression (e.g., prophecy) in an entirely different way than people had used it a hundred years or more before. I suspect that texts like 4QMidrEschat^a II 3 use the word prophecy to imply revelation but without strict limitations on the mode of the revelation. So it is not entirely clear what Collins means when he describes a text like *Pseudo-Daniel^{a-b} ar* as a "prophecy." It may very well have been understood by the Qumran Essenes or Hellenistic Jews as a "prophecy," but that does not make it the best description we can use as historical literary critics. In other words, we would not consider Jeremiah or Amos to be the best literary models with which to read Dan.

One cannot know for certain if the revelation presented in the text is the result of a dream, vision, audition, or physical discovery. The strongest possibility seems to be that Daniel interprets a text of some kind in order to present Belshazzar with the apocalyptic review of history. Several fragments indicate this possibility. Daniel appears before Belshazzar and his officials and is apparently tasked with solving some mystery. After praying to God for assistance, the text reports in (4Q243 6 2–4=CE 20–22): "And upon it was written . . . Daniel who . . . and the writing was fo[und]." Later in (4Q243 28 1–2=CE 43–44) the text reports that a text is given, "[to D]aniel and he rea[d the names] . . . [Phineha]s, Abish[ua]."

---

[26] Jassen, *Mediating the Divine*, 279–308.

Though Collins and Flint do not transcribe 4Q243 28 in the same way that I do, they believe that 4Q243 6 raises three possibilities concerning the mode of revelation. Daniel apparently read and interpreted a text before Belshazzar. This interpretive action could find parallels in a scene from 4QPrEsther[a] ar (4Q550). It might represent the reading of a book of Enoch. Finally, it could depict Daniel correctly deciphering a "heavenly tablet." The first possibility seems less likely. In 4QPrEsther[a] ar 3–7 the servants of a distressed Persian king find a scroll sealed among the records of Darius I that makes pronouncements about his successors.[27] The document is not, however, a revelation and does not give a detailed account of history.[28] It does mention a noble Jewish exile (4QPrEsther[d] ar I 1–7), but it is unclear how he functions in the text. It also seems unlikely that Daniel expounds upon a book of Enoch. As DiTommaso, argues, "The fact . . . that his name is mentioned in the portion of 4Q243/244 that contains the *ex eventu* review of history would seem to argue against the view that the text which contains the review was written by him."[29] Given the ostensible content of the revelation in *Pseudo-Daniel*[a–b] *ar*, the third possibility seems most likely. If so, one can be confident that a heavenly being mediated the revelation (tablets) to a human recipient. The heavenly tablets motif presumes as much. DiTommaso posits that Daniel might interpret the lost tablets of Adam. He bases this suggestion on a late tradition from an already late text called the *Cave of Treasures*.[30] In the earliest versions of the *Cave of Treasures*, which are already quite late in relation to 4Q243/244, the tradition of the tablets of Adam is not present.[31] There is a far more compelling tablet-tradition from which it is possible that 4Q243/244 borrows: the heavenly tablets tradition mentioned by Collins. Moreover, one can push the analysis of the tablet tradition in 4QpsDan[a–b] ar further than Collins has done.

The concept of the heavenly tablets was relatively widespread in Hellenistic Judaism, as well as in other Hellenistic cultures. Heavenly tablets serve as a conduit through which divine revelation given before the great flood (and consequently lost in the flood) could be transmitted to later generations. For example, in the *Babyloniaca* of Berossus, one finds an account of the *apkallu* Oannes (a prediluvian sage appearing in half-human, half-fish form) instructing humans in the knowledge of civilization on behalf of the gods. The text is preserved in part by Eusebius: "Berossos says

---

[27] Cf. Parry and Tov, eds., *Additional Genres and Unclassified Texts*, 6–7.
[28] Cf. 4QPrEsther[b–f] ar.
[29] DiTommaso, "4QPseudo-Daniel[a–b] (4Q243–4Q244)," 129.
[30] DiTommaso, "4QPseudo-Daniel[a–b] (4Q243–4Q244)," 29–30.
[31] A. S.-M. Ri, *Commentaire de la Caverne des Trésors* (Turnhout: Brepols, 2002). Cf. the discussion in the fourth chapter of Lorenzo DiTommaso, *The Book of Daniel and the Apocryphal Daniel Literature* (SVTP 20; Leiden: Brill, 2005).

that this monster spent its days with men, never eating anything, but teaching men the skills necessary for writing and doing mathematics and for all sorts of knowledge: how to build cities, found temples, and make laws . . ."[32] This knowledge was inscribed on tablets that Kronos (Enki) commanded Xisouthros (i.e., Utnapishtim or Atrahasis) to bury in the city of Sippar before the great deluge. Xisouthros disappears after disembarking from the boat, but a disembodied voice from the heavens commands those remaining to go to Sippar and dig up the tablets in order to redistribute the heavenly knowledge first delivered to humans by the wise fish monster Oannes.[33] Prediluvian knowledge is *only* available to later generations by divine revelation. The disembodied voice in the sky is the deity directing humans to the source of knowledge that taught their ancestors.

The heavenly tablets tradition is also found in Jewish literature from the Hellenistic period including *Jubilees* and *1 Enoch*.[34] In *Jubilees*, the revelation to Moses on Sinai is reworked so that the angel of the presence reveals to Moses the contents of the pre-existent heavenly tablets.[35] "Now you,

---

[32] Gerald Verbrugghe and John Wickersham, *Berossos and Manetho Introduced and Translated: Native Traditions in Ancient Mesopotamia and Egypt* (Ann Arbor: University of Michigan Press, 1996), 44.

[33] Verbrugghe and Wickersham, *Berossos and Manetho*, 50–1. For a more in depth discussion of these passages see Russell Gmirkin, *Berossus and Genesis, Manetho and Exodus: Hellenistic Histories and the Date of the Pentateuch* (London: T & T Clark, 2006), esp. 92–119. I do not agree with Gmirkin that all of the Mesopotamian material found in Gen 1–11 must have been derived from Berossus post 278 B.C.E. (see Gmirkin, 139). Some "biblical" manuscripts (including an Exod scroll) from Qumran date to the 3rd century B.C.E.. See James VanderKam and Peter Flint, *The Meaning of the Dead Sea Scrolls: Their Significance for Understanding the Bible, Judaism, Jesus, and Christianity* (San Francisco: HarperSanFrancisco, 2002), 20–33. The oldest copy of Gen derives from the middle of the second century B.C.E., but twenty-four distinct manuscripts are attested and since the mss present a text relatively close to the MT and the SP, one may logically infer that the text of Gen was already highly stable by the time it reached Qumran. See Vander-Kam and Flint, *The Meaning of the Dead Sea Scrolls*, 104. Moreover, while there was no biblical canon even by the time the Essenes lived at Qumran (and probably not until at least the second century CE), there is evidence that the Pentateuch was already treated as an authoritative collection of scripture. For example, 4QGen–Exod^a and 4QpaleoGen–Exod^l are both texts in which Gen and Exod were collected together in the same scroll. It would appear difficult to explain all of this evidence in a scenario where Gen 1–11 could not have been written before 278 B.C.E..

[34] Cf. Robert Kraft, "Scripture and Canon in Jewish Apocrypha and Pseudepigrapha," in *Hebrew Bible / Old Testament: The History of Its Interpretation* (ed. Magne Saebo; Göttingen: Vandenhoeck & Ruprecht, 1996), 205, n. 17.

[35] On the heavenly tablets in the *Book of Jubilees*, see Florentino García Martínez, "The Heavenly Tablets in the Book of Jubilees," in *Studies in the Book of Jubilees* (ed. Matthias Albani, et al.; vol. 65 of *TSAJ*; Tübingen: Mohr Siebeck, 1997), 243–60. See also Shalom Paul, "Heavenly Tablets and the Book of Life," in *Divrei Shalom: Collected Studies of Shalom M. Paul on the Bible and the Ancient Near East 1967–2005* (vol. 23 of *CHANE*; Leiden: Brill, 2005), 59–70. Published previously in Shalom Paul, "Heavenly Tablets and the Book of Life," in *The Gaster Festschrift* (ed. David Marcus; New York: Ancient Near Eastern Society, 1974), 345–53. James

Moses, write down these words because this is how it is written and entered in the testimony of the heavenly tablets (ጽላተ ሰማይ ṣᵉllāt samāy) for the history of eternity" (*Jub.* 23:32).³⁶ This verse helps to contextualize other mentions of tablets in the prologue and in 50:13. The content of the revelation in *Jubilees* is attributed more to the tablets than to Moses. As Kraft puts it, "Moses is not usually depicted as independently involved, and the impression is that everything is tightly controlled by the heavenly authorities and tablets (see 23:32, 50:13), which are reflected in the instructions given to humans."³⁷ Indeed, Hindy Najman has pointed out how the *Book of Jubilees* attempts to preempt the Mosaic Torah by using the heavenly tablets motif to locate its own revelation prior to Sinai (prior to the creation of the world!).³⁸ "If pentateuchal laws owe their authority to the tradition of the heavenly tablets, then extra-pentateuchal laws recorded on the tablets have just as much authority as pentateuchal laws."³⁹ The discussion of the calendar in *Jub.* 6:35–38 illustrates the point. *Jubilees* also depicts other prominent personalities such as Enoch, Noah/Shem, Abraham, and Jacob receiving revelations about the contents of the tablets.⁴⁰

In the *Astronomical Book* (*1 En.* 72–82), Enoch reports that an angel commands him, "Enoch, look at the tablet(s) of heaven; read what is written upon them and understand (each element on them) one by one. So I looked at the tablet(s) of heaven, read all the writing (on them), and came to understand everything."⁴¹ In the *Epistle* (*1 En.* 91–107), Enoch recounts what he has learned from the heavenly tablets, "I now I swear to you, righteous ones, by the glory of the great one and by the glory of his kingdom; and I swear to you (even) by the Great One. For I know this mystery; I have read the tablets of heaven and have seen the holy writings, and I have understood the writing in them; and they are inscribed concerning you."⁴²

Scott, *On Earth as in Heaven: The Restoration of Sacred Time and Sacred Space in the Book of Jubilees* (JSJSup 91; Leiden: Brill, 2005), esp. 75, 211–2.

³⁶ Trans. VanderKam, *The Book of Jubilees*, 149.

³⁷ Kraft, "Scripture and Canon," 206.

³⁸ Hindy Najman, "Interpretation as Primordial Writing: Jubilees and its Authority Conferring Strategies," 30 (1999): 379–410, esp., 391. On the same topic, see Martha Himmelfarb, "Torah, Testimony, and Heavenly Tablets: The Claim to Authority of the Book of Jubilees," in *A Multiform Heritage: Studies on Early Judaism and Christianity in Honor of Robert A. Kraft* (ed. Benjamin Wright; Atlanta: Scholars Press, 1999), 19–29.

³⁹ Najman, "Interpretation as Primordial Writing: Jubilees and its Authority Conferring Strategies," 391–2.

⁴⁰ Cf. Kraft, "Scripture and Canon," 206.

⁴¹ *1 Enoch* 81:1-2. Trans. E. Isaac, "1 Enoch," in *OTP I* (ed. James Charlesworth; New York: Doubleday, 1983), 59.

⁴² *1 Enoch* 103:1. Isaac, "1 Enoch," 83. On the use of heavenly tablets in *1 Enoch* 93:2b, see VanderKam, *Enoch and the Growth*, 150.

An especially important text for understanding the concept of the heavenly tablets in Hellenistic Judaism is 4QAges of Creation A (4Q180). This text specifically ties the heavenly tablets to a narration of the course of history in epochs:[43]

1. An interpretation concerning the ages which God made: an

age for walk[ing   ]

2. and is to come. Before he created them he ordained [their]

works [ ]

3. an age to its age; and it was engraved upon tablets (חרות) [   ]

4. [ ] the ages of their rule. This is the order of [   ][44]

A. Lange notes that, "4Q180 1 3–4 links the idea of a pre-existent order with the heavenly tablets motif by quoting Exod. 32:16 (והוא חרות על לחות). The predestined and pre-existent order of the world was inscribed on the heavenly tablets and revealed to Moses on Mount Sinai in the form of the Torah."[45] Lange emphasizes that in the fusing of the sapiential idea of the pre-existent order of the world with the motif of the heavenly tablets and the Torah, the pre-existent order is described in terms of epochs – a feature reminiscent of the historical reviews in many apocalypses.[46]

In Jewish writings from the Hellenistic Period, access to information from prediluvian times was apparently restricted to divine revelations that occurred most frequently in association with the heavenly tablets tradition. The notion that the heavenly tablets contained the predestined, epochal history of the world is also common in Jewish writings from the Hellenistic Period. *Pseudo-Daniel*[a–b] *ar* contains a revelation that encompasses prediluvian, postdiluvian, and eschatological history. Moreover, several lines indicate that the revelation is based on some kind of writing. Therefore, it is a reasonable conclusion that the inscriptions interpreted by Daniel were heavenly tablets – texts that are by their very nature "mediated by an otherworldly being." The only way for the Daniel of 4QpsDan[a–b] ar to know about Enoch is through heavenly tablets. One concludes, then, that the

---

[43] *Jub.* probably makes the same move. See VanderKam, *The Book of Jubilees*, 149.

[44] Trans. J. M. Allegro with N. Gordon in Donald Parry and Emanuel Tov, eds., *Exegetical Texts* (*DSSR*; Leiden Brill, 2004).

[45] Armin Lange, "Wisdom and Predestination in the Dead Sea Scrolls," *DSD* 2 (1995): 353. Cf. also Armin Lange, *Weisheit und Prädestination: Weisheitliche Urordnung und Prädestination in den Textfunden von Qumran* (vol. 18; Leiden: Brill, 1995), 275–81.

[46] Lange, "Wisdom and Predestination in the Dead Sea Scrolls," 353.

mode of revelation in 4QpsDan^{a-b} ar accords well with the *Semeia* 14 definition of apocalypse.[47]

Before moving on to the spatial and temporal aspects of the *Semeia* 14 definition of the genre apocalypse, one more note about the mode of revelation in 4QpsDan^{a-b} ar is worth considering. Like other Jewish historical apocalypses, most of the words composed by a Hellenistic Jewish writer are placed in the mouth of a figure respected for his piety or skill (e.g., Daniel, Enoch, Baruch, Ezra). In this case the figure is the supposed 6th century Judahite exile/Babylonian-educated diviner Daniel.[48] The way in which *Pseudo-Daniel's* revelation in invested with the authority of the figure Daniel distinguishes it from other "apocalyptic" texts (not literary apocalypses) found at Qumran. Collins highlights the Essenes/Sectarians' view of the investiture of revelation: "In the Dead Sea sect, authority was vested in the Teacher of Righteousness and his successors. He is the one in whose heart God has put the source of wisdom for all those who understand (1QH 10:18 = 2:18). To him, 'God has disclosed all the mysteries of the words of his servants the prophets' (1QpHab 7:4)."[49] In other words, the apocalyptic community at Qumran (and ostensibly all Essenes) had no need to employ the authority of a venerable sage or prophet in their literature when they had the Teacher of Righteousness. The investiture of authority functions differently in 4Q243/244. In 4Q243/244, the investiture of authority functions in the same way as texts like the Book of Daniel, 1 Enoch, 4 Ezra, etc., and serves as one more indication that 4QpsDan^{a-b} ar is best read with other

---

[47] Collins and Flint do not go this far but agree that the contents of the text almost certainly represent a divine revelation. See Collins and Flint, "4Qpseudo-Daniel^a ar," 135. For them it is possible that Daniel is expounding a book of Enoch. This possibility seems unlikely, however, given the putative context of the revelation in *Pseudo-Daniel*. The mere mention of Enoch does not indicate that the text might expound a book of Enoch. Many other important figures are named. There is a near certainty that Moses was named in the text even though it is not extant (see above 4QpsDan^a ar 12). Other figures known to have received revelations in other Jewish text, e.g. Noah, Belshazzar) are also mentioned.

[48] This feature of the text is sometimes described as pseudonymity. I agree with DiTommaso, however, that 4Q243/244 is not a pseudepigraphon. DiTommaso, "4QPseudo-Daniel^{a-b} (4Q243–4Q244)," 115. There are very few Jewish texts from the Hellenistic period that one could describe as pseudepigraphic in the sense of, for example, Pseudo-Hecataeus. Bernstein has pointed out some of the problems with terms like pseudepigraphon – especially as these terms are applied to the Dead Sea Scrolls. Moshe Bernstein, "Pseudepigraphy in the Qumran Scrolls: Categories and Functions," in *Pseudepigraphic Perspectives: The Apocrypha and Pseudepigrapha in Light of the Dead Sea Scrolls* (ed. Esther Chazon and Michael Stone; vol. 31 of *STDJ*; Leiden: Brill, 1999), 1–26. 4QpsDan^{a-b} ar would fit into Bernstein's category "convenient pseudepigraphy," i.e., "the work in anonymous and individual pseudepigraphic voices are heard within the work" (25). There is no indication in the text that Daniel claims to have written it. The text simply uses the figure of Daniel to invest its revelation with authority.

[49] Collins, *Apocalypticism in the Dead Sea Scrolls*, 153.

apocalypses and not prophetic or "apocalyptic" texts, not *Pesharim* or *Milhamah*.

After mode of revelation, the second major element of the *Semeia* 14 definition of the genre apocalypse concerns a distinct concept of space-time. Apocalypses bear witness to an imagined cosmos that includes not only earth, but a heavenly world. More specifically, apocalypses envision interaction between the two worlds. The distinct spatial aspect of apocalypses may be observed in 4QpsDan[a-b] ar in a feature common to many apocalypses: a robust interaction with the angelic world. The word מלאך is not preserved in *Pseudo-Daniel*[a-b] *ar*, but demons are explicitly mentioned. As we saw in the chapter on *Apocryphon of Jeremiah C* above, a strict separation of angels and demons in terms of Hellenistic Jewish literature is unwise.

The most significant passage in terms of interest in the angelic/demonic world is found in the overlapping manuscripts 4Q243 13+4Q244 12 (CE 46–49). The passage describes the Babylonian exile and explains it as a punishment from God for Judah's transgressions. Among the most terrible of Judah's sins is their offering of child sacrifices to שידי טעותא "the demons of error." The expression "demons of error" is treated in more detail below but a few comments are in order here.

Several biblical texts, mostly from Jeremiah and the Psalms, bear witness to a similar tradition, i.e., human sacrifice as a leading cause of the Babylonian exile.[50] Jeremiah claims that these sacrifices were made to Baal and implies that some of the sacrifices were made to YHWH.[51] In precisely the same (putative) historical context, *Pseudo-Daniel*[a-b] *ar* designates the recipient of Israelite human sacrifices as "the demons of error." Thus the writer of *Pseudo-Daniel*[a-b] *ar* effectively translates some of the former gods of the Israelite pantheon (e.g., Baal, etc.) not into gods of the "Canaanite" pantheon as in Deut, but into demons. That demons would be inserted intentionally into a familiar Israelite/Jewish narrative tradition about the exile in a way that altars the tradition significantly is an impressive sign of the evolving and increasing interest in the world of angels and demons. In other words, the use of demons in the specific historical context of the late

---

[50] Cf. Jer 7:30–31, 19:5 32:35. 2 Kgs 23:10 describes Josiah's destruction of the *tophet* or site of human sacrifice in the valley of *Ben-Hinnom* during his late 7th century religious reforms. Three passages whose putative context does not explicitly address the exile nevertheless refer to it obliquely and in retrospect: Lev 18:21, 20:2–5, 1 Kgs 11:7. The closest biblical parallel to the 4QpsDan[a-b] ar passage is Ps 106:37–8.

[51] I contend that sacrifices were not made to a god named *Molek* and that the supposed divine name *Molek* is a misinterpretation of a technical term for human sacrifice derived fom the root הלך. See Bennie H. Reynolds III, "Molek: Dead or Alive? The Meaning and Derivation of מלך and *mlk*," in *Human Sacrifice in Jewish and Christian Tradition* (ed. Armin Lange, et al.; Leiden Brill, 2007), 133–50.

seventh century B.C.E. marks a shift in the metaphysics normally associated with Jewish historiography of the period. The review of history in 4QpsDan[a-b] ar is not *mere* earth-history, but cosmos history in which another, supernatural world parallels and sometimes interacts with the earthly realm.

The third aspect of the *Semeia* 14 definition of apocalypses concerns time. Apocalypses almost always disclose a transcendent reality that is temporal in that it envisions eschatological salvation. This feature is not easy to locate in the text, but hints of it may be preserved. Most fragments from the text are very small and permit only the most modest results from material reconstruction. Therefore, the relative placement of fragments can create or erase an eschatological period. As Collins and Flint suppose, however, some fragments do seem to present an eschatological scenario reasonably clearly. When one begins with the definite knowledge that the course of the Hellenisitic period is included in the text, lines such as, "and the l[and] will be filled . . . all all their decayed carcasses" CE 65–6 (4Q243 25 3–4) and "at] this [time] the elec[t] will be gathered" CE 73 (4Q243 24 2) appear to indicate eschatological events. A gathering of the elect would seem to be out of place in other contexts such as the Babylonian Exile. Descriptions like "remnant" (שְׁאֵרִית) are typical of language used to describe those God has chosen out of the ashes of exile – a group with whom to start anew (cf. Jer 23:3).

I indicated above that locating an eschatological period/war in *Pseudo-Daniel[a-b] ar* is dependant on the subjective process of arranging manuscript fragments. Nevertheless, two fragments suggest the presence of a final eschatological period (including a final battle) at the end of the text's historical review. For example, in CE 65–66 (4Q243 25 3–4) one finds, "and the l[and] will be filled . . . and all their decayed carcasses (כֹּל שלדיהוֹן)." The reference to "the l[and]" is almost certainly a reference to Palestine, but this passage seems an unlikely reference to an event such as the Babylonian capture of Jerusalem in 586 B.C.E. since in other, unambiguous descriptions of the events of 586 elsewhere in the text, the fate of the people is clearly articulated as exile, not massacre (cf. CE 46–49=4Q243 13+4Q244 12).

There is also a description of the gathering of the elect and a punctilliar point in history after which the course of events will be different: "at] this [time], the elect will be gathered . . . the peoples will be from [that] day" (CE 73–74=4Q243 24 2–3). The gathering of the elect surely has eschatological connotations and the following line indicates a break in history. The implication is that the "peoples" will act or exist in a way that they have not previously done after a certain day. Finally, after what may be a description of seventy years of suffering, the text claims that, "with his mighty hand and he will save them." This line resonates with a part of the description of the *eschaton* in Dan 12:1b: "At that time your people shall be delivered." 4QpsDan[a–b] ar goes on to describe what appears to be the advent of a "holy kingdom" after a battle between חסינין "the mighty ones" and ומלכות עממ[י]א "the kingdom of the peoples" in CE 70–71 (4Q243 16 3–4).

There is only one line in *Pseudo-Daniel[a–b] ar* that could be construed as a reference to resurrection and eternal life. "[At] this [time], the elect will be gathered" (CE 74=4Q243 24 2) sounds like a reference to resurrection, but it is probably not since the next line seems to indicate that a turning point is supposed to occur on Earth: "the peoples will be from [that] day" (CE 74=4Q243 24 3). The combination of these passages appears to indicate an eschatological period including a final battle and a time of reward. The fragmentary nature of the text makes a final judgment difficult, but 4QpsDan[a–b] ar appears to meet the third basic criteria of the Collins/*Semeia* 14 definition of apocalypses.

The Text of Pseudo-Daniel[a–b] ar

Before analyzing the language in *Pseudo-Daniel[a–b] ar*, I provide a fresh transcription and translation. While I agree with the vast majority of Collins and Flint's work, I hope to have made some small improvements on their critical edition. Below is my transcription and translation followed by brief notes only for those readings on which I disagree with Collins and Flint. The Hebrew transcriptions are not scaled to reflect the physical line lengths, etc., of the manuscripts. Moreover, not every line of the text is represented below. If, for example, the manuscript reveals that space for a line is present but no visible/legible letters are present, I have not included an open line. Ostensibly, a good combined reconstruction would make blank lines moot. Either way, the text was certainly longer than the reconstruction that appears below. Readers are cautioned that a considerable amount of text is missing and that hardly any of the choices in the ordering of the fragments are based on material reconstruction. Overlaps are underlined.

4Q243–244[52]

4Q243 2 1–2=CE 1–2

1 דֿניאל קודֿ]ם

2 בלשצֿרֿ

4Q244 1–2 1–4=CE 3–6

3 [קודם רב̇ בני מלכא ואׄשריׄא עׄ°]
4 [ר] [אקיׄםׄ]
5 [וכמה ו°°]
6 מ[לכא מס°]

4Q243 7 2–3=CE 7–8

7 [כשדיא °° בני]
8 [אורחת °]

4Q243 4 1=CE 9

9 מ[ל]כ[א יתמרה[°] לֿ]

4Q243 8 2–3=CE 10–11

10 י[שראל גברין]
11 [דׄי לא לשניה

4Q244 4 1–2=CE 12–13

12 [קדים א°]
13 [אמר דניאלֿ]

4Q243 1 1–3=CE14–16

14 שאיל דניאל לממר בדֿיׄל

---

[52] This transcription and translation is based on the one in my 2004 UNC M.A. Thesis, "4QPseudo-Daniel[a–b] ar and the Development of Jewish Apocalyptic Literature." This edition reflects several changes.

15   אלהך [○] ומני○ [53]
16   יצלה ו[54]

4Q243 5 1=CE 17

17   [דניאל]

4Q243 3 1–2=CE 18–19

18   איתי
19   מלכא

4Q243 6 2–4=CE 20–22

20   [ובה כתיב]55

---

[53] Collins and Flint translate אלהך as "your god." The form is unusual. One expects אלהך. Three explanations are possible. First, the ending כה could reflect the full orthography for the 2ms suffix found in some Hebrew texts from Qumran. But there are no other examples of this orthography (with any preposition) in the manuscript. Second, the writer could have used an archaic form of the word with a final vowel (signifying the accusative/dative case). The fact that the word is written in paleo-Hebrew could hint to this possibility. Third, the ה could just be a directive particle (i.e., "locative" ה). Grammarians used to suppose that the locative ה was a derivative of the old accusative case ending, but Ugaritic provides evidence of both the locative particle and the case ending functioning simultaneously. Most Hebrew examples attest to the locative ה, but some words like ארצה and לילה probably preserve the old case ending. See Waltke and O'Connor, An Introduction to Biblical Hebrew Syntax, 127–8, 85–6. It seems more likely that the writer of a Persian period/Hellenistic period text would have used the directive ה. Thus, I have rendered "to your God." One wonders if it would be possible to reconstruct, "pray to your god" given the context as well as the assumption that there are a limited number of actions one would perform "to your god." On the use of paleo-Hebrew at Qumran, see K. Matthews, "The Background of the Paleo-Hebrew Texts at Qumran," in The Word of the Lord Shall Go Forth (ed. C Meyers and M O'Connor; Winona Lake: Eisenbrauns, 1983), 549–68.

[54] The verb צלה in line three is a pe'al imperfect 3rd person masculine singular. Collins and Flint render it as a simple future but I prefer to see it as jussive. This form occurs one other time at Qumran in the Genesis Apocryphon (1Q20 20:23). Cf. Collins and Flint, "4Qpseudo-Daniel[a] ar," 98–9. My choice is based on the assumption that Nebuchadnezzar is issuing a statement concerning Daniel. While the king might have been cordial, his request was not likely optional. It is sometimes possible to see morphological evidence for the 3ms jussive (i.e., י ending rather than ה or א, cf. Dan 5:12). But these forms are comparatively rare. See Rosenthal, A Grammar of Biblical Aramaic, 56.

[55] This fragment was not originally published by Milik. The second word of line two is derived from the root כתב. Collins and Flint insist that some remnants of ink exist directly after the ב. They speculate that it could be an א and contends that this would render the verb a feminine pe'il form. One assumes they mean the plural form since the singular is always כתיבת. The plural form is still not without its problems since it should be rendered כתיבה. It is possible to interchange א and ה as the definite article. Here, however, the ה would not function as the article. My

21 [דניאל די י]
22 והש[תכח כתי]ב בה[56]

4Q243 9 1–2=23–24

23 [לחנוך]
24 [ל]ל‎ל‎[

4Q243 23 1–2=CE 25–26

25 [ברח כ]ל
26 [מ]על[ ]לא

4Q244 8 2–4=CE 27–29

27 [מן בתר מבולא]
28 [נוח מן לובר] טור
29 [ ]קריה[

4Q244 9 2=CE 30

30 [א מגדלא רו]מה

---

reading of the fragment rules out the next letter being a ו. A ת or נ seem equally unlikely as they would directly connect to the leg of the bet (for examples of this phenomenon, see fragment 16 for a ת connected to a ב and fragment 27 for a נ connected to a ב). There may not actually be more letters attached to the word, however, even if there were; one can be guaranteed that the form is either a pe'al passive participle or a pe'il form of some sort. A plural form (as Collins and Flint apparently suggest) seems unlikely since the ostensible subject of the verb is singular. The most likely reading is a pe'al passive participle since the phrase seems to suggest a state rather than an action (i.e., one can imagine the words fitting into a sentence such as this one: "He looked at the scroll and upon it was written . . ."). Given ובה and the fact that כתב is clearly in the passive voice, one can hardly imagine how the phrase is *not* describing a state. The form is attested several times at Qumran: 4Q530 2ii:6, 12:19; 4Q533 3:2, 3:3; 4Q537 1+2+3:3, 1+2+3:5; 4Q550 1:6. Interestingly, all of these fragments are from the *Book of Giants* – a work that could have a close relationship with both the 4QpsDan[a–b] ar manuscripts as well as the book of Daniel. See Stuckenbruck, "Daniel and Early Enoch Traditions in the Dead Sea Scrolls," 368–86.

[56] Three radicals remain of a word that precedes the כתיב in line 4. The only viable candidate is the lexeme שכח. See Hoftijzer and Jongeling, *DNWSI*, 1132–3. Collins and Flint propose the first-person form אשתכח but do not attempt to translate it. Cf. Collins and Flint, "4Qpseudo-Daniel[a] ar," 101. The problem with a first person form here is that the *hithpe'el* (or, *hithpa'al*) is passive. The reading would be, "I was found, written." There might be a better alternative. I suggest the form is a bi-form of the *hithpe'el* perfect 3ms (Collins and Flint *may* have this form in mind but do not specify). A case of metathesis has occurred producing השתכח from התשכח. There can be no guarantee about the identity of the subject of this clause, but one candidate stands out: the writing inscribed on the scroll or tablet interpreted by Daniel, i.e., "And (it) was found written [on it] . . ." See the similar construction in 4QPrEsther[a] ar, פתיחת קרית השתכח כתיב בה "It was opened, it was read, it was found written in it."

4Q243 10 2–3=CE 31–32

31 [ ]ל גדלא ושלח֯[
32 ל[ב֯קרה בבנין]

4Q244 13 1=CE 33

33 [ובד֯ר אנון]

4Q243 35 1–2=CE 34–35

34 [ ]ן אגרה [
35 ד[י֯ ארעא]

4Q243 11ii 2–3=CE 36–37

36 [מצרין ביד ח֯]זקה[57]
37 [שלטן בארא֯]ע֯

4Q243 12 1–5=CE 38–42

38 שנין אר[ב֯ע֯ מאה ומ֯ן]
39 [צ֯°הקו ויתין ס°גוא]
40 [מע֯ברהון ירדנא ויבדד[קו[58]

---

[57] מצרין ביד in line 2 is unambiguous. The letter following ביד is extremely difficult to decipher. A long, straight down-stroke is visible. There does not appear to be any horizontal strokes along the bottom line (ruling out נ ב כ and מ). Possible candidates are ר ח ה and ת. The slight horizontal mark of ink on the top left corner of the down-stroke seems to indicate a ח. When this is coupled with the frequency with which the "mighty hand" motif is used to describe YHWH's action *vis a vis* Israel in Egypt, the likelihood of the letter ח and consequently the word חזקה become significantly higher. I explored the "mighty hand" motif in the Hebrew Bible and the Dead Sea Scrolls in a paper presented at the 2007 IOQS meeting in Ljubljana, Slovenia: Bennie H. Reynolds III, "Arrogance as Virtue or Vice? The Expression ביד רמה in the Hebrew Bible and the Dead Sea Scrolls." I have expanded the paper into a study of the legacy of the Holiness School in Hellenistic Judaism and am currently revising it for publication.

[58] מעברהון is a interesting form of עבר ("to pass over, through"). Collins and Flint apparently take it as a pa'el (active or passive?) participle with an unusual indicator of person and number (הן instead of מעברין). See Collins and Flint, "4Qpseudo-Daniel[a] ar," 105. The normal form of the word (if a pa'el masculine plural participle as they seem to suggest) would be מעברין for both the active and passive voices. I suggest another possibility. It is a haph'el active participle (masculine singular) with a 3rd masculine plural suffix. Like their suggestion, this would not be what one would call a "normal" form. It seems to have fewer problems though. The lack of the pre-formative ה after the מ occurs from time to time and should be no surprise in this first-guttural verb. Indeed, with first-א verbs, this is the norm. See Rosenthal, *A Grammar of Biblical Aramaic*, 51–2. Next, since the context is almost certainly the exodus, it makes sense that a masculine

41	[ובניהון]
42	[ויתי]ן

4Q243 28 1–2=CE 43–44

43	לד[ניאל וקר]א שמיא[59]
44	פינח[ס אביש]וע

4Q243 39 1=CE 45

45	נד[א סנא]

4Q243 13 + 4Q244 12=CE 46–49

46	ב[חרו בני ישראל אנפיהון מן]אנפי אלוהין
47	דב[ח]ין לבניהון לשידי טעותא ורגז עליהון אלוהין וא [ ]
48	למנתן אנון ביד נבכדנצר מלך בבל ולאחרבא ארעהון מנהון מן די ש[ ]
49	[ ] ומאתא[כל] בני גלותא]ₒ

4Q243 34 1–2=CE 50–51

50	[מן משכנו]תא[60]
51	[מקד]שא

4Q243 21 1–2=CE 52–53

---

singular subject would cause the בני ישראל to cross the Jordan (YHWH or Moses would be acceptable candidates). My reading of the last word of line 3 (ויבלקו) is new. Collins and Flint read יובלא. This reading seems unlikely since "the Jordan" is not in construct form. Since the verb בלק is possible (epigraphically speaking) and since that verb means "to destroy" or "to lay waste" (precisely the action that ostensibly followed the crossing of the Jordan in the Hebrew Bible), it seems like a better option.

[59] The נ and י are poorly preserved, but legible under magnification. The bottom horizontal stroke of the נ can be identified and to top hook of the י can be seen under magnification. For the right-most tip of the ק, see 4Q243 40 2. Collins and Flint reconstruct only וק. See Collins and Flint, "4Qpseudo-Daniel[a] ar," 116–7. The key to determining the word is the letter that follows: ר. For the length of the down-stroke of the ר relative to a ק, see 4Q243 24 2. I propose that some document (possibly the one that has already been mentioned by 4QpsDan[a–b] ar) is given to Daniel and he reads it to interpret its meaning.

[60] Collins and Flint read משכנא, but I do not think the final letter of line two can be an א. The א they point to in frg. 26 2 does not seem as straight as they characterize it and it is not long enough. See Collins and Flint, "4Qpseudo-Daniel[a] ar," 119. A safer reading is a ו. The form must be a plural. Similar plural forms of the word are attested among the Scrolls: משכנות in 1QpHab 2 15, 3 2, משכנותיך in 4QMiscellaneous Rules 1 6, and משכנותי in 4QBeatitides 29 3.

52	[מֹלך שׁנין]
53	[בלכרוס]ºº

4Q243 19 1–4=CE 54–57

54	[שׁ]נִין]
55	[רוֹהִס בי]
56	[וס שׁנִין ת]לת
57	וִ[יֹמללין]

4Q243 22 1–3=CE 58–60

58	בֹ[ר ושׁמה]
59	מֹ[ללין להון תרין][61]
60	וִ[מֹללוֹ][62]

4Q243 20 1–3=CE 61–63

61	[ס בֹר מֹל]כֹא
62	שׁנ[ין עשׂרין]
63	[די מל]כֹא

4Q243 25 2–4=CE 64–66

64	[לֹהו עד יש]
65	[ותתמלא א]רעא[63]
66	[כֹל שׁלדיהוֹןֹ]

4Q243 33 1=CE 67

67	שׁ[בקו אוֹר]חת

---

[61] The first ל as well as the י and ן of מללין are legible under magnification. My reading is heretofore unrecognized. The noun תרין ("two") describes the subject of the clause. Thus, "Two (men, angels, scholars, ?) were speaking to them."

[62] I propose that the subject of the verb in line three should be a 3mp (taking the cue from להון in line two). That group has been spoken to and now they speak (possibly even "and they replied").

[63] תתמלא is a hithpa'al imperfect 3rd feminine singular from מלא. Beyer's suggestion of ארעה to follow makes particularly good sense since the subject of תתמלא must be a feminine singular noun. Furthermore, the ו prefixed to the verb lets us know that this cannot be a case of a verb following its subject. The word that follows the verb *is* the subject and it is a I-א feminine singular noun. This information reduces considerably the number of lexemes that could be said to "be filled." Indeed, ארעא seems to be the only choice.

4Q243 16 1–4=CE 68–71

68	[אָנוֹן שָׁבְעִין שְׁנִין נֹ[⁶⁴
69	בִּי[דָה רַבְּתָא וִיוֹשַׁע אֲנ[וֹן⁶⁵
70	[חַסִינִין וּמַלְכוּת עַמְמִ]יָּא
71	[מִיָּא מַלְכוּתָא קַדִּ]ישְׁתָא

4Q243 24 1–5=CE 72–76

72	בְּנֵי רַשׁ[עָ יֹטְעוֹ[ן תוּן⁶⁶
73	בְּעִדָּנָא [דְּנָה יִתְכַּנְשִׁין קְרִיאִ]ן
74	[עַמְמַיָּא וֶלֱהֱוֵה מִן יוֹם] הוּא
75	[שִׁין וּמַלְכֵי עַמְמַיָּא]
76	עַ[בְדִּין עַד יוֹם

4Q243 38 1=CE 77

77	[אִיֹר]

4Q243 26 1–3=CE 78–80

78	יְסַ[וֹף מְנוּנִיֹה]וֹן⁶⁷

---

⁶⁴ Milik's reading of "seventy years" is preferable here. Collins and Flint dissent: "4Qpseudo-Danielᵃ ar," 108–9. Only the ש and ב are really questionable. The only letter that realistically could be read instead of the ב would be a נ. Since the word שנין follows and is unambiguous, a נ seems unlikely. The word in question is almost certainly a number (since שנין follows). Thus, the options can be easily pared down. Even if there were no ink from the ש or ב, there would only be one cardinal number one could reconstruct from עין: שבעין. For אנון at the beginning of the line, cf. fragment 13. I do agree with Collins and Flint, however, that this reference need not have adopted the 70 years motif from Daniel. Various 70-year motifs are well attested. See Christian Wolff, *Jeremia im Früjudentum und Urchristentum* (Berlin: Akademic Verlag, 1976), 113–16.

⁶⁵ The first letter of the line is either ד or ר. The horizontal line with left-tick is unmistakable. I find the ד to be much more likely given the words that follow. This marks the second usage of the "mighty hand" motif in this manuscript.

⁶⁶ Collins and Flint follow Milik in the reconstruction of אטעו. See Collins and Flint, "4Qpseudo-Danielᵃ ar," 114. It may be possible to improve on this reading as well as their translation "the sons of evil have led astray." The PAM photos reveal (using magnification) that the left-most down-stroke of the (presumed) א descends too far. One might also make an adjustment based on conventional syntax. The subject should follow the verb unless there is sufficient context to demand otherwise. I suggest that the two visible down strokes are those of the ו and the י respectively. The form of the word is thus an imperfect from the verb טעה/י. It is probably a 3ms, but it may also include a 3ms suffix.

⁶⁷ While only two letters of the first word are extant, there are only several real possibilities to reconstruct. Collins and Flint do not attempt any reconstruction. The lexeme must be a third-פ

79 [די לא מנין]
80 יש[ראל]

      4Q243 2 1–2=CE 1–2

1 Daniel before
2 Belshazzar

      4Q244 1–2 1–4=CE 3–6

3 Before the nobles of the king and the Assyrians
4 [ ]
5 And how
6 O (or, the) king

      4Q243 7 2–3=CE 7–8

7 The Chaldeans who . . . the sons of
8 path

      4Q243 4 1=CE 9

9 O [K]i[n]g, let him be cast in[to

      4Q243 8 2–3=CE 10–11

10 Israel, men
11 which cannot be changed

      4Q244 4 1–2=CE 12–13

12 East
13 Daniel said

      4Q243 1 1–3=CE14–16

14 Daniel inquired saying, "On account of . . .[68]

---

root. I propose the word is a pe'il 3rd masculine singular from יסף and represents "their numbers" as a collective. Some confirmation for my view may be found in the masculine singular participle used in the next line (מנין) to refer to a plural subject. Other possible roots (that would still have to be pe'il masculine singular forms) are חלף "to pass by" and תקף "to be strong, strengthen."

[68] The verb שאל fits into a common syntactical formula that often opens new sense units in Aramaic or Hebrew (i.e., verb of speech in the imperfect or sometimes perfect followed by the subject followed by verb of speech in the infinitive). For this reason, my translation is a bit different from that of Collins and Flint. They argue that conventional Aramaic syntax must be ignored because of the probability that the speaker in the second line is not Daniel. This is presumed because line 2 reads, "your god" and they consider there to be insufficient space to switch speakers. See Collins and Flint, "4Qpseudo-Daniel^a ar," 98–9. This seems to be an unnecessary conclusion since there is an entire column length between lines 1 and 2. The form of שאל does not occur

15 your God and a number
16 let him pray and

                                        4Q243 5 1=CE 17

17 Daniel

                                        4Q243 3 1–2=CE 18–19

18 There is [a god in heaven who reveals mysteries?]
19 The King (or, O, King)

                                        4Q243 6 2–4=CE 20–22

20 And upon it was written
21 Daniel who
22 and the writing was fo[und]

                                        4Q243 9 1–2=CE 23–24

23 To Enoch
24 to

                                        4Q243 23 1–2=CE 25–26

25 he escaped
26 the entrance

                                        4Q244 8 2–4=CE 27–29

27 From after the flood
28 Noah from [mount] Lubar
29 The city

                                        4Q244 9 2=CE 30

30 The tower, whose height

                                        4Q243 10 2–3=CE 31–32

31 The tower and he cast
32 To] inspect a building[

                                        4Q244 13 1=CE 33

33 And he scattered them

---

elsewhere among the Scrolls and is otherwise attested only twice: once in the Palestinian Midrashim (*Bereshit Rabba* 906:2) and once in the Palestinian Talmud (*Pesikta de Rav Kahana* 393:12). See Michael Sokoloff, *A Dictionary of Jewish Palestinian Aramaic of the Byzantine Period* (Baltimore: Johns Hopkins Press, 2002), 532–3.

4QPseudo-Daniel^{a–b} ar

                              4Q243 35 1–2=CE 34–35

34 The letter (or, his reward)
35 Of the land

                              4Q243 11ii 2–3=CE 36–37

36 Egypt, with a mighty hand
37 dominion in the land

                              4Q243 12 1–5=CE 38–42

38 Hundred and from
39 and he gave
40 their crossing of the Jordan and [they] laid was[te]
41 and their children
42 [   ]

                              4Q243 28 1–2=CE 43–44

43 [to D]aniel and he rea[d the names]
44 [Phineha]s, Abish[ua]

                              4Q243 39 1=CE 45

45 which he hates

                              4Q243 13 + 4Q244 12=CE 46–49

46 <u>the sons of Israel chose their presence rather than</u> the presence of God
47 sacrificing their sons <u>to the demons</u> of error and God became angry with them and
48 to give them into the hand of Nebuchadnezzar king of Babylon and to make <u>their land</u> desolate <u>of them</u> because
49 and [all] the exiles went

                              4Q243 34 1–2=CE 50–51

50 from the tabernacle
51 the temple

                              4Q243 21 1–2=CE 52–53

52 He w]ill rule ... years
53 Balakros

                              4Q243 19 1–4=CE 54–57

54 years

55   [name of Greek ruler ending in "-ros"?]
56   for thir[ty (or, three or thirteen)] years
57   and they will speak

                                            4Q243 22 1–3=CE 58–60

58   A son and his name (is)
59   two . . . were speaking to them
60   and they spoke

                                            4Q243 20 1–3=CE 61–63

61   s, son of the king
62   twenty years
63   of the kingdom

                                            4Q243 25 2–4=CE 64–66

64   until
65   and the l[and] will be filled
66   and all their decayed carcasses

                                            4Q243 33 1=CE 67

67   They [l]eft the wa[y

                                            4Q243 16 1–4=CE 68–71

68   70 years
69   with his mighty hand and he will save them
70   the mighty ones and the kingdom of the peoples
71   the holy kingdom (or the former kingdoms)

                                            4Q243 24 1–5=CE 72–76

72   [the sons of evi[l] and [th]ey will str[ay]/err
73   at] this [time], the elect will be gathered
74   the peoples will be from [that] day
75   and the kings of the peoples
76   doing until that day

                                            4Q243 38 1=CE 77

77   light

                                            4Q243 26 1–3=CE 78–80

78   their numbers
79   who were innumerable
80   Israel

Language in 4QPseudo-Daniel[a–b] ar

L. DiTommaso has argued that the language of 4Q243/244 is significantly different than all other historical apocalypses. "4Q243/244's review of history is presented *en clair*. This is radically different from the highly cryptic language of the visions of Dan 7–12 and of the dream interpretation of Dan 2."[69] It is unfortunate that DiTommaso does not give a definition of what he means by "cryptic." Standard definitions of cryptic in English always involve concealment or hiding. As we have already seen, the "symbolic" language of apocalypses like Dan 2, 7, 8, and the *Animal Apocalypse* is hardly hiding anything because of the underlying structures in which the symbols participate and because of the traditions and motifs within which the symbols are embedded. On the other hand, the explicit language found in Dan 10–12 and the *Apocryphon of Jeremiah C* does not point beyond itself, but it is often considerably more opaque than, for example, the use of beasts or horns. DiTommaso is correct that 4QpsDan[a–b] ar uses explicit language, but this feature is more widespread than he claims. In the analysis that follows I attempt to show that the language in 4Q243/244 is consistent with that found in Dan 10–12 and the *Apocryphon of Jeremiah C*. The language is always explicit – but it is often also cryptic and sometimes group-specific. The expressions do not point beyond themselves, but they are sometimes unintelligible outside of highly-specialized interpretative contexts (i.e., "in-group" contexts).

Descriptions of Deities, Angels, and Demons
The god of Israel is mentioned explicitly on two separate occasions in the texts. A third use may also be reconstructed. The first use apparently occurs in the prologue during a conversation between Daniel and the Babylonian king Belshazzar: 𐤀𐤋𐤄𐤊 (4Q243 1 2=CE 15). While there are no syntactical clues that the first use of the word "God" refers explicitly to the God of Israel as opposed to other Gods, the use of paleo-Hebrew (Phoenician) script to write the name leaves little doubt that YHWH is intended. As I indicated above, there is a second-person, masculine, singular suffix attached to the noun as well as either the archaic final vowel ה (signifying

---

[69] DiTommaso, "4QPseudo-Daniel[a–b] (4Q243–4Q244)," 115.

the accusative/dative case) or the directive/locative ה suffix.[70] The latter possibility is vastly more likely. Neither grammatical feature is part of conventional Aramaic and the use of the Paleo-Hebrew script is unlikely an emulation of, for example, an 8th century Syrian script. The use of Paleo-Hebrew among certain Jewish groups, especially during the Hasmonean Period, probably best explains the usage here and thus helps contextualize the unusual grammar as an appropriation from Hebrew.

Paleo-Hebrew was used by Hasmoneans on their coins, perhaps as a claim to legitimate independance.[71] In other words, the last time the script was widely used in Judea was before the fall of the Judean monarchy. Paleo-Hebrew script is sometimes used to write the tetragrammaton in biblical quotations found in Essene compositions.[72] In some Essene texts Paleo-Hebrew is also used to write the name El in biblical quotations.[73] The use of Paleo-Hebrew in *Pseudo-Daniel*$^{a-b}$ *ar* cannot be explained on analogy with the Essene texts since 4QpsDan^{a-b} ar also uses regular script and orthography to spell the same name later in the text. In the combined edition above (line 47) the God of Israel is written אלוהין. The passage describes God's anger at Judah for religious infidelity and the consequent punishment of the Babylonian exile. It is not possible in this context that the word is used to describe a god(s) other than the God of Israel.

The name probably also appears in combined edition line 46. In the context of line 47, it strains credulity to imagine an object other than אלוהין being reconstructed: ב[חרו בני ישראל אנפיהון מֹן] אנפי אלוהין "the children of Israel [ch]oose their presence rather than [the presence of God]."[74] Thus, the use of Paleo-Hebrew in 4QpsDan^{a-b} ar is not an attempt to avoid writing and/or pronouncing a name of God. The name אלוהין, regardless of its orthography or script, does not point beyond itself in any way. It is an explicit name for the God of Israel. The only other example of liminal beings found in the text is a group of demons called "demons of error."

Within the main body of the revelation, the expression שידי טעותא "demons of error" (CE 47=4Q243 13 + 4Q244 12) is used to name the putative

---

[70] Grammarians presumed that the locative ה was a vestige of the old accusative ending until the discovery of the Ugaritic texts proved this theory wrong (i.e., both particles are used in the some of the same Ugaritic texts and it is demonstrable that they are not identical). Cf. Waltke and O'Connor, *An Introduction to Biblical Hebrew Syntax*, 127–8, 85–6.

[71] Yaakov Meshorer, *A Treasury of Jewish Coins from the Persian Period to Bar Kokhba* (Nyack, NY: Amphora, 2001), 23–59. Cf. also Yaakov Meshorer, *Jewish Coins of the Second Temple Period* (Tel Aviv: Massada, 1967). See also Yigal Ronen, "The First Hasmonean Coins," 50 (1987): 105–7.

[72] E.g., 1QpHab I 1, IV 17, VI 14, X 7, 14, XI 10, XII 17. Other examples among the *Pesharim* are found in 1QpZeph, 4QpPs^a, 4QMidrEschat^e?, 1QpMic, and 4QpIsa^a.

[73] E.g., 1QpMic 12 3.

[74] Cf. Collins and Flint, "4Qpseudo-Daniel^a ar," 107.

"foreign" deities that played a part in the pre-exilic cult of Israel, e.g., *Ba'al*, *Asherah*, etc. The expression is not found elsewhere in Aramaic or cognate languages, but a linguistic analysis of each component word and an analysis of the constellation of related motifs surrounding it (human sacrifice, child sacrifice, and exile as a punishment for improper sacrifice) help to put the expression in its proper context.[75]

טעותא is a feminine, singular, determined noun derived from the root טעי/ו.[76] The basic meaning of the root is "to err, stray." The semantic range of the word may be divided into two categories: 1) concrete (i.e., non-religious) and 2) figurative (i.e., religious) uses. The root almost always refers specifically to religious unfaithfulness or cultic errors in post-Biblical Hebrew and Judean Aramaic.[77] For example, 4QApocryphon of Levi[b] ar (4Q541) speaks of a future time when the Great Sea will turn red, books of wisdom will be opened, and a teacher of wisdom will come.[78] טעי/ו is used to describe the generation of the teacher: "His term of office will be marked by lies and violence [and] the people will go astray (יטעה) in his days and be confounded" (4Q541 9i 7).[79] It is this focus on religious/cultic infidelity that the lexeme brings to the expression "demons of error."

---

[75] For a full linguistic study of the expression שידי טעותא and its function in the motifs of 4QpsDan[a–b] ar, see Reynolds, "What Are Demons of Error?," 593–613. I take the opportunity to note here that one of the texts I used in my linguistic treatment of טעיון appears no longer relevant in light of Hanan Eshel's reading of a cursive ש where Maurice Baillet read a ט in the text. Removing this text from my evidence does not change my results as several other reliable examples remain. Nevertheless, it is regrettable that I did not locate Eshel's article before publication of my own. See Hanan Eshel, "6Q30, a Cursive Šin, and Proverbs 11," *JBL* 122 (2003).

[76] Evidence concerning the final consonant of this root is ambiguous. Evidence for an original III-ו is as prevalent as evidence for an original III-י. The ambiguity is found not only in several dialects of Aramaic but also in other Semitic languages. Wellhausen held that apart from a few exceptions, III-י and III-ו roots ultimately derive from bilateral roots. See Julius Wellhausen, *Skizzen und Vorarbeiten VI* (Berlin: J. Reimer, 1889), 255ff. While Gesenius pointed out that Wellhausen's view may not be taken as a general principle because of exceptions he found in Biblical Hebrew, he admitted that Wellhausen's view is undoubtedly correct in many cases. See Gesenius et al., *Gesenius' Hebrew Grammar* (Oxford: Clarendon Press, 1957), 207. I find Wellhausen's view helpful for explaining this root – especially given the large degree of conflicting evidence in the forms attested. The Akkadian evidence suggests a bilateral root. See J. Black et al., *A Concise Dictionary of Akkadian* (SANTAG 5; Wiesbaden: Harrassowitz Verlag, 2000), 413. I am unconvinced that there could have been two originally distinct roots behind the word *a la* the case of ענה in Biblical Hebrew. I.e., one may observe distinctions in orthography but never in meaning with טעי/ו.

[77] Cf. Reynolds, "What Are Demons of Error?," 598–604.

[78] This text is not related to the Aramaic Levi Document. See Greenfield et al., The Aramaic Levi Document: Edition, Translation, Commentary, 31–2.

[79] Transcription by É. Puech. Trans. E. Cook, "4Q541 (4QapocrLevi[b]? ar)," in *Parabiblical Texts* (ed. Emanuel Tov and Donald Parry; vol. 3 of *DSSR*; Leiden Brill, 2005), 447.

שד is a bilateral root that is most likely an Akkadian loanword and is elastic in meaning.[80] For example, the *šdyn* in the Balaam text from *Deir Alla* are synonymous with the *'lhn* and indicate the generic council of El familiar from prologue to Job (i.e., בני אלהים).[81] The same word is used to describe the rogue, malevolent forces that act in the physical world of human beings in text like the *Book of Tobit* (i.e., *Asmodeus*, cf. 4QTobit[b] ar 4ii 13). The latter usage shares strong similarities with the *šedū* of Iron Age Akkadian texts such as the loyalty oaths of *Esarhaddon*.[82] When combined with the word טעותא and contextualized with three specific motifs (human sacrifice, child sacrifice, and exile as a punishment for improper sacrifice), a distinct meaning is created.[83] These demons are not the troublesome, mischievous spirits that meddle in the everyday affairs of humans such as the Akkadian *šedū* or Tobit's *Asmodeus*. They are not the generic divine council of El as depicted in, for example, the Balaam text from *Deir Alla*. They are not fallen angels run amuck. There is no indication that the term שידי טעותא was used to indicate cult objects made by craftsman as in Deutero-Isaiah or *Jubilees*.[84] Instead, the expression demons of error functions in the same context as the use of demons in Ps 106:37–8: "They sacrificed their sons and their daughters to demons (לַשֵּׁדִם). And they spilled the blood of the innocent – the blood of their sons and their daughters, whom they sacrificed to the idols of Canaan. And the land was defiled with blood." This passage mirrors the accusations of child sacrifice found in, for example, Jer 19:4–5:

Because the people have forsaken me, and have profaned this place by making offerings in it to other gods whom neither they nor their ancestors nor the kings of Judah have known; and because they have filled this place with the blood of the innocent, 5 and gone on building the high places of Baal to burn their children in the fire as burnt offerings to Baal, which I did not command or decree, nor did it enter my mind.

In both Ps 106 and *Pseudo-Daniel*[a-b] *ar*, former gods of the Israelite pantheon are transformed not into Canaanite gods (as in Deut), but into demons. In other words, שידי טעותא is a description of some "foreign" gods that played a part in the pre-exilic cult of Israel. The expression perhaps reflects a theological world in which the very conception of a god other than YHWH is unintelligible. Gods of old are demoted in status and trans-

---

[80] Koehler and Baumgartner, eds., *The Hebrew and Aramaic Lexicon of the Old Testament*, 2: 1417. Reynolds, "What Are Demons of Error?," 604–10.

[81] Hackett, The Balaam Text from Deir Alla, 29.

[82] Cf. Simo Parpola and Kazuko Watanabe, eds., *Neo-Assyrian Treaties and Loyalty Oaths* (*SAA*; Helsinki: Helsinki University Press, 1988), 49.

[83] Reynolds, "What Are Demons of Error?," 610–13.

[84] Cf. Isa 44:19, 4QJubilees[a] II 11.

formed into lesser liminal beings. The language used here is explicit. Demon is not a metaphor or a trope of any kind. It is difficult even to understand it as a euphemism since there is no evidence that the writer would believe the demons could actually be gods. It does not point beyond itself or require interpretation (if Daniel interprets a heavenly tablet then the description is itself an interpretation). The language used to describe heavenly beings is different than what one finds in the symbolic apocalypses where they are normally described as humans or stars.

Descriptions of Persons

Like *Apocryphon of Jeremiah C*, several explicit descriptions found in *Pseudo-Daniel*[a-b] ar probably belong to a narrative introduction/prologue that is not part of the revelation proper. Included in this category are at least four mentions of the figure Daniel (דניאל 4Q243 2 1,3 1, 6 3, 4Q244 4 2) and one of the Babylonian king Belshazzar (בלשצר 4Q243 2 2). The name of Daniel is also found once in the body of the revelation (4Q243 28 1).

The oldest "historical" figure preserved in the revelation is חנוך Enoch (CE 23=243 9 1). The description of Enoch is considerably different than what one finds in the *Animal Apocalypse*. We saw above that the *Animal Apocalypse* uses pairs of conventional association (e.g., animals are used to represent humans). Beyond this basic system, the *Animal Apocalypse* used tropes like metaphor to describe figures by their basic characteristics. For example, Enoch is described as part of a group of the descendants of Seth (i.e., the history revealed to Enoch is one in which he is involved). The group is depicted as "pure-white cattle" (ኦላሀመተ ጸዐዳ 'alehemate ṣa'ada) in *1 En.* 85:9. The description of Enoch in *Pseudo-Daniel*, however, does not point beyond itself. An explicit description is used: his personal name.

Another figure whose description departs from his most well known version (Gen) is נוח Noah (4Q244 8). Noah is described with his personal name – unlike the kind of description used to name him in the *Animal Apocalypse*: חד מן תוריא [חוריא] "one of the white oxen" (4Q206 4i 13–14). Like the biblical Noah, this figure is named specifically in the context of a deluge, but unlike the biblical Noah, this figure is named in association with לובר ([Mount] Lubar) rather than אררט Ararat (Gen 8:4).

Milik (followed by García-Martínez and Collins and Flint) noted that the references to Noah and Mt. Lubar were not taken from Gen, but perhaps *Jub.* (5:28, 7:1, 17, and 10:15) or the *Genesis Apocryphon* (*1QapGen*

XIII:10–13).⁸⁵ The situation may be even more complex. If DiTommaso is correct that 4Q243/244 must have been written after the collection of Dan 1–6 or 2–6 was established but before the Hellenistic religious reforms of Antiochus, then there is a problem. Most agree that Jubilees should be dated between 160 and 110 B.C.E.. VanderKam places the text between 160 and 150 B.C.E..⁸⁶ It was probably written too late to have influenced 4QpsDan^{a-b} ar. The *Genesis Apocryphon* in its final form (first century B.C.E.?) was probably also written too late to influence *Pseudo-Daniel*.⁸⁷ But a large section of the *Genesis Apocryphon* containing a Mt. Lubar tradition may derive from the third century B.C.E.: *The Book of the Words of Noah*.⁸⁸ Since there is no direct evidence that the Lubar tradition (or any other material) from 4QpsDan^{a-b} ar influenced *Jubilees* or the *Genesis Apocryphon*, it may be that the *Book of the Words of Noah* was a source for *Pseudo-Daniel*.

There is no scholarly consensus about the the *Book of the Words of Noah*. (See the more significant engagement with the *Book of the Words of Noah* in chapter 3 above). Pieces of it or references to it may be found in *Jubilees*, *1 Enoch*, 4QMess ar (?), *The Genesis Apocryphon*, and *Aramaic Levi*.⁸⁹ It is not possible to establish an exact date for the composition of the *Book of the Words of Noah* but references in other works can help establish a *terminus a quo*. For the purposes of this chapter, it is necessary only to indicate a pre-Maccabean date. References in the *Book of Watchers* dis-

---

⁸⁵ Milik, "Prière de Nabonide et autres écrits d'un cycle de Daniel," 412. Martínez, *Qumran and Apocalyptic. Studies on the Aramaic Texts from Qumran*, 140–1. García-Martínez points out that Lubar also appears in 6QpapGiants ar (6Q8 26 1) and *Epiphanius, Adv. Haer*. 1.1.4. Context is severely limited in the former. Cf. John J. Collins and Peter Flint, "4Q243–244," in *Qumran Cave 4 XVII: Parabiblical Texts, Part 3* (ed. James VanderKam; vol. 22 of DJD; Oxford: Clarendon Press, 1996), 149.

⁸⁶ James VanderKam, *The Book of Jubilees* (Sheffield: Sheffield Academic Press, 2001), 17–21. Cf. the discussion in Segal, *The Book of Jubilees*. Crawford places the date slightly further back in the second century (170–150 B.C.E.). Crawford, *Rewriting Scriptures in Second Temple Times*, 61–2. Cf. also Hanneken, "The Book of Jubilees among the Apocalypses," 141–5.

⁸⁷ Crawford argues for a first century date. See Crawford, *Rewriting Scriptures in Second Temple Times*, 106. Falk argues for a slightly earlier date: "the latter half of the second century B.C.E. to the first half of the first century B.C.E.." Cf. E. Y. Kutscher, "Dating the Language of the Genesis Apocryphon," *JBL* 76 (1957): 288–92. Falk, *The Parabiblical Texts*, 29.

⁸⁸ Lange argues that the *Book of the Words of Noah* from the *Genesis Apocryphon* should be assigned a third century date. Lange, "The Parabiblical Literature," 312–3. Cf. Morgenstern et al., "The Hitherto Unpublished Columns of the Genesis Apocryphon," 30–54.

⁸⁹ It may not be that all of these works include the same information or even excerpts from the same documents. For example, it is conceivable that before some of the disparate Daniel traditions came together in the Book of Daniel, different pieces could have been quoted as the "Book of Daniel." Thus, while it need not be a problem that quotations in *The Genesis Apocryphon* and *Aramaic Levi* seem to be about different topics, neither would it be a problem for two completely different documents to be quoted. Neither scenario would indicate, as some have suggested, that a *Book of Noah* never existed.

cussed by García Martínez easily establish such a date.[90] For example, García Martínez notes how in *1 En.* 10:1–3, "Noah suddenly appears as a personage already known, and the whole passage is an announcement of the deluge that has no connection with what precedes or follows it."[91] If García Martínez is also correct about 1) the relationship of the *Book of Noah* to 4QMess ar and 2) the fact that the *Book of the Words of Noah* was common source for both *Jubilees* and *The Genesis Apocryphon* (as opposed to a linear relationship), then a date in the 3rd century would be safe. Morgenstern, Qimron, and Sivan argue that the language of the text places it in the third century and Lange points out that its reception in *Sibylline Oracles* 3 and 1QM I–II point to the same conclusion.[92] Thus, the *Book of the Words of Noah* was probably written early enough to be a source of or influence on *Pseudo-Daniel*$^{a-b}$ *ar*.[93] Even if the source of *Pseudo-Daniel's* Noah tradition cannot be settled conclusively, an important conclusion can still be made. I argued in chapter five that the language of *Apocryphon of Jeremiah C* is often borrowed from Jewish Scripture (i.e., Jer, Dan, Nah, and Deutero-Isa). 4QpsDan^{a-b} ar bears witness to traditions and motifs familiar from Jewish scripture, but the expressions used by 4QpsDan^{a-b} ar are departures from those used in, for example, Gen. These departures indicate its language is derived from other sources. Based on the language found in this text, one could conclude that texts like *Jubilees* or the *Book of the Words of Noah* might have held an equal, higher or more authoritative status for the writer of 4QpsDan^{a-b} ar than the "biblical" books that contain the same traditions.

Daniel is probably mentioned explicitly in the revelation in 4Q243 28 1. In the fragment, he apparently reads a list of names of pre-exilic high priests. Names extant in the text are *[ס[ינח Phineas and אבישו]ע/* Abishua (4Q243 28 2). Phineas is mostly a reconstruction, but the ס is clear and since Phineas was the father of Abishua and appears in similarly close proximity in other lists of priests (1 Chron 6:4–5, 50, Ezra 7:5, 1 Esd 8:2, 4 Esd 1:2) there is little doubt about whether the reconstruction is legitimate.

---

[90] Martínez, Qumran and Apocalyptic. Studies on the Aramaic Texts from Qumran, 26–30.
[91] Martínez, Qumran and Apocalyptic. Studies on the Aramaic Texts from Qumran, 29.
[92] Morgenstern et al., "The Hitherto Unpublished Columns of the Genesis Apocryphon," 30–54. Lange, "The Parabiblical Literature," 313.
[93] The text of *Pseudo-Daniel*$^{a-b}$ *ar* raises important questions about canonical history and the concept of authoritative literature. From a tradition- and motif-historical point of view, *Pseudo-Daniel*$^{a-b}$ *ar* seems to indicate a fluid matrix of traditions and motifs that are not strictly governed by any text-based standards. That is, while the tradition of the deluge might have been an authoritative narrative for religious formation, it is not clear that the version in Gen was preferred over other accounts found in *Jub.* or the *Book of Noah* during Second Temple times. I explored this topic in a paper presented at the 2010 IOQS meeting in Helsinki, Finland: "Whose History? The Sources for Ex Eventu Prophecies at Qumran and the Authority of 'Biblical' Books."

Mark Fretz notes that, "In the post-exilic Jewish community, Ezra's authority was legitimized by proof of descent through the high priest Abishua."[94] It is unclear whether this concern about Ezra's authority is present in *Pseudo-Daniel*.

The overlapping fragments 4Q243 13 and 4Q244 12 provide the largest continuous block of text in the manuscripts. They contain the name נבכדנצר Nebuchadnezzar, modified by the title מלך בבל "king of Babylon." 4QpsDan[a-b] ar agrees with the Book of Jeremiah in casting Nebuchadnezzar as a servant/tool of YHWH – even using the same language. One may compare 4Q243 12 + 4Q244 13 3 למנתן אנון ביד נבכדנצר "to give them into the hand of Nebuchadnezzar" with Jer 27:6: אנכי נתתי את־כל הארצות האלה ביד נבוכדנאצר "I have given all these lands into the hand of Nebuchadnezzar" (cf. Jer 22:25, 29:21, 32:28, 44:30, 46:26). There is no attempt to mask the identity of the Mesopotamian king. The language used to describe him is explicit and does not point beyond itself. This description is a significant departure from descriptions of kings in part one of this study.

Perhaps the most enigmatic explicit description in *Pseudo-Daniel*[a-b] ar is found in 4Q243 21: בלכרוס Balakros. Milik proposed that the name Balakros refers to Alexander Balas.[95] As García-Martínez and Collins and Flint have noted, such a proposal seems gratuitous in light of the many references to actual figures named Balakros.[96] Alexander Balas would not even be the only figure named Balas mentioned in Hellenistic sources. Josephus discussed a certain Βαλας (king of Sodom) in *Antiquities* 1.171. So even if Balakros is an alternate spelling of Balas, one could not assume that Alexander Balas was the only candidate in a sweep of history that begins in primeval times. If one took בלכרס as a misspelling, there would still be several problems isolating Βαλας as the intended name. The names of much closer "misspellings" can be found. For example, Josephus mentions a Βαλακος (king of Moab) some 13 times (*Antiquities* 4.102, 104, 107, 112, 112, 118, 119, 124, 126, 126, 127). Josephus also mentions other figures close in name such as Βαλατορος (*Antiquities* 1.157), which is alternately spelled Βαλαζωρος (*Apion* 1.124), and Βαλαδας (*Antiquities* 10, 30, 31, 34; cf. Isa 39:1). These figures are not Hellenistic, but the review of history in 4Q243/244 contains much more than just the Hellenistic period.

Collins and Flint note that three officers of Alexander the Great bore the name Balakros.[97] In my judgment the most reasonable candidate would be

---

[94] Mark Fretz, "Abishua," in *Anchor Bible Dictionary* (ed. David Noel Freedman; New York: Doubleday, 1992), CD-ROM.

[95] Milik, "Prière de Nabonide et autres écrits d'un cycle de Daniel," 407–15.

[96] See Collins and Flint, "4Qpseudo-Daniel[a] ar," 137, 50. Similarly, Martínez, *Qumran and Apocalyptic. Studies on the Aramaic Texts from Qumran*, 145.

[97] Collins and Peter Flint, "Pseudo-Daniel," 150.

Balakros of Cilicia. After his decisive defeat of Persia at Issos (333 B.C.E.), Alexander the Great left Balakros in charge of Cilicia (cf. Arrian 2.12.2, Diodorus 18.22.1).[98] Of the known figures named Balakros, he would have the nearest geographical and chronological proximity to the writer of 4QpsDan[a-b] ar. Part of another Greek name might be found in 4Q243 19 2, but only four letters are extant: רהוס. The identity of this figure is entirely speculative, but Collins and Flint suggest that the use of the ה might indicates an Aramaic rendering of a double-*rho* in Greek.[99] According to them an example of this type of name could be Pyrrhus (King of Epirus 319–272 B.C.E.).

Some titular descriptions have already been mentioned above. For example, Nebuchadnezzar is described as מלך בבל "the King of Babylon." Within the main body of the revelation, at least one and possibly two kingdoms (מלכו]תא) 4Q243 18i–ii 1–2) are mentioned in a context that appears to fall after the Tower of Babel, but before the sojourn in Egypt and Exodus. Sons (or children) are mentioned on several occasions without sufficient context to make more meaningful comments (cf. 4Q243 27 1, 12 4, 22 1). Once in the context of the Hellenistic period a בר מל]כא "son of the king" is mentioned. This type of expression, contrary to claims made by L. DiTommaso, mirrors the representation techniques found in Dan 10–12 and the *Apocryphon of Jeremiah C*. It is not unique to *Pseudo-Daniel*. For example, a description of events concerning Seleucus II Callinicus and his sons Seleucus III Ceraunus and Antiochus III the Great in Dan 11:8b–10 reads, "For some years he shall refrain from attacking *the king of the north*; then the latter shall invade the realm of *the king of the south*, but will return to his own land. *His sons* shall wage war and assemble a multitude of great forces" (emphasis added). The language is entirely explicit, but it is also cryptic. The fact that this language is not encoded with the images familiar from Dan 2, 7, 8 or the *Animal Apocalypse* does not mean that it provides more tools for interpretation. It provides less.

The expression בני גלותא "exiles" is used in 4Q243 13 + 4Q244 12 4 to describe those that Nebuchadnezzar carried from Jerusalem after razing the city in 586 B.C.E.. The same Aramaic expression is used in Ezra 6:16 and Dan 2:25, 5:13, and 6:14 as a title for Jews deported to Babylon.[100] It was

---

[98] Waldemar Heckel, "The Politics of Distrust: Alexander and His Successors," in *The Hellenistic World: New Perspectives* (ed. Daniel Ogden; London: Classical Press of Wales, 2002), 84.

[99] See Collins and Flint, "Pseudo-Daniel," 111, 150.

[100] The expression מנים גולתו "the number (i.e., group) of its captivity" in 4Qpap psEzek[e] (4Q391 77 2) may be synonymous with the בני גלותא since Israel is mentioned in the same fragment, but the text's state of preservation is so terrible that little can be said with confidence. I presume that the writer has inadvertently placed the masculine rather than feminine plural ending

probably originally present in 4QPrNab ar 1–3 4. Formulaic speech makes the reconstruction highly plausible.[101] One may draw an important distinction between the way that 4QpsDan$^{a\text{-}b}$ ar and *Apocryphon of Jeremiah C* on the one hand and Essene texts on the other use exile terminology. Whereas the first group of texts (e.g., Ezra, etc.) always use exile terminology to refer to the events of 586 B.C.E., other "apocalyptic" texts found at Qumran use exile terminology to describe themselves. The expressions גולת המדבר "exiles of the desert" and גולת בני אור "exiles of the sons of light" in 1QM 1 2–3 are synonymous, but are set in the Hellenistic period and are probably self-descriptions of Essenes.[102] The *Pesher Habakkuk* shares the view that the Qumran-Essenes desert home was an exile: "Its interpretation concerns the Wicked Priest, who pursued the Teacher of Righteousness to consume him in the heat of his anger at his place of exile." (אבית גלותו 1QpHab 11 4–6). The description בני גלותא thus provides one more argument why 4Q243/244 should not be considered an Essene text.

Three enigmatic adjectival group-descriptions are found in the eschatological section of the text. קריאין (the elect), חסינין mighty ones (4Q243 16 3), and מלכותא קד[ישתא a holy kingdom (4Q243 16 4) are found in the same fragment. The fragment describes how, at the conclusion of a 70 year period, God gathers the elect (קריאין) and the gentiles and their rulers are destroyed. The expression קריאין is at first glance similar to an expression from the *Apocryphon of Jeremiah C* (ק[ריאי השם). But the meaning of the expression in the *Apocryphon of Jeremiah C* is not applicable here. "Those called by name" in the *Apocryphon of Jeremiah C* are not located in the eschatological portion of the text, but clearly in the pre-exilic portion.

While an eschatological meaning (i.e., "elect" rather than "called") is not common for the plural participle of 13 (Hebrew קרא), Collins and Flint are correct to translate it that way in light of the imperfect יתכנשין that precedes it and the expression עַמְמִיא הוא]ולהוה מן יום] "The peoples will be from [that] day" in the next line (4Q243 24). Collins and Flint compare the expressions with ones found in the *Apocalypse of Weeks* and the *Damascus Document*. In the *Apocalypse of Weeks* Enoch describes the subject of the revelation (derived from the heavenly tablets and communicated to him by angels) as, "Concerning the children of righteousness, concerning the elect of eternity" (*1 En.* 93:2). Only a few words are preserved of the Aramaic text and "elect" is not one

---

on מן. This seems a far more plausible answer than to assume מנים to be stringed-instruments a la Ps 150:4.

[101] See Frank Moore Cross, "Fragments of the Prayer of Nabonidus," *IEJ* 34 (1984). Collins and Flint, "4QPrayer of Nabonidus ar," 91.

[102] Only the final form of 1QM should be described as an Essene text. Earlier literary strata are probably not Essene.

of them. Milik reconstructs בחירי עלמא. The Ethiopic text (ኅሩያን ዓለም, *ḥeruyān 'ālamu*) appears to indicate that Milik's choice of vocabulary parallels the cognate lexemes used in the Ethiopic translation. But the *Apocalypse of Weeks* clearly offers a time table of history that concludes with the judgment of the wicked and the advent of a new heaven in which the righteous live peacefully forever (cf. *1 En.* 91:15–18).

In the *Damascus Document* a group described as בחירי ישראל "the chosen of Israel," and קריאי השם "those called by name" are mentioned in an interpretation of Ezek 44:15: "The priests and the Levites and the sons of Zadok who maintained the service of my temple when the children of Israel strayed far away from me, shall offer the fat and the blood." Each group mentioned in the Ezekiel passage is isolated and re-contextualized: "The priests are the converts of Israel who left the land of Judah; and (the Levites) are those who joined them; and the sons of Zadok are the chosen of Israel, "those called by name," who stood up at the end of days" (CD IV 1–4). Like the elect in the *Apocalypse of Weeks*, "those called by name" in the *Damascus Document* are specifically associated with the *eschaton*. They are those "who stood up at the end of days." Especially in the *Damascus Document*, "those called by name," is a cryptic, group-specific term. It is only intelligible within a highly-specialized community of interpretation.

A similar construction is found in 1QM. In the instructions for the organization of battle formations and war trumpets in column three, the writer declares, "On the trumpets for the assembly of the congregation, they shall write, "Those Called by God" קרואי אל (1QM 3 2). The designation קרואי אל is the most general moniker to be written on a trumpet. For example, in line three "The Princes of God" (נשיאי אל) is to be written on the trumpets of the more exclusive group; "chiefs" (ה[ס]רים). Other trumpets are inscribed for individual battle formations, those slain in war, etc.[103] Thus, in the version of the *War Scroll* read/written/redacted by Essenes, the entire Qumran group is referred to as "those called by God." The expression is, for all intents and purposes, a synonym for עדה. For reasons articulated at the beginning of this chapter, it is not likely that *Pseudo-Daniel*[a–b] *ar* was written by Essenes. Therefore, while קריאין is the *kind* of expression used by Essenes to describe themselves, it is highly unlikely that the expression is meant to invoke the Essenes. Instead, it is a term (like many other Essene terms) that only takes on specific meanings in highly specialized contexts. For example, it is unlikely that the Essenes or any other group had a special association with the expression "called by God" in Hellenistic Ju-

---

[103] Trumpets are designated for times (.i.e., the time of pursuit, the time of ambush, the time of return, etc) as well as for groups.

daism. Presumably more than one group of Jews considered themselves to be "called by God" on an exclusive basis. The only way an individual would be able to know without doubt who was intended by the term קריאין would be to be one of the קריאין. The expression can perhaps be illuminated by Eco's conception of the symbolic mode – the expression cannot support a definitive interpretation outside of a highly specialized reading community. In other words, monikers such as Pharisees and Essenes carried specific connotations that Hellenistic Jews could have understood regardless of their narrative context. A description like "the elect" is far more malleable and only takes on a definitive meaning within a closed context. The use of the term "elect" in 4QpsDan[a–b] ar indicates that like the *Apocryphon of Jeremiah C* and Dan 10–12, the text was produced for limited community – indeed, expressions like "elect" help to construct a limited community. Non-symbolic apocalypses contain a large amount of explicit language that might have been understood by anyone. Personal names clearly restrict interpretative options for the reader. But only one or two in-group expressions need be inserted into a text filled with otherwise explicit language in order to transform the text into an in-group text.

The "mighty ones" (חסינין) are more enigmatic. They play a role in God's victory and the subsequent establishment of the "holy kingdom" at the end of days (4Q243 16 3–4, cf. CE 64–76). The root חסן is a comparatively rare lexeme connoting "power" or "strength." It is notable that all three examples from the Hebrew Bible are from the Book of Daniel. To my knowledge the substantive in 4Q243 is the only such form preserved in Judean Aramaic.

The first example from the Book of Daniel occurs when Daniel interprets Nebuchadnezzar's dream of the statue in chapter 2. Daniel begins the less-than-comforting interpretation with a formal introduction that lavishes praise on the king: "You, O King, to whom the God of heaven has given the kingdom, the power (חסנא), the might, and the glory . . ." (2:37). The second example is found in Dan 4:30. Nebuchadnezzar experiences another dream and it is also interpreted by Daniel. The implications of this dream are more dire than the those of the last dream. Nebuchadnezzar discounts Daniel's doom-interpretation and says to himself while surveying his kingdom, "Is this not magnificent Babylon – which I have built as a royal capital by my mighty power (בתקף חסני), for my glorious honor?" (4:30). The third example derives from Dan 7:22. The text uses the root as a verb to describe how the קדישין "holy ones" seize power (הֶחֱסִנוּ) with the advent of the Ancient of Days.[104] A similar scenario appears to obtain in *Pseudo-Daniel's* description of the advent of the *eschaton*:

4Q243 16 1–4=CE 68–71

68 70 years

69 with his mighty hand and he will save them

70 the mighty ones (חסינין) and the kingdom of the peoples

71 the holy kingdom (מלכותא קד[ישתא)

In the lines above two groups are distinguished: the "mighty ones" and the "kingdom of the peoples."[105] One presumes that the victory of the mighty ones leads to the establishment of the "holy kingdom" (i.e., the opposite of "the kingdom of the peoples"). Like "the elect" (קריאין), the description "mighty ones" (חסינין) appears to be a group-specific term. These terms do not have the limited semantic range of terms like "Pharisee," but they are terms that only function properly with a highly specialized context that is not open to the majority of the population. These kinds of descriptions are different than the symbolic descriptions of people and groups encountered in apocalypses such as Dan 2, 7, 8, and the *Animal Apocalypse*. In those cases, descriptions of people or groups always pointed beyond themselves by means of categorical associations (i.e., animals=people or people=angels). The symbolic descriptions do not presume a group-specific context. To the contrary, it is the conventional associations and the motifs and traditions in which they are embedded that make them accessible to the largest possible Jewish audience. The language in *Pseudo-Daniel's* review of history is hardly unique. The same type of language is used in Dan 10–12 and the *Apocryphon of Jeremiah C*.

---

[104] The same vocabulary may be employed in 4QpapVision[b] ar 20 3 (4Q558): מלכותה חס]ינה. See Parry and Tov, eds., *Additional Genres and Unclassified Texts*, 144. In another apocalypse, the *Book of Giants* (4Q531 22 3), the giant Ohya uses the root חסן to describe his own strength – a strength he laments as insufficient to defeat the angels in heaven. Its basic meaning in the Hebrew Bible is "fortress," but three instances appear to resemble or even appropriate Aramaic meanings. In Ps 89:89 it is used to describe and Praise YHWH, "YHWH, God of hosts, who is mighty (חסין) like you?" In this case, it does not simply appropriate an Aramaic meaning, but an Aramaic form. In the first of Isaiah's indictments of Judah and Jerusalem, the lexeme functions as a foil to אביר. YHWH, "the mighty one of Israel (אביר ישראל) promises that, "the mighty (החסן) shall become like tinder and their work like a spark" (Isa 1:24, 31 NRSV). Finally, in Amos 2:9, YHWH describes his destruction of the Amorites, who were, "strong as oaks (חסן הוא כאלונים)."

[105] See more on the "kingdom of the peoples" in the next section below.

Descriptions of Ethno-Political Groups

אשריא Assyrians (4Q244 1–2 2) and כשדיא Chaldeans (4Q243 7 2) are mentioned in the context of the literary prologue.[106] It is not clear that these explicit titles actually refer to ethnically/geographically distinct peoples. It is likely that "Assyrians" is used as general designation for "Mesopotamians." The relative stability of meaning for the lexeme אשור in the Hebrew Bible gives way to considerably more diversity in the Jewish literature of the Hellenistic Period.[107] It rarely indicates the Neo-Assyrian Empire in the Hellenistic Period. More often it indicates Seleucid Syria or functions as a general designation for Mesopotamia/Mesopotamians.[108] The last meaning is found in *Pseudo-Daniel*. In other words, why would the text describe Daniel as appearing, "before the nobles of the king and the Assyrians," if the king in whose court he functions is Belshazzar (cf. 4Q244 1–2 1=CE 3)? Conflation of Assyrians and Babylonians can also be found in the third and fourth *Sibylline Oracles*, *Judith*, and *4 Maccabees*.

Assyrians are mentioned twice in the third Sybilline Oracle. The first comes in a list of seven kingdoms: "As time pursued its cyclic course the kingdom of Egypt arose, then that of the Persians, Medes, and Ethiopians, and Assyrian Babylon (Ἀσσυρίης Βαβυλῶνος), then that of the Macedonians, of Egypt again, then of Rome." In this list Assyria and Babylon are coterminous – a point reinforced by the second use of Assyria in the oracle. Lines 265–294 describe the Babylonian exile and later restoration of Jerusalem, but it is not Babylon to which the residents of Jerusalem are deported. "And you will surely flee, leaving the very beautiful temple, since it is your fate to leave the holy plain. You will be led to the Assyrians (Ἀσσυρίους) and you will see innocent children and wives in slavery to hostile men" (3:266–270). Assyrians and Babylonians are treated as synonymous. A similar meaning appears to obtain in the Fourth Sibylline Oracle.

The four kingdoms motif familiar from several ancient Near Eastern/Mediterranean texts is employed in the Fourth Sybilline Oracle. Within

---

[106] Assur deviates from traditional Aramaic orthography in favor of Hebrew orthography. Three other examples of Assyria(ns) in Aramaic texts from Qumran follow traditional Aramaic orthography, i.e., ת (אתור) instead of ש (אשור). A papyrus manuscript of Tob describes the Neo-Assyrian Empire as אתור 4QProto-Esther^e ar (4Q550 4) uses אתור to describe the territory of Mesopotamia. 4QApocryphon of Daniel ar (4Q246 i 6) uses the expression מלך אתור to describe a Seleucid king.

[107] Cf. Bennie H. Reynolds III, "אשור," in *Theologisches Wörterbuch zu den Qumrantexten* (vol. 1; ed. H. J. Fabry and U. Dahmen; Stuttgart: Kohlhammer-Verlag, 2011), forthcoming.

[108] Cf. Bennie H. Reynolds III, "Lost in Assyria: Lexico-Geographical Transmogrifications of *Assur* in Jewish Literature of the Hellenistic Period," under revision for publication. Most Hebrew examples are found in 1QM. Hanan Eshel, building on work done by Eleazar Sukenik and David Flusser, has demonstrated that the *Kittim of Ashur* is a reference to Seleucids in the *War Scroll*. Cf. Eshel, "The Kittim in the War Scroll and in the Pesharim," 29–44.

this literary framework, Assyria is used as the first kingdom: "First, the Assyrians (Ἀσσύριοι) will rule over all mortals, holding the world in their dominion for six generations from the time when the heavenly God was in wrath with the cities themselves and all men, and the sea covered the earth when the Flood burst forth." It is clear from the description of Ἀσσύριοι that it cannot designate only the Neo-Assyrian empire. The dominion of this Assyria begins immediately after the great flood in the Fourth Sibylline Oracle. Since Babylonians are never mentioned one may assume that Ἀσσύριοι refers to "Mesopotamians" in general.

Assyrians and Babylonians are also described as synonymous in Judith 12:13: "So Bagoas left the presence of Holofernes, and approached her and said, 'Let this pretty girl not hesitate to come to my lord to be honored in his presence, and to enjoy drinking wine with us, and to become today like one of the Assyrian women (θυγάτηρ μία τῶν υἱῶν Ασσουρ) who serve in the palace of Nebuchadnezzar.'" This usage of "Assyrian" closely parallels that of 4QPseudo-Daniel[a-b] ar where Assyrian Nobles are functionaries in the court of Belshazzar.

Precisely the same idea is expressed in 4 Maccabees 13:9 where one brother encourages the others with the example of Shadrach, Meshach, and Abednego familiar from Daniel: Brothers, let us die like brothers for the sake of the law; let us imitate the three youths in Assyria (Ἀσσυρίας) who despised the same ordeal of the furnace." The only difference between this passage and the previous ones is that it uses Assyria as a geo-political term, not an ethnonym. In all of these cases it appears that Assyria and Assyrians are general designation for Mesopotamia and Mesopotamians.

While Assur had a flexible semantic range in Jewish literature from the Hellenistic Period, it is categorically different than the kinds of descriptions used to depict ethno-political groups in the symbolic apocalypses. The description does not point beyond itself. It is entirely explicit whether it refers to the Neo-Assyrian Empire, to Seleucid Syria, or to Mesopotamia. The language does not participate in an underlying system of conventional associations in the same way that, for example, animals or metals are used to describe nations in symbolic apocalypses.

Within the revelation proper, מצרים Egypt (4Q243 11ii 2) is mentioned in the context of the Exodus. The use of the "mighty hand" motif as well as the description of the crossing of the Jordan (ירדנא 4Q243 12 3) in the next fragment indicates that the Exodus motif is present.[109] Thus Egypt does not connote the same meaning in *Pseudo-Daniel*[a-b] *ar* that it does in *Apocry-*

---

[109] For the association between the mighty hand motif and the Exodus tradition, see Reynolds, "Arrogance as Virtue or Vice? The Expression ביד רמה in the Hebrew Bible and the Dead Sea Scrolls."

phon of Jeremiah C. Both are explicit, but the former intends Egypt of the Late Bronze Age/Early Iron Age while the latter intends the Ptolemaic Empire. The overlapping fragments 4Q243 13 and 4Q244 12 also use the explicit description בני ישראל "Children of Israel" to name the residents of Judah on the eve of the Babylonian destruction of Jerusalem in 586 B.C.E..

In the eschatological section of the text the expression [מלכות עממי]א "a kingdom of the peoples" (4Q243 16 3) is used to describe a gentile nation. A similar and related expression is also found in the eschatological section of the text: מלכי עממיא kings of the peoples (4Q243 24 4). A Hebrew version of the expression, מלכי העמים "kings of the peoples" is used in the *Damascus Document* in a passage that condemns the so-called "princes of Judah" (Maccabees?) with an interpretation of Deut 32:33: "Their wine is serpents' venom, and the head of the cruel, harsh asps." The writer interprets this passage to mean, "The serpents are the kings of the peoples מלכי העמים and the wine their paths and the asps' head is the head of the kings of Greece" (CD-A 8 10–11=CD-B 19 22–24).[110]

Both the "kingdom of the peoples" and the "kings of the peoples" in 4QpsDan[a–b] ar are presumably Greek (Seleucid). עם cannot designate all of the people of Israel or Judah in this context because מלכות עממי]א is contrasted with the "elect" קריאי[ן elect.[111] A similar scenario appears in the eschatological predictions of 4QapocrDan ar ii 2–8 (4Q246), or, "Apocalypse of the Son of God:"

Like the comets that you saw, so will be their kingdom (מלכותהן). They will reign only a few years over the land, and all will trample – one people will trample another people (עם לעם ידוש) and one province (will trample) another province *vacat* until the people of God (עם אל) arise, then all will rest from warfare. Their kingdom will be an eternal kingdom, and all their paths will be righteous. They will judge the land justly and all will make peace. War will cease from the land and every province will pay homage to it. The great God will be their help. He himself will fight for them, placing peoples (עממין) under their control.[112]

The *Apocryphon of Daniel* is an apocalypse in which Daniel interprets the dream of a king – presumably based on help from YHWH in a vision of his own.[113] Cross argues that the designation מלכותהן "their kingdom" in II 2

---

[110] The Hebrew expression is apparently also used in 4Q299 60 4, but the fragment is not preserved well enough to contextualize the words.

[111] Neither of these phrases is used in the Book of Daniel, though the term עממיא is used seven times. In every case it designates gentiles and in all but one case it appears in the same speech formula: כל עממיא אמיא ולשניא, "all peoples, nations, and languages," cf. Dan 3:4, 7, 31, 5:19, 6:26, 7:14.

[112] Lit. "He will place peoples into his hand" (עממין ינתן בידה)

[113] There is considerable debate about this text and in particular its enigmatic ברה די אל "Son of God." I am inclined to agree with Frank Cross and John Collins that the "Son of God" figure is a

refers back to "the king of Assyria [and] (the king of) [E]gypt" in I 6, since the symbol used to represent "their kingdom" is dual or plural: רסיא "the comets." The use of עממין at the end of the text presumably includes the kingdoms represented by comets, but also others. The contrast drawn between the מלכות עממ[יא and the קריא[ין] in 4QpsDan[a–b] ar seems to reflect the same distinction made between מלכותהן and עם אל the *Apocryphon of Daniel*.

Similar scenarios and terminology may be found in another fragmentary apocalypse from Qumran: 4QNJ[a] (4Q554). *New Jerusalem[a]* recounts a heavenly journey, apparently based on Ezek 40–48, in which the visionary is given a guided tour of an ideal or eschatological temple and its environs.[114] Unlike some other heavenly journeys, *New Jerusalem* appears to include a historical section that details the *eschaton*. It describes the rise and fall of one kingdom after the other, forecasting that, "They shall do evil to your descendants until the time at which . . ." (4Q554 3iii 20). The text breaks off before describing the final eschatological reversal, but it appears to use the term עממין similarly to 4QpsDan[a–b] ar and the *Apocryphon of Daniel*: ויעב[דון] בהון עממין "And the people will commit against them" (4Q554 3iii 22).

Jewish Messiah. The other main position holds that the figure is a Syrian king or otherwise "antichrist" figure. I cannot imagine that a Jewish writer would describe a Syrian king as בר עליון. See Frank Moore Cross, "The Structure of the Apocalypse of 'Son of God' (4Q246)," in *Emanuel: Studies in Hebrew Bible, Septuagint, and Dea Sea Scrolls in Honor of Emanuel Tov* (ed. Shalom Paul, et al.; vol. XCIV of *VTSup*; Leiden: Brill, 2003), 151–8. John J. Collins, "The 'Son of God' Text from Qumran," in *From Jesus to John: Essays on Jesus and New Testament Christology in Honour of Marinus de Jonge* (ed. M. de Boer; vol. 84 of *JSNTSup*; Sheffield: Sheffield Academic Press, 1993), 65–82. (*Idem*, chapter 7 of Collins's *The Scepter and the Star*). For the alternate position originally espoused by Milik, see J.T. Milik, "Les modèles araméens du livre d'Esther dans la grotte 4 de Qumrân," *RevQ* 15 (1992). See also David Flusser, "The Hubris of the Antichrist in a Fragment from Qumran," *Imm* 10 (1980). E. Cook, "4Q246," *BBR* 5 (1995): 43–66. A middle ground is perhaps held by F. García Martínez who sees the figure as eschatological, but not a royal messiah. Martínez, *Qumran and Apocalyptic. Studies on the Aramaic Texts from Qumran*, 162–79. Florentino García Martínez, "Two Messianic Figures in the Qumran Texts," in *Technological Developments on the Dead Sea Scrolls* (ed. Donald Parry and Stephen Ricks; Leiden: Brill, 1996), 14–40.

[114] Collins, "Apocalypticism and Literary Genre in the Dead Sea Scrolls," 417–8. But see Lorenzo DiTommaso, *The Dead Sea 'New Jerusalem' Text* (TSAJ 110; Tübingen: Mohr Siebeck, 2005). He argues that the Aramaic *New Jerusalem* text is an historical apocalypse, not an otherworldly journey. There are some problems with this thesis. Like Tigchelaar, I am not entirely convinced that the city of Jerusalem in *NJ* is a normal "residential" city. Eibert Tigchelaar, "Review of *The Dead Sea New Jerusalem Text: Contents and Contexts* by Lorenzo DiTommaso," *DSD* 15 (2008): 405–6.

Raw Data from Pseudo-Daniel[a-b] *ar*

Citation		Description	Description-Type
4Q243 9 1	חנוך	Enoch	Explicit
4Q244 8 2	נוח	Noah	Explicit
4Q243 18i–ii 1	מלכו]תא	(the) kingdom	Titular
4Q243 18i–ii 2	מל]	King/kings/kingdom	Titular
4Q243 27 1	בני	The sons of	?
4Q243 11ii 2	מצרים	Egypt	Explicit
4Q243 12 4	בניהון	Their children	Titular
4Q243 28 1	ד]ניאל	Daniel	Explicit
4Q243 28 2	פינח]ס	Phineas	Explicit
4Q243 28 2	אביש]וע	Abishua	Explicit

4Q243 13 + 4Q244 14 1	בני ישראל	The children of Israel	Explicit
4Q243 13 + 4Q244 14 2	אלוהין	God	Explicit
4Q243 13 + 4Q244 14 2	שידי טעותא	The demons of error	Adjectival
4Q243 13 + 4Q244 14 3	נבכדנצר מלך בבל	Nebuchadnezzar, king of Babylon	Explicit/ Titular
4Q243 13 + 4Q244 14 4	בני גלותא	The exiles	Titular
4Q432 21 2	בלכרוס	Balakros	Explicit
4Q243 22 1	ב[ר	A son	?
4Q243 20 1	בר מל[כא	The son of the king	Titular
4Q243 20 3	מל[כא	The king	Titular

4Q243 25 4	כל שלדיהון	All their decayed carcasses	Adjectival
4Q243 16 3	חסינין	The mighty ones	Adjectival
4Q243 16 3	מלכות עממ]יא	A kingdom of the peoples	Titular/ Adjectival
4Q243 16 4	מלכותא קד]ישתא Or קד]מאה	The holy kindom Or The first/former kindom	Adjectival/ Titular
4Q243 24 2	קריאי]ן	The elect	Titular
4Q243 24 3	עממיא	The peoples	Titular
4Q243 24 4	מלכי עממיא	The kings of the peoples	Titular
4Q243 26 2	די לא מנין	(those) who were innumerable	Adjectival
4Q243 26 3	יש[ראל	Israel	Explicit

Findings From Chapter Six

One

While *Pseudo-Daniel^{a-b} ar* provides considerably less data than Dan 10–12 or the *Apocryphon of Jeremiah C*, it exhibits the same type of language. Unlike the symbolic apocalypses in part one of this study, it does not use language that points beyond itself. The revelation does not require interpretation because, like Dan 10–12, the revelation *is* the interpretation. Therefore, in terms of the distinctions of Artemidorus/Oppenheim highlighted in chapter one, *Pseudo-Daniel^{a-b} ar* falls into the non-symbolic category. It uses explicit language to describe deities, angels/demons, and humans (both individuals and groups).

Two

In chapter five we saw that much of the non-symbolic language in the *Apocryphon of Jeremiah C* is derived from Jewish scripture (i.e., Jer, Dan, Nah, and Deutero-Isa) even if it is used in ways that depart from those antecedents. *Pseudo-Daniel^{a-b} ar* also uses terminology familiar from Jewish scripture. But in some cases *Pseudo-Daniel^{a-b} ar* narrates events familiar from scripture based on variant traditions. In other words, *Pseudo-Daniel^{a-b} ar* narrates events known from the books of Genesis and Exodus (e.g, the exodus from Egypt), but uses sources other than Genesis and Exodus. For example, the text uses the name Noah (נוח), but apparently derives its Noah tradition from a text such as the *Book of the Words of Noah* rather than Genesis. The mention of Lubar instead of Ararat makes this clear. Thus, the language of *Pseudo-Daniel^{a-b} ar* appears to exhibit interaction with a variety of traditions normally associated with texts from the Hebrew Bible. It is unclear whether the language of *Pseudo-Daniel^{a-b} ar* indicates that it is attempting to usurp the authoritative status of (proto-) biblical books such as Genesis or if it merely considered the pluriform Noah traditions that obtained in the Hellenistic Period to have equal authority. More research on *Pseudo-Daniel^{a-b} ar* could further illuminate its ideological program.

Three

While the language used in *Pseudo-Daniel^{a-b} ar* is never symbolic, it is sometimes cryptic or opaque. I suggest that some of the expressions may be in-group terms. One of the characteristics of the language found in chapter five is that it is polemical. It contrasts different groups of people.

This type of contrast is not unique, but one gets the impression that unlike, for example, the contrast between the חָכָם "wise" and the כְּסִיל "fool" in the Book of Proverbs, the groups contrasted in *Apocryphon of Jeremiah C* are not merely schematic. One finds instances of this contrast in *Pseudo-Daniel*[a-b] *ar*. For example, with the advent of the *eschaton*, the חסינין "mighty ones" are contrasted with ומלכות עממ[יא "the kingdom of the peoples." Unlike monikers such as "Essene" or "Pharisee" that carried specific connotations across literary and contextual boundaries, terms like קריאין "the elect" cannot support a definitive interpretation outside of highly specific contexts. Numerous groups could have considered themselves "the elect," but it is unlikely that numerous groups considered themselves "Pharisees." Josephus outlines several distinct characteristics of Pharisees and those not bearing the characteristics would have found it difficult to claim Pharisaic identity in the eyes of others. On the other hand, groups like "the elect" or "the mighty ones" could not have commanded such rigorous associations in the eyes of most Jews in the Hellenistic Period. In other words, descriptions such as יחד "community" or מורה הצדק "The teacher of righteousness" probably only signified specific referents within a highly specific context of Essene communities. Similarly, expressions like המצדקים from Dan 10–12 and the *Apocryphon of Jeremiah C* and קריאין from 4QpsDan[a-b] ar probably only carried specific meanings within exclusive groups. The presence of group-specific terminology in 4QpsDan[a-b] ar, like the other non-symbolic apocalypses, points to the possibility that the text envisions and /or linguistically constructs a limited audience. Ironically then, the data indicate that while symbolic apocalypses appear to have been crafted with a large, general audience in mind, non-symbolic apocalypses appear to have been crafted with group-specific interests.

Chapter Seven

Conclusions

With this study I have attempted to perform a systematic analysis of the language of ancient Jewish historical apocalypses by analyzing the *dramatis personae*, i.e., deities, angels/demons, and humans (both individuals and groups), used in the historical reviews found in the Book of Daniel (2, 7, 8, 10–12) the *Animal Apocalypse* (*1 En.* 85–90), 4QFourKingdoms$^{a\text{-}b}$ ar, the *Book of the Words of Noah* (1QapGen 5 29–18?), the *Apocryphon of Jeremiah C*, and 4QPseudo-Daniel$^{a\text{-}b}$ ar. I do not summarize the brief findings from each chapter here. Instead, I offer five conclusions that synthesize the findings from each chapter. Each of the five conclusions points to one overarching thesis: the data available from the Dead Sea Scrolls fundamentally alter our picture of the language used in ancient Jewish apocalypses. In what follows I first list the individual conclusions and then discuss each one.

1. While some apocalypses encode historical actors in symbolic cipher, others use explicit, realistic language. In other words, there is such a thing as a non-symbolic apocalypse.
2. Among those apocalypses that utilize symbolic language, a limited and stable repertoire of symbols-types is used.
3. Among the apocalypses that utilize symbolic language, it appears that rather than hiding information or obscuring a private message, the symbols used in ancient Jewish apocalypses function to embed exegetical tools within the text. In other words, not only do they not attempt to hide information from outsiders, they actually provide *extra* information and attempt to make the text intelligible to a wide audience.
4. Non-symbolic apocalypses often utilize language that, while explicit and realistic, obscures their referents in a way that symbolic language does not. In other words, while the symbolic language used in apocalypses often contains within itself the very codes needed for interpretation, non-symbolic language often presents concepts that are "hidden in plain sight."

With reference to work already done on in-group language in texts from Qumran as well as U. Eco's concept of the symbolic mode I argue that non-symbolic apocalypses contain group-specific language that indicates a limited audience.

5. The variety of language within ancient Jewish historical apocalypses indicates that they derive from diverse social settings. No one quarter of Hellenistic Judaism should be described as "apocalyptic" in the Hellenistic Period.

Conclusion 1
The intellectual seed for this study is the typology used in DJD 39 to describe Jewish historical apocalypses found among the Dead Sea Scrolls.[1] In chapter one I called attention to the way that Armin Lange and Ulrike Mittmann-Richert divide historical apocalypses into two categories: "symbolic" and "non-symbolic." Lange's division serves as the starting point for this study because these categories denote more than a helpful way to organize the texts found at Qumran. They use the data recovered from Qumran to reorganize how we understand the genre apocalypse in the Hellenistic Period – even if the some implications of this reorganization are not apparent from the list itself. The bifurcation of texts into the categories "symbolic" and "non-symbolic" cuts against the grain of most scholarship dedicated to ancient Jewish apocalypses. In the history of research I summarized nearly two hundred years of scholarship and noted how virtually every student of Jewish apocalypses has proclaimed that symbolic language is a standard feature – a *sine qua non* – of all apocalypses.

Lange and Mittmann-Richert do not base their categories on a radical reinterpretation of the evidence, but on the new data provided by the Dead Sea Scrolls. In light of the new data found among the Dead Sea Scrolls and the basic incongruence between the generic categories in DJD 39 and the history of scholarship on ancient Jewish apocalypses, I framed this study as systematic analysis of the language used in Jewish historical apocalypses 333–63 B.C.E.. The first task for this study was to come up with a critical account of the distinction between symbolic and non-symbolic for the language of apocalypses.

For my basic definition of what constitutes symbolic/non-symbolic language in apocalypses, I turned to analyses of a literary genre closely related to Ancient Jewish apocalypses: dream reports. Specifically, I turned to the work of the Greek diviner/writer Artemidorus of Daldis and the Viennese

---

[1] Lange and Mittmann-Richert, "Annotated List of the Texts from the Judean Desert Classified by Genre and Content," 120–1.

born and educated Assyriologist Leo Oppenheim. Their analyses of dream reports are relevant for this study for two reasons: 1) the generic similarity of apocalypses and dream reports, and 2) the antiquity of the categories.

Oppenheim divides dream reports with revelatory value into two basic categories: message dreams and symbolic dreams. According to Oppenheim, message dreams are characterized by direct, explicit communication between a deity and a dreamer. Symbolic dreams, on the other hand, required the dreamer to seek interpretation. Oppenheim's description of symbolic language agrees with the one proposed by Artemidorus, but it does not capture an important aspect of Artemidorus' definition. What Oppenheim describes as a "symbolic" dream, Artemidorus describes as an "allegorical" (ἀλληγορικοί) dream. Artemidorus does not describe the Greek practice of *allegoresis* (from ἀλληγορέω) here. *Allegoresis* names a strategy for interpretation (e.g., Philo's allegorical interpretation of Gen), while allegory (ἀλληγορία) names a mode of text production, "a description of one thing under the image of another."[2] The latter concept is reflected in the standard English definition of allegory: a story with (at least) two levels of meaning.[3] The most famous example of this type of literature in English is probably John Bunyan's *Pilgrim's Progress* (1678).[4] So for Artemidorus, the significance of allegorical (symbolic) dreams is not only that they require interpretation (Oppenheim), but that they are constructed in a way that some or all of the words have two layers of meaning. Thus, in the examples of dreams used in chapter one, the mountain in the dream of Gilgamesh is clearly not (only) a real mountain, but something else. The cows or ears of wheat in Gen 41 are clearly not (only) cows or ears, but something else. A reader's interpretation of the cows or ears as something else is hardly a mere reader-response. The two levels of the story are intentionally built into the text. Many of Philo's interpretations (*Allegoresis*) of Genesis are decidedly not. But the use of the term allegory in English is problematic since it normally refers to an entire piece of literature and not an individual element therein. Therefore, in order to be more precise in my description of what is "symbolic" about symbolic apocalypses, I integrate the definitions of Oppenheim and Artemidorus. Descriptions used in ancient

---

[2] H. G. Liddell, An Intermediate Greek-English Lexicon Founded Upon the Seventh Edition of Liddell and Scott's Greek-English Lexicon (Oxford: Clarendon Press, 2001), 37.

[3] Cuddon, ed., *Dictionary of Literary Terms and Literary Theory*, 20–3.

[4] Cuddon summarizes the tale as follows: "This is an allegory of Christian Salvation. Christian, the hero, represents Everyman. He flees the terrible City of Destruction and sets off on his pilgrimage. In the course of it he passes through the Slough of Despond, the Interpreter's House, the House Beautiful . . . and finally arrives are the Celestial City . . .The whole work is a simplified representation or similitude of the average man's journey through the trials and tribulations of life on his way to Heaven. Cuddon, ed., *Dictionary of Literary Terms and Literary Theory*, 20–1.

Jewish apocalypses are symbolic if they point beyond their basic, plain-sense meaning and require a visionary to seek interpretation. Revelations in which visionaries and heavenly beings carry on direct, explicit conversations are not symbolic. I apply this definition to most, though not every, text that might reasonably be labeled an apocalypse from the period 333–63 B.C.E.. The resulting picture of historical apocalypses is highly similar to, though not precisely the same as, the list produced by Lange and Mittmann-Richert in DJD 39. Below I provide the chart used by Lange and Mittmann-Richert followed by my own chart. In my chart an asterisk* is placed by those texts I analyze. My chart is larger because I consider apocalypses from the Hebrew Bible itself as well as some texts listed by Lange and Mittmann-Richert under other genres (I note that they would not necessarily disagree with their placement in this chart since genres are not existential entities. In other words, some texts can reasonably fit into more than one genre).

Lange and Mittman-Richert:[5]

Symbolic Apocalypses	Non-Symbolic Apocalypses
Book of Dreams (*1 En.* 83–90)	4QHistorical Text A (4Q248)
4QapocrDan ar (4Q246)	*Apocryphon of Jeremiah* A, B?, C^{a-f} (4Q383, 384, 385a, 387, 388a, 389–90, 387a)
4Q FourKingdoms^{a-b} ar (4Q552–553)	4QpsDan^{a-b} ar (4Q243–244)
	4QpsDan^C ar (4Q245)
	Words of Michael (4Q529, 6Q23?)

---

[5] Lange and Mittmann-Richert, "Annotated List of the Texts from the Judean Desert Classified by Genre and Content," 141–2.

Reynolds:

Symbolic Apocalypses	Non-Symbolic Apocalypses
Daniel 2*	Daniel 10–12*
Daniel 7*	4QPseudo-Daniel[a-b] ar (4Q243–244)*
Daniel 8*	*Apocryphon of Jeremiah A–C* *
Animal Apocalypse *	*Apocalypse of Weeks*
4QFourKingdoms[a-b] ar (4Q552–553)*	4QWords of Michael ar (4Q529, 6Q23)
Book of the Words of Noah (second dream of Noah)*	4QVision[a] ar (4Q556)?
Book of Giants (dream of Hahyah)	4QVision[c] ar (4Q557)?
4QapocrDan ar (4Q246, i.e., "Aramaic Apocalypse")	*Vision of the Earth's Destruction* (*Book of Dreams*)
4QpapVision[b] ar (4Q558)?	4QHistorical Text A (4Q248)

The basic difference between symbolic and non-symbolic apocalypses can be seen in the Book of Daniel alone. In Dan 7 and 8, the visionary experiences dreams/visions of animals. It is clear, however, that the animals represent more than mere animals. The meaning of the animals is unintelligble to Daniel so an angel interprets their meaning for him. The inclusion of heavenly interpretations distinguishes symbolic apocalypses from symbolic dream reports. The interpretation of symbolic dreams is normally external to the dream experience. Thus apocalypses that use symbolic ciphers always hover somewhere between symbolism and realism. The non-symbolic apocalypses, however, are quite close to the form of non-symbolic dream reports. For example, in Dan 10–12, the visionary carries on a clear, explicit conversation with a heavenly being from beginning to end. He never has to ask for interpretation since he receives direct communication. This vision model is much closer to Oppenheim's "message dream" (reflected in the dreams of Nabonidus and Samuel discussed in chapter one). In light of the larger evidence pool provided by the Qumran library, the distinction between symbolic and non-symbolic apocalypses now seems rudimentary. But the analysis of each term used to describe actors in historical apocalypses has led to other, less anticipated results.

Conclusion 2
It became obvious relatively early in my research that my basic definitions of symbolic and non-symbolic language were not capable of fully explaining the language encountered in Jewish historical apocalypses. But only once the texts were segregated in this way were some of the finer distinctions visible. The descriptions of deities, angels/demons, persons, and groups in symbolic apocalypses are not drawn from a diverse or varied pool of terms. Symbolic apocalypses use a limited and stable stock of symbol-types. These symbol types tend to have conventional associations that are sometimes limited to one text, but more often obtain across the entire genre during the Hellenistic Period. For example, humans are almost always used to represent angels and animals are almost always used to represent humans. In other words, while there is always a surface-level association based on the allegory present in any given symbolic apocalypses (i.e., the little horn of Dan 7 represents Antiochus IV Epiphanes), there are also much deeper structures/associations present in each apocalypse.

These deeper structures within the symbolic language of apocalypses cannot be properly described or explained with reference to only the symbolic/non-symbolic typology of Artemidorus/Oppenheim. The conventional associations that often appear on the level of symbol-types prompted me to turn to the work of F. de Saussure and C. Peirce – the founders of Structuralism and Semiotics. The conventional associations/structures that I found in symbolic apocalypses are not the same as the "deep" structures highlighted by most Structuralists – in the case of apocalypses such a deep, binary structure might be the opposition between heaven and earth or light and darkness. But the categories used by Structuralists can provide a nomenclature to better describe the conventional pairs one observes in apocalypses because they force one to consider the implications of symbolic language beyond the significance of any particular symbol/referent combination. It alerts one to more fundamental features of discourse in Jewish writing from the Hellenistic Period. I highlighted that the basic concept of symbol developed (independently) by de Saussure and Peirce have been applied outside the fields of linguistics and mathematics. Roland Barthes's work on fashion and Jonathan Culler's work on the (French) novel are notable examples. But perhaps the best analogy for this study is Claude Levi-Strauss's work on totemism, i.e., the phenomenon by which certain tribes are associated or described with certain animals.

For Levi-Strauss, to explain a given totem is to understand its place in a system of signs – not merely its particular connection to the culture/group it names.[6] In other words, if one culture is named bear, another fish, and another hawk, it is important to understand the relationships between bears, fish, and hawks at least as much as it is important to understand the relationship between a particular group and "bear."[7] Indeed the totality of the symbolic system at work is what allows one to understand how a single example functions. In terms of Jewish symbolic apocalypses, this might mean that in order to understand properly the relationship between a little horn and Antiochus IV Epiphanes, one cannot merely attempt to analyze what might be held in common between the horn and Antiochus, but between the little horn and all other symbols in Dan 7 as well as other apocalypses. Therefore in chapters two and three I considered not only how each individual symbol names its referent, but if and how patterns of representation emerge when one considers the relationship between the symbols themselves. A series of conventional relationships emerged that are not entirely different from De Saussure's concept of the symbol in language or Peirce's concept of the symbol in mathematics and philosophy. For example, π is a conventional description of the number 3.14159. There is nothing about π from which one could logically deduce the number 3.14159.

---

[6] By reading into the social structure of several native peoples a basic opposition between nature and culture, Lévi-Strauss describes the relationships between particular tribes and their "totems" in a series of possible relationships. For him, the very idea of totemism is the unfortunate result of an overly simplistic imagination of the relationship between a given tribe and an animal or plant type. "The totemic illusion is thus the result, in the first place, of a distortion of a semantic field to which belong phenomena of the same type. Certain aspects of this field have been singled out at the expense of others, giving them an originality and a strangeness which they do not really possess; for they are made to appear mysterious by the very fact of abstracting them from the system of which, as transformations, they formed an integral part." Lévi-Strauss, *Totemism*, 18.

[7] Lévi-Strauss, *Totemism*, 15–31, esp., 28–9.

One only understands the relationship because of convention. Similarly, there is nothing that allows one to deduce a relationship between stars and angels or animals and humans. It is a conventional relationship. By analyzing all symbols in all historical apocalypses, a series of conventional relationships emerged. Several of these conventional pairs are found in multiple texts across the genre. There is, then, a limited and stable repertoire of symbol-categories in ancient Jewish historical apocalypses. As noted in chapters one and two, A. Lange has already performed an initial investigation into the systems at work behind apocalyptic symbols.[8] He called attention to the use of flora and fauna to represent humans and stars and humans to represent angels and humans in Daniel and the *Animal Apocalypse*.[9] I have been able to enlarge and sharpen our image of the deeper structures involved in symbolic language. Below I list the limited and stable repertoire of symbols-types used in ancient Jewish apocalypses as well as the conventional associations in which they participate. I anticipated that by considering a larger evidence pool than Lange I would discover a much larger number of conventional associations within the symbolic language of Jewish apocalypses. As the chart below shows, however, I have added only a few additional symbol types. This limited and stable repertoire of symbols that obtains in all symbolic apocalypses has serious implications for the contexts in which these texts were read. This leads to conclusion 3 below.

Symbol-Type	Referent
Humans	Angels
Stars	Angels
Animals -Horns	Humans (both individuals and groups)

---

[8] Lange, "Dream Visions and Apocalyptic Milieus," 27–34.
[9] Lange, "Dream Visions and Apocalyptic Milieus," 28–31.

Trees	Humans (both individuals and groups – though predominantly individuals)
-branches	
Metals	Humans (ethno-political groups, i.e., kingdoms only)

Conclusion 3
The presence of conventional symbolic systems – often embedded within literary motifs with wide cultural cache, e.g., the four kingdoms motif – affects how one interprets the function of any one particular symbol. The view of H. H. Rowley remains popular today – especially among non-specialists. He held that the writers of apocalypses used symbols as a means of hiding resistance-communities from imperial overlords and protecting them from reprisal.[10] Rowley viewed the language of apocalypse as similar to that used by the resistance in German occupied Europe during World War II. His own socio-historical location makes his interpretation entirely understandable. I pointed out that one of the most influential theorists of our day, James C. Scott, has essentially also argued that communities of resistance use tools such as language to produce a "hidden transcript."[11] This hidden transcript would agree with the basic thesis of Rowley (and Hanson). I do not merely reject Rowley's thesis, I suggest its opposite. The symbols used in apocalypses do not hide anything. They provide additional information that explicit, realistic descriptions alone cannot provide. For example, instead of describing Antiochus IV Epiphanes with his personal name or with a title such as "King of the North," both of which are completely neutral, Dan 7 describes Antiochus as a "little horn." Within the description of a ferocious beast with many horns, the description of Antiochus as a "little horn" is almost certainly a slight – a way to disparage Antiochus. The swipe at Antiochus is not simply a general one since the description of him as a little horn serves to contrast him with other horns (Greek kings). In other words, Antiochus is the worst of the Greek kings in Palestine. Indeed, it is on account of the small horn that the fourth beast

---

[10] Rowley, The Relevance of Apocalyptic, 50.
[11] Something like a "hidden transcript" may be found in the non-symbolic apocalypses, but, as I point out, in those cases it is incidental. In other words it seems unlikely that the language is *designed* to keep others out even if it has that practical effect.

ultimately loses its life: "I watched then because of the noise of the arrogant words that the horn was speaking. And as I watched, the beast was put to death, and its body destroyed and given over to be burned with fire" (Dan 7:11). The description of Antiochus as a little horn does not hide or obscure his identity. It tells one more than his personal name or title alone could. Symbolic apocalypses were not designed for a small group of insiders, but rather for general public consumption. This conclusion is indicated by the limited repertoire of symbol categories, the regularity of conventional associations within these categories, and the widespread motifs within which symbolic language is often embedded. One need only compare the variety of symbol types in Ancient Neast Eastern dream reports or even the visions found in the prophetic texts of the Hebrew Bible with the symbols used in apocalypses in order to measure just how regular and consistent are the symbol types found in ancient apocalypses. The symbol types found in Artemidorus alone are legion. On the other hand, the chart above catalogs only a small number of symbol types for all Jewish historical apocalypses written between 333 and 63 B.C.E.. The implications of this type of language are significant. The language of symbolic apocalypses contains within itself sufficient exegetical tools for use by a broad swath of Hellenistic Jewish culture. Symbolic apocalypses appear to have been constructed in order to appeal to the largest possible audience. Ironically, the opposite appears to be true for non-symbolic apocalypses.

Conclusion 4
An unexpected problem with the language of several apocalypses manifested itself in my analysis of the texts in chapters four, five, and six. None of these apocalypses are symbolic in terms of the primary criterion appropriated from Artemidorus/Oppenheim. They do not use descriptions that point beyond themselves/require interpretation. Dan 10–12, *Apocryphon of Jeremiah C*, and 4QpsDan[a–b] ar all use descriptions whose meanings are exhausted by a plain-sense reading. In other words, they mean what they say. This stands in contrast to symbolic apocalypses in which an animal might not be used to describe an animal, but something else that the animal represents. In an ironic twist, however, the non-symbolic language of apocalypses like Dan 10–12 is sometimes more occluded than the "symbolic" language found in a text like Dan 7. Whereas the symbolic apocalypses often contain deeply embedded exegetical tools based on conventional and (relatively) simple allegories that include widespread motifs, non-symbolic apocalypses sometimes use language that is unintelligible when divorced from highly specialized interpretative contexts or communities. Recent work on the Essene texts from Qumran has attempted to isolate features

such as polemical language, dualistic language, and particular exegetical strategies as reflective of efforts to construct identities in a group-specific context.[12] Similarly, the language of non-symbolic apocalypses often serves to build cohesion and identity among those who are "in the know." This notion of semiosis might be usefully applied to several of the explicit descriptions found in non-symbolic apocalypses. For example, the expression מַצְדִּיקֵי הָרַבִּים "those who lead many to righteousness" in Dan 12:3 is open to various meanings in a way that the beasts in Dan 7 and 8 are not. The beasts in Daniel are governed by their participation in a system of conventional pairs as well as their participation in an allegory as well as common literary motifs. "Unlimited semiosis" in U. Eco's terms is ultimately not possible for the beasts in Dan 7–8 despite the fact that sometimes outrageous interpretations have been suggested. A different situation obtains with "those who lead many to righteousness." The meaning of the expression is governed only by its immediate literary context. One gets the distinct impression that the only way to know the identity of "those who lead many to righteousness" is to be one of them. Similar expressions are found in *Apocryphon of Jeremiah C* and 4QPseudo-Daniel[a-b] ar. Expressions such as מרישיעי ברית "those who act wickedly against the covenant" (4Q385a 5a–b 9=4Q387 3 6) and קריאין "the elect" (4Q243 16 4) do not point beyond themselves nor does the visionary require an interpretation for them. The opaque and apparently exclusive language found in non-symbolic apocalypses suggests that they were intended for much more limited audiences than their symbolic counterparts. The function of this language appear to be the creation and sustaining of what Michael Barkun calls the "microcosm" of apocalypticism. A foundational principle of apocalypticism is the highlighting (or more likely, linguistic construction) of the dualism between a righteous microcosm and an evil macrocosm. It is difficult to find examples of groups that sustain an apocalyptic worldview without this crucial distinction. It is notable, in addition, that none of the three non-symbolic apocalypses appears to reflect the same social group. The writer of *Apocryphon of Jeremiah C* certainly borrowed from Dan 10–12, but also from several other texts.

A related issue requires further research. In several cases distinct symbolic and non-symbolic apocalypses have been brought together in the same piece of literature. This situation obtains in the Book of Daniel and in 1 Enoch's *Book of Dreams*. Whether or not one text might have been used

---

[12] Several relevant examples can be found in Martínez and Popović, eds., *Defining Identities: We, You, and the Other in the Dead Sea Scrolls. Proceedings of the Fifth Meeting of the IOQS in Groningen*. The contributions of Grossman, Newsom, and Nickelsburg are discussed in chapters five and six.

intentionally to contextualize or interpret the other is not clear. It seems clear that regardless of the editor's intentions, the proximity of Dan 10–12 to Dan 2, 4, 7, and 8 probably led multiple generations of scholars to describe the language of Dan 10–12 in terms of the language found in Daniel's symbolic apocalypses.

Conclusion 5

A final observation that may be drawn from the group-specific language used by some apocalypses is that the phenomenon of apocalypticism and the production of literary apocalypses seem to have been a widespread phenomenon and not just the product of one or more small fringe groups. The language found in symbolic apocalypses appears to suggest that these texts were designed for wide use among Jews of the Hellenistic Period. At the same time the group-specific language of the non-symbolic apocalypses appears to indicate that some apocalypses were the domain of more limited target-audiences. Moreover, the diversity of in-group terms indicates that Dan 10–12, *Apocryphon of Jeremiah C*, and 4QPseudo-Daniel^{a-b} ar could point to at least three distinct in-groups in which apocalypses were read. There are obvious continuities between these groups, but the ways in which identity is constructed in each text indicates that they were probably not the domain of only one or two groups.

Numerous large and small Jewish groups appear to have produced literature that we may refer to as apocalypses. Apocalypse is thus simultaneously a mainstream and a fringe movement – a literature for poor and wealthy, for powerful and powerless alike.[13] This conclusion comports with the picture of modern apocalypticism painted in the most recent sociological analyses.[14] Modern apocalypticism seems not united by a particular social or economic stratum within society, but by a peculiar ideology – millenarianism: the belief in the imminent end of the world. This ideology explains the unlikely common ground created by, for example, the respective expectations of the return of Jesus and the Twelfth Imam by American evangelicals and Iranian Shiites.[15] Reading apocalypses is not the domain

---

[13] Cf. Stephen Cook, *The Apocalyptic Literature* (Nashville: Abingdon, 2003), 1–38, 62–87.

[14] Cf. Thomas Robbins and Susan Palmer, eds., *Millennium, Messiahs, and Mayhem: Contemporary Apocalyptic Movements* (New York: Routledge, 1997). Michael Barkun, *A Culture of Conspiracy*. Stephen Stein, ed., The Encyclopedia of Apocalypticism 3: Apocalypticism in the Modern Period and the Contemporary Age (New York: Continuum, 1998).

[15] Especially instructive is the diverse compilation of millenialists in Robbins and Palmer, *Millenium, Messiahs, and Mayhem*. See also the sometimes humorous stories surrounding the beliefs and lives of several American figures gathered together in Bart Ehrman, *Jesus: Apocalyptic Prophet of the New Millenium* (Oxford: Oxford University Press, 1999), 3–19. The contrast of

of one kind of social group in the modern world and it was apparently not in Hellenistic Judaism either. Therefore, one will probably search in vain for "apocalyptic" Judaism if one imagines by that expression a limited and specific social group or even a marginal strain within the larger society. Instead, the apocalypses from Qumran have sufficiently enlarged and changed our pool of evidence to show that apocalypticism is an ideology that affected different elements of Hellenistic Judaism in different ways with different results.

If the language of apocalypses can point to the varied social contexts behind the texts, one might ask if they also help to precisely identify specific social groups behind the texts. I mentioned in chapter five that there are some indications that *Apocryphon of Jeremiah C* might have been a Pharisaic text. But this is far from clear. In general I do not think that there is enough evidence to support connecting any of the texts studied here to a specific group within Second Temple Judaism. Moreover the impulse to use these texts to create place-holders for social groups that are unknown to us from other sources (e.g., "Danielic Judaism," or "Enochic Judaism" or "Pseudo-Danielic Judaism," etc.) seems to me imprudent.[16] It is enough for now to acknowledge the continuities and diversity within Second Temple Jewish thought reflected in the genre apocalypse. The texts studied here paint a picture of a topsy-turvy, sometimes monstrous world. This world produces real and quantifiable suffering, but is ultimately a façade behind which exists a cosmos where time and space is ordered precisely and properly. The origins and end of the chaotic world are imagined differently in many of the texts studied here and reflect different hopes, fears, prejudices, and virtues. These texts embody the paradox of Jewish identity during the Second Temple Period reflected in the scholarly debates that modulate between categories such as "common Judaism" and "Judaisms."

Edgar Whisenant, Hal Lindsey, and William Miller in terms of their education and social positions is all the more surprising in light of their similar beliefs about the apocalypse.

[16] See also Collins, "'Enochic Judaism' and the Sect of the Dead Sea Scrolls," 283–99.

Bibliography

Jerome's Commentary on Daniel. Translated by Gleason Archer. Grand Rapids: Baker Book House, 1956.
"lamassu." Pages 60–6 in *The Assyrian Dictionary of the Oriental Institute of the University of Chicago.* Edited by M. Civil, Ignace Gelb, Leo Oppenheim, and Erica Reiner. Chicago: The Oriental Institute, 1973.
"aladlammû." Pages 286–7 in *The Assyrian Dictionary of the Oriental Institute of the University of Chicago.* Edited by Ignace Gelb, Benno Landsberger, Leo Oppenheim, and Erica Reiner. Chicago: The Oriental Institute, 1964.
"Saussure." Pages 6–15 in *Modern Literary Theory: A Reader.* Edited by Philip Rice and Patricia Waugh. New York: Arnold, 1996.
Abegg, Martin, ed. *The Dead Sea Scrolls Concordance. Volume One: The Non-Biblical Texts from Qumran.* Leiden: Brill, 2003.
Aharoni, Yohanan. *Arad Inscriptions.* Jerusalem: Israel Exploration Society, 1981.
———. "Arad: Its Inscriptions and Temple." *BA* 13 (1968): 2–32.
Albani, Matthias. *Astronomie und Schöpfungsglaube: Untersuchungen zum astronomischen Henochbuch* Neukirchen-Vluyn: Neukirchener 2000.
———. "The Downfall of Helel, the Son of Dawn: Aspects of Royal Theology in Isa 14:12–13." Pages 62–86 in *The Fall of the Angels.* Edited by Christoph Auffarth and Loren Stuckenbruck. Leiden: Brill, 2004.
Albertz, Rainer. *Der Gott des Daniel: Untersuchungen zu Daniel 4–6 in der Septuagintafassung sowie zu Komposition und Theologie des aramäischen Danielbuches.* Vol. 131, Stuttgarter Bibelstudien. Stuttgart: Verlag Katholisches Bibelwerk, 1988.
Albright, William F. "The North-Canaanite Epic of 'Al'êyân Ba'al and Môt." *JPOS* 12 (1932): 185–208.
Alexander, Philip. "The Demonology of the Dead Sea Scrolls." in *The Dead Sea Scrolls after Fifty Years: A Comprehensive Assessment.* Edited by Peter Flint and James VanderKam. Leiden: Brill, 1999.
Anderson, Francis and David Noel Freedman. *Hosea*, AB 24. New York: Doubleday, 1980.
Anderson, Gary and Michael Stone. *A Synopsis of the Books of Adam and Eve.* Second Rev. Ed. Vol. 17 of SBLEJL. Atlanta: Society of Biblical Literature, 1999.
Anderson, Jeff. "From 'Communities of Texts' to Religious Communities: Problems and Pitfalls." Pages 351–55 in *Enoch and Qumran Origins: New Light on a Forgotten Connection.* Edited by Gabriele Boccaccini. Grand Rapids, MI: Eerdmans, 2005.
Angel, Andrew. *Chaos and the Son of Man: The Hebrew Chaoskampf Tradition in the Period 515 B.C.E. to 200 CE.* London: T&T Clark, 2006.
Artemidorus. *The Interpretation of Dreams (Oneirocritica).* Translated by Robert White. Park Ridge, NJ: Noyes, 1975.
Aruz, Joan, Prudence Harper, and Francoise Tallon. *The Royal City of Susa.* New York: The Metropolitan Museum of Art, 1993.
Assefa, Daniel. *L'Apocalypse des animaux (1 Hen 85–90) une propagande militaire? Approches narrative, historico-critique, perspectives théologiques.* Vol. 120 of JSJSup. Leiden: Brill, 2007.
Assman, Jan. *Death and Salvation in Ancient Egypt.* Ithaca: Cornell University Press, 2005.

Austin, Michael. *The Hellenistic World From Alexander to the Roman Conquest. A Selection of Ancient Sources in Translation*. 2nd Augmented Ed. ed. Cambridge: Cambridge University Press, 2006.

Avigad, N. and Y. Yadin. *A Genesis Apocryphon: A Scroll from the Desert of Judah: Description and Contents of the Scroll, Facsimiles, Transcription and Translation of Columns II, XIX–XXII*. Jerusalem: Magnes Press, 1956.

Bagnall, R. S. and P.S. Derow. *The Hellenistic Period. Historical Sources in Translation*. Oxford Oxford University Press, 2003.

Baillet, Maurice. *Qumrân grotte 4.III (4Q482–4Q520)*, Vol. VII of DJD. Oxford: Clarendon, 1982.

Bainbridge, W. S. *A Sociology of Religious Movements*. New York: Routledge, 1997.

Baines, John. "Writing, invention and early development." Pages 882–5 in *Encyclopedia of the Archaeology of Ancient Egypt*. Edited by Kathryn Bard. London: Routledge, 1999.

Barkun, Michael. *Disaster and the Millenium*. New Haven: Yale University Press, 1974.

———. *A Culture of Conspiracy: Apocalyptic Visions in Contemporary America*. Berkeley: University of California, 2003.

Bartelmus, R. "Die Tierwelt in der Bibel II: Tiersymbolik im Alten Testament – examplarisch dargestellt am Beispiel von Dan 7, Ez 1/10, und Jer 11, 68." Pages 283–306 in *Gefärten und Feinde des Menschen. Das Tier in der Lebenswelt des alten Israel*. Edited by B. Janowski, U. Neumann-Gorsolke, and U. Glessmer. Neukirchen-Vluyn: Neukirchener Verlag, 1993.

Barthes, Roland. *Elements of Semiology*. New York: Hill and Wang, 1967.

———. *Système de la mode*. Paris: Seuil, 1967.

Baumgartner, W. "Ein Vierteljahrhundert Danielforschung." *ThR* 11 (1939).

Beaulieu, Paul-Alain. "The Sippar Cylinder of Nabonidus (2.123A)." Pages 310–13 in *The Context of Scripture*. Edited by William Hallo and K. Lawson Younger. Leiden: Brill, 2003.

Bedenbender, Andreas. *Der Gott der Welt tritt auf den Sinai : Entstehung, Entwicklung und Funktionsweise der frühjüdischen Apokalyptik*. Vol. 8 of ANTZ. Berlin: Institut Kirche und Judentum, 2000.

Beebee, Thomas. *The Ideology of Genre: A Comparative Study of Generic Instability*. University Park, PA: Penn State University Press, 1994.

Bengtsson, Håkan. *What's in a Name? A Study of the Sobriquets in the Pesharim*. Uppsala: Uppsala University Press, 2000.

Bennett, Patrick. *Comparative Semitic Linguistics: A Manual*. Winona Lake: Eisenbrauns, 1998.

Bentzen, Aage. "Daniel 6: Ein Versuch zur Vorgeschichte der Märtyrlegende." in *Festschrift A. Bertholet*. Edited by Walter Baumgartner, Otto Eisenfeldt, Karl Elliger, and Leonhard Rost. Tübingen: Mohr, 1950.

Bergen, Theodore. *Fifth Ezra: The Text, Origin, and Early History*. Vol. 25 of SBLSCSS. Atlanta: Scholars Press, 1990.

Berlin, Andrea. "Archaeological Sources for the History of Palestine: Between Large Forces: Palestine in the Hellenistic Period." *BA* 60 (1997): 2–51.

Bernstein, Moshe. "Angels at the Aqedah: A Study in the Development of a Midrashic Motif." *DSD* 7 (2000): 263–91.

———. "From the Watchers to the Flood: Story and Exegesis in the Early Columns of the Genesis Apocryphon." Pages 39–63 in *Reworking the Bible: Apocryphal and Related Texts at Qumran. Proceedings of a Joint Symposium by the Orion Center for the Study of the Dead Sea Scrolls and Associated Literature and the Hebrew University Institute for Advanced Studies Research Group on Qumran, 15–17 January, 2002*. Edited by E. Chazon, D. Dimant, and R. Clements. Vol. LVIII of STDJ. Leiden: Brill, 2005.

———. "Pseudepigraphy in the Qumran Scrolls: Categories and Functions." Pages 1–26 in *Pseudepigraphic Perspectives: The Apocrypha and Pseudepigrapha in Light of the Dead Sea Scrolls*. Edited by Esther Chazon and Michael Stone. Vol. 31 of STDJ. Leiden: Brill, 1999.

———. "Noah and the Flood at Qumran." Pages 199–231 in *The Provo International Conference on the Dead Sea Scrolls. Technological Innovations, New Texts, & Reformulated Issues*. Edited by D. Parry and E. Ulrich. Vol. 30 of STDJ. Leiden Brill, 1999.
Beyer, Klaus. *Die aramäischen Texte von Toten Meer*. Göttingen: Vandenhoeck & Ruprecht, 1984.
Bilbija, Jovan. "Review of Scott Noegel, Nocturnal Ciphers: The Allusive Language of Dreams in the Ancient Near East." *ZAW* 98 (2008): 138–42.
Binst, Olivier, ed. *The Levant: History and Archaeology in the Eastern Mediterranean*. Cologne: Könemann, 2000.
Black, J., A. George, and N. Postgate. *A Concise Dictionary of Akkadian*, Vol. 5 of SANTAG 5. Wiesbaden: Harrassowitz Verlag, 2000.
Black, Matthew. "The Apocalypse of Weeks in the Light of 4QEn^g." *VT* 28 (1978): 464–9.
———. *Apocalypsis Henochi Graece*. Leiden: Brill, 1970.
———. *The Book of Enoch, or, 1 Enoch: A New English Edition with Commentary and Textual Notes*. Vol. 7 of SVTP. Leiden: Brill, 1985.
Blasius, Andreas. "Antiochus IV Epiphanes and the Ptolemaic Triad: The Three Uprooted Horns in Dan 7:8, 20 and 24 Reconsidered." *JSJ* 37 (2006): 521–47.
Blum, Erhard. "Formgeschichte – A Misleading Category? Some Critical Remarks." Pages 32–45 in *The Changing Face of Form Criticism for the Twenty-First Century*. Edited by Marvin Sweeney and Ehud Ben Zvi. Grand Rapids: Eerdmans, 2003.
Boccaccini, Gabriele. *Beyond the Essene Hypothesis: The Parting of the Ways between Qumran and Enochic Judaism*. Grand Rapids: Eerdmans, 1998.
———. *Middle Judaism: Jewish Thought, 300 B.C.E. to 200 C.E.* Minneapolis: Fortress Press, 1991.
———. *Roots of Rabbinic Judaism: An Intellectual History from Ezekiel to Daniel*. Grand Rapids: Eerdmans, 2002.
Bottéro, Jean. *Religion in Ancient Mesopotamia*. Chicago: University of Chicago Press, 2001.
Brady, Monica. Prophetic Traditions at Qumran: A Study of 4Q393–391. Ph.D. Diss.: University of Notre Dame, 2000.
Braulik, Georg. "Das Deuteronomium und die Geburt des Monotheismus." Pages 115–59 in *Gott, der einzige: zur Entstehung des Monotheismus in Israel*. Edited by Ernst Haag. Freiburg im Breisgau: Herder, 1985.
Brekelmans, C. "The Saints of the Most High and Their Kingdom." *OTS* 14 (1965): 305–29.
Briant, Pierre. *From Cyrus to Alexander. A History of the Persian Empire*. Winona Lake: Eisenbrauns, 2002.
Brown, T. *Justin's history of the world from the Assyrian monarchy down to the time of Augustus Cæsar; being an abridgment of Trogus Pompeius's Philippic history, with critical remarks upon Justin*. London: D. Midwinter and H. Clements, 1719.
Brownlee, William H. "The Wicked Priest, the Man of Lies, and the Righteous Teacher: The Problem of Identity." *JQR* 73 (1982): 1-37.
Brunner-Traut, Emma. "Epilogue: Aspective." Pages 421–46 in *Principles of Egyptian Art*. Edited by Oxford Griffith Institute, 1986.
———. *Frühformen des Erkennens: Aspektive im Alten Ägypten*. Darmstadt: Wissenschaftliche Buchgesselschaft, 1992.
Budin, Stephanie Lynn. *The Myth of Sacred Prostitution in Antiquity*. Cambridge: Cambridge University Press, 2008.
Burstein, Stanley. *The Hellenistic Age from the Battle of Ipsos to the Death of Kleopatra VII*. Cambridge: Cambridge University Press, 1985.
Campbell, Antony. "Form Criticism's Future." Pages 15–31 in *The Changing Face of Form Criticism for the Twenty-First Century*. Edited by Marvin Sweeney and Ehud Ben Zvi. Grand Rapids: Eerdmans, 2003.
Campbell, Jonathan. *The Use of Scripture in the Damascus Document 1–8, 19–20*. Vol. 228 of BZAW. Berlin: de Gruyter, 1995.

Camping, Harold. *Time Has an End: A Biblical History of the World 11, 013 BC–AD 2011.* New York: Vantage Press, 2005.

Caquot, André. "Sur les quatre Bêtes de Daniel VII." *Semitica* 5 (1955): 10.

Caragounis, C. "History and Supra-History: Daniel and the Four Empires." Pages 387–97 in *The Book of Daniel in the Light of New Findings*. Edited by Adam van der Woude. Vol. CVI of BETL. Leuven: Peeters, 1993.

Carey, Greg. *Ultimate Things: An Introduction to Jewish and Christian Apocalyptic Literature*. St. Louis: Chalice Press, 2005.

Carmignac, Jean. "Qu'est-ce que l'apocalyptique? Son emploi à Qumrân." *RevQ* 10 (1979): 3–33.

———. "Description du phénomène de l'Apocalyptique dans l'Ancient Testament." Pages 162–70 in *Apocalypticism in the Mediterranean World and the Near East*. Edited by David Hellholm. Tübingen: Mohr Siebeck, 1983.

Chandler, Daniel. *Semiotics: The Basics*. London: Routledge, 2002.

Charles, R. H. *A Critical and Exegetical Commentary on The Revelation of St. John*. 1975 [1920]: T&T Clark, 1920.

Charlesworth, James. *The Pesharim and Qumran History: Chaos or Consensus*. Grand Rapids: Eerdmans, 2002.

Clifford, Richard. "The Roots of Apocalypticism in Near Eastern Myth." Pages 3–38 in *The Encyclopedia of Apocalypticism*. Edited by John J. Collins. New York: Continuum, 1998.

Cohen, Margaret. "Traveling Genres." *New Literary History* 34, no. 3 [Theorizing Genres II] (2003): 481–99.

Collins, Adela Yarbro. *Crisis and Catharsis: The Power of the Apocalypse*. Philadelphia: Westminster, 1984.

Collins, John J. *Apocalypse: The Morphology of a Genre*. Vol. 14 of *Semeia*. Missoula, Mont.: Scholars Press, 1979.

———. *The Apocalyptic Imagination: An Introduction to Jewish Apocalyptic Literature*. 2nd ed. Grand Rapids: W.B. Eerdmans, 1998.

———. *The Apocalyptic Vision of the Book of Daniel*, Vol. 16 of HSM. Missoula: Scholars Press, 1977.

———. *Apocalypticism in the Dead Sea Scrolls*. London: Routledge, 1997.

———. "Cosmos and Salvation: Jewish Wisdom and Apocalyptic in the Hellenistic Age." *HR* 17 (1977): 121–42.

———. *Daniel*. Hermeneia. Minneapolis: Fortress Press, 1993.

———. "Jewish Apocalyptic Against Its Hellenistic Near Eastern Environment." *BASOR* 220 (1975): 27–36.

———. "The Place of the Fourth Sibyl in the Development of the Jewish Sibyllina." *JJS* 25 (1974): 365–80.

———. *Seers, Sybils, and Sages in Hellenistic-Roman Judaism*. Leiden: Brill, 2001.

———. "The Symbolism of Transcendence in Jewish Apocalyptic." *BR* 19 (1974): 5–22.

———. "Enoch, the Dead Sea Scrolls, and the Essenes: Groups and Movements in Judaism in the Early Second Century B.C.E." Pages 345–50 in *Enoch and Qumran Origins: New Light on a Forgotten Connection*. Edited by Gabriele Boccaccini. Grand Rapids, MI: Eerdmans, 2005.

———. "The 'Son of God' Text from Qumran." Pages 65–82 in *From Jesus to John: Essays on Jesus and New Testament Christology in Honour of Marinus de Jonge*. Edited by M. de Boer. Vol. 84 of JSNTSup. Sheffield: Sheffield Academic Press, 1993.

———. "'Enochic Judaism' and the Sect of the Dead Sea Scrolls." Pages 283–99 in *The Early Enoch Literature*. Edited by Gabriele Boccaccini and John J Collins. Vol. 121 of JSJSup. Leiden: Brill, 2007.

———. "Introduction: Towards the Morphology of a Genre." in *Semeia* 14. Edited by John J Collins. Missoula: Scholars Press, 1979.

———. "The Jewish Apocalypses." Pages 21–59 in *Semeia* 14. Edited by John J Collins. Missoula: Scholars Press, 1979.

———. "Apocalypticism and Literary Genre in the Dead Sea Scrolls." Pages 403–30 in *The Dead Sea Scrolls After Fifty Years: A Comprehensive Assessment*. Edited by Peter Flint and James VanderKam. Leiden: Brill, 1999.

———. "4Q242 (4QPrNab ar)." in *Additional Genres and Unclassified Texts*. Edited by Donald Parry and Emanuel Tov. Vol. 6 of DSSR. Leiden Brill, 2005.

———. "Stirring up the Great Sea: The Religio-Historical Background of Daniel 7." Pages 121–36 in *The Book of Daniel in the Light of New Findings*. Edited by Adam van der Woude. Vol. CVI of BETL. Leuven: Leuven University Press, 1993.

Collins, John J. and Peter Flint. "4Q243–244." in *Qumran Cave 4 XVII: Parabiblical Texts, Part 3*. Edited by James VanderKam. Vol. 22 of DJD. Oxford: Clarendon Press, 1996.

———. "4QPrayer of Nabonidus ar." Pages 83–93 in *Qumran Cave 4 XVII: Parabiblical Texts, Part 3*. Edited by James VanderKam. Vol. 22 of DJD. Oxford: Clarendon Press, 1996.

———. "4Qpseudo-Daniel[a] ar." in *Qumran Cave 4 XVII: Parabiblical Texts, Part 3*. Edited by James VanderKam. Vol. 22 of DJD. Oxford: Clarendon Press, 1996.

Collins, Matthew A. *The Use of Sobriquets in the Qumran Dead Sea Scrolls*. London: T&T Clark, 2009.

Collon, Dominique. *Ancient Near Eastern Art*. Berkeley: University of California Press, 1995.

Cook, E. "4Q246." *BBR* 5 (1995): 43–66.

———. "4Q552 (4QFour Kingdomsa ar)." in *Additional Genres and Unclassified Texts*. Edited by Donald Parry and Emanuel Tov. Vol. 6 of DSSR. Leiden: Brill, 2005.

———. "4Q541 (4QapocrLevi[b?] ar)." in *Parabiblical Texts*. Edited by Emanuel Tov and Donald Parry. Vol. 3 of DSSR. Leiden Brill, 2005.

Cook, Stephen. *The Apocalyptic Literature*. Nashville: Abingdon, 2003.

Cowley, A. E. *Aramaic Papyri of the Fifth Century B.C.* Oxford: Clarendon, 1923.

Crawford, Sidnie White. *Rewriting Scriptures in Second Temple Times*. Grand Rapids: Eerdmans, 2008.

Cross, Frank Moore. *Canaanite Myth and Hebrew Epic: Essays in the History of the Religion of Israel*. Cambridge: Harvard University Press, 1997.

———. "Fragments of the Prayer of Nabonidus." *IEJ* 34 (1984): 260–4.

———. "Palaeography and the Dead Sea Scrolls." Pages 379–402 in *The Dead Sea Scrolls after Fifty Years: A Comprehensive Assessment*. Edited by Peter Flint and James VanderKam. Leiden Brill, 1998–9.

———. "The Structure of the Apocalypse of 'Son of God' (4Q246)." Pages 151–8 in *Emanuel: Studies in Hebrew Bible, Septuagint, and Dea Sea Scrolls in Honor of Emanuel Tov*. Edited by Shalom Paul, Robert Kraft, Lawrence Schiffman, and Weston Fields. Vol. XCIV of VTSup. Leiden: Brill, 2003.

Cross, Frank Moore and David Noel Freedman. *Studies in Ancient Yahwistic Poetry*. Grand Rapids: Eerdmans, 1997 (1975).

Cuddon, J. A., ed. *Dictionary of Literary Terms and Literary Theory*. Fourth Edition ed. London: Penguin, 1999.

Culler, Jonathan. *Literary Theory: A Very Short Introduction*. Oxford: Oxford University Press, 2000.

———. *Structuralist Poetics: Structuralism, Linguistics and the Study of Literature*. London: Routledge, 1975.

Cumont, Franz. "La Plus Ancienne Géographie Astrologique." *Klio* 9 (1909): 263–73.

Davis, Whitney. "The Origins of Register Composition in Pre-Dynastic Egyptian Art." *JAOS* 96 (1976): 404–18.

Delcor, Mathias. *Le Livre de Daniel*. Paris: SB, 1971.

Delcor, Matthias. "Mythologie et Apocalyptique." Pages 143–77 in *Apocalypses et théologie de l'espérance*. Edited by Lectio Divina. Paris: Les Editions du Cerf, 1977.

Demisch, Heinz. *Die Sphinx: Geschichte ihrer Darstellung von den Anfängen bis zur Gegenwart*. Stuttgart: Urarchhaus, 1977.

Denis, A.-M. *Introduction aux Pseudépigraphes grecs d'Ancien Testament.* Vol. 1 of SVTP. Leiden: Brill, 1970.

Deqeuker, Luc. "The Saints of the Most High in Qumran and Daniel." *OTS* 18 (1973): 108–87.

Derrett, J. Duncan. "The Case of Korah Versus Moses Reviewed." *JSJ* XXIV (1993): 59–78.

Derrida, Jacques. *Margins of Philosophy.* Chicago: University of Chicago Press, 1984.

Dever, William. *Did God Have a Wife? Archaeology and Folklore in Ancient Israel.* Grand Rapids: Eerdmans, 2005.

Dietrich, Manfried, Oswald Loretz, and Joaquín Sanmartín. *The Cuneiform Alphabetic Texts from Ugarit, Ras Ibn Hani and Other Places.* Vol. 8 of ASPM. Münster: Ugarit-Verlag, 1995.

Dillman, August. *The Ethiopic Text of 1 Enoch [Das Buch Henoch, 1853].* Eugene, Oregon: Wipf & Stock, 2005.

Dimant, Devorah. "Between Sectarian and Non-Sectarian Texts: Belial and Mastema." Paper presented at the The Dead Sea Scrolls and Contemporary Culture. Hebrew University, Jerusalem.

———. "The Fallen Angels in the Dead Sea Scrolls and in the Apocryphal and Pseudepigraphical Books Related to Them [Hebrew]." Unpublished Ph.D. dissertation, Hebrew University of Jerusalem, 1974.

———. "Jerusalem and the Temple in the Animal Apocalypse (1 Enoch 85-90) in the Light of the Ideology of the Dead Sea Sect [Hebrew]." *Shnaton* 5-6 (1982): 177–93.

———. *Qumran Cave 4 Parabiblical Texts, Part 4: Pseudo-Prophetic Texts.* Vol. 30 of DJD. Oxford: Clarendon Press, 2001.

———. " Review of A Commentary on the Animal Apocalypse of 1 Enoch by Patrick Tiller." *JBL* 114 (1995): 726–9.

———. "New Light from Qumran on the Jewish Pseudepigrapha - 4Q390." Pages 405–48 in *The Madrid Qumran Congress: Proceedings of the International Congress on the Dead Sea Scrolls.* Edited by J.T. Trebolle Barrera and L.V. Montaner. STDJ. Leiden: Brill, 1992.

———. "4QApocryphon of Jeremiah." Pages 91–260 in *Qumran Cave 4 XXI.* Edited by Devorah Dimant. Vol. 30 of DJD. Oxford: Clarendon Press, 2001.

———. "The Qumran Manuscripts: Contents and Significance." Pages 23–58 in *Time to Prepare the Way in the Wilderness. Papers on the Qumran Scrolls by Fellows of the Institute for Advanced Studies of the Hebrew University, Jerusalem, 1989–1990.* Edited by D. Dimant and L. Schiffman. Vol. 16 of STDJ. Leiden: Brill, 1995.

———. "Two 'Scientific' Fictions: The So-called Book of Noah and the Alleged Quotation of Jubilees in CD 16:3-4." Pages 230–49 in *Studies in the Hebrew Bible, Qumran, and Septuagint Presented to Eugene Ulrich.* Edited by P. Flint, E. Tov, and J. VanderKam. Vol. 101 of VTsup. Leiden: Brill, 2006.

———. "Qumran Sectarian Literature." Pages 483–550 in *Jewish Writings of the Second Temple Period.* Edited by Michael Stone. CRINT. Philadelphia: Assen.

———. "Noah in Early Jewish Literature; Appendix: The So-Called Book of Noah." Pages 144–6 in *Biblical Figures Outside the Bible.* Edited by M. Stone and T. Bergren. Harrisburg, PA: Trinity Press, 1998.

———. "Qumran Sectarian Literature." Pages 483–550 in *Jewish Writings of the Second Temple Period: Apocrypha, Pseudepigrapha, Qumran Sectarian Writings, Philo, Josephus.* Edited by M. E. Stone. Philadelphia: Assen, 1984.

DiTommaso, Lorenzo. "4QPseudo-Daniel[a-b] (4Q243–4Q244)." *DSD* 12 (2005): 101-33.

———. "Apocalypses and Apocalypticism in Antiquity (Part 1)." *CBR* 5 (2007): 235–86.

———. *The Book of Daniel and the Apocryphal Daniel Literature.* Vol. 20 of SVTP. Leiden: Brill, 2005.

———. *The Dead Sea 'New Jerusalem' Text.* VOl. 110 of TSAJ. Tübingen: Mohr Siebeck, 2005.

———. "Review of Ultimate Things: An Introduction to Jewish and Christian Apocalyptic Literature." *RBL* 12 (2007).

Doty, William. "The Concept of Genre in Literary Analysis." Pages 413–48 in *Society of Biblical Literature, One Hundred Eighth Annual Meeting Book of Seminar paper*. Edited by Lane McGaughy. Los Angeles: Society of Biblical Literature, 1972.

Eco, Umberto. *Interpretation and Overinterpretation*. Cambridge: Cambridge University Press, 1992.

———. *The Limits of Interpretation*. Bloomington: Indiana University Press, 1990.

———. *The Role of the Reader: Explorations in the Semiotics of Texts*. Bloomington: Indiana University Press, 1979.

———. *Semiotics and the Philosophy of Language*. Bloomington: Indiana University Press, 1984.

Eddy, K. *The King is Dead: Studies in the Near Eastern Resistance to Hellenism 334–31 B.C.E.* Lincoln: University of Nebraska Press, 1961.

Eggler, Jürg. *Influences and Traditions Underlying the Vision of Daniel 7:2–14: The Research History from the End of the 19th Century to the Present*. Vol. 177 of OBO. Göttingen: Vandenhoeck & Ruprecht, 2000.

Ehrman, Bart. *Jesus: Apocalyptic Prophet of the New Millenium*. Oxford: Oxford University Press, 1999.

Eissfeldt, O. "El and Yahweh." *JSS* 1 (1956): 25–37.

Eldridge, Michael. *Dying Adam with his Multiethnic Family: Understanding the Greek Life of Adam and Eve*. Vol. 16 of SVTP. Leiden: Brill, 2001.

Engberg, Robert. "Megiddo: Guardian of the Carmel Pass." *BA* 3 (1940): 41–51.

Eshel, Esther. "Demonology in the Land of Israel in the Second Temple Period (Hebrew)." Hebrew University, 1999.

———. "Mastema's Attempt on Moses' Life in the "Pseudo-Jubilees" Text from Masada." *DSD* 10 (2003): 359–64.

———. "471b. 4QSelf-Glorification Hymn (=4QH^e frg. 1?)." Pages 421–32 in *Qumran Cave 4.XX*. Edited by E. Chazon. Vol. XXIX of DJD. Oxford Clarendon, 1999.

———. "Possible Sources of the Book of Daniel." Pages 387–94 in *The Book of Daniel: Composition and Reception*. Edited by John J Collins and Peter Flint. Vol. 84 of VTSup. Leiden: Brill, 2001.

Eshel, Hanan. "6Q30, a Cursive Šin, and Proverbs 11." *JBL* 122 (2003): 544–6.

———. *The Dead Sea Scrolls and the Hasmonean*. State Grand Rapids: Eerdmans, 2008.

———. "4Q390, the 490-Year Prophecy, and the Calendrical History of the Second Temple Period." Pages 102–10 in *Enoch and Qumran Origins: New Light on a Forgotten Connection*. Edited by Gabriele Boccaccini. Grand Rapids: Eerdmans, 2005.

———. "The Kittim in the War Scroll and in the Pesharim." Pages 29–44 in *Historical Perspectives: From the Hasmoneans to Bar Kokhba in Light of the Dead Sea Scrolls. Proceedings of the Fourth International Symposium of the Orion Center for the Study of the Dead Sea Scrolls and Associated Literature, 27–31 January 1999*. Edited by D. Goodblatt, A. Pinnick, and D. Schwartz. Vol. 37 of STDJ. Leiden: Brill, 2001.

Falk, Daniel. *The Parabiblical Texts: Strategies for Extending the Scriptures in the Dead Sea Scrolls*. Vol. 63 of Library of Second Temple Studies. London: T&T Clark, 2007.

Fassberg, Steven. "The Linguistic Study of the Damascus Document: A Historical Perspective." Pages 53–67 in *The Damascus Document: A Centennial of Discovery. Proceedings of the Third International Symposium of the Orion Center for the Study of the Dead Sea Scrolls and Associated Literature, 4–8 February 1998*. Edited by Joseph Baumgarten, Esther Chazon, and Avital Pinnick. Vol. 34 of STDJ. Leiden: Brill, 2000.

Festinger, Leon, Henry W. Riecken, Stanley Schachter, eds. *When Prophecy Fails: A Social and Psychological Study of a Modern Group that Predicted the Destruction of the World*. Mansfield Centre, CT: Martino Publishing, 2009 [1956, University of Minnesota].

Fitzmyer, Joseph. *The Aramaic Inscriptions of Sefire*. Vol. 19/A of *BO*. Rome: Editrice Pontifico Instituto Biblico, 1995.

———. The *Genesis Apocryphon of Qumran Cave 1 (1Q20): A Commentary*. 3rd ed. Vol. 18B of *BO*. Rome: Editrice Pontificio Instituto Biblico, 2004.

Flannery-Dailey, Frances. *Dreamers, Scribes, and Priests: Jewish Dreams in the Hellenistic and Roman Eras.* Vol. 90 of JSJSup. Leiden: Brill, 2004.

———. "Lessons on Early Jewish Apocalypticism and Mysticism from Dream Literature." Pages 231–47 in *Paradise Now: Essays on Early Jewish and Christian Mysticism.* Edited by April De Conick. Atlanta: Society of Biblical Literature, 2006.

Fletcher, Angus. *Allegory: The Theory of a Symbolic Mode.* Ithaca: Cornell University Press, 1964.

Flusser, David. "The Four Empires in the Fourth Sybil and in the Book of Daniel." *Israel Oriental Studies* 2 (1972): 148–75.

———. "The Hubris of the Antichrist in a Fragment from Qumran." *Imm* 10 (1980): 31–7.

———. *Judaism and the Origins of Christianity.* Jerusalem: Magnes Press, 1988.

———. *Judaism of the Second Temple Period: Qumran and Apocalypticism.* Vol. 1. Grand Rapids: Eerdmans, 2007.

Foster, Benjamin. "Gilgamesh." Pages 448–50 in *The Context of Scripture. Canonical Compositions from the Biblical World.* Edited by W. Hallo and K. Lawson Younger. Leiden: Brill, 2003.

Fretz, Mark. "Abishua." *Anchor Bible Dictionary.* Edited by David Noel Freedman. New York: Doubleday, 1992.

Freud, Sigmund. *The Interpretation of Dreams.* Translated by James Strachey. New York: Avon Books, 1998.

Frey, Jörg. "Different Patterns of Dualism in the Qumran Library." Pages 275–335 in *Legal Texts and Legal Issues. Proceedings of the Second Meeting of the International Organization of Qumran Studies, Cambridge 1995, Published in Honor of J. M. Baumgarten.* Edited by Moshe Bernstein, Florentino García-Martínez, and John Kampen. Vol. 25 of STDJ. Leiden: Brill, 1997.

———. "Die Bedeutung der Qumrantexte für das Verständnis der Apokalyptik im Frühjudentum und im Urchristentum." in *Apokalyptik und Qumran.* Edited by Jörg Frey and Michael Becker. Paderborn: Bonifatius, 2007.

Fröhlich, Ida. "From Pseudepigraphic to Sectarian" in *RevQ* 21 (2004): 395-406.

———. "Qumran Names." Pages 294–305 in *The Provo International Conference on the Dead Sea Scrolls: Technological Innovations, New Texts, and Reformulated Issues.* Edited by Donald W. Parry and Eugene C. Ulrich. Vol. 30 of STDJ. Leiden: Brill, 1999.

———. *Time and Times and Half a Time: Historical Consciousness in the Jewish Literature of the Persian and Hellenistic Eras*, JSPSup 19. Sheffield: Sheffield Academic Press, 1996.

Frykholm, Amy Johnson. *Rapture Culture: Left Behind in Evangelical America.* Oxford: Oxford University Press, 2004.

Gammie, John G. "The Classification, Stages of Growth, and Changing Intentions in the Book of Daniel." *JBL* 95 (1976): 191–204.

García Martínez, Florentino. *The Dea Sea Scrolls Translated: The Qumran Texts in English.* 2nd ed. Grand Rapids: Eerdmans, 1996.

———. *Qumran and Apocalyptic. Studies on the Aramaic Texts from Qumran.* Vol. 9 of STDJ. Leiden: Brill, 1992.

———. "The Heavenly Tablets in the Book of Jubilees." Pages 243–60 in *Studies in the Book of Jubilees.* Edited by Matthias Albani, Jörg Frey, and Armin Lange. Vol. 65 of TSAJ. Tübingen: Mohr Siebeck, 1997.

———. "Apocalypticism in the Dead Sea Scrolls." Pages 162–92 in *The Encyclopedia of Apocalypticism.* Edited by John J Collins. New York: Continuum, 1998.

———. "Two Messianic Figures in the Qumran Texts." Pages 14–40 in *Technological Developments on the Dead Sea Scrolls.* Edited by Donald Parry and Stephen Ricks. Leiden: Brill, 1996.

Martínez, Florentino García and Mladen Popović, eds. *Defining Identities: We, You, and the Other in the Dead Sea Scrolls. Proceedings of the Fifth Meeting of the IOQS in Groningen.* Vol. 70 of STDJ. Leiden: Brill, 2008.

García Martínez, Florentino and Adam van der Woude. "A 'Groningen' Hypothesis of Qumran Early Origins and Early History." *RevQ* 14 (1990): 521-542.
George, Andrew. *The Babylonian Gilgamesh Epic: Introduction, Critical Edition, and Cuneiform Texts*. Vol. I. Oxford: Oxford University Press, 2003.
Gesenius, Kautsch, and Cowley. *Gesenius' Hebrew Grammar*. 2nd ed. Oxford: Clarendon Press, 1957.
Gibson, J. *Textbook of Syrian Semitic Inscriptions*. 3 vols. Oxford: Clarendon, 1971–82.
Gignoux, Philippe. "L'apocalyptique iranienne est-elle vraiment ancienne?" *RHR* 216 (1999): 213–27.
Gignoux, Phillippe. "L'apocalyptique iranienne est-elle vraiment la source d'autres apocalypses?" *AAASH* 31:1–2 (1986): 67–78.
Ginsberg, H. L. "The Oldest Interpretation of the Suffering Servant." *VT* 3 (1953): 400–4.
Ginsberg, Harold. *Studies in Daniel, Texts and Studies of the Jewish Theological Seminary of America* 14. New York: Jewish Theological Seminary of America, 1948.
Gmirkin, Russell. *Berossus and Genesis, Manetho and Exodus: Hellenistic Histories and the Date of the Pentateuch*. London: T & T Clark, 2006.
Gogel, Sandra Landis. *A Grammar of Epigraphic Hebrew*. Vol. 23 of SBLRBS. Atlanta: Scholars Press, 1998.
Goldstein, Jonathan. *I Maccabees*. Vol. 41 of *AB*. Garden City: Doubleday, 1976.
Goodenough, E. R. *Jewish Symbols in the Greco-Roman Period*. Vol. 37 of Bollinger Series. New York: Pantheon 1958.
Goold, G.P., ed. *Manilius: Astronomica*. LCL. Cambridge: Harvard University Press, 1977.
Gordon, Cyrus. *Ugaritic Textbook : Grammar, Texts in Transliteration, Cuneiform Selections, Glossary, Indices*. Rome: Pontifical Biblical Institute, 1998.
Gowan, Donald. *Daniel*. AOTC. Nashville: Abingdon, 2001.
Green, A. "Mischwesen B." Pages 246–64 in *Reallexikon der Assyriologie und Vorderasiatischen Archäologie*. Edited by Erich Ebeling and Bruno Meissner. Berlin: Walter de Gruyter, 1997.
Green, Anthony. "Hesiodus." in *Brill's New Pauly: Encyclopedia of the Ancient World*. Edited by Hubert Cancik and Helmuth Schneider. Leiden: Brill, 2005.
Greenfield, Jonas, Michael Stone, and Esther Eshel. *The Aramaic Levi Document: Edition, Translation, Commentary*. Vol. 19 of SVTP. Leiden: Brill, 2004.
Greimas, Algirdas Julien. *Narrative Semiotics and Cognitive Discourses*. London: Pinter Publishers, 1990.
———. *Structural Semantics: An Attempt at Method*. Lincoln: University of Nebraska Press, 1984.
Gressman, Hugo. *Altorientalische Bilder zum alten Testament*. Berlin: Walter de Gruyter, 1927.
Grossman, Maxine. "Cultivating Identity: Textual Virtuosity and "Insider" Status." Pages 1–11 in *Defining Identities: We, You, and the Other in the Dead Sea Scrolls. Proceedings of the Fifth Meeting of the IOQS in Groningen*. Edited by Florentino García Martínez and Mladen Popović. Vol. 70 of STDJ. Leiden: Brill, 2008.
Gunkel, Hermann. *Creation and Chaos in the Primeval Era and the Eshchaton*. Grand Rapids, MI: Eerdmans, 2005.
———. *Schöpfung und Chaos in Urzeit und Endzeit*. Göttingen: Vandenhoeck & Ruprecht, 1895.
Hackett, Jo Ann. *The Balaam Text from Deir Alla*. Vol. 31 of HSM. Chico: Scholars Press, 1984.
Hanneken, Todd. "The Book of Jubilees among the Apocalypses." Ph.D. Dissertation, University of Notre Dame, 2008.
Hanson, Paul. *The Dawn of Apocalyptic: The Historical and Sociological Roots of Jewish Apocalyptic Eschatology*. Philadelphia: Fortress, 1975.

———. "Apocalypse, Genre." Pages 27–8 in *The Interpreter's Dictionary of the Bible, Supplementary Volume*. Edited by Keith Crim. Nashville: Abingdon, 1976.
———. "Apocalypticism." Pages 28–34 in *The Interpreter's Dictionary of the Bible, Supplementary Volume*. Edited by Keith Crim. Nashville: Abingdon, 1976.

Hartman, Lars. "Survey of the Problem of Apocalyptic Genre." Pages 329–43 in *Apocalypticism in the Mediterranean World and the Near East*. Edited by David Hellholm. Tübingen: Mohr Siebeck, 1983.

Hartman, Louis and Alexander DiLella. *The Book of Daniel*. Vol. 23 of *AB*. Garden City: Doubleday, 1977.

Heckel, Waldemar. "The Politics of Distrust: Alexander and His Successors." Pages 81–95 in *The Hellenistic World: New Perspectives*. Edited by Daniel Ogden. London: Classical Press of Wales, 2002.

Hengel, Martin. *Judaism and Hellenism: Studies in Their Encounter in Palestine During the Early Hellenistic Period*. 2 vols. Philadelphia: Fortress, 1974.

———. *Judaism and Hellenism: Studies in their Encounter in Palestine during the Early Hellenistic Period*. Philadelphia: Fortress Press, 1981.

Henze, Matthias. *The Madness of King Nebuchadnezzar: The Ancient Near Eastern Origins and Early History of Interpretation of Daniel 4*. Leiden: Brill, 1999.

Herder, J. G. *The Spirit of Hebrew Poetry*. Vol. 1. Burlington: Edward Smith, 1833 [1782].

Hilgenfeld, Adolf. *Die jüdische Apokalyptik in ihrer geschichtlichen Entwickelung: Ein Beitrag zur Vorgeschichte des Christenthums nebst einem Anhange über das gnostische System des Basilides*. Jena: Friedrich Mauke, 1857.

Himmelfarb, Martha. "Torah, Testimony, and Heavenly Tablets: The Claim to Authority of the Book of Jubilees." Pages 19-29 in *A Multiform Heritage: Studies on Early Judaism and Christianity in Honor of Robert A. Kraft*. Edited by Benjamin Wright. Atlanta: Scholars Press, 1999.

Hoftijzer, Jacob and K. Jongeling. *Dictionary of the North-West Semitic Inscriptions* Vol. 1 of HdO 21. Leiden: Brill, 1995.

Hölbl, Günther. *A History of the Ptolemaic Empire*. London: Routledge, 2001.

Horsley, Richard A. *Revolt of the Scribes: Resistance and Apocalyptic Origins*. Minneapolis: Fortress Press, 2010.

———. *Scribes, Visionaries, and the Politics of Second Temple Judea*. Louisville: Westminster John Knox Press, 2007.

Hultgard, Anders. "BAHMAN YASHT: A Persian Apocalypse." in *Mysteries and Revelations: Apocalyptic Studies since the Uppsala Colloquium*. Edited by John Collins and James Charlesworth. Vol. 9 of JSPSup. Sheffield: JSOT Press, 1991.

Husser, Jean-Marie. *Dreams and Dream Narratives in the Biblical World*. Translated by Jill Munro. Sheffield: Sheffield Academic Press, 1999.

Hyatt, J.P. "The Deuteronomic Edition of Jeremiah." Pages 71–95 in *Vanderbilt Studies in the Humanities 1*. Edited by Richmond Beatty, J.P. Hyatt, and Monroe Spears. Nashville: Vanderbilt University Press, 1951.

Isaac, E. "1 Enoch." Pages 5–89 in *OTP* I. Edited by James Charlesworth. New York: Doubleday, 1983.

Jakobson, Roman. "Linguistics and Poetics." Pages 350–77 in *Style in Language*. Edited by T. Sebeock. Cambridge: MIT Press, 1960.

Janowski, Bernd. "JHWH und der Sonnegott: Aspekte der Solarisierung JHWH's in vorexilischer Zeit." Pages 214–41 in *Pluralismus und Identität*. Edited by Joachim Mehlhausen. Gütersloh: Kaiser, 1995.

Janzen, J. Gerald. *Studies in the Text of Jeremiah*. VOl. 6 of *HSM*. Cambridge: Harvard University Press, 1973.

Jassen, Alex. *Mediating the Divine: Prophecy and Revelation in the Dead Sea Scrolls and Second Temple Judaism*. Vol. 68 of STDJ. Leiden: Brill, 2007.

Jeffrey, A. "The Book of Daniel." Pages 339–549 in *The Interpreter's Bible*. Edited by G. A. Buttrick. Nashville: Abingdon, 1956.

Jenni, Ernst. *Die hebräischen Präpositionen: Die Präposition Kaph*. Stuttgart: Kohlhammer, 1994.

Johnson, M. D. "Life of Adam and Eve." Pages 249–95 in *OTP* 2. Edited by J. H. Charlesworth. New York: Doubleday, 1985.

Jokiranta, Jutta. "Social Identity Approach: Identity-Constructing Elements in the Psalms Pesher." Pages 85–109 in *Defining Identities: We, You, and the Other in the Dead Sea Scrolls. Proceedings of the Fifth Meeting of the IOQS in Groningen.* Edited by Florentino García Martínez and Mladen Popović. Vol. 70 of STDJ. Leiden: Brill, 2008.

Jonge, Marinus de. *Pseudepigrapha of the Old Testament as part of Christian Literature: the Case of the Testament of the Twelve Patriarchs and the Greek Life of Adam and Eve.* Leiden: Brill, 2003.

Jonge, Marinus de and Johannes Tromp. *The Life of Adam and Eve and Related Literature.* Sheffield: Sheffield Academic Press, 1997.

Joosten, Jan. "A Note on the Text of Deuteronomy xxxii 8*." *VT* 57 (2007): 548–55.

Josephus. *Jewish Antiquities.* Books I-IV. Translated by H. St. J. Thackaray, LCL. Cambridge: Harvard University Press, 1926.

Junker, H. *Untersuchungen über literarische und exegetische Probleme des Buches Daniel.* Bonn: Peter Hanstein Verlagsbuchhandlung, 1932.

Kamrin, Janice. *The Cosmos of Khnumhotep II at Beni Hasan.* London: Keagan Paul International, 1999.

Keel, Othmar. *Goddesses and Trees, New Moon and Yahweh.* Vol. 261 of JSOTSup. Sheffield: Sheffield Academic Press, 1998.

Keel, Othmar and Christoph Uehlinger. *Gods, Goddesses, and Images of God in Ancient Israel.* Minneapolis: Fortress Press, 1998.

King, Philip and Lawrence Stager. *Life in Biblical Israel.* Louisville: Westminster John Knox, 2001.

Knibb, Michael. *The Ethiopic Book of Enoch: A New Edition in the Light of the Aramaic Dead Sea Fragments*, 2 Vols. Oxford: Oxford University Press, 1978.

Knoppers, Gary. *1 Chronicles, 1–9.* Vol. 12 of AB. New York: Doubleday, 2004.

Kobelski, Paul. *Melchizedek and Melchireša'.* Vol. 10 of *CBQMS.* Washinton: Catholic Biblical Association of America, 1981.

Koch, Klaus. *Daniel.* Vol. XXII/6 of BKAT. Neukirchen-Vluyn: Neukirchener Verlag, 2005.

———. "Der "Menschensohn" in Daniel." *ZAW* 119 (2007): 369–87.

———. *Die Reiche der Welt und der kommende Menschensohn: Studien zum Danielbuch.* Vol. 2 of GA. Neukirchen-Vluyn: Neukirchener Verlag, 1995.

———. *The Rediscovery of Apocalyptic: A Polemical Work on a Neglected Area of Biblical Studies and its Damaging Effects on Theology and Philosophy.* Vol. 22 of SBT. Naperville, Ill.: Alec Allenson, 1970.

———. "Vom profestischen zum apokalyptischen Visionsbericht." Pages 413–46 in *Apocalypticism in the Mediterranean World and the Near East: Proceedings of the International Colloquium on Apocalypticism – Uppsala, August 12–17, 1979.* Edited by David Hellholm. Tübingen: Mohr-Siebeck, 1983.

Koehler, L. and W. Baumgartner, eds. *The Hebrew and Aramaic Lexicon of the Old Testament.* Leiden: Brill, 2001.

Kraft, Robert. "Scripture and Canon in Jewish Apocrypha and Pseudepigrapha." Pages 199–215 in *Hebrew Bible / Old Testament: The History of Its Interpretation.* Edited by Magne Saebo. Göttingen: Vandenhoeck & Ruprecht, 1996.

Kratz, Reinhard. *Translatio imperii. Untersuchungen zu den aramäischen Danielerzählungen und ihrem theologischichtlichen Umfeld.* Vol. 63 of WMANT. Neukirchener: Verlag, 1990.

Kristiansen, Kristian and Thomas Larsson. *The Rise of Bronze Age Society: Travels, Transmissions, and Transformations.* Cambridge: Cambridge University Press, 2005.

Kugel, James. "Which is Older, Jubilees or the Genesis Apocryphon? Some Exegetical Considerations." Paper presented at the The Dead Sea Scrolls and Contemporary Culture. Hebrew University, Jerusalem, 2008.

Kuhrt, Amélie. *The Ancient Near East c. 3000-330 BC.* Vol. 2. London: Routledge, 1995.

Kutscher, E. Y. "Dating the Language of the Genesis Apocryphon." *JBL* 76 (1957): 288–92.

Kvanvig, Helge. *Roots of Apocalyptic: The Mesopotamian Background of the Enoch Figure and of the Son of Man*. Vol. 61 of WMANT. Neukirchen-Vluyn: Neukirchner Verlag, 1988.

Lange, Armin. *Vom prophetischen Wort zur prophetischen Tradition: Studien zur Traditions- und Redaktionsgeschichte innerprophetischer Konflikte in der Hebräischen Bibel*. Vol. 34 of FAT. Tübingen: Mohr Siebeck, 2002.

———. *Weisheit und Prädestination: Weisheitliche Urordnung und Prädestination in den Textfunden von Qumran*. Vol. 18 of STDJ. Leiden: Brill, 1995.

———. "Wisdom and Predestination in the Dead Sea Scrolls." *DSD* 2 (1995): 340–54.

———. "Your Daughters Do Not Give to Their Sons and Their Daughters Do Not Take for Your Sons: Intermarriage in Ezra 9–10 and in the Pre-Maccabean Dead Sea Scrolls. Teil 1." *BN* 137 (2008): 17–39.

———. "Your Daughters Do Not Give to Their Sons and Their Daughters Do Not Take for Your Sons: Intermarriage in Ezra 9–10 and in the Pre-Maccabean Dead Sea Scrolls. Teil 2." *BN* 139 (2008): 79–98.

———. "Divinatorische Träume und Apokalyptik im Jubiläenbuch." Pages 25–38 in *Studies in the Book of Jubilees*. Edited by Matthias Albani, Jörg Frey, and Armin Lange. Tübingen: Mohr Siebeck, 1997.

———. "Dream Visions and Apocalyptic Milieus." Pages 27–34 in *Enoch and Qumran Origins: New Light on a Forgotten Connection*. Edited by Gabriele Boccaccini. Grand Rapids: Eerdmans, 2005.

———. "Kriterien essinischer Texte." Pages 59–69 in *Qumran Kontrovers: Beiträge zu den Textfunden vom Toten Meer*. Edited by Jörg Frey and Hartmut Stegemann. Paderborn: Bonifatius, 2003.

———. "Interpretation als Offenbarung: Zum Verhältnis von Schriftauslegung und Offenbarung in apokalyptischer und nichtapokalyptischer Literatur." Pages 17–33 in *Wisdom and Apocalypticism in the Dead Sea Scrolls and in the Biblical Tradition*. Edited by Florentino García Martínez. Vol. 168 of BETL. Leuven: Peeters, 2003.

———. "The Parabiblical Literature of the Qumran Library and the Canonical History of the Hebrew Bible." Pages 305–21 in *Emanuel: Studies in the Hebrew Bible, Septuagint, and Dead Sea Scrolls in Honor of Emanuel Tov*. Edited by S. Paul, R. Kraft, L. Schiffman, and W. Fields. Vol. XCIV of VTsup. Leiden: Brill, 2003.

Lange, Armin and Ulrike Mittmann-Richert. "Annotated List of the Texts from the Judean Desert Classified by Genre and Content." in *The Texts From the Judean Desert: Indices and An Introduction to the DJD Series*. Edited by Emanuel Tov. Vol. 39 of DJD. Oxford: Clarendon, 2002.

Larson, Erik. "4Q470 and the Angelic Rehabilitation of King Zedekiah." *DSD* 1 (1994): 210–28.

Lebram, Jürgen. *Das Buch Daniel*. Zurich: Theologische Verlag, 1984.

Lenglet, A. "La Structure littéraire de Daniel 2-7." *Biblica* 18 (1972): 243–67.

Leppäkari, Maria. *Apocalyptic Representations of Jerusalem*, Vol. 111 of Numen. Leiden: Brill, 2006.

Leslau, Wolf. Concise *Dictionary of Ge'ez (Classical Ethiopic)*. Wiesbaden: Otto Harrassowitz, 1989.

Lete, Gregorio del Olmo and Joaquín Sanmartín. *A Dictionary of the Ugaritic Language in the Alphabetic Tradition*. 2 vols, Vol. 67 of Handbuch der Orientalisk I. Leiden: Brill, 2003.

Levenson, Jon. *The Death and Resurrection of the Beloved Son: The Transformation of Child Sacrifice in Judaism and Christianity*. New Haven: Yale University Press, 1993.

Lévi-Strauss, Claude. *From Honey to Ashes*. New York: Harper & Row, 1973.

———. *The Naked Man*. New York: Harper & Row, 1981.

———. *The Origin of Table Manners*. New York: Harper & Row, 1978.

———. *The Raw and the Cooked*. New York Harper & Row, 1969.

———. *Totemism*. Boston: Beacon Press, 1963.

Levine, Baruch. *Numbers 1–10*. Vol. 4a of AB. New York: London, 1993.

Levison, John R. *Texts in Transition: The Greek Life of Adam and Eve*. Vol. 16 of EJL. Altanta: Society of Biblical Literature, 2001.

Lewis, Theodore. "The Birth of the Gracious Gods." in *Ugaritic Narrative Poetry*. Edited by Simon Parker. Atlanta: Scholars Press, 1997.

Liddell, H. G. *An Intermediate Greek-English Lexicon Founded Upon the Seventh Edition of Liddell and Scott's Greek-English Lexicon*. Oxford: Clarendon Press, 2001.

Lloyd, Seton. *The Art of the Ancient Near East*. New York: Frederick A. Praeger, 1965.

Lücke, Friedrich. *Versuch einer vollständigen Einleitung in die Offenbarung des Johannes*. Bonn: Eduard Weber, 1852.

Machiela, Daniel. "Each to His Own Inheritance: Geography as an Evaluative Tool in the Genesis Apocryphon." *DSD* 15 (2008): 50–66.

———. "Genesis Revealed: The Apocalyptic Apocryphon From Qumran Cave 1." Pages 205–221 in *Qumran Cave 1 Revisited. Texts from Cave 1 Sixty Years after Their Discovery: Proceedings of the Sixth Meeting of the IOQS in Ljubljana*. Edited by Daniel K. Falk, Sarianna Metso, Donald W. Parry, and Eibert J. C. Tigchelaar (Leiden: Brill, 2010).

Macrobius. *Commentary on the Dream of Scipio*. Translated by William H. Stahl. New York: Columbia University Press, 1952.

Magness, Jodi. *The Archaeology of Qumran and the Dead Sea Scrolls*. Eerdmans: Grand Rapids, 2002.

Matthews, K. "The Background of the Paleo-Hebrew Texts at Qumran." Pages 549–68 in *The Word of the Lord Shall Go Forth*. Edited by C Meyers and M O'Connor. Winona Lake: Eisenbrauns, 1983.

McKane, William. *A Critical and Exegetical Commentary on Jeremiah I. Introduction and Commentary on Jeremiah I-XXV*. ICC. Edinburgh: T&T Clark, 1986.

McLay, Timothy. "The Old Greek Translation of Daniel IV–VI and the Formation of the Book of Daniel." *VT* 55 (2005): 304–23.

Medico, Henri del. "L'identification des Kittim avec les Romains." *VT* 10 (1960): 448–53.

Meshorer, Yaakov. *Jewish Coins of the Second Temple Period*. Tel Aviv: Massada, 1967.

———. *A Treasury of Jewish Coins from the Persian Period to Bar Kokhba*. Nyack, NY: Amphora, 2001.

Mettinger, Tryggve. "Israelite Aniconism: Developments and Origins." Pages 172–203 in *The Image and the Book: Iconic Cults, Aniconism, and the Rise of Book Religion in Israel and the Ancient Near East*. Edited by K. van der Toorn. Leuven: Peeters, 1997.

Meyer, Eduard. *Ursprung und Anfänge des Chistentums*. Stuttgart: Cotta, 1924.

Meyers, Carol. *The Tabernacle Menorah*. Vol. 2 of ASORDS. Missoula: Scholars Press, 1976.

Meyers, Carol and Eric Meyers. *Haggai, Zechariah 1–8*. Vol. 25B of AB. Garden City: Doubleday, 1987.

Mieroop, Marc Van De. *A History of the Ancient Near East ca. 3000–323 BC*. Padstow, Cornwall: Blackwell, 2004.

Milgrom, Jacob. *Leviticus 17–22*. Vol. 3a of AB New York Doubleday, 2000.

Milik, J. T. *The Books of Enoch: Aramaic Fragments of Qumrân Cave 4*. Oxford: Clarendon, 1976.

———. "Le travail d'édition des fragments manuscrits de Qumrân." *RB* 63 (1956): 65.

———. *Ten Years of Discovery in the Wilderness of Judea*. Translated by John Strugnell, SBT. London: SCM Press, 1959.

Milik, J.T. "Les modèles araméens du livre d'Esther dans la grotte 4 de Qumrân." *RevQ* 15 (1992): 383–4.

———. "Prière de Nabonide et autres écrits d'un cycle de Daniel." *RB* 63 (1956).

Montgomery, J. *A Critical and Exegetical Commentary on the Book of Daniel*. ICC. Edinburgh: T & T Clark, 1927.

Morenz, S. "Das Tier mit den Hörnen, ein Beitrag zu Daniel 7 7f." *ZAW* 65 (1951): 151–53.

Morgenstern, M., E. Qimron, and D. Sivan. "The Hitherto Unpublished Columns of the Genesis Apocryphon." *AbrN* 33 (1995): 30–54.

Moscati, Sabatino, ed. *The Phoenicians*. New York: Rizzoli, 1999.

Müller, Hans Peter. "Magisch-mantische Weisheit und die Gestalt Daniels." *UF* 1 (1969): 79–94.

———. "Mantische Weisheit und Apokalyptik." Pages 268–93 in *Congress Volume: Uppsala, 1971.* Edited by P. A. H. de Boer. Leiden: Brill, 1972.

Müller, Karl, ed. *The Fragments of the Lost Historians of Alexander the Great: Fragmenta Scriptorum de Rebus Alexandri Magni, Pseudo-Callisthenes, Itinerarium Alexandri.* Chicago: Ares Publishers, 1979.

Muscarella, O. *Ladders to Heaven: Art Treasures from the Lands of the Bible.* Toronto: University of Toronto Press, 1981.

Myers, Jacob. *I and II Esdras.* Vol. 42 of AB. Garden City: Doubleday, 1974.

Najman, Hindy. "Interpretation as Primordial Writing: Jubilees and its Authority Conferring Strategies." *JSJ* 30 (1999): 379–410.

———. *Seconding Sinai: The Development of Mosaic Discourse in Second Temple Judaism.* Vol. 77 of JSJSup. Leiden Brill, 2002.

Neujahr, Matthew. "When Darius Defeated Alexander: Composition and Redaction in the Dynastic Prophecy." *JNES* 64 (2005): 101–7.

Neusner, Jacob. *The Tosefta: Second Division, Moed (The Order of the Appointed Times).* New York: Ktav Publishing House, 1981.

Newsom, Carol. *The Self as Symbolic Space: Constructing Identity and Community at Qumran.* Vol. 52 of STDJ. Leiden: Brill, 2004.

———. *The Songs of Sabbath Sacrifice: A Critical Edition.* Vol. 27 of HSS. Atlanta: Scholars Press, 1985.

———. "Angels (Old Testament)." Pages 248–53 in *ABD*. Edited by David Noel Freedman. New York: Doubleday, 1992.

———. "Sectually Explicit Literature from Qumran." Pages 167–87 in *The Hebrew Bible and Its Interpreters*. Edited by Baruch Halpern and David N. Freedman. Winona Lake: Eisenbrauns, 1990.

———. "Constructing 'We, You, and Others' through Non-Polemical Discourse." Pages 13–21 in *Defining Identities: We, You, and the Other in the Dead Sea Scrolls. Proceedings of the Fifth Meeting of the IOQS in Groningen.* Edited by Florentino García Martínez and Mladen Popović. Vol. 70 of STDJ. Leiden: Brill, 2008.

———. "Spying out the Land: A Report from Genology." Pages 437–50 in *Seeking Out the Wisdom of the Ancients: Essays Offered to Honor Michael V. Fox on the Occasion of His Sixty-Fifth Birthday*. Edited by Ronald Troxel, Kelvin Friebel, and Dennis Robert Magary. Winona Lake: Eisenbrauns, 2005.

Nickelsburg, George. *1 Enoch 1.* Hermeneia. Minneapolis: Fortress Press, 2001.

———. *Jewish Literature between the Bible and the Mishnah: A Historical and Literary Introduction*. Philadelphia: Fortress, 1981.

———. *Resurrection, Immortality, and Eternal Life in Intertestamental Judaism and Early Christianity*. Vol. 26 of HTS. Cambridge: Harvard University Press, 2006.

———. "Relgous Exclusivism: A World View Governing Some Texts Found at Qumran." Pages I:139–68 in *George W.E. Nickelsburg in Perspective: An Ongoing Dialogue of Learning*. Edited by A. J. Avery-Peck and J. Neusner. Vol. 80 of JSJSup. Leiden: Brill, 2003.

———. "Religious Exclusivism: A World View Governing Some Texts Found at Qumran." Pages 45–67 in *Das Ende der Tage und die Gegenwart des Heils: Begegnungen mit dem Neuen Testament und siener Umwelt: Festschrift für Heinz-Wolfgang Kuhn zum 65. Geburtstag*. Edited by M. Becker and W. Fenske. Vol. 44 of AGJU. Leiden: Brill, 1999.

———. "Polarized Self-Identification in the Qumran Texts." Pages 23–31 in *Defining Identities: We, You, and the Other in the Dead Sea Scrolls. Proceedings of the Fifth Meeting of the IOQS in Groningen.* Edited by Florentino García Martínez and Mladen Popović. Vol. 70 of STDJ. Leiden: Brill, 2008.

Nickelsburg, George and James VanderKam. *1 Enoch: A New Translation*. Minneapolis: Fortress Press, 2004.

Niditch, Susan. *The Symbolic Vision in Biblical Tradition.* HSM. Chico, CA: Scholars Press, 1983.

Niditch, Susan and Robert Doran. "The Success Story of the Wise Courtier: A Formal Approach." *JBL* (1977): 179–93.
Nietzsche, Friedrich. "On Truth and Lie in an Extra-Moral Sense." in *The Portable Nietzsche*. Edited by Walter Kaufmann. New York: Random House, 1980.
Nikelsburg, George W.E. *1 Enoch 1*. Hermeneia. Minneapolis: Fortress Press, 2001.
Noegel, Scott. *Nocturnal Ciphers: The Allusive Language of Dreams in the Ancient Near East.* Vol. 89 of AOS. New Haven: American Oriental Society, 2007.
Noth, Martin. *Das Geschichtsverständnis der altestestamentlichen Apokalyptik*. Geisteswissenschaften 21. Köln: Westdeutscher Verlag, 1954.
———. "The Holy Ones of the Most High." Pages 215–28 in *The Laws in the Pentateuch and Other Essays*. Edited by London: Oliver and Boyd, 1966.
Núñez, Samuel. *The Vision of Daniel 8: Interpretations from 1700 to 1900*. Berrien Springs, Michigan: Andrews University Press, 1989.
Oates, Joan. *Babylon*. London Thames and Hudson, 1986.
O'Leary, Stephen D. *Arguing the Apocalypse: A Theory of Millenial Rhetoric*. Oxford: Oxford University Press, 1994
Olsson, Tord. "The Apocalyptic Activity. The Case of Jamasp Namag." Pages 21–50 in *Apocalypticism in the Mediterranean World and the Near East: Proceedings of the International Colloquium on Apocalypticism, Uppsala, August 12–17, 1979*. Edited by David Hellholm. Tübingen: Mohr Siebeck, 1983.
Olyan, Saul. *A Thousand Thousands Served Him: Exegesis in the Naming of Angels in Ancient Judaism*. Vol. 36 of TSAJ. Tübingen: Mohr Siebeck, 1993.
Oppenheim, Leo. *The Interpretation of Dreams in the Ancient Near East*. Vol. 46.3 of Transactions of the American Philosophical Society. Philadelphia: American Philosophical Society, 1956.
Orlov, Andrei. *The Enoch-Metatron Tradition*. Vol. 107 of TSAJ. Tübingen: Mohr-Siebeck, 2005.
Oshima, Takayoshi and Wayne Horowitz. *Cuneiform in Canaan: Cuneiform Sources from the Land of Israel in Ancient Times*. Jerusalem: Israel Exploration Society, 2006.
Osten-Sacken, Peter von der. *Die Apokalyptik in ihrem Verhältnis zu Prophetie und Weisheit*. Vol. 157 of Theologische Existenz heute. München: C. Kaiser, 1969.
Parker, Simon. "Aqhat." in *Ugaritic Narrative Poetry*. Edited by Simon Parker. Atlanta: Scholars Press, 1997.
Parpola, Simo and Kazuko Watanabe, eds. *Neo-Assyrian Treaties and Loyalty Oaths*. Vol. II of SAA. Helsinki: Helsinki University Press, 1988.
Parry, Donald and Emanuel Tov. *Parabiblical Texts*. Vol. 3 of DSSR. Leiden: Brill, 2005.
———. eds. *Additional Genres and Unclassified Texts*. Vol. 6 of DSSR. Leiden: Brill, 2005.
———. eds. *Exegetical Texts*. Vol. 2 of DSSR. Leiden Brill, 2004.
———. eds. *Texts Concerned with Religious Law*. Vol. 1 of DSSR. Leiden: Brill, 2004.
Paul, Shalom. "Heavenly Tablets and the Book of Life." Pages 345–54 in *Divrei Shalom: Collected Studies of Shalom M. Paul on the Bible and the Ancient Near East 1967-2005*. Edited by Vol. 23 of *CHANE*. Leiden: Brill, 2005.
———. "Heavenly Tablets and the Book of Life." Pages 345–53 in *The Gaster Festschrift*. Edited by David Marcus. New York: Ancient Near Eastern Society, 1974.
Pavel, Thomas. "Genres as Norms and Good Habits." *New Literary History* 34, no. 2 [Theorizing Genres I] (2003): 201–10.
Peirce, Charles. *The Collected Papers of Charles S. Peirce*. Charlottesville: InteLex Corporation 1994.
Perdue, Leo and Brian Kovaks, eds. *A Prophet to the Nations: Essays in Jeremiah Studies*. Winona Lake: Eisenbrauns, 1984.
Perkins, Ann. *The Art of Dura-Europas*. Oxford: Clarendon, 1973.
Perrin, Norman. "Eschatology and Hermeneutics: Reflections on Method in the Interpretation of the New Testament." *JBL* 93 (1974): 3–14.

Peters, Dorothy. *Noah Traditions in the Dead Sea Scrolls: Conversations and Controversies of Antiquity*. Vol. 26 of SBLEJL. Atlanta: SBL, 2008.

Phillips, Mark Salber. "Histories, Micro- and Literary: Problems of Genre and Distance." *New Literary History* 34, no. 2 [Theorizing Genres I] (2003): 211–29.

Philonenko, Marc, Geo Widengren, and Anders Hultgard, eds. *Apocalyptique iranienne et dualisme qoumrânien*. Paris: Maisonneuve, 1995.

Pingree, David, ed. *Dorotheus Sidonus: Carmen Astrologicum*. Leipzig: Teubner Verlagsgesellschaft, 1976.

Pleše, Zlatko. *Poetics of the Gnostic Universe: Narrative Cosmology in the Apocryphon of John*, Vol. 52 of NHMS. Leiden: Brill, 2006.

Poole, Reginald. *Catalogue of Greek Coins: The Ptolemies, Kings of Egypt*. Bologna: A. Forni, 1963.

Popovic, Mladen. *Reading the Human Body: Physiognomics and Astrology in the Dead Sea Scrolls and Hellenistic-Early Roman Period Judaism*. Vol. 67 of STDJ. Leiden: Brill, 2007.

Porteous, Norman. *Daniel: A Commentary*, OTL. Philadelphia: Westminster, 1965.

Porter, Paul. *Metaphors and Monsters: A Literary-Critical Study of Daniel 7–8*. Motala: CWK Gleerup, 1983.

Portier-Young, Anathea. *Apocalypse Against Empire: Theologies of Resistance in Early Judaism*. Grand Rapids: Eermans, 2011.

Puech, Émile, ed. *Qumran Cave 4.XXVII: Textes araméens, deuxième partie: 4Q550–575, 580–587 et appendices*. Vol. XXXVII of DJD. Oxford: Clarendon, 2009.

Qimron, Elisha. "The Distinction between Waw and Yod in the Qumran Scrolls." *Beth Mikra* 18 (1973): 112–22 [Hebrew].

Quinby, Lee. *Anti-Apocalypse: Exercises in Genealogical Criticism*. Minneapolis: University of Minnesota Press, 1994.

Rad, Gerhard von. *Old Testament Theology: The Theology of Israel's Prophetic Tradition*. Translated by trans. D. Stalker. Vol. II. New York: Harper & Row, 1965.

Rahmouni, Aicha. *Divine Epithets in the Ugaritic Alphabetic Texts*, Vol. 93 of HdO I. Leiden: Brill, 2008.

Reid, Stephen Breck. *Enoch and Daniel: A Form Critical and Sociological Study of Historical Apocalypses*. Berkeley: BIBLA, 1989.

Rendtorff, R. "El, Ba'al und Jahweh." *ZAW* 78 (1966): 277–91.

Reynolds, Bennie H. III "Arrogance as Virtue or Vice? The Expression רמה ביד in the Hebrew Bible and the Dead Sea Scrolls." Paper presented at the IOQS 2007, Ljubljana, Slovenia. Currently under revision for publication.

———. "Lost in Assyria: Lexico-Geographical Transmogrifications of *Assur* in Jewish Literature of the Hellenistic Period." Paper presented at SBL 2008, Boston, MA. Currently under revision for publication.

———. "What Are Demons of Error? The Meaning of שידי טעותא and Israelite Child Sacrifices." *RevQ* 88 (2006): 593–613.

———. "אשור." Forthcoming in *Theologisches Wörterbuch zu den Qumrantexten* Vol. 1. Edited by H. J. Fabry and U. Dahmen. Stuttgart: Kohlhammer-Verlag, 2011.

———. "בעל." Forthcoming in *Theologisches Wörterbuch zu den Qumrantexten* Vol. 1. Edited by H. J. Fabry and U. Dahmen. Stuttgart: Kohlhammer-Verlag, 2011.

———. "Molek: Dead or Alive? The Meaning and Derivation of מלך and *mlk*." Pages 133–50 in *Human Sacrifice in Jewish and Christian Tradition*. Edited by Armin Lange, Karin Finsterbusch, and Diethard Römheld. Leiden Brill, 2007.

———. "Adjusting the Apocalypse: How Apocryphon of Jeremiah C Updates the Book of Daniel." Pages 279–94 in *The Dead Sea Scrolls in Context: Integrating the Dead Sea Scrolls in the Study of Ancient Texts, Languages, and Cultures* Vol. 1. Edited by Emanuel Tov, Armin Lange, Matthias Weigold, and Bennie H. Reynolds III. VTSup. Leiden: Brill, 2011.

———. "Identity Crisis: Mapping Daniel Figures and Traditions in Second Temple Judaism." Forthcoming in *The Reception of Biblical Protagonists in Early Judaism*. Edited by Matthias

Weigold and Bennie H. Reynolds III. Book manuscript submitted to Peeters Press for peer review, 2011.

Rhodes, A. B. "The Kingdoms of Men and the Kingdom of God: A Study of Daniel 7:1–14." *Int* 15 (1961): 411–30.

Ri, A. S.-M. *Commentaire de la Caverne des Trésors*. Turnhout: Brepols, 2002.

Robbins, Thomas and Susan Palmer, eds. *Millennium, Messiahs, and Mayhem: Contemporary Apocalyptic Movements*. New York: Routledge, 1997.

Robertson, David. *Linguistic Evidence in Dating Early Hebrew Poetry*. Vol. 3 of SBLDS. Missoula: Scholars Press, 1972.

Robson, E. Iliff. *Arrian*. Vol. 2 of LCL 269. London: William Heinemann LTD, 1933.

Ronen, Yigal. "The First Hasmonean Coins." *BA* 50 (1987): 105–7.

Rosenthal, Franz. *A Grammar of Biblical Aramaic*. 6th revised ed. Vol. 5 of PORTA. Wiesbaden: Harrassowitz Verlag, 1995.

Rowland, Christopher. *The Open Heaven: A Study of Apocalyptic in Judaism and Early Christianity*. New York: Crossroad, 1982.

———. "The Vision of the Risen Christ in Rev. i.13ff: The Debt of an Early Christian to an Aspect of Jewish Angelology." *JTS* 31 (1980): 4–5.

Rowley, H.H. *The Relevance of Apocalyptic*. 2nd ed. London: Lutterworth Press, 1964 [1944].

———. "The Unity of the Book of Daniel." Pages 237–68 in *The Servant of the Lord and Other Essays on the Old Testament*. London: Lutterworth, 1952.

Russell, David. *The Method and Message of Jewish Apocalyptic*. Philadelphia: Westminster, 1964.

Sacchi, Paolo. *Jewish Apocalyptic and its History*. Vol. 20 of JSPSup. Sheffield: Sheffield Academic Press, 1990.

Saussure, Ferdinand de. *Course in General Linguistics*. Lasalle: Open Court, 1986.

Sayler, Gwendolyn. *Have the Promises Failed: A Literary Analysis of 2 Baruch*. SBLDS. Chico: Scholars Press, 1984.

Schäfer, Heinrich. *Principles of Egyptian Art*. Oxford: Griffith Institute, 1986 [1919].

Schäfer, Peter. *The History of the Jews in the Greco-Roman World*. 2nd Revised ed. London: Routledge, 2003.

Schaudig, Hanspeter. *Die Inschriften Nabonids von Babylon und Kyros' des Großen: samt den in ihrem Umfeld entstandenen Tendenzschriften; Textausgabe und Grammatik*. Vol. 256 of AOAT. Münster: Ugarit-Verlag, 2001.

Schniedewind, William. *The Word of God in Transition: From Prophet to Exegete in the Second Temple Period*. Vol. 197 of JSOTSup. Sheffield: JSOT Press, 1995.

Schultz, Brian. "The Kittim of Assyria." *RevQ* 23 (2007): 63–77.

Schulz, Regine and Matthias Seidel, eds. *Egypt: The World of the Pharaohs*. Cologne: Könemann, 2000.

Scott, James. *On Earth as in Heaven: The Restoration of Sacred Time and Sacred Space in the Book of Jubilees*. Vol. 91 of JSJSup. Leiden: Brill, 2005.

Scott, James C. *Domination and the Arts of Resistance: Hidden Transcripts*. New Haven: Yale University Press, 1990.

———. "The Division of the Earth in *Jubilees* 8:11–9:15 and Early Christian Chronography." Pages 295–323 in *Studies in the Book of Jubilees*. Edited by M. Albani, J. Frey, and A. Lange. Vol. 65 of *TSAJ*. Tübingen: Mohr Siebeck, 1997.

Segal, Michael. *The Book of Jubilees: Rewritten Bible, Redaction, Ideology and Theology*. Vol. 117 of JSJSup. Leiden Brill, 2007.

Segert, Stanislav. "Die Sprachenfrage in der Qumrangemeinschaft." in *Qumran-Probleme: Deutsche Akademie der Wissenschaften zu Berlin* Edited by H. Bardtke. Vol. 42 of *Schriften der Sektion für Altertumswissenschaft* Berlin, 1963.

Seters, John Van. *Abraham in History and Tradition*. New Haven: Yale University Press, 1975.

———. *Prologue to History: The Yahwist as Historian in Genesis*. Louisville: Westminser John Knox, 1992.

———. "The Pentateuch." Pages 3–49 in *The Hebrew Bible Today: An Introduction to Critical Issues*. Edited by Steven McKenzie and M. Patrick Graham. Louisville: WJK, 1998.

Sexton, Timothy. "Genre Theory." *American Chronicle*, April 22 2009, electronic access at http://www.americanchronicle.com/articles/view/24975.

Shipley, Graham. *The Greek World After Alexander: 323–30 BC*. London: Routledge, 2000.

Skjærvø, Prods Oktor. "Zoroastrian Dualism." Page forthcoming in *Light Against Darkness: Dualism in Ancient Mediterranean Religion and the Contemporary World*. Edited by Armin Lange, Eric M. Meyers, Bennie H. Reynolds III, and Randall Styers. Vol. 2 of JAJSup; Göttingen: Vandenhoeck & Ruprecht, 2011.

Smith, Mark. *The Early History of God: Yahweh and Other Deities in Ancient Israel*. 2nd ed. Grand Rapids: Eerdmans, 2002.

———. *The Origins and Development of the Waw-Consecutive*. Vol. 39 of HSS. Atlanta: Scholars Press, 1991.

———. "The Baal Cycle." Pages 80–180 in *Ugaritic Narrative Poetry*. Edited by Simon Parker. Vol. 9 of SBLWAW Atlanta: Scholars Press, 1997.

Smith, Morton. "Ascent to Heaven and Deification in 4QM[a]." in *Archaeology and History in the Dead Sea Scrolls*. Edited by Lawrence Schiffman. Vol. 8 of JPS / ASOR 2 of Sheffield Sheffield Academic Press, 1990.

Sokoloff, Michael. *A Dictionary of Jewish Palestinian Aramaic of the Byzantine Period*. Baltimore: Johns Hopkins Press, 2002.

Sparks, Kenton. *Ancient Texts for the Study of the Hebrew Bible: A Guide to the Background Literature*. Peabody, MA: Hendrickson, 2005.

Staub, Urs. "Das Tier mit den Hörnern: Ein Beitrag zu Dan 7.7f." Pages 39–85 in *Hellenismus und Judentum: Vier Studien zu Daniel 7 und zur Religionsnot under Antiochus IV*. Edited by Othmar Keel and Urs Staub. Göttingen: Vandenhoeck & Ruprecht, 2000.

Stegemann, Hartmut. "Die Bedeutung der Qumranfunde für die Erforschung der Apokalyptik." Pages 495–530 in *Apocalypticism in the Mediterranean World and the Near East*. Edited by David Hellholm. Tübingen: Mohr, 1983.

Stein, Stephen, ed. *The Encyclopedia of Apocalypticism 3: Apocalypticism in the Modern Period and the Contemporary Age*. New York: Continuum, 1998.

Steiner, Richard. "The Heading of the *Book of the Words of Noah* on a Fragment of the Genesis Apocryphon: New Light on a "Lost" Work." *DSD* 2 (1995): 66–71.

Stern, Ephraim. *Material Culture of the Land of the Bible in the Persian Period 538–332 B.C*. Jerusalem: Israel Exploration Society, 1982.

Steudel, Annette. *Der Midrasch zur Eschatologie aus der Qumrangemeinde (4QMidrEschat[a.b])*, STDJ XIII. Leiden: Brill, 1994.

———. "אחרית הימים in the Texts from Qumran." *RevQ* 62 (1993): 225–46.

Stone, Michael. "The Book(s) Attributed to Noah." *DSD* 13 (2006): 4–23.

———. *Fourth Ezra*, Hermeneia. Minneapolis: Fortress, 1994.

———. *A History of the Literature of Adam and Eve*. Vol. 3 of SBLEJL. Atlanta: Scholars Press, 1992.

Stone, Michael, Aryeh Amihay, Vered Hillel, eds. *Noah and His Book(s)*. Vol. 28 of EJS. Atlanta: SBL, 2010.

Strathmann, H. "Λαος." in *TDNT 4*. Edited by Grand Rapids: Eerdmans, 1967.

Strawn, Brent. *What is Stronger than a Lion? Leonine Image and Metaphor in the Hebrew Bible and the Ancient Near East*. Vol. 212 of OBO. Göttingen: Vandenhoeck & Ruprecht, 2005.

Stuckenbruck, Loren. *The Book of Giants from Qumran: Texts, Translation, and Commentary*. Vol. 63 of TSAJ. Tübingen: Mohr Siebeck, 1997.

———. "The Book of Daniel and the Dead Sea Scrolls: The Making and Remaking of the Biblical Tradition." Pages 135–71 in *The Hebrew Bible and Qumran*. Edited by James Charlesworth. N. Richland Hills, TX: BIBAL, 2000.

———. "Daniel and Early Enoch Traditions in the Dead Sea Scrolls." Pages 368–86 in *The Book of Daniel: Composition and Reception*. Edited by John Collins and Peter Flint. Leiden: Brill, 2001.

———. "Daniel and Early Enoch Traditions in the Dead Sea Scrolls." Pages 368–86 in *The Book of Daniel: Composition and Reception*. Edited by John J Collins and Peter Flint. Leiden: Brill, 2001.

———. "Reading the Present in the Animal Apocalypse (1 Enoch 85–90)." Pages 91–102 in *Reading the Present in the Qumran Library: The Perception of the Contemporary by Means of Scriptural Interpretation*. Edited by Armin Lange and Kristin De Troyer. Vol. 30 of *Symposium*. Atlanta: SBL, 2005.

Swain, J. W. "The Theory of the Four Monarchies: Opposition History under the Roman Empire." *Classical Philology* 35 (1940): 1–21.

Talmon, Shemaryahu. "The Signification of אחרית and אחרית הימים in the Hebrew Bible." Pages 795–810 in *Emanuel: Studies in the Hebrew Bible, Septuagint, and Dead Sea Scrolls in Honor of Emanuel Tov*. Edited by Shalom Paul *et al*. Vol. 94 of *VTSup*. Leiden: Brill, 2003.

Tester, S. J. *A History of Western Astrology*. Suffolk: Boydell Press, 1987.

Thiel, Winfried. *Die deuteronomitische Redaktion vom Jer 1–25*. Vol. 41 of WMANT. Neukirchen: Neukirchener, 1973.

Thilo, Georg, ed. *Servii Grammatici qui Feruntur in Vergilii Bucolica et Georgica Commentarii*. Lipsiae: Teubneri, 1887.

Tigchelaar, Eibert. "More on Apocalyptic and Apocalypses." *JSJ* 18 (1987): 137–44.

———. "Review of The Dead Sea New Jerusalem Text: Contents and Contexts by Lorenzo DiTommaso." *DSD* 15 (2008): 404–7.

Tiller, Patrick. *A Commentary on the Animal Apocalypse of 1 Enoch*. Vol. 4 of SBLEJL. Atlanta: Scholars Press, 1993.

Tov, Emanuel. *The Dead Sea Scrolls on Microfiche: A Comprehensive Facsimile Edition of the Texts from the Judean Desert*. Leiden: Brill, 1995.

———. *The Septuagint Translation of Jeremiah and Baruch: A Discussion of Early Revisions of the LXX of Jeremiah 29–52 and Baruch 1:1–3:8*. Vol. 8 of HSM. Missoula: Scholars Press, 1976.

———. *Textual Criticism of the Hebrew Bible*. 2nd rev. ed. Minneapolis: Fortress, 2001.

Towner, W. Sibley. *Daniel*. Interpretation. Atlanta: John Knox, 1984.

Tromp, Johannes. *The Life of Adam and Eve in Greek: A Critical Edition*. Leiden: Brill, 2005.

Uehlinger, Christof. "Mischwesen." Pages 817–21 in *Neues Bibel-Lexikon*. Edited by M. Görg and B. Lang. Zürich/Düsseldorf: Benzinger, 1995.

Uffenheimer, B. "*El Elyon*, Creator of Heaven and Earth." *Shnaton* 2 (1977): 20–26.

Uhlig, S. *Das Äthiopische Henochbuch*, Vol. V/6 of JSHRZ. Gütersoh: G. Mohn, 1984.

Ulrich, Eugene. "Daniel." Pages 239–90 in *Qumran Cave 4.XI: Psalms to Chronicles*. Edited by Eugene Ulrich, Frank Moore Cross, Joseph Fitzmyer, Peter Flint, Sarianna Metso, Catherine Murphy, Curt Niccum, Patrick Skehan, Emanuel Tov, and Julio Trebolle Barrera. Vol. XVI of *DJD*. Edited by Emanuel Tov. Oxford: Clarendon, 2000.

Ussishkin, David. *The Conquest of Lachish by Sennacherib*. Tel Aviv: Tel Aviv University Publications, 1982.

VanderKam, James. *The Book of Jubilees*. Vol. 511 of CSCO. Louvain: Peeters, 1989.

———. *The Book of Jubilees*. Sheffield: Sheffield Academic Press, 2001.

———. *Enoch and the Growth of an Apocalyptic Tradition*. Vol. 16 of CBQMS. Washington, D.C.: Catholic Biblical Association, 1984.

———. *An Introduction to Early Judaism*. Grand Rapids: Eerdmans, 2001.

———. "The Textual Affinities of the Biblical Citations in the Genesis Apocryphon." *JBL* 97 (1978): 45–55.

———. "Too Far Beyond the Essene Hypothesis?" Pages 388–93 in *Enoch and Qumran Origins: New Light on a Forgotten Connection*. Edited by Gabriele Boccaccini. Grand Rapids, MI: Eerdmans, 2005.

———. "The Textual Base for the Ethiopic Translation of 1 Enoch." Pages 247–62 in *Working with No Data: Studies in Semitic and Egyptian Presented to Thomas O. Lambdin*. Edited by D. M. Golomb. Winona Lake: Eisenbrauns, 1987.

VanderKam, James and Peter Flint. *The Meaning of the Dead Sea Scrolls: Their Significance for Understanding the Bible, Judaism, Jesus, and Christianity*. San Francisco: HarperSanFrancisco, 2002.

Verbrugghe, Gerald and John Wickersham. *Berossos and Manetho Introduced and Translated: Native Traditions in Ancient Mesopotamia and Egypt*. Ann Arbor: University of Michigan Press, 1996.

Virolleaud, C. *Syria* 30 (1954): 193.

Waltke, Bruce and M. O'Connor. *An Introduction to Biblical Hebrew Syntax*. Winona Lake, IN: Eisenbrauns, 1990.

Wehmeier, G. "עלה." in *TLOT*. Edited by E. Jenni and C. Westermann. Peabody, MA: Hendrickson, 2006.

Wellhausen, Julius. *Skizzen und Vorarbeiten VI*. Berlin: J. Reimer, 1889.

Werman, Cana. "Epochs and End-Time: The 490-Year Scheme in Second Temple Literature." *DSD* 13 (2006): 229–55.

———. "Qumran and the Book of Noah." Pages 91–120 in *Pseudepigraphical Perspectives: Proceedings of the Second International Symposium of the Orion Center for the Study of the Dead Sea Scrolls and Associated Literature, 12–14 January, 1997*. Edited by E. Chazon and M. Stone. Vol. 31 of *STDJ*. Leiden: Brill, 1999.

Westenholz, Joan Goodnick, ed. *Dragons, Monsters, and Fabulous Beasts (דרקונים מפלצות ויצורי פלא)*. Jerusalem: Bible Lands Museum, 2004.

Widengren, Geo. "Les Quatre Ages du Monde." in *Apocalyptique Iranienne et Dualism Qoumrân*. Edited by Marc Philonenko. Paris: Adrien Maisonneuve, 1995.

Wiggerman, F.A. M. "Mischwesen A." Pages 222–46 in *Reallexikon der Assyriologie und Vorderasiastischen Archäologie*. Edited by Erich Ebeling and Bruno Meissner. Berlin: Walter de Gruyter, 1997.

———. "Lamaštu, Daughter of Anu: A Profile." Pages 217–52 in *Birth in Babylonia and the Bible: Its Mediterranean Setting*. Edited by M. Stol. Vol. 14 of *Cuneiform Monographs*. Groningen: Styx Publications, 2000.

Williamson, Hugh. *Isaiah 1–27 Vol. 1: Isaiah 1–5*. ICC. London: T&T Clark, 2006.

Wills, L. M. *The Jew in the Court of the Foreign King*. Minneapolis: Fotress, 1990.

Wolff, Christian. *Jeremia im Früjudentum und Urchristentum*. Berlin: Akademic Verlag, 1976.

Wolters, Al. "Paleography and Literary Structure as Guides to Reading the Copper Scroll." Pages 311–34 in *Copper Scroll Studies*. Edited by George Brooke and Philip Davies. London: Continuum, 2004.

Yadin, Yigael. *The Scroll of the War of The Sons of Light Against the Sons of Darkness*. Oxford: Oxford University Press, 1962.

Yardeni, Ada. "A Draft of a Deed on an Ostracon from Khirbet Qumran." *IEJ* 47 (1997): 233–7.

Zobel. "עֶלְיוֹן" in *TDOT*. Edited by G. J. Botterweck, H. Ringgren, and H.-J. Fabry. Grand Rapids: Eerdmans, 2001.

Index of Ancient Sources

Hebrew Bible

Daniel
2	94–110
2:8	96
2:19	98, 100
2:21	97–8
2:28	96
2:30	99–100
2:34	217
2:43	103
2:44	109
4:7–9[10–12]	204
4:8[11]	205
4:10–13[13–16]	204
4:16	166
4:19[22]	204
4:21	166
4:23[26]	204
4:27[30]	205
4:30	364
5:23	167
7–8	110–20
7	120–44
7:4	178
7:5	123
7:6	125
7:7	25, 127
7:13	151
7:17	151
7:22	151
7:24	146
7:25	151
7:25	98, 129
7:27	151
8	144–57
8:1	144
8:3	145
8:5	146
8:10–11a	152
8:13	150
8:15	144, 151
8:20	145
8:21	149
8:25	145
10–12	225–262
10:5	235
10:16	235
10:18	235
11:1	236
11:2	226, 237
11:3–4	237
11:5	238, 241
11:8–10	361
11:11	240
11:23	243
11:24	243
11:32	227
11:36	228
11:30	180
12:1	231, 341
12:3	84, 246, 385
12:6–7	235
12:11	150

Deuteronomy
4:19	153
32:8–9	195
32:33	368

Exodus
19:6	138
6:2–3	196
29:21	138
32:16	337

Ezekiel
1:10	121
2:1	131
8:14	228
22:27	175
44:15	363

Genesis		Leviticus	
6:4	167	4:23	146
6:13	213–14	16:9–10	301
9:29	168	17:4	292
10:4	249	17:7	292–3
14:8	135	18:26	297
14:18	196		
14:19	196	Nahum	
18:1	202	3:8–10	307, 321
18:3	235		
19:37–38	177	Numbers	
35:9	172	12:8	112
37:26	167	16:2	300
41:1–7	73–74	23:19	131
		24:24	249
Jeremiah			
2:9–10	249	1 Samuel	
5:6	120	3:1–14	72–73
7:18	153	17:43	175
19:4–5	356		
25:26	294	2 Samuel	
27:6	360	22:14	135

Habakkuk		Zechariah	
1:8	175, 180	1:9	235

Hosea		**Dead Sea Scrolls**	
4:13	202		
9:7–8	267	*Damascus Document*	
13:8	124	CD A+B	
		2 13–16	324
Isaiah		4 1–4	363
14	48–49, 153–54	4 1–11a	87
41:2–3	148	6 2–11a	87
14:12–15	154	CD-A	
44:1	302	8 10–11	368
44:5	302	CD-B	
45:1	295	19 22–24	368
49:14	302		
52:13	246	1QMilḥamah (*The War Scroll*, 1Q33)	
53:11	246	1 1–2	244, 305
		1 2–3	362
Job		3 2	363
38:4a, 7	153	9 7–8	137
		12 8	137
Judges		17 6–7	232
7:5	176		
		1QpHab	
1 Kings		7 4	272
15:13	203	7 4	358
		11 4–6	362
2 Kings			
15:17	195		

Index of Ancient Sources

1QSerek haYaḥad	
5 27	62
4Q169	
3–4i 2-3	250
4Q205	
2i 27	172
2i 29	173
4Q206	
4i 13-14	357
4ii 11	167
4ii 17	174, 197
4ii 21	166
4iii 14	174
4Q384	264
9 2	266
4Q530	
2ii + 6–12 2	169
2ii + 6 +7i + 8–11 +12 10	215
4Q531	
22 9-12	169
4QAges of Creation A (4Q180)	
1 3-4	337
1QapGen (*Genesis Apocryphon,* 1Q20)	
5 29–18 ?	207–220
12 17	197
5 29	208
6 11	213
6 14	213
13 9–11a	217
13 8	217
13 11-12	218
4QApocryphon of Jeremiah C	
Text edition	274–87
4Q385a	
4 1-9	277
4 2-4	295
4 6	295, 298
5a-b 7-8	298
5a-b 8-9	299
5a-b 9	304
18i 2	287

4Q387	
1 2	302
1 2-5	293
2ii 5-6	295
2ii 8	295, 297
2ii 11	302
2iii 1-2	296
2iii 5	296
2iii 6-7	296
2iii 6	289–90, 294
3 4-5	298
3 6	287
4 2	287
4Q388a	
7 5	307
7 6-7	289–90
7 9	324
4Q389	
5 2	294
4Q390	319–20
4QApocryphon of Levi^b ar (4Q541)	
9i 7	355
4QAramaic Apocalypse	
(4Q246)	368
4QDan^{a-d}	147
4QFourKingdoms	191–206
4Q552	
3 10	193
3 12	193
2i 5	197
2i 8	198
2ii 3-4	199
2ii 9-10	200
4Q553	
10 2	197
2ii 1-2	198
6ii 3-4	199
4QInstruction^d (4Q418)	
81 4-5	137
4QLevi^b ar	
3–4 7	138
4QMidrEschat^a (Florilegium, 4Q174)	

1 6	137	1:44-46	129
		10:21	300

4QNewJerusalem[a] (4Q554)
3iii 20, 22   369

2 Maccabees
3   242
5:15   244-45
6:1-2   228
6:1-6   129-30

4QPrNab ar (4Q242)
1-3 7-8   102

4QPrEsther[a] ar (4Q550)
1 1-7   334

4 Maccabees
13 :9   367
18 :16   271
18 :23   271

4QPseudo-Daniel[a–b] ar
Text edition   341-53

Pseudepigrapha

4Q243
1 3   354-55, 360
2 4   363
6 2-4   333
16 1-4   365
16 3-4   341, 362
24 2   340-41
24 3   341
25 3-4   340
28 1-2   333

Animal Apocalypse (see also 4Q205-06)
(*1 En.* 85-90)   161-90
89:1   168, 171
89:10-11   172
89:13   173, 174
89:14   173
89:16   173
89:38   173
89:56   177
89:59   169
89:61   169
90:17   169

4Q244
1 2   360
1-2 1   366
13 3   360

Jubilees
10:13-14   207
17:15-16   267
20 :12-13   174
21:10   207

4QText Mentioning Zedekiah
(4Q470)   232-3

Sibylline Oracles
4   109, 143-44

4QTobit[b] ar
4ii 13   356

Hellenstic Jewish Writers

4QpapVision[b] ar (4Q558)
20 3   365n104

Josephus (*Antiquities of the Jews*)
1.128   250
1.171   360
12.3.3   242
12.3.3-4   241

4QWords of Michael ar (4Q529, 6Q23)
1 1   11
1 4-5   233

Classical Sources

Apocrypha

Esdras
2 Esd 1-2   271

Aemilius Sura   107

Artemidorus   62-77
1.1   66
1.2   66

Judith
12:13   367

1 Maccabees
1:1   250

1.2	67	*Pseudo-Callisthenes*	
1.20	67	1.13.8	106n54
2.12	67	*Servius*	106
		Sidonus	149
Herodotus			
2.139	113	**Other Sources**	
Justinus		*Ba'al*	
XXVII.2	239	KTU 1.16:III:6	194
Macrobius (Somn. Scip.)		*Bahman Yasht*	103
1.3.8	66–7		
		Berossus	334–35
Marcus Manilius	149		
		Eusebius	334–35

Index of Modern Authors

Abegg, Martin 244n64, 267n21, 297n100
Albani, Matthias 334n36, 63n138, 153n209, 212n134, 334n35
Albertz, Rainer 33n31, 94n7, 328n17
Albright, William F. 134
Amihay, Aryeh 211n131
Assefa, Daniel 162n5, 163n6, n9–10, 165n14 166n19
Avery-Peck, William 234n130
Avigad, N. 208

Baillet, Maurice 232n18, 354n75
Barkun, Michael 15, 28, 87–88, 90, 261, 324, 384
Baumgartner, Walter 102n32, 103n36, 124n117, 148n193, 286n70, 290n80
Barthes, Roland 83, 380
Bedenbender, Andreas 56–57, 59
Bengtsson, Håkan 85n211
Bernstein, Moshe 209–10, 212–13, 269n26, 290n79, 300n108, 337n48
Black, Matthew 35n38, 162, 163n6, 166n18
Blum, Erhard 30n15
Boccaccini, Gabriele 56, 58–59, 94, 327
Bottéro, Jean 127n126
Brady, Monica 264–65, 273
Braulik, Georg 195n88
Brekelmans, C. 136–37
Briant, Pierre 237n35–36
Brooke, George 150n200
Brownlee, William H. 86n216
Brunner-Traut, Emma 117–19

Carmignac, Jean 52–55, 62–64
Caquot, André 148n193
Charles, R. H. 39–40, 44, 61–62
Charlesworth, James 85n211
Chazon, Esther 197n91, 232n18
Collins, Adela Yarbro 26n6
Collins, John J. 26, 45–56, 61, 64, 78, 96, 98–99, 103, 106–107, 116, 121, 125–26, 132, 136–38, 148, 155, 228–29, 234, 237, 243, 246, 251, 253n74, 268, 272, 328, 330–33, 337, 339–40, 342n53–55, 343n56, 344.58, 345n58–60, 347n64, 66–67, 356, 357n85, 359, 360–61, 367n113, 368n114, 386n16
Collins, Matthew 86–87
Cross, Frank M. 134, 162, 368, 150n200, 152n202, 192n75, 193n78, 362n101, 368n113
Cuddon, J. A. 221n148, 377n3–4
Culler, Jonathan 76, 80, 83, 243, 381
Derrida, Jacques 50n102
De Saussure, Ferdinand 15, 28, 62, 79–81, 83, 93, 158, 221, 380–81
Dever, William 152n203
Dillman, August 167n23
DiLella, Alexander 95–96, 241, 136n162, 147n189, 155n213
Dimant, Devorah 163–64, 170, 174–77, 180, 209–11, 263–68, 273–74, 275n40–41, 276n42, 45, 277n51, 278n62, 279n64–66, 284n68, 285n69, 289n73, 290n78, 291, 295–96, 298–300, 304n114, 307n123, 306, 328n8
DiTommaso, Lorenzo 31n20, 57n125, 329, 334, 338n48, 353, 357, 361, 369n114
Duqueker, L. 117

Eco, Umberto 15, 78, 82n199, 120n98, 141–42, 241, 364, 376, 385
Eddy, K. 105–06
Eggler, Jürg 114, 117n87–88, 128
Ehrman, Bart D. 386n15
Eissfeldt, Otto 193n78
Eshel, Esther 33n29, 138n172, 232n18, 269n27, 290n79
Eshel, Hanan 85n211, 180n65, 250, 264, 266, 308n124, 355n75, 366n108

Fassberg, Steven 150n200
Fitzmyer, Joseph 194n83, 195, 211n130, 212, 216
Flannery-Dailey, Frances 64–65, 110, 112
Flint, Peter 33n29, 102n34, 328n4–5, 329, 334, 338n47, 340–41, 343n53–55, 344n56, 345n58, 346n59–60, 348n64, 66–67, 357, 360–62

Flusser, David 107n58, 244, 250, 295n92, 305–06, 366n108, 369n113
Foucault, Michel 90
Fröhlich, Ida 85n211, 108n64
Frykholm, Amy Johnson 88–89

García-Martínez, Florentino 29, 85n213, 86n216, 208–09, 335n35, 357–60, 369n113
Gibson, John 131n142, 136n164, 166n21
Gmirkin, Russell 335n33
Gordon, Cyrus 248n78
Greimas, A. J. 83
Gressman, Hugo 121n106
Grossman, Maxine 85, 86n214, 247, 323–24
Gunkel, Hermann 26, 44–45, 47, 61, 115

Hackett, Jo Ann 213n141, 356n81
Hanson, Paul 37n42–43, 41, 43, 46–47, 383
Hartman, Louis 96, 136n162, 147n189, 155n213, 241
Hengel, Martin 148n193, 304–305
Herder, J. G. 116
Hilgenfeld, Adolf 39–40, 43–44, 61
Himmelfarb, Martha 336n38
Hoftijzer, Jacob 102n32, 249n78, 344n56
Hölbl, Gunther 180n63, 66, 238n38, 239n44, 240n48, 54, 241n55–56, 248n77, 296n93
Husser, Jean-Marie 66, 112, 114

Jassen, Alex 30, 333
Jokiranta, Jutta 86
Jongeling, K. 102n32, 249n78, 344n56
Joosten, Jan 195n88

Freud, Sigmund 65, 98

Käsemann, Ernst 45
Keel, Othmar 152, 201–02
Koch, Klaus 36, 45–47, 59, 61, 145
Knibb, Michael 166n19–20, 167n23, 172n30, 173n33, 175n40
Knoppers, Gary 147n187, 249n79
Kobelski, Paul 232n18
Koehler, Ludwig 102n32, 103n36, 286n70, 290n80, 356n80
Kratz, Reinhard 96–97
Kugel, James 208n115
Kuhrt, Amélie 200n97
Kutscher, E. Y. 358n87
Kvanvig, Helge 63n138

Lange, Armin 25, 27, 34n36, 35n39, 36, 63, 66n146, 85n211, 123n114, 163n8, 208–09, 212, 263, 265–66, 289n73, 328n9, 337, 358n88, 359, 376, 378, 382
Larson, Erik 233n20
Leslau, Wolf 167n23, 172n30, 178n50
Levenson, Jon 115n83
Lévi-Strauss, Claude 84, 381
Lücke, Friedrich 36–40, 44, 46, 56, 60

Machiela, Dan 35n40, 207n110, 208n115
Magness, Jodi 86n215
McLay, Timothy 34n31, 94n7
Meshorer, Yaakov 354n71
Meyers, Carol 152n203, 157n217, 203
Meyers, Eric 157n217
Mieroop, Marc van de 200n97
Milgrom, Jacob 292n85
Milik, J. T. 162, 172, 328, 343n55, 348n64, 66, 357, 360, 362, 369n113
Mittman-Richert, Ulrike 25, 37, 63, 261, 266, 376, 378
Montgomery, J. A. 116, 127n129

Najman, Hindy 198n93, 336
Newsom, Carol 85, 86n214, 94n5, 137n166, 269n27, 289n73, 323n127, 324n130, 328n8
Nickelsburg, George 165, 179, 231, 163n6, 230n10, 231n12–14, 324n130, 235n131–32
Niditch, Susan 111, 157, 95n9
Nietzsche, Friedrich 50
Noegel, Scott 68n159, 74–77, 103n37

Olsson, Tord 37
Oppenheim, Leo 27, 62–63, 65–70, 72, 74–77, 93, 99, 100, 112–13, 157, 171, 220, 223, 229, 243, 320, 373, 377, 380, 384
Orlov, Andrei 135n159
Osten-Sacken, Peter von der 32n25, 37n42, 43

Parpola, Simo 71n172, 356n82
Peirce, Charles 28, 62, 82–83, 93, 102, 129, 145, 158, 221, 243, 380–81
Perrin, Norman 51, 54, 78, 145
Pleše, Zlatko 221n149
Popovic, Mladen 149n199
Portier-Young, Anathea 41n59
Puech, Émile 107n64, 191, 192n73–74, 197n92, 200n98, 355n79

Qimron, Elisha 212, 359, 150n200
Quinby, Lee 90

Rahmouni, Aicha 134n154, 157 135n158, 194
Reid, Stephen Breck 54
Reynolds, Bennie H. III 235n28, 30, 270n29, 293n87, 299n103, 303n112, 306n121, 329n17, 339n51, 345n57, 355n75, 77, 356n80, 83, 366n107-109
Robbins, Thomas 88n223, 386n14, 15
Rosenthal, Franz 343n54, 345n58
Rowley, H. H. 40-42, 44, 61, 95n10, 383
Russell, David 26n7, 43-47

Sacchi, Paolo 56, 94
Schaudig, Hans-Peter 70n164
Schniedewind, William 30n17
Scott, James C. 41, 383
Skjærvø, Oktor 104n41, 107n58
Sokoloff, Michael 349n68
Stegemann, Hartmut 29
Steiner, Richard 208n211
Stuedel, Annette 97n18-20
Stuckenbruck, Loren 154n209, 163n7, 193n76, 215n144-45, 344n55
Stone, Michael 34n32, 34, 138n172, 211, 234n26
Sukenik, Eliezer 250, 366n108

Talmon, Shemaryahu 97
Thiel, Winfried 266n14
Tigchelaar, Eibert 31n20, 56, 369n114
Tiller, Patrick 162-64, 167, 170, 174, 177-80, 189n69, 190n70, 291
Tov, Emanuel 150n200, 172n32, 191n72, 265n12

Uehlinger, Christoph 101n31, 121n106, 152, 202n102
Ulrich, Eugene 147n190
Ussishkin, David 101n31

VanderKam, James 58, 63n138, 94n3, 162, 163n6, 165, 174n35, 175n38, 207n111, 209n119, 231n14-15, 336n33, 299n105, 335n33, 336n36, 42, 337n43, 358
Van Seters, John 37n45

Waltke, Bruce 297n98, 343n53, 354n70
Weigold, Matthias 211n130
Werman, Cana 209-10, 264, 266-67
Westenholz, Joan Goodnick 117n89, 122n107-09, 123n113, 126n124
Williamson, Hugh 97n17
Wills, L. M. 34n31, 95n9

Wolff, Christian 348n64

Yardeni, Ada 150n200

Index of Subjects

Adam 164–65, 172, 181, 182, 190, 205, 216, 218, 233–34, 334
Akra 228
Aladlammû 122
Alexander Jannaeus 244, 299–300, 305
Alexander the Great 43, 105, 109, 127, 148, 150, 156, 164, 170, 179, 200–01, 226, 237, 238, 250, 254, 289, 291, 304, 308, 360
Alexandria 248, 285n69, 296
Allegoresis 163n9, 164, 337
Allegory 45, 48, 50–51, 100, 115, 124, 163–64, 167, 175
Antiochus III 240–42, 294
Antiochus IV 33, 35, 41–42, 50, 78, 95, 98, 129, 141, 150, 155–56, 180, 228, 236, 238–39, 241–44, 246, 248, 250–51, 255–59, 267, 290–91, 294–97, 303–06, 308, 332, 358, 361, 380–81, 383–84
Apkallu 334
Aram 178, 187
Aramaic 33, 102, 131, 135, 146–47, 149–50, 161, 165–67, 172–75, 191, 196, 207, 212, 328–29, 354–55, 361–62, 164
Aristobulus 298n89, 300
Aristomenes 241
Armageddon 90
Aspective/Aspektische 117–19
Assurbanipal 332
Assyria/Assyrian/s 107, 113, 121, 123, 152, 178, 187, 202, 297, 349, 365–67, 369
Astrologer/Astrology 49, 149
Azazel 231

Ba'al 51, 115, 127, 133, 134, 193n78
Babylon 33, 49–50, 70, 101–02, 107, 109–10, 116–17, 121, 148, 174, 199–201, 204–06, 266, 286, 295, 351, 360–61, 364, 366, 371
Babylonian 70, 114–15, 122–23, 140, 164–65, 169–70, 175, 177–78, 187, 238, 247, 272, 289, 291–93, 295–96, 300–03, 307, 317, 321, 327, 329, 338–40, 353–54, 366–68
Bagoas 367

Balakros 327, 332n24, 351, 360–61, 371
Bear 84, 120, 122–25, 127, 140, 174n36, 175, 381
Belial 170, 232, 244, 251, 267, 270, 290, 305, 319
Belshazzar 144, 327, 329, 332–34, 353, 357, 366–67
Berenice 239, 254–55
Berossus 334, 335n32-33
Birds 101, 178–79, 179n54, 189, 204, 213, 217
Blasphemer 283–84, 295–97, 303, 310, 312

Calendar (& Calendrical) 98, 336
Callinicus 239–40, 255, 361
Canaanite 48, 115, 126, 133–34, 152–53, 155, 163, 196, 221, 228, 339, 356
Cleopatra 256
Covenant (violators of) 14, 232, 243–45, 247, 257, 283–84, 287, 299, 303–05, 314, 322, 324–25, 385
Cyrus 70–72, 147, 237, 252, 295–98, 303, 323

Darius 236–37, 254, 289, 295–98, 303, 334
Day-star 48, 163
Demon 105, 170, 269–70, 290–91, 293, 339, 351, 354–57, 371
Deuternomistic 36, 153, 195, 203, 217, 265, 292, 302, 330
Diadochoi 101, 126, 127, 150, 225, 308
Diviner 62, 69, 71, 74–75, 96, 99, 102, 198, 204, 332–33, 338, 376
Dream 27, 34, 39, 41, 47, 53–54, 62–76, 84, 94–96, 98–100, 102, 110–14, 116, 132, 135, 142–44, 146, 151, 157–58, 161, 165, 169, 223, 227, 261, 272, 320, 329, 333, 353, 364, 368, 376–77, 380
Dualism 13, 29, 245, 385

Egypt (& Egyptian) 74, 101, 106, 113, 117–18, 121, 165, 174–77, 184, 187, 191, 200–01, 206, 230–31, 238–240, 243, 251, 255, 258–59, 266, 281, 284,

286, 295-96, 304, 307-08, 312-13, 316, 321, 323, 351, 361, 366-67, 370, 373
El 115, 133-35, 154, 194, 196, 354, 356
Elohim 196, 270
Elyon 195-96
El Shaddai 196
Enoch 29, 44, 54, 56, 58-60, 165, 169, 181-82, 207, 213, 230-31, 270, 327, 329, 334, 336-38, 250, 357, 362, 370, 385
Eschaton 108-09, 169, 245, 270, 272, 302, 306, 341, 363-64, 369, 374
Esarhaddon 356
Essene 29, 56, 58, 87, 262, 272, 287-89, 307, 324-25, 328, 333, 338, 354, 362-64, 374, 384
Euergetes (Ptolemy III) 238-39, 255, 294
Evangelical 88-89, 386
Exile 102, 169-70, 189, 247, 266, 272, 281, 285, 289, 291-92, 295-96, 300-03, 334, 338-40, 351, 354-56, 361-62, 366, 371

Gabriel 145, 151, 168, 229, 231-33
Genre 15-16, 26, 28-35, 40, 46, 52-56, 59-63, 76, 84, 91, 94, 98, 116, 119, 158, 201, 214, 222-23, 236, 269, 270-71, 330-31, 338, 376, 378, 380, 387
Giants 169, 182, 215
Gilgamesh 71-72, 74, 168-69, 377
Goat 49, 51, 69, 146-49, 151, 155-56, 226
Greece 25-26, 49, 60, 72, 101, 108, 110, 123, 126, 130, 140, 143, 148, 149, 150, 156, 191, 200, 201, 206, 225-27, 229, 236-38, 248, 250, 253-54, 285, 308, 316, 322, 368

Halakhah 86n215, 328
Hasmonean 109, 192, 244, 289n75, 294, 298-300, 303, 305, 332, 354
Heaven 49, 70, 98-100, 108-09, 113, 116, 124, 135-36, 139, 152-54, 156, 167, 179, 182, 189, 196, 197, 204, 213, 229, 237, 254, 261, 269-70, 272, 308, 335-36, 350, 363-64, 380
Heliodorus 242, 257
Holy One 129, 132, 135-39, 150-51, 157, 196, 213, 219, 364
Horns 25, 127-30, 132-33, 141, 145-46, 148-49, 150, 156, 158, 179, 225, 353, 382-83
Hyrcanus, John 244, 294, 298-300, 307
Hyrcanus, Tobias 125
Iraq el-Amir (Qasr el Abd) 125

Jacob 172-73, 184-85, 195-96, 282, 284-85, 293, 301-02, 307, 309, 311, 316, 336
Jason 248, 298-99, 301, 304
Jerusalem 34, 57, 59, 120, 129-30, 150, 152-53, 155, 175, 177, 217, 228, 241-43, 245, 247, 249-50, 272, 284, 286, 289-90, 292-94, 296, 299, 304, 308, 313, 340, 361, 366-67
Jonathan (Maccabee) 244, 248, 294, 299, 300
Judah 96, 120, 129, 173, 177-78, 233, 270, 281, 286, 292, 307, 318, 339, 344, 356, 363, 367-68
Judea 44, 117, 129, 171-72, 200, 227, 243, 251, 354
Judgement 13, 39, 73, 162, 165, 167-68, 193, 204, 230, 271, 301, 363

Kittim 180, 243-44, 248-50, 258, 304-06, 308
Korah 301-02

Laenas, Popilius 180, 348
Lamassu 121-22
Leopard 120, 125-26, 140, 177-78, 187-88, 237
Left Behind 88-89, 324
Lion 46, 50, 82, 116-17, 120-25, 127, 140, 158, 164, 175, 177-78, 187, 202

Mastema 170, 267, 290-91
Mastemot, Angels of 170, 267, 269-70, 284, 290-91, 296, 313, 319
Melchizedek 135, 196
Menelaus 244, 248, 269-70, 284, 290-91, 296, 313, 319
Menorah 203
Mesopotamia/n 45, 72, 77, 106, 113, 121-23, 126, 239, 332-333, 360, 366-67
Messiah 190, 295, 369n113
Messianic 239
Metaphor 46, 61, 76, 78, 82, 119-21, 137, 171, 177, 225, 239, 248, 264
Michael 168, 183, 228-37, 253, 259, 261, 270
Microcosm 87-90
Moab 187, 244, 251, 259, 305, 360
Molek 339n51
Moses 59, 109, 168, 171, 173, 185, 196, 198, 202, 206, 233, 236, 264, 292-93, 297, 300-01, 335-37
Motif 37, 45, 47, 49, 61, 88, 101, 103-09, 116, 128-29

Index of Subjects

Myth/ic 26, 44-53, 83, 88, 115-16, 122, 124, 126, 133-35, 153-55, 159, 163, 170, 221, 228-31, 234-35, 247, 308

Nabonidus 33, 70-71, 74, 102-03, 111, 113-14

Nebuchadnezzar 33, 98, 100-02, 110, 166, 204, 217, 228, 268, 292, 295-96, 329, 351, 360-61, 364, 367, 371

Noah 109, 146, 161, 165, 168-73, 182-83, 205, 207-18, 249, 293, 336, 350, 357, 359, 370, 373

Persia/n 33, 49, 95, 101, 103-07, 110, 122-23, 126-27, 140, 145-46, 148-49, 156, 194, 199-200, 229, 236-38, 248, 251-54, 295-97, 302-03, 307, 334, 366

Pharisee 85, 289n75, 300, 307, 325, 364, 374

Priest 57, 66, 85, 110, 129, 135, 138, 196, 203, 244-48, 284, 286, 289-90, 292-96, 298-301, 304, 307, 313-14, 317-18, 320, 328, 332, 359-60, 362-63

Prophecy 30-31, 36-37, 40-46, 56, 111, 157-58, 244, 251, 272, 306, 331-33

Prophecy (Ex Eventu) 251, 268, 270, 272, 292, 294, 300, 302

Ram 35, 49, 145-49, 151, 156, 162, 172-73, 176, 184-86, 189

Sacrifice 73, 130, 195, 202, 290, 292, 298, 305, 339, 355-59

Sadducee 245

Sargon 48

Semiotics 51, 77-79, 84, 132-33, 135, 158, 221, 380

Sheep 165-67, 169-70, 172-74, 184-190, 197, 236, 298

Sheol 48, 154

Shepherd/s 119, 167, 169, 170, 187-89, 197, 291

Simon (Maccabee) 244, 294, 299-300

Sobriquets 13-16, 84, 86-87

Son of Man (One Like a Human Being) 51, 115, 130, 132-34, 141, 151, 236

Syria 49, 105, 123, 148-49, 191, 195, 200-01, 206, 238, 240, 242, 305, 308, 366-67

Temple 59, 70-71, 74, 128, 130, 137, 146, 150, 152, 155, 165, 175, 177, 228, 242-45, 282, 290, 292, 296, 299, 301, 304, 306, 328, 351, 363, 366, 369

Totem/Totemism 84, 116, 381

Tree 34, 46, 100-01, 103, 107-08, 191-206, 213-222, 226, 230, 239, 270-71, 285, 383

Watchers 162, 165, 171, 182

Wisdom 42, 56, 61, 63n138, 64, 211n126, 246, 337n45

Wolves 173-75, 177-78, 184-85, 187

Zeus 130, 150, 228, 290

Zoroaster 103

Journal of Ancient Judaism. Supplements

V&R

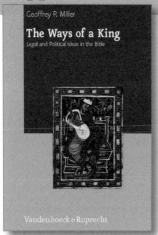

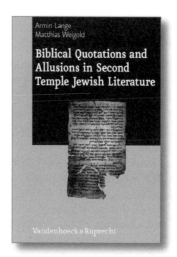

Vol. 7: Geoffrey P. Miller
The Ways of a King
Legal and Political Ideas in the Bible
Translation by Liliane Meilinger.
With a foreword by Shulamit Volkov.
2011. 296 pages, hardcover
ISBN 978-3-525-55034-2

Geoffrey P. Miller argues that the history of the Israelite people from Genesis to 2 Kings contains a well-organized, cogent, and comprehensive set of ideas about political obligation and governmental design.

The Bible explores these issues, not through discursive analysis in the style of Greek philosophy, but rather through careful management of the narrative frame. In this sense the Bible can be considered as one of the earliest political philosophies of the western world.

Vol. 5: Matthias Weigold / Armin Lange
Biblical Quotations and Allusions in Second Temple Jewish Literature
2011. 384 pages, hardcover
ISBN 978-3-525-55028-1

Using new search capabilities of electronic databases this volume presents a comprehensive list of allusions to and quotations of the books collected in the Hebrew Bible in the Jewish literature from the Second Temple period. It is therefore an indispensable tool for everyone interested in ancient Judaism, the Hebrew Bible and its reception.

Vandenhoeck & Ruprecht

Journal of Ancient Judaism. Supplements

V&R

Volume 4: Saul M. Olyan
Social Inequality in the World of the Text
The Significance of Ritual and Social Distinctions in the Hebrew Bible
2011. 240 pages, hardcover
ISBN 978-3-525-55024-3

This volume presents a selection of fifteen essays on social inequalities in the Hebrew Bible dealing with e.g. social status, gender, sexuality, disability, holiness, death and afterlife.

Volume 2: Armin Lange / Eric M. Meyers / Bennie H. Reynolds III / Randall G. Styers (ed.)
Light Against Darkness
Dualism in Ancient Mediterranean Religion and the Contemporary World
2011. 368 pages, hardcover
ISBN 978-3-525-55016-8

Light Against Darkness investigates dualistic thought in ancient Judaism and its cultural environment as well as its reflections in the modern world.

Volume 3: Albert I. Baumgarten / Hanan Eshel / Ranon Katzoff / Shani Tzoref (ed.)
Halakhah in Light of Epigraphy
2011. 303 pages with 16 ill., hardcover
ISBN 978-3-525-55017-5

The contributors examine diversity in halakhic positions, in terms of both exegesis and practice. They explore evidence of halakhic development over the course of the Second Temple period, and of halakhic variety among different groups.

Volume 1: Ruth Sander / Kerstin Mayerhofer
Retrograde Hebrew and Aramaic Dictionary
2010. 258 pages, hardcover
ISBN 978-3-525-55007-6

This dictionary offers an updated list of Kuhn's Hebrew Lemmata from 1958. It includes vocabulary from all Hebrew and Aramaic texts from ancient manuscripts and inscriptions from Palestine dating up to 135 A.D., as well as the Words of Ahikar.

Vandenhoeck & Ruprecht